The British Study of Po
the Twentieth Cent

The British Study of

POLITICS

in the Twentieth Century

EDITORS
Jack Hayward
Brian Barry
Archie Brown

Published for THE BRITISH ACADEMY
by OXFORD UNIVERSITY PRESS

Oxford University Press, Great Clarendon Street, Oxford OX2 6DP

Oxford New York
Auckland Bangkok Buenos Aires Cape Town Chennai
Dar es Salaam Delhi Honk Kong Istanbul Karachi Kolkata
Kuala Lumpur Madrid Melbourne Mexico City Mumbai Mairobi
São Paulo Shanghai Singapore Taipei Tokyo Toronto

Published in the United States
by Oxford University Press Inc., New York

© *The British Academy 1999*

Database right The British Academy (maker)

First published 1999
Paperback binding 2003

British Library Cataloguing in Publication Data
Data available

ISBN 0-19-726924-5

Typeset in Palatino
by J&L Composition Ltd, Filey, North Yorkshire
Printed in Great Britain
on acid-free paper by
The Cromwell Press Limited
Trowbridge, Wilts

Contents

Notes on Contributors

Rodney Barker is Reader in Government at the London School of Economics and Political Science (LSE) where he has taught since 1971. Earlier he studied as an undergraduate at Cambridge, took his PhD at LSE, and was Lecturer in Politics at the University of Wales, Swansea (1967–1971). His publications include *Studies in Opposition* (as editor, 1971), *Education and Politics 1900–1951: A Study of the Labour Party* (1972), *Political Legitimacy and the State* (1990), *Politics, Peoples, and Government: Themes in British Political Thought Since the Nineteenth Century* (1994), and *Political Ideas in Modern Britain In and After the Twentieth Century* (1997).

Brian Barry is Arnold A. Saltzman Professor of Philosophy and Political Science at Columbia University (New York). After studying as an undergraduate and graduate student at Oxford, Professor Barry has taught at a number of universities in Britain, Western Europe and North America. In 1961–62 he was Rockefeller Fellow in Legal and Political Philosophy at Harvard. He has been an Official Fellow of Nuffield College, Oxford, and has held professorial appointments at Essex University, the University of British Columbia, the University of Chicago, California Institute of Technology, and the European University Institute, Florence. He was Professor of Political Science at the LSE from 1987 to 1997 before moving to his present Chair at Columbia. Professor Barry was a Fellow of the Center for Advanced Study in the Behavioral Sciences (1976–77), was elected a Fellow of the American Academy of Arts and Sciences in 1978 and became a Fellow of the British Academy in 1988. His publications include *Political Argument* (1965), *Sociologists, Economists and Democracy* (1970), *The Liberal Theory of Justice* (1973), *Rational Man and Irrational Society?* (with Russell Hardin, 1982), *Democracy and Power* and *Liberty and Justice* (1991) and two volumes of *A Treatise on Social Justice – Theories of Justice* (1989) and *Justice as Impartiality* (1995), both awarded W. J. M. Mackenzie Prize of the Political Studies Association of the UK for best book published in its year.

Vernon Bogdanor, a Fellow of Brasenose College, Oxford, since 1966, has been Professor of Politics at Oxford University since 1996. He was elected a Fellow of the British Academy in 1997 and was appointed CBE for services to constitutional history in 1998. Among his publications are *Devolution* (1979), *The People and the Party System* (1981), *Multi-Party Politics and the Constitution* (1983), *Constitutions in Democratic Politics* (editor, 1988), *The Blackwell Encyclopedia of Political Science* (editor, 1992), *Comparing Constitutions* (with S. E. Finer and Bernard Rudden, 1995), *The Monarchy and the Constitution* (1995), *Politics and the Constitution: Essays on British Government* (1996), *Power and the People: A Guide to Constitutional Reform* (1997), and *Devolution in the United Kingdom* (1999). He is at present editing a volume on British Constitutional History of the Twentieth Century for the British Academy.

Archie Brown has been Professor of Politics at Oxford University since 1989 and a Fellow of St Antony's College since 1971 (Sub-Warden, 1995–97). Before moving to Oxford he studied as an undergraduate and graduate student at LSE and taught at Glasgow University. He was a British Council Exchange Scholar at Moscow University (1967–68) and has been a Visiting Professor of Political Science at the University of Connecticut, Yale (where he gave the 1980 Henry L. Stimson Lectures), Columbia University and the University of Texas at Austin. In the Fall semester of 1998 he was Distinguished Visiting Fellow at the Kellogg Institute for International Studies, University of Notre Dame. Professor Brown was elected a Fellow of the British Academy in 1991. His publications include *Soviet Politics and Political Science* (1974), *The Soviet Union since the Fall of Khrushchev* (co-editor, 1975; 2nd ed., 1978), *Political Culture and Political Change in Communist States* (co-editor, 1977), *Authority, Power and Policy in the USSR* (co-editor, 1980), *Soviet Policy for the 1980s* (co-editor, 1982), *Political Culture and Communist Studies* (editor, 1984), *Political Leadership in the Soviet Union* (editor, 1989), *The Soviet Union: A Biographical Dictionary* (editor, 1990), *New Thinking in Soviet Politics* (editor, 1992), *The Cambridge Encyclopedia of Russia and the Former Soviet Union* (co-editor, 1994) and *The Gorbachev Factor* (1996; awarded W. J. M. Mackenzie Prize of the Political Studies Association).

Tim Dunne is Senior Lecturer in International Politics at the University of Wales, Aberystwyth. He studied as an undergraduate at the University of East Anglia and, as a graduate student, at St Antony's College, Oxford, where he took his MPhil in International Relations and completed his DPhil in 1993. For the latter he was awarded the prize of the British International Studies Association for the best International Relations thesis of its year. After a brief spell as tutor and lecturer in Prague for the Central European University, Dr Dunne moved to Aberystwyth in 1993. Among his publications are *Inventing International Society: A History of the English School* (1998) and *The Eighty Years' Crisis: International Politics, 1919–1999* (co-editor, 1998) and *Human Rights in Global Politics* (co-editor, 1999).

Jack Hayward is Research Professor at the University of Hull and Emeritus Professor of the University of Oxford. From 1993 until 1998 he was Professor of Politics at Oxford University, Director of the University's European Studies Institute and a Fellow of St Antony's College. After studying as an undergraduate and graduate student at LSE, Professor Hayward taught at the University of Sheffield and Keele University and was a Senior Research Fellow at Nuffield College, Oxford before becoming Professor of Politics at Hull (1973–1992). He was Chairman of the Political Studies Association of the UK, 1975–1977, and its President, 1979–1981. He edited the association's journal, *Political Studies*, from 1987 to 1993. Professor Hayward, who was awarded the Chevalier de la Légion d'Honneur in 1996, has been a Visiting Professor at the University of Paris III (1979–1980) and the Institut d'Etudes Politiques (Paris) in 1990–91. He was elected a Fellow of the British Academy in 1990. Among his publications are *Private Interests and Public Policy* (1966), *The One and Indivisible French Republic* (1973), *The State and the Market Economy* (1986), *After the French Revolution* (1991), *De Gaulle to Mitterrand* (editor, 1993), *The Crisis of Representation in Europe* (editor, 1995), *Governing the New Europe* (co-editor, 1995), *Industrial Enterprise and European Integration* (editor, 1995), and *Elitism, Populism and European Politics* (editor, 1996).

Christopher Hood has been Professor of Public Administration and Public Policy at LSE since 1989. After studying at the University of York and Glasgow University, Professor Hood was a Lecturer in Politics at Glasgow and Research Fellow at York before becoming Professor of Government and Public Administration at the University of Sydney, 1986–89. He was Visiting Research Fellow, Zentrum für Interdisziplinäre Forschung, University of Bielefeld in 1982 and 1989 and a Senior Teaching Fellow at the University of Singapore, 1984–85. His publications include *Limits of Administration* (co-editor, 1976), *Big Government in Hard Times* (co-editor, 1981), (with Andrew Dunsire) *Bureaumetrics*

(1981), *The Tools of Government* (1983), *Delivering Public Services in Western Europe* (co-editor, 1988), (with Andrew Dunsire) *Cutback Management in Public Bureaucracies* (1989), (with M. W. Jackson) *Administrative Argument* (1991), *Rewards at the Top* (co-editor, 1994), *Explaining Economic Policy Reversals* (1994), and *The Art of the State* (1998).

Paul Kelly is Senior Lecturer in Government at LSE where he has taught since 1995. After studying at the University of York and at LSE (where he received his PhD), he was Bradley Visiting Research Fellow at the University of Chicago Law School (1987–1990) and Lecturer in Political Theory at the University of Wales, Swansea (1990–1995). Among his publications are *Utilitarianism and Distributive Justice: Jeremy Bentham and the Civil Law* (1990), *The Social Contract from Hobbes to Rawls* (co-editor, 1994), *Impartiality, Neutrality and Justice* (editor, 1998) and *Social Justice from Hume to Walzer* (co-editor, 1998).

Charles King is Assistant Professor of Government at Georgetown University and Ion Ratiu Professor of Romanian Studies in the School of Foreign Service at Georgetown. After studying as an undergraduate at the University of Arkansas, he was a Marshall Scholar at Oxford University and a graduate student of St Antony's College, receiving his MPhil in 1992 and doctorate (for which he was awarded the Walter Bagehot Prize in Government and Public Administration by the Political Studies Association of the UK) in 1995. Before taking up his present appointment at Georgetown University Dr King was J. Arthur Rank and C. A. W. Manning Junior Research Fellow at New College, Oxford, and a Research Associate of the International Institute for Strategic Studies, London. His publications include, *Ending Civil Wars* (1997), *Nations Abroad: Diaspora Politics and International Relations* (co-editor, 1998), and *The Moldovans: Negotiable Nationalism on a European Frontier* (forthcoming).

Geoffrey Marshall has been Provost of the Queen's College, Oxford, since 1993, having been Fellow and Tutor in Politics at Queen's from 1957. Earlier he studied at Manchester University as an undergraduate and took his PhD at Glasgow University where he taught in the Politics Department. He was a Research Fellow at Nuffield College (1955–57) and Andrew Dixon White Visiting Professor at Cornell between 1985 and 1991. Dr Marshall was a member of Oxford City Council, 1965–74, and Sheriff of Oxford, 1970–71. Since 1994 he was been President of the Study of Parliament Group. He was elected to a Fellowship of the British

Academy in 1971. His publications include *Parliamentary Sovereignty and the Commonwealth* (1957), *Some Problems of the Constitution* (with Graeme C. Moodie, 1959), *Police and Government* (1965), *Constitutional Theory* (1971), *Constitutional Conventions* (1984) and *Ministerial Responsibility* (1989).

William L. Miller is Edward Caird Professor of Politics at Glasgow University. He studied as an undergraduate at Edinburgh University and took his PhD at the University of Newcastle. Between 1968 and 1985 (when he moved to his present Chair at Glasgow) he was successively Lecturer, Senior Lecturer and Professor at Strathclyde University. He was Visiting Professor in Politics at Virginia Tech, 1983–84. Professor Miller was elected to a Fellowship of the British Academy in 1994. Among his publications are *Electoral Dynamics* (1977), *The End of British Politics? Scots and English Political Behaviour in the Seventies* (1981), *The Survey Method* (1983), *Elections and Voters* (with Martin Harrop, 1987), *Irrelevant Elections* (1988), *How Voters Change* (co-author, 1990), *Media and Voters* (1991) *Alternatives to Freedom* (editor, 1995), *Political Culture in Contemporary Britain* (co-author, 1996) and *Values and Political Change in Postcommunist Europe* (co-author, 1998). He is currently working on public attitudes to local governance in Britain and on bureaucratic encounters between citizens and junior officials in post-Communist Europe.

Noël O'Sullivan, who studied as an undergraduate at LSE and as a graduate student at Harvard, is Professor of Political Philosophy at the University of Hull. He is the author of *Conservatism* (1976), *Fascism* (1983), *The Problem of Political Obligation* (1986), *The Philosophy of Santayana* (1992) and as editor or co-editor *Revolutionary Theory and Political Reality* (1985), *Terrorism, Ideology and Revolution* (1985), *The Corporate State* (1988), *The Structure of Modern Ideology* (1989), *The Nature of the Right* (1989), *Aspects of India* (1997) and *Political Theory in Transition* (1999). He is currently writing a book on European Political Thought Since 1945.

Jeremy Richardson became Nuffield Professor of Comparative European Politics, Director of the Centre for European Politics, Economics and Society at Oxford University and a Fellow of Nuffield College, Oxford, in 1998. After studying as an undergraduate at the University of Keele and as a graduate student at Manchester University, he taught at Keele between 1974 and 1982 when he moved to the University of Strathclyde as Professor and Head of the Department of

Politics. From 1992 to 1995 he was Professor of European Integration and Director of the European Public Policy Institute at the University of Warwick before becoming Professor of European Public Policy at the University of Essex (1995–98). He has held a number of Visiting Professorships in Norway, Sweden and the USA and was Robert Schuman Distinguished Visiting Fellow, European University Institute, Florence, in 1994. His publications include *The Policy-Making Process* (1969), *Campaigning for the Environment* (co-editor, 1974), *Governing Under Pressure: The Policy Process in a Post-Parliamentary Democracy* (with A. G. Jordan, 1979), *British Politics and the Policy Process* (with A. G. Jordan, 1987), *Government and Pressure Groups in Britain* (with A. G. Jordan, 1987), *Privatization and Deregulation in Canada and Britain* (1990), *Lobbying in the EC* (co-editor, 1993), *Pressure Groups* (editor, 1993), *True Blues: The Politics of Conservative Party Membership* (with Paul Whiteley and Patrick Seyd, 1994), *Managing Policy Change in Britain: The Politics of Water Policy* (with William Maloney, 1995) and *European Union: Power and Policy-Making* (editor, 1996).

Alan Ryan is Warden of New College, Oxford, Professor of Politics at Oxford and Director of the Rothermere American Institute at Oxford University. After studying as an undergraduate at Balliol College, Oxford, he taught at the University of Keele (1963–66) and the University of Essex (1966–69) before returning to Oxford as Tutor in Politics at New College (1969–1988), and as Lecturer in Politics and, from 1978, Reader, at Oxford University. Alan Ryan was Professor of Politics at Princeton University from 1988 until 1996 when he took up the Wardenship of New College. He has held Visiting Professorships at the City University of New York, the University of Texas, the University of California and the University of Witwatersrand, and has been a Visiting Fellow at Australian National University and Mellon Fellow at the Institute for Advanced Study, Princeton. Professor Ryan gave the de Carle Lectures at the University of Otago in 1983. His publications include *The Philosophy of John Stuart Mill* (1970; 2nd ed., 1987), *The Philosophy of the Social Sciences* (1970), *J. S. Mill* (1975), *Property and Political Theory* (1984), *The Blackwell Encyclopaedia of Political Thought* (co-editor, 1987), *Property* (1987), *Bertrand Russell: A Political Life* (1988), *John Dewey and the High Tide of American Liberalism* (1995) and *Liberal Anxieties and Liberal Education* (1998).

Preface

Rather than a conventional disciplinary history, this volume deals with the intellectual response of academics in Britain to the political challenges of the twentieth century. So, the idea from which this book was initially born had no connection with commemorating the centenary of the British Academy, although in the event the timing has proved apposite. It derived in part from a sense that contemporary political scientists in Britain had been rather uninterested in exploring their own past. As they had not sought to demonstrate their pride of ancestry, they could not reproach others with not esteeming them at their own value or distinguishing clearly between those who practise and those who analyse politics in a century that has made severe demands on both practitioners and analysts.

The proposal to undertake a study of the British contribution to the development of political science in the twentieth century was made by Jack Hayward when he chaired the Politics Section of the Academy. The suggestion was to focus on a dozen or so leading figures, but discussion in the Section quickly led to a general preference that the focus should be upon themes and a broader range of scholarship rather than a limited number of personalities. The task of preparing a detailed set of proposals, consisting of the chapter subjects and their suggested authors, was confided to an augmented Section Standing Committee consisting of Archie Brown, John Dunn, Jack Hayward and Adam Roberts, and after several redrafts it received the blessing of the Section. It was agreed that the volume should be edited jointly by Brian Barry, Archie Brown and Jack Hayward and that the Academy should be asked to provide modest financial support to hold three preparatory symposia at which the draft chapters would be discussed. A grant was duly made by the British Academy and contributors were approached.

The timescale adopted merits some comment. The Political Studies Association had produced a twenty-fifth anniversary special issue of its journal *Political Studies* in 1975 but, apart from two or three articles that specifically considered the emerging profession from 1950–75, most of the contributors had other concerns. It was felt that a longer perspective and a sharper focus would be desirable. Hayward's original 'Twentieth Century Founders of British Political Studies' initiative had assumed that, because an excellent study of the nineteenth century already existed in *That Noble Science of Politics* by Collini, Winch and Burrow (Cambridge, Cambridge University Press, 1983) it would not be sensible to go over the same ground. A case could be made, and was made, for going back to the eighteenth century and possibly to the seventeenth century but it was decided that we should concentrate upon the twentieth century on this occasion.

It was also agreed that we should seek some non-British authors so that the British contribution could be seen as others see us. In the event, however, Charles King is the only non-British contributor. One of our initial proposed participants, Stanley Hoffmann, was to our great regret eventually unable to contribute because of a series of health difficulties. We are extremely grateful to Tim Dunne for having stepped in at a very late stage to fill the gap.

Given the broad-based nature of the British study of politics, the scope of the volume was made as wide as possible, with the result that at certain points it overlaps with other disciplines such as philosophy or history. It was not always easy, nor did we deem it desirable, to isolate too pedantically the specifically British contribution, so some latitude was given to authors in how this criterion should be applied to their particular theme.

While the volume endeavours to set out in as balanced a way as possible the varied British contributions to the twentieth century study of politics, it by no means does so uncritically, referring frequently to the objections to the work of this or that writer by other British or foreign scholars. Many of the chapters in this volume illustrate the extent to which Britain has been an 'open society', enriched by the immense intellectual contributions of an élite of exiles, mainly from Continental Europe, escaping from the suppression of liberty that all too frequently prevailed there. So, the 'British contribution' embraces many whose claim to be included derives not from their origin but from their subsequent creative identification with democratic British values, assisted rather than inhibited by not taking them for granted.

The gestation of this volume has been fairly long, having taken some six years from the initial discussion to final publication. A particularly important phase in the preparation of the volume consisted of the three symposia held in the spring of 1997 (the first two at St Antony's College and the last one at the Academy) at which the draft chapters were subjected to searching criticism and comment. In addition to the contributors (not all of whom were able to attend all the symposia) we are extremely grateful to the following colleagues who acted as discussants for one or other of the papers presented at the symposia or participated in the discussion: Erica Benner, John Burrow, David Butler, John Dunn, Rosemary Foot, John Gray, Christopher Hill, Paul Hirst, Jean Leca, Bhikhu Parekh, Guy Peters, Adam Roberts, Alfred Stepan, Paul Whiteley and Robert Wokler.

We wish to record our thanks to Rosemary Lambeth and James Rivington of the Academy for their help and patience as the volume took shape. Finally, we are particularly grateful to Jane Wyatt for carrying the main burden of preparing the typescript with her customary calm and care.

We have endeavoured to make this volume a worthy tribute to our predecessors over the past century, without neglecting the work of our contemporaries. The book provides a conspectus of the development of the academic study of politics for those at present and in the future who are concerned with understanding twentieth century politics in Britain.

Oxford   Brian Barry, Archie Brown, Jack Hayward
November, 1998

1: British Approaches to Politics
The Dawn of a Self-Deprecating Discipline

JACK HAYWARD

Thus the field is indicated for the science of politics: a science dealing with matter so rich and various that from the beginning it has been embarrassed by this weight of wealth.[1]

Political science is just beginning to regain some measure of authority after the acknowledged failure of its confident professions during the first half of the nineteenth century.[2]

The traditionally culture-bound and state-sustaining character of the 'royal science' of politics has set it off from sister social sciences such as economics, which, by virtue of their claim to deductive universality, are better able to achieve a cohesion that is less subject to insularity. This characteristic has been most evident in those totalitarian political systems, such as the former Soviet Union or the Chinese People's Republic, which reduce political education to propaganda and its specialists into exponents of official dogma. At most times and almost everywhere, those who teach or publish their thoughts about politics have been the most exposed to persecution and therefore have the greatest vested interest in the protection offered by liberal safeguards.

The distinctive identity of the British approach to the modern study of politics was formed during the latter part of the nineteenth and early twentieth centuries at a time when the fledgling social sciences were differentiating into separate disciplines and an arm's length relationship

---

[1] Sir Frederick Pollock, *An Introduction to the History of the Science of Politics* (London, Macmillan, [1920 ed.] 1890), p. 8.
[2] G. Wallas, *Human Nature in Politics* (London, Constable, [1929 ed.] 1908) p. 13.

was being developed with the traditional studies of history, law and philosophy. It was also a time when the academic study of politics had not been divorced from its practice and it was considered an advantage to have had personal political experience if one was to describe, analyse and propose improvements in the way politics was actually conducted. Not until the subject was recognized as an autonomous discipline, with its own professionally qualified practitioners, did political zoologists become separated from the denizens of the political zoo. Part of our concern will be to trace some of the vicissitudes of this process by which the specifically academic study of politics parted company from its subject matter and from other disciplines, a self-conscious detachment that has imposed costs as well as affording benefits that have often not been detected, still less evaluated.

If the syndrome of approaches that coexisted within nascent British political science is to acquire some semblance of cultural coherence, we shall have to contrast it with others—notably those of the United States and France—because 'on the recognition of difference depends the significance of the assertion of identity'.[3] However, before these comparisons are made, in an endeavour to show that, despite the pre-existing and enduring differences, British approaches exercised a greater attraction around the turn of the century than they do today, we need to consider some of the prehistory of British political science. We do not do so either in a teleological frame of mind or with the dismissive attitude of those who denigrate their past to flaunt the ephemeral innovations that they have introduced. Such a retrospective glance at our latitudinarian predecessors who, ironically, were much less reluctant to use the appellation 'political science' than their twentieth century successors, may help us to grasp the sources of enduring scepticism about the value of what results from the narrowing that has taken place in the later twentieth century professional pursuit of scientific rigour. It also helps us to understand the implications of the fact that in Britain these older traditions have been adapted rather than repudiated.

A political science without disciplinary frontiers

Before the professionalization of politics as a specialized discipline in the latter half of the twentieth century, writing about statecraft was confined

---

[3] T. H. Green, 'The Word is Nigh Thee' in R. L. Nettleship, ed., *Works* (London, AMS Press, 1885–88) III, p. 225, quoted by W. H. Greenleaf, *The British Political Tradition*, I, (London, Routledge, 1983), p. 9.

merely to part of the activities of philosophers, historians and jurists such as Hobbes, Hume and Bentham, or to politicians and journalists with intellectual inclinations, such as Burke, Bagehot and Bryce. While we shall consider Bryce more closely because he is a transitional figure between political science without political scientists and the professionalization of political studies, those who have studied the discipline's nineteenth century progenitors have detected a 'diffused Burkeanism',[4] reflected in the Whiggish interpretation of British constitutional history as the apotheosis of successful incremental change through piecemeal institutional engineering. Curiously, it was Bagehot, who in *The English Constitution* did such an influential job of demystifying the pieties of the constitutional historians and lawyers, and irreverently stressed that it was the unreflective cast of mind that accounted for the success of those who managed political affairs, who lauds the Whig spirit that pervaded so much of the way the British predominantly approached politics.

> Perhaps as long as there has been a political history in this country there have been certain men of a cool, moderate, resolute firmness, not gifted with high imagination, little prone to enthusiastic sentiment, heedless of large theories and speculations . . . and a steady belief that the present world can, and should, be quietly improved.[5]

A product of the Benthamite University College of London, Bagehot shared something of the great Utilitarian's hostility to 'obsequious quietism' and portentous humbug as well as his desire to reduce politics to a science, but he relied upon the dubious explanatory force of national character, as expressed in commonplace public opinion.

The last British attempt at a self-confidently comprehensive, deductive science of politics was that of Benthamite utilitarianism. Based like Hobbes upon an egoistic hedonism that was to have more enduring success in economics than in politics, Bentham and his leading disciple James Mill purported to have founded a science of legislation. The defeat of Benthamism by the Whig protagonists of the exemplary excellence of the British Constitution was to leave an enduring anti-scientistic mark upon the study of politics in Britain. Macaulay's methodological

---

[4] S. Collini, D. Winch and J. Burrow, *That Noble Science of Politics. A Study in Nineteenth-Century Intellectual History* (Cambridge, Cambridge University Press, 1983), p. 20.

[5] N. St John Stevas, ed., *The Collected Works of Walter Bagehot* (London, *The Economist*, 1965), I, pp. 318–19. On the virtues of English 'stupidity' compared with French cleverness see St John Stevas, *The Collected Works of Walter Bagehot*, IV, pp. 50–3. On Bagehot's shift from national tradition à la Macaulay to national character, see Collini *et al.*, *That Noble Science of Politics*, p. 173; cf. pp. 168–72 for earlier references.

exposure of the a priori attempt to deduce political science from self-interested human nature was the 1829 prelude to the reassertion of an 'inductive' Whig philosophy of British history. The constitution was not a tissue of abuses but a shrine of liberty.

Macaulay managed to bury deductive political science in the name of an inductive political science that turned out to be history under another guise. Empirical political knowledge was to be attained

> by observing the present state of the world,—by assiduously studying the history of past ages,—by sifting the evidence of facts,—by carefully combining and contrasting those which are authentic,—by generalizing with judgement and diffidence,—by perpetually bringing the theory which we have constructed to the test of new facts,—by correcting, or altogether abandoning it, according as those new facts prove it to be partially or fundamentally unsound[6]

History was the repository of enduring political wisdom.

It was the teleological Whig interpretation of English history as the struggle of liberty against despotism, culminating in the seventeenth century conflict between royal absolutism and parliamentary resistance, 'settled' by the mixed system of government born in the 1688 'Glorious Revolution', that became the main foundation of British political culture. However, the credit for the continuity of her unwritten constitution went to the practitioners rather than the theoreticians.

> The perfect lawgiver is a just temper between the mere man of theory, who can see nothing but general principles, and the mere man of business, who can see nothing but particular circumstances . . . But in English legislation the practical element has always predominated, and not seldom unduly predominated, over the speculative . . . Our national distaste for whatever is abstract amounts undoubtedly to a fault. Yet it is, perhaps, a fault on the right side.[7]

Macaulay, both in his criticism and his complacency, still speaks for most of his fellow countrymen, but we would be wrong to believe that this went as far as giving preference to those who *do* over those whose profession it is to *know*, not only in political action but even in matters of political understanding. Bagehot quotes Macaulay's judgement that

---

[6] T. B. Macaulay, 'Mill's Essay on Government: Utilitarian Logic and Politics', *Edinburgh Review*, March 1829, reprinted in J. Lively and J. Rees, eds., *Utilitarian Logic and Politics* (Oxford, Clarendon Press, 1978), p. 128; cf. 101–2, 124, 167–8.

[7] T. B. Macaulay, *History of England* in *Works*, II, pp. 463–4 quoted in Collini *et al.*, *That Noble Science of Politics*, pp. 197–8. The hostility survives in the resistance in Britain to rational choice approaches that recall Benthamism.

the practice of parliamentary debate was likely to impair 'the faculties which are required for close reasoning, or for enlarged speculation' such as would be necessary to produce 'a great original work on political science'.[8]

After its early eighteenth century protagonists such as Defoe and Swift, Walter Bagehot marks the nineteenth century advent of political journalism as an informal instruction in considered political judgement before its transition into an investigative acquisition of muckraking information. Editor of *The Economist* from 1861 to his death in 1877, Bagehot was free of the academic restraint characteristic of those who were increasingly to displace the publicists as the authoritative exponents of political science. His incisive style was usually irreverent and uninhibited, detached and didactic, relying upon aphoristic allusion rather than laboured attempts at systematic but sham scientific demonstration, at which he tried his hand in *Physics and Politics*. The enduring strength of *The English Constitution* (1867) is in his subtle and shrewd, methodological manipulation of the paradoxical complexities of political reality in terms of dichotomies between social stability and change, constitutional dignity and efficiency, governmental inertia and innovation.

Demystification also meant rejecting the Whig celebration of the Constitution as a communion, which was exposed instead as an incongruous imposture, successfully carried off only thanks to anti-intellectual English national character. Bagehot owed to the Whig Burke a sense that the profound mysteries of political culture were far more important than the superficial clarities of constitutional law if one were to account for British political stability and French instability since 1789. 'Only this much is most certain—all men and all nations have a character, and that character when once taken is, I do not say unchangeable . . . but the least changeable thing in this ever-varying and changeful world.'[9] Unlike many other nineteenth century forerunners, Bagehot remains influential because he teaches us in imaginative ways what books with more scientistic pretensions cannot begin to fathom. It is no accident that the two most active parliamentary reformers, responsible notably for establishing Commons specialist committees, Richard Crossman and Norman St John Stevas, were ardent admirers of Bagehot and involved in re-publications of his work.

---

[8] W. Bagehot (ed. N. St John Stevas), *Bagehot's Historical Essays* (London, Dobson, 1965), p. 198.
[9] Ibid. p. 402; cf. 401–9.

Another line of attack upon abstract and deductive utilitarian political science was inspired by the historical jurisprudence of Sir Henry Maine and his onslaught on the Austinian doctrine of law as the command of a sovereign. Together with historians such as Freeman and Seeley, respectively Regius Professors of History at Oxford and Cambridge, Maine sought to provide an empirical legal–historical basis for the study of Comparative Politics. Sir John Seeley's state-centred *Introduction to Political Science* provided an eclectic exposition of the approach, although his debts to Aristotle and to Bagehot in discussing the British Constitution are combined with an attempt to reconcile an impartial political science with a committed Whig patriotism. He stressed 'The importance of adopting the inductive method in politics' as a way of avoiding 'a bastard political science divorced from history'.[10] So defined, a training in politics would fit future imperial administrators with the necessary self-confident skills. Unfortunately, Seeley's prescriptions were directed at running a British Empire that had only another half century to live. In the hands of Edward Freeman, the comparative inductive method incorporated a 'Burkean empiricism which takes the continuity of English history as its political paradigm' and elevates its achievements into 'the culmination of universal history'.[11] The close empirical attention to the classification of political institutions by the development of typologies is an enduring legacy of these predecessors to Bryce and Barker, Herman and Samuel Finer, in their search for pathways through the intimidating mass of historical and contemporary data.

Not least because of the emphasis they placed upon national character as derived from a Whig interpretation of shared British history, dwelling upon the influence of James Bryce and Ernest Barker on a mainstream British approach to politics in the early twentieth century would seem to be especially apposite. Bryce is an important starting point for a number of reasons. He was the first of three British political scientists—Brogan and Laski being the others—who taught the United States major things about their political institutions they did not already know. That this has ceased to be the case for half a century tells us something important about the shift across the Atlantic in the centre of gravity within international political science. Even more than Laski,

[10] D. Wormell, *Sir John Seeley and the Uses of History* (Cambridge, Cambridge University Press, 1980), pp. 128–9; cf. Collini *et al.*, *That Noble Science of Politics*, pp. 225–34.
[11] Collini *et al.*, p. 224.

Bryce was to be both the intimate of Presidents and a prolific contributor to the American press and academic publications. Unlike his predecessors, who 'knew more about the political life of ancient Athens than of modern Washington',[12] the research for Bryce's *The American Commonwealth* (1888) was based, he claimed, only one-sixth on books and documents supplied by American friends and five-sixths on talking to Americans.[13] This book (translated into five European languages) was very highly regarded in the United States, being favourably compared to Tocqueville's masterpiece by Theodore Roosevelt and regarded as an invaluable work of comparative politics by another future American President, Woodrow Wilson.[14]

A close student friend in Oxford of Dicey and T. H. Green, Bryce was appointed by Gladstone to the Regius Chair of Civil Law in 1870, which he held until 1893, long after his election to the House of Commons in 1880. Before developing the empirical study of comparative politics, Bryce concerned himself with comparative law. His intimate friendship with Oliver Wendell Holmes is reflected in a correspondence that lasted half a century, emulated subsequently by Harold Laski. However, from the 1880s (when he briefly served as Under-Secretary for Foreign Affairs in the last Gladstone Government) Bryce's concerns were shifting towards politics. By 1904, when he gave the Godkin Lectures at Harvard on 'The Study of Popular Governments', Bryce—who was a pioneer in the use of census data—advocated the study of institutions based upon observation and comparative analysis leading to probabilistic 'generalization of discerned and recorded fact'.[15] Following the 1906 Liberal landslide, Henry Campbell-Bannerman appointed Bryce to the Cabinet as Chief Secretary for Ireland but from 1907–13 he served as Ambassador in Washington, receiving the unique honour for a foreigner of election as President of the American Political Science Association.[16] On his

---

[12] Ibid. p. 240.

[13] E. Ions, *James Bryce and American Democracy, 1870–1922* (London, Macmillan, 1968), p. 133; cf. H. A. L. Fisher, *James Bryce* (London, Macmillan, 1927), I, p. 238.

[14] Ions, *James Bryce and American Democracy*, pp. 129–31. Wilson's review appeared in *Political Science Quarterly*, 4 (1889), 153–69 and was reprinted in R. C. Brooks, ed., *Bryce's American Commonwealth, Fiftieth Anniversary* (New York, Macmillan, 1939).

[15] Quoted by Ions, *James Bryce and American Democracy*, p. 191. The audience included A. L. Lowell and W. B. Munro, through whom Bryce influenced the American study of comparative government. (Ions, *James Bryce and American Democracy*, pp. 192, 284.) In *The Government of England* (New York, Macmillan, 1908), I, p. vii, Lowell described Bryce as 'the master and guide of all students of modern political systems', while Bryce dedicated *Modern Democracies* to Lowell in 1920.

[16] Ions, *James Bryce and American Democracy*, pp. 198–203, 225.

return to Britain he was created Viscount and took his seat in the Lords in 1914. The 1918 *Bryce Report of the Lords Conference on the Reform of the Second Chamber* anticipated subsequent proposals for the abolition of the hereditary principle, proposing recruitment through regional elections.[17] At a time when the study of international relations had not become separated from political science, Bryce used his British Academy presidential addresses in 1915 and 1916 to promote the idea of a League of Nations championed by his old admirer President Woodrow Wilson.[18]

Having in his youth defended 'popular government' against its critics, Bryce bade farewell with a two-volume comparative study of *Modern Democracies*, both descriptive and analytical, ranging from the Athenian Republic to the Latin American Republics. He deliberately omitted the United Kingdom because he could not be impartial, having followed for 40 years the advice he gave to others that 'The best way to get a genuine and exact first-hand knowledge of the data is to mix in practical politics.'[19] His approach can be summarized in his introductory remarks about the method of enquiry, 'It is Facts that are needed: Facts, Facts, Facts'.[20] Bryce warned against 'hasty inference from a few data', adding:

> Many an error might have been avoided had a body of sound maxims been present to the minds of constitution makers and statesmen; not that such maxims could be used as necessarily fit for the particular case, but that he who had them before him would be led to weigh considerations and beware of dangers which might otherwise have escaped him.[21]

Unlike latter-day political scientists, Bryce could credibly offer advice to statesmen, having been described by Campbell-Bannerman as 'the most accomplished man in the House of Commons. He has been everywhere, he has read almost everything and he knows everybody.'[22] Both more and less would be expected of his professional successors, who decreasingly followed his injunction to take an active part in politics.

In the first half of the twentieth century, academic political scientists such as Ernest Barker, Harold Laski and Sandie Lindsay still bridged the widening gulf between both the humanities and social sciences and

---

[17] Ibid. pp. 242, 283. The Bryce Report was published as Cd 9038 in 1918 (HMSO).
[18] Ibid. pp. 266–73.
[19] J. Bryce, *Modern Democracies* (London, Macmillan, 1920), I, p. 19.
[20] Ibid. p. 13.
[21] Ibid. pp. 18, 22.
[22] Quoted in Ions, *James Bryce and American Democracy*, p. 16.

between political thought and political action. While themselves suffused in the Classical Greek identification of politics and ethics, which came together in an elevated conception of public service, they both wrote for and relied upon the quality press as a medium of political information and education. L. T. Hobhouse could give up his fellowship in Oxford to become a *Manchester Guardian* journalist in 1897, while Barker was not afraid to admit that it was through regular reading of that newspaper that he 'learned such lessons of political wisdom as I have mastered, and acquired the tastes that have since conducted me to a Chair of Politics.'[23]

'Barker appointed himself guardian and interpreter of the national culture' which was based upon a defensive, insular Whig 'reverence for English political institutions', sharing Bryce's concern to trace American institutions to their Whig roots in Britain.[24] In his 1915 study of *Political Thought in England 1848–1914*, Barker emphasizes the Englishness of Herbert Spencer's doctrines in general and *The Man Versus the State* in particular. He traces them to a belief in natural rights based upon religious dissent and economic *laissez-faire*, making explicit what generally remains implicit. The reason that Spencer was 'the thinker who has probably had a greater vogue than any other in the last sixty years' was that

> his philosophy accords with an instinct for individual rights which the course of English history has made almost universal in England. Spencer's philosophy seems to set the stamp of authority on the *prima facie* philosophy of the ordinary man . . . Spencer suited England; and . . . England deserved Spencer.[25]

After going into a prolonged period of decline, his reputation deserved a revival in the 1980s when, in the guise of Thatcherism, many of his precepts were propounded as the new gospel. However, the main reason that his latter day disciples did not acknowledge the origins of their dogmas was that they were now self-evident commonplaces divorced from their progenitor.

---

[23] J. Stapleton, *Englishness and the Study of Politics. The Social and Political Thought of Ernest Barker* (Cambridge, Cambridge University Press, 1994), p. 22 quoting a *Times* 31 December 1931 article.

[24] Stapleton, *Englishness and the Study of Politics*, pp. 12, 35; cf. 4–11, 195–6. On the American debt to English political institutions, see J. Bryce, *The Study of American History* (Cambridge, Cambridge University Press, 1921), pp. 25–6.

[25] Sir Ernest Barker, *Political Thought in England, 1848–1914* (Oxford, Oxford University Press, [rev. ed. 1947] 1915), pp. 111–12; cf. 82ff.

Barker sought to reconcile the normative Idealist philosophy he had imbibed as a disciple of T. H. Green with a concern for the national values of Whig history and the rule of law as the basis of political science.[26] To link a political theory of 'ultimate ends' and legal 'social engineering', Barker offered an empirical and a normative proposition. While political theory studied the interaction of state and society, it was specifically concerned with the state as a legal association and the actual working of the law provided its data. However, to avoid becoming 'merely descriptive politics . . . political theory must ultimately rise to a philosophy of political values and a doctrine of the ultimate ends of organized society. It must, in a word, assume a normative character'[27] so that, like Sir Frederick Pollock in 1890 and Bernard Crick in 1962, a political science that started with Aristotle, ended by returning to him.[28] However, the emphasis progressively shifted in Barker's writings from moral and political philosophy to law.

Barker was impressed by the dominant position of public and constitutional 'legal science' on the European Continent, whereas in Britain the major works of historical jurisprudence by Pollock, Maitland, Vinogradoff and Bryce were simply one of several competing strands in the embryonic science of politics. Maitland turned to Gierke's metaphysical theory of corporate legal personality and the English Common Law to counteract the individualist utilitarianism of Austin and attack the concept of state sovereignty in a way that was to exercise a great influence upon the pluralists. However, as someone who thought that political science was 'either history or humbug', Maitland attacked his mentor Sidgwick's inductivist methodology for improperly attempting to generalize from the diversity of particular historical cases.[29]

The most influential of all publications by the lawyers was A. V. Dicey's 1885 *Introduction to the Study of the Law of the Constitution*, which reverted to a more Austinian view and criticized the relevance of those who sought to reduce law to history and custom as guilty of 'mere antiquarianism'. He sarcastically commented that 'It were far better, as things now stand, to be charged with heresy, than to fall under the

---

[26] J. Stapleton, 'The "National Character" of Ernest Barker's Political Science', *Political Studies*, 37 (1989).

[27] E. Barker, Introduction to O. Gierke, *Natural Law and the Theory of Society* (Boston, Mass., Beacon Press, 1934), pp. xxvii–viii.

[28] Pollock, *An Introduction to the History of the Science of Politics* pp. 2, 134 and B. Crick, *In Defence of Politics* (Harmondsworth, [Pelican ed. 1962], 1964, pp. 21–3, 171.

[29] Collini *et al.*, *That Noble Science of Politics*, pp. 300, 349.

suspicion of lacking historical-mindedness, or of questioning the universal validity of the historical method.'[30] He regarded English political institutions since 1066 as having been characterized by the 'omnipotence or undisputed supremacy throughout the whole country of the central government' and 'the rule or supremacy of law'.[31] While he had some minor reservations about Austin's exposition of the 'dogma' of parliamentary sovereignty, he was careful to stress that it was not deduced from abstract theory but was an inductive generalization based upon 'the peculiar history of English constitutional law'.[32] Although in the century that has elapsed since Dicey's book it has been the subject of much debate among public law professors, notable contributors including Sir Ivor Jennings and E. C. S. Wade, parliamentary sovereignty remains an enduring if contested principle of the study of British constitutional politics.[33]

While Barker identified the British national character with its political institutions, local self-government and voluntary associations, he adopted a moderately pluralist position compared to those who wished to elevate the group into a rival to both the individual championed by Spencer and the state championed by Bosanquet. Barker learned from Maitland that 'whatever else we may say about England, it has certainly been a paradise of groups'[34] but in the search to make both groups and government legally accountable, he preferred Maitland's advocacy of quasi-judicial administrative courts to Dicey's reliance upon parliament. He argued (with a Whiggish concern for balance) that

> The State, as a general and embracing scheme of life, must necessarily adjust the relations of associations to itself, in order to maintain the integrity of its own scheme; to other associations, in order to preserve the equality of associations before the law; and to their own members, in order to preserve the individual from the possible tyranny of the group.[35]

---

[30] A. V. Dicey, *Introduction to the Study of the Law of the Constitution* (London, Macmillan, [8th ed. 1931] 1885), p. 14.

[31] Ibid. p. 179.

[32] Ibid. pp. 68–70. See the comments of S. Collini, *Public Moralists. Political Thought and Intellectual Life in Britain, 1850–1930* (Oxford, Clarendon Press, 1991), pp. 287–301, 326–7.

[33] See 'Exorcising Dicey's Ghost', the Introduction to V. Bogdanor, *Politics and the Constitution. Essays on British Government* (Dartmouth, Aldershot, 1996); cf. C. R. Munro, *Studies in Constitutional Law* (Butterworth, London, 1987), Ch. 5.

[34] E. Barker, 'Maitland as a sociologist', *Sociological Review*, 29 (1937), p. 27, quoted in Stapleton, *Englishness*, p. 72; cf. 87–90.

[35] Barker, *Political Thought*, p. 156.

Following his retirement from his Cambridge Chair of Political Science, Barker championed the British Commonwealth as the international extension of pluralist voluntary association, spreading Whig ideas of Common Law and representative government as adumbrated in the 1931 Statute of Westminster.[36]

Before considering the contributions of the more thoroughgoing advocates of pluralism, G. D. H. Cole and Laski, we need to mention the role of Graham Wallas, the first Professor of Political Science in the London School of Economics and Political Science (LSE), as part of Webb's Fabian Socialist grand design for a meritocratic–technocratic break with the gentleman-amateur Oxford tradition. While Sidney Webb placed an exclusive emphasis upon the instrumental study of institutions, Wallas had started out and in a sense always remained a civic idealist in the Aristotelian mode. He rejected both an Idealist, deductive philosophic abstraction divorced from particular political realities and a Webbian atheoretical empiricism which disjoined piecemeal action from general principles. He wanted to put human beings back into political science, not based on the rationalist behaviouralism of the Utilitarians but upon the non-rationalist psychology of William James, which better fitted his practical experience as a London County Councillor.

> Wallas sought to rebuild political science stripped of ethical assumptions and conclusions, far more limited in its role, but far more effective within these limits. Political science so reconstructed could serve moral ends, but be itself independent of ethics. The political scientist was to be not a philosopher but a social engineer.[37]

While Wallas regarded the competitive civil service as 'the one great political invention in nineteenth-century England' he wanted it to become a more effective problem-solving body of social engineers.[38] This required breaking down the barrier between academic administrative knowledge and practical administrative activity and in serving on the 1912–14 Royal Commission on the Civil Service and as a teacher he

[36] Stapleton, *Englishness*, pp. 99, 110, 186–93. The transformation of the British Empire into the Commonwealth from the 1930s to the 1960s prompted some pioneering studies of colonial administration, in which Margery Perham in Oxford and Lucy Mair at LSE played leading parts, notably by comparing the British and French experience of indirect and direct rule.

[37] M. J. Weiner, *Between Two Worlds. The Political Thought of Graham Wallas* (Oxford, Clarendon Press, 1971), p. 67; cf. 44–6, 61–2, 68.

[38] G. Wallas, *Human Nature in Politics* (London, Constable, [1929 ed.] 1908), p. 249.

anticipated many of the 1968 Fulton Commission recommendations: professionalism, preference for social scientists and a Civil Service Department. He taught many civil servants at the LSE and was elected as the first Fellow of the Institute of Public Administration at its foundation in 1922 but he never wrote a planned book on public administration.[39] His Continental-style vision of a technocrat government by social engineers did not materialize in Britain.

The reception of Wallas's *Human Nature in Politics* was far more favourable in the United States than in Britain, where his arguments for a quantitative behaviouralism were received with scepticism, being turned down by Oxford for the newly-established Gladstone Chair of Politics in 1911. While he tolerated Bryce's comparative study of institutions, he scorned the political philosophers who made 'a conscious or half-conscious attempt to substitute a satisfying picture of that which does not exist for an unsatisfying picture of that which does exist'.[40] An 'honorary American', Wallas preached rather than practised the behaviouralism that was to come into its own in the mid-twentieth century United States. 'He was . . . Moses rather than Joshua: he showed the way out of the desert but he did not himself enter the land of modern political science'.[41] While not himself a pluralist, Wallas made a contribution to its development in Britain by bringing back Harold Laski (his successor to the LSE Chair of Political Science) from Harvard where he had taught from 1916–20. Laski wrote to Holmes after Wallas's death: 'all over the world there are first-rate people in the social sciences who owe their original impulse to him'.[42]

Barker took the chair at Laski's inaugural lecture, having introduced him, when his tutor in Oxford, to the works of Maitland and Figgis.[43] In the second decade of the twentieth century, Harold Laski and G. D. H.

---

[39] Weiner, *Between Two Worlds*, pp. 145–7, 164, 194–5.

[40] Quoted in Collini *et al.*, *That Noble Science of Politics*, p. 368. See his review of Barker's *Political Thought in England*, 'Oxford and English Political Thought', *Nation*, 15 May 1915, 227–8.

[41] Weiner, *Between Two Worlds*, p. 96; cf. 166–74.

[42] M. Howe, ed., *Holmes-Laski Letters* (Cambridge, Mass., Harvard University Press, 1953), II, p. 1401, quoted in I. Kramnick and B. Sheerman, *Harold Laski. A Life on the Left* (London, Hamish Hamilton, 1993), p. 248; cf. 144–6.

[43] Kramnick and Sheerman, *Harold Laski*, p. 59. Barker's laconic opinion of Laski, 'He was too quick to be always accurate'. (Kramnick and Sheerman, *Harold Laski*, p. 60, quoting Barker's *Age and Youth*, pp. 74–5.) Laski gave his daughter Diana the middle name 'Maitland'. (Kramnick and Sheerman, *Harold Laski*, p. 94.) On Figgis, see D. Nicholls, *The Pluralist State. The Political Ideas of J. N. Figgis and his Contemporaries* (Basingstoke, Macmillan, [1994 ed.] 1975).

Cole were the leading exponents of the pluralist attack upon state sovereignty. In this, they followed the medievalist corporatism of the lawyers, Maitland and his disciple Figgis, as well as the anti-Idealist flirtation with pluralism by Lindsay and Barker. R. M. MacIver was also part of this anti-statist revolt but he took pluralism in a sociological direction. He left Britain for Canada in 1915 but, unlike Laski, did not return from the New World.[44]

Laski never completely abandoned pluralism but it was postponed to the post-capitalist period when the coercive state had withered away. Harold Laski's post-pluralist writings—his liberal socialist Fabian tracts of the 1920s and the Marxist writings of the 1930s and 1940s, even his ambitious *A Grammar of Politics* (1925)—took second place to his political and journalistic activism. From his Oxford student days, Laski was a committed socialist, calling for a general strike against the First World War in an anonymous editorial for the *Daily Herald* on 29 July 1914. Before writing regularly for this Labour newspaper in the 1930s (when it was the first daily to sell two million copies in Britain) Laski was involved in editing the *British Worker* during the 1926 General Strike— the year in which he succeeded Wallas as Professor of Political Science.[45] However, his political activities brought him into conflict in the mid-1930s with the Director of the LSE, William Beveridge. Although there was no claim that he did not more than fulfil his academic duties, Laski was compelled to end his weekly column in the *Daily Herald* and reduce his political speaking despite his Bryce-like defence that 'full contact with practical affairs is one of the best ways of understanding the academic problems of politics'.[46] Once bitten, twice shy, Laski would not have welcomed a repeat of the anti-Bolshevik witch-hunt that forced him to abandon his Harvard lectureship in 1920, following his support for the 1919 Boston police strike that elevated Massachusetts State Governor Calvin Coolidge into a prominence that helped him win election as US President.

Laski's view (which he practised, not merely preached) was that an academic should not pretend to be neutral, 'less to avoid his bias than consciously to assert its presence and to warn his hearers against it; above all to be open-minded about the difficulties it involves and honest

---

[44] J. Stapleton, *Academic Political Thought and the Development of Political Studies in Britain, 1900–1950*, University of Sussex, PhD, (1985), pp. 18–23, 57–74.
[45] Kramnick and Sheerman, *Harold Laski*, pp. 243–5; cf. 77.
[46] Ibid. p. 326; cf. 330.

in his attempt to meet them'.[47] The uneasy attempt to preserve a balance between his professional ethic and his political passions led Laski to resist suggestions that he go into parliament. 'He wanted both worlds: the insider's thrill of influencing events and the outsider's capacity to criticize and dissent.'[48] Of the socialist intellectual trio of Tawney, Cole and Laski, Tawney was the most influential scholar, Cole perhaps the most influential ideologically and Laski the most effective publicist and propagandist. Laski and Tawney helped draft the Labour Party manifestos of 1927 and 1928 prior to Ramsay Macdonald winning office in 1929, while Laski drafted the 1931 manifesto following Macdonald's desertion from the Labour Party.

The 1931 crisis played a crucial part in Laski's shift to the Marxist left. Nevertheless, throughout the inter-war years 'Laski was everywhere. He was on royal commissions, at state dinners, at 10 Downing Street, in the popular press and on the radio.'[49] Laski was the darling of the Labour Party constituency associations, topping the poll in elections to the National Executive Committee from 1939 to 1945, the year in which he became party chairman. However, the activist who helped found the Left Book Club and the weekly *Tribune* in the 1930s was ineffectual when it came to back-room ideological steering of a Labour government. 'His real influence and importance waxed when Labour was out of power and waned when it was in power.'[50] This has frequently been the political fate of committed intellectuals, even in countries where they are accorded more esteem than in Britain. Having served for nearly a year from June 1940 as Deputy Prime Minister Attlee's assistant and speech writer, Laski plotted to remove him from the party's leadership both before and after the Labour 1945 victory, which helps explain the tension between the Labour Government and the self-designated guardian of party principles.

Arthur Schlesinger has argued that Harold Laski (almost alone among leading British political scientists to identify himself as a Marxist, albeit an anti-Stalinist) influenced US left-wing thought in the 1930s far

[47] Ibid. p. 333, quoting H. Laski, *The Dangers of Disobedience and other essays* (New York, Harper, 1930), p. 47.

[48] Kramnick and Sheerman, *Harold Laski*, p. 178.

[49] Ibid. p. 287. However, official nervousness about Laski's leftism meant that of 108 BBC wartime broadcasts, 101 were for the Overseas Service—especially those directed to the United States and India where he had many admirers. (Kramnick and Sheerman, *Harold Laski*, p. 457.)

[50] Ibid. p. 435; cf. Ch. 15 *passim* and pp. 481–3.

more than 'any native Marxist'.[51] He had frequently published articles in *New Republic* in the 1920s and regularly lectured in the United States in the 1930s. 'Unlike most left-wing intellectuals . . . Laski loved America' and 'Americans listened to what Laski wrote and said about them.'[52] He championed the New Deal as demonstrating the vitality of democratic government in articles in the United States and in Britain. An extensive correspondence ensued with President Roosevelt and his best-selling advocacy of a strong executive in *The American Presidency* of 1940 was dedicated to Roosevelt. The *American Political Science Review* dubbed it 'as thought-provoking an evaluation of American political practices as has been published in the US in recent decades'; 'it takes its place along with the work of de Tocqueville and Bryce as an acute analysis of American political institutions by foreigners'.[53] Laski had in 1933 written the preface to Denis Brogan's *The American Political System*, in which they had both championed a strong presidency, although by 1954 when Brogan published *An Introduction to American Politics*, he reverted to Bryce's Whig view.[54] Laski's attempt to repeat his earlier success in *The American Democracy* of 1948 failed because of its simplistically Marxist view of the subject. Laski tried to persuade Prime Minster Attlee in 1945 to appoint him Ambassador to Washington, Bryce having 'shown that a scholar politician could successfully interpret and represent Great Britain to the US'.[55] Attlee did not bother to reply, although, as Hugh Dalton—not an admirer—wrote: Laski's 'status in the USA is far higher than in this country'.[56]

The then American Ambassador to the UN, the former academic Daniel Moynihan, observed in 1975 that 'Harold Laski once moulded the minds of so many future leaders' of many of the decolonized anglophone Asian and African states who came to high office after his death.[57]

---

[51] Ibid. p. 390, quoting A. Schlesinger, *The Age of Roosevelt* (Boston, Mass., Houghton Mifflin, 1988), p. 174.

[52] Kramnick and Sheerman, *Harold Laski*, pp. 393, 240.

[53] Quoted in Ibid. p. 402, cf. 398–401.

[54] See the perceptive comments by J. Burrow, 'Some British views of the US Constitution' in R. C. Simmonds, ed., *The US Constitution. The First 200 Years* (Manchester, Manchester University Press, 1989), pp. 130–2.

[55] Kramnick and Sheerman, *Harold Laski*, p. 490, quoting F. Williams, ed., *Twilight of Empire. Memoirs of Prime Minister Clement Attlee* (New York, Barnes, 1962), p. 7.

[56] Kramnick and Sheerman, *Harold Laski*, p. 450, quoting H. Dalton's *The Fateful Years. Memoirs, 1931–35* (London, F. Muller, 1957), p. 149. See also the comment of the Foreign Office reported in Kramnick and Sheerman, *Harold Laski*, p. 458.

[57] Kramnick and Sheerman, *Harold Laski*, p. 320, quoting from *Commentary*, March 1975. On Laski at LSE, see R. Dahrendorf, *LSE. A History of the London School of Economics and Political Science, 1895–1995* (Oxford, Oxford University Press, 1995), pp. 223–32.

His influence upon the Indian political élite was particularly marked, but as a teacher his influence also extended to statesmen such as Moshe Sharett in Israel and Pierre-Elliot Trudeau in Canada. His intellectual impact was of course especially great within the Labour Party: 'among the Labour MPs elected in the landslide of 1945, 67 had once studied with him as either university students, trade unionists in worker education courses or officers in wartime courses'.[58] When he was succeeded at LSE by Michael Oakeshott, his influence there rapidly waned, with Ralph Miliband remaining as an isolated disciple.

Harold Laski was Chairman of the Fabian Society from 1946 to 1948, being both preceded and succeeded by G. D. H. Cole. Together with R. H. Tawney, these two were the leading socialist intellectuals in the inter-war period, when Bernard Shaw and Sidney Webb (who held a chair in Public Administration at LSE) allowed themselves to be blinded by the achievements of Soviet Communism. In their pluralist phase, Laski and Cole were indebted to French syndicalism, but, whereas the legalist Laski particularly followed Duguit in reducing the state to a provider of public services, the libertarian Cole wished to replace it with the worker self-government of guild socialism. 'Laski attacked the state to discredit sovereignty; Cole attacked both to install workers' control.'[59] Cole had been born with the *Fabian Essays* in 1889. 'He inherited this tradition; developed into its *enfant terrible*; then became its leading theoretical and organizational opponent.'[60] Cole repudiated his original attraction to state socialism when he concluded that it would merely shift power from capitalists to bureaucrats. Unlike Barker and Lindsay, who were patriotically reconverted to state loyalty by the First World War, Cole continued to rely upon democratic fellowship expressed through communities of trade unionists. However, the failure

---

[58] Kramnick and Sheerman, *Harold Laski*, p. 587; cf. 586. Among future Labour leaders he encouraged to adopt a political career was a young trade union official, Jim Callaghan. (Kramnick and Sheerman, *Harold Laski*, p. 259.) His former student Krishna Menon was India's first ambassador in London and Mavralankar, the first Speaker of the Indian Parliament, set up a Harold Laski Institute of Political Science in Ahmedabad. Nehru wrote a short preface for an Indian reprinting of Laski's *A Grammar of Politics* in 1956. (Kramnick and Sheerman, *Harold Laski*, p. 589.) His Canadian students spanned the spectrum from the Marxist political theorist C. B. Macpherson to Robert McKenzie, whose *British Political Parties* (London, W. Heinemann, 1955) adopted such a different view to inner party democracy from that of Laski.

[59] A. Wright, *G. D. H. Cole and Socialist Democracy* (Oxford, Clarendon Press, 1979), p. 14. For Barker's critique of guild socialism, see his *Political Thought*, pp. 200–3.

[60] Wright, *G. D. H. Cole and Socialist Democracy*, p. 13. A former extramural politics lecturer, Anthony Wright was elected to parliament as a Labour MP in 1992.

of guild socialism led him from the 1920s into political activism in the Labour movement, just as Laski from the 1930s abandoned pluralism for a liberalized Marxism and a prominent role in the Labour Party.

In a critique of the separation in mid-twentieth century Britain between political thought and political action, Alfred Cobban observed

> Among recent political thinkers, it seems to me that one of the very few, perhaps the only one, who followed the traditional pattern, accepted the problems presented by his age, and devoted himself to the attempt to find an answer to them was Harold Laski . . . Practically alone among political thinkers in Great Britain, he exercised a positive influence over both political thought and action.[61]

Laski at LSE and Cole in Oxford, where he became the first Professor of Social and Political Theory in 1945, also exercised enormous influence upon generations of students. They were on opposite sides when the Political Studies Association was created in 1950, Laski's plea for the title political *science* to be used being rejected in favour of Cole's advocacy of a comprehensive social *studies* emphasis. Cole, who argued that political studies relied on history for its facts and philosophy for its theories, remained opposed to a narrowly positivistic and quantitative political science, declaring in 1954 that 'the deepest insult you can offer me is to call me a "social scientist"'.[62]

Scepticism about the possibility of political science was deeply rooted in the British intellectual tradition, represented notably by the University of Oxford. Writing in 1932, McCallum accurately conveyed both the prevailing attitudes and the state of affairs when he described the study of politics in Oxford in these disenchanted terms. 'The subject is taught by a very few specialists and a large number of philosophers and historians who approach it with varying degrees of enthusiasm or disgust.'[63] In the 1930s, however, they included the future Lord Redcliffe-Maud (chairman of a Royal Commission on Local Government in 1966–9), Patrick Gordon-Walker (a future Labour Cabinet minister) and such distinguished leaders-to-be in the profession as W. J. M. Mackenzie and Sir Kenneth Wheare.[64] The belief that a liberal élite education could

---

[61] A. Cobban, 'The Decline of Political Theory', *Political Science Quarterly*, 68 (1953), 332.

[62] Wright, *G. D. H. Cole and Socialist Democracy*, p. 269; cf. 281. See also G. D. H. Cole, *Essays in Social Theory* (London, Macmillan, 1950), pp. 35–6.

[63] Quoted by D. N. Chester, *Economics, Politics and Social Studies in Oxford, 1900–85*, (Basingstoke, Macmillan, 1986), p. 48.

[64] Chester, *Economics, Politics and Social Studies in Oxford*, pp. 47–8. It was former Politics Tutor Richard Crossman who as minister commissioned the (Redcliffe-Maud) Report of the Royal Commission on Local Government in England, Cmnd 4040, London, HMSO, 1969.

best be acquired through an acquaintance with the political philosophies of Plato and Aristotle, coupled with a knowledge of the history of the political systems of Athens and Rome, survived the Second World War, when mainstream political science was having difficulties in institutionalizing itself.

After the failure to create in the London School a true replica of *Sciences Po* in Paris, with its practical concern to train an élite to serve the state (albeit endowed with radical zeal), the next attempt came with the 1930s creation of Nuffield College in Oxford. The inspiration here was Sandie Lindsay, Master of Balliol College from 1924–49 and the mind behind the creation of the innovative University of Keele in 1950. A teacher of politics in the traditional, classicist manner, Lindsay was concerned to overcome the separation between theory and practice by creating not a Brookings-style institute but a postgraduate college in which there would be a meeting of minds between social scientists and men of action—central and local government officials, politicians and businessmen. Lindsay was convinced that if the traditional separation of political actors and political analysts was breached, this 'could revolutionize the study of contemporary society in England, not only through the high standard of applicable knowledge which it would produce, but even more by the effect it would have in making the theorist and the practical man accustomed to helping and consulting one another.'[65]

Although Cole as Sub-Warden tried in the early 1940s to develop Nuffield College as a centre for research into the problems of post-war reconstruction, he was frustrated in particular by the British disease of official secrecy, which prevented senior civil servants playing any part in this work.[66] We meet here one of the bottlenecks hampering the development of an empirical British political science—lack of access to essential information and the segregation of those who know, but do not write, from those who write, but do not know. So the Oxford reformists, Lindsay and Cole, like their London predecessors the Webbs, failed to institutionalize an applied political science, partly because the acknowledged expertise did not exist on the basis of which they could overcome entrenched official and academic hostility. Not even the upheaval of a world war, in which some of the few teachers of politics acquired

---

[65] D. Scott, *A. D. Lindsay. A Biography* (Oxford, Blackwell, 1971), p. 235; cf. 233–4 and Chester, *Economics, Politics and Social Studies in Oxford*, pp. 68–77.
[66] D. N. Chester, 'Political Studies in Britain: Recollections and Comments', *Political Studies*, 23 (1975), 152.

first-hand experience in government, was able to destroy the barrier between those whose vocations were the *activities* of public administration and political service and those whose vocation was the *study* of politics and administration. As so often happens in Britain, it was in response to external—in this case primarily American—pressure that changes occurred within the academic sphere.

The death of Harold Laski, which prevented him from addressing the inaugural conference of the Political Studies Association in March 1950, marks the watershed between the pre-history of the discipline and its institutionalization in Britain. He had intended to speak on political science but Kingsley Smellie, who replaced him, spoke instead on 'The General State of Political Studies in Great Britain'. Smellie had seconded a proposal by W. A. Robson that the title of the new body should be the 'Political Science Association of the UK' but this was amended (on the proposal of the historian Alfred Cobban) to Political *Studies* Association. When we list some of the names of the sponsors of the new association: Ernest Barker, Denis Brogan, D. N. Chester, G. D. H. Cole, Sandie Lindsay, Michael Oakeshott and E. C. S. Wade, it is clear that the pro-'science' LSE faction was heavily outnumbered.

With this significant terminological battle over, the growing community of British political scientists somewhat suspiciously set out in search of political science. Its development went through three phases. The first decade (1950–60) was marked by a retrospective Whig inclination to complacent description of traditions inherited from the past reflected in the continued teaching of constitutional history and the history of ideas, coupled with a predominantly atheoretical empiricism in the study of political institutions not being seriously threatened by lively but inconclusive debates within political philosophy. This was succeeded by an enthusiastic and optimistic phase of technocratic reformism (1961–74), coinciding with the University expansion of political science and the belief that institutional nostrums could be suggested for national decline. These 15 years of euphoria have been followed since 1975 by a phase of sceptical professionalism, nourished by the failures of the 1960s' ambitions and the reversal of University expansion in the social sciences.

After the (relative) high tide of official interest in the social sciences during the Second World War, from which the economists principally profited, the emergence of an organized international profession under the stimulus of UNESCO with the creation of a Political Studies Association in 1950, meant that there was at last an institutional umbrella under which a variety of allied subjects could shelter. They were loosely enumerated as 'Political Theory and Institutions, Government and Public Administration, Constitutional and Administrative Law, International Relations, International Law and similar subjects'.[67] The product of an uneasy compromise between the founders—with William Robson from the London School and Norman Chester of Nuffield College, Oxford, playing the leading roles—these categories of potential members partly overlapped. In some cases, notably in the instance of the administrative, constitutional and international lawyers, they were—unlike Continental Europe—never to become part of the political studies community. Furthermore, public administration and international relations were in an ambiguous situation, partly sub-sections of a broad-based political studies community and partly autonomous, specialist communities of their own, often with better links to practitioners. The diffident approach of the founders was evident from the recruiting circular send out in 1949: 'It is not suggested that the Association should immediately embark on any ambitious functions or projects.'[68] Despite Laski's clarion-call in a letter to Robson on 22 March 1950 to 'strike out boldly' and 'prepare large-scale plans', members were reassured that they would not be expected to do very much: an annual meeting 'ought to be possible' and 'publication . . . perhaps even of a journal' would be considered, the latter coming into existence in 1953. It was this rather relaxed community of about a hundred scholars who formed the membership of the Political Studies Association in 1950.

The American and French contrasts

If we are to identify what is characteristically British political science, we need to compare it with some of its foreign counterparts, so we shall consider its relationship with the twentieth century transformation that occurred in the American and the French study of politics. Gabriel Almond conveys the patronizing view predominant among the mid- and late-twentieth century American political scientists towards the pre-professional past. 'In the period prior to the First World War,

---

[67] Chester, 'Political Studies in Britain'.
[68] Ibid. Professor F. F. Ridley stated that when he was appointed to a chair of politics in 1966, 'I had to confess that I did not really know what my subject was.' (Ridley, *The Study of Government. Political Science and Public Administration* (London, Allen & Unwin, 1975), p. 14.)

American scholars still viewed themselves as provincials. In the inter-war years, and in such an innovating centre as the University of Chicago, Merriam still urged his most promising students to spend a postgradu-ate year in Europe', but thanks to the emigration of German social scientists there was little need subsequently to do so any longer.[69] In the 1930s, Almond recalled that although 'we had the occasional foreign visitor such as Harold Laski or Herman Finer, who lectured on European Politics, we had no foreign area studies to speak of, and no dissertations focused on the European area'.[70] However, 'In the 1940s–1950s there was a widely shared view that the United States and Britain stood alone in the world as trustees for humane civilization' and this was still reflected in Almond and Verba's *The Civic Culture* of 1963.[71] In subsequent years, the self-sufficiency of American political science as the discipline's superpower inordinately increased. Dismissing the classic political thin-kers, who had occupied a hallowed place in the study of politics, Almond went as far as to assert with self-confidence bordering on arrogance that 'Michael Walzer (1983) has a better grasp of the concept of justice than does Plato and with respect to rigor [and insight as well] Robert Dahl (1989) gives us a better theory of democracy than does Aristotle'.[72] We have come a long way from 1950 when the American Political Science Association advocated 'responsible party government' on the British parliamentary model in preference to American

---

[69] G. Almond, 'Political Science: the History of the Discipline' in R. E. Goodin and H.-D. Klingemann, eds., *A New Handbook of Political Science* (Oxford, Oxford University Press, 1996), p. 76; cf. 77.

[70] G. A. Almond, 'A voice from the Chicago School' in H. Daalder, ed., *Comparative European Politics. The Story of a Profession* (London, Pinter, 1997), p. 54.

[71] Ibid. p. 57.

[72] Ibid. p. 51. The unconsciously ethnocentric nature of Almond's choice of Walzer's *Spheres of Justice* (New York, Basic Books, 1983) perhaps reflects the fact that 'Walzer argued that political philosophy was embedded in the way of life of a specific community, that it was primarily concerned to articulate the latter's self-understanding and that it was necessarily municipal in its scope' (B. C. Parekh, 'Political Theory: Trends in Political Philosophy' in *New Handbook*, p. 509; cf. 514.)

The other Almond reference is to Robert A. Dahl's *Democracy and its Critics* (New Haven, Yale University Press, 1989), who does not adopt the same haughty attitude to the past as Almond. In 'A Brief Intellectual Biography', Dahl recalls the English pluralists and Laski's preface to Duguit's *Law in the Modern State* as being at the source from which he 'probably started down the road towards a "pluralist" interpretation of democratic politics'. (Daalder, ed., *Comparative European Politics*, p. 71.) Dahl also acknowledges that the term 'polyarchy' had been coined before he and Lindblom adopted it in *Politics, Economics and Welfare* (1953), but they had been unaware at the time that it had been used earlier by Althusius and by Ernest Barker in his *Greek Political Theory*, p. 294. (Daalder, ed., *Comparative European Politics*, p. 78, note 3.)

presidential government. Even Almond has to confess that on occasion he and his colleagues were rediscovering the insights of Seeley and Hintze.[73] By the 1990s he was fighting a rearguard battle against the rational choice school, determined to consign the work of his generation to the same historical dustbin in which he had dumped that of his predecessors.

Despite the fact that American behaviouralism had some roots in the British empirical tradition and that Wallas was one of its pioneers, British political science largely ignored transatlantic developments as long as it could. By the end of the 1950s, this was becoming increasingly difficult and the uncompromisingly negative response in the shape of Bernard Crick's *The American Science of Politics* appeared in 1959. It has not really been improved upon since then. The attempt to model political science methodologically upon the natural sciences was based on six tenets: that there were discoverable uniformities in human behaviour; they could be confirmed by empirical tests; the methods by which data were acquired and analysed should be as quantitative as possible; theory should be empirical and predictive rather than philosophical and historical; value-free research was possible and desirable; the search for a macro-theory common to the social sciences took precedence over applied research into issues of reform.

Even before the behavioural revelation had reached its apotheosis in the early 1960s, Crick had criticized its tendency to inhabit 'a bleak and barren world of abstract and arbitrary concepts', 'content to ignore the major problems of politics so long as they can appear to be scientific'.[74] Reassuring his British colleagues a decade before the disenchantment of the late 1960s, that they need not jump on a bandwagon that had stopped rolling, Crick detected 'some signs that the advocacy of a science of politics has now lost its earlier momentum and its dominance even may be in question', notably because of the 'pragmatic realization that the science of politics has not and cannot "deliver the goods" amidst the frustrations of world politics'.[75]

---

[73] Almond, 'A voice from the Chicago School', p. 64. For a less ethnocentric American view, see D. Apter, 'Comparative Politics, Old and New' in Goodin and Klingemann, eds., *A New Handbook*, Ch. 15. See the supplement to the September 1950 issue of *American Political Science Review* for the report of the Committee on Political Parties: 'Towards a More Responsible Two-Party System'.

[74] B. Crick, *The American Science of Politics* (London, Routledge, 1959), pp. 208, 231.

[75] Ibid. pp. 228, 246.

To understand Crick's negative response—a more articulate and thought-out repudiation but representative of the majority allergy to the abstract scientism of the methodologies propounded—it is necessary to read his subsequent tract *In Defence of Politics*, with its vehement reassertion of a liberalized version of the Aristotelian conception of the study of politics. In it he protested against the fact that 'in recent years the growing tendency in the university study of politics has been to make the criteria for research and study not political importance, but various notions of methodological impeccability'.[76] As William Riker put it, 'traditional methods . . . can produce only wisdom and neither science nor knowledge. And while wisdom is certainly useful in the affairs of men, such a result is a failure to live up to the promise in the name of political science'.[77] Ironically, given the Fabian attempt to create a school of applied social science, it was as a Lecturer at the London School that Crick championed Aristotle and Tocqueville against those who wished to substitute predictive scientific laws for understanding.[78] However, to demonstrate some of the weaknesses of American political science was not to vindicate the strength of British 'political studies', and by 1975 Crick was to confess 'I am a bit fed up with *political science*' and suggested that it was time to accept the interdisciplinary implications of being parasitic upon history and philosophy.[79]

If American political science established its bona fides by breaking away from descriptive historical studies, French political science had to break away from the domination of public law. Léon Duguit spoke for the jurists when he peremptorily asserted in an 1889 pre-emptive strike: 'Political phenomena are those which are related to the origin and functioning of the State: they are essentially judicial phenomena . . . and this alleged political science is nothing other than constitutional law.'[80] The initial attempt at a breakthrough came with the establishment in 1871–2 of the *Ecole libre des sciences politiques*, founded, in Emile

---

[76] Crick, *In Defence of Politics* p. 190; cf. 23, 171.

[77] W. H. Riker, *A Theory of Political Coalitions* (New Haven, Conn., Yale University Press, 1962), p. viii. More generally, see D. M. Ricci, *The Tragedy of Political Science. Politics, Scholarship and Democracy* (New Haven, Conn., Yale University Press, 1984), for a sceptical critique of this view. See especially pp. 139–41 and Ch. 5 *passim* on 'The Behavioral Persuasion'.

[78] Crick, *American Science*, pp. 224–6.

[79] B. Crick, 'Chalk-dust, Punch-card and the Polity', *Political Studies*, 23 (1975), 180.

[80] L. Duguit, 'Le Droit constitutionnel et la Sociologie', *Revue Internationale de l'Enseignement*, (1889), quoted by P. Favre, 'France' in W. G. Andrews, ed., *International Handbook of Political Science* (Westport, Conn., Greenwood Press, 1982), p. 166 note.

Boutmy's words, 'with the aim of training for the good of the Nation and the service of the State, men who combine with general culture precise economic and political knowledge as well as a character and civic sense which are above reproach'.[81] Despite the influences of those who thought Germany should be the model after proving its prowess in the 1870 Franco-Prussian War, it was the ultra-Anglophile Protestant, liberal conservative milieu around Boutmy and Taine that shaped the destinies of the political sciences (note the plural with its suggestion of political *studies*) in France. Initially, 'political science' as such played a very modest part in its teaching, the use of the plural (political *sciences*) being indicative of the fact that law and history as well as other social sciences such as economics dominated the syllabus. However, from the start, what was in 1945 to become the *Institut d'Etudes Politiques* relied almost entirely on part-time teachers, may of them drawn from government and industry rather than from among academics, ensuring close links with practical activity. This result was further reinforced by the 1945 creation of the ENA (most of whose products are recruited from *Sciences Po* and hold many of the senior posts in the civil service and both public and private finance and industry, as well as politics) which has meant that while university political science is regarded as 'a discipline whose practical utility and scientific legitimacy appear limited', its role within *Sciences Po* ensures that it enjoys 'a privileged relationship with power'.[82]

Boutmy's conception was close to the comprehensive, comparative, historical and inductive approach fashionable in the Whig tradition, by contrast with the economic and legal deductivism dominant in France.[83] This crossroads conception of the political sciences gave it a somewhat indeterminate character at a time when in France other social science disciplines such as sociology, under the guidance of Durkheim, were strictly defining their boundaries as a way to assert their identity. Like the historian Elie Halévy, 'anglophilia was the main characteristic of Boutmy's liberalism. It might even be said that the "English model" is a constant element in his political thought'.[84] In the Liberal–Conservative

---

[81] Quoted by J. Chapsal, 'L'Institut d'Etudes Politiques de Paris' in *Revue de l'Enseignement Supérieur*, special issue on political science, (October–December 1965), p. 113.

[82] Favre, 'France', p. 161.

[83] P. Favre, *Naissances de la Science Politique en France (1870–1914)* (Paris, Fayard, 1989), p. 89; cf. 24–6, 33–5.

[84] G. Quagliarello, *Politics Without Parties. Moisei Ostrogorski and the Debate on Political Parties on the Eve of the Twentieth Century* (Aldershot, Avebury, 1996), p. 6; cf. 49.

Right-Centre of French politics, the British model of party organization was popular in the 1890s, while on the Socialist Left German Social Democracy was more attractive.[85] Boutmy conducted a sustained correspondence with James Bryce but it was the relationship between Bryce and Ostrogorski, a Russian émigré who first studied at the *Ecole* and wrote his thesis there, prior to preparing his *magnum opus* on *Democracy and the Organization of Political Parties* (1902), that is of more specific concern. Their contrasting views reflect the British and French conceptions of political parties at the turn of the century, based in part on their pioneer field work on American political parties.

Whereas Ostrogorski concentrated upon the similarities between political parties in the United States and Britain, arguing that British parties were becoming like their corrupt American counterparts, Bryce emphasized their differences. This was intended by Bryce to 'quash contemporary fears of the inevitable americanization of English political life. It also aimed to support the use of a rigorous comparative method which could evaluate the importance of institutions and the environment in which they operated'.[86] The conservative historian Lecky had argued in 1899 that Bryce's analysis of the American spoils system was an inevitable democratic evil and Ostrogorski adopted the same view. For good measure, he added (in the spirit of the anti-democrat Taine) that party government was leading to a debasement of the political class and the sacrifice of minorities to public opinion, with party unity and the pursuit of power becoming ends in themselves. Bryce rejected Ostrogorski's attempt to use comparison to arrive at a general theory that neglected the institutional context. As Bryce had put it in an 1867 essay on 'The Historical Aspect of Democracy' against those who misused comparative history to attack popular government:

> we are forbidden to argue loosely and hastily from the circumstances of one state or nation to those of another, or from those of a nation at one period of its growth to the same nation at some other period. We are warned against confounding names with things, and essentials with accidentals; against supposing when we find in different ages and countries two institutions bearing a certain external resemblance to one another, that

[85] R. Huard, *La Naissance du Parti Politique en France* (Paris, Presses de la Fondation Nationale des Sciences Politiques, 1996), pp. 223, 228–30, 293.
[86] Quagliarello, *Politics Without Parties*, p. 115. Bryce wrote the preface to the English edition of Ostrogorski's *Democracy and Organization of Political Parties* (London, Macmillan, 1902), I, pp. xxxix–xlvii.

they are necessarily the same, and that the results which flowed from the one may be expected to flow also from the other.[87]

It was not Ostrogorski but André Siegfried who, as the founding father of French electoral geography, left an enduring imprint upon political science at *Sciences Po*. Ardent Anglophile, he was offered the Chair of British Political Economy in 1910, publishing a series of popular books on Britain after having failed to win a seat in parliament. His eloquent lectures sustained interest in Britain first at *Sciences Po* and then from 1933 at the *Collège de France*, but it was the post-Second World War revival of interest in his more introspective 1913 *Tableau politique de la France de l'Ouest* that has retrospectively established this admirer of Jules Verne's *Round the World in 80 Days* as the Phileas Fogg of French political science.[88]

By the second half of the twentieth century, a Jean Blondel would seek to '"Americanize" European political science—beginning with British political science', notably through the 1970 creation of the European Consortium for Political Research (ECPR).[89] Blondel's proselytization for American political science from Britain can be contrasted with Giovanni Sartori's harshly critical attitude as an Italian exile in the United States, because in America

> theory became largely atrophied into mere research design . . . By the end of the 1970s it was very clear to me that American political science had entered a path that I neither would or could accept: the pattern of excessive specialization [and thus narrowness], excessive quantification and, by the same token, a path leading—in my opinion—to irrelevance and sterility.[90]

---

[87] Quagliarello, *Politics Without Parties*, pp. 117–18 quoting Bryce, 'The Historical Aspect of Democracy' in G. Brodrick, ed., *Essays on Reform* (London, Macmillan, 1867), p. 241. More generally, see Quagliarello, *Politics Without Parties*, pp. 111–21. For the objections by Wallas to Ostrogorski, see Quagliarello, *Politics Without Parties*, pp. 102–7. Goldwin Smith (who, like Dicey, was one of the 1867 essayists) had left Oxford for the United States, where he supported Ostrogorski's analysis, (Quagliarello, *Politics Without Parties*, pp. 122–5) whose arguments follow those made earlier by Goldwin Smith, whereas Lowell develops Bryce's counter-arguments (Quagliarello, *Politics Without Parties*, p. 129; cf. 130–51).

[88] Favre, *Naissance*, Chs. 8–10 *passim*.

[89] J. Blondel, 'Amateurs into Professionals' in Daalder, ed., *Comparative European Politics*, p. 117 and Ch. 11 *passim*.

[90] G. Sartori, 'Chance, luck and stubbornness', in Daalder, ed., *Comparative European Politics*, pp. 96, 98–9. Sartori describes Samuel Finer's attempt to get him elected in 1976 as John Plamenatz's successor as Chichele Professor of Political Theory in Oxford (Sartori, 'Chance, luck and stubbornness', pp. 97–8).

The attitudes of leading Continental political scientists towards British work receded from their favourable disposition in mid-century, to an increasing attraction towards the American alternative. Stein Rokkan began his distinguished career with a thesis on David Hume, translations into Norwegian of works by Bertrand Russell and Harold Laski and a year at LSE in 1950–51 but felt he only became a political sociologist once he came under the spell of the Michigan Survey Research Centre.[91] While Klaus von Beyme reacted against his Heidelberg predecessor Dolf Sternberger's 'devoted Anglophile views' and 'the uncritical Anglomania of many scholars of the older generation', notably towards the British model of parliamentary government,[92] Hans Daalder's response in The Netherlands was much less dismissive. His mentor Jan Barents not only encouraged him to read the work of Lindsay and Barker;

> I had learnt from Barents the joy and value of reading British memoirs and biographies long before I went to the LSE. I married insights obtained from these sources with the more structurally-oriented teachings on British government and administration by Ivor Jennings, W. A. Robson, Norman Chester and others.[93]

His supervisor, William Robson, took Daalder to the annual Political Studies Association conference and the first Editor of *Political Studies*, Wilfrid Harrison, worked 16 hours with him over a weekend to get an article into shape, claiming that 'he rewrote his own articles on average nine times. I remember telling this later to S. E. Finer, who reacted with a characteristic exclamation: "What nonsense. If I can manage in five redrafts, he should be able to do so in seven!"'[94] A post-doctoral year

---

[91] H. Daalder, 'Europe's Comparatist from the Norwegian Periphery: Stein Rokkan 1921–1979' in Daalder, ed., *Comparative European Politics*, pp. 26–8.

[92] K. von Beyme, 'Walking on two legs: comparative politics in East and West' in Daalder, ed., *Comparative European Politics*, pp. 206–8. Arendt Lijphart has written of R. T. Mckenzie's ability to communicate a fascination with British politics through his *British Political Parties*. 'Under his influence, I became a strong admirer of the elegant simplicity of the Westminster model and the excitement of the political game under its rules. Although I have become an advocate of the consensus model of democracy—the very opposite of the Westminster model—I still think that the British-style political game is the more attractive spectator sport.' ('About Peripheries, centres and other autobiographical reflections' in Daalder, ed., *Comparative European Politics*, p. 244). Lijphart expresses his indebtedness to Sir Arthur Lewis' *Politics in West Africa* (London, Allen & Unwin, 1965) as the pioneer consociationalist, although he did not actually use the term.

[93] H. Daalder, 'A Smaller European's Opening Frontiers' in Daalder, ed., *Comparative European Politics*, p. 230; cf. 228.

[94] Ibid. p. 229.

in the United States in 1960–61 led Daalder to adopt a more American orientation towards comparative politics, which he helped to spread in Europe through the ECPR from 1970.

The defence of a distinctive study of politics

What was happening meanwhile in the realm of political philosophy? Peter Laslett famously declared in 1956 that 'for the time being anyway, political philosophy is dead' and Richard Tuck echoed this obituary by asserting that no major works had been published between those of Sidgwick and Rawls.[95] While Brian Barry dismisses as 'oracular literature' the claims in this pre-Rawlsian interlude of all other works than Isaiah Berlin's essay on 'Two Concepts of Liberty', Bhikhu Parekh in the same volume championed the claims of the anti-rationalist Oakeshott and the anti-historicist Popper, adding that Berlin's essay 'has spawned more critical literature than any other contemporary work including Rawls' *A Theory of Justice*'.[96] Parekh argues that the 1950s and 1960s were 'thinker-centred', the 'decades of prima donnas and gurus. Hardly any of the major thinkers engaged in a critical dialogue with others or even referred to them', in contrast to the controversy-suffused post-1970s.[97] Let us look briefly at some of the leading mid-century figures.

The Whiggish, liberal–conservative values that were to shape the political science environment from 1950 were expounded most forcefully from outside the emerging profession. In the early and mid-century, Bertrand Russell—whose impact was felt far outside Britain and the university milieu—switched from philosophical to political writing and activity. Though he had only a limited impact at the time, the economist Hayek, who left LSE for Chicago in 1950 and the logician Karl Popper who came to LSE in 1946, developed a form of methodological individualism that was to become very influential. Hayek's anti-scientism and Popper's rationalistic, hypothetico-deductive model of scientific method, united in their attack on historicism, pointed in different directions (respectively relying upon the market versus

---

[95] P. Laslett's introduction to Laslett, ed., *Politics, Philosophy and Society* (Oxford, Blackwell, [1st series] 1956), p. viii; cf. R. Tuck, 'History' in R. Goodin and P. Pettit, eds., *A Companion to Contemporary Political Philosophy* (Oxford, Basil Blackwell, 1993), p. 72.

[96] B. Barry, 'Political Theory, Old and New' in Goodin and Klingemann, eds., *A New Handbook*, p. 537 and note; B. Parekh, 'Political Theory: Traditions in Political Philosophy', *A New Handbook*, p. 504.

[97] Parekh, 'Political Theory: Traditions in Political Philosophy', pp. 505; cf. 513.

incrementalist, piecemeal, social engineering). Nevertheless, they shared a strong commitment to liberal values, forcefully expounded in Popper's *The Open Society and its Enemies* (1945) and Hayek's *The Constitution of Liberty* (1960). Other voices at LSE that were marginal to political science, such as the anthropologist–sociologist–philosopher Ernest Gellner, made important contributions, notably to the study of nationalism. However, Laski's Chair of Political Science was occupied by Michael Oakeshott, who did not merely embody different political preferences from his predecessor. With his somewhat sceptical idealization of the incomparability of national tradition, the introvert Oakeshott appealed to a tiny group of mainly British scholars, whereas the extrovert Laski had enjoyed an international audience for his optimistic and universalist teaching.

Oakeshott rejected attempts by both rationalists and empiricists to found political knowledge of anything other than history. In his 1951 inaugural lecture on 'Political Education', Oakeshott argued that 'what we are learning to understand is a political tradition' from which the complexities had been summarily abbreviated, whereas 'we have not resources outside the fragments, the vestiges, the relics' of our national tradition.[98] That Whig tradition was above all exemplified in John Locke's *Second Treatise of Civil Government*, which was misconstrued by American and French rationalists 'as a preface to political activity. But so far from being a preface, it has all the marks of a postscript and its power to guide derives from its . . . brilliant abridgement of the political habits of Englishmen.'[99] He concluded that 'The study of other people's politics, like the study of our own, should be an ecological study of a tradition of behaviour, not an anatomical study of mechanical devices or the investigation of an ideology.'[100] While this retrospective contemplation of one's own national political culture reinforced insular proclivities within British political science, it inspired little creative work. However, W. H. Greenleaf's four-volume essay in retrieval of *The British Political Tradition* can be regarded as a sustained attempt to apply Oakeshott's conception to the study of the nation's political history.[101]

Oakeshott's arresting image of political activity as sailing a boundless sea, without destination and with the minimal ambition of keeping

---

[98] M. Oakeshott, *Rationalism in Politics* (London, Methuen, 1962), pp. 130, 126; cf. 125.
[99] Ibid. pp. 120–1.
[100] Ibid. p. 121.
[101] W. H. Greenleaf, *The British Political Tradition* (London, Methuen, 1993), I, p. 87.

afloat, provoked rejection by many, notably W. J. M. Mackenzie, who as Professor of Government at Manchester from 1948 was to be one of the main architects of British political science in its years of expansion.[102] However, the historian Alfred Cobban, in his 1953 reflections on 'The decline of political theory' went further, gloomily speculating upon whether directionless drift betokened that a great tradition was coming to an end, having been sentenced to death by the linguistic philosopher T. D. Weldon in his *Vocabulary of Politics* (1953). He noted that 'politicians have on the whole ceased to discuss general principles', while, as an esoteric academic discipline, political theory had 'become disengaged from political facts'.[103] The attempts to develop a value-free discipline led to an attempt to reduce political theory to either history or science. 'Mostly what is called political science', Cobban acerbically concluded,

> seems to me a device, invented by university teachers, for avoiding that dangerous subject politics, without achieving science. Taken at the highest valuation, political science can give us guidance of the greatest possible importance in achieving the objects we want to achieve; it cannot help us to decide what those objects should be, or even what they are.[104]

Despite Crick's 1959 anathema against the behaviouralism of American political science, British political studies had meanwhile begun to adopt in a piecemeal and incremental fashion many of the theoretical, quantitative and substantive concerns of American political scientists but without their concomitant theoretical self-consciousness. The British response to American political science was a classic case of dynamic conservatism: changing enough so as to keep things basically the same. Particularly when it was associated with a roseate view of the working of the British political system—a view encouraged by much American political science writing into the 1960s—the emphasis upon how successful the pragmatic British capacity for gradualist compromise was in ensuring that 'the more things change, the more they remain the same', gave way by the end of the 1960s to attacks on 'pluralist stagnation'.[105] The pervasive 'What's wrong with Britain' syndrome, based upon its relative economic decline and its loss of great power status internationally, meant that a certain style of teaching and writing that exuded a sense of political legitimation rather than critical political

---

[102] W. J. M. Mackenzie, *Explorations in Government* (London, Macmillan, 1975), Ch. 2.
[103] A. Cobban, 'The decline of political theory' p. 331; cf. 322, 336.
[104] Ibid. p. 335.
[105] D. Kavanagh, 'An American Science of British Politics', *Political Studies*, 22 (1974), 264.

analysis, ceased to be fashionable. Comparative studies first of political sociology, then political development, later of political economy, were clearly less concerned with celebrating consensus and instead high- lighted social divisiveness, stagnation and poor economic performance.

The fear of world war in its two manifestations and their aftermaths, imparted an impetus to the study of the international dimension of politics. Twentieth-century British international relations had distin- guished early protagonists in Norman Angell and Alfred Zimmern but it is with E. H. Carr and Hedley Bull that the study came of age. In reaction against rooting the discipline in the idealistic pursuit of peace, Carr's *The Twenty Years' Crisis* in 1939 developed the realist, power- centred approach from a historical standpoint, which subsequently was given a much more dogmatic American exposition by Hans Morgenthau in his 1948 *Politics Among Nations*. Hedley Bull's *The Anarch- ical Society* of 1977 adopted a much more circumspect, non-behaviour- alist approach, with less pretension to social scientific authority and more recourse to history, law and philosophy. Adam Roberts, a repres- entative of this 'English School of International Relations', has identified five features that distinguish it from its American big brother. First, different national historical experiences shape contrasting interpreta- tions of the world. Second, there is a philosophical emphasis upon the unique character of anarchical international society. Third, there is a distrust of the capacity of grand, legalistic schemes to reshape interna- tional relations. Fourth, there is a preference for national interest over ideology as a guide to state behaviour. Fifth, there is a scepticism about national self-determination as the basis of a new international order in an era characterized by decolonization and decommunization.[106]

In the late 1950s and early 1960s, some of the most lively work in British political science was being done under the leadership in Manchester of W. J. M. (Bill) Mackenzie and the Keele of S. E. (Sammy) Finer, although both of them started their academic careers in Oxford and Finer ended his career there. They had strong reservations about political science as conceived in the United States, which some such as Jean Blondel (ex-Keele) and Richard Rose (ex-Manchester) were to attempt to establish in the Universities of Essex and Strathclyde respec- tively. Mackenzie's sympathetically sceptical attitude towards the

---

[106] A. Roberts, *The Evolution of International Relations*, unpublished paper to the Royal College of Defence Studies, London, 14 January 1997, p. 10. More generally, see S. Smith, ed., *International Relations: British and American Perspectives* (Oxford, Basil Blackwell, 1985).

scientific aspirations of the professionalized study of politics preferred to 'let questions of methodology arise incidentally out of questions of substance'.[107] He admitted that 'It is intellectually impossible to disregard the Americans: one is forced to take up a position in relation to them, even at the risk of losing intellectual independence.'[108] Unlike those such as George Catlin, who left Britain at the end of the 1920s to preach in the United States the adoption of a natural science model for political science, Mackenzie was much more circumspect towards scientism, adopting a standpoint that was closer to, if less acerbic than, that of Sartori. While conceding that American political scientists were better 'trained to organize their material in a disciplined way' by comparison with their British counterparts, Mackenzie predicted that the British emphasis on the state compared to its neglect by American political science marked 'the revival of an old fashion which is due to come round again'.[109] Against ambitious transatlantic claims to propound 'overarching theory', Mackenzie argued that 'in describing and explaining politics we carry a bag of different intellectual tools, using each tool for its own job and not worrying too much about a general theory of tools'.[110] As Mackenzie (who more than most of his colleagues had familiarized himself not merely with the behavioural but other methodological approaches) put it in 1975: 'I see "the discipline" as a group of people rather than as a set of principles, as a continuing debate rather than as an enquiry in the style of natural science . . . methodology comes after practice not before it.'[111] This conception of a community of different if critical scholars, writing individual books rather than contributing to a cumulative advance of authoritative knowledge, was associated with an inability to acquire that status of advisers to public policy makers achieved by 'in and outer' American political scientists or the old boy network of *Sciences Po* and ENA in France.

Another British critic of the behavioural revelation, S. E. Finer, retrospectively recalled that in 1954 he had explicitly rejected the claim that a scientistic

---

[107] W. J. M. Mackenzie, *Politics and Social Science* (Harmondsworth, Penguin, 1967), p. 43; cf. 17–19, 42.
[108] Ibid. p. 68.
[109] Ibid. pp. 68, 323–4.
[110] Ibid. p. 64.
[111] Mackenzie, *Explorations*, p. xxxii. For Mackenzie's influence at Manchester, see R. Rose, 'The Art of Writing about Politics' in Daalder, ed., *Comparative European Politics*, pp. 133–5.

theory is possible for Political Behaviour. Nor therefore is there the slightest reason to assume that unless our General Theory has the completeness and mathematical certainty of Mechanics we shall have failed to make Politics a 'science'. The error lies in assuming that no 'scientific theory' is worthy of that name unless it permits us to predict with a near mathematical certainty. But Biology cannot do this: it must accept 'mutations' and 'freaks' as unpredictable intrusions. Its predictions are short-term and have a low degree of probability. It is a science not so much because it can predict with certainty but because it can offer reasons and causes from events once those events have happened. It is an *explanatory* body of knowledge. So, though to a lesser extent, is Economics; and so too, it seems, is Politics likely to be.[112]

That assessment has worn well. Political scientists have the capacity to offer some hindsight, a little insight and almost no foresight.

The major formative influence on Sammy Finer was his elder brother Herman, who left LSE for the United States but championed the classic comparative institutional approach in his *Theory and Practice of Modern Government* (1932). From this, the younger Finer learned that governmental institutions were the heart of the subject; that comparison was the best means of finding the regularities across space and time that would allow probabilistic explanations, testable by historical evidence; above all that 'Politics was not a dependent variable'.[113] While Sammy Finer was prepared to learn from American political scientists in the selection of areas of research interest, such as legislative behaviour or pressure groups, he resisted their reductionism and their amnesia about past work and their neglect of the historical databank. His comparative study of military intervention in politics—*The Man on Horseback*—was a highly original work about a pervasive but neglected phenomenon. He was old-fashioned in that 'He did not need research grants or research assistants but relied upon a good library, his formidable memory and his own sharp mind.'[114]

---

[112] S. E. Finer, 'Political Science: an idiosyncratic retrospect of a putative discipline', *Government and Opposition*, 15/3–4, Summer–Autumn 1980, p. 361; cf. 354–62.

[113] D. Kavanagh, 'The fusion of history and politics: the case of S. E. Finer' in Daalder, ed., *Comparative European Politics*, p. 21; cf. 16–17.

[114] Kavanagh, 'The fusion of history and politics', p. 19; cf. 20–5. For other general reviews of Finer's work, see Dennis Kavanagh's 'Personality, Politics and Government' in D. Kavanagh and G. Peele, eds., *Comparative Government and Politics. Essays in Honour of S. E. Finer* (London, Heinemann, 1984), Ch. 1; the special issue of '*Government and Opposition*, 29/5, (1994) on 'S. E. Finer'; H. Berrington, 'Samuel Edward Finer, 1915–1993', *Proceedings of the British Academy: 1995 Lectures and Memoirs*, (1996), 347–64; and J. Hayward, 'Finer's Comparative History of Government', *Government and Opposition*, 32 (1997), 114–31.

In a 1997 essay on Carl Friedrich, Klaus von Beyme incautiously claimed that 'Nobody today would dare to deal with all the political systems in history.'[115] This was to underrate Sammy Finer, whose rebuttal of this claim also appeared in 1997. The boldness of Finer's concern for grand comparison culminated in his massive posthumous *History of Government from the Earliest Times* (1997) which has five interrelated themes: state-building, military formats, religious belief systems, social stratification and time span.[116] Having been an early and vigorous critic of the ahistorical approach to state-building characteristic of the behavioural 1960s in American political science, in his final work he argued that only by generalizing from pre-European polities could we distinguish the territorial characteristics of states. Finer settled on two variables to clarify governmental forms: how far rulers had created a standardized central administration and the extent to which a homogeneous culture, language and law were established. For most of history, Finer argued, military organization has been crucial to the founding of political regimes and their survival. The 'coercion–extraction' cycle has been central not merely to supporting armed forces but in the creation of a permanent civil service. He went on to argue that only when the prevailing belief system, social stratification and political institutions were congruent did political institutions achieve enduring stability. However, Finer is careful in his comparative history to avoid allowing his trajectory of inventions with a future and of dead-ends from degenerating into a teleology. It will be the task of subsequent thematic essays to show how far a distinctive British view has persisted into the globalized late twentieth century and whether Finer's *History of Government* is the last trump reasserting an old institutionalism or the resounding affirmation of the potentialities of a new, historical institutionalism within British political science.

---

[115] K. von Beyme in Daalder, ed., *Comparative European Politics*, p. 14.

[116] S. E. Finer, *The History of Government from the Earliest Times* (Oxford, Oxford University Press, 1997), see especially the 'Conceptual Prologue', I, pp. 1–96.

2: Contextual and Non-Contextual Histories of Political Thought

P. J. KELLY

The study of past political ideas and theories has been a central part of the academic study of politics since it began to take a definite shape in the latter part of the nineteenth century. But the real consensus on the importance of studying the history of political thought belies deep divisions over the object, point and method of studying political ideas from the past—divisions that are often both personal and occasionally bloody. It would be possible to provide an account of the origin of the study of the history of political thought in terms of personal antagonism and institutional politics. In recent decades these divisions have resurfaced with the historical revolution associated with the 'Cambridge School' of historians of political thought.[1] The high profile that the 'Cambridge' historians have won for an 'historical' approach might suggest that the British experience of the study of the history of political thought has been one that has led to the triumph of 'history' over less sophisticated approaches to the past.

One has to be wary in speaking of the history of political thought as this already seems to entail a particular method of enquiry. Indeed it is precisely this common sense assumption which in part explains the ease with which the 'Cambridge School' has been able to spread its influence within the field. Furthermore, this explains why the different and often

---

[1] I. Hampsher-Monk, *A History of Modern Political Thought: Major Thinkers from Hobbes to Marx* (Oxford, Basil Blackwell, 1992), p. ix, and N. J. Rengger, *Political Theory, Modernity and Postmodernism* (Oxford, Basil Blackwell, 1995), p. 11.

antagonistic positions of Pocock, Skinner and Dunn are often lumped together as a single school. Any form of enquiry that claims to be 'historical' must obviously be judged by means of criteria derived from the discipline of history, in which case philosophers and moralists whether conservative, liberal or Marxist who ransack the past for some 'practical' purpose can be dismissed as bad 'historians', whose views and 'scholarship' do not deserve serious consideration. But the history of political thought is also primarily an *object* of enquiry and not simply an activity, and conceiving of it in this way leaves open the issue of how best we are to understand the writings of past thinkers and what role their study should play in the study of politics or any conception of political science as a distinct field of enquiry.[2]

If one conceives of the history of political thought in this latter way, then there is no obvious implication that the best or only way of studying it is with the methods of the 'historian' rather than say the moral philosopher, or even literary critic, assuming an non-controversial account of these methods can be given. Indeed, a survey of the development of the genre of British histories of political thought shows that they have been written by authors who often saw themselves as either 'moral philosophers' and moralists, students of literature, or professional 'historians' more narrowly conceived.[3]

[2] See J. Dunn, 'The Identity of the History of Ideas', reprinted in J. Dunn, *Political Obligation in its Historical Context* (Cambridge, Cambridge University Press, 1980), pp. 13–28, 'What is living and what is dead in the political theory of John Locke?', in J. Dunn, *Interpreting Political Responsibility* (Cambridge, Polity Press, 1990), pp. 9–25, and J. Dunn, *The History of Political Thought and Other Essays* (Cambridge, Cambridge University Press, 1996); J. G. A. Pocock, 'The history of political thought: a methodological enquiry' in P. Laslett and W. G. Runciman, eds., *Philosophy, Politics and Society, Series II* (Oxford, Basil Blackwell, 1962), pp. 183–202, *Politics, Language and Time* (London, Methuen, 1972), and *The Machiavellian Moment* (Princeton N. J., Princeton University Press, 1975), and Q. Skinner, 'Meaning and Understanding in the History of Ideas', *History and Theory*, 8 (1969), 199–215, 'Conventions and the Understanding of Speech Acts', *Philosophical Quarterly*, 20 (1970), 118–38, and 'Some Problems in the Analysis of Thought and Action', *Political Theory*, 2 (1974), 277–303. For a comprehensive review of Skinner's methodological position, together with critical essays and Skinner's response see J. Tully, ed., *Meaning and Context: Quentin Skinner and his Critics* (Cambridge, Polity Press, 1988).

[3] It is simply a *non-sequitur* to criticize a philosophical reconstruction of Hobbes's alienation contract by saying 'yes, but it's not Hobbes's argument'. For this assumes that the text only has one meaning, that authorial intentions should be privileged over all other matters in textual interpretation, and that the only interesting questions 'political theorists' should ask of the past is what did the author mean in acting in this way. Issues of authorial intention might well be highly significant, but they are not obviously the only interesting issues, nor do they have an obvious priority over any reading of a text by a past political theorist.

In subordinating epistemological and methodological questions about the nature of historical enquiry to an account of the history of political thought as an object of enquiry, I do not mean to suggest that such theoretical positions are unimportant. It remains true that the methodological and historiographical writings of Pocock, Skinner and Dunn and their critics have had a significant impact on our ideas about the way in which past political thought should be studied and its importance to the wider study of politics. In this chapter I want to leave aside, as far as possible, the 'historians' debate' about how to study the past and focus instead on how the history of political ideas has been approached in the context of British political science. This has the consequence that the discussion will range over commentators who are explicitly *not* historians.

The argument of this chapter is simple. It claims that the current British approaches to the study of past political thought have domestic origins in the development of the study of politics in British Universities, especially Oxford, Cambridge and LSE. Section I accounts for different approaches to the study of political ideas in British political science by invoking differing conceptions of what the history of political thought is, and differing conceptions of the point of studying these divergent objects of enquiry. This section shows how institutional history is connected to the development of a *genre*, and how this history has not been dependent on the direct import of Continental or American intellectual fashions or personalities. Section II delineates the three main British approaches to the study of the history of political ideas in the postwar period. I shall seek to show that, underlying the different philosophical presuppositions and concerns of each approach, is a distinctive set of presuppositions that justifies the claim that there is a 'British' contribution to the study of the history of political thought.

A plurality of approaches: the emergence of the history of political thought

In an important essay on the contribution of history to the development of modern political science, Richard Tuck argues that the significance of the return to 'history' among some political theorists is a response to the resurgence of normative political theory in the shape of post-Rawlsian political philosophy. Because Rawls offered the renewed possibility of reasoning about fundamental political values, in a way that had not been available since the time of Sidgwick's *Methods of Ethics* in the 1870s, there was no longer the need to rely on the study of past political thinkers as a source of the political values that political science could apply in the shaping of its broader enquiries.[4] There is much in Tuck's suggestion, but it suffers from the weakness of assuming a rather homogenous view of the history of political thought.

It is certainly true that one reason why political scientists turned to the thought of great political thinkers of the past was to derive some 'practical' lesson about basic political values. This was true of Ernest Barker, whose Cambridge Inaugural Lecture identifies the study of politics as a part of 'moral philosophy', in which the thoughts of great political thinkers played a significant role.[5] Harold Laski, in his LSE Inaugural Lecture, similarly maintains that the study of political thought from the Greeks to Bentham, Mill and the Idealists is central to any understanding of the realm of the political.[6] Barker and Laski were not, however, simply offering the study of the canon of great political thought as a substitute for what in a post-Rawlsian world is called normative political theory. Rather, they were proposing it as largely constitutive of the study of politics itself. To assume that the study of past political ideas was largely devoted to the recovery of perennial values presupposes a unity of purpose amongst practitioners of the history of political thought and a stable conception of the canon of great political thinkers. But if one returns to the emergence of the academic study of politics in the latter part of the last century, and slightly earlier still, to the emergence of textbook histories of political thought, one can see that this picture is too simple. The object of study was deeply contested. Similarly, while there was some agreement on the centrality of the study of a canon, whatever its content, there was very little agreement as to *why* this should be studied, let alone how.

The idea of a single canon of great political theorists which forms the subject matter of the history of political thought (whether in its historical or philosophical guise) is a relatively modern invention.[7] The study of

---

[4] R. Tuck, 'The Contribution of History', in R. E. Goodin and P. Pettit, eds., *A Companion to Contemporary Political Philosophy* (Oxford, Basil Blackwell, 1993), pp. 72–89.

[5] E. Barker, *The Study of Political Science and its Relation to Cognate Studies* (Cambridge, Cambridge University Press, 1928), p. 39.

[6] H. J. Laski, 'On the Study of Politics', in P. King, ed., *The Study of Politics: A Collection of Inaugural Lectures* (London, Frank Cass, 1977).

[7] The best account of the development of the genre in Britain is D. Boucher, *Texts in Context* (Dordrecht, Martinus Nijhof, 1985), pp. 73–98 and 'Philosophy, History and Practical Life: the emergence of the history of political thought in England', *The Australian Journal of Politics and History*, 35 (1989), 220–238; also important are S. Collini, D. Winch and J. Burrow, *That Noble Science of Politics* (Cambridge, Cambridge University Press, 1983), and J. Stapleton, *Englishness and the Study of Politics: The Social and Political Thought of Ernest Barker* (Cambridge, Cambridge University Press, 1994).

some of the individual texts which compose the canon has its roots in the development of an interest in history as a prelude to philosophising which can be traced at least to Kant and Hegel. The study of Classics in the ancient universities also contributes the idea of a canon of great thinkers, but even there the content of the canon was far from uncontroversial. Yet the idea of a distinct history of political thought in English is no older than Robert Blakey's *The History of Political Literature From the Earliest Times* (1855).[8] Blakey's two volumes were originally to form part of a much longer eight-volume 'History of Social and Political Philosophy From the Time of Charlemagne to the French Revolution in 1790'. This larger project never saw the light of day, but Blakey was able to excerpt his own research from it, to compose his two-volume history. Blakey's history was as its title suggests a history of 'political literature' covering political thought very broadly, including as it does Scripture, ballads, newspapers, dramas, satires as well as political philosophy. Indeed, it is not inappropriate to say, echoing Skinner, that Blakey's concern was a history of political *utterance*. There was, in Blakey's time, no self-selecting canon of texts. Even the great works of political philosophers such as Hobbes owe their incorporation into our contemporary canon of political theorists largely to their rediscovery by Benthamite philosophic radicals in the early part of the nineteenth century.[9] Other, to us obvious, candidates were either still living authors such as J. S. Mill and Marx (living in obscurity to all but members of the International Working Men's Association), or Continental thinkers such as Hegel, who were only beginning to make inroads into British philosophical thought with the Idealists in the latter part of the nineteenth and early twentieth century. Indeed any account of the composition of the canon of 'great' political thinkers cannot be detached from that of the development of academic political studies since the late nineteenth century.

Histories of political thought in Britain were generally textbooks and these were written to serve the institutional requirements of the emerging field of political studies. Thus, with the institutionalisation of the academic study of politics there was an obvious tendency to see the

---

[8] R. Blakey, *The History of Political Literature from the Earliest Times* (London, Richard Bentley, 1855). For a more comprehensive survey of the emergence of the genre of 'histories of political thought', see Boucher, 'Philosophy, History and Practical Life', on which I have drawn heavily in this section.

[9] Sir William Molesworth retired from radical politics in 1838 specifically to edit what was the first edition of the English works of Thomas Hobbes. See Sir William Molesworth, *Hobbes, The English Works*, 11 vols. (London, Longman, Brown and Green, 1839–45).

study of past political thought as an essential component of that study. But this institutionalisation gave voice to a distinct plurality of claims. At Oxford the influence of Idealists such as T. H. Green on writers such as John MacCunn,[10] Barker and—indirectly through Barker—Laski, gave rise to a conception of the canon as being comprised of great political philosophers. For Green, as with other Idealists, the analysis and criticism of past philosophers such as Spinoza, Hobbes, Locke and Rousseau served as an important prelude to his own philosophising on the nature of political obligation.[11] The engagement with the history of political thought in this case taken to comprise political philosophy and not more general political literature, was seen as a branch of moral philosophy and a way of addressing important issues of political practice by appeal to the philosophical analysis of moral principle. However, given Green's Idealist metaphysics he was certainly not of the view that reflection on these past thinkers was a source of perennial truths or answers to political questions. Thinkers of the past may well have had a moral to impart to us, but for Green, and historians of political thought influenced by him, this was not a crude moral that freed one from the need to do one's own political theorizing. The Idealist-inspired approach does, however, deny a categorical separation between the study of thinkers from the past and doing what is now called normative political philosophy, although it makes the point of past study an intellectual preparation for political philosophising through both conceptual clarification, and by providing a philosophical account of the origins of problems of political theory. This view is certainly reflected in Barker's own view of the history of political thought as a branch of moral philosophy.[12] The method employed in such theorizing was largely the logical analysis of arguments that were separable from speculation on the social context of the authors or linguistic conventions. Barker supplements his enquiry with a reflection on the context of thought in some of his studies, but he too, particularly in works such as *The Political Thought of Plato and Aristotle*,[13] is largely concerned with the philosophical analysis of arguments.

---

[10] J. MacCunn, *Six Radical Thinkers: Bentham, J. S. Mill, Cobden, Carlyle, Mazzini, T. H. Green* (London, Edward Arnold, 1907).

[11] T. H. Green, 'The Principles of Political Obligation', in P. Harris and J. Morrow, eds., *T. H. Green: Lectures on the Principles of Political Obligation and Other Writings* (Cambridge, Cambridge University Press, 1986).

[12] E. Barker, *The Study of Political Science and its Relation to Cognate Studies*, p. 39.

[13] E. Barker, *The Political Thought of Plato and Aristotle* (New York, Dover, [1959] 1906).

The influence of the Idealists extended beyond those who subscribed to their philosophical and practical agenda and it gave rise to the emergence of the dominant 'political theory' approach at Oxford which extends through writers such as J. D. Mabbot, E. F. Carritt, John Plamenatz, Sir Isaiah Berlin, to contemporary political theorists such as John Gray, David Miller, Alan Ryan, G. A. Cohen and most recently Jonathan Wolff, all of whom pursue the study of past thinkers as part of the activity of normative political theory, and not as pure 'historical' enquiry. This 'political theory' approach disguises considerable differences in that some use it purely as a means of conceptual clarification prior to doing normative theorizing, e.g. Plamenatz, whereas others such as Mabbott and Carritt see engagement with thinkers of the past as a way of addressing the legitimacy of the modern state. Mabbott, for instance, sees a progressive development of the state and its accompanying conception of citizenship as being paralleled by a progressive development in the theoretical defence of state legitimacy and conceptions of the individual subject. This 'onward and upward' account of political theory, with each generation building upon what went before, he likens to the ascent of the tower of St Stephen's Cathedral in Vienna.[14] In this way the correct approach to the history of political ideas is one which privileges philosophical engagement, as this explains the point of including the history of political thought in the politics curriculum. What also emerges with the development of 'political theory' is the attempt to distinguish political theorists and philosophers among past exponents of political ideas from other kinds of political thought. This distinction is never very clearly worked out, but the institutional division between the study of political thought and institutions, allowed political theorists and historians of political theory to distinguish their object of enquiry, from that of the ideas of pamphleteers and political actors whose contribution is to the shaping of political and legal institutions.

The view from Oxford was not, however, one in which the history of political thought was shaped solely by the philosophical concerns of political theorists. The six volumes of the Carlyle brothers' *A History of Medieval Political Theory in the West*[15] were written with a deliberate indifference to present political concerns in a way that any contemporary 'Cambridge historian' could admire.

---

[14] J. D. Mabbott, *The State and the Citizen* (London, Hutchinson, 1947), p. 9.
[15] A. J. and R. W. Carlyle, *A History of Medieval Political Theory in the West*, 6 vols. (Edinburgh, Blackwood, [6th impression] 1970).

The Cambridge experience was different from that of Oxford. Sir John Seeley's influence on the composition of the Historical Tripos gave a significant place to political philosophy, most notably as found in Sidgwick's *Elements of Politics*[16] which remained a set text right into the 1920s, as part of Seeley's concern to make the study of history a 'school of statesmanship'. Sidgwick's *Elements* was not devoid of discussions of past political philosophers such as Aristotle, Hobbes, Locke, Hume, Bentham, Paley and J. S. Mill, but it is not intended as anything other than a work of what would now be called normative political theory. The irony of Seeley's advocacy of the study of a largely ahistorical form of political theory as part of the study of history was not lost on either his colleagues or subsequent historians. The place of the history of political thought within this conception of the study of politics became a source of considerable and passionate disagreement between the legal historian F. W. Maitland on the one hand and Henry Sidgwick, Alfred Marshall and Seeley on the other.[17] Maitland was hostile to the broad speculative reading of philosophical works and preferred the study of politics through the analysis of legal documents as a means to understanding political institutions: political science was for Maitland 'either history or humbug'. This is a view that certainly finds an echo in Oakeshott, as well as in the utterances of the 'Cambridge School'. That said, Maitland's influence on the teaching of the history of political thought at Cambridge and on subsequent scholars was significant and contributed to a significant alteration to received conceptions of the history of political thought. It is Maitland's legacy that shaped the way in which the history of political thought was approached at Cambridge by subsequent generations. As well as authoring many influential essays Maitland brought Continental conceptions of historical scholarship to the study of the history of political thought through his translation of Otto Gierke's *Political Theories of the Middle Ages*,[18] and his subsequent influence on the work of J. N. Figgis, author of *The Divine Right of Kings* and *Political Thought from Gerson to Grotius, 1414–1625*.[19]

---

[16] H. Sidgwick, *Elements of Politics* (London, Macmillan, 1891).

[17] On the early history of political science at Cambridge see S. Collini, 'A Place in the Syllabus: Political Science at Cambridge', in Collini, Winch and Burrow, *That Noble Science of Politics*, pp. 341–63, and M. Goldie, 'J. N. Figgis and the History of Political Thought in Cambridge', in R. Mason, ed., *Cambridge Minds* (Cambridge, Cambridge University Press, 1994), pp. 177–92.

[18] O. Gierke, *Political Theories of the Middle Ages*, trans. F. W. Maitland (Cambridge, Cambridge University Press, 1990).

[19] J. N. Figgis, *The Divine Right of Kings* (Cambridge, Cambridge University Press, 1896) and *Political Thought From Gerson to Grotius, 1414–1625*, (Cambridge, Cambridge University Press, 1907).

The latter of these works was written as a companion to a lecture course and it further illustrates how the conception of the canon of political thought varies depending upon the author's conception of the scope and nature of political inquiry.

Figgis, who was to have a profound impact on English pluralist thought, used the study of the doctrine of the divine right of kings to explain the emergence of the sovereign state. This could not be traced back to the medieval period, as it was a response to claims for papal supremacy found in the antecedents of the Protestant Reformation. Once absolute supremacy had been assumed by the monarch, it could just as easily be assumed by Parliament and thus the modern state. In tracing the emergence of the modern state, Figgis's canon of political thinkers consisted of minor writers 'without charm or brilliance, or overmuch eloquence, voluminous, arid, scholastic'[20] engaged in ecclesiastical disputes.

But it would be a mistake to see Figgis's historical studies as having no practical purpose. He certainly was not concerned to draw crude morals from the past, and was careful to let the past speak for itself. Yet at the same time the recovery of the origins of modern state sovereignty helped undermine any claims for its absolute necessity. It opened up alternative possible forms of political organisation that do not entail centralised sovereign power or acknowledge the real personality of associations that exist between the individual and the state. Mark Goldie has drawn parallels between Figgis's historical enquiries and those of the contemporary Cambridge historian Quentin Skinner's own work on the emergence of the modern state in the early modern period. Both are first and foremost historians, but the crucial point is that their historical enquiries both challenge and contribute to political theorizing by uncovering the contingency of our present political institutions and their accompanying discourses and by recovering discourses that have been submerged by the dominance of the modern state.

Figgis and Maitland have a different conception of the object of study from that held by political philosophers influenced by the Idealists or even Sidgwick. Nevertheless, both groups see the study of past political ideas as having a role in the study of politics more generally, either as a prelude to, or source of, problems for political theory or as a substitute to normative political theory. For those influenced by Maitland and Figgis, the history of political thought was not obviously a branch of moral philosophy, nor was it simply the broad range of political literature that Blakey and other historians of literature covered. Instead Maitland and

---

[20] Figgis, *Political Thought From Gerson to Grotius*, p. 3.

Figgis have a conception for the canon of political thought which undermines any idea of a simple separation between political theory and the history of political institutions, an idea which certainly shaped the study of politics at Oxford but was also part of the vision of Seeley, Sidgwick and Alfred Marshall. Figgis and Maitland saw the study of political institutions as the study of political thought, but it was political thought about institutions, authority and power, rather than conceptions of the good life for man or morality. In short, the study of history was the study of political thought—but not necessarily the history of moral philosophy or something called normative political theory (a species of study of which Maitland was particularly dismissive). Thus, what separates the perspectives of Idealist-inspired historians and Maitland-inspired historians such as Figgis is not simply a difference in terms of the method but also in terms of the object of enquiry.[21] This is reflected in the disagreements between the heirs of the 'moral philosophers' and the heirs of Figgis and Maitland in the guise of the 'Cambridge School'. Perhaps even more influential in the long term than the Cambridge School's methodological writings will be their challenge to a First XI conception of the history of political thought.

No single perspective gained a dominant position across British university departments of Government or Politics, and this ensured that the canon of political thought studied in courses on the history of political thought was always controversial, with claims being made for great political philosophers, minor historical figures, traditions of thought or whole political ideologies, or a mixture of all of these, as the appropriate object of study. Where stability arose this was as much to do with institutional pressures as with any significant agreement on the nature and content of political enquiry.[22] Histories of political thought—even those of Figgis, the Carlyles, J. W. Allen, Phyllis Doyle or George Catlin[23]—were written primarily to serve courses. Hence there was an

---

[21] I should point out at this stage that although Barker acknowledges this influence of the Idealists in his view of political theory as a branch of moral philosophy, he was also profoundly influenced by the work of Maitland and Figgis, as indeed was Laski, at least prior to his conversion to Marxism.

[22] J. G. Gunnell takes a similar view about the development of the history of political thought as taught in the United States, despite the best efforts of Straussians and others to give a permanent structure to the canon of great political philosophers. See J. G. Gunnell, *The Descent of Political Theory: The Genealogy of an American Vocation* (Chicago, University of Chicago Press, 1993), pp. 251–78.

[23] J. W. Allen, *A History of Political Thought in the Sixteenth-Century* (London, Macmillan, 1928), P. Doyle, *A History of Political Thought* (London, Jonathan Cape, 1937), and G. E. C. Catlin, *The Story of the Political Philosophers* (New York, McGraw Hill, 1939).

inevitable pressure to constitute the canon to reflect those courses, and to draw on texts which students could obtain easily. Of course as textbooks become available they also influence the content of courses and the composition of the canon becomes more stable. This institutional pressure tends to a convergence on certain major figures, such as Plato and Aristotle, Hobbes and Locke, but it still leaves considerable room for diversity. The canon is only ever a compromise holding position between contending groups and approaches.

In assessing the continuing role of the history of political thought in the study of politics within Government or Politics departments, it is significant that amongst all of these plural voices it is rare to find any that regarded the study of the history of political thought as having no practical purpose and thought of it as being of purely detached historical interest. Nevertheless, this practical purpose is also something that is controversial. For some, such as Phyllis Doyle, the history of political thought is the source of perennial questions which each generation has to address; for others it is as a prelude to normative theorizing—a kind of intellectual deck-clearing operation. For positivists such as Catlin, whose approach was shaped by his experience teaching in the United States and Canada, the study of political ideas was a means of recovering and analysing ideals and values that could then be factored into a naturalistic science of politics. Figgis offers a history of—and challenge to—the dominant institutional preconceptions of politics.

The conception one held of the point of studying the history of political thought determined the appropriate method of enquiry. Was it to recover the discrete and particular voices of now-dead debates? Or was it to engage as equals in some timeless conversation with the greats of the past armed only with logic, in which those past thinkers can have as much to learn from us as we from them? An alternative would be to adopt a similar conversational perspective, but one in which we have all the learning to do from the wisdom of the ancients. Or finally, following Laski's turn towards Marxism in the 1930s, we could view the history of political thought as a branch of the sociology of knowledge, whose object is to explain the origins and developments of the ideological forms that shape current political debates.[24] All of these practical perspectives provide a reason for regarding the study of the history of political thought as a central (if not the major) component of the study of politics, and not as an activity that is better hived off into history departments.

[24] See H. J. Laski, *The Rise of European Liberalism* (London, George Allen & Unwin, 1936).

One thing that is clear from the account so far is that the development of approaches to the study of the history of political thought shares the general experience of British Political Science, which, as Jack Hayward has pointed out, has been largely insular and not subject to the claims of imported hegemonic methodologies.[25] Unlike the American experience, the study of history of political thought in Britain has not been transformed by the influx of émigré scholars such as Strauss (though he did briefly pass through Britain), Arendt, Voeglin and Marcuse (and many others of differing political persuasions) all of whom brought their experience of anti-positivist debates in Weimar in the 1920s to confront the 'behavioural revolution' in post-war American political science.[26] Thus the development of the three main British perspectives on the history of political thought in the post-war period are continuations of the 'political theory' and 'historical' approaches that have been discussed already, rather than incorporations of Continental and North American methodological preoccupations.

The history of political thought: a British perspective?

Although the study of the history of political thought continues to allow for diversity of approach to the object, method and point of enquiry, three conceptions of the history of political thought have come to dominate the study of past political thinkers in British universities and in overseas universities whose faculties are populated by British-trained graduates. These approaches are 'political theory', most closely associated in post-war Oxford with the work of John Plamenatz and Isaiah Berlin, the 'historicism' of Michael Oakeshott which has influenced two generations of LSE graduates and the 'linguistic' contextualism of Quentin Skinner. In identifying these three main approaches I recognize that there are many other thinkers such as E. P. Thompson or Raymond Williams who have used the political literature of the past in radically different ways. I have concentrated on these three perspectives because for good or ill they comprise the dominant discourse of the history of political thought in the post-war period. My primary concern with these approaches is not with their precise delineation nor with an historical

[25] J. Hayward, 'Cultural and contextual constraints upon the development of political science in Great Britain', in D. Easton, J. G. Gunnell and L. Graziano, eds., *The Development of Political Science* (London, Routledge, 1991), pp. 93–107.
[26] Gunnell, *The Descent of Political Theory*, pp. 251–78.

account of their emergence, but rather with showing that despite their obvious differences they all contribute to a distinctive British perspective on the study of the history of political thought. This perspective comprises: first, a hostility to any single naturalistic methodology for political science; second, an associated assertion of human agency over structure in attempts to explain political ideas or political discourse; and, third, a recognition of a continuity between the study of the history of political thought and political theory or philosophy. Each of these perspectives is pretty general, but they are not vacuous for they distinguish a British perspective. This approach avoids Continental philosophical fashions, whether Marxist or structuralist, and North American attempts to draw substantive morals about the good life from contemplating the tradition of great texts, such those of Strauss or Wolin.

Despite having diverse origins in particular debates, these perspectives can be seen as offering a response to the kind of ideological reading of the history of political thought that came to dominate the work of Harold Laski in the late 1930s and 1940s, and which is exemplified in the work of his student the Canadian political theorist C. B. Macpherson. Macpherson's *The Political Theory of Possessive Individualism*,[27] employs a Marxist sociology of knowledge to explain the arguments of the seventeenth-century political theories of Hobbes and Locke. The very different forms of argument of Hobbes and Locke are shown by Macpherson to exhibit a significant similarity which can be explained in terms of their respective roles in theorizing the emergent social formation of modern capitalism. Macpherson's argument is certainly not the direct concern or starting point of each of these perspectives, as any adequate account of the emergence of Cambridge 'linguistic' contextualism would also have to include the 'historians' debate. Nevertheless, Macpherson's attempt to reduce political thought to a Marxian sociology of knowledge, with its reductionist approach to language and discourse, subordination of human agency to causal structure, as well as its implications for all political theory as merely a function of social and economic interests, provides a useful starting point.

Plamenatz's view of the study of the history of political thought is rather more mundane than that of Macpherson, but no less valuable for that. Instead of reading the works of past thinkers for some answers to

[27] C. B. Macpherson, *The Political Theory of Possessive Individualism: Hobbes to Locke* (Oxford, Clarendon Press, 1962).

grand questions about how one should live or as moments in the development of ideological forms, they are to be read for a pedagogical purpose. As part of an education in political theory and as preparation for theorizing about 'political' matters, we can gain conceptual clarity and a clearer understanding of some fundamental political principles by analysing the arguments of great thinkers from the early modern period including Machiavelli and Hobbes. Plamenatz's work, along with that of his predecessor as Chichele Professor of Social and Political Thought at Oxford, Isaiah Berlin, are clear examples of that form of political theorizing associated with Oxford, which maintains a continuity between the history of political thought and normative political theory.[28] Plamenatz's method was simply a careful reading of the text (over and over again) and the employment of basic logical tools such as the principle of non-contradiction. In effect it is the application of the methods of 'Oxford' philosophy in both its realist and logical positivist/ordinary language guises to the arguments of past thinkers. His underlying vision of the subject is a conversation among equals with thinkers of the past, where they might have as much to learn from us as we from them. What this position presupposes is the 'realist' view that arguments have an identity and autonomy. This identity is distinct from 'authorial intention' and cannot be reduced to historical context as Marxists and other 'sociologists of knowledge' claim. Certainly, context forms part of the study of past thinkers, but ultimately for Plamenatz it does not determine the arguments which are the chief object of study.

In *Man and Society* and his last work (on Marx), Plamenatz focuses on the way in which human nature is shaped by social relationships. These relationships are constituted (at least in part) by the way in which men think about human nature. This is the issue alluded to in the title of his most famous work. Of course, ideas are shaped by context, as indeed are our own political ideas. Political theory must always bear that in mind and not offer its conclusions as universal timeless prescriptions. But, equally, that shaping does not rule out agency and the ability to think novel thoughts. The danger of both 'hegemonic ideologies' and some crudely reductionist methods in political science is that they do not allow for the subtle ways in which human agency defies overdetermination.

---

[28] Both Plamenatz and Berlin deny that they are 'historians' in any narrow disciplinary sense. See J. P. Plamenatz, *Man and Society*, 2 vols. (London, Longman, 1963), I, p. i, I. Berlin, interview, in R. Jahanbegloo, *Conversations with Isaiah Berlin* (London, Peter Halban, 1991).

Although Plamenatz was not hostile to a naturalistic political science, or to the contextualisation of thought as ideology, he robustly defended the view that neither position precludes the possibility of normative political theorizing, the autonomy of arguments, and the relative autonomy of those who make them. Though it is perhaps stretching the point, there is a parallel between Plamenatz's defence of the autonomy of arguments which defy overdetermination by context and ideological formation, and Quentin Skinner's focus on speech-acts. The latter emphasizes the possibility of novelty and discursive innovation as opposed to structuralist approaches to political language which emphasize normal discourse. At any rate, Plamenatz's approach to the history of political thought mirrors a view of human agency and freedom that is carefully poised between libertarianism and determinism.

Isaiah Berlin's writings, though differing from the more austere analytical style of Plamenatz, share with his Oxford colleague a common general approach to the value and point of the study of the writings of past political thinkers. In some respects they may be said to share a common method, in that neither pays much overt attention to the method of historical enquiry. Recently it has become commonplace to trace the outlines of a version of pluralist liberalism in Berlin's writings.[29] It remains a matter of controversy how developed such a theoretical position is. But it is undoubtedly true that Berlin has used his reflections on the history of political thought to delineate the outline of a plausible political theory that can respond to the modern condition of pluralism about ultimate and incommensurable ends. In this respect, he is like Plamenatz in exemplifying the continuity between the history of political thought and political theory. His essays on 'Equality' and 'Two Concepts of Liberty'[30] in particular, combine conceptual clarification with reflections on the emergence of two ways of conceiving the problem of freedom in a way that is not wholly dissimilar from that of Plamenatz or other 'political theorist' approaches to past thought. Similarly, he has focused much of his attention on undermining the determinist theories of history that underlie Marxist accounts of political ideology such as Macpherson's. This forms part of an affirmation of human agency by maintaining the relative autonomy of political theory from its social and

---

[29] See J. Gray, *Isaiah Berlin* (London, Harper, 1995) and C. Galipeau, *History, Pluralism and Liberty: a Study of Isaiah Berlin's Political Thought* (Oxford, Clarendon Press, 1993).
[30] I. Berlin, *Concepts and Categories* (Oxford, Oxford University Press, 1980), pp. 81–102, and *Four Essays on Liberty* (Oxford, Oxford University Press, 1969), pp. 118–172.

political context. Political ideas emerge within certain cultures, and understanding their emergence can help us understand the ideas themselves; but this is not the same as asserting that those ideas are caused by forces outside of a people's conscious response to their predicament and their reading of the human condition. There are no iron laws in history and all accounts of historical inevitability can be shown to be bogus.[31] Connected to Berlin's obvious commitment to the history and defence of a modern conception of 'negative' or liberal freedom and his assault on unfalsifiable historical teleologies is a theme that underlies much of the post-war defence of the study of the history of political thought; this is that it serves to undermine the pretensions of any narrow conception of political enquiry. For Berlin, the engagement with past texts is justified because it provides us with evidence of human genius and originality which defies reduction to some common theory of human behaviour and action. Furthermore, Berlin has always been careful not to focus his attention on any narrow agenda of political issues. His enquiries are not simply concerned with the agenda of contemporary moral philosophy, nor with the institutional history of the modern state. Instead the subject matter of his enquiries remains broad and deliberately ill-defined. For it is by continually reassessing the boundaries of the concept of the political, that the study of the history of political thought contributes to the study of politics.

The influence of the 'political theory' approach of Berlin and Plamenatz outside Britain is difficult to estimate. Berlin has a wide international reputation, and both Plamenatz and Berlin supervised many graduates who went on to hold university posts throughout the English-speaking world. However, neither is really associated with a school, nor do they have disciples. That said, their approach is mirrored in the approach of American scholars such as George Kateb, Judith Shklar, Stephen Holmes and Nancy Rosenblum. These scholars are all concerned with the historical emergence of *political* liberalism, which has come to dominate much American political philosophy since John Rawls. Their historical enquiries have attempted to undermine conservative, Straussian and more recently communitarian claims that liberalism is a substantive moral position alien to the constitutional tradition of the United States. To this extent these American scholars have a more

---

[31] Berlin, 'Historical Inevitability', *Four Essays on Liberty*, pp. 41–117, and 'The Sense of Reality', *The Sense of Reality: Studies in Ideas and their History* (London, Chatto and Windus, 1996), pp. 1–39.

obvious political objective than the more cautious scepticism of Berlin or Plamenatz.

While it is somewhat easy to find a recognition of the continuity of normative political theory and the history of political ideas, and both a clear defence of freedom and human agency and a denial of deterministic historical teleologies in Plamenatz and Berlin, the work of Michael Oakeshott poses difficulties of a different order. Michael Oakeshott, Laski's successor as Professor of Political Science at LSE, was a singular political philosopher who published little directly on the history of political thought, merely an introductory essay to an edition of Hobbes' *Leviathan* and a series of posthumously published lectures delivered at Harvard in the 1950s.[32] Despite this, he has exerted an enormous influence on the study of the history of political thought through a long-running seminar on the history of political thought and through his lecture course on the history of political thought. This influence extends throughout the English-speaking world through the large number of graduate students who passed through that seminar. However, Oakeshott's hostility to anything so vulgar as a 'methodology' means that it is difficult to point to departments with an Oakeshottian character, in the way in which one can point to Straussian departments in the United States or Canada.

The most distinctive features of Oakeshott's position are his criticism of the view that the history of political thought is continuous with some form of practical enquiry called political theory or moral philosophy, and the denial of the view that the historian's task is to explain causally the structure and development of an argument by relating it to social and political context.

For Oakeshott, normative political theory has no place in the study of politics. It is merely a form of political activity—ideology in the crude sense of being the political programme of some sectional or party interest. Consequently, whatever the history of political thought is, it is not political theory by other means. Those who thought it was included past thinkers such as Bentham, Mill, St Simon or Marx, and contemporaries such as Rawls. These are merely 'Rationalists' trying to foist an unachievable 'Utopian blueprint' onto an unsuspecting public by dressing it up in the guise of a spurious philosophy.[33]

---

[32] M. Oakeshott, *Hobbes's Leviathan* (Oxford, Basil Blackwell, 1946) and *Morality and Politics in Modern Europe: The Harvard Lectures*, S. R. Letwin ed. (New Haven, Conn., Yale University Press, 1993).

[33] M. Oakeshott, *Rationalism in Politics and other essays* (London, Methuen, 1962) and *Morality and Politics in Modern Europe*.

But to leave the matter here would be a caricature of Oakeshott's subtle approach to the philosophy of history and its implications for the history of political thought. Unlike Berlin and Plamenatz, who adopt a broadly realist metaphysics, Oakeshott is a sceptical idealist. This philosophical perspective is set out in *Experience and its Modes*.[34] For Oakeshott, experience is a single connected whole, of which conscious mind, the external world, and the individual are merely partial abstractions. Understanding this manifold of experience requires the adoption of one of two positions, either a particular standpoint or the understanding of the whole in its totality. The former perspective is Oakeshott's 'modes' of understanding, (practice, science and history), while the latter is the perspective of philosophy, which is concerned to comprehend unabstracted experience. This entails that philosophy's task is to map experience onto these three (subsequently four, with the addition of poetry) 'modes' of understanding and to delineate the boundaries between them. Philosophy can have no practical wisdom to deliver, as it is a purely second-order form of enquiry. It is for this reason, rather than a simple ideological hostility to 'interventionist' liberalism, that Oakeshott cannot allow space in his intellectual map for normative political theory: it is simply 'practice' masquerading as knowledge and a category mistake.

History as a distinct and autonomous mode of enquiry views the totality of experience from the past. What this means is that history is a way of understanding the totality of present experience. There is no external perspective called 'the past' against which the historian's enquiries can be compared. Therefore, in order to distinguish what history is we focus not on the object of enquiry, but rather on criteria internal to a certain kind of activity. The activity is that of historians, and the example Oakeshott gives of the kind of historian he has in mind is F. W. Maitland.[35] It follows from this map of experience that the 'historical' mode of enquiry is conceptually distinct from the 'scientific' mode. It is for this reason that 'historical' enquiry must eschew appeal to causality, since causal explanations involve a category mistake, in the same way that normative political theory does.

Where does this leave the history of political thought? Clearly it rules out two perspectives: the kind of 'political theory' approach found in

[34] M. Oakeshott, *Experience and its Modes* (Cambridge, Cambridge University Press, 1933).
[35] Oakeshott sets out to delineate this activity in the essay 'On the Activity of Being an Historian' in *Rationalism in Politics*, and in *On History* (Oxford, Basil Blackwell, 1983).

Plamenatz and Berlin, and the sociology of knowledge as practised by Laski and many Marxists. The most interesting implication of Oakeshott's theory is that it extends the object of enquiry beyond the scope of political thought as theory. The object of enquiry is past political thought associated with the emergence and development of a distinct political tradition; and this includes not only philosophers but ideologues and pamphleteers. In this way, Oakeshott's teaching converges with that of his hero Maitland. Certain 'great' political thinkers (such as Plato, Augustine, Hobbes and Hegel) can be distinguished as philosophers— rather than mere thinkers—because they are concerned with the presuppositions of experience. The study of such 'great' thinkers remains important but is devoid of practical interest. Oakeshott himself had much to say on Hobbes, but it was left to disciples such as W. H. Greenleaf to show in works such as the multi-volume *The British Political Tradition*, what an Oakeshottian history of political thought might look like.

Although Oakeshott's hostility to normative political theory puts him at odds with 'political theorists', what is most crucial in understanding his position is in its implications for the nature of the history of political thought and its relation to the wider study of politics. Oakeshott's conception of the science of politics echoes Maitland's: it is either 'history or humbug'. In this respect, the history of political thought broadly conceived is not merely a bulwark against, but a rival to, any naturalistic science of politics, or deterministic sociology of knowledge. And the study of the few genuine 'greats' is important because it shows through their exemplification of the presuppositions of forms of experience that the subject matter of naturalistic sciences of politics is unnecessarily restrictive. In this way there is a connection between studying the history of political thought and studying politics, in that (as with Maitland) the two are not distinct activities.

Where Oakeshott's position is closest to that of the other British perspectives is in its hostility to the dominance of naturalistic and positivist conceptions of political science methodologies. In this way the history of political thought offers itself as an alternative conception of political enquiry, and a challenge to fashionable views of what the study of politics should be about. In this respect, although the substance of Oakeshott's position differs radically from that of theorists such as Plamenatz and Berlin, the effect is the same: to undermine Marxist and other sociologies of knowledge, and by implication assert the autonomy of ideas. Oakeshott has less to say on the matter of freedom and agency. That said, both his assault on ideological or contextual determination of thought, and his defence of the autonomy of practical life and politics from both history and science provide good grounds for claiming that, as with Berlin and Plamenatz, an ideal of freedom underpins his philosophy of history and conception of political inquiry.

The precise origins of perhaps the most significant contemporary British voice in the study of the history of political thought, the 'Cambridge School', are complex and diverse. But all the 'Cambridge School' historians take a stand against the kind of reductionist Marxism of Macpherson, although they take an equally robust line on the historically insensitive textualism of Oxford political theorists such as Plamenatz. It is not my intention here to give an exhaustive summary of the subtle though significant differences between the works of Pocock, Skinner and Dunn, nor am I primarily concerned with providing an assessment of their methodological prescriptions. Instead, as with the other perspectives, I will address the implications of a 'Cambridge' approach for the value of the study of the history of political thought, and its implications for the study of politics more generally.

In doing this I will focus largely on the work of Quentin Skinner. In doing so I acknowledge that I am doing a considerable disservice to the equally important and distinctive work of Dunn and Pocock, to say nothing of influential Cambridge historians such as Peter Laslett. The advantage of focusing on Skinner is that his methodological writings have attracted particular attention. Moreover he is often seen, rightly or wrongly, as being the most prescriptive. My aim will be to show that, despite his obvious differences with the other perspectives, his views about the connection between the study of the history of political thought and the broader study of politics and political theory, constitute a significant commitment to what I have identified as a British approach to the history of political thought.

Despite the manifesto pledge to provide a 'history of political thought with a genuinely historical character',[36] Skinner has in recent publications tempered the perception of some injudicious followers that such an approach would make the history of political thought an irrelevance in the politics curriculum. A good case can be made for arguing that the significance that Skinner (and Dunn, particularly in recent works)[37] attach to the history of political thought is as a response to

[36] Q. Skinner, *The Foundations of Modern Political Thought* (Cambridge, Cambridge University Press, 1978), I, p. xi.

[37] J. Dunn, *The History of Political Thought and other essays* (Cambridge, Cambridge University Press, 1996) and *Interpreting Political Responsibility* (Cambridge, Polity Press, 1990).

those who would purge the politics curriculum of anything but positivistic and narrowly naturalistic conceptions of political science. Rather than wishing to hive off the study of the history of political thought into history departments, he has increasingly stressed the consequences of his particular conception for the study of politics. However, the redirection of the object of enquiry that Skinner is keen to advocate has been partially obscured by too narrow a focus on his own methodological prescriptions about uncovering the historical meaning of past texts.

Building both on the speech-act theory of Austin and Grice, and on R. G. Collingwood's philosophy of history, Skinner attempts to redirect attention from the artificially-constructed arguments of interpreters such as Plamenatz and Berlin to the utterances of the authors themselves. The meaning of an author's utterance is not best understood in terms of what the propositional content of his argument is, but rather in terms of what the author was *doing* in using language in a certain way. This presupposes the centrality to the study of a past text or language of questions concerning what an *author* meant. We confront Hobbes, or Bentham or James Harrington, by asking: what was he doing in arguing or writing in a particular way? The whole object of enquiry becomes the actions (albeit speech actions) of past thinkers and not the apparently separable prepositional content of an argument. This approach links the understanding of political arguments with understanding the thoughts and actions of political agents, since both thought and action are connected.

One might concede to Skinner that this is an interesting set of questions, but still deny its priority over other ways of understanding an author's argument. But Skinner's point is to deny that there is this alternative perspective. This is not merely to re-emphasize the point that we have to do our thinking for ourselves and leave the past to its own devices. It is to assert the dialogical character of political thinking: arguments, values and the character of human institutions are not static statements of how the world is, because the way the world is is constituted by the arguments of political agents. Focusing on authorial intentions and utterances is not merely an option: it is offered as the only way in which we can understand the intentional actions of political agents. A monological approach to politics, as a neutral description of how the human world works, is not simply inadequate. It mistakes what politics is about. But more fundamentally, it fails to recognize the way in which the object of our enquiries and the way in which we can understand them is constituted dialogically.

Skinner concedes that the reading of past texts and discourses contains an element of interpretative construction, but this is constrained by a residual realism about intentions and the historical past. These intentions can only be recovered by re-entering the discursive practices in which the author was operating, and reconstructing the conceptual frameworks in which his concerns become intelligible. It is perhaps no surprise that Skinner has devoted recent attention to the rhetoric of Hobbes's *Leviathan*, perhaps the paradigmatic example of a monological science of politics and the basis of modern political science models of man.[38]

A preoccupation with the intricacies of Skinner's speech-act theory can divert attention from the strong Collingwoodian influence that shapes his understanding of history—that it is not merely as a means of recovering the past, but a means of understanding human action. And there is a good case for claiming that it is this Collingwoodian influence and its assertion of agency that makes Skinner ultimately hostile to those more structuralist approaches to the language of politics such as Foucaultian genealogy and *Begriffsgeschichte* of Reinhart Koselleck, Otto Brunner and Werner Conze. They either deny subjective agency or else diminish it by emphasizing the ways in which language moulds or speaks through an author. For Skinner, in contrast, we focus on the way in which authors mould and shape language as speech.

This is not to claim that he is wedded to anything so simplistic as a conception of the agent free from any constitutive ties to community, context and spheres of discourse. Equally, however, this recognition should not be taken to overdetermine the subject to the point of her disappearance or denial. It is interesting that, while Skinner is undoubtedly sympathetic to some continental approaches, his historical researches tend to emphasize the ways in which language changes and the ways in which authors subvert the stable patterns of normal discourse. This, for example, contrasts with Pocock's concern with normal language, which places much less emphasis on agency, subjectivity and originality, and far more emphasis on structure.

It is perhaps no surprise that Skinner, like the main figures in the other three perspectives, draws out from historical discoveries a defence of a distinctive ideal of freedom. This is not the 'negative' idea of free-

---

[38] Q. Skinner, *Reason and Rhetoric in the Philosophy of Hobbes* (Cambridge, Cambridge University Press, 1996).

dom as non-interference that we find in Berlin and Plamenatz, or that is implicit in Oakeshott's conception of 'civil association'. Instead it is a republican ideal of freedom which connects strands of negative liberty with a conception of self-rule that is usually associated with Berlin's account of 'positive' liberty. This is not to say that Skinner has after all become a political theorist, and that his historical researches are only political theory by other means. But it does show (as with Figgis) that historical researches, properly conceived, have a contribution to thinking about politics and normative political theory.

John Dunn, whose work is less tainted by a prescriptive 'methodology' than Skinner's or Pocock's, has been particularly keen to emphasize the centrality of an historically informed approach to past political ideas to the broader study of politics. In particular, Dunn has been keen to claim that reflecting on the history of political thought is crucial, in order to prevent our understanding of politics becoming fossilized by inadequate theoretical approaches. We can learn form the past, but as with the other approaches discussed, this lesson is a negative one, rather than the recovery of some solution to the problem of living well.

Skinner has adopted a more cautious line in merely arguing that the history of political thought, properly conceived, can inform the horizons of political theory, remaining more circumspect than Dunn on its relation to the wider study of politics. Even on the relationship with political theory Skinner is cautious. He certainly does not want to suggest that one can only theorize about liberty by engaging with Hobbes, Bentham and Richard Price. But, as the example of Philip Pettit's recent work on republicanism[39] shows, a more historically informed understanding of the sources of modern political languages and conceptual vocabularies can open up fruitful avenues of enquiry for political theorists and political scientists. These possibilities are obscured by reading the text of the past simply in terms of a static political agenda shaped by our own dominant political vocabulary of state, sovereignty, rights and law.

Like Figgis and Maitland before him, Skinner has devoted his historical attentions to the development of the juridical state and its consequent conceptual vocabulary and distinctions, including freedom as the absence of interference. In tracing this development Skinner has also explored those alternative discourses that the hegemony of the juridical

---

[39] P. Pettit, *Republicanism: A Theory of Freedom and Government* (Oxford, Clarendon Press, 1997).

state have drowned out, such as the civic republican tradition which has been a preoccupation of J. G. A. Pocock,[40] and from which Skinner's own concern with republican liberty emerges. The conception of freedom associated with this version of republicanism is neither freedom as 'non-interference' nor a positive conception of freedom with its communitarian implications, but rather freedom as non-domination. This again mirrors the conception of the subject that underpins his conception of language and agency, which draws a fine balance between structure and agency, but which does not dispense with the subject in ways familiar in French post-structuralist thought or even in *Begriffsgeschichte*.

Of all three perspectives, the international influence of the 'Cambridge School' is easiest to measure. Skinner, Dunn and Pocock have trained large numbers of graduates in the English-speaking world, but have also extended that influence to Europe and even Japan where there is great interest in the history of western political ideas. The Cambridge 'blue book' series of *Texts in the History of Political Thought* has also extended Skinner's influence, although not all of the many editors would subscribe to any common methodological orthodoxy. John Pocock has also extended the influence of his own peculiar brand of linguistic contextualism through the seminar programme in 'The History of British Political Thought' at the Folger Library at Johns Hopkins University. Dunn's international influence has less of an institutional character than that of Skinner or Pocock. He has also been more studious in avoiding the accumulation of a school of disciples or giving birth to a method. Nevertheless, from his position at King's College, Cambridge and from the many overseas posts he has held, he has continued to shape the minds of subsequent generations of scholars with his commitment to the moral imperative of understanding past thought in an historically informed way.

Conclusion

The parallels I have drawn between the three most significant British approaches to the study of the history of political thought undoubtedly

---

[40] Q. Skinner, 'Machiavelli on the Maintenance of Liberty', *Politics*, 18 (1983), 3–15, 'The Idea of Negative Liberty', R. Rorty, J. B. Schneewind, and Q. Skinner, eds., *Philosophy in History* (Cambridge, Cambridge University Press, 1984), 'Pre-Humanist Origins of Republican Ideas', G. Bock, Q. Skinner and M. Viroli, eds., *Machiavelli and Republicanism* (Cambridge, Cambridge University Press, 1990). For the influence of Skinner's recovery of Civic Republicanism, see P. Pettit, *Republicanism*.

obscure many significant differences, not least because I have chosen to play down the incompatible philosophical presuppositions each makes about meaning and understanding, language and truth. Nevertheless, there is a parallel between, on the one hand, the preoccupation with freeing the language of the history of political thought from over-determination by theories of ideology, by naturalistic conceptions of political explanation or by structuralist conceptions of language, and, on the other, a deep-seated British scepticism about approaches to politics which deny freedom and agency at some level. Whether this deep-seated intuition can be given an adequate philosophical grounding is another matter, but it does continually re-emerge, albeit in different ways, in the defences each perspective on the history of political thought offers for its centrality to the study of politics.

   In claiming that the history of political thought functions as the conscience of the British science of politics, I am not drawing any parallels with the way in which Strauss or Wolin[41] offered conceptions of the history of political thought as an alternative to the 'behavioural revolution' in American political science. For in none of these British perspectives does the history of political thought have a substantive moral to teach about how to live one's life or purport to find trans-historical universal values. The one common value that all share is freedom and agency. But even here, the moral is a negative one consistent with the scepticism all share towards theories of explanation that undermine agency or narrowly prescribe its content. This is a peculiarly 'modernist' position, and it is no doubt definitive of the 'institutional' orientation of British perspectives on the history of political thought that all are concerned with early and late modern political thought from Machiavelli and Hobbes. This contrasts instructively with the way in which Strauss and, even to some extent, Wolin are concerned with the ancients and with issues of living well and human flourishing—a set of issues that is largely alien among British historians of political thought. Whatever wisdom is to be found in these British perspectives on the history of political thought, it remains the wisdom of the 'moderns'.

Acknowledgements.   An earlier version of this chapter was presented at the University of York and at LSE. I am grateful to Susan Mendus, Matt Matravers,

---

[41] S. Wolin, *Politics and Vision: Continuity and Innovation in Western Political Thought* (Boston, Mass., Little, Brown, 1961).

Duncan Iveson, Brian Barry, Richard Noble, Cillian McBride for their comments. I am particularly grateful for the insightful comments of John Dunn at the British Academy symposium. Although I have not even attempted to respond to all his penetrating suggestions I have benefited from them all the same.

3: Visions of Freedom
The Response to Totalitarianism

NOËL O'SULLIVAN

Perhaps the one safe generalization that can be made about political philosophy is that its greatest products have been the offspring of times of crisis. This, at any rate, appears to be the main lesson to be learned from a glance at the history of western political thought during the past two and half thousand years. The fratricidal chaos that marked the approaching fall of the order of the polis, we are reminded,

> impelled the work of Plato and Aristotle. The break-up of Christendom and the religiously motivated civil strife of post-Reformation Europe gave rise to the work of Hobbes and Bodin. The shock waves of the French Revolution, in combination with the transforming power of industrialization . . . created the circumstances in which Saint-Simon, Comte and their contemporaries set out to build the positive science of society to which they gave the name of sociology.[1]

What holds good of the western tradition of political thought in general holds good, it may plausibly be suggested, of British[2] political theory in the present century in particular. In this case, crisis took the form of the advent of totalitarianism. It was this challenge, above all,

---

[1] D. Levy, *Realism: An Essay in Interpretation and Social Reality* (Manchester, Carcanet, 1981), p. 1.

[2] For present purposes, 'British' political theory will be defined in an extended sense that includes contributions specifically directed to the context of British debate about the social order by contributors with significant personal commitments to this country. One of the best indications of a 'significant personal commitment' is a tenured academic appointment in Britain. This definition is sufficiently flexible for it to cover thinkers who have influenced the course of post-war British theory, regardless of whether they were British by birth, or even of whether they possessed British citizenship at the time when relevant parts of their work were published.

which provoked the few attempts that have been made in Britain since the time of T. H. Green and Bosanquet to situate politics within a broader vision of the human condition itself. In the absence of those attempts, what would remain is a series of restricted analyses of individual concepts, critiques of ordinary language usage, or discussions of problems of method. These latter concerns are not, of course, to be disparaged: important examples of each can immediately be cited by any student of the subject. All, nevertheless, are devoid of the element of vision essential for viewing politics *sub specie aeternitatis*, in the manner of classical political thought.

The purpose of the present chapter is to consider four of the most influential visions which characterized the response to totalitarianism, and in particular the various concepts of limit they provide, since those are the basis of the opposition which each vision sought to oppose to the totalitarian ideal. The first vision which will be considered is the positivist one of Karl Popper, for whom the logic of scientific method offers the only genuine knowledge of man and society. The second great vision is that of Berlin, who abandons positivism and instead presents the human condition in tragic terms, on the ground that it is intrinsically characterized by a plurality of incommensurable and conflicting values. Yet a third vision is offered by Hayek, who sympathizes with Popper's positivism but attempts to go a step further by situating positivism in a naturalistic portrait of the human condition. Finally, there is the 'civil' vision of Michael Oakeshott, which is ultimately grounded in a radical, anti-reductionist conception of human freedom.

The positivist vision: Popper's 'laboratory liberalism'[3]

The least satisfactory of the four visions is Karl Popper's, in which the concept of limit is presented in terms of an ideal of rational morality and politics based on Popper's 'fallibilist' theory of scientific method. The difficulties this view presents may be brought out by examining the concept of the 'open society' which lies at the heart of his political thought.

The open society is one in which the whole of human existence is treated as an opportunity to conduct an endless process of experimenta-

---

[3] For a useful introduction to K. Popper, see J. Shearmur, *The Political Thought of Karl Popper* (London, Routledge, 1996).

tion, in the course of which no aspect of life must remain uncriticized. This ideal obviously links Popper to J. S. Mill. There is, however, a crucial difference, which is that Mill thinks of the process of experimentation as one in which citizens are ceaselessly pursuing truth, whereas Popper thinks of it instead as a process whose outcome, ideally at least, is the endless avoidance of error. The essence of this process, more precisely, is commitment to a scientific procedure of trial and error that eschews verification and is instead content with the modest and viable goal of falsification of hypotheses through a process of trial and error. The details of this fallibilist concept of scientific method are less relevant in the present context than the fact that Popper believes that his account of scientific method is applicable to both the natural and the social sciences, and that he characterizes the open society in terms of its commitment to this method.

It is from this standpoint that Popper interprets the totalitarian experience. Totalitarians are defined as those who have attempted to apply non-fallibilist philosophies to politics. Unfortunately, such an analysis results in little more than the demonizing of a collection of completely disparate thinkers—notably Plato, Hegel and Marx—in order to present them as forebears of Hitler. This simplistic account of the origins of totalitarianism has been the target of so many critics that it would be tedious to mention more than one of the earliest and most eminent. Not long after the publication of *The Open Society and its Enemies*, G. R. Mure wrote that many good men would sympathize with Popper's liberal sentiments,

> but nobody who has seriously studied the works of [his] alleged enemies [of the open society] could think Dr. Popper a reliable historian of philosophy. One would say, indeed, that he had flung scholarship to the winds in the pursuit of his thesis, could one be sure that he had any to fling; but his accounts of Aristotelean and Hegelian doctrine could only be defended from the charge of deliberate caricature on the plea that they are founded on an almost complete ignorance of the originals.[4]

The gross oversimplification which vitiates Popper's account of totalitarianism is not, however, confined to the critical side of his thought: the same oversimplification reappears in his portrait of the 'open society', his alternative to the total state. Here, simplification takes the form of the laboratory analogy referred to above. The result of this analogy is to imbue Popper's political thought with the same utopian characteristic

---

[4] G. R. Mure, 'The Organic State', *Philosophy*, 24 (1949), 206.

that marks the totalitarian regimes against which his attack is directed. This is the elimination of politics in favour of planning. What takes the place of politics in the open society is the purely technical task Popper calls 'social engineering'. Popper believes, of course, that there is all the difference in the world between totalitarian planning and social engineering, because he assumes that the open society is synonymous with a liberal society. His ground for this assumption, however, is not clear. In fact, the position of liberty in the open society appears to be rather precarious, since there is little to warrant Popper's assumption that effective social engineering will coincide with a commitment to liberty. What makes Popper's vagueness about this crucial issue especially disturbing is his express refusal to set limits to the range and scope of reformist political projects, provided that governments carry them out on a piecemeal basis.[5] What is especially noteworthy here is Popper's apparent indifference to such concerns of classical liberal theory as the rule of law and the separation of powers: matters of this kind have no place in the open society.

Ironically, then, Popper's attempt to convert his revised version of positivism into a more secure basis for opposition to totalitarianism than any previously available served only to divorce the concept of limit from the traditional institutional checks upon power once associated with it. In practice, what this meant was that his vision of the open society ultimately rested on little more than an uncritical faith in piecemeal social engineering—a faith completely at odds with, for example, Hayek's conviction that even piecemeal planning was the road to serfdom. Popper was lucky, however: his faith in social engineering chimed in with the post-war faith in planning expressed in the social democratic ideal of the middle way, and therefore added for a time to his reputation as a political thinker, rather than detracting from it.

Berlin and the tragic vision

Popper led political theory into the blind alley of positivism. Berlin's great merit, in the first instance at least, lies in his attempt to extricate it from this blind alley and to ground the concept of limit instead in a version of the tragic vision. In the course of this enterprise Berlin displays a range of philosophical and literary sympathy rarely rivalled by

---

[5] K. Popper, *The Poverty of Historicism* (London, Routledge, 1961), p. 68.

his contemporaries. He also displays a wisdom often denied to those contemporaries, in the form of a profound sense of the ineliminable tensions at the heart of the human condition—a sense which contrasts markedly with the complacent ethos of post-war social democratic thought. It is in this connection that Berlin rightly sought, above all, to remind contemporaries that the friends of 'true' or 'positive' liberty were not defending civil (or 'negative') freedom, but pursuing ends all too likely to destroy it. Although these are admirable achievements, Berlin's deployment of the tragic vision nevertheless suffers from several major flaws. Before these can be identified, however, it is necessary to consider his concept of pluralism in more detail.

Berlin's pluralism is best approached by recalling the principal target against which it is directed. This is the monism which he regards as 'the central current of western thought'.[6] The essence of monism is the belief that all genuine human values can be harmonized within a single ideal of individual and social perfection. Since the time of Plato, Berlin maintains, this belief has been so powerful that it has concealed from sight a possibility which is so painful that western thinkers have rarely been willing to contemplate it, even at the present day. This is the possibility 'that there might exist ends—ends in themselves in terms of which alone everything else was justified—which were equally ultimate, but incompatible with one another, that there might exist no single universal overarching standard that would enable a man to choose rationally between them'.[7]

This then is the idea which inspires Berlin's value pluralism. The core of value pluralism, as he interprets it, is the threefold contention that values are multiple, incommensurable and in potential conflict. Berlin compresses all three ideas into the following formulation:

> Pluralism . . . [is] a truer and more humane ideal than the goals of those who seek in the great, disciplined, authoritarian structures the ideal of 'positive' self-mastery by classes, or peoples, or the whole of mankind. It is truer, because it does at least recognize the fact that human goals are many, not all of them commensurable, and in perpetual rivalry with one another . . . It is more humane because it does not (as the system builders do) deprive men, in the name of some remote, or incoherent, ideal, of much that they have found to be indispensable to their life as unpredictably self-transforming human-beings.[8]

---

[6] I. Berlin, 'The Originality of Machiavelli', in Berlin, *Against the Current* (London, Oxford University Press, 1981), p. 68.

[7] Ibid. p. 69.

[8] I. Berlin, *Four Essays on Liberty* (London, Oxford University Press, 1969), p. 171.

Although Berlin defends this position with great learning and subtlety, he never succeeds in overcoming three major difficulties presented by it. The first concerns the implausible picture of the relation between the self and the world which Berlin's value pluralism appears to take for granted. The basis of this picture is an asocial concept of the individual which has recently been the object of a powerful attack by communitarian critics of liberalism. Long before the communitarian onslaught, however, Bhikhu Parekh noted that:

> Berlin's view of man seems to be underpinned by an unarticulated conception of the natural or pre-social man characteristic of the Contractualist thinkers. Like them, he assumes that men somehow come to possess the liberty to do everything they like. Since the organization of society on such a basis is not possible, he asks how much of their liberty they should give up. As he says, social life involves 'giving up some of our liberty to preserve the rest'. This is a strange view of liberty. It implies that an individual enters society already possessed of liberty, that his liberty is infinite, that it can be broken into bits, and that men in civil society are like traders investing in the common political pool portions of their liberty that are as small as they can get away with in order better to preserve the remainder. Like the Contractualists, Berlin assumes that men derive liberty from nature, not from society, but does not ask if the assumption is valid.[9]

Even if Berlin's excessively abstract concept of the individual is ignored, however, a second major difficulty lies close to hand. This is a basic inconsistency between the moral relativism towards which his value pluralism inexorably seems to point, and the moral absolutism upon which he tends to fall back when he is, for example, discussing fascism.[10] Berlin's relativist tendency is evident, for instance, when he stresses, in a way reminiscent of existentialist contemporaries on the Continent, that arbitrary choice is the only way of coming to terms with the fact that

> ends equally ultimate, equally sacred, may contradict each other, that entire systems of value may come into collision without possibility of rational arbitration, and that not merely in exceptional circumstances, as a result of abnormality or error—the clash of Antigone and Creon or in the story of Tristan—but . . . as part of the normal human situation.[11]

---

[9] B. Parekh, *Contemporary Political Thinkers* (Oxford, Martin Robertson, 1982), p. 46.
[10] M. Ignatieff, 'Understanding Fascism?', in E. and A. Margalit, eds., *Isaiah Berlin: a Celebration* (London, Hogarth Press, 1991), pp. 135–45.
[11] Berlin, 'The Originality of Machiavelli', pp. 74–5.

Berlin's inability to come to terms with relativism is evident, however, when he refers, in 'Two Concepts of Liberty', to 'the moral validity—irrespective of the laws—of some absolute barriers to the imposition of one man's will on another'.[12] It is evident, likewise, when he insists, towards the end of the same essay, that there are natural, wholly objective frontiers to liberty—frontiers, that is,

> not artificially drawn, within which men should be inviolable, those frontiers being defined in terms of rules so long and widely accepted that their observance has entered into the very conception of what it is to be a normal human being, and, therefore, also of what it is to act inhumanly or insanely; rules of which it would be absurd to say, for example, that they could be abrogated by some formal procedure on the part of some court or sovereign body.[13]

The rejection of 'artificial' frontiers, along with the concepts of 'sanity', of 'humanity' and 'normality' invoked here, suggest a moral absolutism for which Berlin's philosophy provides no philosophical justification.

Closely related to this incoherence in Berlin's philosophy of value is a further difficulty, created in this case by his well-known distinction between negative and positive liberty. Negative liberty is freedom from interference by others in whatever one wants to do. This liberty is regarded by Berlin as the foundation of human dignity, although he emphasizes that it is only one of a range of competing values between which a choice must be made. Positive liberty, by contrast, means the power to live in accordance with one's higher self. Positive liberty is therefore compatible with the imposition, either by persuasion or coercion, of some purpose or ideal regarded as good because it facilitates the realization of that self. This latter kind of liberty is thus potentially the road to serfdom in Berlin's eyes, since it constitutes a door through which despotism may enter into the heart of modern liberal democracy. Nevertheless, Berlin does not maintain that positive liberty is invariably unacceptable, but only that it inevitably entails the sacrifice of negative liberty, and the consequent diminution of human dignity.

The problem presented by this view may be brought out by considering the concept of negative liberty more closely. To be precise, this concept enshrines a hard core of romantic anarchism at the very heart of Berlin's political thought. It does so because, if negative liberty means freedom from interference by others, it becomes possible to reject

[12] Berlin, *Four Essays on Liberty*, p. 166.
[13] Ibid. p. 165.

civilization itself, on the ground that it inevitably entails subjection to non-voluntary restraints imposed by others. This may sound a preposterous suggestion, not least because Berlin himself was a profoundly civilized man. Berlin's anarchic impulse, however, is all too apparent in his fundamental suspicion of all institutionalization, which he instinctively tends to regard as an intrinsic threat to the area of free will which negative liberty is intended to protect. This suspicion is evident, above all, in Berlin's inability to theorize adequately the institution most vital for the implementation of the liberal pluralist position he himself upholds, which is the rule of law.

For Berlin, law is an intrinsic restriction upon the area of free choice required by negative liberty, rather than a defence of that area. He does not, of course, maintain on this account that there should be no law, but that is by the way: what is of significance for present purposes is his assertion that liberty and law are intrinsically opposed. 'Every law', he writes,

> seems to me to curtail *some* liberty, although it may be a means to increasing another. Whether it increases the total sum of attainable liberty will of course depend on the particular situation. Even a law which enacts that no one shall coerce anyone in a given sphere, while it obviously increases the freedom of the majority, is an 'infraction' of the freedom of potential bullies and policemen. 'Infraction' may, as in this case, be highly desirable, but it remains 'infraction'.[14]

The confusion entailed by Berlin's view of law as a necessary curtailment of some liberty or other was subsequently brought out by H. L. Hart in *The Concept of Law*, one of the landmarks of post-war British political theory. In that work Hart maintained that constitutional law (to which he gave the name primary rules) does not curtail an activity but defines a status, namely that of citizenship, together with the system of governmental offices which that status ultimately entails. Likewise, much contractual law does not curtail the activity to which it relates, but simply makes that activity possible. The marriage contract, for example, would be impossible without the body of law which defines what constitutes a binding contract. Hart's non-coercive theory of law was later to be taken a stage further by Michael Oakeshott, when he distinguished between the formal, essentially non-directive (and hence 'non-curtailing') character of law in civil association, in which it takes the form of impersonal rules, and the fundamentally directive character of

[14] Berlin, *Four Essays on Liberty*, p. xlix, fn. 1 (italics in the original text).

law in what he termed enterprise association, where law takes the form, not of rules, but of orders and commands addressed to specific groups of individuals.

Berlin's confusion about the nature of law, it may be noticed, is symptomatic of a more general confusion about the nature of sovereignty. This confusion consists in his definition of sovereignty as unlimited authority,[15] in a sense which treats this as synonymous with unlimited *power*. The outcome of this confusion is a serious misinterpretation of the role of sovereignty in the thought of Hobbes, the first modern theorist of civil association.

Hobbes, Berlin writes, is to be praised for his candid admission that sovereignty enslaves: 'he [Hobbes] justifies this slavery, but at least did not have the effrontery to call it freedom'.[16] The most striking feature of Hobbes' thought, however, is that he does *not* make the candid admission with which Berlin credits him. In fact, Hobbes could not possibly make it, because he does not consider that sovereignty enslaves. Far from destroying freedom, Hobbes regards sovereignty as protecting the very pluralism to which Berlin himself is committed. Sovereignty in its civil mode does this, for Hobbes, not by creating negative freedom, but by creating *civil* freedom. Sovereignty in civil association, in a word, is not the destruction of pluralism by despotism, as Berlin assumes, but is on the contrary the means by which legitimacy and pluralism are reconciled. Sovereignty in its civil form permits this reconciliation for two reasons. On the one hand, it does not consist, *pace* Berlin, of orders and commands promulgated by power, but of rules which do not impose substantive restraints upon the aims and purposes of subjects. On the other, as Hobbes makes clear, sovereignty does not consist of *unlimited* authority, as Berlin assumes, but consists, rather, of *final* authority (final, that is, in relation to the claims of both internal subjects and external challengers).

It is now time to turn to the most problematic aspect of Berlin's work. This relates not so much to what he actually says, as to the perspective from which he says it. To be precise: Berlin fails to distinguish clearly between the ethical and the political standpoints.

As Hobbes makes clear in his portrait of the state of nature, the political standpoint relates to *the existence of a plurality of agents each of whom is concerned to pursue a self-chosen life, and none of whom may claim to*

---

[15] Ibid. p. 163.
[16] Ibid. p. 164.

possess an intrinsically privileged position of command in relation to the others.
Berlin, however, is not so much concerned with a plurality of *agents*, as
with the incommensurability and incompatibility of what he sometimes
terms 'forms of life', sometimes 'ends', sometimes 'systems of values',
and most commonly, just 'values'.[17] It is the relationship between these
forms of life or values, then—that is, the *ethical* problem—that interests
him, rather than the nature of the political bond that is capable of
holding a plurality of agents together.

The fact that Berlin's perspective is ethical rather than political
explains, in particular, the most extraordinary omission in his writings.
This is his systematic failure to confront the principal difficulty created
by his own doctrine of pluralism. That difficulty concerns the problem of
legitimacy—the problem, that is, of how the diversity of values he
favours is to be contained by means other than coercion. As Berlin's
inability to theorize the concepts of law and sovereignty has already
indicated, what he lacks is any means for making a distinction between
mere coercion and authority. Unless that problem is addressed, however,
it is of course impossible to develop a coherent concept of the state, as
opposed to that of a mere power system. The reason why Berlin fails to
address this problem—the problem, that is, of legitimacy—is not far to
seek. It stems from a tendency, characteristic of liberal thinkers at large,
to offer a reductionist analysis of the political—an analysis, that is,
which sees the political entirely from the moral standpoint of the individual faced by the burden of choice. This, then, is the principal weakness of Berlin's vision: the fact, that is, that it is not properly political at
all.

Hayek and the vision of a Darwinian natural order[18]

For Hayek, the opposition to totalitarianism mounted by Popper and
Berlin suffer from a crucial flaw. This is their failure to appreciate that a
free political order requires a free economy or, what is the same thing,
that a free society is inevitably a capitalist one. Hayek's principal aim is
to make good this flaw by re-situating post-war British political theory

---

[17] See, for example, 'The Originality of Machiavelli', in Berlin, *Against the Current*. 'Forms of
life' are referred to on e.g. p. 78; 'systems of value' on e.g. p. 74; 'ends' on p. 78, and 'values'
at many points.
[18] For a useful bibliography, see C. Kukathas, *Hayek and Modern Liberalism* (Oxford, Oxford
University Press, 1990). More recently, see A. Gamble, *Hayek* (Oxford, Polity Press, 1996).

within the broader context of a comprehensive socio-economic philosophy. By doing so, he seeks to anchor the post-war theory of limited politics more firmly in the nature of reality itself. Despite this socio-economic difference of emphasis, however, Hayek continues to share with Popper and Berlin the quest for unassailable theoretical foundations for liberty. Like them, that is, he seeks a knock-down theoretical critique of totalitarianism, and an absolute justification for liberal-democracy. Not surprisingly, he also encounters, like them, the problems which *hubris* creates for political philosophy.

For Popper, the principal danger facing the post-war world came from the survival in Marxist form of the totalitarian conviction that it is possible to discover laws of history which enable the structure of society to be completely reshaped. For Berlin, it came from the survival of monistic political creeds incompatible with value pluralism. For Hayek, by contrast, the principal danger facing the west has deeper roots than either Popper or Hayek realizes: he traces it to an all-pervasive rationalism which cuts completely across ideological divisions, being as much a mark of liberalism as of Marxism. What makes rationalism especially dangerous is that it increasingly tends to mask itself in the guise of a social and political idealism which claims to offer social justice while being in reality the road to serfdom.

Rationalist doctrine rests on two assumptions. One is the 'constructivist' assumption that all social order is the product of conscious human design.[19] The second, closely related rationalist assumption is that consciously designed order is intrinsically superior to order which is the outcome of spontaneous, organic evolution. The political expression of these rationalist assumptions is an unlimited faith in planning, of which totalitarianism is merely one possible form. It is to this vision that Hayek opposes his own vision of the Great Society, which is a social order based on recognition of the natural, spontaneous and unplanned nature of the sources of integration in social life. In the Great Society, the only legitimate limit upon the spontaneous order is the purely formal rule of law, which permits the unimpeded evolution of this order by refusing to impose upon it some overall ideology or shared purpose. Hayek, it may be noted, disclaimed originality for this insight, acknowledging Adam Smith, David Hume and Tocqueville as amongst his forebears in appreciating the spontaneous basis of the Great Society. Above all, he

---

[19] F. Hayek, *New Studies in Philosophy, Politics, Economics and the History of Ideas* (London, Routledge & Kegan Paul, 1978), pp. 4–5.

credited Bernard Mandeville with being the first to recognize clearly that although society is *made* by man, it is not, and cannot be, *designed* by him.[20]

To Hayek's credit, he spoke out against the uncritical post-war faith in planning at a time when it was unfashionable to do so. Nevertheless, three major problems are presented by his critique. The first concerns his conviction that there is an iron link between any and every kind of planning and totalitarianism. In fact, the precise nature of this link is never made clear. Hayek relies more upon a priori dogma than on empirical evidence, for example, when he attributes the rise of totalitarianism to a desire for rational planning of the economic order. Critics have not been slow to point out that it is impossible to explain the quasi-religious inspiration behind either Nazi or communist ideological fanaticism in such terms.[21] What is no less problematic, however, is Hayek's assumption that the post-war welfare state must inevitably end in totalitarianism. It must do so, he maintains, because the welfare state automatically destroys the rule of law by imposing upon society a set of substantive purposes. That criticism, however, is easily met by critics who point out that the welfare state does not typically operate through orders and commands, but works principally through progressive taxation, which is quite compatible with the rule of law.

The second problem presented by Hayek's critique of planning concerns his reliance on an economic model derived from an earlier stage of capitalist society. This model presupposes a clear state/society distinction which oversimplifies the complex relationship between the state and the economy in advanced industrial societies.[22] In particular, Hayek assumes that the economic order is separable from the political order in a greater degree than is the case in an era of large corporations.[23]

The third, and philosophically most serious, problem presented by the critique of planning relates to the concept of the spontaneous order which Hayek opposes to that of the planned society.[24] The spontaneous

---

[20] Ibid. p. 253.

[21] For example, J. Shklar, *After Utopia* (Princeton, Princeton University Press, 1957).

[22] See, for example, the review of the principal criticisms of Hayek's economic theory in Ch. 3, P. Dunleavy and B. O'Leary, 'The New Right', *Theories of the State* (London, Macmillan, 1987), pp. 72–135.

[23] Dunleavy and O'Leary, *Theories of the State*, pp. 274–6, for a brief review of the nostalgic element in the economic theory of the Austrian School.

[24] 'Whenever we speak of the economy of a country, or of the world, we are employing a term which suggests that these systems ought to be run on socialist lines and directed according to a single plan so as to serve a unitary system of ends.' *Law, Liberty and Legislation*, vol. 2, p. 108.

order, he stresses, is not merely a device for organizing production and consumption, as the description of it as a mere economy or market would suggest. It is, rather, a sophisticated information system for the synthesizing of a body of knowledge which is dispersed amongst a mass of separate individuals. Not only can this dispersed knowledge never be extracted from those who possess it and placed at the disposal of a unitary central authority: it cannot even be formulated into a body of explicit propositions. This epistemological argument against economic planning is the most persuasive part of Hayek's work. Even if we ignore possible objections and decide to accept it, however, what is questionable is how far it actually serves Hayek's purpose.

To be precise, what is questionable is Hayek's assumption that an unregulated spontaneous order will automatically issue in liberal democratic institutions. The historical evidence suggests, to the contrary, that the outcome is just as likely to be despotism. But if that is so, the epistemological argument boomerangs, since, instead of underpinning the case for non-intervention in the spontaneous order, it can equally well be used to demonstrate the need for interventionism in the interest of creating and maintaining liberal institutions. Hayek himself implicitly acknowledges this by arguing that extensive rational constitutional and financial reform is necessary, partly in the interest of reinvigorating the spontaneous order, and partly to protect democracy against an inherent tendency to soft finance, which he regarded as the ultimate source of inflation. Ironically, the fact that Hayek is so concerned with such reform has exposed him to the charge of ultimately doing little more than replace one kind of rationalism with another.[25]

Hayek's critique of planning creates even more difficulty, however, when he carries his quest for an absolute philosophical foundation from which to oppose totalitarianism beyond epistemology into ontology. The ontology he adopts takes the form of a version of Social Darwinist[26]

---

[25] See, for example, C. Kukathas, *Hayek and Modern Liberalism* (Oxford, Oxford University Press, 1990), esp. Ch. 6.

[26] Hayek endeavours to rebut this charge, on the ground that, although Darwinists did indeed stress the importance of natural selection of the most able individuals in free competition, his own concern is with 'the competitive selection of cultural institutions . . . My problem is not genetic evolution of innate qualities, but cultural evolution through learning.' The trouble is that Hayek frequently blurs the distinction he makes here by speaking of cultural institutions as natural formations, in order to stress that they are not, and cannot become, the creatures of conscious human design. In particular, what he failed to contemplate was the possibility that the spontaneous order might produce prosperity, but with a diminishing number of jobs.

philosophy, according to which man is an organism engaged in the same process of evolutionary adaptation to his environment that governs the survival of all organisms, except that, in man's case, the struggle is complicated by the fact that part of his environment is a complex social order. Unfortunately, the result of this naturalistic philosophy is that the core concept of liberalism, which is of course the idea of freedom, is eliminated from Hayek's thought. This is because naturalistic philosophy finds it impossible to acknowledge freedom as the defining characteristic of man. Hayek's difficulty in this respect emerges most clearly in *The Sensory Order*, in which he stressed that the physical and mental dimensions of human existence 'are . . . identical and that to postulate a separate set of terms for the mental order would be redundant'.[27] In other words, man is deprived of any characteristic, such as freedom, which would create a significant discontinuity in the overall structure of existence.

What may now be made explicit is the paradoxical outcome of Hayek's search for an absolute philosophical foundation for liberalism. This is that his attempt to distinguish between the spontaneous order, on the one hand, and the political order, on the other, inevitably reproduces the difficulties created by Marxist attempts to distinguish between the material base and the ideological superstructure of society.

Just as Marxism downgrades the state in relation to the material base, for example, so Hayek downgrades it in relation to the spontaneous order in so far as he denies any intrinsic value to political institutions. The political order, that is, has a purely functional value, which it acquires in so far as it contributes to the unimpeded evolution of the spontaneous order. The functional perspective, however, makes it impossible to deal with the ethical problem posed by the state's coercive dimension. Strictly speaking there is, indeed, no concept of the state in Hayek's work, since it is impossible for him to distinguish it in principle from a more or less valuable coercive system.

The structural similarity between Hayek's version of liberalism and Marxism extends beyond their mutual rejection of the autonomy of the political order, however. Just as Marxism dismisses nationalism as a form of false consciousness, for example, so also Hayek dismisses it as merely an atavistic echo of an earlier, tribal stage of social development. Such echoes, he believes, are wholly out of place in today's world, where

---

[27] F. Hayek, *The Sensory Order* (London, Routledge & Kegan Paul, 1952), p. 40.

they serve only to impede rational adjustment to the spontaneous order of the Great Society.[28]

Hayek goes a step beyond Marxism, however, when he attempts to dismiss Marxism itself, along with all forms of socialism, as an instance of the same kind of atavistic response to modernity as nationalism represents. Socialism at large, that is to say, he regards as merely echoing sentiments appropriate to pre-modern tribal society, and wholly inapplicable to the modern world. This view is positively misleading, however, in so far as it involves maintaining that the ideal of community *as such* is atavistic. What *is* defensible is the more modest proposition, that socialism is atavistic and totalitarian *in so far as it demands the conversion of the state itself into a community.* But Hayek is not content with that.

There are, however, two further major problems created by Hayek's unqualified hostility to socialism, both of which were forcefully brought out some years ago by Irving Kristol, one of the leading American critics of market liberalism. The first is that Hayek's animosity towards social-ism blinds him to one of the most important dangers faced by liberal democracy in advanced industrial society. This is the possibility, Kristol remarked, that the real enemy of the liberal order *'is not so much socialism as nihilism'.*[29] This latter danger, which has been taken up by contem-porary communitarian critics of the free market such as John Gray,[30] stresses that the market ideal tends to destroy all the integrating institu-tions of society by encouraging attitudes which are wholly insensitive to the non-instrumental presuppositions of morality, on the one hand, and communal identity, on the other.

The second major problem identified by Kristol is a further outstand-ing example of the way in which Hayek's hostility to socialism blinds him to fundamental aspects of contemporary social life. In this case, Hayek's blindspot concerns the need for a legitimating myth that would render the inequalities of market society acceptable.[31] In practice, an appropriate myth would have to take the form of a theory of distributive justice that provides generally acceptable criteria for deciding who gets what. Hayek, however, dismisses the whole concept of 'social justice' as

---

[28] See M. Forsyth, 'Hayek's Bizarre Liberalism', *Political Studies*, 36 (1988), 235–250, pp. 246–7.

[29] I. Kristol, 'Capitalism, Socialism and Nihilism', *The Public Interest*, 31 (1973), 12.

[30] John Gray's later view of Hayek may be found in, for example, 'Hayek as a Conserva-tive', *Post-liberalism* (London, Routledge, 1993), pp. 32–9.

[31] I. Kristol, '"When virtue loses all her loveliness"—some reflections on capitalism and "the free society"', *The Public Interest*, 21 (1970).

totally unacceptable, for two reasons. One is that the concept has no objective meaning, but possesses only a purely rhetorical significance. Hayek's other objection is that the concept requires that every man should be materially rewarded according to his moral merit. In practice, however, no-one (except God) can ever know for certain what a man's moral merit is, and there is any case no objective way of determining what material reward would correspond to it. Any attempt to match material rewards to moral merits must therefore involve the arbitrary imposition of a single set of values upon society by an authoritarian government, endowed with power to pronounce who deserves what.

It is important to notice the precise reason why Hayek feels able to reject the quest for social justice with such complete confidence. This is not, it should be stressed, because he is a defender of the minimal state. On the contrary, he is quite prepared to accept state intervention to supply public goods which the market cannot provide, although he is firmly opposed to conferring a monopoly of those goods on the state. The reason for Hayek's confident rejection of the need to legitimate social inequalities is, rather, that he feels able to rely on a widespread mood of fatalism to make the economic and social hazards and inequalities of modern industrial society acceptable. Such fatalism, Hayek assumes, is borne of recognition that these hazards and inequalities result entirely from the operation of impersonal forces, and therefore cannot appropriately be assessed in moral terms. At this point, however, Hayek is wholly at odds with the dominant culture of modernity.

He is at odds with it because that culture is not merely 'constructivist', as Hayek himself notes, but also 'voluntarist'. This means, as Agnes Heller and Ferenc Fehér have observed, that the dominant conception of individual identity is in terms of the 'total indeterminateness of the person [and] the absence of fate . . . The person is the maker of his/her life, and in this sense is a *self-made man* or a *self-made woman* . . . At least in our imagination', the authors add, 'there are no limits to the possibilities for our "shaping the world"'.[32] In a culture of this kind, to which any concept of fatality is completely alien, Hayek's attempt to divorce the ideal of a free society from that of a just society is hardly likely to win mass support, since the sense of fatality which would make the divorce acceptable is wholly lacking.

There are, then, two major problems confronting even the most

---

[32] A. Heller and F. Fehér, *The Postmodern Political Condition* (Cambridge, Cambridge University Press, 1991), p. 17.

sympathetic student of Hayek's work. The first is philosophical and concerns, as has been seen, the limitations of naturalism as a source of the foundations Hayek seeks for liberalism. The problem, to be precise, is that a naturalistic philosophy has no ethical vocabulary, and therefore deprives Hayek not only of a coherent concept of liberty, but also of a coherent concept of the state, which can only appear as a power system, from the standpoint of naturalism. The second problem is political rather than philosophical, and arises from Hayek's denial that the Great Society can have a moral basis. Even if that is philosophically correct, it was too hard a saying to win acceptance in the increasingly idealistic mood of the 1960s. On the one hand, then, Hayek has failed to satisfy the demands of philosophers; on the other, he has also failed to satisfy politicians searching for easily digestible ideas with mass appeal. Falling as it does between those extremes, the fate of his vision has been to provide ideological cannon fodder for new right intellectuals.

It is time to consider, finally, a thinker whose vision was for long dismissed as of interest only to romantic conservatives determined to ignore at all costs the post-traditional character of western modernity. He is Michael Oakeshott.

Oakeshott and the 'civil' vision

Although Oakeshott's philosophy, like that of the three thinkers already considered, was developed in the shadow of totalitarianism, his response is distinguished from theirs by its profoundly sceptical nature. This scepticism was originally presented in *Experience and its Modes* (1933), in the form of the claim that there is no absolute or unconditional truth to be found anywhere in human experience, which is always and inevitably 'modal' or specific. Despite subsequent shifts of philosophical emphasis, Oakeshott never abandoned that doctrine. Accordingly, he always refused to engage in the search for an absolute vantage point, whether in epistemology, ontology or ethics, from which to oppose totalitarianism. Although Oakeshott did not refer to Popper, Hayek and Berlin by name, he indicated in *On Human Conduct* (1975) that those who do pursue that search merely manifest the understandable (albeit philosophically indefensible) disposition of human beings 'to be disconcerted unless they feel themselves to be upheld by something more substantial than the emanations of their own contingent imaginations'.[33]

---

[33] M. Oakeshott, *On Human Conduct* (Oxford, Clarendon Press, 1975), p. 80.

Instead of searching for an absolute vantage point from which to oppose totalitarianism, Oakeshott sought instead to develop a theory of the limited state by reformulating the central concern of classical political thought, which is the ideal of civil association.[34] Before that could be done, however, he considered it was necessary to prepare the ground in two ways. The first, which constituted common ground with Hayek, was by demolishing the rationalist mentality which he believed not only inspired totalitarianism but had come to pervade modern western culture at large. In Oakeshott's mature political thought, however, the concept of rationalism disappears, and the enemy becomes instead 'telocratic' or, in the phrase he finally preferred, 'managerial' politics. Managerial politics is incompatible with freedom because it imposes a single purpose on the whole of society.

It is true that, despite his broader philosophical scepticism, Oakeshott's critique of rationalism sometimes suggests that he did at one stage envisage the ultimate task of political philosophy in much the same way as Popper, Hayek and Berlin, in the very general sense that he seemed, like them, to be seeking a privileged philosophical position from which to deliver a decisive blow against the totalitarian challenge. In *Rationalism in Politics* (1962), for example, he appeared at times to assume the privileged epistemological standpoint of a self-appointed guardian of tradition gifted with mysterious insight into what he termed its 'intimations', in order to castigate ideological (or what he called 'rationalist') politics. This, as is well known, did not take him very far, mainly because his critique proved too much, by demonstrating that *all* politics are necessarily traditionalist in character. This meant that his argument ceased to be a viable way of trouncing rationalist enemies of the limited state, since they turned out to be unwitting traditionalists, in his sense of the term. In *On Human Conduct*, however, the conditionality of all experience was reasserted, and the earlier play which Oakeshott had made with the concepts of rationalism and tradition was completely abandoned.

What now concerned Oakeshott was a second, more profound problem which required to be dealt with by way of prolegomena to political theory proper. This problem, which constitutes the most extraordinary deficiency of contemporary western culture, is the continuing lack, after

---

[34] Oakeshott's principal writings from what may be termed his middle period (that is, from the 1940s until roughly the end of the 1960s) are contained in *Rationalism in Politics* (n.e. Indianapolis, Liberty Press, 1991).

two and a half thousand years of philosophy, of a coherent discourse in which to describe what a human agent is. Oakeshott's quest for an adequate vocabulary in which to theorize agency comprises the first part of *On Human Conduct*, and may alternatively be described as the quest for a vocabulary in which to theorize the nature of freedom.

The reason why we lack such a vocabulary is that the western philosophical tradition has succumbed from the beginning to a tendency to think of agents as things or substances of some sort (the Christian conception of the soul is one example; and Descartes' identification of the subject with a mysterious spiritual substance is another, more recent, example). One of Oakeshott's central philosophical aims was to break with this age-old tendency to theorize the nature of agency in the language of objects. In this respect he was, of course, in line with philosophers such as Heidegger, Sartre, Wittgenstein, Berdyaev and Ryle, all of whom recognized the need for a non-reductive concept of freedom, or self-hood, or agency.

It is against the background of this wider inquiry into the nature of freedom that Oakeshott worked out the concept of civil association as the most fitting form of political organization for those who, having risen to consciousness of their freedom, embrace it either with delight (as Oakeshott himself did), or else accept it with more or less resignation (as Sartre, for example, did).

Civil association in this sense, Oakeshott emphasizes, is best understood as the appropriate response to a specifically modern western problem, which is the problem of legitimacy. Since legitimacy is the central concern of Oakeshott's political thought, it is vital to appreciate precisely how he interprets that problem. It may be formulated thus: *how can membership of a non-voluntary association (the state) be made compatible with a self-chosen life for people who have different concepts of the good and complicated identities, involving membership in a multiplicity of associations?* It is to this problem, then, that the concept of civil association provides an answer. This has been stressed because the civil model, characterized in terms of the problem of legitimacy, cannot provide, and does not aspire to provide, a complete theory of the modern state. In particular, it does not, for example, clarify the conditions for creating and maintaining civil association itself.

For purposes of brevity, and at the expense of disregarding the subtlety of Oakeshott's thought, the main features of his revised model of civil association may be characterized by means of the following seven propositions.

In the first place, civil association offers freedom in the sense that choice is not constrained by directives or orders or commands, but only by rules which specify formal conditions to be observed in all conduct. Civil association consists, in fact, entirely of rules, in the form of laws, together with the conditions necessary for making those rules, adjudicating them, and securing compliance with them.

Secondly, the rules of civil association are not intended to serve any extraneous purpose, interest or ideology. They are, that is, non-instrumental rules. In so far as the rules may be said to 'do' anything, it is to create, and thereafter maintain, an identity, which is that of membership in civil association. In this respect, they are a bit like the rules of grammar, which do not require one to speak about any particular topic, but define what is involved in speaking about any topic at all.

Thirdly, the rules of civil association are obligatory only because they are acknowledged as authoritative; and what makes them authoritative is that they are the outcome of an acknowledged procedure. The distinctive character of the concept of authority developed by Oakeshott in connection with civil association becomes obvious when what he is implicitly denying is noticed, which is that rules have to possess independently valid rational grounds for them to be obligatory. They neither have to possess such grounds, nor do they have to possess a functional or utilitarian value of any kind.

The fourth characteristic of civil association also concerns the nature of authority, and is to the effect that acknowledgement of the authority of the rules of civil association does not entail personal *approval* of them by citizens, or approval of their outcomes, or approval of those who make the rules. Lest this should appear to be little more than a formula for despotism, it must immediately be added that Oakeshott is fully aware that there will inevitably be disapproval of the rules and a desire to change not only them but, on occasion, the legislators who make them. He is quite explicit, in fact, in insisting that it is part of the nature of the civil model to provide procedures not only for discussion of what rules should be made, but also for expressing disapproval of them once made, and beyond that, for changing them, as well as the procedures in accordance with which they are made. It is therefore possible, within the civil model, to go a considerable way towards accommodating the republican arguments which have inspired the political position characteristic of the third phase of political theory which will be considered below.

Fifthly, civil association entails, by its very nature, a distinction between 'public' and 'private' life, not in the sense of there being intrinsically different kinds of acts (as Mill thought), or intrinsically different spheres in which acts occur (as Arendt believed), but in the sense that there are two dimensions to every act, namely a public dimension, in so far as every act can be seen from the standpoint of compliance or non-compliance with the rules of civil association, and a private dimension, in so far as every act is the successful or unsuccessful pursuit of some substantive purpose on the part of a particular agent.

Sixthly, civil association is an inclusive mode of association, in the sense that its rules do not exclude the simultaneous enjoyment of relationships other than the civil one itself. The only relationships they exclude are those which are *incompatible* with them; they do not exclude relationships which are only *different* from them.

Finally, Oakeshott accepts that it is impossible to give a full account of civil association in terms of merely making and implementing a system of formal rules. In this connection, he makes two important qualifications. The first is that civil association must include provision for an activity that goes beyond the activities of legislating and adjudicating. This is the activity of ruling, which is the executive activity of providing specific directives to particular groups or individuals to do particular acts in the interest of maintaining the civil order as a whole.[35] The second qualification is Oakeshott's recognition that there will inevitably be situations in which civil government acquires a purposive or 'managerial' character. Above all, when a civil association is threatened with dissolution or destruction, as in time of war, 'or when (in a lesser emergency) *cives* [citizens] are deprived of the shelter or amenity of a civil order, in such circumstances that judicial remedy is unable to restore the situation', then the 'common concern' may become a 'common purpose', and rulers may become managers of its pursuit. Oakeshott immediately adds, however, that 'For rulers to become managers even of an undertaking such as this, and for subjects to become partners or role-performers in a compulsory enterprise association such as this, is itself a suspension of the civil condition.'[36]

These then are characteristics of civil association. Unfortunately, Oakeshott's hostility to what he termed managerial politics was so great that it tended to have a paralysing effect on his willingness to speculate about the kind of policies necessary to implement the model

[35] Oakeshott, *On Human Conduct* (Oxford, Clarendon Press, 1975), p. 144.
[36] Ibid. pp. 146–7.

in contemporary European states. He gave no indication, in particular, about how the 'loyalty' which is the bond of solidarity amongst members of civil association might be fostered and sustained.[37] The result of this inability to propose any way of softening the conflict between the liberal and democratic sides of modern western politics was that Oakeshott increasingly tended to despair of modern politics at large. The last work published during his lifetime, for example, included an essay called 'The Tower of Babel' (1983) in which he presented modernity as so deeply permeated by an instrumental mentality that civil association is completely replaced by a Baconian version of managerial politics in which the whole of social life is organized for economic purposes.

Nevertheless, Oakeshott's work on civil association constitutes the most rigorous post-war attempt to define clearly the concept of the limited state which western liberal democracies opposed to totalitarianism. The weakness, as was indicated, is Oakeshott's apparent indifference to the question of how the kind of social order necessary for the civil ideal to prosper is to be created.

Conclusion

The question which inevitably arises from a review like the present one is whether anything of continuing relevance for the contemporary world emerges from the four visions considered, or whether the totalitarian challenge to which they were a response has severely restricted their wider applicability. It may be said immediately that the one which has suffered most in this respect is undoubtedly Popper's positivist vision of the open society, largely because his naïve faith in the possibility of scientific politics and of rational planning failed to take account of the realities of conflict and power. Setting this profoundly anti-political vision to one side, then, attention will be focused on the relevance of the remaining three.

Of these, Hayek's vision appears at first sight to be the one of most obvious continuing relevance, in view of the widespread acceptance (in varying degrees) of his critique of planning, on the one hand, and his defence, on the other, of the rationality and efficiency of the market as a mode of economic organization, as well as its contribution to civil and political freedom. The economic emphasis which constitutes Hayek's

---

[37] Oakeshott, *On Human Conduct*, pp. 201–2.

strength, however, is also his weakness, since he has little appreciation of the continuing power of nationalism, on the one hand, or, on the other, of the 'politics of difference' which has put identity at the fore of contemporary political debate.

It is in the latter connection that Berlin's vision has recently acquired a renewed relevance. His commendably sceptical attitude towards liberal rationalism, manifest in remarkable essays on such thinkers as de Maistre, Tolstoy and Sorel, paved the way for his relatively early recognition of the continuing importance of nationalism in the post-war world. If Berlin is open to qualified criticism in this respect, it is only on the ground that he tended to suggest that nationalism was likely to be more important outside the western world than within it, and therefore failed to integrate it fully into contemporary liberal democratic theory.[38]

Berlin's meditations on nationalism, however, have endowed his own distinctive vision of the free society with a wider relevance that still remains to be noticed. In the course of reflecting on the defence of cultural particularity characteristic of early theorists of nationalism such as Herder, Berlin was led to abandon the assumption of cultural uniformity which had hitherto characterized much liberal democratic theory. He thereby laid the foundation for a revised version of pluralism capable of accommodating a multicultural society. More generally, the same affirmation of particularity at the expense of the dominant liberal stress on universality carried Berlin's version of value pluralism beyond the consensus politics of the early post-war decades in a way that anticipated the contemporary quest for a politics of difference. Like Hayek, then, albeit for different reasons, Berlin's vision transcends its original Cold War context.

Finally, it may be suggested that it is the civil vision advanced by Oakeshott that is likely to be the one of most enduring relevance, for three reasons. The first is the philosophical modesty with which he supports it, revealed above all in his sceptical rejection of the claim that the political philosopher can ever enjoy a privileged position from which to advance absolute claims of any kind. Despite his early confidence in the ability of philosophy to pass judgement on ideology, Oakeshott's dominant view was more consistent with his insistence, already noticed, on the modal character of experience. By this he meant

---

[38] 'It would not, I think, be an exaggeration to say that no political movement today, *at any rate outside the western world*, seems likely to succeed unless it allies itself to national sentiment.' Berlin, *Against the Current*, p. 355 (italics added).

in effect that we never see, and never can see, the world 'as it really is in itself', but inevitably view it from specific standpoints which entail, so to speak, always viewing it through various kinds of spectacles. The categories which constitute those spectacles are what he termed 'modes of experience'. Such modes are potentially infinite in number but in practice may be restricted to the practical, scientific, historical and (he later added) the aesthetic modes, on the ground that these are the only kinds of experience in which logically coherent and non-reducible criteria of relevance have thus far been established.

Although we can never step outside modal experience (that is, we can never remove the spectacles through which we view experience), what we *can* do is become conscious of modality. We can, that is, examine the spectacles (i.e. categories) we are using and become conscious in that way of how they determine our interpretation of experience, even though we cannot take them off and gaze on absolute reality. It is to this activity of turning our critical gaze back on the modality of our experience that Oakeshott gives the name philosophy. Philosophy, in other words, is what would now be called a reflexive activity. For Oakeshott, it is the only *fully* reflexive activity.

This sceptical characterization of philosophy not only distinguishes Oakeshott from Popper, who elevated scientific knowledge to the status of supreme knowledge, but also from Berlin, who makes an absolute ethical claim on behalf of the incommensurability and incompatibility of values, and Hayek, whose naturalistic philosophy entails an absolute claim about the role of spontaneity in the creation of universal order. For Oakeshott, by contrast, the purely reflexive nature of philosophy confines it to a sustained meditation on the ethical and political implications of the fact that we have become a diverse and complex people and desire, for the most part, to live self-chosen lives.

Although this (as has been seen) means that Oakeshott follows classical political thinkers in placing the problem of legitimacy at the centre of modern political philosophy, it does not mean, as is sometimes supposed, that his model of civil association is necessarily incompatible with social justice, or other social ideals. What it means is only that such ideals are not viewed in terms of their abstract merits but are seen, rather, in terms of their contribution to civil association itself.

The second enduring aspect of the civil vision is Oakeshott's insistence on the autonomy of the civil relationship. It is a relationship, that is, which can, amongst a politically creative people, transcend religion, race, gender, class and nationality. The third is his claim on behalf of the inclusive character of that relationship, on the ground that it is the only one whose formal character renders it capable of accommodating the diversity of modern social life in a non-coercive way. It must be repeated, however, that civil association cannot provide a complete account of the state, as Oakeshott himself sometimes seems to wish that it could. It is inevitably only one aspect of the theory of the state, because its emphasis is formal and procedural—and there are of course dimensions of polit-ical life which cannot possibly be dealt with by rules (as admirers of Carl Schmitt are not slow to point out).

A patient reader may at this point finally insist that the most impor-tant objection to the various visions of freedom has not yet been con-fronted. This objection comes from theorists of globalization. Those visions, it is maintained, have simply been rendered irrelevant by the 'chronic intensification' of admittedly long-established patterns of inter-connectedness, now

> mediated by such phenomena as the modern communications industry and new information technology, and the spread of globalization in and through new dimensions of interconnectedness: technological, organiza-tional, administrative and legal, among others, each with its own logic and dynamic of change.[39]

It should also be stressed that more plausible versions of globalization theory do not suggest that either nationalism or the nation-state are likely to disappear: what is argued is only that growing interconnected-ness makes the assumptions of the traditional vocabulary of political thought increasingly difficult to apply, based as that vocabulary is on a concept of state impermeability which no longer fits the facts.

Impressive though the literature on globalization may be, I shall end by siding with the sceptics who query the ultimate value of the concept itself. Paul Hirst, for example, concludes that:

> Globalisation is a myth, unsustained by the evidence . . . The world remains international rather than global . . . Both alone and in concert with others, the nation state can still guide economic forces . . . Globalisa-tion is the ideology of a pessimistic era which leaves us standing helpless before the future.[40]

---

[39] D. Held, 'Democracy and the Global System', in D. Held, ed., *Political Theory Today* (Cambridge, Polity Press, 1991), pp. 222–3.

[40] P. Hirst, 'Globaloney', *Prospect* (February 1996), 33.

It would seem, then, that although none of the four visions offers a means of completely accommodating subsequent developments in political theory, three at least not only remain suggestive in fundamental respects but have indeed already been incorporated in varying degrees into liberal democratic political theory.

Acknowledgement.   A draft of this chapter was greatly improved by the comments of Bhikhu Parekh. Responsibility for the final version is of course entirely my own.

4: The Critique of Individualism

ALAN RYAN

The organization of this Chapter is as simple as its arguments: some critiques of individualism fall naturally to other chapters in this volume—one on pluralism and another on visions of freedom—so I concentrate here on the thought that 'rational, economic man' may be a useful figment of the economists' imagination but is not a useful figment of the social and political theorist's imagination. My case is essentially that this is not a methodological matter; methodological issues are largely irrelevant to the critique of individualism, and it is substantive questions about what kind of moral and political creatures we are and should be that have animated theorists for the past hundred years. So, after some prefatory remarks about the strength of individualism in British political thought, I begin out of chronological order with a brief discussion of the post-1945 debate over the virtues of 'methodological individualism' and its supposed political implications. The argument then begins in earnest with the late nineteenth-century and early twentieth-century Idealist critique of the 'narrow individualism' that Idealists believed underlay utilitarianism and earlier forms of liberalism; I move on to other early twentieth-century critiques of the assumption that human beings are naturally, or essentially, rational egoists; I briefly mention some British contributions to the Marxist critique of rational economic man, and end with a very short discussion of communitarianism. The so-called 'liberal-communitarian debate' has been a somewhat confused American recapitulation of the arguments of late nineteenth-century Idealists, both British and American, so I go into it no more deeply than I need to do to support the claim that it is the latest stage in a long, and not always clearly structured, debate.

I do not spread my net wider in order to embark on a discussion of the usefulness of rational choice theory in political science, even although this is an issue that has preoccupied political science departments in the United States. Some of the questions that argument over rational choice theories raise were answered, although rather glancingly, in earlier debates; more to the point, however, rational choice theorists have been concerned with the explanation of voting behaviour, committee behaviour, aspects of international relations, and the like, rather than with the issues debated by political theorists in the sense understood here. Normative questions have emerged, to the extent that they have emerged at all, in the course of an explanatory enterprise different from anything discussed here. I begin with some introductory observations— negative in nature but not in tone—about the strength of a certain sort of individualism in British political thought.

Introduction

There is little in the tradition of British social and political thought to sustain a thorough-going anti-individualism. Hobbes's *Leviathan* is a paradigm of methodological individualist virtue, whatever defects it might otherwise possess; Locke's individualism may be thoroughly misunderstood by some recent commentators, but it was certainly an ethical individualism.[1] To find a condemnation of individualism as opposed to mere selfishness or rebelliousness or wilfulness, we need to turn to Edmund Burke's *Reflections on the French Revolution*. There we certainly find an argument against the adequacy of the psychology of 'rational economic man' as a basis for citizenship, or even as a basis for the perception of our everyday moral obligations. A man who lamented that 'the age of chivalry is dead' and deplored the arrival of the 'sophists, economists, and calculators' was certainly convinced that the rational calculation of individual advantage was a poor foundation for a political order. Whether it made Burke a moral collectivist is another question. Burke declined, as he famously said, to 'set each man to trade upon his

---

[1] I have in mind Michael Sandel's association of liberalism with an exaggerated concern for 'choice'. See M. Sandel, *Liberalism and the Limits of Justice* (Cambridge, Cambridge University Press, 1982). This seems wrong; whatever one might say about Locke's views on religion, it is not that they displayed a consumerist concern with choice.

own stock of reason', because he feared that in most men that individual stock was small. They should draw upon the bank and capital of the ages, and more locally, they should draw upon the prejudices of their own community. Was this to subscribe to a collectivist theory of reason, or of social and political action? The answer is surely not. Burke was a professed disciple of Adam Smith, and his understanding of the workings of a more *laissez-faire* economy than the one that had so far emerged in late eighteenth-century Britain was highly sophisticated. He had no problem embracing the thought that individuals were enmeshed in both cultural and economic settings that were sustained by the actions of individuals even though they were not the object of those individuals' intentions.

Burke certainly held an 'organic' view of society; he emphasized the importance of the way we are socialized into the mores of our own society so as to form the values and beliefs that he labelled 'prejudice' and defended as an indispensable second nature. Within that framework, however, he also argued that there were areas of social life in which men both did and should behave as self-interested maximizers of their own welfare; and he could do so all the more confidently because he thought that under favourable conditions their socialization into the ordinary morality of their country would ensure that they were selfish only where they should be, and would be without damaging their capacity for altruistic behaviour. It was right to insist that there were spheres of action where men could properly be motivated by secular, calculating considerations, only because they could be relied on to know when other forms of motivation were required. To the extent that Burke held a collectivist view of social rationality, it was not in the form of an attachment to a free-standing sociological or philosophical theory, but in the form of a religious conviction; society possessed a kind of collective wisdom only because the fate of society was in God's hands. Burke did not suggest that there were supra-individual entities, social or other, which possessed a moral value higher than that of individuals; he did not ask his readers to sacrifice themselves for the race or the nation. Although Burke took it for granted that an ordinary patriotic Englishman or Irishman would in fact risk death in battle, or work himself to death in order to provide for his family and friends, this was simply a fact about what would motivate properly socialized individuals, not evidence that 'the family' or 'the nation' or 'Britain' represented a moral ideal to which we should sacrifice ourselves.

Nor did the late nineteenth century see the creation of British versions of the racial nationalism to be found in France. There is no British equivalent of Gobineau, let alone of Maurras or Barrès; the mythic conception of the proletariat and its destiny, much admired by Sorel, and identified in Russell's *German Social Democracy* as the religious core of Marxism, was not prominent in British Marxism.[2] British writers sometimes echoed Durkheim's insistence that the individual is the creation of society, and that individuality is a facet of society's self-expression, but the political ethic that that sociological claim sustained was an individualist ethic, just as Durkheim's own sociology of morals grounded an individualist ethics and politics. Durkheim's politics were those of a Third Republic liberal; and his ethics were Kantian. This frequently surprises readers of Durkheim, but it ought not to do so.

Since it is a matter that illuminates what follows, and does much to explain the fuzziness of many of the debates about individualism, it is worth pausing to distinguish quite sharply between what one might call the logical or methodological holism of an adequate sociological explanation on the one hand, and moral and political collectivism on the other.[3] Sociological explanations of whatever phenomena we have it in mind to explain must attempt to show how those phenomena are rooted in our membership of social groupings such as the family, the village, the work-group, or the nation; but to show that there is, or may be, a sociological explanation of a modern society's attachment to ethical individualism or to liberal-democracy is not to suggest that these attachments are not what they seem, and certainly not that those who hold these allegiances are in some way deluded. What such explanations offer is an account of why these allegiances are particularly apt to modern societies such as our own. Indeed, the purpose of providing such an account is commonly to strengthen the argument for ethical individualism and its political embodiment. The thought is simple enough; we may be less moved by philosophical argument in favour of ethical individualism than by circumstantial considerations.

Durkheim was particularly concerned to provide a sociological explanation of what he took to be the distinguishing mark of moral obligation—the feeling of its irresistibility. Kant had explained moral obligation by representing our moral and political judgements as commands issued by the noumenal self, and it was this explanation that Durkheim resisted. But the thought that what could not be ascribed

---

[2] B. Russell, *German Social Democracy* (London, Allen & Unwin, [1965] 1895).

[3] See S. Lukes, *Durkheim* (London, Allen Lane, 1969).

to the deliverances of the noumenal self must be understood as the result of our socialization into a modern society did nothing to suggest that the insights themselves were other than those that had been understood as the deliverances of Kantian reason. The fuzziness that almost inevitably complicates the discussion of individualism, however, returns when we ask whether there is not *some* effect on the content of the political ethic. The interpreter of Durkheim must concede that the replacement of metaphysics by moral sociology makes some difference, that there is what one might call a conceptual pressure exerted by the preferred form of explanation. Durkheimian sociology represents individuals as in need of social support and assistance in a way in which Kant's own account of a similar political ethic does not. Nor is it surprising that Durkheim advocated social and economic arrangements of a broadly liberal–socialist kind that Kant would mostly have rejected. (I say 'mostly' to accommodate the fact that although Kant was an 'absolutist' over private property in insisting that individuals must have a right to own and dispose of their own property, he was surprisingly utilitarian in his approach to what governments might allow by way of publicly owned entities such as schools, hospitals, and even monasteries.)

In a British setting, one might think of Fabian socialism as determinedly anti-individualist and collectivist. 'Bourgeois, benevolent, and bureaucratic', as Beatrice Webb described herself and Sidney, are not adjectives that suggest a strong commitment to an ethical individualism. Yet, the obsession with organization that Fabianism certainly connotes was underpinned by a desire for justice for individuals. The avowed goal, to be secured by replacing the egoistic competition of the marketplace by a socialist organization of production and distribution, was to secure *justice*, understood as giving each individual what he or she deserved as a result of their contribution to the common weal. What this suggests, of course, is the difficulty of deciding what is and is not consistent with ethical individualism. The Fabians thought a large measure of economic collectivism essential for national efficiency, and in that sense were certainly not economic individualists. How far this meant that they were not ethical individualists is another matter. In that it is the common weal that sets the standards by which we should judge our individual conduct, we are faced with a form of communitarianism; yet on the other hand, the sustaining idea is that we cannot live easily with ourselves except in a just society, and this I take to be an individualist (or, as I shall soon say, a 'personalist') ideal.

So, one guiding thread in what follows is that the 'critique' of individualism is a critique in the sense that that term bears in Kant's critiques. The aim of a critique is to understand what the strengths and limitations are of what is put under inspection; just as Kant's inspection of the strengths and weaknesses of pure reason showed, not that reason was powerless and delusive, but that it had to be kept within its proper bounds if it was not to lead us astray, so the critique of individualism— to the extent that one can think of it as a continuing thread of argument—does not issue in the claim that no form of individualism is acceptable, but in the thought that what individualism entails for what areas of human activity needs careful analysis so as to decide when particular attitudes and ambitions are and are not acceptable.

Methodological individualism

I turn now to the post-war argument between Sir Karl Popper and his 'methodological individualist' allies on the one side, and the critics of methodological individualism on the other. The 'methodological holism' of Idealist philosophy and most forms of sociology is consistent with a broadly individualist stance in political ethics. Sometimes the social or cognitive whole which sociologists—and, as we shall see, Idealist philosophers and social theorists—invoke to explain the structure within which behaviour is meaningful has dramatic features. The whole history of human culture is invoked by Hegel's *Phenomenology of Spirit* to sustain some very large claims about the way in which the hidden purpose of human history lies in the liberal culture of post-French Revolution Europe. If Hegel's own philosophy provides too rich an intellectual diet, the naturalistic version of a not-dissimilar story told by John Dewey or Jürgen Habermas yields the simpler conclusion that 'modernity' dictates, or strongly presses us towards, the acceptance of a legal structure built on individual rights, and a political structure built on representative democracy.

The argument of Karl Popper's *The Open Society and Its Enemies* and *The Poverty of Historicism* makes the conjunction of methodological holism and a respect for individual rights look either impossible or at least grossly mistaken. For one of Popper's claims in those books—the books were described by Popper himself as his 'war work'—was that the totalitarian regimes of Nazi Germany and Stalin's Soviet Union rested on a holistic methodology, and that methodological and political virtue and vice went hand in hand. On the face of it, this was an odd view for Popper to adopt, since his principle of the logical discontinuity between facts and decisions, with ethical stances belonging firmly in the latter camp, suggested that almost any philosophical view might coexist with almost any political attachment. This, of course, was Russell's view, and it led Russell to insist that strictly speaking there could be no such thing as political philosophy. Philosophy was not a realm of choice; politics was a realm of nothing else. But Popper held that 'methodological individualism' was a useful solvent of the assorted forms of nonsense on which both communist and fascist regimes had rested.

The argument is a brief one. On Popper's account of them, fascism and communism rested on the thought that 'the race' or 'the proletariat' or some other 'whole' was more real than the individuals we actually see around us. He conceded that this view was not without some support. People who are serving in an army really do act as they do 'because' they are in an army, and in that sense the behaviour of the parts—the soldiers—is explained by the whole—the army. Still, this does not show that there is any sense in which the army is prior to the soldiers, nor that the locution of explaining something 'as a whole' makes any great sense. There is no such condition as that of being able to invoke *all* the features of whatever it is we are explaining, and in that sense any ambition to know 'the whole' must remain frustrated. Whether this argument cuts much ice against the political positions that Popper intended is another matter.

The history of arguments about 'methodological individualism' after Popper put the terms into circulation was not inspiring. For one thing, it became increasingly obscure who or what the 'individuals' invoked in an explanation are supposed to be. 'The median voter' is not ontologically exactly on all fours with our neighbour Mrs. Jones. But if the notion of the 'individual' is to embrace whatever appears in the theory as 'the consumer' or 'the voter' or whatever, the contrast between individuals and holistic entities seems to have vanished, or at any rate to have been thinned out rather drastically. Indeed, it turns out to be disarmingly simple to recast almost everything that Marx wished to say about the inevitable transition from one mode of production to another into exactly the terms that Popper and his followers demanded. Enthusiasts for methodological individualism did not suggest that history should be explained as a conspiracy in which particular individuals made everything happen. What they appealed to was what Popper baptized as 'situational logic'. Given their situation and their wants and beliefs, rational actors—not narrowly self-interested and fully-informed actors, but people who knew what they wanted and had coherent beliefs about the world they were faced with—would find that a particular action was 'the thing to do'; when they did it, and the various persons involved in whatever the situation was interacted with one another, the result was not something each of them wanted, let alone something that all of them wanted, but it was explicable as the outcome of their all acting in the way they rationally ought. Feudalism may have collapsed because it suited so many landowners to compound for the military services they owed their feudal superiors by paying cash so that mercenaries could be hired. Since they needed cash, they had an incentive to alter the leases their tenants enjoyed and to turn them into more modern forms of cash rental. Once the process had started, the brighter and more productive tenants began to make real profits and so had money to invest; this they might do by leaving the land entirely and going into small manufacturing or trade in the towns, or by buying land from their financially strapped landlords and creating in the process a new class of capitalist farmer.

Whether or not this process took place is a question of fact. That the explanation proceeds throughout in terms of the strategies pursued by rational agents, and the unanticipated consequences of their doing so, is incontrovertible. There is thus nothing in Marxism that links it logically to the espousal of an improper form of methodological holism. There is a form of holism to which it must be attached, and that is the holism involved in taking sociological explanation seriously at all. What does this consist in? Surely in the hypothesis that methodological individualism is acceptable as the demand that we should be able to trace the phenomena for which are offering an explanation in a step-by-step way through the actions and reactions of the people whose behaviour is involved. The phenomenon of the declining rate of profit would—had it not turned out to be a myth—have been explained in terms of each entrepreneur having an incentive to maximize profits; whenever someone got ahead of his competitors, they would instantly switch into whatever had given him an advantage, so driving down the extra profits he had momentarily made. Eventually, there would be no further moves to be made, and each competing capitalist would try to undercut all the others, with the ultimate result that all would be operating at a minimal level of profit. Now, *if* the process were like this, the holism of Marxism would amount to the claim that the motivation and beliefs of the participants in this self-destructive process were dictated to them by their participation in this economic system. It would not be 'human nature' that drove them, but the imperatives of the economic system. To disbelieve in the Marxist account of historical change it is enough to believe that Marx was in fact wrong, both about the way a capitalist economy works, and about the trends he observed during his own lifetime. There is no need to believe either that the logic of the explanations he wanted to offer was incoherent, or that unacceptable political allegiances were implicit in that logic. To put it differently, methodological individualism is persuasive when it is the demand for adequately filled-out explanations, and its claims are obscure when it is more than that. In any event, it does not represent a contentious (or even an uncontentious) form of ethical or political individualism, and its further discussion would for present purposes be an adventure into a cul-de-sac.

The Idealist critique

The critique of individualism wears much the same appearance for the past hundred years. The underlying grounds of the critique vary a good deal, however, according to the different authors' philosophical or sociological commitments. At its simplest, the critique is this: the fully-informed, wholly rational calculator of economic theory is nowhere to be found in the real world; not only do we in fact have imperfect knowledge of the outside world, we do not have the well-ordered preferences that rational economic man must have. To the extent that we sometimes approximate to the condition of the idealized economic agent, it is in very special situations—either in the laboratory or in the stock market, for instance. Economic theory starts with the assumption that economic actors are essentially what Marx called *Träger*, that is, the bearers of those characteristics required for economic analysis to analyse their behaviour successfully. If economic theory can be formulated only if economic actors are utility maximizers acting selfishly, the bare fact that people often act unselfishly is enough to show that moral and political theory must be interested in something other than economics, and particularly in the way in which people are socialized into the qualities that make them adequate moral agents and decent citizens. Now, if this is the essence of the critique, it need not amount either to the claim that economic theory is ill-founded, nor to the claim that 'ethical individualism' is an error, nor to the claim that the rights of the individual are of no account in politics. What it must amount to is a meta-ethical claim: for instance, that we are so essentially part of a community that even individualist ideals must—in some fashion—be a collective as well as an individual possession.

The origins of the modern critique of individualism—from our 'political thought in the past century' perspective—lie in philosophical Idealism. I mean by this that the transformation of the Idealist critique into a more naturalistic, and broadly sociological, critique of the sort advanced by John Dewey in the United States and L. T. Hobhouse in Britain amounted to a seamless transition from a philosophical mode of argument that now seems hopelessly old-fashioned to a more naturalistic mode of argument with which we are familiar in the work of American neo-pragmatists and Jürgen Habermas.[4] What the Idealists rejected was what they saw as an atomistic conception of the person, in which the biography of the self was reduced to a string of momentary thoughts, sensations and appetites, and in which happiness for the individual is a mathematical sum of the accumulated instances of felt pleasure. F. H. Bradley, T. H. Green, and Bernard Bosanquet all claimed that happiness is something that attaches to a whole life, that what we seek is our satisfaction as persons, and that personality involves not only a sustaining link throughout the individual life but membership in a community of similar selves. F. H. Bradley was perhaps the most philosophically distinguished of the English idealists, but also the least interested in politics. Green and Bosanquet, on the other hand, were influential, not only in academic life, but in British politics more widely. It is sometimes said that Green's expansive liberalism, and his own moral impact on students, and thence by descent on the students his own students taught, was one of the formative influences on the modern British welfare state. Although he had been dead some years by the time R. H. Tawney and William Beveridge went up to Oxford, Green's spirit might unsuperstitiously be said to have permeated the place still. It is arguable that Bosanquet's influence on the practice of the welfare state was greater still. Bosanquet was deeply involved in the Charity Organisation Society (COS), an organization that may have had a greater effect than Green's philosophy in setting the tone of the welfare arrangements eventually made by government; Bosanquet combined his career as a philosopher with what most people would consider a second full-time career in the COS.

---

[4] On Dewey, see A. Ryan, *John Dewey and the High Tide of American Liberalism* (New York, W. W. Norton, 1995); on Hobhouse, see S. Collini, *Liberalism and Sociology* (Cambridge, Cambridge University Press, 1979); on Habermas, see T. McCarthy, *Habermas and Critical Theory* (Cambridge, Mass., MIT Press, 1986).

Knowing that Green was a liberal and that Bosanquet was a good deal more conservative in his political allegiances, it is tempting to think that this must be reflected in a more individualist political ethic in Green and a more collectivist political ethic in Bosanquet. In fact, this is not how the difference emerges. Bosanquet was a pupil of Green's, and learned the ethos of public service from him. The beginning of wisdom starts with the observation that Green was more nearly a Kantian than a Hegelian. Green certainly held the fundamental Idealist tenet that the world is ultimately ruled by intelligence; since the world is intelligible, he thought, it must be the product of intelligence. But, he did not hold the Hegelian view that only the whole is ultimately real. Bosanquet did, and it is that doctrine that gives Bosanquet's *Philosophical Theory of the State* its apparently collectivist flavour. For, the natural interpretation of Bosanquet's moral holism is that individuals should give the state the benefit of the doubt when their best judgement of what they ought to do is at odds with what the state requires. Bosanquet rejected the complaint that his views were in any sense collectivist, however. Certainly, it would have been hard to square either economic or ethical collectivism with the goals of the COS, for its aim was to organize the charitable efforts of the better-off in such a way that the worse-off who were in receipt of their charity would be enabled to find and hold employment, to manage their household budgets efficiently, and in one way and another to advance from a position of dependency to one of self-reliance. The COS has had an unfortunate reputation for distinguishing between the 'deserving' and 'undeserving' poor by reference to the 'deserving' being more amenable to reform and improvement than the undeserving. In fact, that is a shading of the truth. The 'deserving' were not so much the virtuous poor as those who were able to get back on their own feet with a minimal amount of help.

All the same, Bosanquet was not a liberal in the way that Green was. The fact emerges in the different focuses of their best known writings on politics. It is not surprising that Green's *Lectures on the Principles of Political Obligation* became something like a liberal Bible.[5] One reason is that Green took the search for individual freedom as the starting point of his inquiry His slightly unnerving essay 'On the Different Senses of 'Freedom' as Applied to Will and to the Moral Progress of Man' was printed as a preface to the *Lectures* when they were extracted from the

---

[5] T. H. Green, *Lectures on the Principles of Political Obligation* (London, Longmans, Green, 1917).

main body of his *Works*, and that suggests Green's approach. Green's question was not only whether we can recognize an obligation to obey the powers that be and yet remain free agents, but in what ways the state could positively further the task of *making* us free agents. His answer came close to providing a liberal and Kantian account of the withering away of the state; the closer the state's laws came to requiring us to do what an autonomous, morally rational person would will in any event, the closer we would come to reconciling law and liberty. Paradoxically, however, the achievement of this in actuality would occur at the moment at which we would have taken our own moral perfection as our goal, and in that way transcended the political condition entirely.[6] One of the key words in Green's own account of this vision, however, is 'organization', and this gives a clue to one way in which what Green is providing is an immanent critique of an old-fashioned individualism.

Older individualism was associated in Green's mind with both the utilitarian and the social contract tradition—anyone who doubts whether it could have been may reflect on the way John Rawls's *Theory of Justice* relies on the same moral psychology as the utilitarianism it criticizes.[7] Both contractualism and utilitarianism began with a vision of 'finished' single individuals, who were supposed to be fully-informed, who had clear preferences but no moral convictions, and who must construct for themselves a political ethic and institutional arrangements justified by that ethic. Freedom for such individuals could not be anything else than being left to get on with pursuing their own ambitions. Organization would be a constraint not a liberation, and would at best have an instrumental value; that is, rational persons would accept constraints for the sake of the goals the constraints enabled them to achieve. Green's ethics, like those of all the writers I shall mention in these first two sections, are what I have called 'personalist'; that is to say they begin from the thought that the bare biological individual is considered only as the raw material for ethical growth, and ethical growth is explained as personal development; Green, like Bosanquet in Britain and Dewey in the United States, was impressed by the extent to which we *become* persons only as the result of learning how to order our thoughts and desires so as to shape them into the materials of a whole life. Satisfaction as a person was, they all agreed, something distinct from a sum of felt pleasures.

---

[6] Green, *Lectures on the Principles of Political Obligation*, pp. 24–5.
[7] J. Rawls, *A Theory of Justice* (Cambridge, Mass., Harvard University Press, 1971).

It is an easy move from this thought to an emphasis on 'organiza-tion'. Green's acknowledgment that utilitarianism had marked a stage of moral advance, even if it had rested on an implausible moral psychology, allowed him to claim that the misrepresented moral goal was self-satisfaction, in a sense diametrically opposite to that which 'self-satisfied' usually possesses. A hundred years later, this thought has been redescribed by Charles Taylor and others in terms of 'second-order desires'.[8] Where the psychology of 'rational economic man' suggests that happiness is a matter of satisfying one preference after another, Green and other Idealists and their successors rely on the thought that the satisfaction we aim at is that of satisfying the desires which we *wish* to have, not those that happen to move us at any particular moment. It is not surprising that Green took the drunkard surrounded by gin shops as his paradigm of a modern form of slavery. While the drunk surely wants the drink he is swilling down, he wishes at the same time that he did not want it.

The free man is the man with his psyche so organized that what he wants is what he would ideally want if he were rational, well-informed, and in complete command of himself. It is this conception of the free individual that is common to all forms of personalist ethics, and the difference between more and less liberal versions of its associated politics rests on different understandings of the extent to which what we ordinarily count as the activities of government can assist in the development of such a personality. This is a view with many modern adherents, of whom Charles Taylor is the best known. Both Taylor and Harry Frankfurt emphasize 'second-order desires', which is to say that they emphasize the importance of our endorsing, or, at any rate, whole-heartedly accepting, the desires on which we act. Acting against our second-order desires is quite plausibly described as being a slave to our (first-order) desires, and it is the freedom that consists in not being so enslaved that they write about.

One way in which Green remained a Kantian was in describing the state's work as that of hindering hindrances to the good life. Of course, an expansive enough understanding of what hindrances the state might remove would make liberals indistinguishable from conservatives on the one hand and socialists on the other; but Green's own account of these

---

[8] H. Frankfurt, *The Importance of What We Care About* (New York, Cambridge University Press, 1988); C. Taylor, 'What's Wrong with Negative Liberty?', in A. Ryan, ed., *The Idea of Freedom* (Oxford, Oxford University Press, 1979).

matters ran no such risk. In his essay, 'Liberalism', Ronald Dworkin argues that all legitimate democracies are committed to treating their citizens with 'equal concern and respect', as individual persons with lives to lead according to their own conception of the good life. He then distinguishes conservatives from liberals in terms of the degree of confidence they place in the individuals who are engaged in this project. Conservatives do not trust us to come to reasonable conclusions and manage our own moral enterprises, and therefore accept a degree of paternalism that outrages liberals; liberals trust in our capacity to operate as autonomous creatures, and therefore refrain from supervising us where conservatives think good sense requires it.[9] By the same token, one might think that socialists hold that the risk of our being crushed and exploited by our competitors means that the common ownership of the means of production promotes freedom, even if it deprives us of the chance to acquire vast fortunes; conservatives reverse the estimate of the benefits and burdens of private property rights. Green was almost a liberal in the terms suggested by Dworkin, but not quite. For Green, the crucial element was the need to preserve the voluntariness of our acceptance of our own conception of the good. Here again, the difference between an economic and an ethical and political interest in the autonomy of the agent becomes clear. The 'economic' interest in voluntariness is that a voluntary choice is a good indicator of the preferences of the agent whose choice it is; if we wish to satisfy preferences, voluntariness is the best guide we have to our success in doing it. It does not, however, feature in the assessment of the goals of action. That is exactly what it does do in Green's and indeed in any other ethics with a Kantian background.

Bosanquet did not differ from Green on the main point at issue. He did, however, go further down the path that Dworkin suggests as the path taken by the conservative. A recent student of the political theory of Idealism, Professor Simchoni, has argued that the characteristic aim of Idealism was to pursue a *via media* between tempting but inadequate conceptions of social relations. Contractarian models of social life were inadequate on one front, and theories that represented individuals as essentially passive creations of a social whole were inadequate on the other. On her account of the Idealists, Green performed the appropriate balancing act more delicately than Bosanquet, whose wish to emphasize

[9] R. Dworkin, 'Liberalism', in S. Hampshire and B. Williams, eds., *Public and Private Morality* (Cambridge, Cambridge University Press, 1972).

the priority of the whole over the part led him to exaggerate the dependency and underrate the capacity for autonomy of the individual.[10] This is perhaps an injustice to Bosanquet, but there is certainly something to the charge. The issue between them may, however, have been less a philosophical one than a matter of social and political judgement. Green was readier than Bosanquet to believe that there is such a thing as moral progress and he held that it characteristically occurs when individuals find the demands of conscience set them at odds with their society's existing positive morality and its embodiment in the local laws. Bosanquet, in contrast, was quicker than Green to think that dissenters were muddled or wicked rather than prophets of a new vision.

The interest of the Idealists lies today less in their affinities with Hegel or his latter-day *epigone* than in their affinities with subsequent sociological theorists. A transitional figure in the movement from a 'pure' philosophical stance to a form of social theory more thoroughly infused with the findings of social science was D. G. Ritchie, who was interested in combining the insights of Hegel with those of Darwin, something that was much on the mind of John Dewey on the other side of the Atlantic.[11] The problem about effecting a union of the two was obvious enough. The attraction of Hegel's philosophy was that it operated in the same moral and intellectual space as traditional religion. The Absolute might have been an austere and excessively impersonal substitute for God, but the thought that the ascent to the Absolute was the modern version of the age-old philosophical quest to see the world as God might see it, was irresistible. The obvious drawback was that Hegel's own version of this programme was notoriously opaque, and the difficulty that Hegel attempted to overcome remained firmly in place: traditional religion was intelligible but incredible, and attempts to save it from empirical discrediting only made it unintelligible. Evolutionary theory on the other hand suffered from its scientific virtues. Being concerned only with explaining how the world came to contain the various animal species that it did, it could say nothing about the moral excellence or lack of it that this process generated. If evolutionary theory is well founded, it provides an excellent explanation of why the world contains the species it contains, and it does nothing more than that. This

[10] A. Simchoni, *The Political Theory of English Idealism*, DPhil. thesis (Oxford, 1981).

[11] J. Dewey, 'From Hegel to Darwin', in *Middle Works* (Carbondale, Ill., Southern Illinois University Press, 1985).

was the gist of T. H. Huxley's famous Romanes Lecture on 'Ethics and Evolution'; Huxley made the simple point that what made plants, animals, or people good at surviving in their environment was an entirely different sort of question from that of what made them beautiful, admirable or virtuous, and after a hundred years it still appears that Huxley had the better of the argument with his critics.[12] It was this difficulty in the attempt to extract moral and political lessons from evolutionary theory that every Idealist thinker could point to in distinguishing the pretensions of philosophy from those of sociology and biology. Yet, the temptation to 'naturalize' Hegelianism was all but irresistible. In the United States, it yielded Dewey's pragmatism; in Britain, it produced L. T. Hobhouse's liberal sociology.

Ritchie was more nearly a collectivist in economic matters than his fellow-Idealists; indeed, he was briefly a member of the Fabian Society. Like all the Idealists, however, his fundamental allegiance was to a rather loose evolutionism, according to which social development could be measured by the increasing harmonization of individual and social aims, and in a broad sense by an increase in the capacity of both society and the individual to achieve their goals. Thin though this is, it is strikingly like the last words of Talcott Parsons on the subject some 30 years ago. It is nonetheless sufficient to cast doubt on 'narrow individualism' as an adequate basis for social and political life. It does not do this by arguing head-on that nobody was ever accurately described in the terms of rational economic man, since even Ritchie and Hobhouse were content to agree that, within appropriate limits, the economist's picture of how the economy functioned was correct. Nor did they wish to insist too hard that nobody could live their whole lives with nothing more in their psyche than that minimal equipment. It was rather that they wished to be able to bracket the assumptions of economic theory, as if to say that the liberating effect of casting off the old constraints on social and economic life had been mildly intoxicating, so that thinkers had run away with the idea that mankind really were as they seemed to be in some narrowly commercial transactions, and that things would go more smoothly the less they were interfered with. Then, they could draw the familiar moral: for a society to function while operating the institutions of the free market, it had to have in place all manner of educative and disciplining mechanisms that would prevent the social fabric from un-

---

[12] T. H. Huxley, 'Evolution and Ethics', in Huxley, *Evolution and Ethics and other essays* (London, Macmillan, 1894).

ravelling. It is a familiar point today, and was made perhaps somewhat less neatly a century ago than it has been made since. Still, the simple point that people could not operate a market if others did not trust them, and that others would not trust them if it seemed that they would be trustworthy only as long as it was obviously in their immediate interest to be so, was one that was understood long before the idea of the 'Prisoners' Dilemma' got into circulation.

The sociological turn

Hobhouse was a political theorist in the traditional sense, but he was also the first Professor of Sociology in a British university. He is also something of a counter-example to my suggestion that once a political theorist takes a sociological turn, he or she is almost bound to have a certain distance from an individualist perspective on politics. Or rather, he forces me to clarify the different ways in which a contrast between an individualist and a collectivist political theory might be taken. The sense that most writers at the turn of the century would have had in mind referred to government action in the economy. The sense in which Hobhouse began as more of a collectivist than he later became, is that he was initially more optimistic about the likely results of government intervention. Or, to put it simply, he began as a socialist and ended as a liberal. Indeed, his best-known work may well be *The Metaphysical Theory of the State*, which drew a direct connection between the political philosophy of Hegel and the wickedness of subsequent German militarism. It was also an unkind thrust at Bernard Bosanquet's *Philosophical Theory of the State*. Hobhouse claimed that the Zeppelins he could see dropping bombs on London as he wrote were the consequence of the German attachment to Hegelianism.[13] But he was himself a good, if rebellious, student of Idealism, and an articulate exponent of the view that a critique of individualism was an essential element in the refurbishment of liberalism.

Hobhouse inherited from his philosophy tutors two thoughts, to which he added some more empirically-founded anxieties of his own. The first was that moral progress consisted in the growth of harmony. This was a central tenet, not only of his political theory in the narrower sense, but of his longer scholarly works, such as *Morals in Evolution*. But

---

[13] L. T. Hobhouse, *The Metaphysical Theory of the State* (London, Allen & Unwin, 1918).

Hobhouse was always careful to insist that he had in mind the existence of a latent harmony, not an actual one; the world as it existed was in fact disjointed and full of conflict, and there was nothing to be gained by pretending it was not so; nor was there any merit in asking people to accept that all is right with the world when it manifestly is not. Not unlike Dewey, whose English counterpart he in many ways was, Hobhouse acknowledged the creative role of forms of conflict that fell short of civil war. Then he insisted that its creative role was to drive us to create more harmonious forms of psychic and social order. The second part of his inheritance cut to some extent across the emphasis on harmony. For this was the claim that humanity had experienced a form of moral education in human history, of an unplanned and only retrospectively intelligible kind, of which the result was that we had come to understand that we might take control of our own existence.

That second strand in the argument makes Hobhouse what I have been claiming that 'new liberals' characteristically were. The goal of politics remained the liberal goal of individual emancipation. The usual commonplaces about the impossibility of 'absolute freedom' were taken for granted—although not so much so that they were not mentioned in lectures on *The Individual and the State*; and Green's insistence that the state could not *make* us good citizens, let alone virtuous individuals by compulsion, was rewritten in a more sociological and less Kantian vein. The state in its nature was clumsy and coercive; it therefore ought to do only those things that would cure the grosser ways in which we got in one another's way. In other words, the state was well designed for hindering hindrances, but ought to tread carefully when it came to enforcing particular conceptions of the good life. Since this sounds exceedingly like a milk-and-water view of politics, it is worth recalling what it is *not* endorsing. It is not endorsing a Nozick-like, natural rights-based, defence of the night watchman state, nor lending to *laissez-faire* a particular moral legitimacy.[14] Hobhouse was emphatic that the moral basis of property rights—which he treated in an evolutionary fashion in a famous essay on the subject[15]—lay in their contribution to our freedom. This meant that property which we used ourselves was on a very different moral footing from property that we used when we hired other

[14] R. Nozick, *Anarchy, State and Utopia* (New York, Basic Books, 1974).
[15] 'The Evolution of Property in Fact and Idea', in J. Meadowcroft, ed., *Liberalism and Other Writings* (Cambridge, Cambridge University Press, 1994), pp. 176–98.

people's labour in order to secure a profit. This was not the traditional liberal version of what has often been thought to be a distinctively Marxian thought; that is, it was not an attempt to allow the state to expropriate surplus value, but to allow the state to defend the liberty of the employee. The consequence was that it was always in principle legitimate for the state to step in and regulate the activities of investors and employers, and that it could do so, in principle, without being unnerved by the cry that it was attacking liberty when it was reducing inequality and reducing the power of employers over their employees. It might be in practice that the clumsy instrumentalities of the state did not much advance freedom by intervention, in which case even mildly socialist versions of new liberalism would be a mistake; but in principle, they might do good, and if they did, they were right.

Conversely, Hobhouse's emphasis on a 'common good' might in principle have led to a more illiberal politics than any he accepted. Today, American writers of a communitarian persuasion affect to believe that they are offering a powerful criticism of liberalism when they insist that citizens ought to be motivated by a concern to promote a, or the, common good, and that social institutions should be remodelled in such a way as to bring up young people to be so motivated. The second side of this, Hobhouse, like Green, argued all his life. What I have called the personalist ethic was emphatic that persons lived in communities whose goals they shared. The thought that this might license an attack on liberalism would have been thought quite mad. There were, after all, pre-modern societies that ensured that their members shared the common goals of those societies; Athens did not flinch at poisoning Socrates; the Romans did not flinch at executing the soldier who mocked the auguries. Medieval Europe did not flinch at burning heretics. The sense in which Hobhouse's ethics were sociologically formed and rested on a critique of individualism was that Hobhouse supposed that a liberal society could be created in which individuals learned the arts of living in such a society and acquired a loyalty to it. Against 'narrow' individualism, he insisted that a sense of individuality was an historical and social achievement rather than a gift of nature—something that he thought we all know perfectly well, but forget when we are engaged in theorizing. But this meant that the difference between Hobhouse and, say, Mill lay only in a new self-consciousness about the history of modern consciousness—and even there a case can certainly be made for saying that Mill knew, even if he did not bring to the forefront of his argument, everything that

Hobhouse wanted to emphasize.[16] The individuality that he thought it should be the object of a modern society to promote was not unlike what Mill was seeking.

Since that needs little argument, it is perhaps worth emphasizing one way in which what Hobhouse wanted was not wholly like what Mill was seeking. It will illustrate my earlier suggestion that the sociological turn colours, even though it does not dictate, the political theory with which it is associated. Hobhouse said, and clearly very much meant, that his talk of harmony was not intended to suggest that harmony had been achieved. Harmony was the latent goal of social progress, but it was not an achieved fact. Still, there is no doubt that this perspective yields something rather different from *On Liberty*. Mill thought that individuals needed to learn a certain stubbornness and resistance to social pressure; to that extent, his attachment to the idea of social harmony, and even to an ideal of individual harmony, was weaker than Hobhouse's. Whether one ascribes the difference between Mill and Hobhouse to the effect of Idealism on Hobhouse or to Hobhouse's taste for evolutionary sociology is perhaps immaterial. Either influence would have had much the same effect. To my mind, it is probably impossible to guess, simply because the effect of Idealism was to render its adherents receptive to the naturalistic interpretation of their existing views that was embodied in sociology. Dewey's autobiographical account of the way the distinctively philosophical features of Hegel's search for absolute knowledge 'dropped away' conveys the essence of the process quite well.

Wilder figures than Hobhouse held similar views. Bertrand Russell's *Principles of Social Reconstruction* were, he told Ottoline Morrell, intended to show 'the spark of the divine' within each individual, but the content of those splendidly utopian essays is entirely secular, and for the most part represents the 'new liberalism' pushed to an extreme—but an extreme of moral ambition rather than anything institutionally astonishing. But what is worth extracting from it is something less visible in Hobhouse, and strikingly more visible in Graham Wallas's *Human Nature in Politics*.[17] This is the attack, not on the 'finished' quality of the individuals presupposed in utilitarian liberalism, but on the 'intellectualist' assumptions that underlay it. Wallas did not, as we often do today, split out assumptions that might be productive in economics from

---

[16] I. W. Müller, *John Stuart Mill and French Thought* (Urbana, Ill., Illinois University Press, 1956).

[17] G. Wallas, *Human Nature in Politics* (London, Constable, 1908).

those that were illuminating in politics. He thought that economics had itself become institutional and historical in response to the obvious shortcomings of pure theory. What he *did* insist was that the old under-pinnings of the theory of representative government were mistaken, because they supposed a degree of rationality on the part of individuals at all levels that did not, and could not, exist. He and Russell both absorbed something of what had animated the American pragmatists. Individuals were not driven by rational calculation so much as by impulse and instinct. It was therefore part of the art of politics to ensure that they were driven by benign and freedom-promoting impulses rather than blind rage or blind terror. In Russell's case, this was part of his campaign against the First World War, and he was pretty shameless about offering a sketch of human nature geared to the purpose. Human beings were not calculating creatures, and they did not try to maximize pay-offs to themselves. They were driven by impulses; once satisfied, an impulse generally disappeared for the moment, and we sought to satisfy some other impulse. Russell thought it worth dividing impulses into two types, the creative and the possessive. Possessive impulses drive us to acquire things that cannot be shared with others, especially property and power; creative impulses lead us to pursue goals where competition is not inevitable. My theorem makes it no less likely that you, too, will discover an interesting truth or two. It takes little wit to see that in the middle of a war between rival imperialist powers, the reduction of possessive impulses and the encouragement of creative impulses would have seemed a very good thing. Wallas was not so concerned with immediate political needs. He was more interested in what one might call 'democratic disappointment', the way people had striven to make the British political system more democratic, had succeeded, but had not got what they expected from democratization. The explanation lay partly in the mechanics of government, in the fact that unelected bureau-crats must play a large part in determining policy, so that what emerged as government policy might be very far from what either electorates or politicians wanted. But some lay in the consequences of our attachment to symbolic and emotive aspects of the political system. There is in Wallas's pages no suggestion that we should, so to speak, succumb to irrationality and luxuriate in its pleasures. Indeed, he was an enthusiast for efficiency, no friend to imperial wars, and a humanitarian. He was also a surprisingly influential voice in undermining faith in rationality, at least in the sense of an untroubled conviction that human beings are by nature rational.

Anti-self-interested rational man

Although it is true enough that the Idealists and their more sociologically-minded successors were insistent on the need for unselfish behaviour, and were to some degree—Bosanquet excepted—egalitarians, it was left to R. H. Tawney and A. D. Lindsay to turn the critique of individualism they had learned in their youth into a defence of democratic socialism. Tawney's attack on the psychology and politics of unfettered capitalism in *The Acquisitive Society* and his later, more measured, book on *Equality* was a great deal fiercer than Lindsay's work on *The Modern Democratic State.* Nonetheless, they had it in common that their vision of a successful modern society looked back to the social cohesion of Puritan England rather than forward to the post-capitalist utopia of Marxism. One ought not to exaggerate that nostalgia; Tawney's *Religion and the Rise of Protestant Capitalism* is notably less inclined to give Puritanism the benefit of the doubt than Weber's *Puritan Ethic* was. Weber was intrigued by the way in which a society that (as he thought) was genuinely attached to other-worldly goals nonetheless brought into existence secular, calculating, self-interested economic order. Tawney was more inclined to believe that they had worldly ambitions in plenty, although ones that their religious beliefs helped to legitimate.

The model of a democratic community in Lindsay's eyes was the Quaker congregation. It was a paradigm of the sort of society in which power was dispersed absolutely equally. It was governed by the attempt of all concerned to converge upon a common view of the community's needs, and it was scrupulous about not moving in ways that violated individual consciences. Such a society is vulnerable to erosion by the sort of person described in standard rational-choice theory. Selfish, rational people will parasite on the self-restraint of others, and may behave in all manner of duplicitous ways if they are confident of the honesty of others. It is one of the long-standing puzzles of rational choice theory to explain how a principled moral concern for honesty could spread through a society of rational egoists; on the face of it, honesty requires us to forego the advantages of duplicity in just the same way as the heroes of Prisoners' Dilemma games are required to forego the advantages of ratting on such promises as they might make, and every problem that besets 'solutions' to Prisoners' Dilemma problems besets solutions to the problem of making honest people out of rational self-interested actors.

Neither Lindsay nor Tawney were much interested in pursuing these arguments. One might think that this was surprising, at any rate in Lindsay's case, since Lindsay was a philosophy tutor in Oxford and Glasgow, and wrote a good deal about Kant, Mill, and Plato. The truth, however, is that even as a philosopher Lindsay wrote in a discursive, historical, and rather sociological fashion—it was the aptness of a philosophical vision to the social conditions of its time that occupied his attention. Tawney was, in the same way, a moralist rather than a moral philosopher. For our purposes, therefore, they matter because they were part of the same movement of thought that I have already described. The interest of their views, however, is greater than that, because one aspect of what they wanted to say tied the social equality they sought to the ideal of personality that they promoted. Here, too, one might draw a connection with Mill's insistence in *The Subjection of Women* that only when children are brought up in egalitarian conditions will they develop an unforced and spontaneous concern for the interests of others. But, one can see in the context of Tawney's work that this, although true enough, does not cover the case that the ethical socialists wished to make. For that case was not—perhaps sadly—directed to the question of how we behave in close relationships. Rather, it was directed towards the moral disgrace of a society in which some lived so luxuriously that they were probably unhealthy, and less happy than they would have been in more modest circumstances, while others lived lives of cramped poverty, and above all insecurity. Such an existence was inconsistent with self-respect.

And here, once more, we find the personalist understanding of individuality returning to the centre of the stage. The claim is not that the individualism that Tawney and Lindsay repudiated could not find room for such an idea as that of self-respect, say; but finding room for it, as one can see from the efforts that Mill makes in *Utilitarianism*, is a strenuous undertaking. Tawney, on the other hand, just takes for granted that without self-respect nobody will find life worth living. It then becomes possible to scrutinize social and economic relationships for their success or failure in preserving the self-respect of all parties. The argument for a more egalitarian society is couched in personalist terms; and the argument is what we should expect: *bad* individualism is the self-interested striving to gain advantages over other people, while *good* individualism is the search for a common project that will satisfy our own temperament and call out or own abilities, while allowing us to engage with other persons as equals. Mill could have said as much as an account of the ideal social outcome, but of course Mill was more concerned in the meantime to emphasize the need to stand up for our own spiky, quirky, and *unco*-operatve qualities against the tendency of modern societies to impose a coerced intellectual and moral uniformity. Tawney would not have agreed that Mill had chosen the right place to start the argument. Or perhaps, one should say that he would not have thought that Mill had correctly diagnosed the causes of oppression and mutual distrust. If the problem was not so much the illiberal tendencies of modern democracy as the stifling effect of economic and social inequality, the place to start was with liberating the energies that a hierarchical and inegalitarian economic and social order suppressed. Oddly enough, Barrington Moore offered a more aggressive version of that thought some 50 years later when he observed that a revolutionary would wish for Lenin first and Mill next.[18] That may have been a foolish thought in some respects: it passes too lightly over the overwhelming probability that if we get Lenin first we shall not get Mill ever. But the thought that Mill begged the question against those who wanted more economic equality first, and wanted it for essentially liberal reasons, is not itself at all foolish.

A topic that has only marginal relevance here is the impact of a Marxist view of history and politics on this sort of argument. The British contribution to Marxism belongs to the history of British historical writing rather than to the history of political theory. Because the British role in Marx's own account of the origins of capitalism was largely confined to its having been the first example of capitalist industrialization, Marx himself was not on the face of it especially interested in the relationship of his doctrines to British political philosophy. His concern was with the advances he (thought that he) had made in the sphere of political economy. British Marxism had impressive achievements to its credit in cultural analysis and literary theory; and its impact on the writing of history has been enormous and, on the whole, beneficial. Its impact on political theory was neither. To the degree that writers whose interest lay in such issues as the transition from feudal to capitalist property relations allowed themselves moral and methodological commentary, it was to insist, first on the methodological holism implicit in Marxism, and second on the need to reverse our usual moral perspectives. Where we are usually inclined to assess the virtues of the futures offered us by reformists and revolutionaries alike in terms of what we now want, the Marxian ethic set us the task of being worthy of our future.

[18] B. Moore *et al.*, *A Critique of Pure Tolerance* (Boston, Mass., Beacon Books, 1968).

What there is no evidence of in British political thought is a principled disposition to see the proletariat as the bearer of the meaning of history in such a way as to imply that individuals might properly be required to subordinate their interests to that meaning. Class loyalty was often enough demanded, but almost invariably in terms of our duty to meet the demands of justice. The interest of Marxist theory, however, is greater than that suggests. For the problem faced by the Marxist insistence on the way in which habits and beliefs are framed by social conditions is that it undermines the Marxist belief that Marxism provides a determinate account of social change. Marxists criticize the assumptions of nineteenth-century economists on the grounds that the rational economic agents in which it deals are the products of a capitalist order, and not its begetters. Yet the dynamics of a capitalist economy are the result of individual actors pursuing profit, or maximizing their incomes, in a rational and well-informed way. It is this assumption that allows their behaviour to be predicted, at any rate within the terms of the theory. This raises obvious puzzles about how the behaviour of non-rational (perhaps 'expressive' or religiously-motivated) and non-fully informed actors can be predicted in the way Marxism seems to suggest it has to be for the Marxist theory of history to succeed. The behaviour of rational, self-interested calculators is predictable, simply because there is in most situations a single best strategy which they *should* pursue, and which we assume that they therefore *will* pursue. For actors not so situated, it is not so clear that there is some single best line of conduct that they ought, rationally, to pursue. It is perhaps this fact that has meant that most British Marxist historians have been quite modest in their ambitions. That is, they have been interested in explaining the way in which capitalism in fact came about, rather than the way in which it had to come about.

Indeed, to the extent that their work has borne on the subject of this essay, some of the most distinguished work has trodden a delicate line between accepting the implications of the view that history is largely the record of the doings of *collective* actors, especially classes, and a concern for the lives of individual members of those classes. Edward Thompson's *The Making of the English Working Class*, for instance, is firmly in the tradition of earlier works such as Raymond Postgate's *The Common People*, and that tradition begat the 'History Workshop' movement which was not only moved by a wish to recover the record of the ways in which working people had striven to shift the balance of advantage between themselves and the possessing classes in their own favour, but even more by a wish to rescue from oblivion the experience of individuals whose lives were as likely to suffer from the condescension of Marxist historians as from the condescension of bourgeois historians. It need hardly be said that this attitude is light-years away from the strain in Marxism that originated in Hegel's observation in his *Philosophy of History* that history was a 'slaughterbench', and that such rationality as it displayed was to be recovered with hindsight and by the philosopher. A sentimental, but not wholly inaccurate, observation is that British historians have never wanted to rise to the theoretical level of some of their European counterparts, a complaint levelled at Edward Thompson some 20 years ago, and worn by him as badge of pride thereafter.[19] The point, of course, was that what his critics took to be the deliverances of high theory, he took to be yet another excuse for ignoring the realities of individual human existences.

A coda on communitarianism

To conclude, let me recapitulate the simple point I have been making throughout, by returning to the argument misleadingly labelled 'the communitarian critique of liberalism'.[20] The argument has largely been a North American one, and it was sparked off by John Rawls's path-breaking *A Theory of Justice*, a book that drew on the social contract tradition of theorising about the foundations of a liberal constitutional and economic order to explicate and reinforce a view of a just social order that drew both on modern ideas about the value of a welfare state and on older, Kantian ideas about the need to treat individuals as the holders of inviolable rights. Rawls was clear that this was a 'hypothetical contract', that is, that we were asked to think what people *would* have done if they had been asked to contract with one another about the terms of social co-operation when they were deprived of the knowledge on which they would have to rely to drive an unfair bargain. Critics could not therefore complain, as their predecessors had done two hundred years before, that human beings never signed such a contract. What they could complain of was perhaps two things: the first was that Rawls relied too heavily on the idea that mankind was more naturally rational

---

[19] E. Thompson, *The Poverty of Theory* (London, Merlin Press, 1978); P. Anderson, 'The Peculiarities of the English', in Anderson, *Arguments Within English Marxism* (London, New Left Books, 1980).
[20] S. Mulhall and A. Swift, *Liberals and Communitarians* (Oxford, Basil Blackwell, 1992).

self-interested and self-centred than he ought, and the second that this sort of model smuggles into its conclusions the idea that we are self-contained creatures, whose social relationships are inessential to our conception of ourselves and the purpose of our lives. As arguments against Rawls's own work, neither of these two points is impressive. The third part of *A Theory of Justice* was devoted to the question of how an actual society might live according to the principles that the book had developed. The conception of society that Rawls there appealed to was that of a social union of social unions, or in more recent terminology, a community of communities.

Communitarian critics of Rawls have also argued that justice is not the central virtue of social life. If human beings are not self-centred, we have less reason to worry about protecting ourselves from the ill-will or exploitation of others, and less occasion to worry about the justice of the terms of social co-operation. The argument then may move towards the positive claim that we are social creatures whose conception of our interests and whose aspirations for our lives are formed by our upbringing in, and our membership of, a community whose understanding of the purpose of existence and of the nature of our aspirations is what gives sense to our own view of these. It is easy to see that in the United States of the 1980s it is tempting to respond to the greed and exploitation so visible in the economic realm by insisting on the virtues of community attachment. What is less obvious is that this is a criticism of *liberalism*. One might wish to say, indeed, it is hard to avoid saying, that what a liberal should aim to create is a liberal community, and that it is hard to imagine an isolated individual living as a liberal. But this, after all, is what earlier critics of 'narrow individualism' have always said. What communitarians oppose is not liberalism, for almost all of them are liberals of one stripe and another, but the modern version of 'narrow individualism'.

The critique of individualism is not an attack on ethical systems that placed the individual's welfare and moral well-being at the centre of the assessment of the health of society and its political arrangements. It has been all along a reminder of what we know: that individual character takes time and a proper environment to develop; that the rational, self-interested actor of economic analysis is not the basic unit of analysis, as though we were egoists first and only later and reluctantly tack on our moral and political attachments and sentiments; that because the political order controls and regulates the economic system, it is not possible in analysing and prescribing for the political system to 'bracket off' all those features as we legitimately do in economics. The continuity between the Idealist critique and the more sociologically-based critique of the next generation, and the continuity between them and ourselves, reflects the continued persuasiveness of the 'new liberal' consensus that academic circles, and the common human habit of reading whatever theories we embrace in such a way as to incorporate our existing moral convictions. The emphasis on political pluralism, the wish to render work not only better paid but more 'meaningful', the fear of both the over- and the under-active state, the wish to reconcile moral egalitarianism with the recognition of intellectual merit and economic productivity—all these were old allegiances that did more to shape the interpretation of new ideas than the new ideas did to shape them. Like many other ideas that migrated to the United States and Canada, these have flourished there. Not only did John Dewey incorporate them into the renovated liberalism that he constructed between the 1880s and 1940, they have made subsequent appearances in the widely-read work of Michael Walzer, Charles Taylor, and Richard Rorty. Like the thinkers who have developed them, these ideas are now not distinctively British or American, but part of the intellectual and political resources of a community that embraces both shores of the North Atlantic and its offshoots all over the globe.

5: Pluralism, Revenant or Recessive?

RODNEY BARKER

What is it, where and why did it go, and why has it come back?

Sir Ernest Barker once performed the rare trick of proposing two completely different interpretations of contemporary politics in a single article.[1] His original version analysed the pincer movement of international interconnectedness and internal diversity which appeared to challenge, even to marginalize, the centralized sovereign national state. Groups were increasingly fulfilling functions which the state had previously performed, and pluralism, not just as an account of social character, but more importantly as an account of and prescription for both politics and government which rejected both simple individualism and comprehensive collectivism, was in the ascendant.

The argument neatly identified both aspects of pluralism. In both its principally normative British early twentieth- and late twentieth-century versions, and its late mid-century North American and British version, pluralism constructed a description and an analysis of politics which was built on the actions, both self-creating and self-motivating, of groups and associations. The common denominator for all pluralists, both North American and British, although not necessarily the unifying or dominant characteristic, has been a belief in the dissemination of power and a dilution of the power of central government. This made it critical of much liberalism, conservatism, and socialism, although its

[1] E. Barker, 'The Discredited State', *Political Quarterly* (1915).

advocates have usually found a place at some point on the existing political spectrum: in Britain generally towards the radical left, in North America towards optimistic liberalism. But these rough triangulations are no more than rough, and the history of pluralism, and the thinking of pluralists, continually escape from, and render of only limited use, such generalizations.

Ernest Barker having thus pinpointed the international and the sub-national, the normative and the descriptive aspects of pluralism, was given cause to think again by the outbreak of war. The same article, by the time it was published, contained the additional and totally contrary observation that 'We have forgotten that we are anything but citizens, and the state is having its high midsummer of credit'.[2] The obituary was premature, since pluralism continued to flourish until the 1920s.[3] But the general observation was accurate enough. By the end of the first quarter of the chronological twentieth century the pluralist assault on the sovereign state had almost completely evaporated. Its protagonists were either, like J. N. Figgis, dead and lacking any disciples or successors, or, like Cole and Laski, had gone over to the enemy and, bar a few pious reservations,[4] had become enthusiastic supporters of collectivism. With the possible exception of Bertrand Russell and a few advocates of various forms of workers' control, British pluralism had changed from a dissident challenge to an historical memory.[5]

Yet by the 1980s the pluralist strain in British political thinking had proved itself to be one of the century's great recessive themes, and was established as a major web of reference for those who, for a variety of reasons and from a variety of perspectives, were increasingly disturbed

---

[2] E. Barker, 'The Discredited State', *Political Quarterly*, p. 121.

[3] It lingered for even longer than that. M. Tyldesley, 'The House of Industry League: Guild Socialism in the 1930s and 1940s', *Labour History Review*, 61 (1996), 309–321.

[4] This view is disputed by W. H. Greenleaf. W. H. Greenleaf, 'Laski and British Socialism', *History of Political Thought*, 2 (1981).

[5] There is a large number of studies of British pluralism. The principal ones are S. T. Glass, *The Responsible Society: the Ideas of the Guild Socialists* (London, Longman, 1966); D. Nicholls, *The Pluralist State: the Political Ideas of J. N. Figgis and His Contemporaries* (London, Macmillan, [2nd ed.] 1994); A. W. Wright, *G. D. H. Cole and Socialist Democracy* (Oxford, Clarendon Press, 1979); N. Carpenter, *Guild Socialism: An Historical and Critical Analysis* (New York, D. Appleton & Co., 1922); W. Y. Eliott, *The Pragmatic Revolt in Politics* (New York, Macmillan, 1928); K. C. Hsiao, *Political Pluralism* (London, Kegan, Paul, Trench, Tubner & Co., 1927); H. M. Magid, *English Political Pluralism* (New York, Columbia University Press, 1941). Nicholls' *The Pluralist State* contains useful bibliographical notes. For a sceptical note, see S. Collini, *Public Moralists: Political Thought and Intellectual Life in Britain 1850–1930* (Oxford, Clarendon Press 1991).

by the relentless centralization of state power and the frailty of political restraints on government. David Nicholls used the ideas of Figgis as a platform from which to denounce contemporary trends in government, Paul Hirst both anthologized Figgis, Laski, and Cole as neglected voices of continuing relevance and set out his own version of a pluralist polity, while John Keane used thematic quotations from Figgis[6] to introduce his own defence of a pluralist alternative. The context of this reappearance has been identified by both Nicholls and Hirst as the radical changes in the relative powers of central state and subordinate organizations and associations after 1979.[7] Whether or not this shift was linked solely to the government of Margaret Thatcher, Nicholls and Hirst reflect a widely current assumption that the years from the late 1960s to the early 1990s saw a shift in the balance of state power of historical significance.[8] At the same time, the end of the Cold War and the collapse of East European and Soviet communist regimes removed the institutional framework which had sustained simple ideological polarization. This was accompanied both by the disappearance of orthodox socialism and conservatism, and by a diversity of thinking around and beyond a much looser

---

[6] Nicholls, *The Pluralist State*; P. Hirst, ed., *The Pluralist Theory of the State: Selected Writings of G. D. H. Cole, J. N. Figgis, and H. J. Laski* (London, Routledge, 1989); P. Hirst, *Associative Democracy: New Forms of Economic and Social Governance* (Cambridge, Polity Press, 1994); J. Keane, *Democracy and Civil Society* (London, Verso, 1988).

[7] Nicholls, *The Pluralist State*; Hirst, ed., *The Pluralist Theory of the State*. The judgement of David Nicholls, *The Pluralist State*, while conceding some of the claims of the supporters of the Conservative government, is also clear in deploring the assault on intermediate associations.

> The Thatcher regime of the 1980s purported to be critical of state bureaucracy and in favour of decentralisation in a number of spheres. The claim was that devolution and the introduction of so-called internal market mechanisms would bring more 'customer choice' in such matters as education and health. What in fact has happened is that small units have indeed been given more power but so has Whitehall; it is the middle levels of county, municipality and region which have been throttled.

The small units, whether locally managed schools or hospital trusts, were relatively powerless in the face of central government departments. (x).

> Whether the state is more or less powerful than it was in the pre-Thatcher era may be debated, that its role has changed is incontrovertible. Equally apparent is the decline in power and independence of the various intermediate institutions in the country. (xi)

[8] Vernon Bogdanor sets a broader context, while still making Margaret Thatcher the main protagonist. V. Bogdanor, *Politics and the Constitution: Essays on British Government* (Aldershot, Dartmouth, 1996).

division between left and right.[9] It became easier to be anti-collectivist at the same time as being democratic, to want a radical distribution of power but favour neither state nor market as its progenitor, or to revolt simultaneously against the power of capital and the power of central government. It was easier to deny the existence of any simple common good without falling back deferentially on the existing contours along which individual well-being was distributed.

Not all the responses in these new times were pluralist: there was a broad range from revolutionary defensiveness to constitutional assertiveness.[10] But the pluralist solution was the most radical. It was also governmental not economic, proposing government, and the politics of government, where the New Right had proposed markets and utilitarian self-interest; and proposing functional subsidiarity, government at the lowest level possible, rather than central unitary power, where many radicals and those on the left had concentrated on changing the methods and quality of representation, while retaining the size and functions of central power virtually untouched.

---

[9] R. Barker, 'Why Are There No More Socialists or Conservatives?', *Contemporary Politics*, 1 (1995), 129–33 ; R. Barker, 'Political Ideas Since 1945, or How Long Was the Twentieth Century?', *Contemporary British History*, 10 (1996), 2–19; R. Barker, 'A Future for Liberalism or a Liberal Future?' in J. Meadowcroft, ed., *The Liberal Political Tradition: Contemporary Reappraisals* (Aldershot, Edward Elgar, 1996); R. Barker, *Political Ideas in Modern Britain in and After the Twentieth Century* (London, Routledge, 1997). Although Anthony Giddens has argued that we have now moved 'beyond left and right', his use of the terms is to describe old socialism and old conservatism, and the view presented here is less at odds with Giddens's argument than the terminology might suggest. A. Giddens, *Beyond Left and Right* (Cambridge, Polity Press, 1994); A. Giddens, 'Brave New World: The New Context of Politics' in D. Miliband, ed., *Reinventing the Left* (Cambridge, Polity Press, 1994).

[10] From the middle 1980s onwards, the constitution emerged from the obscurity of legal and political exegesis of a rather remote kind, to become a topic of increasing discussion by those who sought to reform British government, and to do so in the light of defensible principles derived from identifiable but eclipsed or smothered features of British public life. See for example: A. Barnett, C. Ellis, and P. Hirst, eds., *Debating the Constitution: New Perspectives on Constitutional Reform* (Cambridge, Polity Press, 1993); T. Benn and A. Hood, *Common Sense—A New Constitution for Britain* (London, Hutchinson, 1993); M. Evans, *Charter 88: A Successful Challenge to the British Political Tradition?* (Aldershot, Dartmouth, 1995); K. D. Ewing and C. A. Gearty, *Freedom Under Thatcher: Civil Liberties in Modern Britain* (Oxford, Clarendon Press, 1990); C. Graham and T. Prosser, eds., *Waiving the Rules: the Constitution under Thatcherism* (Milton Keynes, Open University Press, 1988); Institute for Public Policy Research, *A Written Constitution for the United Kingdom* (Poole, Mansell, Cassell, 1993); A. Marr, *Ruling Britannia: The Failure and Future of British Democracy* (London, Michael Joseph, 1995); P. McAuslan and J. F. McEldowney, *Law, Legitimacy and the Constitution* (London, Sweet & Maxwell, 1985); M. Rustin, 'Citizenship and Charter 88', *New Left Review*, 191 (1992), 37–42; Bogdanor, *Politics and the Constitution*.

British pluralism as a doctrine of government

Yet despite the re-introduction of pluralist ideas at the end of the 'short' twentieth century,[11] British pluralism[12] still remains relatively unknown, and likely to be confused with its North American namesake, if it is recognized at all.[13] This social, or intellectual, invisibility has been accentuated by the fact that there was in Britain from the 1950s a development of analytical, political pluralism in the study of the contribution of groups to public policy.[14] The irony is that this work of W. J. M Mackenzie, S. E. Finer, Robert McKenzie and their successors drew on North American and north European work on the contribution of groups to political representation and the negotiation of government policy,[15] while neglecting, being unaware of, or not using the work of, British writers who, from a different perspective, had identified the group nature of political life at the beginning of the century. This later British study of groups, while it has had until the 1980s more impact on political science in Britain, was a less distinctive contribution. Not all pluralist thinking which has taken place in Britain has been, in this sense 'British'. In making the distinction between this transatlantic pluralism and British pluralism, no conceptual cleansing is intended. The purpose is merely to distinguish a form of pluralism where a distinctive British

[11] The term is Eric Hobsbawm's: E. Hobsbawm, *Age of Extremes: The Short Twentieth Century 1914–1991* (London, Michael Joseph, 1994).

[12] I have used the term 'British pluralism' rather than the more familiar 'English pluralism'. Since one of the several elements of dispersal of central state power which pluralists in the United Kingdom have proposed, has been to local, regional, and sub-national-state communities, 'English' is inappropriately blind to the existence of Northern Ireland, Wales, and Scotland, and is the nationalist equivalent of talking of 'men' when we mean 'people'.

[13] Nicholls, *The Pluralist State* comments tartly on this unfamiliarity. The distinction between North American pluralism and British pluralism has often been obscured despite, or perhaps because of, an English sniffiness towards American imports (the bourbon syndrome) which has led to their origin, when their use cannot be disputed, being glossed over, and hence their distinctiveness obscured. This may be only the latest example of two nations divided by a common language. However, some attention is now being given to British pluralism among North American political theorists seeking for solutions to contemporary difficulties. A. I. Eisenberg, *Reconstructing Political Pluralism* (Albany, NY, State University of New York Press, 1995); K. McClure, 'On the Subject of Rights: Pluralism, Plurality and Political Identity' in C. Mouffe, ed., *Dimensions of Radical Democracy: Pluralism, Citizenship, Community* (London, Verso, 1992). McClure, however, subsumes British pluralism under the label 'Anglo-American', giving as its exponents Barker, Laski, Bentley and Follett. McClure, pp. 113–114.

[14] See the discussion in Jeremy Richardson's chapter in this volume, pp. 183 ff.

[15] See Richardson, pp. 184, 186 (this volume).

contribution has been made, from an area of work where British contributions have been elements in an international or trans-national discussion. Since, moreover, the British contribution to this trans-national, political pluralism is dealt with by another contributor to this volume,[16] I have not discussed it further, and have used the term 'British pluralism' to refer only to the fundamentally, but not exclusively, normative tradition which I have already identified.

David Nicholls has pointed to the distinguishing characteristics which mark off all the exponents of this British pluralism from the later North American, and British, variety. North American pluralism 'far from abandoning the pork-barrel state' sees politics 'as a contest for its appropriation'.[17] It thus leaves the unitary state untouched. British pluralism by contrast, rather than describing the varied activities of groups and associations as contributions to the formulation of universal and uniform policies for pursuing the common good, denies the existence of such a good.[18] Paul Hirst, equally usefully, has drawn attention to a feature which all forms of British pluralism share, and which distinguishes them from the North American variety of the second half of the century: the latter is political, the former governmental.[19] The distinction between political pluralism and governmental pluralism provides a useful gauge for setting limits to a discussion of the particularly British recessive pluralist theme. It makes it easier to set on one side not only political pluralism,[20] but normative and philosophical pluralism as well. This is not to deny that there are affinities between governmental, political, and normative pluralism, nor that they can be usefully discussed. But it is in the creation of an argument for governmental pluralism that a distinctive British contribution has been made. A concentration on this particular contribution, further, draws attention both to the circumstances in which pluralism has emerged, and to the problems which it has faced. Both of these arise from its claim to be not principally a doctrine of society or of politics, but of government. Pluralism in its distinctively British version is a doctrine about how and by

---

[16] See Richardson, Chapter 7 (this volume).

[17] Nicholls, *The Pluralist State*, p. 134.

[18] Ibid. p. 134.

[19] Hirst, ed., *The Pluralist Theory of the State*.

[20] What I have termed 'governmental pluralism' is from time to time called 'political pluralism', even by those such as Nicholls who insist on the distinctiveness of the British version. I have avoided this usage, in that 'political pluralism' could quite properly refer to a pluralist analysis of politics of the kind carried out by Dahl and his associates and successors.

whom people should be ruled, and while it may be useful to use the word governance rather than government to distinguish the forms of rule with which it is concerned from central, sovereign government,[21] whichever term is employed distinguishes pluralism from both its North American title-sharer, and from arguments which are principally about politics and the political contribution of groups and associations to the formation of policy by the centralized national state.[22] Pluralism, as a doctrine of government, sets limits to what the national state may do, and simultaneously gives governing functions to associations.[23] This, for Figgis, was the fundamental reason for the opposition of the imperial Roman state to Christianity: 'the State demanded and the Church could not yield an unlimited allegiance'.[24]

In one final but essential respect British governmental pluralism differs from trans- or mid-Atlantic pluralism. The latter is principally descriptive or analytical, despite the preferences which have been attributed to it and the ideological function with which it has been charged.[25] The former is in the first place a doctrine about how government should

---

[21] See for instance the discussion in R. A. W. Rhodes, 'The New Governance: Governing without Government', *Political Studies*, 44 (1996), 652–67.

[22] British pluralists have taken pains to distinguish and distance themselves from ethical pluralism. For Figgis there was 'the ultimate criterion of love', while for others there was the belief that 'the maximization of liberty should be the principle end of political activity'. Nicholls, *The Pluralist State*, pp. 20–21. But the normative and radical or reformist agenda of British pluralism, and its concern as much with government as with politics, distinguishes it from a simple explanatory or analytical political pluralism. The latter, at its most basic, consists of no more than the sensible but unstartling observation that political actors are normally most accurately seen as less than the whole of society, but more than a single individual or collaboration of single individuals, and that political divisions and alliances are generally more complex than simple divisions into proletarians and capitalists, Protestants and Catholics, north and south, would suggest.

[23] A New Liberal such as Hobhouse, on the other hand, while valuing diversity, saw it as contributing to a higher harmony. There would be unitary government, and intermediate associations were regarded with suspicion as sources of oppression of the individual.

[24] J. N. Figgis, 'Church and State' (1912) in Nicholls, *The Pluralist State*, p. 161.

[25] Paul Hirst makes an effective case for Robert Dahl as an advocate of a pluralist politics in a critical review of those who have presented North American pluralism as little more than a justification of the existing distribution of power. P. Hirst, *Representative Democracy and its Limits* (Cambridge, Polity Press, 1990). Dahl is treated similarly as a contributor to a normative pluralism by A. I. Eisenberg, *Reconstructing Political Pluralism* (Albany, NY, State University of New York Press, 1995). Dahl himself, one of whose early articles was a discussion of workers' control in Britain, returned to the subject with the argument, in 1985, that liberty required economic democracy, which could not be achieved via the market, but required self-governing industrial enterprises. R. A. Dahl, 'Workers' Control of Industry and the British Labour Party', *American Political Science Review*, 41 (1947); *A Preface to Economic Democracy* (Cambridge, Polity Press, 1985).

be carried on, even if this is one prong of a two-pronged attack, the other of which is a critical analysis of existing constitutional and governmental arrangements.

'Original' pluralism

The original British pluralists, Figgis, Cole, Laski and Russell have some-times been distinguished from one another by their respective concerns with social, economic, or constitutional pluralism. But more important than the differences of emphasis between them was the clear distance which each placed between what they were arguing for and the view of sovereignty shared by all the other major strands of political thinking.[26] Figgis argued for the rights of associations, in particular churches, to govern their own affairs. Cole argued for the government by producers of their own economic activity. Laski drew on the work of both to attack the very idea of sovereignty both within the territory of existing states and in relations across their borders. Russell endorsed all these arguments, in particular the guild socialist version of workers' control, and pursuing themes from Kropotkin and Belloc, as well as from Cole and the guild socialists, argued that independent agencies were necessary to check the power of the central state and to ensure freedom and creativity.[27]

There were differences amongst the first generation of British plur-alists in the way in which they envisaged the character and responsib-ilities of the national state. Figgis saw the state itself as 'composed of a number of associations and groups',[28] whereas for Laski the state was itself just one more association. But all were agreed in seeing the sover-eign state as increasingly inappropriate for the needs of a modern society or for the flourishing of liberty. Laski applied this point externally as well as internally, as Ernest Barker had done, but where Barker had simply seen the state diluted in a wider international community, Laski saw in addition a global pluralism in which

> All bodies which seek influence in the modern world, the co-operators, the
> trade unionists, the chambers of commerce, are driven to organize

---

[26] Hsiao goes so far as to see them breaking with a dominant tradition of state theory running back to Aristotle. Hsiao, *Political Pluralism.*

[27] B. Russell, *The Practice and Theory of Bolshevism* (New York, Simon & Schuster, [repr. 1964] 1920); Russell, *Principles of Social Reconstruction* (London, Allen & Unwin, 1916); Russell, *Roads to Freedom: Socialism, Anarchism, and Syndicalism* (London, Allen & Unwin, 1918).

[28] Nicholls, *The Pluralist State*, p. 78.

themselves internationally in the search to make their influence felt. More and more they are winning positions in which the State finds itself compelled to take account of their power.[29]

So not only was the state to be in some instances subordinate to organizations such as the League of Nations, but those who on one occasion would act as its citizens, would, on another, act as members of bodies whose membership cut across, indeed ignored, the boundaries of states, and which were constituted on quite other criteria.

Community and association

Within this British governmental pluralism, a distinction exists between pluralism of communities, and pluralism of associations. British pluralism has affinities with, and is inter-tissued with, decentralization and localism and David Nicholls, commenting on the reappearance of interest in non-Statist forms of socialism and political and governmental life in the 1980s, cites syndicalism, guild socialism, Proudhon, Kropotkin and Morris.[30] Proudhon was for Harold Laski a major source of inspiration. But not only should syndicalism be set on one side as not a pluralist doctrine at all, but a tactic of collectivist state-seizure—and the early British pluralists did set it aside in this way—but the three anarchists cited can be distinguished from, for instance, guild socialists by a fundamental difference in the character of their pluralist vision. Although not primarily concerned with government at all, as defenders of the life of small groups they were also advocates of those groups having governing functions. But for Proudhon, Kropotkin, and Morris the most important social unit, and the one in which people lived virtually the whole of their social life, was the community, small, local, and face-to-face. It was a community characterized by creative production under the control of the producers, but had a life wider than mere production. For the guild socialists, on the other hand, and for other British pluralists, the pluralities which society contained were associations not communities. They accounted for a part, but only a part, of the lives of their members. Those individual persons, although their lives were expressed and shaped through their membership of associations, were not understood or defined either wholly or principally by any single association. It was

---

[29] H. J. Laski, *A Grammar of Politics* (London, Allen & Unwin, 1925), pp. 235–6.
[30] Nicholls, *The Pluralist State*, p. xi.

for this reason that the State, (and writers such as Figgis consistently capitalized the word), had to deal with associations as real persons. They should do so, not because associations were real and individuals unreal or lacking wholeness or unqualified to enjoy rights, but because the individual as treated under representative democracy or individualist liberalism was either unique, and therefore representable only by himself or herself, or abbreviated in a way which ignored or distorted much or most of the identities which membership of associations expressed and cultivated.[31]

The disappearance and reappearance of pluralism

The submergence of pluralism in collectivism in the thinking of Laski has been well and often gleefully documented.[32] But Laski's transition was shared by pluralism as a whole. It is possible to see early twentieth-century British pluralism as performing a transitional function, and by its own ambivalence facilitating the politicization of activities which had previously lain outside, or only athwart, politics. It played a part consequently in the expansion rather than contraction of the sphere of the central sovereign state.[33] Partly this was a matter of opportunism, partly of the absence of any clear or feasible strategy for achieving a pluralist state. Whether or not the post-1918 state was considered to be undesirable or an enemy of liberty, it was the only available instrument for the achievement of the broad aims of social and economic reform or manipulation which pluralists such as Laski and Cole sought.[34] And while a pluralist future might still have been desired in the long term, the

[31] So, for instance, David Nicholls comments that the early twentieth-century British pluralists 'argued that a true understanding of human nature recognises individuality indeed, but as manifesting itself and maturing within the context of a multitude of different associations and communities, families, churches, sporting and cultural societies, trade unions, civil associations, universities and schools.' Nicholls, *The Pluralist State*, p. xx.

[32] H. A. Deane, *The Political Thought of Harold J. Laski* (New York, Columbia University Press, 1955).

[33] I discuss this more fully in *Political Ideas in Modern Britain in and After the Twentieth Century*, and in 'Harold Laski' in W. Euchner, ed., *Klassiker des Sozialismus* (Munich, C. H. Beck, 1989).

[34] Hirst argues that Laski is consistent in that his commitment is to equality and democratic freedom, and that when circumstances make the collectivist state seem the most appropriate means of pursuing those goals, he supports the collectivist state. But for Laski, learning from Duguit, the state was never more than an instrument, so this caused him no problems. P. Hirst, 'Introduction', *The Collected Works of Harold Laski*, 10 vols, (London, Routledge, 1997).

convenient short term stretched further and further ahead. This was to be as much a problem for pluralists at the end of century as for their predecessors, although different in context and detail.[35]

The combination of unchecked centralized state power with liberal economic policies at the end of the 'short' twentieth century encouraged thinkers on the left to look further afield for appropriate responses. Post-socialist pluralists took up themes from both early twentieth-century pluralism and early twentieth-century new liberalism. But was there anything other than mere contingency in the role of recessive themes in political thinking in the 1990s? Was the use made of British political thinking from the first quarter of the century any more than a use of what happened to be around? Did pluralists at the close of the twentieth century depend on those recessive themes, and did those themes make any effective demands? Even if the answer to both those questions is 'no', it may still be possible to argue that because of the use of recessive themes, pluralism at, and after the end of, the 'short' twentieth century had one particular character, and not another. One simple but clear and important difference between early twentieth-century British pluralism and the re-emerged pluralism of the century's end, is that the second generation was able to draw not only on the same sources as Laski and his contemporaries, but in addition to read those sources in the light of Laski's arguments, and to read Laski, Cole, Figgis and Russell in addition. The sources on which re-established pluralism could draw were to that extent richer and more diverse. The pluralism of the 'short' twentieth-century's end was in this way formed from a recessive theme, rather than being a revenant approximation of its earlier form.

This does not however fully explain clear differences of emphasis between British pluralism at its first and second appearances. For Laski the principal concerns were the fulfillment of a democratic momentum which had got under way in the nineteenth century, and the development of an efficient form of government for an increasingly complex modern society.[36] For the pluralists of the second appearance, the

---

[35] Paul Hirst comments on civil society and new social movements in similar vein at the end of the century: 'Ultimately, activists are bought off by seeking decisions, special programmes, laws or funding from the state.' Hirst, *Representative Democracy and its Limits*, p. 6.

[36] As Gregor McLennan neatly observes, the pluralism of Laski and his contemporaries 'was as much a critique of the emerging orthodoxy of representative democracy as it was a critique of statism'. G. McLennan, *Pluralism* (Buckingham, Open University Press, 1995), pp. 32–3.

principal concerns were the defence and cultivation of diversity and freedom. For the first generation of pluralists, or at least for Laski and Cole, society was divided, but it was not fragmented, and the major divisions were given a stability by the presence of class. The working classes were, correspondingly, to be the principal beneficiaries of pluralist reorganization. At the close of the century, by contrast, class had been demoted to one more dimension in an unpredictable diversity of social identities. The appropriateness of a single focus, and the attraction of collectivism by the back door, was correspondingly reduced.

British governmental pluralism was not the only theme employed in the reaction against uniform collectivism. One branch of left and radical response at the close of the twentieth century drew on North American rather than British, and on social rather than political, pluralism. Mike Rustin's *For a Pluralist Socialism*[37] was an argument for a reform of representation, rather than of government, as were the arguments of Rowbotham, Segal, and Wainwright.[38] Rustin's argument, in particular, went little beyond a class centred advocacy of representational pluralism, and was severely critical even of the kind of multi-issue, multigroup socialism which Rowbotham, Segal, and Wainwright argued for in collections such as *Beyond the Fragments*. They, too, however, argued for the interdependence of causes and collaborations, rather than for their diversity. The pluralist re-working of Hayek by Hilary Wainwright[39] occupied an interesting intermediate position.

The renewed advocacy of workers' government of industry on the other hand, by writers such as David Miller,[40] and the comprehensive governmental pluralism advocated by Paul Hirst[41] and John Keane,[42] drew on a more indigenous tradition of pluralist thinking. Both David Nicholls and Paul Hirst have seized on governmental pluralism as providing material for a response to the growth of unitary state power and the renewed or intensified assertion of sovereignty,[43] whilst similar

---

[37] M. Rustin, *For a Pluralist Socialism* (London, Verso, 1985).

[38] S. Rowbotham, L. Segal and H. Wainwright, *Beyond the Fragments* (London, Merlin Press, 1979).

[39] H. Wainwright, *Arguments for a New Left: Answering the Free Market Right* (Oxford, Basil Blackwell, 1994).

[40] D. Miller, *Market, State, and Community: Theoretical Foundations of Market Socialism* (Oxford, Clarendon Press, 1989).

[41] Hirst, *Representative Democracy and its Limits; Associative Democracy: New Forms of Economic and Social Governance*, (Cambridge, Polity Press, 1994).

[42] Keane, *Democracy and Civil Society.*

[43] Nicholls, *The Pluralist State*; Hirst, *Associative Democracy.*

proposals have been made by Keane, although entitled civil society rather than governance or state.[44] 'Associative democracy' as described by Paul Hirst is a radical alternative to social democracy, liberal markets, or republican citizenship. It seeks the vitalities of markets without the snowdriftings of power which they create. It proposes welfare without bureaucracy, and democracy without collectivism. It recommends variety without intolerance, and individual autonomy without the oppression of others. It aims to reward initiative, but not to stigmatize bad luck.

Drawing first on Cole, then on Laski and Proudhon, Hirst argues that economic, producer pluralism is futile without a pluralism of governance. More is demanded, in other words, than a simple division or devolution of a state which remains coherent, comprehensive, and collectivist. The activity of authoritative organization has itself to be from the bottom up, or at least from half-way up in the form of associations. A federal judicial and regulatory structure will be, together presumably with defence and policing, all that is left of collectivism.

---

[44] The difference is largely one of nomenclature, although Hirst has taken issue with those such as Keane who have advocated a strengthened civil society because it is an attempt to check or influence, rather than fragment and re-distribute state functions. But the precise proposals of Keane and Hirst and Nicholls differ far less than do the names which they attach to them. Hirst describes writers such as Keane as 'relying upon an active organised civil society to act as a check upon *and a substitute for* the state' (my italics). Hirst, *Representative Democracy and its Limits*, p. 3. But a substitute for the state presumably has the function of governing, and it is difficult to see that it differs in a significant way from the associative democracy proposed by Hirst. The distinction fades even further when Hirst writes that pluralism

> offers a way for the state and civil society to interpenetrate, whilst restricting the scope of state power and its capacity to dominate civil society. Pluralism in this sense creates the space for an active civil society of associations freely formed of citizens and allows those self-governing associations to undertake a greater part of the tasks of social life.

Hirst, *Representative Democracy and its Limits*, p. 8. Similar differences existed amongst the first generation of British pluralists, and Alan Ryan comments on Russell that he

> takes no interest in the creation of legal obstacles to government misbehaviour; he does not suggest a Bill of Rights, for instance. On the whole, Russell assumes throughout that what checks government is the power of social groups rather than the provisions of the legal system, and that what gives social groups their power is the strength of opinion among their members. Only voluntary associations whose morale is strong enough to resist government bullying can really limit the power of governments; that such groups exist is clear enough—the Welsh miners took on Lloyd George in the middle of a war and won.

A. Ryan, *Bertrand Russell. A Political Life* (London, Allen Lane, 1988) p. 76.

Hirst's associative democracy thus employs a pluralism of roles or identities, rather than of either communities or classes. This is what the early pluralists such as Figgis did, but not what the 'socialist' or 'class' pluralists of the new urban left attempted. For them there was a plurality of groups, but people did not enjoy, to any significant degree, plural identity. Like the first generation of British pluralists, Hirst's account is a mixture of pointing to the inadequacies of the existing condition of things, and the advantages of a pluralist solution, and trusting to a mixture of old-order breakdown and popular common-sense to arrive at a new and better arrangement of things. The 'existing doctrines of social organization are bankrupt'; there are problems about how to provide and pay for social services; and 'it is implausible that sophist-icated and individuated publics' will put up with things for much longer.[45] The identification of a constituency for pluralism is thus left rather general. Certainly there is no group, role or association which performs for pluralism the role that the proletariat performed for Marx, or the electorate in alliance with public administrators for the Fabians. Laski had a joint constituency in the electorate and the working class organized through the trade unions. The end of century pluralists, while avoiding the creeping collectivism towards which this alliance could nudge, lacked on the other hand the potential support which it offered. There was a positive reason for renouncing some forms of such support. Unlike associations, communities involve 'the danger of "communal-ism", that different social projects will become self-enclosed and self-valuing, encompassing the whole life of their members. That is the first step towards antagonistic pluralism'.[46]

Pluralism, postmodernism, and multiculturalism

The reappearance of the recessive theme of governmental pluralism is only one feature of the diversity of political thinking at the end of the twentieth century. There are apparent similarities or affinities with post-modernism and with multiculturalism, to the extent that sceptics have dismissed postmodernism as no more than pluralism warmed up. But postmodernism, in versions such as that presented by Richard Rorty, commits people to a value dualism, on the one hand above the fray and recognizing the contingency of everything, on the other deriving all their

---

[45] Hirst, *Associative Democracy.*
[46] Hirst, *Representative Democracy and its Limits*, p. 18.

values from historical contingency. Pluralism, both in its early version and in Hirst's contemporary version of associative democracy, assumes a conscious and independent ability to move between roles and hence across the boundaries of contingency, but does not provide the vantage point of private irony from which the whole operation can be overseen.

There are affinities as strong, if not stronger, between arguments for multiculturalism and pluralism. Not only does pluralism accommodate a variety of associations and identities beyond the economic and political, but the first impetus for early twentieth-century British pluralism, well before Laski took up the issue, was for religious self-government. On the other hand, one major response to the existence of cultural, ethnic, religious and national diversity within existing states has been to propose reforms of representation, the entrenchment of rights, and federalism, of which only the third shares anything with pluralism, and of which the first two are by implication a rejection of its analysis and proposals.[47]

Religion of greater importance than production

One of the principal areas where first wave pluralists sought to apply pluralist principles was work. Trade unions, industrial unions, or guilds were an essential component of the pluralism of Laski, and the main component of the pluralism of Cole. Workers' control and guild socialism were not proposals for just worker or co-operative capitalism. Workers would exercise governmental functions in the setting of professional qualifications, the regulation of professional conduct, and the self-government of their members in those aspects of their lives which related to their economic or productive function. There was a difference, however, between an advocacy of productive self-government, the pure pluralist governmental position, and the advocacy of a distinctive productive input into the process of unitary state policy-making. Nicholls places Cole on the non-pluralist side of this divide.[48] The distinction is important, since it divides those whose broad purpose was to enhance

---

[47] See for instance W. Kymlicka, *Multicultural Citizenship: A Liberal Theory of Minority Rights* (Oxford, Clarendon Press, 1995).

[48] 'Cole was significant as a guild socialist but, as we shall see, was hardly a pluralist at all. He believed, throughout the tergiversations of his early work, in functional representation at a central parliament or assembly of some kind.' Cole 'attached little importance to group personality and to the need for groups to manage their own affairs and live their own lives.' Nicholls, p. 3.

the representativeness of a state which remained centralized and, in its effects on its subjects, homogenizing, and those for whom human purposes were diverse, and who in consequence wanted to imbue that diversity with the functions of governing rather than to transcend diversity in a government which was uniform and comprehensive.

Although our most recent sighting of pluralism was economic, a guild socialism or a workers' control fading into nostalgia or revolutionary hopefulness, it should be remembered that the emergence of pluralism at the beginning of the twentieth century was religious, and that its re-emergence at the close of the 'short' twentieth century has an equally important religious dimension. Although the demand for producers' pluralism has both persisted and been reiterated,[49] it is at the very least likely that one of the principal forms of pluralism at the end of the twentieth century will be religious, a development that would have appealed to Figgis, although not necessarily in a way that he would either have appreciated or expected. The importance of religion for the first manifestation of British pluralism has been obscured despite Laski's use of religious examples, particularly the Free Church of Scotland case, and despite his debt to Figgis. It has been masked because of Laski's translation of these instances and arguments into a secular context: religion provided a metaphor or an example for the secular world.

The postmodern, multicultural, or fluid society to which pluralist ideas are now applied is one characterized, as the Prince of Wales is only one of many to point out, not by faith, but by faiths. Whereas the first expression of pluralism argued for a distinction between church and state, the second argues for a distinction between church and church. So first generation pluralism, as Nicholls neatly puts it, was inspired by the unifying hopes of idealism: 'the hands are often the hands of Léon Duguit, but the voice is unmistakably that of T. H. Green'.[50] The second generation, by contrast, was inspired by an acceptance and valuing of diversity. The most tangible post-twentieth-century example of pluralism is the claim of religious groups, in particular Muslims of a pro-Iranian tendency, to govern themselves and other members of their community. Hence the so-called 'Muslim Parliament', which raises again

---

[49] R. Barker, 'Guild Socialism Revisited?', *Political Quarterly*, 46 (1975); Miller, *Market, State, and Community*. Paul Hirst, too, both in his *The Pluralist Theory of the State* and in his *Associative Democracy* gives a major place to self-governing associations of producers.
[50] Nicholls, *The Pluralist State*, p. 85.

precisely those questions of the relationship between the autonomy of a group or association from the central state, and the autonomy of those whom the leaders, controllers, or representatives of the group claim as its members.

Pursuing an occupation may be exclusive, but it is not incompatible with the existence of other occupations. Holding a religious faith, on the other hand, may, but not must, involve believing that everyone else ought to hold that faith. Relativism and self-confidence sit uncomfortably together, and it is difficult to say both that our characteristics are valuable, and that yours are just as good. This view is complemented by a division of the world into believers and non-believers. The language of Christianity, but not only of Christianity, is suffused with images of this: sheep and goats; he who is not with me is against me; wise and foolish virgins; saved and damned. Plumbers feel no similar antipathy towards lorry drivers, whatever else they may think about them. They neither wish to convert them into plumbers, nor to exclude them, nor to create a society in which there are no lorry drivers. The language of enemies is endemic to religion, in a way that it is not to occupation. The only instance of such language in occupational identity, class, has had a most unsuccessful history in dividing British politics or political thinking into us and them.

The record of diverse religious affiliations is too varied to be the basis for anything more than a guess as to the balance of probabilities in any pluralist future. But at the very least there is some ground for thinking that the further apart believers are, the less they are likely to see each other as threats.[51] A multi-faith society might be more tolerant than a multi-sect one.

The problem of authority within the group

Pluralism as a doctrine of government takes power from the central unitary state, and gives it to associations. It reverses the process which liberals such as Hobhouse saw as conducive, possibly necessary, to individual liberty. Those who are sceptical about its claims argue that in empowering religious leaders, or governing bodies, pluralism

---

[51] Although there is plenty of evidence to suggest the contrary possibility, from the civil wars of the former Yugoslavia, to the vision of a world divided by faith-associated civilizations of Samuel Huntington, S. P. Huntington: *The Clash of Civilizations and the Remaking of World Order* (New York, Simon & Schuster, 1996).

subordinates other members of the group, particularly women and children.[52] Supporters of pluralism such as Hirst have been aware of this problem,[53] but advocates of the power of groups have sometimes given substance to this criticism, rather than deflected it. Mandell Creighton defined the rights claimed by the church as the rights of parents to give their children a church education.[54] There is a similarity of the point at

[52] 'Critics of "collective rights" in this sense often invoke the image of theocratic and patriarchal cultures where women are oppressed and religious orthodoxy legally enforced', Kymlicka, *Multicultural Citizenship*, p. 36. Thus Salman Rushdie argued that in supporting the demand for separate schools for the daughters of Muslim families, the Labour Party was ignoring both the rights and the opinions of the young women themselves, and 'delivering them into the hands of the Mullahs'. S. Rushdie, 'In Good Faith' *The Independent on Sunday* (4 February 1990).

Laski observed, in his discussion of Duguit, that states do not do things, only particular officials do them. Duguit denies personality to the state, the 'action of the state means, in cold fact, simply that certain officials have carried out the order of a minister; there is nothing in that which gives use to any personality differing from that of those concerned in the conception and performance of the order'. H. Laski, 'Introduction' to L. Duguit, *Law in the Modern State*, translated by F. and H. Laski (New York, B. W. Huebsch, 1919), p. xix. But what applies to the personality of the state, applies equally to that of associations. One of the concerns of those who have not advocated governmental pluralist solutions to multi-culturalism has been precisely the possibility of groups or cultures within the state oppressing those whom they claim as their members. Thus Kymlicka argues that 'rights should not allow one group to dominate other groups; and they should not allow a group to oppress its own members'. It cannot be 'morally legitimate for a group to oppress its own members in the name of group solidarity, religious orthodoxy, or cultural purity'. Kymlicka, *Multicultural Citizenship*, pp. 194, 198. There remains, of course, the problem of who is to decide who are the group's members.

[53]   Certainly, the Rushdie affair should give any intelligent pluralist advocate pause for thought. There are in every modern western country social forces and associations that would ruthlessly exploit the freedoms given them within a pluralist state and yet refuse to accept the rights or legitimacy of others. The more fanatical in the Muslim community offer only a conspicuous example, for there are other more established groups and associations equally likely to abuse such freedom. What forms would such abuse take? Firstly, the attempt to expand at the expense of other groups, and, secondly, the attempt to dragoon and subjugate the individuals who form their members.

Tolerance and respect are needed to counter this tendency, but state power will be necessary when they are insufficient. Hirst, *Representative Democracy and its Limits*, pp. 16–17. Hirst is thus not guilty of the charge levelled at him by Eisenberg in *Reconstructing Political Pluralism*, p. 25.

[54] M. Creighton, *The Church and the Nation*, p. 72, quoted Nicholls, *The Pluralist State*, p. 84. There are two different kinds of association here, the voluntary one which adults join and which they are free to leave, and the family, where for children membership is not a matter of choice, and where they are under the control of their parents in a way and to a degree which is qualitatively different from the relationship between an association and its members.

issue here, with the debate over human rights and national cultures on a world level.

When Nicholls writes of associations and their members he uses the word 'authority'. It may not be the most appropriate, since it is difficult to see what authority there could be except the permission of the members. When he describes Figgis as insisting that the state allow associations to exercise authority over their members it is not clear what permission is involved, or what restriction might be imposed, save for the crucial one which he mentions of expulsion or refusal of admission.[55] The answer to this objection is that associations must be self-governing, and that the central state should exercise oversight to see that this is so. A democratic state might do so—a despotic one would not, and so the success of the pluralist enterprise depends not on pluralism alone, but on democracy. One objection to this solution is that pluralists treat the central state as inimical to liberty, and thus transfer functions from it to groups, yet as soon as the possibility of group tyranny arises, they appeal precisely to that state which apparently had hitherto been untrustworthy. Yet if the state is suspect when exercising functions itself, but reliable when supervising the exercising of those functions by others, why might not the reverse be just as likely?

As if in recognition of the difficulty, the account given of the problem by both pluralists and their contemporary admirers is both careful and unhelpful.

> One matter on which Figgis's theory is not sufficiently detailed is the extent to which the state is justified in intervening in the affairs of a group to prevent the persecution of individuals, or to maintain justice. He does not seem to have been fully aware of what Dicey called 'the paradoxical character' of the right of association. He would certainly have said that the presumption is always that the individual has freely chosen to join the group, and however absurd its rules may appear to the outsider, the state should not, under normal circumstances, intervene.[56]

Laski is even less helpful, and deserves Nicholls's dismissive observation, 'he avoided a detailed discussion of the respective spheres of the state, the group and the individual, arguing that this should be left to "the test of the event", whatever this may mean.'[57]

---

[55] Nicholls, *The Pluralist State*, p. 84.

[56] Ibid. p. 83.

[57] Ibid. p. 86, quoting H. Laski, *Studies in the Problem of Sovereignty* (New Haven, Conn., Yale University Press, [repr. London, 1968] 1917) p. 23.

Despite his support of pluralist solutions, Nicholls is well aware of the problem:

> A more valid criticism of these pluralist writers would be that they failed to take seriously the challenge to individual freedom which might come from the group itself, and therefore hardly considered the criteria according to which the state might properly intervene in the internal affairs of a group to secure the rights of individual members. In general they believed that so long as the individual was formally free to leave the group, then any discipline to which he submitted was voluntary and not a matter with which the state should interfere. But there may be economic and social pressures which make it practically impossible for the individual to leave the group, and in this situation the only hope for the individual might be some kind of external intervention. An obvious example would be the 'closed shop' situation, where to leave the union would involve losing a job.[58]

Laski was equally ready to seize the bull by the horns, and if necessary put it through the mincer of the idealist state to turn out suitable social democratic beefburgers. While his early writings had depended on the assumption that the identity of groups was self-evident, once he began to make proposals for identities and activities which were not self-evident, because not yet in existence, the problem of defining groups emerged. The theory of function seemed to solve this problem, but it brought the state in its knapsack. The performance of function could not, in a post-capitalist world, be placed wholly beyond the control of society and hence of the state. Function was after all something that had meaning only with reference to a society broader than the immediate group of functionaries.

> To give the schools to the teachers, the postal service to the postal workers in full ownership is a solution that only a few of the more extreme enthusiasts have claimed . . . They recognize that society has its place in every human equation, and that, as a consequence, it has a right to an indirect control over everything that is related to a social function . . . Where common problems arise, they must be settled by common decision. The state, in some form or other, must persist to protect the common interest, and it must retain a certain measure of power for that purpose.[59]

As to strikes, they may be necessary when a group of workers is attempting to assert its interests, but once it has been given professional status, they can no longer be justified, although Laski is a bit veiled about this:

---

[58] Nicholls, *The Pluralist State*, pp. 90–1. Eisenberg has taken up this point and applied it to sexual and racial subordination, Eisenberg, *Reconstructing Political Pluralism*, pp. 17–20.
[59] H. J. Laski, *Authority in the Modern State* (New Haven, Conn., Yale University Press, 1919) pp. 351–2.

It is surely obvious that the privilege of autonomy logically implies the acceptance of the purpose for which that responsibility is given. Once the professional group is given the means of independent action, it must be fully and stringently responsible for the causes of its acts . . . For the narrowness of their responsibility is, for the moment, simply a weapon forged to meet a special industrial situation. Once the cause for that narrowness is removed, there is not (*sic*) reason for such restriction to continue. The state could not confide the interests of society to men who would not accept the responsibilities of their trusteeship.[60]

Strikes, in other words, while acceptable as a response to capitalism, will be out of place in a functionally organized social democratic society.

Nicholls is in two minds over the issue, or at least aware that the early British pluralists were in two minds. He writes that it is 'perfectly possible to envisage a pluralist state composed largely of groups whose organization is centralized and hierarchical, with little place for the participation of their members in the policy and management of the group'.[61] Because the justification for pluralism is, however, the maximization of liberty, pluralists 'cannot totally ignore' such a threat to individual liberty, lest they be accused of 'handing over the individual from one tyranny to another' and accepting in the group the concentration of power to which they objected in the state.[62]

Both the Free Church of Scotland case and the history of the trade unions raise exactly these problems. In insisting that there be ballots for strikes was the Thatcher government, whatever else it may have been up to, not extending just that democratic self-government of associations of which pluralists approve? Which *existing* churches or religious bodies could a democratic state accept as being governed by their members? What, for instance, would be a pluralist solution to the problems of the Anglican Church over gay or female priests? It would not presumably offer much comfort to those who followed the Gummer/Widdecombe line on tradition and authority, but where would it place the right to decide the present character and doctrine of the church?

Figgis's answer to this is clear, at least in the case of the medieval church. The conflict between Pope and Emperor was not a tension within a dual system, but a contest for supremacy between two hierarchies both of which were organized around the Roman law idea of supremacy. But he adds a further reason for not seeing the medieval

---

[60] Ibid. p. 353.
[61] Nicholls, *The Pluralist State*, p. 111.
[62] Ibid. p. 111.

church as expressing the sort of views he is himself advocating: 'When the liberty of the Church is claimed, it almost always denotes the liberty of the hierarchy, not that of the whole body.'[63]

On the other hand, although Figgis's preference was for a participatory rather than an hierarchic church, it was nonetheless a church where authority was exercised over its members. 'What we must assert, are bound to assert, cannot help asserting if we have thought out our principles is this. The Church *has* real rights and true authority over all its members the moment they become such.'[64]

Pluralists face a problem when the distribution of power within the association gives no more freedom, or less freedom, to individuals than does the state. For Nicholls the true pluralist solution can only come from within the group:

> What most of the pluralists rejected was the idea that the state should interfere with groups in order to protect the interests of members, and impose upon the group the kind of polity which it thinks best. The really effective claim for freedom and for a devolution of power within the large associations must come from within and not from outside. Only if it comes from the members themselves will it be likely to lead to a real change for the better; if it comes from the state nothing but state absolutism can result.[65]

If associations are to be self-governing, are they of necessity to be self-policing? Is one glimpse of the pluralist future the private North American housing estate with its own enforcement agents? Would pluralists communities have their own regulations and their own punishments? One of the failures of British pluralism, at both its first and its second appearance, was to avoid this central question. Laski's avoidance of the matter was facilitated by his use of a definition of the state—and of government since he frequently used the terms interchangeably—which did not mention force or coercion at all. Quoting Alfred Zimmern, he defined the state as 'a territory over which there is a government claiming unlimited authority'.[66] The ability of the state to

---

[63] J. N. Figgis, *Churches in the Modern State* (London, Longmans, Green & Co., 1913), anthologized in Hirst, ed., *The Pluralist Theory of the State*, p. 120.

[64] J. N. Figgis, 'The Church and the Secular Theory of the State' in Nicholls, *The Pluralist State*, p. 158.

[65] Nicholls, *The Pluralist State*, p. 13.

[66] H. Laski, 'The Pluralistic State' in *The Foundations of Sovereignty and other essays* (London, Allen & Unwin 1921), reprinted in Hirst, ed., *The Pluralist Theory of the State*, p. 185. The quotation from Zimmern is from A. E. Zimmern, *Nationality and Government* (London, Chatto & Windus, 1918) p. 56.

govern was described by him wholly in terms of consent, which thus both elided the distinction between the state and other associations, and made it easier to pass over the problem of securing assent within groups:

> It is a matter of degree and not of kind that the State should find for its decrees more usual acceptance than those of any other association. It is not because of the force that lies behind its will, but because men know that the group could not endure if every disagreement meant a secession, that they agree to accept its will as made manifest for the most part in its law.[67]

If so, the dreams of the radical pluralists and the dreams of the libertarian individualists—the anarcho-capitalists—look as though they are getting pretty close to one another. If, on the other hand, the pluralist association is self-regulating by consensus and moral pressure, it may threaten all the horrors of small town life.[68]

The experience of the last two centuries in Britain has in general been one of national pressure to dissolve the oppressions and restrictions placed by associations on their members. There are clear reasons why this may have been so. Insofar as open discussion is a solvent of oppressive orthodoxy, the public sphere has been wider than the sphere of the group or association, and appeal to reason or conscience has thus been beyond the group to the wider society. Analogously, the defence or assertion of individual rights in Britain has frequently been advanced in the closing years of the twentieth century by appeal from the law or courts of the United Kingdom to the European level, and to the European Commission and Court of Human Rights. But there is no necessity in this equation of wider and larger rights, more free, more egalitarian, or more just. One of the motives which led many Norwegians to vote against accession to the European Union was that both the culture and the institutions of Norway were seen as more progressive and egalitarian, particularly in regard to gender, than those of Europe.

Feminism as a test of pluralism?

One strand within both modernism and postmodernism presents a particular challenge to a re-emerged pluralism. How far can pluralism accommodate, or be accommodated by, feminism? None of the 'constituencies',

---

[67] H. J. Laski, *Studies in the Problem of Sovereignty* (New Haven, Conn., Yale University Press, 1917) p. 17.

[68] As Eisenberg points out in her distinction between the aggregative and developmental functions of groups. Eisenberg, *Reconstructing Political Pluralism*.

associations, or functional groups normally cited in pluralist discussion take account of the particular character of gender, or of the unpaid domestic production by women. This of course raises the important but tangential question of whether there are institutional forms which are implied by, or sustaining of, a social and political life which transcends, or seeks to transcend, gender, or whether all democratic institutions are equally deficient but equally capable of transformation. If the former, then pluralism may or may not meet the feminist requirement, if the latter then it may, but is in principle no more and no less likely to do so than any other kind of institutional arrangement. It has recently been argued by Judith Squires that there are constitutional implications, or applications, of a recognition of difference, an argument which could involve feminism approaching pluralism. But the constitutional solution proposed for recognizing political variety is not constitutional dispersal, but constitutional safeguards.[69] At present the credentials of pluralism with regard to one of the major innovations within, and challenges to, political thinking thus remain untested. It has not evidently failed, but nor has it made any major contribution.

Why bother?

A major problem for pluralists of the second generation is one which lay just as firmly in the path of the British pluralists of the first decades of the century. Even granted that a pluralist society and governance would be desirable, or conducive to human flourishing, or freer, or more in accord with vital aspects of human social nature, how is one to get from here to there? Is it entirely a matter of depending on advocacy and persuasion? The elaboration of constitutional or institutional arrangements which would cultivate and sustain pluralism is not an answer to this question, but merely a displacement of it to a further level. For how are such institutions to be introduced or created?[70] One answer is that if

---

[69] J. Squires, 'Liberal Constitutionalism, Identity and Difference', *Political Studies*, 43 (1995).

[70] Constitutional speculation however generally proceeds on the double assumption that the exercise is worthwhile, but that the intended benefits will be difficult or impossible to achieve, or to achieve in the foreseeable future, or to achieve in a foreseeable manner. Thus the discussion amongst the contributors to the *Political Studies* special issue on Constitutions are bold on general aims and principles, but cautious on outcomes, *Political Studies*, 44 (1996), Special Issue, R. Bellamy and D. Castiglione, eds., *Constitutionalism in Transformation: European and Theoretical Perspectives*. The editors are guardedly optimistic in their view of the circumstances under which 'political scientists and theorists' can 'play a constructive role in shaping the politics of the future'. *Political Studies*, 44 (1996), 416.

we can never do any more than attend upon the flow of history, then all political thinking, and not just pluralism, is fruitless.

Political thinking is worth pursuing because one to some extent sets the agenda; the Hayek view of consequences is thus incorrect. What happens may not be the result of any single will, or any wills acting in concert, but the result of many actions and identities, and the mirror of none of them. But individual actions, and individual thought, nonetheless contribute to making some things possible, or more possible, and others impossible, or less possible. The history of pluralism is itself an illustration of this. It did not at the time have the effects its proponents hoped for, and its subsequent history is not what they might have expected. It is nonetheless closer to what they hoped for, even if neither the circumstances of its being so, or the manner in which it re-emerged, were ones they might have expected or even been able to envisage. This is something on which Figgis commented, saying of the Roman conception of the state,

> An ideal which Charles the Great, Otho the Great, Pope Sylvester II, Henry of Luxemburg were content even to try to realize cannot be dismissed as of no influence on the lives of men. If it was not realized, it at least caused people to do what they would otherwise have left undone and ruled their imaginations.[71]

Circumstance, contingency, prediction

Whether or not pluralism would be the most appropriate outcome for our contemporary society, it in no way follows that it is the most likely outcome. The circumstances of the re-appearance of pluralism are both similar and dissimilar to those of its first appearance. The national sovereign state seemed on both occasions to be caught in an eroding pincer, trans-national society on the one hand, formerly subordinate regions or associations on the other. On the first occasion the international dimension was provided by trade and commerce, on the second by the European Union.[72] The example of the original circumstances

---

[71] Figgis, *Churches in the Modern State*, anthologized in Hirst, ed., *The Pluralist Theory of the State*, p. 119.

[72] It is not as odd as it seems that prescriptive pluralism has developed in the most unitary and centralized of states if it is seen as an antibody or reaction. The unitary and centralized character of the government of the United Kingdom has been thrown further into relief by the growing frequency of comparison with the other states of the European Union, but the contrast has sustained calls for change.

might suggest that prediction is rash, that one should remember the example of Sir Ernest Barker, and not be too cocky.

What are the reasons for doubting the likelihood of a pluralist future? The movement of technology, information, and organization in the contemporary world facilitates both more convenient decentralization and easier centralization. It is possible, in the industrial world, to work from home; it is equally possible to be scrutinized at home. Pluralism is gaining ground in Europe and the United Kingdom as industrial, class society is slowly being both eclipsed and criticized in those countries. In the rest of the world, despite the existence of communal, national, ethnic and religious divisions, the dominant pressure is precisely for industrialization, modernism, collectivism, and against pluralism and liberalism.

What are the reasons for doubting the congeniality of a pluralist future? Pluralism may claim to solve the dispute between communitarianism and liberalism, freeing communitarianism from being inclusive and comprehensive, and saving liberalism from atomistic abstraction. But if pluralism is a doctrine of government, is it not open to Oscar Wilde's jibe that the trouble with socialism was that it did 'cut into one's evenings so dreadfully'[73] and to the accusation that liberty depends not in the proliferation of government, but in its limitation? Another objection, although not a novel one, is that pluralism would lead to confusion, conflict, even violence. The defenders of pluralism are not always reassuring on this point. David Nicholls writes

> There will certainly be occasions on which individuals will find themselves torn between loyalty to one group and loyalty to another. There will inevitably be friction in a pluralist state. People will have to make up their minds what they will do in cases of conflict. Perhaps the state will itself intervene, and side with one group against another on the particular issue; normally citizens will accept the decisions of the state, because they accept the importance of there being some generally recognized machinery for maintaining order and settling disputes. But they may on particular occasions refuse to accept the ruling of the state, and disobey, or even take to arms.[74]

---

[73] This is a particular instance of the wider claim that political change, socialist or radical, is unlikely to be worth the effort for large sections of the population. Russell made this observation about the likelihood of Marxist revolution in 1896, and it was reformulated in the following century by Przeworski. B. Russell, *German Social Democracy* (London, Allen & Unwin, 1896); A. Przeworski and J. Sprague, *Paper Stones: A History of Electoral Socialism* (Chicago, University of Chicago Press, 1986); D. S. King and M. Wickham-Jones, 'Review Article: Social Democracy and Rational Workers', *British Journal of Political Science*, 20 (1990).

[74] Nicholls, *The Pluralist State*, p. 14.

Conclusion

Identity

Is the pluralism which I have discussed a particularly British contribution to twentieth century political science and political thinking? Doubt may be cast on the claim when attention is drawn to the influence of Continental European thinkers on leading British pluralists: Gierke on Maitland, Duguit on Laski. To this it can be answered that intellectual traditions or cultures are not autonomous or self-generating. It is precisely because they are not, that communication and cross-fertilization is possible between them. Their distinctiveness lies, as it does with sexual reproduction, not in philoprogeniture, but in the particular unique results of differing origins or influences, none of which are exactly mirrored in the end result. Being open to and influenced by global or cosmopolitan thinking does not compromise particular identity—it can be a condition of it. Hence the fact that British political science, particularly through the medium of the English language, is part of a far wider intellectual community, does not dilute its distinctiveness. It is one of the conditions of it, just as Latin was at one and the same time the means of giving unity to Christendom, and of enabling its different peoples to develop their own religious, political, and cultural identities. The French language does not turn a Quebecois into a Parisian.

Can pluralism be called a contribution to the study of politics, given the varied provenance of those who expounded it? The work of J. N. Figgis might seem a particular problem here. Can a priest whose principal concern is the status of the church, be allowed past the customs post of political science? The answer is that the object of enquiry is not a series of individual biographies or even the thinking of discrete individuals, but the debate or discussion to which they can be seen to have been contributing.

Change

There are three familiar metaphors used to explain intellectual change. The first, that of standing on giants' shoulders, is optimistic and teleological, and sees intellectual activity as an incremental progression towards fuller and more accurate information and understanding. The second is of a continual round of forgetting and remembering, where both permanent loss and remorseless progress are illusions. The third is the pessimistic or at least sceptical reverse of the giants' shoulders progressive optimism: history repeats itself in increasingly less worthy forms, as tragedy, or as farce. What each one of these metaphors fails to bring to the course of pluralism is a simultaneous recognition of both continuity, and change and difference, or a view of political thinking which is committed to a belief neither in progress nor in decline. It is for this reason that I have used the metaphor of recessive themes, rather than of revenance. Revenants are pale shadows of earlier realities, whereas the metaphor of the recessive gene can draw, cautiously, on the image of sexual reproduction to accommodate continuity or originality.[75]

Consequences

A discussion of the contribution of a particular piece of political thinking cannot easily avoid the obligation to say something about its significance. Such significance can be attributed either by placing some value on the activity, or by assessing clear and evident effects: by considering consequences, in other words, either in the sight of God—political science triumphant—or in the sight of the living body of political scientists—political science militant. Whichever test of significance is adopted, one feature of employing the metaphor of the recessive gene to give an account of the two careers of British pluralism is that, as with all aspects of sexual reproduction, creation rather than simple reproduction is involved, and a degree of unpredictability, congenital unpredictability as one might say, is built into the use of the analogy. And whether or not the reappearance of a recessive theme in political thinking is dependent on a receptive historical context, once it has reappeared, we view both current and past thinking from a changed vantage point. Twenty years ago, we would not have been writing of pluralism so much as writing off pluralism. But now strands in the past—pluralism itself, or religious thinking—are being accorded a greatly enhanced significance.[76]

First generation pluralism was worked out within a structure of thinking which led people to assume that the personal ends of men

---

[75] There is of course a danger in a metaphor which can accommodate too much. The more it accommodates, the less it distinguishes.

[76] And not only in Britain. See for instance Eisenberg, *Reconstructing Political Pluralism*; K. McClure, 'On the Subject of Rights: Pluralism, Plurality and Political Identity' in Mouffe, ed., *Dimensions of Radical Democracy*.

and women could be described by reference to general and objectively identifiable human needs, which people had in their various capacities as parents, workers, householders, etc. They needed freedom in the pursuit of these ends, but the purpose of the pluralist prescription was to facilitate the achievement of this freedom, not to respond to the absence of any common ends. The situation of pluralism at the close of the twentieth century is quite different. It begins by recognizing a diversity of individual ends, which are not necessarily in conflict with one another, but which cannot be subsumed under any one principle either. Not only cannot individual ends be predicted, but it is an interference with the freedom of people to pursue their own ends, to try to predict what they might choose. That is up to them, and the governance they exercise over the various aspects of their own lives.

Because of the contribution of Laski and Cole, and the presence of guild socialism as a major application of pluralist doctrine, pluralism has been treated as a radical, left wing, or socialist doctrine.[77] But, although many of its exponents were socialists or developed a particularly socialist form of pluralism, the doctrine is not in itself readily locatable on either left or right. David Nicholls has no difficulty in drawing affinities between pluralism and Oakeshott's conception of civil association.[78] Even the socialist pluralists put forward arguments which made their position at least ambivalent in terms of the conventional alliances of political thinking. Laski could comment approvingly on how 'the whole tendency in England, indeed, has been to place a decreasing confidence in any final benefit from government action'.[79] Pluralism is neither socialist, nor conservative, nor liberal, although it has affinities at different points with all three. It even sits uneasily on a scale of left to right. Its reappearance indicates how far the old morphology of political thinking has been transcended.[80]

---

[77] Even with socialism, it was recessive at the time, and subsequently underplayed or disregarded in accounts of socialist thinking. Even so perceptive a commentator as Kymlicka deals with 'minority rights in the socialist tradition' from the starting point of a consideration of Marx and Engels on nationality, and arrives at the market socialism of contemporaries such as David Miller without considering the specific attention which thinkers such as Laski gave not only to minority nations and nationalities, but to the whole range of particular and minority associations and groups.

[78] Nicholls, *The Pluralist State*, p. xvii.

[79] Laski, 'Introduction' to Duguit, *Law in the Modern State*, pp. xxxi–xxxii.

[80] Similarly indicative, writers such as Vernon Bogdanor argue, is the growing and growingly divisive presence of argument about Europe which is, also, about sovereignty and subsidiarity. Bogdanor, *Politics and the Constitution*, pp. 136, 135–62.

6: Comparative Politics[1]

VERNON BOGDANOR

The British tradition

How is one to estimate what is of significance in British twentieth-century contributions to a subject so protean as 'comparative government' which, on one definition, could include almost the whole of political science? Writing in 1964 of the United States, Somit and Tannenhaus pointed to a 'curious lack of consensus in recognizing great contributions to political science', a lack of consensus which, they believed, resulted 'less from divergent standards of judgement than from a pervasive conviction that there are few men in the profession who have made truly significant contributions'.[2]

In fact, it is the 'divergent standards of judgement' which are likely to prove a greater obstacle than the conviction that there are few great men or women in the discipline. For, at the end of the twentieth century there is much less of a consensus on what political scientists ought to be doing than there was at the beginning. There is little agreement between different universities in Britain on what the foundations of the discipline should be; nor is there any set of agreed basic textbooks. There is no consensus amongst students of comparative government as to the problems which should be regarded as solved nor the areas which would repay further investigation. There is not even agreement on which are the current problem areas.[3] The study of comparative

[1] I am grateful to Rodney Barker, Brian Barry, Archie Brown, Jack Hayward and Michael Steed for their penetrating criticisms of earlier drafts. But I alone am responsible for any mistakes.
[2] A. Somit and J. Tannenhaus, *American Political Science: A Profile of a Discipline* (New York, Atherton Press, 1964), p. 76.
[3] G. Sjöblom, 'The Cumulation Problem in Political Science: An Essay in Research Strategy', *European Journal of Political Research*, 5 (1977), 3.

government can thus hardly be said to resemble even a well-established social science such as economics, let alone a natural science such as physics or mathematics. Perhaps it could be better compared to the study of biology before Darwin, where it was necessary to collect information and provide taxonomies before law-like generalizations could be produced; or perhaps, alternatively, it is not a science at all in the sense of a discipline capable of producing law-like generalizations, but a human science, an interpretative discipline. Whatever its status, the current chaotic state of comparative government bears more resemblance to the state of historical studies than it does to any of the sciences. Whether this state of affairs is one that should comfort political scientists or annoy historians is not wholly clear.

Any evaluation of British political science in the twentieth century must begin with a frank recognition that British political scientists have produced no 'grand theory'. There are no Almonds, Deutsches or Eastons amongst British political scientists. Indeed, the majority view amongst British political scientists remains sceptical if not downright hostile to such work. British political scientists have been more sympathetic to middle-range theories—theories comparing a number of countries by means of new explanatory concepts, such as 'cleavage structure', 'consociational democracy' and 'polarized pluralism'. Yet, not only are there no Almonds, Deutsches or Eastons among British political scientists, there are no Lipsets and Rokkans, Lijpharts or Sartoris either, although a number of British political scientists have produced valuable criticisms of, or variations upon, the work of these original thinkers.

Viewed through this perspective, the contribution of British political science in the twentieth century is bound to seem unremarkable. In a recent handbook of world political science, amongst the four most frequently cited authorities on political institutions and the four most frequently cited on comparative politics, there were no British names at all. Indeed, there was only one book by a British political scientist— Brian Barry—amongst the 32 books most frequently cited.[4]

That is not the only criterion, however, by which British political science should be judged. Indeed it may be that the criteria adopted in the Goodin/Klingemann handbook already presuppose a certain conception of political science which the majority of British political

---

[4] R. E. Goodin and H.-D. Klingemann, eds., *A New Handbook of Political Science* (Oxford, Oxford University Press, 1996), pp. 35–6, 31–2.

scientists have disdained. It is generally assumed that this disdain is a sign of parochialism or insularity. Yet the prospectus and the promise of grand theory—whether systems theory, functionalism or rational choice theory—have been far greater than their achievement. These approaches have been unable to provide a foundation for political science in the form of laws, other than those deriving from very general conditions of human rationality, nor have they been particularly successful in explaining the working of particular political systems.

In its aversion to grand theory, British political science reflects tendencies which lie deep in British intellectual life. For the same aversion to over-arching theory, to general laws and to scientism, the application of principles derived from the natural sciences in disciplines where they do not belong, can be seen in many other intellectual disciplines. In philosophy, the dominant figures in the post-war years were Ryle, Austin and the later Wittgenstein, all of whom were hostile to general philosophical theories which, they believed, were all too often a product of intellectual laziness or confusion, paying as they did insufficient attention to the diverse purposes which language served. In jurisprudence, similarly, H. L. A. Hart drew attention to the diverse functions of law, to which insufficient attention had been paid due to excessive concentration on just one function of the law, that of deterring criminal behaviour. In literary criticism, F. R. Leavis proclaimed himself hostile to literary theory and declared that ideology, whether Christian or Marxist, had no role to play in the 'common pursuit of true judgement',[5] which resulted from the felt experience of 'life', something undefinable and unanalysable, but nevertheless fundamental. In history, Namier and A. J. P. Taylor emphasized not ideals or ideology, which they saw as reflections of psychological needs, but the contingent and the unforeseen. No politician, whether Bismarck, Lloyd George or Hitler, went so far as one who did not know where he was going. In political theory, Britain, alone amongst the major countries of Europe, had no indigenous Marxist tradition. It lacked also a Weber, Durkheim, Pareto or Parsons, or indeed, until recently at least, any sociological theory of a general kind. For the development of sociological theory has often been a response to Marxism. Lacking the one, British sociologists saw no need to develop the other. Significantly, British intellectuals, with Mill being the prime

---

[5] F. R. Leavis, *The Common Pursuit* (London, Chatto & Windus [Penguin Books ed. 1962] 1952) p. v. The phrase 'the common pursuit of true judgement' was taken by Leavis from T. S. Eliot's essay, *The Function of Criticism*.

exception, never thought sociologically about Ireland in the way that Weber thought about East Prussia. In political theory, Berlin and Popper stressed the importance of rendering human aims concrete, condemning ideological conceptions of the good. A central theme of Berlin's work indeed is the attempt to show that it is logically impossible to reconcile conflicting human ideals, an important part of Berlin's defence of pluralist society.

British political science is a product of that same intellectual culture. If there is a central tendency to the discipline as it has developed in Britain in the twentieth century, it lies in the aversion to positivism, understood as the doctrine that the model of the natural sciences constitutes the only valid form of knowledge, with facts being the only possible object of knowledge. British political scientists have not needed to be reminded of Alasdair Macintyre's parable.

> There was once a man who aspired to be the author of the general theory of holes. When asked 'What kind of hole—holes dug by children in the sand for amusement, holes dug by gardeners to plant lettuce seedlings, tank traps, holes made by roadmakers?' he would reply indignantly that he wished for a *general* theory that would explain all of these. He rejected *ab initio* the—as he saw it—pathetically commonsense view that of the digging of different kinds of holes there are quite different kinds of explanations to be given; why then he would ask do we have the concept of hole? Lacking the explanations to which he originally aspired, he then fell to discovering statistically significant correlations; he found for example that there is a correlation between the aggregate hole-digging achievement of a society as measured, or at least one day to be measured, by econometric techniques, and its degree of technological development. The United States surpasses both Paraguay and Upper Volta in hole-digging. He also discovered that war accelerates hole-digging. There are more holes in Vietnam than there were. These observations, he would always insist, were neutral and value-free. This man's achievement had passed totally unnoticed except by me. Had he however turned his talents to political science, had he concerned himself not with holes, but with modernization, urbanization or violence, I find it difficult to believe that he might not have achieved high office in the APSA.[6]

The achievement of British political scientists should be judged in terms of the aims which they have set themselves, their conception of the discipline. The best way of evaluating that achievement is by pointing to

---

[6] A. Macintyre, *Against the Self-Images of the Age* (London, Duckworth, 1971), p. 260. See also Ch. 8 of A. Macintyre, *After Virtue* (London, Duckworth, 1981), 'The Character of Generalizations in Social Science and their lack of Predictive Power'.

some representative figures in the development of the subject, seven characters in search of a discipline. In what follows, a 'British' political scientist is taken to be someone whose best work has been done in Britain, rather than a native or naturalized British citizen. Work on Eastern Europe, on developing countries and on democratization is excluded.[7] No claim is made that the seven characters chosen are *the* major figures in the development of the discipline—although the work of Ostrogorski, S. E. Finer and Rose displays elements of great originality, amounting perhaps to genius—only that the seven are representative of major trends in British political science. All of them, moreover, pioneered a particular approach to the discipline. They are originators as well as representative figures.[8]

Ostrogorski

Modern Democracies by James Bryce in 1921 is commonly said to have been the first scholarly book to have been published on comparative government in Britain in the twentieth century. It was, however, preceded by a remarkable work by a Russian émigré, Moisei Ostrogorski, *Democracy and the Organisation of Political Parties*, published in 1902.[9] Ostrogorski's book was in fact sponsored by Bryce who had encouraged him to write it, in the hope that it would serve to test his theory of political parties. The book contained a preface in which Bryce commented that

> Although political parties are as old as popular government itself, their nature, their forces and the modes in which they have been organized have received comparatively little attention from historians or from writers on what is beginning to be called political science. Something has been said, and by no one perhaps as well as by Edmund Burke, upon the theory and aim of Party, and the functions which it ought to discharge; and historical accounts, though seldom either full or philosophical, have been given of the development and career of the two great parties in England and in the American Union. But no one has, so far as I know, produced any treatise containing a systematic examination and description of the structure of

[7] In a recent survey article, Page also included non-native Britons and excluded Eastern Europe, developing countries and democratization, from his purview. E. C. Page, 'British Political Science and Comparative Politics', *Political Studies*, 37 (1990), 439–40.

[8] Three of those selected—Ostrogorski, Rose and King—are not British, but their best work was written in Britain, and was shaped by British influences.

[9] M. Ostrogorski, *Democracy and the Organisation of Political Parties*, 2 vols, (London, Macmillan, 1902).

parties as organizations governed by settled rules and working by established methods.'[10]

Bryce had noticed this lacuna when he had come to write *The American Commonwealth*, but had found no book on which he could draw; and this had struck Ostrogorski also. Parties had been in their formative stage in the United States in the 1830s when Tocqueville wrote *Democracy in America*, and Tocqueville had failed to appreciate their significance. Ostrogorski, however, had, according to Bryce, filled the gap in analysis. He was 'both scientific in method and philosophical in spirit'.[11]

Ostrogorski began by citing Tocqueville's aphorism, 'Il faut une science politique nouvelle à un monde tout nouveau'. In Ostrogorski's view, this new science was developed not solely through the study of institutions, of political *forms*, but by analysing the political *forces* which lay behind them, the forces of 'social and political psychology', what today would be called political culture.[12]

Ostrogorski was the first to ask general questions about political parties, the first to ask if there were any general statements which could be made about the development of parties in democracies. How, in particular, were parties affected by the coming of universal suffrage? Ostrogorski's answer was similar to that later to be given by Michels and Weber. It was, that behind a democratic façade, parties were essentially oligarchic structures, barely accountable to their members. Work on political parties for many years consisted of little but variations on this central theme first adumbrated by Ostrogorski.

Ostrogorski's book is a comparative study of the organization of political parties in Britain and the United States. For these were the two advanced democracies displaying the trajectory which other democracies too would take. Ostrogorski's conclusion was that the promise of liberalism, the dominant ideological force in both societies, was being undermined by party organization and by the growing power of professional party politicians. The nineteenth century had held out the prospect of the triumph of the free and autonomous individual, but, by the end of the century, the individual was able to wield but a shadow of his sovereignty. 'It would, in truth', Ostorgorski concluded, 'be difficult to find in the history of human societies a more pathetic drama than

---

[10] Ostrogorski, *Democracy and the Organisation of Political Parties*, I, p. xxix.
[11] Ibid. I, p. xiii.
[12] Ibid. I, p. li.

the ruin of so many generous aspirations, of so many noble efforts, of such high promise and expectations'.[13] The growth of party organization was not inevitable, however. It resulted from ideological, not technological trends, from certain ways of thinking, which it lay in the power of men to change. There were two factors, Ostrogorski believed, which determined the existence of every political community, 'its culture, both intellectual and moral, and its political methods'.[14] But a society's political methods flowed from its culture. Ostrogorski believed that for every political arrangement or form 'an inside is indispensable'.[15] That 'inside' was the set of ideas which sustained the structure of authority. So it was that 'victory over political formalism, if it is to be genuine, must be won first of all in the mind of the elector'. Democracy had 'carried the *habeas corpus* by force, but the decisive battle of democracy will be fought on the *habeas animum*'.[16]

Ostrogorski has generally been regarded as a pioneer of modern political science. Yet his legacy had often been distorted by modern commentators. Robert McKenzie, for example, set up a straw man whom he called Ostrogorski who, he claims, believed that 'MPs as individuals and the parties in parliament were almost certain to become the slaves of the mass party organizations outside Parliament'. Ostrogorski believed precisely the opposite. McKenzie thinks that he is refuting Ostrogorski when he concludes that, 'effective control of the affairs of the Conservative Party remains in the hands of the Leader thrown up by the parliamentary party'.[17] Yet that is precisely what Ostrogorski himself believed. David Butler hailed Ostrogorski in 1958 'not only as the first serious student of British parties, but also as an illustration of the possibility of separating description and analysis'.[18] Ostrogorski, however, cast the whole of his analysis within a framework of liberal indivdualism. He was in no sense a modern positivist. The true philosophical basis of Ostrogorski's approach was long obscured by S. M. Lipset's bowdlerized abridged edition of *Democracy and the Organisation of Political Parties* which made him appear as a forerunner of American political science, rather than as the protagonist of a form of individualist liberalism which has had hardly any successors. For,

[13] Ibid. II, p. 608.
[14] Ibid. II, p. 601.
[15] Ibid. II, p. 560.
[16] Ibid. II, p. 728.
[17] R. T. McKenzie *British Political Parties* (London, Heinemann, 1955), pp. 9, 637.
[18] D. E. Butler, *The Study of Political Behaviour* (London, Hutchinson, 1958).

although Ostrogorski's book was the product of 15 years of close observation of Britain and the United States, he interpreted the facts very much in the light of his commitment to a rather Whiggish and traditional liberalism. This liberalism predisposed him to regard party not as an inevitable concomitant of democracy, but as an almost accidental growth. Indeed, he seemed to believe that an advanced democracy could operate without organized parties at all. That was little more than wishful thinking on his part.

Ostrogorski has hardly been read since his death—'There are uncut pages in the seventy-two-year-old first and only edition of his major work in university libraries, and there is remarkably little scholarly writing on him', complained two writers on him in 1975.[19] A Russian who spent only a short period of time in Britain, Ostrogorski yet displays qualities which may be said to characterize much later British political science. There was, indeed, a deep elective affinity between Ostrogorski and Britain; and he sent a signed copy of his last work, published in Russian in 1916, *The Constitutional History of England in the last Half-Century* 'To the Reading Room of the British Museum from an old reader'.[20]

Bryce

James Bryce was the first British subject to be asked to give the presidential address to the American Political Science Association, in 1909. In 1921, a year before his death, he published *Modern Democracies*, of which he said that 'the most flattering thing that anyone could think to say was that it was a very large book to have been written by an eighty-three year old'.[21]

Bryce wrote in his Preface,

---

[19] R. Barker and X. Howard-Johnston, 'The Politics and Political Ideas of Moisei Ostrogorski' in *Political Studies*, 22 (1975), 415. This article offers a most valuable short exposition of Ostrogorski's life and ideas.

[20] G. Ionescu, 'Moysey Ostrogorski' p. 145. In J. A. Hall, *Rediscoveries: Some Neglected Modern European Political Thinkers* (Oxford, Clarendon Press, 1986). See also, G. Quagliarello, *Politics Without Parties* (Avebury, Aldershot, 1996), although this is an unsatisfactory work in many ways.

[21] S. Collini, D. Winch and J. Burrow, *That Noble Science of Politics: A Study in Nineteenth Century Intellectual History* (Cambridge, Cambridge University Press, 1983), p. 237. On p. 236, the authors commit the solecism of referring to Bryce as an 'Englishman'. He was of course an Ulsterman, born of a Scottish father and a Northern Irish mother.

Many years ago, at a time when schemes of political reform were being copiously discussed in England, mostly on general principles, but also with references usually vague and disconnected, to history and to events happening in other countries, it occurred to me that something might be done to provide a solid base for argument and judgement by examining a certain number of popular governments in their actual working, comparing them with one another and setting forth the various merits and defects which belonged to each. As I could not find that any such comparative study had been undertaken, I formed the idea of attempting it.[22]

Before *Modern Democracies*, there had been a number of valuable books on particular foreign systems, the most important of which were J. E. C. Bodley's *France* and Bryce's own *American Commonwealth*; but *Modern Democracies* was the first scholarly work published in Britain which attempted to compare a range of democratic systems.[23]

Bryce believed that modern democracies could not be analysed on the same basis as the democracies of the ancient republics, but required a more modern method of inquiry. This 'method of inquiry' was

known as the Comparative Method. That which entitles it to be called scientific is that it reaches general conclusions by tracing similar cases, eliminating those disturbing influences which, present in one country and absent in another, make the results in the examined cases different in some points and similar in others. When by this method of comparison the differences between the workings of democratic government in one country and another have been noted, the local or special conditions, physical or racial or economic, will be examined so as to determine whether it is in them that the source of these differences is to be found. If not in them, then we must turn to the institutions and try to discover which of those that exist in popular governments, have worked best . . . When allowance has been made for the different conditions under which each acts, it will be possible to pronounce upon the balance of consideration, which form offers the best prospect of success.[24]

The method proposed by Bryce was, in fact, very much like J. S. Mill's 'method of agreement and difference', as outlined in Book III, Chapters 8 to 10 of his *System of Logic* (1843).[25] It cannot be said, however,

---

[22] J. Bryce, *Modern Democracies* (London, Macmillan, 1921), 2 vols; I, p. vii.

[23] J. E. C. Bodley, *France* (London, Macmillan, 1898), 2 vols; J. Bryce, *The American Commonwealth* (London, Macmillan, 1888), 2 vols. The influence of both works has been far-reaching. In *Crisis and Compromise*, first published in 1964, Philip Williams declared that he had found Bodley 'invaluable for French politics and society in 1900' (Garden City, New York, Anchor Books edition, Doubleday and Co., 1966), p. 504; and he quoted extensively from Bodley in his first chapter, 'The Basis of French Politics'.

[24] Bryce, *Modern Democracies*, I, p. 20.

[25] I owe this point to Brian Barry.

that Bryce actually applies this method. For *Modern Democracies* proceeds, not on the basis of institutions, but by means of a country-by-country analysis. It examined two Continental democracies, France and Switzerland, two Atlantic democracies, the United States and Canada, and the two Australasian democracies, Australia and New Zealand. Bryce deliberately omitted Britain because, as an ardent Liberal, he felt that he could not offer an impartial treatment of his native country.

Bryce chose what he thought of as stable democracies. Like most British political scientists until the 1970s, however, his perspective was dominated by the Anglo-Saxon individualist democracies. He did not look closely at the more corporatist and collectivist democracies to be found in the Scandinavian countries or in Belgium and the Netherlands. His sample of democracies, therefore, was biased in favour of the adversarial democracies, containing as it did just one example of a consensual democracy—Switzerland. This had important consequences for the development of British political science. For it meant that the idea of a social cleavage and its relationship to party was not perceived for many years to come. 'Democracy' came to be equated with the practices of Britain, the United States and Australia, not with those of Belgium, the Netherlands and Norway.

In his preface to *Modern Democracies*, Bryce declared that 'The book is not meant to propound theories'. He took the view that the greatest obstacle to the study of comparative government lay in a lack of factual knowledge about other systems of government. 'There were', he went on, 'two methods of handling the subject', which presented themselves.

> One, that which most of my predecessors in this field have adopted, is to describe in a systematic way the features of democratic government in general, using the facts of particular democracies only by way of illustrating the general principles expounded. The other method, commended by the examples of Montesquieu and Tocqueville, keeps him in a closer touch with the central concrete phenomena of human society making it easier for him to follow reasonings and appreciate criticisms, because these are more closely associated in memory with the facts that suggest them.[26]

Although not seeking to propound theories, Bryce concluded his book with some 'considerations' applicable to democratic governments in general. For 'the value' of political science, he believed,

---

[26] Bryce, *Modern Democracies*, I, preface, p. ix, p. 6.

consists in tracing and determining the relation of these tendencies (of human nature) to the institutions which men have created for guiding their life in a community. Certain institutions have been found by experience to work better than others; i.e. they give more scope to the wholesome tendencies, and curb the pernicious tendencies. Such institutions have also a retroactive action upon those who live under them. Helping men to goodwill, self-restraint, intelligent co-operation, they form what we call a solid political character, temperate and law-abiding, preferring peaceful to violent means for the settlement of controversies. Where, on the other hand, institutions have been ill-constructed, or too frequently changed to exert this educative influence, men make under them little progress towards a steady and harmonious common life. To find the type of institutions best calculated to help the better and repress the pernicious tendencies is the task of the philosophic enquirer, who lays the foundations upon which the legislator builds.[27]

Democracy, Bryce believed, depended upon a lively and well-informed public opinion; it required an efficient and accountable bureaucracy and a lively system of local government. The value of the book, however, lies not in these 'considerations', trite as they may seem today, nor in Bryce's rather unsophisticated view of the purpose of the study of comparative government. It lay rather in the detailed investigation of individual political systems, an investigation carried out, as *The American Commonwealth* had been, as much through personal investigation and inquiry as by reflection on already published work.

The most fundamental of Bryce's assumptions was the liberal one that democracy was becoming the norm and that all human societies were tending towards it. He referred to 'the almost universal acceptance of democracy as the normal and natural form of government . . . Men have almost ceased to study its phenomena because these now seem to have become part of the established order of things'.[28]

That was a judgement which, amidst the turmoil afflicting Continental Europe, perhaps only a British writer would have dared to make in 1921. Bryce's choice of countries was indeed skewed towards those nations which, with the exception of France perhaps, already provided examples of stable democracy. His view of an 'ideal democracy' was, Graham Wallas believed, 'the kind of democracy which might be possible if human nature were as he himself would like it to be, and as he was taught at Oxford to think it was'.[29] No less than Ostrogorski

---

[27] Ibid. p. 11.
[28] Ibid. p. 4.
[29] G. Wallas, *Human Nature in Politics* (London, Constable, 1908), p. 127.

did Bryce allow his approach to be conditioned by his fundamental commitment to liberal values in politics.

Bryce was writing in the aftermath of the Soviet revolution, of the failed German and Hungarian revolutions, and on the eve of the Fascist revolution in Italy. None of this is mentioned in *Modern Democracies*. Yet, during the years following the book's publication, violent upheaval left the political structure of hardly any European state intact. Only Britain, Switzerland and the Nordic states, remained immune from upheaval. In Europe, at least, stable democracy was by no means the norm in the years between the wars. Seven years after *Modern Democracies* appeared, Agnes Headlam-Morley published a short book entitled *The New Democratic Constitutions of Europe* in which she studied a very different set of countries from those chosen by Bryce—Weimar Germany, Czechoslovakia, Yugoslavia, Poland, Finland and the Baltic states. Her conclusion was that

> although democratic in form, they (i.e. the new democracies) show abundant signs of the total reaction that has taken place against the individualistic Liberalism on which were based the democratic constitutions of the 19th century . . . The complete failure of parliamentary government in Italy; the discontent it has aroused in other countries, the difficulties with which the practice of self-government has been faced in many of the new states, the steady pressure of the socialistic opinion demanding above all things, efficiency; all these have combined, since the establishment of these constitutions to produce a rapid reaction against this belief in the absolute value of democracy.[30]

The disintegration of the great European empires, the Czarist, the Habsburg and the Hohenzollern, was leading not to the spread of liberalism or democracy, but to a new form of populistic dictatorship, whether Communist, Fascist or National Socialist, forms of government for which there was no room in the liberal philosophy to which Bryce was heir. Bryce's failure, then, was not one of method, but of perception. For all his vaunted empiricism, he simply failed to notice what was happening in the Europe of his time.

Herman Finer

In 1921, the year in which *Modern Democracies* appeared, a short book on comparative politics was published. It was called *Foreign Governments at*

---

[30] A. Headlam-Morley, *The New Democratic Constitutions of Europe* (London, Oxford University Press, 1928).

Work and its author was a young assistant lecturer at the LSE, Herman Finer. From one point of view, *Foreign Governments at Work* was a standard country-by-country introductory textbook, containing as it did chapters on France, Germany and the United States. The book discerned five main influences on government, those of 'race', history, a dominant personality, imitation and 'lastly, . . . the consistent working out of new theories of government and experiment', theories which had deeply influenced the governments of the USSR and Weimar Germany.[31]

But there was something new in Herman Finer's book, an analytical index which enabled the reader to consult topics such as 'Second Chambers', 'Electoral Methods', etc., and refer to the treatment given to them in different chapters. 'In that way one can study the institutions of a country as a single system, and then study the similar institutions in different countries.'[32]

This can be seen as a challenging statement of future intentions. For it presaged not only Herman Finer's own contribution to the study of comparative government, but provided the germ of an idea later to be utilized in a much more sophisticated way by Herman's younger brother, S. E. (Sammy) Finer in his book, *Five Constitutions*, published in 1979.[33] The five constitutions were those of the United States, the Federal Republic of Germany, the Fifth Republic of France, the Constitution of the USSR, and the Constitution of Britain, on which Finer contributed a long discursive essay.[34]

The crucial original feature of *Five Constitutions*, however, lay in its analytical index. The book in fact contained two indexes, one which was traditional, with the topics listed in alphabetical order, but in a manner facilitating cross-comparison between provisions in different constitutions. The other index was analytical. Sammy Finer broke down the components of governance into the categories normally used by political scientists, and cross-indexed them accordingly. Thus, the analytical index is broken down into eleven categories—constitutions, federations, local government, dependencies, the legislative branch, executive

---

[31] H. Finer, *Foreign Governments at Work* (Oxford, Oxford University Press, 1921), pp. 14–19.
[32] Ibid. p. 5.
[33] S. E. Finer, *Five Constitutions* (Harmondsworth, Penguin Books, 1979).
[34] S. E. Finer, V. Bogdanor and B. Rudden, *Comparing Constitutions* (Oxford, Clarendon Press, 1995). A revised edition, *Comparing Constitutions*, by V. Bogdanor and B. Rudden, published in 1995, substituted the constitution of the Russian Federation for that of the USSR and included extracts from the European Convention of Human Rights together with the Treaty of Rome and its main amending treaties, the Single European Act and the Maastricht Treaty on European Union.

branch, judicial branch, emergency powers, external relations and defence, citizens and the state and constitutional offences. Each category is in turn then subdivided.

The analytical index is far more than a juxtaposition of information, for its purpose is to display the conceptual logic of different political systems. It is thus an indispensable tool of analysis and a method which could be extended to the analysis of families of constitutions, or, for example, to the constitutions of the 15 member states of the European Union. That could probably only be achieved through collaborative work as the comparative analysis of even five constitutions is an arduous task.

S. E. Finer's method offers a way of pursuing the analysis of constitutions. This method remains in its infancy. It is often said that other forms of analysis have superseded the analysis of constitutions, and that such analysis is in any case less important for political scientists than analysis of the real underlying factors of the political world. In truth, however, the comparative analysis of constitutions has barely begun, and the most important contributions towards it have been made by British authors—Herman Finer, whose chapter on constitutions in *The Theory and Practice of Modern Government*, was drawn upon by K. C. Wheare in his classic *Modern Constitutions*, and S. E. Finer.[35]

Herman Finer's main contribution to the study of comparative government came in his massive two-volume work, *The Theory and Practice of Modern Government*, first published in 1932 and reprinted in an enlarged version in 1949. The product of immense erudition—its author immodestly claimed that it was 'founded upon *all* the available material, primary sources and secondary works'—its material was drawn chiefly from the experience of Britain, France, Germany and the United States.[36] Finer, however, treated his material, not after the fashion of Bryce country by country but topic by topic, analysing each set of institutions for all the countries together. There are thus sections on parliaments, the executive and the civil service, as well as chapters on the separation of powers, constitutions and federalism. Local government, on which Finer wrote extensively, and the judiciary were left for later volumes, never in fact to be completed. Nevertheless, Finer's work was indeed, as he declared, 'truly comparative, and this affords the basis for sound generalization . . . Against the loss of the all-dimensional relative sense,

[35] H. Finer, *The Theory and Practice of Modern Government* (London, Methuen, [1946 ed.] 1932), K. C. Wheare, *Modern Constitutions* (London, Oxford University Press, 1951).
[36] Finer, *The Theory and Practice of Modern Government*, p. vii. Emphasis added.

there is the great gain of analysis and immediate comparison—clearer revelation of the uniformities of human nature in government'.[37]

Finer's aim was to display the conceptual logic behind alternative structures of government. Sensitive to history as he was, his analysis was neither mechanistic nor reductionist. He was far too aware of the cultural diversity of the systems which he was studying and of the sheer contingency of political life to believe that government could be anything other than an active agent in politics, rather than a mere mechanism converting 'inputs' into 'outputs'. While the descriptive material in the book is now, inevitably, outdated, the method of inquiry and the laying bare of the logic of different forms remain achievements of permanent value. Perhaps little read by modern political scientists, Herman Finer's influence has been filtered through political scientists of the successor generation, such as Wheare. Alone of British political scientists in the field of comparative government between the wars, Finer's work remains alive and of relevance. The work of contemporaries who overshadowed him, such as Laski and Cole, seems, by contrast, now largely of merely historical interest.

S. E. Finer

S. E. (Sammy) Finer's ambition had always been 'to be like my brother'.[38] There is indeed a remarkable intellectual continuity between the two men. Sammy learnt from his brother three things:

> 1. Politics is not a natural science, but it can be a disciplined and systematic study. This is best achieved by looking for patterns of uniformities and regularities across time and space. The comparative approach is the nearest approach to a scientific method.
> 2. All generalizations are limited. A good grasp of history is essential for understanding the context and antecedents of political institutions—and for testing general statements.
> 3. It is more useful to adopt a problem-oriented approach than to seek some grand theory of politics.[39]

---

[37] Ibid. pp. viii–ix.

[38] S. E. Finer, 'Political Science: An Idiosyncratic Retrospect of a Putative Discipline', in 'A Generation of Political Thought', *Government and Opposition*, 15 (1980), 346. See also the *festschrift*, D. Kavanagh and G. Peele, eds., *Comparative Government and Politics* (London, Heinemann, 1984), and the special issue of the journal, *Government and Opposition*, 29 (1994), devoted to Finer's memory.

[39] D. Kavanagh, 'The Fusion of History and Politics: The Case of S. E. Finer', in H. Daalder, ed., *Comparative European Politics: The Story of a Profession* (London, Pinter, 1997), pp. 16–17.

Herman Finer, however, like Ostrogorski and Bryce, had restricted his comparisons to liberal democratic states. His brother determined to develop a typology which could be applied to *all* states.

Sammy Finer came late to comparative politics. His first book was a historical biography, the life of the great nineteenth-century civil service reformer, Edwin Chadwick; he then moved on to public administration and local government in Britain. It was not until the age of 47 that he published his first work in comparative government, *The Man on Horseback*. This was a pioneering and wide-ranging account of the role of the military, analysing and comparing the level of military intervention by relating it to the political culture of different countries. Finer sought to show that the most important causes of military intervention were not military but political, relating as they did to conditions in the society in which the military operated. Military intervention, Finer believed, rested on the level of political culture, on the extent of public approval for the procedures for transferring power, i.e. legitimacy, and the width of the political public, the extent to which there were strong social organizations such as trade unions, churches, political parties, etc. With strong legitimacy and a wide political public, a society had a 'mature' political culture; with weak legitimacy and a narrow political public, a society had a 'minimal' political culture. Finer distinguished between three types of military regime, the direct, the indirect where the military ruled through a civilian government, and the dual. Military rule, moreover, could be either continuous or intermittent.[40] *The Man on Horseback* displayed many aspects of Finer's technique, in particular his concern to understand a complex reality through straightforward and parsimonious typologies which, nevertheless, contained massive explanatory power.

Finer's next book on government, *Comparative Government*, was published in 1970.[41] The value of this book lies less in the sections on Britain, the United States, etc., than in its attempt to categorize all the governments of the world, 'with the most economical set of distinctions' on the basis of 'three criteria of comparison and contrast'. These were, first, the extent to which the mass of the public were or were not involved in the governmental process, the *participation–exclusion* dimension; second, the extent to which the mass public obeyed their rulers out

---

[40] S. E. Finer, *The Man on Horseback: The Role of the Military in Politics* (London, Pall Mall Press [2nd rev. ed., 1988] 1962), pp. 245 and 149 ff.

[41] S. E. Finer, *Comparative Government* (London, Allen Lane [Penguin edition, 1974] 1970).

of commitment or fear, the *coercion—persuasion* dimension; and third, the extent to which the rulers reflected the actual and current values of the ruled, rather than sacrificing them in the interests of continuity or future values, the *order—representativeness* dimension.[42]

Finer used these criteria to deploy a typology of the world's governments in five categories—the liberal-democratic state, the totalitarian state, the façade-democracy, the quasi-democracy and the military regime. The notion of a 'façade-democracy' was derived from Pareto whose writings Finer had edited.[43] It is defined as

> a system where liberal-democratic institutions, processes and safeguards are established by law but are in practice so manipulated or violated by a historic oligarchy as to stay in office. The structure of the government is usually collegiate but for a time it may be superseded by an individual autocratic ruler using similar methods to perpetuate himself.[44]

Examples were taken from Argentina, Mexico, Iran under the Shahs, Iraq before 1958 and Spain before 1931. This particular structure was linked to social correlates, 'what we might call 'the old oligarchy' or 'the old autocracy', as contrasted with the neo-oligarchy and neo-autocracy of the *quasi-democracy*'.[45] The quasi-democracy was a one-party state which was not, however, totalitarian, a predominant form of government at the time in Africa, in Mexico and, until 1945, in Turkey. These five types, Finer believed, covered all the known varieties of governmental forms. He sought to use this typology as a 'basis for explaining what forms arise in what given circumstances and, . . . predicting what vicissitudes or alterations a given form may undergo should circumstances change in named respects'.[46]

Finer's posthumously published *History of Government from the Earliest Times* is an astonishing work in range and depth overcoming as it does the parochialism of both time and space.[47] In this book, Finer succeeded in producing a typology which covered every government

---

[42] Ibid. p. 440.

[43] S. E. Finer, ed., *Pareto: Sociological Writings* (London, Pall Mall Press 1966).

[44] S. E. Finer, *Comparative Government*, p. 442.

[45] Ibid. p. 442.

[46] Ibid. p. 40.

[47] S. E. Finer, *History of Government from the Earliest Times* (Oxford, Oxford University Press, 1997). See, for short expositions of Finer's *History*, S. E. Finer, 'Perspectives in the World History of Government—A Prolegomenon', *Government and Opposition*, 18 (1983); J. Hayward, 'Finer's Comparative History of Government', *Government and Opposition*, 32 (1997) and H. Berrington, 'Samuel Edward Finer, 1915–1993', in *Proceedings of the British Academy*, (1996), 359–61.

since the dawn of human history. He identified four different types of polity, the Palace type, where legitimacy lies with the ruler, the Forum type, where it lies with the ruled, the Church, and the Nobility, using combinations of these types and sub-types to categorize every known system of government. Finer's *History* is likely to be recognized as one of the most important works produced by a British political scientist this century.

Sammy Finer's main contribution, then, to the study of comparative government lay in the development of typologies. It would be foolish to dismiss such an activity as nothing more than a refined form of stamp collecting. One might as well dismiss the work of Linnaeus as beetle labelling or the human genome project as mere counting. For classification forms an essential part in the development of any scientific discipline. It leads to the development of typologies which in turn suggest correlations and uniformities requiring explanation. 'Linnaeus didn't just codify; he unmasked'.[48] In the social sciences, apart from economics, laws are derived inductively, not deductively as in the physical sciences.[49] Thus, the development of typologies is a necessary preliminary to the discovery of laws. Indeed, the formulation of laws, whether in the physical or the social sciences, inherently presupposes correct classification.

An emphasis on classification marks, perhaps, an early stage in the development of a discipline.

> The development of a scientific discipline may often be said to proceed from an initial 'natural history' stage, which primarily seeks to describe the phenomena under study and to establish simple empirical generalizations concerning them, to subsequent more and more 'theoretical' stages, in which increasing emphasis is placed upon the attainment of the empirical subject matter under investigation.[50]

Political science is, of course, a young discipline. Its successes so far lie less in the development of laws or of a body of settled doctrine than in conceptual analysis and classification. Moreover, classification is bound to play a larger role in political science than it does in a more quantitatively-based discipline such as physics or economics. Thus, even someone holding a positivistic conception of the social sciences would be

---

[48] S. J. Gould, *Dinosaur in a Haystack: Reflections in Natural History* (London, Jonathan Cape, 1996). p. 420.

[49] M. H. Lessnoff, *The Structure of Social Science: A Philosophical Introduction* (London, Allen & Unwin, 1974).

[50] C. G. Hempel, *Aspects of Scientific Explanation* (New York, Free Press, 1965), pp. 139–40.

hard put to deny that the work of Sammy Finer marks a vital stage in the development of the modern discipline.

Philip Williams

It could be argued that comparative politics is quite different from the intensive study of one particular country. Therefore, it may be suggested, it is misleading to cite British political scientists who have written on foreign countries such as Denis Brogan or Philip Williams, as engaged in comparative politics. For this would have the absurd consequence that, if *The American Political System* or *Crisis and Compromise* had happened to be written by American or French authors, they would not count as 'Comparative Politics'; while, because they have been written by British authors, they do so count.[51]

But this dichotomy between comparative politics and single-country studies is drawn too sharply. British political scientists have generally taken the view that it is best to move from the particular to the general, to understand one system thoroughly before proceeding to comparison; and then to compare just a few countries which are not too dissimilar. The procedures of American political science tend to be quite different, beginning with generalizations which are then applied to individual countries as instances. British political science tends of course to the inductive, while American tends to the deductive.

Comparative government must depend upon studies of individual countries. Moreover, as Rose has pointed out, 'A single-nation study can be implicitly comparative if it uses concepts applicable elsewhere'.[52] Brogan's book, *The American Political System* was said to have fallen 'like a coruscating rocket'. It

> virtually re-discovered America for a generation of British readers as a country to which the reach-me-down axioms of Anglo-Saxon political theory did *not* apply, where the historic pieties were overloaded with a very antithetical set of actualities, whose successes and failures demanded assessment in the light of their distinctive circumstances, not by Old World criteria, respectful or dismissive.[53]

---

[51] D. W. Brogan, *The American Political System* (London, Hamish Hamilton, 1933); P. M. Williams, *Crisis and Compromise* (1964) (Garden City, NY, Anchor Books, 1966).
[52] R. Rose, 'Comparing Forms of Comparative Analysis', *Political Studies*, 39 (1991), 447.
[53] H. G. Nicholas, 'Denis William Brogan, 1900–1974', *Proceedings of the British Academy* (Oxford, Oxford University Press, 1977), p. 400.

Philip Williams was described in his British Academy obituary as a scholar 'who was perhaps in Oxford and beyond the most important single influence on the study of modern comparative institutions to emerge since the Second World War'.[54] *Crisis and Compromise*, Williams's classic analysis of the Fourth French Republic is, moreover, a book which could probably only have been written by a British scholar. This is so for two reasons. First, parliamentary government is understood in terms of the British model in which parliament, while it neither makes law nor seeks to dominate the executive, is, nevertheless, sufficiently powerful to be able to subject the executive to effective scrutiny. This system may be contrasted with a *mitregierung* parliament of the German type, and with a *régime d'assemblée*. It is the model of a—perhaps idealized—House of Commons. Williams's admiration for *Hugh Gaitskell*, the subject of his massive biography, published in 1979, and arguably the best biography of any modern politician published since the war, derived from Gaitskell's being, in Williams's view, an exemplar of the ideal *parliamentary* statesman, a man who could apply to ideals passionately held the tools of reasoned argument and debate.[55]

Second, the discursive approach, combining as it does history with sociology, is perhaps distinctively British. As David Caute noticed in his review of *Crisis and Compromise*, the technique involved 'approaching the evidence along three different but converging lines of inquiry: the parties, the institutions, the system'. It combined the social scientist's 'horizontal' understanding of the multiplicity of forces at work in a single society at a given time, with the historian's sensitivity to 'vertical' development in time. For this reason, concluded Caute, *Crisis and Compromise* 'must rank as one of the classics of modern political science'.[56]

The final chapter of *Crisis and Compromise* contains one of the earliest examples of cleavage analysis being used to explain the behaviour of political parties and applied to the investigation of a particular political system. The book was published three years before the Lipset/Rokkan *Introduction*, and it did not use cleavage analysis systematically.[57] It

[54] D. Johnson, 'Philip Maynard Williams', *Proceedings of the British Academy* (Oxford, Oxford University Press, 1986), p. 551.

[55] P. M. Williams, *Hugh Gaitskell* (London, Jonathan Cape, 1979).

[56] D. Caute 'Crisis, Compromise and Democracy in France', *Oxford Magazine*, 29 April 1965, 297–8.

[57] S. M. Lipset and S. Rokkan, eds., 'Introduction', *Party Systems and Voter Alignments* (Free Press, Glencoe, 1967).

introduced, however, a constitutional/anti-constitutional cleavage, which is absent in Lipset and Rokkan, and also emphasized, as Lipset and Rokkan were to do, the massive importance of the inheritance of past cleavages.

In his analysis, Williams concluded that 'The constitution of the Fourth Republic was . . . a characteristic symptom rather than a basic weakness of the French democratic state'.[58] The Fourth Republic regime had been

> remade in 1946 in order to destroy the bad old ways; but before long the System reappeared. This return (not persistence) of traditional attitudes and methods suggests that the problem of adapting the political mechanism to social change lay not in the faults of character of two very different sets of men, or the institutional weaknesses of two constitutions devised for quite different ends, but deep in the historical and sociological structure of France.[59]

Thus, explanations based either on institutions or on specific socio-economic factors were incomplete. Williams's fundamental proposition is that the instability of French politics was due less to her institutions or to those who sought to manage them than to the historical and social position in which France found herself. His position had been stated as early as 1954 when he had declared that

> the real French problem is one of majorities, not of institutions. The difficulty lies in deep sociological and historical fissures which split up the French electorate into a series of separate compartments having little mental or physical contact with one another.[60]

The weakness of this explanation was that it seemed to involve a kind of historical determinism. The assumption in the first edition of *Crisis and Compromise*, published as *Politics in Post-War France*, was that the Fourth Republic system, bad as it was, would nevertheless go on for ever.[61] In *Crisis and Compromise*, Williams was honest enough to admit that he had 'seriously overestimated the stability of a regime which had yet to face a political and emotional challenge as grave as the Irish question in Britain, or the problem of the South in the United States'.[62] There is, however, no place in the categories of explanation in *Crisis and*

---

[58] P. M. Williams, *Crisis and Compromise* (1964), p. 6.
[59] Ibid. p. 33.
[60] Ibid. p. 484.
[61] Williams, 'Problems of Fourth Republic France' in *Political Studies*, 2 (1954), 42.
[62] Williams, *Politics in Post-War France* (London, Longmans Green, 1954).

Compromise, let alone in *Politics in Post-War France*, for the phenomenon of leadership, or of de Gaulle, who seems to emerge as a *deus ex machina* from nowhere at the end of the book. But few if any political scientists in any country have been able to account for that characteristically twentieth-century phenomenon, the emergence of charismatic leadership.

Richard Rose

Richard Rose's first book, *Politics in England*, was originally published as part of a series of works on different countries exemplifying the functionalist approach. It began, challengingly, with the statement that only a comparativist would have made, 'In the study of comparative politics, England is important as a deviant case'.[63] Yet the functional categories were so general that, of themselves, they provided little illumination of British politics, and the book concluded with a rather breathless institutional analysis of a highly traditional kind. Later editions of *Politics in England* gave less and less priority to the functionalist approach and more emphasis to the orthodox analysis of institutions.

The progress of successive editions of *Politics in England* mirrors that of Rose's intellectual development. An American with vast knowledge of, and sympathy with, the diverse trends of American political science, he had, nevertheless, and perhaps against his conscious inclinations, become socialized into many of the presuppositions of British political science.[64] The bulk of Rose's vast output has been concerned with the testing of hypotheses. The outcome, however, has been not a general theory of politics but a heightened sensitivity to the way in which politics in one society differs from politics in another.

---

[63] R. Rose, *Politics in England* (Boston, Mass., Little Brown, 1964) and (London, Faber, 1965), p. 1. See also Rose, 'England: a Traditionally Modern Culture', in L. W. Pye and S. Verba, eds., *Political Culture and Political Development* (Princeton, Princeton University Press, 1965), pp. 83–129, and Rose, 'Politics in England', in G. A. Almond and B. Powell, eds., *Comparative Politics Today: A World View* (Boston, Mass., Little, Brown, 1974), pp. 131–91, pp. 149–209, 3rd ed. 1984, 136–96, 4th ed. 1988, 143–208, 5th ed. (New York, Harper Collins 1992) 6th ed. 1996, pp. 154–209 for further attempts to explain English politics in functionalist terms.

[64] An important influence was that of W. J. M. Mackenzie, Professor of Politics at Manchester University, where Rose was a lecturer from 1961 to 1966, who helped to disseminate the findings of American political science in Britain. 'From Bill Mackenzie I learned to puzzle about what others took for granted or ignored'. Rose, 'The Art of Writing about Politics' in Daalder, ed., *Comparative European Politics*, p. 135.

The 'England' in the title of *Politics in England* is significant, for Rose was the first British political scientist to appreciate that the techniques of comparative study could be applied to Britain itself. He was the first to grasp that Britain, far from being a nation-state was a multinational polity.[65] This insight resulted in three important books on the United Kingdom, an edited volume and numerous papers.[66] The genesis of his major book on Northern Ireland, *Governing without Consensus*, Rose has declared, stemmed from 'a theoretical concern with questions of political legitimacy. Within a universe of western nations, Northern Ireland is distinctive in being partially legitimate; this led to the decision to treat it as a deviant case'.[67]

Rose's first explicitly comparative work, however, was *People in Politics: Observations across the Atlantic*, an introduction to political sociology, based on lectures delivered at Cambridge.[68] This too was based on functionalist categories, yet as with *Politics in England*, these categories seemed too general to yield much explanatory power. The book's main concern indeed is with specificity. Why, asks Rose, is a given political outcome 'inconceivable' in one culture but perfectly 'conceivable' in another? Why, for example, in the 1960s might the nationalization of public utilities have seemed a 'conceivable' policy in Newham but not in New Haven?

In 1974, Rose edited an important collection, *Electoral Behaviour: A Comparative Handbook*, dedicated 'to Stein (Rokkan) with whom there is no comparison'.[69] Previously, Rose, in collaboration with Derek Urwin had carried out empirical investigations testing the Lipset/Rokkan 'freezing hypothesis' and operationalizing the strength of the various Lipset/Rokkan cleavages. He had come to the conclusion, contrary to the *Marxisant* tendencies of the times that not class but communal strains posed the greatest threat to the state. Class, by contrast, was a late

[65] R. Rose, 'The United Kingdom as a Multi-National State', Occasional Paper No. 6, Survey Research Centre, University of Strathclyde, Glasgow, 1970. See also Rose, 'The United Kingdom as an Intellectual Puzzle' in D. Jaensch, ed., *The Politics of New Federalism* (Adelaide, Australasian Political Studies Association, 1977), 21–34.

[66] R. Rose, *Governing without Consensus: An Irish Perspective* (London, Faber, 1971); *Northern Ireland: A Time of Choice* (London, Macmillan, and Washington, DC, American Enterprise Institute, 1976) and P. Madgwick and R. Rose, eds., *Understanding the United Kingdom: The Territorial Dimension in Government* (London, Longmans, and London, Macmillan, 1982). Rose's paper in this book is entitled, 'Is the United Kingdom a State? Northern Ireland as a Test Case'.

[67] Rose, 'Comparing Forms', p. 455.

[68] R. Rose, *People in Politics: Observations across the Atlantic* (New York, Basic Books and London, Faber, 1970).

[69] R. Rose, ed., *Electoral Behaviour: A Comparative Handbook* (New York, Free Press, 1974).

cleavage, at its strongest in Protestant societies marked by religious homogeneity. Where it was important, this was so by default, in the absence of other social divisions.[70] *Electoral Behaviour* was based very much on Rokkan's work and sought to carry forward a systematic comparison of electoral behaviour through a uniform theoretical framework across a group of countries by means of cleavage analysis. The countries compared were divided into three groups—Continental Europe—Belgium, Germany, Italy and The Netherlands—Scandinavia—Finland, Norway and Sweden, and the Anglo-American democracies—Australia, Canada, the United States, the United Kingdom and Ireland. Each chapter contained a historical account, describing the development of society, the economy and culture, together with the party system; an account of the legal and other provisions relating to elections; comprehensive data relating to elections; and an analysis of the relationship between the various cleavages identified by Lipset and Rokkan. Through tree analysis, an attempt was made to grade the influence of various explanatory variables in each country. The variables were the Lipset/Rokkan cleavages—class, religion, urban/rural and geographical location. At the end of the book, a single table was produced summing up the comparative effect of social structure on partisanship in 16 countries. *Electoral Behaviour* was, in the words of Alain Lancelot, 'a major step forward in the development of the discipline'.[71] Since that time, Rose has turned his attention to other problems, but Derek Urwin has continued Rokkan's work, not so much in the areas of party politics or electoral behaviour, but in the field of territorial identity and in a comparative study of the politics of agrarian defence.[72]

[70] R. Rose and D. W. Urwin, eds., 'Social Structure, Party Systems and Voting Behaviour', special issue of *Comparative Political Studies*, 2 (1969), 47. See also R. Rose and D. W. Urwin, 'Persistence and Change in Western Party Systems since 1945' in *Political Studies*, 18 (1970), 287–319; R. Rose and D. W. Urwin, 'Regional Differentiation and Political Unity in Western Nations', Sage Professional Papers in Contemporary Political Sociology (London and Beverly Hills, 1975); R. Rose 'Modern Nations and the Study of Political Modernization' in S. Rokkan, ed., *Comparative Research across Cultures and Nations* (Paris and The Hague, Mouton, 1968), pp. 181–228 and Rose, 'Party Systems, Social Structure and Voter Alignments in Britain: A Guide to Comparative Analysis' in O. Stammer, ed., *Parteiensysteme, Parteiorganisationen und die Neuen Politischen Bewegungen* (Berlin, Free University, 1968), pp. 318–84, for further work inspired by Rokkan.

[71] A. Lancelot, 'Comparative Electoral Behaviour', *European Journal of Political Research*, 3 (1975), 414.

[72] S. Rokkan and D. W. Urwin, eds., *The Politics of Territorial Identity: Studies in European Regionalism* (Beverly Hills, Calif., Sage 1982); S. Rokkan and D. W. Urwin, eds., *Economy, Territory, Identity: The Politics of West European Peripheries* (Beverly Hills, Calif., Sage, 1983); and D. W. Urwin, *From Ploughshare to Ballotbox: The Politics of Agrarian Defence in Europe* (Oslo, Universitetsforlaget, 1980).

In his later work, Rose has analysed what governments actually do, asking himself why it is that public policy outcomes vary in different liberal democracies. He has concerned himself with the problem of 'overload', with 'big government', fiscal stress and the welfare state, and the influence of 'inheritance', the impact of past commitments on current public policies.[73] Rose's work has throughout been based on the operationalizing of concepts and rigorous empirical testing. Although, in his empirical approach, he is at the opposite end from the ideologue, his later work nevertheless fits in with an intellectual atmosphere of neo-liberalism and scepticism towards the state.

It has been said that it would take an ordinary mortal a lifetime just to copy out J. S. Bach's music. It is not too much of an exaggeration to say, similarly, that it would take an ordinary mortal much of a lifetime to read and appraise the whole of Rose's work, so vast has been his output. By 1996, he had authored or co-authored 31 books, edited or co-edited a further 21, and written 212 journal articles and chapters in books.[74] Yet this vast output has not been at the expense of quality. There is, indeed, little of Rose's work which does not contain original thoughts. That the United Kingdom is a multinational polity is not the only insight, obvious only with hindsight, that we owe to him.

Anthony King

Anthony King, a Canadian based in Britain, has, like Rose, ranged widely. But he has primarily concerned himself with two areas of comparative government. The first is the analysis of commonly used concepts in politics such as 'party' and conceptual frameworks such as 'executive–legislative relations'. King's 'sceptical reflections' on the role of party offer a precise definition and detailed discussion of the different meanings and functions of 'party', a topic which had, until then, surprisingly, received little detailed discussion, and has been little followed up.[75] His work on executive–legislative relations has been primarily

---

[73] See, *inter alia*, R. Rose, *Big Government: The Programme Approach* (London and Beverly Hills, Sage, 1984), R. Rose and T. Karran, *Taxation by Political Inertia* (London, Allen & Unwin, 1987), R. Rose, *Lesson-Drawing in Public Policy: A Behavioural Analysis* (London and Newbury Park, Calif., Sage, 1989), and R. Rose and P. L. Davies, *Inheritance in Public Policy: Change without Choice in Britain* (New Haven, Conn., and London, Yale University Press, 1994).
[74] I am grateful to Richard Rose for sending me a bibliography of his work.
[75] A. King, 'Political Parties in Western Democracies: Some Sceptical Reflections', *Polity*, 2, (1969), 111–141.

designed to show that they are in reality modes of conflict within and between political parties.[76] The traditional language of the separation of powers tends, he believes, to conceal the real political differences between countries.

> It seldom makes sense to speak of executive–legislative relations. Rather, there are in each political system a number of distinct political relationships, each with its own 'membership', so to speak, and each with its own dynamics and structures of power. If we wish to understand the real world of politics better, it is these separate relationships that we should seek to identify and study. The traditional separation-of-powers language is not only unhelpful most of the time; it is a positive hindrance to understanding. It blurs distinctions that ought not to be blurred and distracts attention from important political phenomena.[77]

'We need', therefore, 'to think behind' the Montesquieu formula.[78] King cites three modes, the intra-party mode, the opposition mode and the non-party or private members mode. Combinations of these modes give rise to a large number of possible relationships—up to 75 combinations are identified in West Germany. King uses his schema to distinguish between different combinations of the various modes in Britain, France and West Germany. The conceptual framework devised by King in terms of inter- and intra-party relationships forms a powerful tool of analysis in place of the stale categories inherited from Montesquieu.

The second area which King has concerned himself with is the comparative analysis of the tasks of government, of what governments do, both in an analysis of 'overload' and in a comparative European/ American study of the size and shape of the public sector in five advanced democracies.[79] Much of this work has been influenced by the school of public policy analysis in the United States.[80] King has asked why it is that the scope of the public sector is less and public

---

[76] A. King, 'Modes of Executive–Legislative Relations: Great Britain, France and West Germany' in *Legislative Studies Quarterly*, 1 (1976), 11–34. Reprinted in P. Norton, ed., *Legislatures* (Oxford, Oxford University Press 1990), pp. 208–236. Citations are from the Norton volume. See also A. King, 'Executives' in F. I. Greenstein and N. W. Polsby, eds., *Handbook of Political Science*, V (Reading, Mass., Addison Wesley, 1975).

[77] King, 'Modes of Executive–Legislative Relations', pp. 235–6.

[78] Ibid. p. 208.

[79] King, 'Ideas, Institutions and the Policies of Governments: A Comparative Analysis', *British Journal of Political Science*, 3, 291–313 and 409–23; and King, 'Overload: Problems of Governing in the 1970s', *Political Studies*, 23, 285–96.

[80] See, for an early example of the work of this school, T. Dye, *Politics, Economics and the Public: Policy Outcomes in the American States* (Chicago, Rand McNally, 1966), cited by King, p. 409.

expenditure lower in the United States than in Europe. He locates the answer, not in different concentrations of social power, or the strength of interest groups, nor in constitutional factors such as federalism or the separation of powers, but in ideology. King's answer, a striking confirmation of the work of Louis Hartz, is that it is ideas about the role of government which are crucial. In the United States, ideas about the role of government legitimate neither a broad public sector nor high public expenditures.[81]

> It is our contention that the pattern of American policy is what it is, not because America is dominated by an elite (though it may be); not because the demands made on government are different from those made on governments in other countries; not because American interest groups have greater resources than those in other countries; not because American institutions are more resistant to change than those in other countries (though they probably are); but rather because Americans believe things that other people do not believe and make assumptions that other people do not make. More precisely, elites, demands, interest groups and institutions constitute neither necessary nor sufficient conditions of the American policy pattern; ideas, we contend, constitute both a necessary condition and a sufficient one.[82]

Work of this kind has proved highly fruitful and has been taken up by a number of political scientists, most notably Peter Flora in his programme on the Historical Indicators of Western Democracy (HIWED) programme, and Gösta Esping-Andersen.[83]

King, however, concludes his own analysis by suggesting that to his basic question 'Only outline answers can be given, . . . partly because in many cases the relevant history has not been written; political scientists seldom concern themselves with the past of present policies; historians often fail to ask the questions that political scientists would'.[84] It is a call for comparative history as a preliminary to comparative political science. That comparative history has yet to be written for the twentieth century although Finer's *History of Government* is a powerful analysis of previous times.

---

[81] L. Hartz, *The Liberal Tradition in American Politics* (New York, Harcourt Brace, 1955).

[82] King, 'Ideas, Institutions and the Policies of Governments', p. 423.

[83] See, for example, P. Flora, ed., *Growth to Limits. The Western European Welfare States since World War II* (Berlin, De Gruyter, 1986); G. Esping-Andersen, *The Three Worlds of Welfare Capitalism* (Oxford, Polity Press, 1990).

[84] King, 'Ideas, Institutions and the Policies of Governments', p. 302 fn.

Conclusion: The British approach

It is peculiarly difficult to determine what is lasting in political science. In the *New Handbook of Political Science*, over three-quarters of the works cited were published in the last 20 years, and over 30 per cent in the last five years. Less than one in ten were published before 1960, the year in which *The American Voter* was published. Such judgements, however, display the tyranny of the present in a most extreme form. What is published later is seen as inevitably more 'professional' and therefore better than what has come before. It is historicism with a vengeance.[85] The judgements of the present will not necessarily be endorsed by posterity. In 1964, Harold Laski was the only non-American name to appear in a ranking of the great men of American political science. He would be unlikely to secure a very high ranking today.[86]

This chapter has examined seven characters in search of a comparative politics, Ostrogorski, the Whig, Bryce, the liberal, Herman Finer, the comparativist, S. E. Finer, the Paretian realist, Philip Williams, the parliamentary democrat, Richard Rose, the social scientist and Anthony King, the sceptic. While British political scientists may not have originated grand theory—what Richard Rose has called landless theory—or even middle-ranging theories, their contribution to the development of the discipline in the twentieth century can be seen, nevertheless, to have been a powerful one.[87] Has it also been distinctive? Page has argued that it has not, for

> If one frames the question of where comparative politics would be without us, then the answer is probably that it would not be anywhere very different to where it is now. There are no single leaps in the comparative approach to politics in the post-war period which can be directly attributed to British political scientists writing comparative studies. In fact, there are probably no single leaps in the field taken as a whole.[88]

Page's assumption is that political science is a discipline like the natural sciences or perhaps economics where a discovery can advance the subject only by a few years at most. Yet, to the extent that political

---

[85] Goodin and Klingemann, *New Handbook of Political Science*, p. 16.
[86] Somit and Tannenhaus, *American Political Science*, p. 66.
[87] R. Rose, 'Institutionalising Professional Political Science in Europe: A Dynamic Model', *European Journal of Political Research*, 18 (1990), 597.
[88] E. Page, 'British Political Science and Comparative Politics', *Political Studies*, 38 (1990), 440–1, 451.

science is an interpretative discipline, one cannot be at all sure that, for example, Finer's explanatory typologies, or King's analysis of executive–legislative relations, would have been rapidly discovered had their authors never existed. And would any political scientist other than Finer have had the courage to write a *History of Government from the Earliest Times*?

British political science derives, fundamentally, from two basic influences. The first is that of Dicey who sought to display the conceptual logic of the British Constitution, to discover what it was that distinguished the British Constitution from codified constitutions. The second is that of Bagehot who, with Ostrogorski, sought to understand political 'forms' through the analysis of political 'forces'. By explaining politics in terms of 'national character', Bagehot made it easy for the modern social scientist to dismiss him as antediluvian. It is, however, only his terminology that is old-fashioned, not his analysis. For he was groping towards something very much like the modern notion of 'political culture', basic elements of which were those norms and values which affected behaviour. These fundamental influences have proved powerful enough to affect even those such as, perhaps, Richard Rose and Anthony King, who, émigrés from across the Atlantic, have sought to 'professionalize' the discipline and make it more like its counterpart in the United States. Social scientists, no less than others, find it difficult to escape from an inherited national style which is powerful enough to socialize those who seek to imbue it with elements of other traditions. The tenacity of the past is a familiar theme of much modern political science. British political scientists have not needed Freud or Proust to remind them that the past still exists as part of the present. It is, indeed, the extent of the overlap between political science and history which is so remarkable, and perhaps peculiar to Britain.

British political science has been carelessly and inaccurately stereotyped. Two main charges have been made against it. First, it has been accused of legal formalism. British political scientists failed, so it has been suggested, to investigate the real working of political institutions due to an obsession with legal analysis. The second charge is that British political science has concentrated on the study of institutions to the exclusion of the investigation of political behaviour. Neither charge can be sustained.

In Britain, by contrast with many European countries, the study of politics was not part of the work of Faculties of Law, whose main concern, until recently at least, has been with the vocational training of lawyers, with private rather than public law. Partly for this reason, the work of British political scientists has been marked by a positive *disinclination* to expressing matters of political organization in legal terms. It is hard, therefore, to understand how Eckstein could claim that there was in Britain 'some tendency toward turning the study of politics into the study of public law'.[89] For the vitality of the tradition of British political science may be constrasted with, for example, the dominant tradition in French political science which was indeed highly legalistic. It was as a result of their lack of interest in public law indeed that British political scientists found themselves at a disadvantage when they were called upon, in the 1970s, to analyse constitutional problems, both in Britain and in other democracies.[90]

The work of the founding fathers of British political science— Bagehot, Ostrogorski and Bryce—could almost be defined by a concern to get behind legalistic 'forms' so as to investigate real 'forces', the socio-political realities. No doubt there have been some second-rate authors of textbooks who remained content with a merely legal description of political systems, but a national contribution to the development of a discipline is not to be defined by its second-raters.

The founding fathers of British political science were deeply sensitive to the conceptual bases of particular political systems. It is for this reason that the best of the older work is still of permanent value. It would be absurd to suggest that the work of Wheare on federal government, of Williams on France, of Finer on comparative government and the involvement of the military in politics, or of Rose on the multinational character of Britain is irrelevant because published before 1980.

Nor is it correct to say that British political scientists have been guilty of a concern with institutionalism at the cost of the study of political behaviour. Ostrogorski's explicit concern was to get behind institutional 'forms' to study cultural 'forces'. That is true even of Bryce, a more conservative scholar. His book, *Modern Democracies*, contains chapters on 'The Press in a Democracy', on 'Party', on 'Traditions', 'The People', and 'Public Opinion' and he subjected all of these notions to comparative analysis.

British political scientists, moreover, have been eclectic. They have rarely concentrated on just one form of analysis because it seems

---

[89] H. Eckstein, 'A Perspective on Comparative Politics', in H. Eckstein and D. Apter, eds., *Comparative Politics; A Reader* (New York, The Free Press, 1963), p. 32.
[90] N. Johnson, *In Search of the Constitution* (Oxford, Pergamon Press, 1976).

fashionable. This had its advantages when the promise of grand theory was found to be unrealizable. The British approach, that intellectual advances in political science are more likely to be made along a narrow front has been less ambitious than that of many American practitioners of the subject, but perhaps no less fruitful.

The trouble with being fashionable, as Oscar Wilde once pointed out, is that one becomes so quickly out of date. The *New Handbook* discovers a return in recent years to the analysis of institutions, of 'the legacy of history' and of ideas. British political science has never lost its concern with such factors.[91] As Hayward has put it, in Europe, there was never a need to 'bring the state back in'. For the state had never been taken out.

> We felt that we did not need to 'bring the state back in' because our theoretical paradigms had always accepted that the organizational structures of the state could autonomously act upon society and were not simply a 'black box' for processing societal inputs and outputs. This was because, in our empirical work on European politics, we were constantly brought face to face with governments that were active, not passive, even if they were acting within societal constraints. Given the international dominance of American political science, it was a welcome sign for European political scientists that methodological pressures and premises that threatened to distort research by the imposition of inappropriate paradigms would ease and the transatlantic divergence of presuppositions would decrease. By adapting rather than abandoning traditional approaches, European political science had provided a continuity of scholarship that would once again be recognized as within the mainstream of comparative politics.[92]

Fashionable opinion is thus rather like the hunted hare. If one remains in the same place for long enough, it will catch up in the end.

Two other accusations commonly made against British political science—that it is insular and that it is a mere derivative of American political science—cancel each other out. It can in fact be argued that the best of British political science has been acutely sensitive to the needs of other societies. In 1945, K. C. Wheare provided the classical analysis of federalism, which remains, over 50 years later, the starting-point for any consideration of the subject. Brian Chapman began the comparative

---

[91] Goodin and Klingemann, *New Handbook of Political Science*, pp. 17, 19.

[92] J. Hayward, 'Between France and universality: from implicit to explicit comparison', p. 147, in H. Daalder, ed., *Comparative European Politics*. This book contains a valuable autobiographical account of their work in comparative European politics by Jean Blondel, Richard Rose, Jack Hayward, Gordon Smith and Vincent Wright, as well as a chapter on S. E. Finer by Dennis Kavanagh.

analysis of the civil service by analysing the very different traditions of public service prevailing on the Continent. W. J. M. Mackenzie was the first to understand that the needs of ethnically divided societies could only be met by a conscious departure from the Westminster Model.[93] American political science, by contrast, has often taken an undifferentiated or globalist view of the world, while the tendency of French political science as of French politics has been towards the assimilationist.

The best of British political science has concerned itself with asking the question—what is special and distinctive about the particular countries or set of countries being studied. Only after that question had been answered, could the work of synthesis begin. Thus, British political science at its best has combined deep historical knowledge with breadth of perspective.

That combination is increasingly difficult to achieve in an intellectual environment which encourages analysis but not synthesis. Today, as Rose has noticed,

> A young professional submitting a journal article will be expected to write about an established topic, review a mass of familiar literature and carry out research in professionally recognized ways. The insistence on professional standards can raise the average level of performance but it also constricts the field of vision, discouraging tackling big themes or novel or deviant topics.[94]

In Britain, the main threat to political science lies not in its being insufficiently 'professional', but in the bureaucratization of universities and of research, a process that is bound to prove detrimental to creative work. There has, in addition, been a certain loss of intellectual self-confidence in Britain, parallel perhaps to that loss of national self-confidence which remains the most striking feature of British post-war politics. This loss of self-confidence persuades many to abandon what is both distinctive and valuable in the British approach to political science. That, however, would be a pity. For there is an indigenous British approach to the study of politics, a definite intellectual tradition, and one that is worth preserving.

---

[93] K. C. Wheare, *Federal Government* (London, Oxford University Press, 1945), B. Chapman, *The Profession of Government* (London, Allen & Unwin, 1959), W. J. M. Mackenzie, *Free Elections* (London, Allen & Unwin, 1958), Mackenzie, 'Representation in Plural Societies', *Political Studies*, 2 (1954), 111–31 and Mackenzie, 'The Export of Electoral Systems', *Political Studies*, 5 (1957), 132–53.

[94] Rose, 'Institutionalizing Professional Political Science in Europe', p. 598.

'If social scientists think about form', Richard Rose has argued, 'it is usually in terms of mathematics and closed deductive theories. To me, form is aesthetic, a creative discovery of what is behind or beneath what we see and count'.[95] The best of British political science has always sought to live up to this precept.

[95] R. Rose, 'The Art of Writing about Politics', p. 129 in Daalder, ed., *Comparative European Politics*.

7: Pressure Groups and Parties
A 'Haze of Common Knowledge' or the Empirical Advance of the Discipline?

JEREMY RICHARDSON

Introduction: the study of intermediary organizations

The study of pressure groups, parties and social movements by British political scientists this century has been firmly anchored in the strong empirical traditions of the discipline as a whole. Perhaps as an inevitable consequence of this tradition, relatively few works by British authors can be said to have broken new ground theoretically or methodologically leading to their adoption, or adaptation, internationally. This is not to suggest that very good work has not been done or that British political scientists (especially in the fields of interest groups and political parties) have not achieved international recognition for their work. In a sense, the scholars have travelled much better than their works in that they have been active participants in the international political science community, yet their analyses have tended not to structure the way future research is conducted by overseas scholars. Few British studies seem to have changed the intellectual map of these sub-disciplines beyond these shores. This may be because studies in all three categories have tended to be somewhat parochial (focusing on Britain) and 'risk-averse' in the sense that a cautious attitude to innovation has emerged as the dominant research style. Hence, the self-reproduction of studies is rather common. There has also been a tendency (with notable exceptions such as Richard Rose—see later) to focus on the tactics of influence (for groups), and organization and office holding (for parties), rather than on analysing the effects that these institutions have on policy outcomes or on theorizing about the relationship of these institutions to the concept of power and its distribution.[1]

Despite this, there has been (and still is) a lively and very productive community of scholars and a very large *corpus* of empirical works has been amassed. Moreover, if one places this work in the context of the general theme of the study of intermediary or 'linkage' organizations between the state and society, there has been a steadiness of purpose, a degree of continuity and a considerable advance of empirical knowledge about the ways in which these intermediary organizations are organized and operate. Unfortunately, British scholars have tended not to bring the study of intermediary organizations together, for example in the way that Sam Beer did in 1965 in his study of British parties and pressure groups.[2]

Part One: Pressure groups

> Readers of Professor Hancock's autobiography will remember that he refers to Disraeli's gambit—'How is the old complaint?'—and says that if he ever meets a young political scientist whose name he has forgotten he opens conversation by asking 'How is the conceptual framework?'[3] The subject of 'pressure groups' raises so many issues of social and political theory that one is tempted to treat it primarily as an excuse for the discussion of concepts. I think, however, that it would be unwise to push logical analysis very far until some attempt has been made to state the facts of the situation, and this is the primary object of this paper.[4]

The early works

British political scientists were extremely slow to recognize the study of pressure groups as a legitimate field of study. However, since the mid-1950s British scholars have been productive, especially in the field of empirical studies, and have gained some recognition in Western Europe. The relative lack of theoretical focus has meant that few, if any, British pressure group scholars could claim that they have influenced work outside Europe, particularly in the United States. For example, the

---

[1] I am grateful to Brian Barry for suggesting this point in his comments on an earlier draft.
[2] S. Beer, *Modern British Politics. A Study of Parties and Pressure Groups* (London, Faber & Faber, 1965).
[3] K. Hancock, *Country and Calling* (London, Faber & Faber, 1955), p. 223.
[4] W. J. M. Mackenzie, 'Pressure Groups in British Government', *British Journal of Sociology*, 6 (1955), 133–148.

important edited volume on *Policy Change and Learning: An Advocacy Coalition Approach* (published in the series 'Theoretical Lenses on Public Policy' in 1993) lists only three works on pressure group systems by British authors.[5]

As in so many fields of British political science, W. J. M. (Bill) Mackenzie proved to be one of the most perceptive and earliest to identify new fields of study which others then followed. He also captured the essential spirit of British pressure group studies—a belief that research should be firmly grounded in empirical analysis, prior to the development of concepts and theories. His reasons for suggesting pressure groups as a new field of study (he was addressing a meeting of the British Sociological Association) were academic interest in other countries and the then state of British parties. On the latter, he noted that 'since 1949 we have entered a phase in which party programmes seem relatively unimportant'.[6] In a telling passage, some four years before the publication of Charles Lindblom's classic article, 'The Science of Muddling Through',[7] he referred to British post-war politics as 'a continuous process of adjustment and not as a contest between alternative principles'.[8] He noted that academic studies also reflect changes in the 'real' world of politics. Thus, Sidney and Beatrice Webb, in their *Constitution of a Socialist Commonwealth of Great Britain* (1920) had identified forces *outside* parties (such as trade unions and professional associations) as important.[9] Prior to 1914, Mackenzie argued, 'the more sophisticated and rebellious were agreed in regarding British parties, like American parties, as empty bottles bearing different labels, into which any political mixture might be poured'.[10] After 1920, with the emergence of the Labour Party as a political force, scholarly analysis focused more on what Finer much later described as 'adversary politics'.[11]

Mackenzie set the tone of British pressure group studies for the next two decades by emphasizing politics as a continuing social process. He did so by drawing attention to the classic American studies of pressure

---

[5] P. A. Sabatier and H. C. Jenkins-Smith, eds., *Policy Change and Policy Learning. An Advocacy Coalition Approach* (Boulder, Col., Westview Press, 1993).

[6] Mackenzie, 'Pressure Groups in British Government', p. 133.

[7] C. Lindblom, 'The Science of Muddling Through'. *Public Administration Review*, 19 (1959), 79–88.

[8] Mackenzie, 'Pressure Groups in British Government', p. 133.

[9] S. and B. Webb, *Constitution of a Socialist Commonwealth of Great Britain* (Cambridge, Cambridge University Press, 1920).

[10] Mackenzie, 'Pressure Groups in British Government', p. 134.

[11] S. E. Finer, *Adversary Politics and Electoral Reform* (London, Anthony Wigram, 1975).

groups—namely A. F. Bentley's 1908 book, *The Process of Government*[12] and the 1951 restatement of that approach by D. B. Truman, in *The Governmental Process*.[13] In Britain, as elsewhere in Europe, the study of pressure groups was, according to Mackenzie, in contrast to the United States *'wrapped in a haze of common knowledge'* (emphasis added).[14] In an attempt to lift some of this haze, he suggested a clear *definition* of the field of study. His definition of 'the field of organised groups possessing both formal structure and real common interests, in so far as they influence the decision of public bodies', has stood the test of time.[15] It is sobering to re-read his analysis. What many of us later thought we discovered had in fact been identified by Bill Mackenzie in 1955! Thus he noted (as an ex-wartime civil servant himself) that:

> it is almost commonplace that any public body has its penumbra of organized groups which form part of its particular public. Perhaps this is most familiar in the middle levels of administration . . . each Permanent Secretary in Whitehall has to know a good deal about the troops of big and little associations which move within and around his Ministry: in a sub-department the attendant retinue may be quite small and it is the civil servant's job to know it intimately.

So struck was he by the empirical evidence from such sources as the official *Committee on Intermediaries*, which had reported in 1950,[16] that he used the term *'clienteles* of decision-makers at various levels', nearly a decade in advance of its more famous use by Joseph Lapalombara in 1964.[17] Mackenzie's thrust, nearly a quarter of a century before the publication of *Governing Under Pressure*[18] in 1979 was to de-emphasize the importance of the Cabinet, Parliament and political parties as the focus of pressure group involvement on the policy process. Anticipating a flood of sectoral case studies over the next 30 years, he noted that one way of organizing research would be to focus on particular sections of 'the administration' and the associated group activity.[19] On internal

---

[12] A. F. Bentley, *The Process of Government* (first published 1908, but see edition edited by Peter Odergard, The Belknap Press of Harvard University, 1967).

[13] D. B. Truman, *The Governmental Process: Political Interests and Public Opinion* (New York, Knopf, 1951).

[14] Mackenzie, 'Pressure Groups in British Government', p. 134.

[15] Ibid. p. 137.

[16] *Report of the Committee on Intermediaries* (Cmd 7904, March 1950, HMSO).

[17] J. La Palombara, *Interest Groups in Italian Politics* (Princeton, NJ, Princeton University Press, 1964).

[18] J. J. Richardson and A. G. Jordan, *Governing Under Pressure. The Policy Process in a Post-Parliamentary Democracy* (Oxford, Martin Robertson, 1979).

[19] Mackenzie, 'Pressure Groups in British Government', p. 138.

structure he, again, seemed ahead of his time when he suggested that pressure groups were often run by 'a new type of entrepreneur or broker, the man who makes a living by finding and focusing common interests and grievances and pressing them in the right way'.[20] Only much later have we come to use the term 'movement entrepreneur'[21] and to see some groups as marketing organizations,[22] although this is clearly what Mackenzie had in mind.

Finally, Mackenzie produced a very sensible and useful classification of method (or types) of pressure—from persuading MPs to act as spokesmen for groups in the Commons, to pressure on political parties, appeal to public opinion and, (again, anticipating later works), emphasizing the importance of good information and the appeal to reason (as the Webbs, too, had noted). As he put it 'there is a vast area of decision in which politicians are concerned mainly to acquire a reputation for being right, and they too are very thankful to anyone who can keep them out of trouble'.[23] Similarly, what he termed 'administrative necessity', (a phenomenon later given great emphasis by Sammy Finer in his pathbreaking *Anonymous Empire*[24]), was seen as a driving force bringing groups and government together (giving, for example, 'a rather syndicalist look' to one sector of the health service). Mackenzie observed that 'it is often tactically important for the government to unify the experts and interests concerned in a problem, so as to be able to make a bargain which will stick (perhaps) so as to be able to shift the burden of responsibility to their shoulders if the scheme breaks down'.[25] Such observations, new at the time, are now commonplace with much current emphasis on the role of so-called epistemic communities in advising decision-makers in conditions of uncertainty,[26] and the diffusion of power in the 'new' system of governance.[27]

---

[20] Ibid. p. 140.

[21] R. Schmitt, 'Organisational Interlocks Between New Social Movements and Traditional Elites: The Case of the West German Peace Movement', *European Journal of Political Research*, 17 (1989), 583–98.

[22] For a discussion of groups as marketing organizations see J. Richardson, 'The Market for Political Activism: Interest Groups as the Challenge to Political Parties', *West European Politics*, 18 (1995), 116–39; G. Jordan and W. Maloney, *The Protest Business? Mobilizing Campaign Groups* (Manchester, Manchester University Press, 1997), G. Jordan and W. Maloney, 'How Bumblebees Fly: Accounting for Public Interest Participation', *Political Studies*, 44, 668–685.

[23] Mackenzie, 'Pressure Groups in British Government', p. 144.

[24] S. E. Finer, *Anonymous Empire* (London, Pall Mall Press, 1958).

[25] Mackenzie, 'Pressure Groups in British Government', p. 145.

[26] P. Haas, 'Introduction: Epistemic Communities and International Policy Co-ordination', *International Organization*, 46 (1992), 1–35.

[27] For a discussion of the governance concept see R. A. W. Rhodes, 'The New Governance: Governing Without Government', *Political Studies*, 44 (1996), 652–67; R. A. W. Rhodes, *Understanding Governance* (Buckingham, Open University Press, 1996).

Mackenzie's awareness of American developments became more apparent from 1956 when Samuel Beer wrote a series of articles on pressure groups and parties in Britain.[28] Beer's empirical findings were similar to those of Mackenzie, but he placed them in a somewhat broader cultural context. He laid great emphasis on the consensus in British politics as a cultural backdrop for pressure group activity. Thus, to Beer 'the present convergence of party policy expresses this consensus on new values and ideology. Not only does this consensus affect the intrinsic nature of the interests asserted and provide an integrating framework within which the electoral competition and the struggle of pressure groups is carried on; it also has a somewhat similar function with regard to the balance of social forces'.[29] Beer's 1956 article was important, not so much for the broader conclusions about the changes in the party system and the emerging consensus, but, perhaps, because he legitimized a new area of study. His oft-quoted passage, 'if we had some way of measuring political power, we could quite possibly demonstrate that at the present time pressure groups are more powerful in Britain than in the United States' was an important signpost for British scholars.[30] Thus, when *Political Quarterly* brought together those few British scholars then working on pressure groups (in an important special issue of the Journal in 1958) it was no surprise that R. T. (Bob) McKenzie opened with a quotation from Beer's 1956 article. As McKenzie (a Canadian by birth) noted, it was strange that pressure groups had been ignored by British scholars when Sir Ivor Jennings, in his classic study of Parliament published in 1938, had first pointed the way in his comment that much legislation was derived from organized interests.[31]

Clearly, by the mid 1950s, pressure group studies in Britain were about to burgeon and Bob McKenzie's analysis proved as influential as Bill Mackenzie's. Bob McKenzie mounted a defence of pressure groups as a counter to the growing concern by contemporary political commentators about the relationship between groups and democracy. McKenzie's views on groups cannot be dissociated from his authoritative analysis of political parties (discussed later). He totally rejected the view of parties as having the exclusive function of canalizing and transmitting the will of the citizenry to their elected representatives, who then

[28] S. H. Beer, 'Pressure Groups and Parties in Great Britain', *American Political Science Review*, 50 (1956), 1–23.

[29] Ibid. p. 20.

[30] Ibid. p. 3.

[31] Sir Ivor Jennings, *Parliament* (Cambridge, Cambridge University Press, 1939), p. 503.

proceed to transmute it into positive law.[32] In a passage which became the classic statement of the role of groups in the British political system he argued:

> I have suggested that any explanation of the democratic process which ignores the role of organised interests is grossly misleading, I would add that it is hopelessly inadequate and sterile in that it leaves out of the account the principal channels through which the mass of the citizenry brings influence to bear on the decision-makers whom they have elected. In practice, in every democratic society, the voters undertake to do far more than select their elected representatives; they also insist upon their right to advise, cajole, and warn them regarding the policies they should adopt. This they do, for the most part, through the pressure group system.[33]

To McKenzie, therefore, there was no doubt that 'pressure groups, taken together, are a far more important channel of communication than parties for the transmission of political ideas from the mass of citizenry to their rulers'.[34] Thus, Bill Mackenzie and Bob McKenzie in Britain, and Sam Beer in the United States, effectively placed pressure-group studies if not at the centre stage of British political science, at least on it—a place they have occupied since.

McKenzie's important article was followed in the special issue of *Political Quarterly* by four academic studies of types of groups and one 'practitioner' view from George Strauss, writing as an MP and former minister. At least three of these studies also became classics in Britain. They were Peter Self and Herbert Storing's study of 'The State and the Farmer',[35] Sammy Finer's study of 'Transport Interests and the Roads' Lobby'[36] and Allen Potter's study of what he termed 'Attitude Groups'.[37] Self and Storing's study (subsequently expanded in their 1962 book)[38] has certainly stood the test of time in terms of its relevance to the study of agricultural policy-making. Thus, today their concern about the symbiotic nature of the relationship between the National Farmers Union and the Ministry of Agriculture (now the Ministry of Agriculture, Fisheries and Food) could have been written amidst the

---

[32] R. McKenzie, 'Parties, Pressure Groups and the British Political Process', *Political Quarterly*, 29 (1958), 9.
[33] Ibid. p. 9.
[34] Ibid. pp. 9–10.
[35] Ibid. pp. 17–27.
[36] Ibid. pp. 47–58.
[37] Ibid. pp. 72–82.
[38] P. Self and H. Storing, *The State and the Farmer* (London, George Allen & Unwin, 1962).

1996–7 crisis over BSE in cattle. Thus they observed that '"Partnership" in agriculture, whatever its specific advantages, has on the whole been much too close to be really healthy for either partner', and that 'Government by anxious compromise is not an inspiring process'.[39] These broader conclusions about the effects of groups on the ability of government to introduce policy change were reflected in many subsequent British case studies. However, there has been a developing focus in more recent work on groups and policy change, with a new recognition that groups might now be less important than some of the early writers assumed.

Finer's contribution to the special issue of *Political Quarterly* is especially interesting in this regard, as he was very conscious that a lobby could be well-financed and busy, but could run up against forces which made success difficult. Thus, he did recognize the need to address the difficult question of outcomes, although did not take the enquiry very far conceptually. However, having outlined the structure of the pro-roads lobby, he noted that, at least up to 1954, it had 'no success whatsoever',[40] largely because the Government simply lacked the necessary financial resources to meet the lobby's demands. As Finer describes it, the situation changed in the lobby's favour after 1954, but the policy change could only partly be attributed to the work of the roads lobby. Finer's conclusion is fascinating if we set it alongside current more conceptual policy analysis literature. He pointed out that there had been a phenomenal increase in the number of cars on Britain's roads with a continued rapid increase expected. As Finer put it, 'In these circumstances, what else can the government do but plan new roads?'[41] How would we write this up today? John Kingdon's more conceptual approach refers to the 'inexorable march of problems' as a key factor in the agenda-setting process.[42] Do we really say the same thing more effectively now than did Finer and his generation?

Finally, in terms of the 'landmark' special issue of *Political Quarterly*, Potter's study of what he termed 'attitude groups' was important because it was the precursor of a small but important group of subsequent empirical studies of those groups thought to be weaker in terms of their political influence—namely those groups 'which either advocate

---

[39] P. Self and H. Storing, 'The Farmers and the State, *Political Quarterly*, 29 (1958), 27.

[40] S. E. Finer, 'Transport Interests and the Roads' Lobby', p. 56.

[41] Ibid. p. 58.

[42] J. Kingdon, *Agendas, Alternatives and Public Policies* (New York, HarperCollins, [2nd ed.] 1995).

policies more or less beneficial to particular sections of the community or in other ways organise people with common attitudes'.[43]

The pathbreaking 1958 special issue of *Political Quarterly* preceded the publication of the first British book-length studies of pressure groups. Sammy Finer's classic *Anonymous Empire*[44] and John Stewart's study of the role of *Pressure Groups in Relation to the House of Commons*[45] were published in the same year. Finer's study soon became the standard work and went into two reprints and a second and enlarged edition in 1966. In fact, *Anonymous Empire* grew out of a still unpublished study which Finer had conducted of railway nationalization. Quite why this study was never published is a slight puzzle, as the manuscript was virtually complete.[46] It appears that Finer became so excited by the discovery of so much interest group activity (the conventional wisdom when he started the study had been that Britain did not have a dense pressure-group system) that he became convinced that a general introductory text was needed. He was right, of course, and had the skill to write a consciously 'accessible' study. Thus, *Anonymous Empire* was addressed to the 'general public' (enabling him, as he put it, largely to dispense with 'the usual "critical apparatus" of citations and footnote references'. Those were the days!)

Why was *Anonymous Empire* so important at the time and why did it stand the test of time for so long? Basically, Finer had an excellent eye for new fields of study (he later wrote a pioneering work on the military in politics, for example) and amassed a body of empirical material which enabled him to make well-founded observations on how the pressure group system was organized and how groups participated in the policy-making process. He described the world as it was, almost without overt use of what we would now see as essential theories and concepts. He was also able to present this material in a very catchy way—such as his characterization of many pressure group public campaigns as 'fire brigade' campaigns, used when a group had failed to exercise influence in

---

[43] A. Potter, 'Attitude Groups', *Political Quarterly*, 29 (1958), 72. Since Potter's pioneering work there have been some excellent case studies of what he called attitude groups. The two best examples are P. Lowe and J. Goyder, *Environmental Groups in Politics* (London, Allen & Unwin, 1983) and P. Whiteley and S. Wynyard, *Pressure for the Poor* (London, Methuen, 1987).

[44] S. E. Finer, *Anonymous Empire, A Study of the Lobby in Great Britain* (London, Pall Mall Press, 1958), p. 173.

[45] J. D. Stewart, *British Pressure Groups, Their Role in Relation to the House of Commons* (Oxford, Clarendon Press, 1958).

[46] This author has the only copy, donated by Sammy Finer, his doctoral supervisor.

the crucial early stages of policy making and faced a parliamentary defeat. Perhaps his most perceptive and long-lasting observation— again grounded in empirical observation—was that the whole system of British administration assumed the co-operation of what he chose to term 'the lobby'. As he put it, 'the outcome has been an ever-closer interdependency of the interest groups and Whitehall. Each *needs* the other'. For example, he saw the National Health Service as 'another striking example of administrative dependency on a private body. Without the active co-operation of the profession . . . it is difficult to see how the service could be provided at all . . . The National Health Service is astonishingly "syndicalist" in structure'.[47] Again, we see in this early work a recognition of the phenomenon later described in slightly different terms, such as Tony King's 1975 analysis of governmental 'overload' in which he argued that one of the causes of overload was the increase in 'dependency relationships' between government and groups;[48] the concept of 'policy community' formulated by Richardson and Jordan in 1979;[49] 'resource dependency' analyses formulated by Rhodes in 1988;[50] the neo-corporatist literature of the 1980s, such as Alan Cawson's edited volume of studies of meso-corporatism in 1985[51] and the current influential analysis of governance by Rhodes.[52]

John Stewart's very scholarly study had less impact than Finer's much shorter study because it was primarily concerned with only one aspect of lobbying—that of the House of Commons—when the general consensus was (and still is) that Parliament was probably the least important of the opportunity structures used by British pressure groups. Also, like Finer, Stewart's study was firmly anchored in the empirical tradition and did not set out to advance or generate theory. Alan Potter's *Organized Groups in British National Politics*, published in 1961,[53] became, alongside Finer, one of the standard works on pressure groups. His study, too, was essentially empirical and descriptive but was a very professional contribution to the new field of study.

[47] S. E. Finer, *Anonymous Empire* pp. 30–1.
[48] A. King, 'Overload: Problems of Governing in the UK in the 1970s', *Political Studies*, 23 (1975), 284–96.
[49] Richardson and Jordan, *Governing Under Pressure*, p. 74.
[50] R. A. W. Rhodes, *Beyond Westminster and Whitehall, The Sub-Central Governments of Britain* (London, Unwin Hyman, 1988), p. 42.
[51] A. Cawson, ed., *Organized Interests and the State, Studies in Meso-Corporatism* (London, Sage Publications, 1985).
[52] Rhodes, *Understanding Governance*.
[53] A. Potter, *Organized Groups in British National Politics* (London, Faber, 1961).

These studies laid the foundation for what has become a very productive sub-discipline in British political science, all the more so because in the following three decades scholars have tried to link the specific study of pressure groups to broader observations about the policy process. For example, by the late 1970s there was an established 'industry' of pressure group studies, such as Richard Kimber and Jeremy Richardson's edited volume of case studies in 1974,[54] Maurice Kogan's study of the role of interest groups in educational policy making,[55] Ken Newton's pioneering study of local pressure-group activity in Birmingham,[56] Frank Castles' study of pressure groups and political culture,[57] Tony Barker's study of the local amenity movement,[58] David Coates' study of teachers' unions as pressure groups,[59] Timothy May's study of trade unions as pressure groups,[60] Philip Lowe and Jane Goyder's study of environmental groups,[61] and a classic study of the Confederation of British Industry by Wyn Grant and David Marsh (considered by some to be one of the best British studies of groups to date).[62]

Thus, in 1978, Wyn Grant was able to draw upon some of these and other studies (particularly of environmental groups) to develop a new typology of pressure groups[63]—something of a preoccupation of British political scientists to this day. Grant rejected many of the earlier attempts at classification and suggested a seemingly straightforward distinction between 'insider' and 'outsider' groups. Though later qualified by subsequent writers,[64] the distinction has become a generic term. Whatever its limitations, the utility of Grant's classification was that it focused on

[54] R. Kimber and J. J. Richardson, eds., *Pressure Groups in Britain* (London, Dent, 1974).

[55] M. Kogan, *Educational Policy-Making: A Study of Interest Groups and Parliament* (London, Allen and Unwin, 1975).

[56] K. Newton, *Second City Politics* (Oxford, Oxford University Press, 1976).

[57] F. G. Castles, *Pressure Groups and Political Culture* (London, Routledge & Kegan Paul, 1967).

[58] A. Barker, *The Local Amenity Movement* (London, Civic Trust, 1976).

[59] D. Coates, *Teachers' Unions and Interest Group Politics* (Cambridge, Cambridge University Press, 1972).

[60] T. C. May, *Trade Unions and Pressure Group Politics* (Farnborough, Saxon House, 1975).

[61] P. Lowe and J. Goyder, *Environmental Groups in Politics* (London, Allen & Unwin, 1983).

[62] W. Grant and D. Marsh, *The CBI* (London, Hodder & Stoughton, 1977).

[63] W. Grant, 'Insider Groups, Outsider Groups and Interest Strategies in Britain', University of Warwick, Department of Politics Working Papers, 19 (May 1978).

[64] For a discussion of the insider/outsider group distinction see W. Maloney, G. Jordan and A. McLaughlin, 'Interest Groups and Public Policy: The Insider/Outsider Model Revisited', *Journal of Public Policy*, 14 (1994), 17–38.

the power of the state to determine the status and role of groups, under certain circumstances, and also the choice groups have in their form of relationship with the state. In a sense, studies in the late 1970s and early 1980s lost sight of this issue and became rather preoccupied with that category of pressure group/state relations which Grant had termed 'insider' status. It is to studies which both emphasized the intensity of group/state involvement and characterized the nature of the British polity in these terms, that we now turn.

Policy communities and policy networks as the dominant paradigm

Although pressure-group studies had become a very well-established branch of British political science by the mid 1970s, it could not be claimed that these studies had changed the way that the majority of British political scientists analysed the British polity.[65] The main focus was still on the parliament, the cabinet, elections and political parties as the traditional institutions of democracy through which the polity was governed. This began to change in the late 1970s, however, an indicator being the publication of *Governing Under Pressure* in 1979. The sub-title of this book was a conscious attempt by the authors to signal that there had been fundamental changes in the nature of the British political system in the post-war period of consensus politics.[66] As Bill Mackenzie had noted much earlier, academic studies do tend to track changes in the real world, particularly shifts in the distribution of power in society. In sub-titling their book 'The Policy Process in a Post-Parliamentary Democracy', Richardson and Jordan tried to re-focus attention away from the traditional institutions of study to a different world of power—essentially the 'private management of public business', as they put it. The core argument of *Governing Under Pressure* was a simple enough idea which arose out of a body of empirical work conducted by the authors with Richard Kimber in the 1970s. Following in the British empirical tradition, they had observed the close relationship between groups and government and that policy change seemed to be a depen-dent variable of this relationship. Thus, out of empirical observation came the linked notions of '*sectorization*' of policy, and policy making via '*policy communities*'. As Judge noted in 1993, and Dowding in 1995,

---

[65] R. Rose, ed., *Studies in British Politics A Reader in Political Sociology* (London, Macmillan, 1976) listed 36 articles on pressure groups by British authors.
[66] Richardson and Jordan, *Governing Under Pressure*.

the notion of 'community' was descriptive rather than definitional[67] and was a metaphor rather than a model.[68] It had no grand pretensions to being a new *theory* of British politics. Its purpose, as Judge correctly observed, was to contrast established models of parliamentary government with a new reality of 'a myriad of interconnecting, interpenetrating organisations (and of) *policy communities* of departments and groups, the practices of co-option and the consensual style'.[69]

The concept of policy communities soon became (and, in the form of network studies has remained) fashionable in British political science. Why? As Wyn Grant later commented, 'as an analytical proposition, the idea of policy communities clearly provides a good fit with the available empirical evidence on how decisions are made in British government'.[70] Thus, 'policy communities' as an approach helped shift the focus of British policy studies because it reflected the strong empirical traditions of the discipline—theorizing should be well grounded in empirical observation—and because it appeared to capture the realities of post-war British politics. It was also a genuinely independent British approach. As its co-author, Grant Jordan, later observed 'there was no straight-line application of US ideas [about sub-government and iron triangles] to a British context. Instead, there was a description of British policy making structures—with a later recognition of US precedents'.[71] (Indeed, it was only many years later that Grant Jordan and his Aberdeen colleagues discovered that the term 'policy community' had also been coined by Jack Walker in 1974 in the United States, some years before *Governing Under Pressure* was written).[72]

This is not to say that these new developments in British political science were entirely autonomous. For example, Richardson and Jordan were influenced by Heclo and Wildavsky's study of the public expenditure process in Britain, which had referred to Whitehall politics as

[67] D. Judge, *The Parliamentary State* (London, Sage, 1993), p. 121.

[68] K. Dowding 'Model or Metaphor? A Critical Review of the Network Approach', *Political Studies*, 43 (1995), 136–58.

[69] Judge, *The Parliamentary State*, p. 121, quoting Richardson and Jordan, p. 74.

[70] W. Grant, *Pressure Groups, Politics and Democracy in Britain* (London, Philip Allen, 1989), p. 31.

[71] A. G. Jordan, 'Sub-Governments, Policy Communities and Networks: Refilling the Old Bottles?' *Journal of Theoretical Politics*, 2 (1990), 325.

[72] A. G. Jordan, W. Maloney and A. McLaughlin, 'Assumptions About the Role of Groups in the Policy Process. The British Policy Community Approach', Aberdeen, British Interest Groups Project, 1993.

'village life',[73] by work conducted by Johan P. Olsen in the Norwegian 'Power Project' based in Bergen,[74] by Stein Rokkan (also of Bergen) and by the analysis of the European polity by Robert Kvavik (also Norwegian) and Martin Heisler.[75] Thus, in so far as external influences were important in bringing about this intellectual shift, they were more Scandinavian than American in origin. Later work[76] drew more upon American scholars—particularly Hugh Heclo's seminal study of Washington politics in which he launched the idea of issue networks[77]—and took more account of the fact that empirical observations in so many other countries had produced similar conclusions about the nature of the modern polity.

The strength of the British empirical tradition carried the simple unrefined concept of policy community forward. As Judge comments, 'the concern for descriptive accuracy has led a whole generation of British scholars to follow'.[78] This concern is still very much alive in the 1990s and now utilizes a large body of much more systematic literature on policy networks which has considerably refined and developed the original simple metaphor of policy community. (Indeed it has largely replaced it amongst a newer generation of British and other Western European political scientists).[79] Though at times the debate about different definitions of networks has not been terribly productive,[80] there is no doubt that the work, particularly of Rod Rhodes, (together with David Marsh), has become a very influential body of literature in British, and to an increasing extent, European policy studies. Thus, Rhodes' formulation of the network concept had immediate appeal to students of

---

[73] H. Heclo and A. Wildavsky, *The Private Government of Public Money* (London, Macmillan, 1974), pp. 76–118.

[74] Richardson had spent several months in Bergen during 1975 and was greatly influenced by Johan P. Olsen's work there.

[75] M. Heisler and R. B. Kvavik, 'Patterns of European Politics: The European Polity Model', in M. Heisler, *Politics in Europe* (New York, David MacKay, 1974).

[76] For example, see A. G. Jordan and J. J. Richardson, 'The British Policy Style on the Logic of Negotiation? in J. Richardson, ed., *Policy Styles in Western Europe* (London, Allen & Unwin, 1982), pp. 80–110 and A. G. Jordan and J. J. Richardson, *Government and Pressure Groups in Britain* (Oxford, Clarendon Press, 1982).

[77] H. Heclo, 'Issue Networks and the Executive Establishment' in A. King, ed., *The New American Political System* (Washington, DC, American Enterprise Institute, 1974).

[78] Judge, *The Parliamentary State*, p. 121.

[79] However, for an interesting use of the policy community concept in the field of industrial policy see J. Hayward 'The Policy Community Approach to Industrial Policy' in A. Rustow and Kenneth P. Erickson, eds., *Comparative Political Dynamics. Global Research Perspectives* (New York, HarperCollins, 1991), pp. 381–407.

[80] Judge, *The Parliamentary State*, p. 121.

multi-level governance in the EU and has become one of the main analytical tools in the analysis of a multi-level EU.[81]

Rhodes' work is well grounded in empirical studies—initially in central/local relations.[82] The original 'Rhodes Model' now has a number of variants but rests on Benson's 1982 definition of a policy network as a 'complex of dependencies and distinguished from other . . . complexes by breaks in the structure of resource dependences'.[83] The crux of Rhodes' development of the policy community/policy network approach is to focus on resource dependencies—that 'networks have different structures of dependencies, structures which vary along . . . key dimensions'.[84] This led to a classification of types of networks—such as professional, inter-governmental, and producer networks, etc.[85] One of the most recent versions of the 'Rhodes Model' is to be found in the book of network case studies which he and David Marsh edited in 1992.[86] In the introduction to a further re-formulation of the 'model', they point to a growing divergence of view between Grant Jordan, on the one hand, who has drawn increasingly on the American literature on networks and on a whole range of theoretically informed American literature,[87] and Rhodes who emphasizes that the British literature on networks owes a great deal to non-American sources.[88] This, at times tedious, debate cannot be covered here[89] but it is

---

[81] C. Ansell, C. Parsons and K. Darden, 'Dual Networks on European Regional Development Policy', *Journal of Common Market Studies*, 35 (1997), 345–75.

[82] For example, see R. A. W. Rhodes, *The National World of Local Government* (London, Allen & Unwin, 1986) and R. A. W. Rhodes, *Beyond Westminster and Whitehall, The Sub-Central Government of Britain* (London, Unwin Hyman, 1988).

[83] J. K. Benson, 'A Framework for Policy Analysis', in D. Rogers, D. Whitten and Associates, *Interorganization Co-ordination* (Ames, Ia., Iowa State University Press, 1982), pp. 137–70, cited in Rhodes, *Beyond Westminster and Whitehall*, p. 77.

[84] Rhodes, *Beyond Westminster and Whitehall*, p. 77.

[85] See ibid. pp. 78–81.

[86] D. Marsh and R. A. W. Rhodes, eds., *Policy Networks in British Government* (Oxford, Clarendon Press, 1992).

[87] See Jordan, 'Sub-Governments, Policy Communities and Networks: Refilling the Old Bottles?', 2.

[88] For example, the work by researchers at The Science Centre (WZB) in Berlin in the 1970s produced some excellent conceptualizations of the network approach which were very influential in Britain. See K. Hanf and F. Scharpf, eds., *Interorganisational Policy Making: Limits to Coordination and Central Control* (London, Sage Publications, 1978), especially Hanf's Introduction, pp. 1–15.

[89] See A. G. Jordan, W. A. Maloney and A. M. McLaughlin, 'Characterising Agricultural Policy-Making', *Public Administration*, 72 (1994), 505–26. M. D. Kavanagh, D. Marsh and M. Smith, 'The Relationship Between Policy Networks at the Sectoral and Sub-Sectoral Level: A Response to Jordan, Maloney and McLaughlin', *Public Administration*, 73 (1995), 627–9). G. Jordan and W. A. Maloney, 'Policy Networks Explained: A Comment on Kavanagh, Marsh and Smith', *Public Administration*, 73 (1995), 630–63.

perhaps worth noting that empirical research in all developed western societies—whether by political scientists, sociologists, psychologists or organization analysts—has generally identified networks as important in making public and organizational decisions. Similar approaches seem to have emerged relatively independently in many intellectual *milieux* throughout the world.

The corporatist interlude and reactions to the network approach

It is not surprising that the emergence of corporatism as an intellectual fashion, sparked by Philippe Schmitter's classic article 'Still the Century of Corporatism' in 1974, should also have influenced British scholars.[90] Wyn Grant had worked closely with Philippe Schmitter in Chicago, Berlin and Florence, with Wolfgang Streeck in Berlin and Florence, and was part of the International Institute of Management project on business interest associations. This brought together North American and European scholars. Corporatism was undoubtedly a 'foreign import'. However, the British version of the imported intellectual fashion was also subject to the British intellectual 'style', especially in scholarly work by the historian Keith Middlemass. His impressive and detailed volume on the politics of industrial society outlined what he termed the 'corporate bias' in British politics.[91] He describes how what were once interest groups outside the formal constitution, became 'governing institutions, existing thereafter as estates of the real'. It was not a system of corporatism that had emerged, however, 'but one where a corporate bias predominates'. Independently of *Governing Under Pressure*, he painted the same image of the British political system. Corporate bias was 'inseparable from the decline of party and parliamentary politics . . . By 1945 it had replaced, for all *practical* purposes, classical democratic theory as it had been understood in 1911'.[92] As Wyn Grant notes in his introduction to his edited volume, the revival of interest in corporatist explanations was an attempt to understand the process by which groups were transformed into what Middlemas had termed 'governing institutions'.[93]

The most effective and oft-cited (both within and outside the United Kingdom) work from this corporatist period is probably Alan Cawson's,

---

[90] W. Grant, ed., *The Political Economy of Corporatism* (London, Macmillan, 1985).

[91] K. Middlemas, *Politics in Industrial Society, The Experience of the British System Since 1911* (London, André Deutsch, 1979).

[92] Ibid.

[93] W. Grant, 'Introduction' in W. Grant, ed., *The Political Economy of Corporatism*, p. 2.

Corporatism and Political Theory,[94] published in 1986. However, it seems fair to characterize the period when corporatism and its variants became fashionable as an interlude because it did not fundamentally change the way that the policy process was perceived and it failed to capture the changing realities of British politics after 1979. In fact, it led to a rather sterile debate between British pluralists and corporatists, although Cawson himself was at pains to point out that pluralism and corporatism were ideal types and that 'political theory should recognize the coexistence of pluralist and corporatist processes, and engage the task of specifying the relationship between the two concepts'. In his conclusion, he identified the key task for corporatist writers as the need 'to specify where corporatism is likely to develop, and conversely where interest politics is likely to remain open and competitive'.[95]

One of the most effective critics of those British political scientists who claimed to have identified some form of corporatism in Britain was Grant Jordan. In a still widely cited (in Britain and abroad) article published in 1981, 'Iron Triangles, Woolly Corporatism and Elastic Nets', he argued that what the corporatist writers saw in British politics was 'the order of segmentation, inter-sectoral bargaining, limited access, voluntary groups'.[96] As he noted, there had been much talk of the corporate state in the late 1970s but few of the corporatist writers had claimed to have found it in operation.[97] In contrast to the corporatists, Jordan was keen to emphasize the utility of the network approach as 'at least the notion (of network) implied disaggregated power, extended links, a developing complexity in policy making reflects reality (in the area of political administration)'.[98] In a series of more recent articles, he, William Maloney and Andrew McLaughlin have drawn upon a wide range of American group literature and continue to emphasize the importance of consultation in the British policy process.[99] In a break with British tradition, Jordan and Maloney have also recently studied the logic of membership (rather than the logic of influence) via surveys of two British groups—Amnesty International and Friends of the Earth.[100]

---

[94] A. Cawson, *Corporatism and Political Theory* (Oxford, Basil Blackwell, 1988), p. 148.

[95] Ibid. p. 148.

[96] A. Grant Jordan, 'Iron Triangles, Woolly Corporatism and Elastic Nets: Images of the Policy Process', *Journal of Public Policy*, 1 (1981), 113.

[97] Ibid. p. 113.

[98] Ibid. p. 121.

[99] W. A. Maloney, A. G. Jordan and A. McLaughlin, 'Insider Groups and Public Policy: The Insider/Outsider Model Revisited', *Journal of Public Policy*, 14 (1994), 37.

[100] Jordan and Maloney, *The Protest Business?*

In a critique of what they see as flaws in the Olsonian analysis, they have argued that rational choice analysis must subsume non-material incentives. They also point to the importance of group activity in shaping the preferences of potential members and in stimulating membership.

Two important criticisms have emerged from the long period of dominance by the network approach. One is that emphasizing the identification and description of policy networks and the ubiquity of consultation underestimates the power of the state. For example, Martin Smith has correctly argued that network analysis needs balancing with a recognition of state autonomy and a greater concern with power. He has argued that the state can act according to its own preferences. Even when state action and group demands appear to coincide, policies 'are often developed because of the interests of state actors'.[101] He cites the poll tax or community charge which was introduced despite the opposition of most interest groups. Similarly, Richardson is now inclined to see consultation as often more about detail than about core policy change and has emphasized the fact that post-1979 politics has been quite different from the politics described in *Governing Under Pressure*, published just as Mrs Thatcher came to power. He too has emphasized the power of the state in setting agendas and determining what consultation is about[102] and, in work with Geoffrey Dudley, William Maloney and Wolfgang Rüdig, the role of forces exogenous to entrenched policy networks in bringing about policy change.[103] Rhodes and Marsh[104] have also placed emphasis on the importance of factors exogenous to policy networks. Indeed, this might be the future direction of British studies of pressure groups, i.e. how does the group system respond to exogenous change and under what conditions does policy change emerge in the absence of consensus?

Keith Dowding's critique of the network approach, from the rational choice perspective has been one of the most important and most widely

---

[101] M. J. Smith, *Pressure Power and Policy, State Autonomy and Policy Networks in Britain and the United States* (London, Harvester Wheatsheaf, 1993), p. 49.

[102] See J. Richardson, 'Doing Less by Doing More, British Government 1979–93', *West European Politics*, 17 (1994), 178–197.

[103] See J. Richardson, W. Maloney and W. Rüdig, 'The Dynamics of Policy Change: Lobbying and Water Privatisation' *Public Administration*, 70 (1992), 157–75; G. Dudley and J. Richardson, 'Why Does Policy Change Over Time? Adversarial Policy Communities, Alternative Policy Arenas and British Trunk Roads Policy 1945–95', *Journal of European Public Policy*, 3 (1996), 63–83 and G. Dudley and J. Richardson: 'Arenas Without Rules and the Policy Change Process: Outsider Groups and British Roads Policy', *Policy Studies*, 46 (1998).

[104] R. A. W. Rhodes and D. Marsh, 'New Directions in the Study of Policy Networks', *European Journal of Policy Research*, 21 (1992), 193–97.

cited recent contributions to British pressure group studies. It might yet turn out to be a watershed finally marking the intellectual fatigue of policy community and network analysis in Britain. Dowding's central thesis is that policy network began as a metaphor and may only become a theory by developing along the lines of sociological network analysis, something which he considers is of limited potential.[105] Noting that 'network analysis has become the dominant paradigm for the study of the policy-making process in British political science', he sees network approaches as failing 'because the driving force of explanation, the independent variables, are not network characteristics *per se* but rather characteristics of components within the networks'.[106] Thus, to Dowding, the network metaphors are heuristically useful (all that the early British proponents intended) but they are 'incapable of explaining transformation'.[107] The difficulty is that many would see the rational choice approach which he advocates as no more likely to explain transformation and policy change than conventional network analysis.[108]

Comparative and European Union studies

The preceding discussion has been almost exclusively concerned with the British contribution to the study of British pressure groups. This reflects the main thrust of British pressure group studies this century. Fortunately, there have been some notable exceptions. For example, Graham Wilson (although for some years now at the University of Wisconsin, Madison) has been one of the few British political scientists to become a recognized authority for *comparative* work on pressure groups. Starting with the publication of his study of agricultural politics and policies on Britain and the United States in 1977,[109] he has produced

---

[105] K. Dowding, 'Model or Metaphor? Critical Review of the Policy Network Approach', *Political Studies*, 43 (1995), 136–7.

[106] Ibid. p. 137.

[107] Ibid. p. 139.

[108] Rational choice perspectives and their weaknesses (especially the Olsonian approach) have produced some useful British contributions. For example see R. Kimber's revised version of his article, first published in *World Politics*, 33 (1981), 'Interest Groups and the Fallacy of the Liberal Fallacy' in J. Richardson, ed., *Pressure Groups* (Oxford, Oxford University Press, 1993), pp. 38–48; and, for some useful empirical data on why people join public interest groups, see A. G. Jordan and W. A. Maloney, 'How Bumble Bees Fly; Accounting for Public Interest Participation', *Political Studies*, 44 (1996), 668–85 and Jordan and Maloney, *The Protest Business?*

[109] G. K. Wilson, *Special Interests and Policymaking: Agricultural Politics and Politics in Britain and the United States* (London, John Wiley, 1977).

well-recognized studies of unions in American national politics,[110] an overview of interest groups and the United States[111] and, more recently, an excellent general comparative text.[112]

Similarly, other British authors have made a major contribution to the understanding of foreign pressure-group systems, reflecting a strong British tradition of the study of other Western European states. Particularly notable in this category are studies by Jack Hayward of the French interest group system. He has characterized the French and British pressure group system as 'best analysed—depending upon the type of actor and policy issue involved—in the context of the typology of endemic conflict, concerted politics and domination, with the possibility that any particular predicament can be tackled at different phases by methods appropriate to more than one of these models'.[113] In France, groups can be as much *pressured* by the state as they apply pressure on the state themselves. Similarly, Kenneth Dyson's study of the German interest group system has also become one of the standard works, cited regularly outside Britain. Dyson, too, emphasized the complexity of state/group relations—sometimes, exhibiting a style of consensus building and interdependence of state and society and at others emphasizing a more authoritarian style of imposition based on a conception of state vs. society.[114] Interestingly, the very basic and simple concept of 'policy style', in which the relationship between the state and groups was one of only two variables, was a British concept which did manage to travel reasonably well and was applied especially in the 1980s. For such a simple idea, this is perhaps odd, yet it was a concept which had some comparative potential (when comparative policy studies seemed becalmed) and hence it was utilized outside the United Kingdom as well as within it.

Finally, we turn to an area of pressure group studies where British analysts have possibly had their greatest impact internationally—the role of pressure groups in the European Union. British political scientists

---

[110] G. K. Wilson, *Unions in American National Politics* (London, Macmillan, 1979).

[111] G. K. Wilson, *Interest Groups in the United States* (Oxford, Oxford University Press, 1981).

[112] G. K. Wilson, *Interest Groups* (Oxford, Basil Blackwell, 1990).

[113] J. E. S. Hayward, 'Pressure Groups and Pressured Groups in Franco-British Perspective', in D. Kavanagh and G. Peele, eds., *Comparative Politics. Essays in Honour of S. E. Finer* (London, Heinemann, 1984), pp. 100–101; See also J. E. S. Hayward, *The State and The Market Economy in France. Industrial Patriotism and Economic Intervention in France* (Brighton, Wheatsheaf Books, 1986).

[114] K. Dyson, 'West Germany: The Search for a Rationalist Consensus', in J. Richardson, ed., *Policy Styles in Western Europe* (London, Allen & Unwin, 1982), p. 18.

seem to have achieved a position of international authority and influence significantly greater than with their earlier studies of mainly British pressure groups.[115] In a sense, this is puzzling as it cannot be claimed that these British studies are heavily theoretical, have generated new generic concepts, or have applied new methodologies. Indeed, in so far as they draw upon 'grand theory', it tends to be American. However, at the less ambitious conceptual level, it is the case that British scholars have utilized existing British network approaches to reasonably good effect (although this is not without its British critics).[116] For example, John Peterson's evaluation of the utility of network approaches at the European level is very widely cited in Europe and the United States.[117] Similarly, other British scholars have made a significant contribution to the understanding of the effects on pressure-group organization and behaviour of shifts in the locus of power to Brussels, the linkages between the Commission and the European and national level interest group systems, and the role and organization of European level associations.

Their success possibly rests on a British strength—namely a tradition of good empirical research directed towards the development of accurate characterizations of the political process, rather than formulating over-arching theories to be later tested empirically. From the outset of the EC, British writers such as Emil Kirchner, Alan Butt Philip, and Wyn Grant were some of first to describe and analyse the emerging pressure group system in the EC.[118] They were later joined by a number of British scholars now specializing in the study of the European policy process—such as Justin Greenwood, Sonia Mazey, John Peterson, Jeremy

---

[115] As one leading American pressure group scholar expressed it to this author, 'as far as British contribution to the (general) pressure group literature is concerned . . . most American scholars read pluralism and corporatism as the classic literatures, and many of the key authors are American . . . when it comes to "transnational" interest groups, the key authors are almost all British' (private correspondence 3 April 1997).

[116] See H. Kassim 'Policy Networks and European Union Policy Making: A Sceptical View' *West European Politics*, 17 (1994), 15–27.

[117] J. Peterson, 'Decision-making in the European Union: towards a framework for analysis', *Journal of European Public Policy*, 2 (1995), 69–93.

[118] See A. Butt Philip, *Pressure Groups in the European Community* (London, University Association for Contemporary European Studies, 1985). E. Kirchner, *Trade Unions as Pressure Groups in the European Community* (Farnborough, Saxon House, 1977). E. Kirchner, 'Interest Group Behaviour at the Community Level' in L. Hurwitz, ed., *Contemporary Perspectives on European Integration* (London, Aldwich, 1980). W. Grant, *Pressure Groups, Politics and Democracy in Britain* (London, Philip Allan, 1986), pp. 90–111. W. Grant, 'Industrialists and Farmers: British Interests in the European Community', *West European Politics*, 1 (1978).

Richardson and others—all of whom could be said to have added considerably to the stock of knowledge on the role of pressure groups in the European policy process.[119] These studies quickly became part of the standard literature on the European Union policy process and the broader process of European integration used by analysts in the United States and Western Europe.

British scholars of groups in the European Union have also benefited greatly from being more integrated into a large international community of European Union scholars and this has undoubtedly assisted them in having an impact beyond the United Kingdom.

Also, studies of the European policy process are relatively 'young'. Hence, data gathering and preliminary characterizations of processes gain greater currency than when a field of study has developed a bedrock of empirical material on which theorists can build. The European Union is still a polity in the making and, hence, empirically-driven studies can make a significant impact internationally. Moreover, Continental and American scholars are more interested in the European Union as a polity than they are in Britain as a polity. The real test for the British scholars is whether they can develop a more theoretically sophisticated approach which links interest group studies to theories of European integration and polity building at the supranational level.

Part Two: Political parties

> the spirit and force of party has in America been as essential to the action of the machinery of government as steam is to a locomotive engine; or to vary the simile, party association and organisation are to the organs of government what the motor nerves are to the muscles, sinews, and bones of the human body. They transmit the motive power, they determine the directions in which the organs act.[120]

---

[119] For example see J. Greenwood, J. Grote, and K. Runit, eds., *Organized Interests and the European Community* (London, Sage Publications, 1992). S. Mazey and J. Richardson, eds., *Lobbying in the EC* (Oxford, Oxford University Press, 1993). A. McLaughlin and J. Greenwood, 'The Management of Interest Representation in the European Union', *Journal of Common Market Studies*, 33 (1995), 143–56. J. Peterson, 'Decision-Making in the European Union: Towards a Framework for Analysis', *Journal of European Public Policy*, 2 (1995), 69–96. D. Coen, 'The Evolution of the Large Firm as a Political Actor in the European Union', *Journal of European Public Policy*, 4 (1997), 91–108.

[120] J. Bryce, *The American Commonwealth*, III, (London, Macmillan, 1888), p. 321.

The early works

British political scientists have been very active investigators of political parties. Starting with James (later Lord) Bryce's study of the American Commonwealth in 1888, there has been a long tradition of party studies—from power within parties through to the role of parties in government and, more recently, as declining institutions for political activism. Thus, compared with British pressure-group studies, the history of work on parties is both longer and more wide ranging. For example, there are very few British studies of non-British pressure groups but very many excellent British studies (by specialists in the study of the politics of foreign political systems—not reviewed here due to lack of space—of, particularly, Western European parties, but also of Communist and post-Communist, Developing World and (to a much lesser extent) American parties.[121] In fact the total output this century is enormous. The record is of good, professional, but largely empirical, research, with rather few (although more than in the field of pressure-group studies, it must be said) British writers being able to claim that they have written works that have helped shape the way that parties are studied elsewhere or have formulated concepts and theories that have been widely applied outside Britain. If one thinks of pioneering conceptually-based works in the field of political parties, it is names such as Michels, Duverger, Sartori, Kirchheimer, Pizzorno, Lipset, Rokkan, Dahl, Epstein, Lijphart, von Beyme, Downs, Kitschelt, Lawson and Merkl that spring to mind, rather than British scholars.[122] With only a few notable exceptions—

---

[121] Space precludes a review of this very large body of literature by British scholars on parties in Western Europe, the former Communist states, and the developing world. Many British scholars have achieved international recognition for their expertise in particular countries, for example, and this work often includes work on political parties. (See Chapter 6 of this volume, 'Comparative Politics'.) It is invidious to select from this impressive list, but it would certainly include work on France by such scholars as Malcolm Anderson, Byron Criddle, John Frears, Martin Harrison, Jack Hayward, Howard Machin, Peter Morris, Phillip Williams, Vincent Wright; on Germany by Kenneth Dyson, Nevil Johnson, Stephen Padgett, William Paterson, Geoffrey Pridham, Geoffrey Roberts, Gordon Smith; on Italy by Percy Allum, Martin Bull, Phil Daniels, Mark Donovan, David Hine, Paul Furlong; on Spain by Richard Gillespie, Paul Heywood; on The Netherlands by Ken Medhurst; on Scandinavia by John Madeley; on the former Communist states by Archie Brown, Leonard Schapiro, Stephen White and William Iordoff; on Latin America Alan Angell, Laurence Whitehead and Joe Foweraker.

[122] See for example: G. Sartori, *Parties and Party Systems—A Framework for Analysis*, I, (Cambridge, Cambridge University Press, 1976) p. 370. M. Duverger, *Political Parties, Their Organization and Activity in the Modern State*, (translated by B. and R. North) (London, Methuen & Co, 1954), p. 370. H. Daalder, 'The Comparative Study of European Parties

such as the work of Richard Rose, Derek Urwin, Alan Ware and Ian Budge[123]—has the British contribution achieved genuinely international recognition and influenced work overseas. For example, in Peter Mair's invaluable collection of key party and party system studies in Western Europe only two of the reprinted articles (out of 24) are from Britain.[124]

The reasons for this relative lack of impact—notwithstanding a critical mass of party studies by British scholars—are similar to the relative failure of British interest group studies to achieve very much international impact. First, party studies have tended to follow the British empirical, descriptive tradition, with relatively little effort and resources being put into theory building and conceptualization. Secondly, there has been a tendency to concentrate on office holding and organization rather than on power. Hence, British studies of parties have probably travelled abroad only marginally better than British studies of pressure groups. In those cases where they have, the authors have had considerable experience outside the United Kingdom.

The British study of British political parties was dominated for decades by one classic book—Robert McKenzie's *British Political Parties*, first published in 1955.[125] In the second edition, published in 1963, the

and Party Systems, An Overview', in H. Daalder and P. Mair, eds., *Western European Party Systems: Continuity and Change* (London, Sage Publications, 1983), pp. 1–28. H. Kitschelt, *The Transformation of European Social Democracy* (Cambridge, Cambridge University Press, 1994). A. Lijphart, 'Typologies of Democratic Systems', *Comparative Political Studies*, 1 (1968), 3–44. L. D. Epstein, *Political Parties on Western Democracies* (New Brunswick, J. J. Transaction Books, 1980). R. Dahl, ed., *Political Opposition on Western Democracies* (New Haven, Conn., Yale University Press, 1966). O. Kirchheimer, 'The Transformation of Western European Party Systems', in J. La Palombara and M. Weiner, eds., *Political Parties and Political Development* (Princeton, Princeton University Press, 1966), pp. 177–200. A. Pizzorno, 'Interests and Parties in Pluralism', in S. Berger, ed., *Organized Interests in Western Europe, Pluralism, Corporatism, and the Transformation of Politics* (Cambridge, Cambridge University Press, 1981), pp. 247–84. A. Downs, *An Economic Theory of Democracy* (New York, Harper, 1957). K. Lawson and P. Merkl, eds., *When Parties Fail* (Princeton, NJ, Princeton University Press, 1988). K. von Beyme, *Political Parties in Western Democracies* (Aldershot, Gower, 1985). R. Michels, *A Sociological Study of the Oligarchic Tendencies of Modern Democracy* (first published 1911, but see the 1962 edition, introduced by S. M. Lipset, New York, Free Press, 1962). S. M. Lipset and S. Rokkan, eds., *Party Systems and Voter Alignments* (New York, Free Press, 1967).

[123] Peter Mair has been excluded from this study as he is Irish and has spent a large proportion of his professional life in The Netherlands, after periods at Strathclyde and Manchester.

[124] P. Mair, ed., *The West European Party System* (Oxford, Oxford University Press, 1990).

[125] R. McKenzie, *British Political Parties* (London, Mercury Books, [2nd rev. ed.] 1963).

publishers could rightly claim that the book 'remains the only full-scale analysis of the power structure of the two major British political parties since the publication of Ostrogorski's *Democracy and the Organization of British Political Parties,* in 1902'.[126] We will return to his work later, but it is important to note that, although McKenzie is really the father of British studies of parties, even he did not face totally virgin territory. Indeed, it could be argued that much of McKenzie's analysis had been preceded by that of Ostrogorski some 50 years before.[127] For example, McKenzie's introductory chapter has much to say about Ostrogorski's book (translated from the French and published in Britain in 1902) and his alleged theory that British parties would be subject to the kind of control attempted by Joseph Chamberlain and the Birmingham caucus, who wanted popular control by the constituency parties of their elected representatives.[128] Indeed, McKenzie's central thesis—which was to be dominant for decades—was that Ostrogorski's predictions were not fulfilled, at least as far as the Liberal and Conservative Parties were concerned. As McKenzie argued, 'the leaders of those two older parties had recognized the principal danger against which Ostrogorski preached as soon or sooner than he did'.[129] However, Ostrogorski was something of a 'straw man' in McKenzie's analyses. Thus, Barker and Howard-Johnstone argue that Ostrogorski had, in fact, claimed that the Conservative Party remained in the hands of the leader who had emerged from the parliamentary party. Rather politely, they point out that some of the views about Ostrogorski's work held by McKenzie (and others such as Lipset) were either incorrect or, if true, 'sufficiently far from the whole truth to involve serious distortion'.[130]

A rival interpretation to Ostrogorski's work was James Bryce's *American Commonwealth,* first published in 1888. This provided a detailed account of the American political system at work, including party machines and their operation in the United States.[131] In writing his three-volume study of American politics, he could find 'no author who has set himself to describe impartially the actual daily working of

---

[126] M. Ostrogorski, *Democracy and the Organization of Political Parties,* I, (London, Macmillan, 1902).

[127] I am grateful to Rodney Barker for drawing my attention to this point. However, see the comments in the preceding chapter, p. 151–4.

[128] M. Ostrogorski, quoted by McKenzie, *British Political Parties,* p. 9.

[129] McKenzie, *British Political Parties,* p. 9.

[130] R. Barker and X. Howard-Johnson, 'The Politics and Political Ideas of Moisei Ostrogorski', *Political Studies,* 22 (1975), 416.

[131] Bryce, *The American Commonwealth,* II.

that part of the vast and intricate machine which lies outside the Constitution, nor, which are more important still, the influences which sway the men by whom this machine has been constructed and is daily manipulated'.[132] Bryce analysed the convergence of the two main parties in America and likened the remaining differences (of 'spirit and sentiment') of the Republicans and Democrats to the differences between the Tories and the Liberals in England at that time.[133]

Although McKenzie quotes Bryce's introduction to Ostrogorski's first edition approvingly, Bryce probably had little influence on McKenzie's own work. Much more important was Robert Michels' *Political Parties: A Sociological Study of The Oligarchical Tendencies of Modern Democracy*, first published in English in 1915.[134] The notion of an 'iron law of oligarchy' was an important concept underpinning McKenzie's largely empirical study of British parties. Other British writers on parties, such as Harold Laski,[135] were generally dismissed by McKenzie as being wrong in their analysis (as, indeed, they were). In one passage McKenzie derides Laski for suggesting that Attlee could attend the Potsdam Conference after polling day in 1945 (but before the election result was known). McKenzie comments that 'Laski then revealed a really extraordinary misconception of the working of the Labour Party when it is in office by adding . . . "the Labour Party cannot be committed to any decisions arrived at, for the Three-Power Conference will be discussing matters which have not been debated either in the Party Executive or at meetings of the Parliamentary Party"'.[136]

This leads us, naturally, to a discussion of McKenzie's own work, as his jibe at Laski contains the crux of McKenzie's own analysis of the distribution of power within British parties. McKenzie's book is regarded as a pioneering and monumental work, certainly still cited regularly today and of enormous importance in the study of British political parties. Why was it so important? Rather like Finer's *Anonymous Empire* in the field of pressure-group studies (though altogether a much weightier volume), McKenzie achieved prominence because he had the foresight, and analytical capabilities, to see a new field and to write about it in a way which made sense of reality. But he also had a

---

[132] Ibid. II, p. 322.

[133] Ibid. II, pp. 348–53.

[134] R. Michels, *Political Parties: A Sociological Study of the Oligarchical Tendencies of Modern Democracy* (New York, Free Press, 1962).

[135] H. Laski, *Democracy in Crisis* (London, Allen & Unwin, 1933).

[136] McKenzie, *British Political Parties*, p. 330.

very clear 'line' which others (fans and critics alike) could grasp and utilize. His central thesis was that

> the distribution of power within British political parties is primarily a function of cabinet government and the British parliamentary system . . . whatever the role granted in theory to the extra-parliamentary wings of the parties, in practice final authority rests in both parties within the parliamentary party and its leadership. In this fundamental respect the distribution of power within the two major parties is the same.[137]

Influenced by Schumpeter's *Capitalism, Socialism and Democracy*,[138] McKenzie rejected the classical definition of the democratic process and saw the essential role of the electorate as not reaching decisions on specific issues of policy but deciding which of two or more competing teams of potential leaders should make the decisions.[139] McKenzie's broad characterization of the British political process was a system in which parties played a *relatively* unimportant role in the actual policy process and in which pressure groups were a more important and effective linkage mechanism between citizens and ruling élites. This clear 'line' has proved to be the benchmark against which every study of British political parties has been measured ever since. Whether or not subsequent scholars have accepted the McKenzie thesis, he was the originator of a series of studies of internal party politics and processes in British parties, to which we now turn.

Internal party processes

One of the peculiarities of the work by British political scientists on British parties has been the heavy preference for studies of the Labour Party. This strong bias is especially puzzling in view of the fact that it is the Conservatives who have been in office for the majority of the period since the Second World War, when British political science has been at its most productive. There *are* studies of the Conservatives, Liberals and, indeed, of the brief life of the Social Democratic Party but they are few and often by historians rather than political scientists.[140] It partly reflects political balance within the profession and the view (mistaken, as the

---

[137] Ibid. p. 635.
[138] J. A. Schumpeter, *Capitalism, Socialism and Democracy* (London, Unwin Books, [10th impression] 1965).
[139] McKenzie, *British Political Parties*, p. 646.
[140] J. Vincent, *The Formation of the Liberal Party 1857–1868* (London, Constable, 1966).

authors of *True Blues*[141] demonstrated in 1994) that the Conservative
Party was not accessible to political science researchers. Also, as
Whiteley *et al.* suggest, the fact that McKenzie's analysis became almost
hegemonic for so long also played its part, by arguing so strongly on the
basis of his exhaustive research, that the analysis of power in the Conservative Party was of little importance.[142] The continuation of the lively
debate within the Labour Party over the respective roles of the Conference and the Parliamentary Labour Party (PLP) was no doubt also
influential in attracting the attention of political science researchers—
after all, it appeared to be an issue of real importance in the real world.
Finally, the delayed development of policy studies in British political
science (eventually given much greater prominence by Richard Rose at
Strathclyde) might have contributed to the preoccupation with parties as
institutions of politics rather than of government.

Important studies of the origins of the Labour Party were produced
by G. D. H. Cole in 1948[143] and by Henry Pelling in 1961.[144] Much of this
historical analysis is concerned, quite naturally, with the relationship
between the Labour Party and the trade unions. A good example of
this focus is Martin Harrison's *Trade Unions and the Labour Party Since
1945*, published in 1960.[145] Subsequently, in a prophetic passage (in
terms of the New Labour Party led by Mr Blair) he commented that
'the Labour Party has never been exclusively a trade union party, and
has never considered itself simply the political arm of the industrial
movement'.[146] Although not solely focused on the Labour Party *per se*,
Henry Pelling's *A History of British Trade Unionism*[147] is an important
source, as is the book by David Marsh, analysing changes in the relationship between unions and the Labour Party in the 1980s.[148] Some of the
studies of the Labour Party have, of course, had a conscious Marxist or

---

[141] P. Whiteley, P. Seyd and J. Richardson, *True Blues, The Politics of Conservative Party Membership* (Oxford, Clarendon Press, 1994).

[142] Ibid. p. 3, quoting McKenzie, *British Political Parties*, p. 258.

[143] G. D. H. Cole, *A History of the Labour Party from 1914* (London, Routledge & Kegan Paul, 1948).

[144] H. Pelling, *A Short History of the Labour Party* (London, Macmillan, [St Martin's Press, 1993] 1961).

[145] M. Harrison, *Trade Unions and the Labour Party Since 1945* (London, George Allen & Unwin, 1960).

[146] M. Harrison, 'Trade Unions and the Labour Party' in R. Kimber and J. J. Richardson, eds., *Pressure Groups in Britain: A Reader*, (London, J. J. Dent & Co., 1974), p. 80.

[147] H. Pelling, *A History of British Trade Unionism* (London, Penguin Books, [4th ed.] 1987).

[148] D. Marsh, *The New Politics of British Trade Unionism, Union Power and the Thatcher Legacy* (London, Macmillan, 1992), pp. 139–163.

neo-Marxist stance and this has reduced their influence. For example, Laski and Miliband both produced studies which did not really influence the way other analyses were conducted or advance the discipline.[149] Miliband's central purpose was to analyse the consequences for the Labour Party of its commitment to parliamentary politics. It was a polemic designed to explain why the Labour Party has not succeeded in creating a radically different social order—concluding, in the second edition in 1972, that, on balance, Labour was unlikely to be turned into a socialist party.[150] Of more importance has been Lewis Minkin's detailed and scholarly study of the role of the Labour Party Conference and of the relationship between trade unions and the Labour Party, which also throws light on the conduct of intra-party processes. Although generally supporting the McKenzie thesis of concentration of power in the hands of the Parliamentary leadership, he provided a much more nuanced view of internal policy making in the Labour Party than did McKenzie.[151]

Really good analytical or theoretical studies of power within the Conservative Party are almost impossible to find. Richard Kelly's *Conservative Party Conferences* is an attempt to redress the balance of McKenzie's work by claiming that party members are more influential than he suggested. It is, therefore, useful, but it could not claim to break new ground conceptually or to have amassed so much empirical data as really to change the way in which the intra-party policy process in the Conservative Party is judged.[152] His contribution is that he points to a conference *system* in the Conservative Party via which Conservative Party leaders sound out activists throughout the year—with at least one party conference taking place somewhere in the country each week—and the importance of informal channels of influence within the Party.[153] Robert Blake's history of the Conservative Party, *The Conservative Party from Peel to Thatcher*, is essentially a

---

[149] H. Laski, *Democracy in Crisis* (London, George Allen & Unwin, 1933). R. Miliband, *Parliamentary Socialism. A Study of the Politics of Labour* (London, Allen & Unwin, 1961).

[150] R. Miliband, *Parliamentary Socialism. A Study of the Politics of Labour* (London, Merlin Press, [2nd ed.] 1972), p. 372.

[151] L. Minkin, *The Labour Party Conference. A Study on the Politics of Intra-Party Democracy* (London, Allen Lane, 1978), p. 317. See also L. Minkin, *The Contentious Alliance* (Edinburgh, Edinburgh University Press, 1992).

[152] R. Kelly, *Conservative Party Conferences* (Manchester, Manchester University Press, 1989).

[153] Ibid. p. 184.

descriptive account.[154] Both Philip Norton[155] and Andrew Gamble[156] have also made important contributions to our understanding of the Conservative Party and Conservatism, as does Greenleaf's study of Conservative Ideology.[157]

All of these intra-party studies, especially of the Labour Party, are well researched, professional (particularly those by Minkin), detailed and informative, but it is doubtful if even their authors would see them as designed to advance theory building. They add, successfully, to the stock of empirical knowledge of the parties. Also of the descriptive, but important, *genre* of party studies are works by Michael Pinto-Duschinsky and Malcolm Punnett. Both authors deserve more credit than they have received for conducting meticulous and scholarly studies of two key aspects of political parties largely ignored by British political scientists, yet often studied outside Britain—namely the financing of parties[158] and the selection processes of party leaders.[159]

An attempt to be more innovative—both in terms of research method and the formulation of theories of participation and activism—is the first of a series of studies of party activism developed by Patrick Seyd and Paul Whiteley. *Labour's Grass Roots, The Politics of Party Membership*, is the first quantitative and detailed study of party members and marks the emergence of studies of British Parties from the shadow of McKenzie. It provided new socio-economic data on the party members, the factors that lead them to join the Party, their attitudes and beliefs, and the extent of their activism beyond simply joining.[160] This study is important for two reasons. First, it provides a mass of unique empirical data on members and their activities. On these grounds alone, it has been widely cited in Britain and abroad. Secondly, they have tried to set their empirical research in the context of a more conceptual approach to the study of activism in society. In that sense, their work is quite different to the

---

[154] R. Blake, *The Conservative Party from Peel to Thatcher* (London, Fontana Press, 1985).

[155] See P. Norton, *Conservative Dissidents* (London, Temple Smith, 1978); P. Norton and A. Aughey, *Conservatives and Conservatism* (London, Temple Smith, 1981); P. Norton, 'The Conservative Party from Thatcher to Major', in A. King, ed., *Britain at the Polls* (Chatham NJ, Chatham House, 1992), pp. 29–62.

[156] A. Gamble, *The Conservative Nation* (London, Routledge & Kegan Paul, 1974).

[157] W. H. Greenleaf, *The British Political Tradition*, II, (Methuen, London, 1983).

[158] M. Pinto-Duschinsky, *British Political Finance, 1830–1980*, (Washington DC, American Enterprise Institute, 1981) and 'Trends in British Party Funding', *Parliamentary Affairs*, 42 (1989), 197–212.

[159] R. M. Punnet, *Selecting the Party Leader* (Brighton, Harvester Wheatsheaf, 1992).

[160] P. Seyd and P. Whiteley, *Labour's Grass Roots, The Politics of Party Membership* (Oxford, Clarendon Press, 1992).

party studies which preceded them.[161] Thus, in their first study, they formulated what they termed a 'general incentive theory' of activism which sought to explain the 'paradox of participation'—namely that only approximately seven per cent of the electorate are party members in Britain and only approximately two per cent are actually activists.

Starting with Mancur Olson's theoretical argument, which suggests that there is a problem in explaining why some people do actually join parties and become active, they suggest that a wider range of incentives needs to be considered than traditional Olsonian logic would suggest.[162] They argue that two types of selective incentives—process and outcome incentives—help explain the paradox of participation. Thus, process incentives refer to motives for participation which are not linked to outcomes—'the political process can be interesting and stimulating in itself, without regard to the outcomes of the process'.[163] Their work was followed by a study of the Conservative Party, published in 1994.[164] This replicated and extended the earlier Labour study and used the incentives model to explore the data (produced from a survey of 3,919 party members, of whom 63 per cent replied in a usable form). Again, the study produced unique empirical data, particularly on the decline in numbers and ageing profile of the Conservative Party in 1990s Britain— revealing it as an essentially geriatric 'mass' party.

The lasting value of the corpus of work by Seyd and Whitely, how- ever, might rest on the extent to which their general incentives model proves to be a theoretical approach which is transferable to other studies outside Britain. Essentially, the decline in activism is explained by changes in the incentives for political action. The theoretical model suggests that 'distinct factors are at work in explaining why people support a particular party by joining it, or by becoming active once they have joined. These are selective and collective incentives, group efficacy, and affective or expressive attachments to the party'.[165] Basic- ally, so the argument runs, if individuals are influenced in their decisions to participate by incentives, then a decline in participation in parties

---

[161] See, however, the work by Alan Ware (cited in notes 177–179), which is an earlier attempt to develop a more conceptual approach to the study of participation and activism in terms of incentives.

[162] Seyd and Whiteley, *Labour's Grass Roots*, p. 59.

[163] Ibid. p. 59.

[164] Whiteley *et al.*, *True Blues*.

[165] P. Whiteley and P. Seyd, 'The Dynamics of Party Activism in Britain—A Spiral of Demobilisation?' *British Journal of Political Science*, 28 (1998), 113–137.

must be explained by a decline in these incentives. The key to the acceptability and transferability of this model rests, of course, on other scholars' acceptance of the rational choice approach (albeit in a significantly modified form) which underpins it.

A much earlier and very notable exception to the generally atheoretical approach of British scholars to the study of the internal process of political parties is, of course, the work in the 1960s by Richard Rose on followers and leaders, and factions and tendencies within parties.[166] Rose drew attention to the fact that McKenzie tended to ignore followers when he wrote about leaders and Rose produced evidence (contrary to Duverger's predictions) that all constituency parties were not in the hands of extremists. He also suggested that there were many all-party, consensual issues. His ideas were developed in his major, internationally-recognized book, *The Problem of Party Government*, published in 1974 (by which time Rose had written over half a million words on political parties, since he began studying them in 1953).[167] Rose pointed out the importance of 'policy parties' within electoral parties. He argued that 'in order to understand the role of party in government, one must consider how policy parties predominate in the victorious electoral party, as well as which electoral party wins a parliamentary majority'.[168] In a passage which could have been written following Mr Blair's capture of the Labour Party in the 1990s, Rose argued that 'the realignment of policy groups within and across electoral lines has been as significant, if not more significant, than changes in government caused by general elections'.[169] The value of this work was that it focused on the difficult question of policy change and the fact that the 'surface cohesion' of British parties disguised a much greater capacity for policy change, over time.[170] The notion of policy parties was linked by Rose to the question of leadership and this led him to question one of McKenzie's central theses. Thus, one of Rose's many contributions was to point out that McKenzie placed too much emphasis on retention of office as an indication of power and not enough on policy-making as an indicator of

---

[166] See R. Rose, 'The Political Ideas of English Party Activists', *American Political Science Review*, 56 (1962), 360–71, R. Rose, 'Complexities of Party Leadership', *Parliamentary Affairs*, 16 (1963), 257–73.

[167] R. Rose, *The Problem of Party Government* (London, Macmillan, 1974).

[168] Ibid. p. 319.

[169] Ibid. p. 319.

[170] Ibid. p. 335.

power. Thus, if a leader could not affect the outputs of government, he was no more than a figurehead.[171]

As suggested earlier, Richard Rose was an early convert to the need to study *public policy* and this led him to a much more rounded and perceptive view of the role of parties in the political system as a whole, than produced by earlier (or, indeed, later) party scholars. Hence, a great value of *The Problem of Party Government* was that it set the study of parties in a much broader context and was underpinned by interesting ideas. It was an innovative study which said much about the *obstacles* to party government and the ways in which party government might be strengthened.[172] Rose's broader public policy process perspective led, naturally, to a consideration of the impact of parties on public policy, a topic to which we turn in the next section.

Before doing so, however, it is important to note other examples of important exceptions to the empirical/historical tradition as outlined earlier. For example, Anthony King's 1969 article on political parties in Western democracies was a sceptical review of existing party studies and of the six major functions which had been claimed for political parties in the literature. His hunch was that parties were less important than often claimed, but the main thrust of the article was that future research should focus on the *function* being claimed for parties, rather than solely on the parties themselves, and on clarification of theory.[173] King's approach was, therefore, deviating from the central theme of British studies of parties—namely parties as institutions worthy of study in their own right, rather than as one of many institutions in the political system as a whole. A similar concern with theory building can be found in Derek Urwin's work (influenced by Richard Rose and Stein Rokkan with whom Urwin collaborated). For example, a 1973 article[174] and his 1980 book, *From Ploughshare to Ballot Box*[175] are both cited still. The latter was a broadly based study of agrarian politics in Europe and is probably a unique British contribution to the study of the formation of new political parties and their subsequent behaviour and fortunes. It was a

---

[171] Ibid. p. 355.

[172] See particularly Chapters XV and XVI of Rose, *The Problem of Party Government*, pp. 379–480.

[173] A. King, 'Political Parties in Western Democracies. Some Sceptical Reflections', *Polity*, 2 (1969), 111–41.

[174] D. W. Urwin, 'Political Parties, Societies and Regimes in Europe: Some Reflections on the Literature', *European Journal of Political Research*, 1 (1973), 179–204.

[175] D. W. Urwin, *From Ploughshare to Ballot Box, The Politics of Agrarian Defence in Europe* (Oslo, Universitetsforlgatet, 1980).

fine mixture of empirical data and conceptualization. Somewhat earlier, Jean Blondel had published an article on party systems, classifying them into six types.[176] As with scholars such as Rose and Urwin, Blondel's work is uncharacteristically *comparative*—something which has undoubtedly increased the appeal of their work outside Britain and which has ensured that they continue to be cited.

Finally, we turn to a more recent body of literature—produced by Alan Ware—which also has a more comparative and conceptual approach. His study of the breakdown of party organization in the United States, 1940–80 is interesting both as an empirical study and for its analysis of party activism in terms of incentives—preceding work by Patrick Seyd and Paul Whitely by some years.[177] The careful balance between empirical work and theorizing was seen in his early book on the Denver Democrats, which had formulated a theory of intra-party democracy, explaining why parties need to be internally democratic and centralized, and why their policies should as far as possible be determined by party activists.[178] The relationship between parties and democracy in the modern state became the central theme of a subsequent book—*Citizens, Parties and the State*, published in 1987,[179] reassessing the contributions made by parties to the advancement of democracy. As Ware himself notes, empirical studies of institutions (such as parties) and theoretical studies had tended to diverge since the days of Ostrogorski and Michels. The central thrust of the book was that parties have not quite fulfilled their potential as agents of democracy, although they have made an important contribution—for example their role as intermediaries in the liberal democratic state.

Parties and public policy

The critical mass of British public policy researchers, which emerged in the 1970s and 1980s, has tended to see political parties as relatively unimportant in the policy process. As a result, there have been relatively few works which have party and policy-making as their central focus.

[176] J. Blondel, 'Party Systems and Patterns of Government in Western Democracies', *Canadian Journal of Political Science*, 1 (1968), 180–203. See also J. Blondel and M. Cotta, eds., *Party and Government* (London, Macmillan, 1996).

[177] A. Ware, *The Breakdown of Party Organisation, 1940–1980* (Oxford, Clarendon Press, 1985).

[178] A. Ware, *The Logic of Party Democracy* (London, Macmillan, 1979), p. 70.

[179] A. Ware, *Citizens, Parties and the State* (Cambridge, Polity Press, 1987). See also Ware's textbook *Political Parties and Party Systems* (Oxford, Oxford University Press, 1996).

Rose is, again, a notable exception to this trend. His volume, *Do Parties Make A Difference?*, first published in 1980 (and in an expanded second edition in 1984) has become the standard work in Britain, widely cited abroad, on the relationship between parties and public policy making.[180] In answer to the question posed in his title, Rose concluded that 'British parties are not the primary forces shaping the destiny of British society; it is shaped by something stronger than parties'.[181] Amongst these forces was a relatively consensual electorate and powerful secular trends—'necessity more than consensus is the explanation for similarities in behaviour'.

He, therefore, rejected the 'adversary model' of British politics (see later). Drawing on Stein Rokkan's famous phrase, 'votes count but resources decide', Richard Rose characterized the British political system as a moving consensus. As he pointed out, Reginald Bassett had been an early exponent of the theory that British politics was essentially consensual. Thus Bassett wrote in 1935, 'The practical exigencies of government necessitate avoidance of the dramatic reversals of policy which might follow from the alternation of parties in power; and the violent oscillations alleged to result from the system—do not in fact occur'.[182] Bassett had also anticipated the so-called 'spatial competition' theories of today, usually attributed to Anthony Downs' classic study (see later). Thus, Bassett noted that electoral competition had consequences for the policies adopted by parties—'extremist politics or movements, on one side or the other, have always led to a transference of support on the part of the steadying and balancing elements of the centre'.[183]

This was, of course, in sharp contrast to Sammy Finer's later characterization of British politics in terms of the adversary 'model'.[184] Finer claimed that, since 1945 especially, British public life had been conducted as a stand-up fight between two adversaries for the favour of the lookers-on. In a famous passage, he commented that 'the alternation of first one major party and then another over the last generation, but particularly since 1964 when the polarization between the Labour and Conservative parties became far more pronounced than before is on the whole inimical to the good conduct of the nation's affairs'.[185] In a thesis quite

---

[180] R. Rose, *Do Parties Make A Difference?* (London, Macmillan, [2nd ed.] 1984).
[181] Ibid. p. 146.
[182] R. Bassett, *The Essentials of Parliamentary Democracy* (second and revised edition, with an introduction by Michael Oakeshott, London, Frank Cass 1964), p. 76.
[183] Ibid. p. 77.
[184] S. E. Finer, ed., *Adversary Politics and Electoral Reform*.
[185] Ibid., Chapter 1, p. 12.

contradictory to that formulated by Rose, Finer argued that 'since Party A alternates with Party B, the left of centre policies of the first alternate with the right of centre policies of the second so that, according to the distance between these two poles of policy, so the discontinuity in national policies over time is exaggerated'.[186] Finer's work was important in that it possibly misled some people in Britain, and rather more abroad, into accepting what Rose has successfully demonstrated to be false. However, it was a useful reminder that party politics in Britain had two distinct faces—adversary rhetoric and the accommodation to reality which public policy analysts such as Rose charted.

A much more recent and more rigorously comparative approach to the role of parties in public policy is the work of so-called 'spatial theorists' such as Ian Budge. With David Robertson and various international colleagues, he has analysed the spatial competition between parties (following Anthony Downs' pioneering work in his book, *An Economic Theory of Democracy*). Budge co-authored (with Richard Hofferbert) an important 1990 article on American party platforms[187] which demonstrated the existence of strong links between post-war election platforms and governmental outputs. In a large comparative research project covering 19 democracies, often cited outside the United Kingdom, Budge, Robertson and Hearl (collaborating with an international team of researchers) analysed the electoral programmes and manifestos of parties in liberal democracies since the Second World War. The project has produced much data on the nature of differences between parties in a wide range of countries, particularly in terms of the meaning of Left and Right in party politics and the possibilities of grouping parties into 'families' of parties.[188] The project is unusual in the context of British studies of political parties in being both comparative and quantitative. Budge's theoretical work has drawn on this empirical data and he has formulated a spatial theory of party competition. The theory aims to predict party behaviour when parties have to decide on policy in the absence of reliable information

---

[186] S. E. Finer, ed., *Adversary Politics and Electoral Reform*, pp. 13–14.

[187] I. Budge and R. I. Hofferbert, 'Mandates and Policy Outputs: US Party Platforms and Federal Expenditures', *American Political Science Review*, 84 (1990), 111–31.

[188] I. Budge, D. Robertson and D. Earl, eds., *Ideology, Strategy and Party Change: Spatial Analyses of Post-War Election Programmes in Nineteen Democracies* (Cambridge, Cambridge University Press, 1987).

about the effects of those decisions on voting—essentially using cognitive theories to explain behaviour.[189] Budge has also made important contributions to the study of coalition formation (in work with Hans Keman,[190] with M. J. Laver,[191] and with Hans-Dieter Klingermann and Richard Hofferbert).[192] This work reflects a desire to address the bias in party studies which has emphasized the behaviour of parties in elections rather than in government. In his work with Hans Keman, it is argued that parties are more significant actors than often suggested and might be *the* significant actors within parliamentary democracies.[193]

Party competition and coalition behaviour have also been the subject of two other British studies which have received some international recognition. Thus, in 1976 David Robertson published *A Theory of Party Competition* in which he constructed a model or empirical theory of the party competitive process. The essence of his theory was a critique of some of the weaknesses in Downs' theory of party competition—for example, he argued that it is not true that there can never be a cost involved on taking up a vote-maximizing position.[194] Geoffrey Pridham's work on a theoretical framework for coalitions is also a rather 'deviant' case in terms of British studies. Thus, he has proposed a multi-dimensional inductive framework for the analysis of coalitions, 'revolving strictly around the role of political parties as coalitions actors within the context of their party systems'.[195]

Minor parties

All of the works cited so far have been concerned with established mass parties, mostly in Britain. There have, however been a few studies of

---

[189] I. Budge, 'A New Spatial Theory of Party Competition: Uncertainty, Ideology and Policy Equilibria Viewed Comparatively and Temporally', *British Journal of Political Science*, 24 (1994), 443–67.

[190] I. Budge and H. Keman, *Parties and Democracy. Coalition Formation and Government Functioning in Twenty States* (Oxford, Oxford University Press, 1990), p. 189.

[191] M. J. Laver and I. Budge, eds., *Party Policy and Government Coalitions* (New York, St Martin's Press, 1992).

[192] H.-D. Klingermann, R. Hofferbert and I. Budge, *Parties, Policies and Democracy* (Boulder, Col., Westview Press, 1994).

[193] Budge and Keman, *Parties and Democracy. Coalition Formation and Government Functioning in Twenty States*.

[194] D. Robertson, *A Theory of Party Competition* (London, John Wiley, 1976).

[195] G. Pridham, ed., *Coalition Behaviour in Theory and Practice* (Cambridge, Cambridge University Press, 1986).

transient or minor parties. In the former category, the most notable study is the volume on the Social Democratic Party by Ivor Crewe and Anthony King—*SDP: The Birth, Life and Death of the Social Democratic Party*.[196] This is an extremely detailed and perceptive account of the SDP over its seven-year history and contains a wealth of information on the trajectory of a transient political party. However it tends to adhere to the British empirical tradition of party studies. In contrast, the work of Wolfgang Rüdig, John Curtice, and Mark Franklin (formerly) at Strathclyde University, on Green Parties, draws more directly on theories of party systems—such as Lipset and Rokkan's work on cleavages cited earlier—and more recent theoretical literature on new cleavages in society. They have explored the question of whether Green Parties are merely 'flash parties' or are likely to be a more enduring phenomenon. Breaking with the dominant British tradition, they test a number of plausible theories predicting relative stability or relative volatility of Green Party support.[197] They concluded that 'conventional expectations that Green voting would gain durability from being grounded in a stable, value-based cleavage are hardly fulfilled in Western Europe', but suggested that the Greens could capitalize on the possible emergence of an ecological cleavage in society.[198]

The study of nationalist parties in Britain also deserves some mention. Of particular note is work by Jack Brand, James Mitchell and James Kellas. All of these studies have contributed to the stock of knowledge on the Scottish National Party and the nature of Scottish nationalism.[199] The recent work by Brand *et al.* is especially interesting in that it sets the empirical data in the context of theoretical approaches to the study of relative deprivation, identity and new social movements.

Social movements

There has been relatively little interest in social movements by British political scientists, in contrast to their European and American

---

[196] I. Crewe and A. King, *SDP: The Birth, Life and Death of the Social Democratic Party* (Oxford, Oxford University Press, 1995).

[197] M. Franklin and W. Rüdig, 'On the Durability of Green Politics, Evidence from the 1989 European Election Study', *Comparative Political Studies*, 28 (1995), 417.

[198] Ibid., pp. 433–34. See also W. Rüdig, M. N. Franklin and L. G. Bennie, 'Up and Down with the Greens. Ecology and Party Politics in Britain 1989–92', *Electoral Studies*, 15 (1996), 1–20.

[199] For example see, J. Brand, *The Nationalist Movement in Scotland* (London, Routledge, 1978); J. Kellas, *The Scottish Political System* (London, Cambridge University Press, 1973); and especially, J. Brand, J. Mitchell, and P. Surridge, 'Social Constituency and Ideological Profile: Scottish Nationalism in the 1990s', *Political Studies*, 42 (1994), 616–29.

colleagues. Indeed, the whole question of political participation outside institutional structures such as parties and interest groups is seriously under-researched, making it difficult to find good, systematic, empirical (let alone theoretical) studies of participation. One such exception is the 1992 study of *Political Participation and Democracy in Britain*, by Parry, Moyser and Day.[200] They conducted a survey of 1,600 people in England, Scotland and Wales as well as an additional 1,600 men and women and 300 leaders in selected and contrasting local communities. The pioneering study produced a wealth of data on citizen participation—the extent of citizen activity, the social profile of participation, and the impact of participation—and concluded that Britain was a long way from participatory democracy

The Parry *et al.* project was, however, not specifically on social movements. The latter were the focus, however, of Wolfgang Rüdig's comparative research on anti-nuclear movements. He has argued that the most fruitful approaches for the analysis of social movements are likely to be a reinterpretation of relative deprivation theories, combined with resource mobilization theories.[201] He has also conducted comparative research on peace and ecology movements in Western Europe, analysing commonalities and differences across national boundaries in terms of cycles of protest, their social basis, the structures of movements and their forms of action and political impact.[202] Together with James Mitchell, Jeremy Chapman and Philip Lowe, he has also reviewed the study of social movements by social scientists in Britain. Their conclusions echo the theme of this chapter. Thus, they comment that 'while such research elsewhere has been set in an established framework of social movement

---

[200] G. Parry, G. Moyser and N. Day, *Political Participation and Democracy in Britain* (Cambridge, Cambridge University Press, 1992).

[201] W. Rüdig, *Anti-Nuclear Movements: A World Survey of Opposition to Nuclear Energy* (London, Longman, 1990), p. 50.

[202] W. Rüdig, 'Peace and Ecology Movements on Western Europe', *West European Politics*, 11 (1988), 26–39. See also, W. Rüdig, 'Maintaining a Low Profile: The Anti-nuclear Movement and the British State', in H. Flam, ed., *States and Anti-Nuclear Movements* (Edinburgh, Edinburgh University Press, 1994), pp. 70–100. W. Rüdig, 'Between Moderation and Marginalisation: Environmental Radicalism in Britain', in B. Taylor, ed., *Ecological Resistance Movements* (Albany, NY, State University of New York Press, 1995). W Rüdig, 'Nuclear Power: An International Comparison of Public Protest in the USA, Britain, France and West Germany', in R. Williams and S. Mills, eds., *Public Acceptance of New Technologies* (London, Croom Helm, 1986), pp. 364–417. W. Rüdig, 'Between Moderation and Marginalisation: Environmental Radicalism in Britain', in B. R. Taylor, ed., *Ecological Resistance Movements: The Global Emergence of Radical and Popular Environmentalism* (Albany, NY, State University of New York Press, 1995), pp. 219–240.

theory, in Britain disparate accounts have rarely been integrated into a more generalised theory . . . the reasons for this may partly lie in the atheoretical inclination of much of British social sciences'.[203] Few political science exceptions are identified in their review, although Jack Brand's study of Scottish nationalism is noted as being unique amongst studies of nationalism for its use of social movement theory.[204]

While Rüdig has concentrated on social movements in Western Europe, Joe Foweraker has focused on social movements in Spain[205] and, more recently, Latin America. As with Rüdig's work, Foweraker is unusual in that he combines a theoretical perspective with empirical work.[206] He emphasizes the overwhelming presence of the state in the political economics of Latin America, which creates a specific political and cultural context for social movement activity.[207] This, he argues, is quite different to the context of most social movement theory. Thus, he has made an important contribution to the study of social movements on societies where the problems facing citizens are not post-industrial, but where the basic issue is how to consume enough to survive.

Interestingly, sociologists in Britain are currently engaged in a debate about *their* contribution to the study of social movements. In a recent review in *Sociological Review*, Paul Bagguley has suggested that 'there is no institutionalised sociology of social movements in Britain comparable to those of mainland Europe and N. America'.[208] However, he also reports that the recently formed British Sociological Association group on Protest and Social Movements had nearly 100 members by early 1997. Also, his review possibly underestimates the large volume of work conducted by Chris Rootes.[209] In political science, British scholars have

---

[203] W. Rüdig, J. Mitchell, J. Chapman and P. D. Lowe, 'Social Movements and The Social Sciences in Britain', in D. Rucht, ed., *Research and Social Movements. The State of the Art in Western Europe* (Frankfurt, Campus Verlag, 1991), pp. 121–48.

[204] Brand, *The Nationalist Movement in Scotland*.

[205] J. Foweraker, *Making Democracy in Spain. Grass-Roots Struggle in the South 1955–75* (Cambridge, Cambridge University Press, 1989).

[206] For example see J. Foweraker, *Theorizing Social Movements* (London, Pluto Press, 1995).

[207] Ibid. p. 31.

[208] See P. Bagguley 'Beyond Political Sociology? Developments in the Sociology of Social Movements', *Sociological Review*, 45 (1997), p. 147 and C. Rootes, 'The future of social movement research: reply to Bagguley', unpublished paper (1998), Centre for the Study of Social Movements, University of Kent at Canterbury.

[209] C. Rootes, 'The New Politics and the New Social Movements; accounting for British exceptionalism', *European Journal of Political Research*, 22 (1992), 171–191. C. Rootes, 'The Political System, the Green Party and the Environmental Movement in Britain', *International Journal of Sociology and Social Policy*, 12 (1992), 216–29. C. Rootes and H. Davis, eds., *A New Europe? Social Change and Political Transformation* (London, UCL Press, 1994). C. Rootes,

been rather active within the European Consortium for Political Research in recent years and so both sociology and political science might be set to make a bigger contribution in the future.

Conclusion: Does the 'haze of common knowledge' obscure analysis of power?

The central paradox in reviewing the contribution of British political scientists to our understanding of these intermediary institutions is that (with the exception of social movements) both the number of scholars and the output has been considerable yet the international impact has been relatively modest. Why should this be so?

Two explanations seem plausible. First, with a few notable exceptions, the centre of gravity of these studies has coincided with the centre of gravity of British political science as a whole—it is largely atheoretical in its research style. Bill Mackenzie's advice in the 1950s—that theorizing should await robust and systematic empirical evidence—has been followed to a fault by most of us! Those British scholars who have deviated from this research style have, almost without exception, gained experience outside Britain or have received much of their early training abroad. Working with overseas scholars and being involved in cross-national projects seems to have encouraged them to be less risk averse and to take the chance of theorizing, generalizing and developing new concepts and approaches.

A second possible explanation is that studies in these three fields have tended to focus on *activities* (of groups and social movements) or on *office-holding* (parties) and have been much less interested in power as a concept. Thus we know a great deal about the organization and activity of the pressure-group system—essentially about *tactics* of influence. In contrast we know relatively little about the effects that this activity has

'Introduction', in Rootes and Davis, eds., pp. 1–12. C. Rootes, (with Richardson) ed., *The Green Challenge: the Development of Green Parties in Europe* (London and New York, Routledge, 1995). C. Rootes, 'Britain: Greens in a Cold Climate', in Richardson and Rootes, eds., *The Green Challenge: the Development of Green Parties in Europe*, pp. 66–90. C. Rootes, 'Environmental consciousness, institutional structures and political competition in the formation and development of Green parties?', in Richardson and Rootes, eds., *The Green Challenge: the Development of Green Parties in Europe*, pp. 232–252. C. Rootes, 'A New Class? The Higher Educated and the New Politics', in L. Mahew, ed., *Social Movements and Social Classes: the Future of Collective Action* (London, Sage Publications, 1995), pp. 220–235. C. Rootes, 'Shaping Collective Action: Structure, Contingency and Knowledge', in R. Edmondson, ed., *The Political Context of Collective Action* (London, Routledge, 1997).

on outcomes in terms of public policy or the distribution of power in society. Similarly, the weight of party studies has tended to be concerned with parties as organizations and the mechanics of office holding, with little on the place of parties in the system of government as a whole. Thus, the power dimension is largely absent from many of the party studies.

Quite why these two traits should have developed is difficult to explain. However, if this analysis is correct, it might explain a second paradox—namely that British political scientists in these fields are regarded as very expert and professional, yet their work tends not to have shaped how others have approached the subject. As scholars we know a lot about groups and parties, for example, but tend not to 'write up' that knowledge in a form that is easily transported across boundaries (either national or disciplinary). We ourselves, perhaps, find difficulty in escaping the 'haze of common knowledge' as Bill Mackenzie put it, in order to develop theories and concepts that can be utilized in different national contexts. Even when theories or concepts are suggested they tend to be underplayed, perhaps reflecting a British cultural trait for understatement. Moreover, their originators tend not to further develop and refine their own concepts over a long period of time.[210] Thus, British participation in international conferences, for example, is quite high, reflecting international respect for the knowledge base developed by British scholars, yet the theories and concepts which underpin those conference tend not to be British. Had we focused more on the key concept of power—and less on activity and organization—and had we been prepared to risk criticism for suggesting theories which might be proved wrong by subsequent empirical evidence, our studies might have had greater impact.

Acknowledgements. In preparing this chapter, I benefited greatly from advice from the following: Tony Barker, Jack Brand, Keith Dowding, Geoffrey Dudley, Wyn Grant, David Judge, Tony King, Peter Mair, William Maloney, Sonia Mazey, Mick Moran, Wolfgang Rüdig and Paul Whiteley. I owe a special debt to Pat Seyd and Phil Daniels and, above all, to Richard Rose, whose knowledge of British Political Science in its international context is unmatched. Finally, I wish to thank the Editors of the volume for their advice, help and encouragement. Responsibility for the (near-impossible!) task of selection and analysis of material included in the review remains, however, with me.

---

[210] An interesting exception is the work on the network concept by Rod Rhodes, who has consistently developed the concept over many years. It has, as a result, become more 'transportable'.

8: Electoral Systems, Elections and Public Opinion

WILLIAM L. MILLER

Throughout the twentieth century, the content and focus of British research on elections and public opinion was influenced by the changing political agenda of the day, but its quantity and style—and to some degree its focus as well—were more influenced by economic and technical factors: the increasing availability of funds and rapid advances in the technology of research particularly from the 1960s onwards. Economic and technical factors were positively related: serious public opinion research was almost impossibly expensive at the start of the century but advances in technology had made it relatively inexpensive by the end. Even the quality, the achievements, were as much a matter of technology and method as of substance: what distinguished the end of the century from the start was not so much the accumulated store of knowledge about electoral behaviour and public opinion, important though that was, but an ability to investigate quickly, easily, frequently, and in great detail which simply did not exist at the start. The ability to investigate is especially important because the study of political opinion and behaviour is at least as much about complexity, variation and change as about simplicity, uniformity and continuity. Mechanical laws of political behaviour, even recast as 'empirical regularities', have not only proved difficult to discover and prone to decay,[1] but also limited in scope and significance.

---

[1] A good example is the 'Cube Law' originally proposed to the Royal Commission on Electoral Systems by J. Parker Smith in 1909. It held that the proportions of seats won by parties in parliament were in the same ratio as the cubes of their popular votes. It depended upon the accidents of social and political polarization which no longer apply. See D. Butler,

A lost generation

Throughout the nineteenth century the great questions about elections in Britain were 'who should vote?', 'what power should their elected representatives wield?' and, to a much lesser extent, 'how should the votes be counted?' British writers made important contributions to the discussion of these questions but they approached them from a moral, philosophical, mathematical and, above all, a speculative, perspective. There was relatively little interest in hard facts, in evidence, in a scientific approach which was left to other, related disciplines such as public health or sociology. Thus, for example, the material condition of the poor was researched by increasingly scientific methods[2]—but not their political opinions. Public opinion, in the narrow sense of the opinions of the minority who enjoyed the right to vote could be inferred, inaccurately as we now know, from their votes; and public opinion in the broader sense of the whole adult population, including the vast majority excluded from the franchise, could be inferred, also inaccurately as we now know, from their propensity to riot and rebel. But it was not measured. To a degree that did not matter: the nineteenth-century public was governed, it did not participate in government so its propensity to riot and rebel was perhaps more important than its preferences.

But the twentieth century was the century of democracy in Britain. The supremacy of the elected House of Commons over the non-elected upper house was established in 1911 and universal adult suffrage was established, in principle, if not quite in practice, by 1918.[3] After that, Britain at least approximated a popular democracy for the first time in its history. Yet it was another 30 years before the first serious attempt was

---

British General Elections Since 1945 (Oxford, Basil Blackwell, 1989), pp. 50–52. The limited conditions in which it applies were set out in M. G. Kendall and A. Stuart, 'The law of cubic proportions in election results', *British Journal of Sociology*, 1 (1950), 183–97, although the article did not make for easy reading. More accessibly, see P. J. Taylor, G. Gudgin and R. J. Johnston, 'The geography of representation: a review of recent findings' in B. Grofman and A. Lijphart, eds., *Electoral Laws and their Consequences* (New York, Agathon, 1986).

[2] See H. Mayhew, *London Labour and the London Poor: A Cyclopaedia of the Condition and Earnings of Those that Will Work, Those that Cannot Work, and Those that Will Not Work* (London, Griffin and Bohn, 1862); C. Booth, *Life and Labour of the People of London*, (London, Macmillan, 17 vols, 1892–97); S. Rowntree, *Poverty: A Study of Town Life* (London, Longmans, 1902); or A. L. Bowley, *Livelihood and Poverty* (London, Bell, 1915).

[3] It was not until 1928 that legislation was passed which gave women the vote at the same age as men, namely 21.

made to investigate the political opinions and behaviour of this newly enfranchised public. For a generation after 1918, British students of elections clung to the moralistic and mathematical perspectives of the nineteenth century.[4] In the twentieth century there was less need to defend or advocate democracy in Britain itself than there had been in the nineteenth, but the rise of fascism on the Continent provided a new reason for debating democracy's virtues and vices. And within Britain the continuing use of several different electoral systems helped to encourage some debate about the proper mechanisms for realizing mass democracy. But a scientific approach, focused on the search for empirical evidence rather than abstract reasoning, hardly got under way until after the Second World War.

That was certainly the view of those who were most active in the immediate post-war years. Writing in 1953, David Butler lamented that 'the British electoral system has been much neglected in academic study . . . [and] too largely left to propagandists in the weary argument over proportional representation . . . *an electoral bibliography is astonishingly void of solid fare'* [my emphasis]. Indeed, he added,

> this absence of academic attention perhaps helps to account for the fact that on the few occasions when the electoral system has been the subject of parliamentary debate there has been so little informed factual comment; *discussion has not been so much abstract . . . as vague* [my emphasis again].[5]

Some of those most involved in advocating proportional representation agreed with him. Lakeman and Lambert noted, in 1955, that

> during the further century that has elapsed since [the time of J. S. Mill] there has been a vast extension of parliamentary government but comparatively little study of its electoral foundations. John H. Humphreys'

---

[4] Even J. F. S. Ross for example could not avoid the temptation to classify electoral systems into what he called the 'civilized' (proportionate) and the 'uncivilized' (majoritarian) and then devote much space to advocating 'reforms'. However, he also did a great deal of objective statistical analysis, including postal surveys to analyse the age, education and occupation of MPs; statistical analyses of patterns of contest; and a quantitative study of the exaggerative properties of the British electoral system, using graphical methods which were developed very much later by the American Douglas Rae and others. See J. F. S. Ross, *Parliamentary Representation* (London, Eyre and Spottiswood, 1943); and J. F. S. Ross, *Elections and Electors: Studies in Democratic Representation* (London, Eyre and Spottiswood, 1955).

[5] D. Butler, *The Electoral System in Britain since 1918* (Oxford, Oxford University Press, 1953), 'Introduction'.

Proportional Representation, published in 1911, remains the only comprehensive work of its kind produced in Britain.[6]

The same was true for research into electoral behaviour and public
opinion. Many of the concepts on which British and American public
opinion research later focused—as well as the methods it used—were
foreshadowed by Graham Wallas at the turn of the century. His *Human
Nature in Politics*, first published in 1908, was reprinted or reissued
another nine times over the next 40 years, which was both a testimony
to the innovative concepts that Wallas had put forward in 1908 and a
reflection of the discipline's lack of empirical vitality. The foreword
contributed to the 1948 edition, extravagantly claimed it as 'the most
original and important contribution to be made to political thought by
an Englishman in this century' but then lamented the lack of 'any
notable progress' since 1908.[7]

Wallas attacked the 'rationalist fallacy' in political thinking. While he
himself believed in the virtue of 'enlightened self interest', he regarded it
as something unnatural, which could be attained only by 'conscious and
systematic effort'. He wished to refocus the attention of political
scientists onto 'such political impulses as personal affection, fear,
ridicule, the desire for property', and onto such aspects of institutions
as 'symbols' and 'recognition'. Having been particularly impressed by
the use of quantitative methods in sociological surveys of poverty in
Britain, he advocated the replacement of 'qualitative' by 'quantitative'
methods in the study of politics as well. Paradoxically, however, his own
book was a literary plea for other people to use quantitative methods.

It was not until after the second world war that Wallas' ideas were
put into practice.[8] The founding of *Political Studies* in 1953 with a mission
statement that committed the journal to the new behaviouralist
approach, followed by the *British Journal of Political Science* in 1971,
and *Electoral Studies* in 1982, indicated a belated ambition to do so.
The initial spread of electronic computing in the late 1950s, the Wilson

---

[6] E. Lakeman and J. D. Lambert, *Voting in Democracies: A Study of Majority and Proportional Electoral Systems* (London, Faber & Faber, 1955), p. 23. Humphreys served from 1905 to 1946 as Secretary of the Proportional Representation Society and published two important books which were both (internationally) comparative and factual: J. H. Humphreys, *Proportional Representation: A Study in the Methods of Election* (London, Methuen, 1911); and J. H. Humphreys, *Practical Aspects of Electoral Reform* (London, P. S. King, 1923).

[7] G. Wallas, *Human Nature in Politics* (London, Constable, [4th ed.] 1948), p. xiii.

[8] Wallas was one of only two Britishers (the other was Laski) to be footnoted in Michigan University's classic survey study, *The American Voter*.

Government's creation of the Social Science Research Council (SSRC), later the Economic and Social Research Council (ESRC) in the 1960s, and the information revolution in the 1980s and 1990s provided the funding and the technology.

At the same time, the world outside Britain increasingly attracted the attention of British electoral and public opinion researchers. In contrast to the first half of the century, there were a lot more elections, and a lot more publics whose political opinions and electoral behaviour were worth researching. Western Europe was no longer dominated by fascism, the decolonization of the British Empire produced a rash of sometimes short-lived democracies that had a special interest for British researchers and, as the century drew to a close, democratization in southern and eastern Europe produced new opportunities for electoral and public opinion research on Britain's doorstep.

Electoral systems

British authors writing about electoral systems, especially the British electoral system, have always found it difficult to avoid the feeling that they were addressing a Royal Commission on reform.[9] The first detailed and dispassionate account of the new fully democratic system set up in 1918 was provided 35 years later by David Butler.[10] He refocused attention away from moralistic assessments and onto a factual description of the origins and workings of the system. Much later, Vernon Bogdanor extended Butler's work on the origins of the system by tracing its development back into the nineteenth century and Robert Blackburn updated the description to the end of the twentieth.[11] Although both slipped back into a more moralistic posture on occasion, they retained Butler's concern for detailed and objective description.

Earlier, Enid Lakeman and James Lambert had tried to combat what they termed 'the disposition among some politicians, often based on prejudice and ignorance, to rest satisfied with their institutions merely

---

[9] See, for example, S. E. Finer, ed., *Adversary Politics and Electoral Reform* (London, Wigram, 1975); developed further in S. E. Finer, *The Changing British Party System 1945–1979*, (Washington, American Enterprise Institute, 1980).

[10] Butler, *The Electoral System in Britain since 1918*.

[11] V. Bogdanor, *The People and the Party System: The Referendum and Electoral Reform in British Politics* (Cambridge, Cambridge University Press, 1981); V. Bogdanor, *Multi-party Politics and the Constitution* (Cambridge, Cambridge University Press, 1983); R. Blackburn, *The Electoral System in Britain* (London, Macmillan, 1995).

because they have acquired the sanctity of tradition', by pointing to infrequent but totally inexcusable failures of the British first-past-the-post (FPTP) electoral system—at the 1886 British election and the 1948 South African—when the minority won even in an essentially two-party (or two-coalition) contest with grave consequences for the state in each case. They sought to inform the British about the alternatives by reviewing the operation of different electoral systems in many parts of the world, including a dozen European and Scandinavian countries, Ireland, Malta, and all the major Commonwealth Countries. From this review they deduced that proportional representation (PR) systems did not lead to an 'inordinate multiplicity of parties or to unstable government'. They recognized a correlation between PR systems and such tendencies, but argued that 'in no country previously free from them have these disadvantages developed as a result of changing to a proportionate system'.[12] That was a more complex, and more significant, conclusion than could easily be drawn from a statistical analysis based simply upon correlations.

British authors were notably sensitive to the importance of technical details, national idiosyncrasies and historical settings, illustrated for example in *Democracy and Elections: Electoral Systems and their Consequences* which was jointly written by 12 British, and one former British, authors.[13] They were clearly as interested in the exception as in the norm. Most chapters focused on the operation of an electoral system in a single country and, although important general tendencies associated with different kinds of electoral system were uncovered, the authors urged 'humility in generalising', warned 'that one should be sceptical about attributing fixed qualities to electoral systems', and suggested that electoral systems had different effects at different times—more when a party system was in the process of formation, for example, and less at other times. For the authors, these were more important conclusions than the general tendencies that they uncovered.

---

[12] E. Lakeman and J. D. Lambert, *Voting in Democracies: A Study of Majority and Proportional Electoral Systems* (London, Faber & Faber, 1955). Later editions were published with a revised title and solely under Lakeman's name: E. Lakeman, *How Democracies Vote: A Study of Majority and Proportional Electoral Systems* (London, Faber & Faber, [3rd ed. 1970, 4th ed. 1974]). Conclusions quoted from pp. 226–7 of the 1974 edition.

[13] V. Bogdanor and D. Butler, eds., *Democracy and Elections: Electoral Systems and their Consequences* (Cambridge, Cambridge University Press, 1983). Other comparative studies of electoral systems by British authors include A. McLaren Carstairs, *A Short History of Electoral Systems in Western Europe* (London, Allen & Unwin, 1980); and R. A. Newland, *Comparative Electoral Systems* (London, Arthur McDougall Fund, 1982).

Other volumes in the same style, also co-edited by David Butler, although with a more multi-national team of authors, looked in similar depth at the use of referendums around the world.[14]

British authors wrote extensively, and well, from a moral, philosophical and historical perspective. Their work was clearly about the real world, with all its peculiarities and problems. They wrote much less from a purely abstract analytic perspective. The most comprehensive cross-national comparative statistical analyses of electoral systems and their effects were not written by British authors.[15] Nonetheless there were some useful British contributions in this area. In a series of short but devastatingly pointed statistical analyses, Richard Rose drew attention to the proportionality achieved by plurality systems of election, the disproportionality that occurred under some nominally proportional systems,[16] and the lack of correlation between electoral systems and economic performance.[17] Naturally enough, there was a particular interest in statistical analysis of the arithmetical consequences of Britain's 'first past the post' plurality system in which the location of votes was as important as their number, and an interest more generally in the spatial organization of elections.[18]

[14] D. Butler and A. Ranney, eds., *Referendums: A Comparative Study of Practice and Theory* (Washington, DC, American Enterprise Institute, 1978); and *Referendums Around the World: The Growing Use of Direct Democracy* (London, Macmillan, 1994).

[15] The most influential cross-national statistical analyses of electoral systems include D. Rae, *The Political Consequences of Electoral Laws* (New Haven, Conn., Yale University Press, 1967); G. Bingham Powell, *Contemporary Democracies: Participation, Stability and Violence* (Cambridge, Mass., Harvard University Press, 1982); R. Taagepera and M. S. Shugart, *Seats and Votes: The Effects and Determinants of Electoral Systems* (New Haven, Conn., Yale University Press, 1989); and A. Lijphart, *Electoral Systems and Party Systems: A Study of Twenty-Seven Democracies 1945–1990* (Oxford, Oxford University Press, 1994)—none of them by British authors. Interestingly, in contrast to Lakeman and Lambert who criticized the 'sanctity of tradition' which disposed British politicians against changing their electoral system, Taagepera and Shugart warned that the costs of transition might exceed the benefits to be gained from switching to an alternative system.

[16] R. Rose, 'Elections and electoral systems: choices and alternatives' in Bogdanor and Butler, *Democracy and Elections*, and 'Electoral systems: a question of degree or of principle?' in A. Lijphart and B. Grofman, eds., *Choosing an Electoral System: Issues and Alternatives* (New York, Praeger, 1984).

[17] R. Rose, *What are the Economic Consequences of Proportional Representation?* (London, Electoral Reform Society, 1992).

[18] For example P. J. Taylor and G. Gudgin, 'The myth of non-partisan cartography: a study of electoral biases in the English Boundary Commissions', *Urban Studies*, 13 (1976), 13–25; G. Gudgin and P. J. Taylor, *Seats, Votes and the Spatial Organisation of Elections* (London, Pion, 1979); R. J. Johnston, *Political, Electoral and Spatial Systems: An Essay in Political Geography* (Oxford, Oxford University Press, 1979).

Mathematical approaches could be more usefully applied to the study of electoral systems than to the study of electoral behaviour.[19] Indeed, purely mathematical treatments of electoral systems enjoyed a resurgence of popularity towards the end of the century under the title of 'public choice theory', and Iain McLean could claim that, of the 'two economists [who] wrote the works which are the starting-points for all modern discussions of the problem', one was the British economist Duncan Black.[20] Black rediscovered the lost conclusions of an earlier British mathematician, Charles Dodgson (better known under his pseudonym, Lewis Carroll, as the author of *Alice in Wonderland*), including the deceptively simple but important paradox that even though each individual voter can rank three policy options in order of his or her preference, the electorate as a whole may be unable to place them in a clearly definable preference order by means of majority voting.[21]

Similarly, moral and philosophical approaches also remained relevant. Elections were a *principal*, and certainly the *distinctive*, mechanism of democracy. The study of electoral systems was often based upon implicit models of democracy, and it could therefore be useful to make these models explicit.[22] But more than that, British writers were particularly good at seamlessly combining philosophical and historical perspectives to produce accessible and thought-provoking discussions of actually existing electoral systems. In one short book, W. J. M. Mackenzie reviewed not just such standard academic issues as party proportional representation, but also the very practical problems of communal representation, recognition and non-recognition of political parties, the 'exclusion of frivolous candidates', 'administration and adjudication', intimidation, corruption and the influence of money and then developed an influential 'pathology' of elections—'muddled

---

[19] For a recent British oriented review of the many approaches to the study of electoral systems see A. Reeve and A. Ware, *Electoral Systems: a Comparative and Theoretical Introduction* (London, Routledge, 1992).

[20] The other was the American, Kenneth Arrow, whose most celebrated book *Social Choice and Individual Values* (New York, Wiley, 1951) was published a few years earlier than Duncan Black's *The Theory of Committees and Elections* (Cambridge, Cambridge University Press, 1958), although after many of Black's articles had already appeared.

[21] Carroll had himself rediscovered the lost conclusions of earlier writers. See I. McLean, *Public Choice* (Oxford, Basil Blackwell, 1987), p. 10.

[22] As in D. Held, *Models of Democracy* (Oxford, Polity Press, 1987).

elections', 'stolen elections', 'made elections' and 'elections by acclamation'.[23]

Mackenzie's interest in the influence of money on elections was later pursued in depth by Michael Pinto-Duschinsky whose research showed, amongst much else, that the British Labour Party was much less disadvantaged than previously thought, once proper account was taken of implicit subsidies from the state (including free time on radio and television) and from trade unions and their officials;[24] and by Ron Johnston whose analysis of constituency expenditures showed that although money went particularly 'to places where victory was [already] probable or possible', 'in many contexts, one party could gain a vote advantage [at a British election] by spending more'.[25]

Elections

There is an important difference between the study of electoral behaviour and the study of elections themselves. The most distinctively British contribution was the founding, in 1945, by R. B. McCallum and A. Readman of what later became known as the 'Nuffield Series' of election studies,[26] subsequently continued by H. G. Nicholas in 1950,[27] and thereafter by David Butler—at first alone, and later with successive co-authors Richard Rose, Anthony King, Michael Pinto-Duschinsky and

---

[23] W. J. M. Mackenzie, *Free Elections: An Elementary Textbook* (London, Allen & Unwin, 1958). Other notable examples include P. Pulzer, *Political Representation and Elections in Britain* (London, Allen & Unwin, 1967); A. H. Birch, *Concepts and Theories of Modern Democracy* (London, Routledge, 1993) and his earlier *Representative and Responsible Government* (London, Allen & Unwin, 1964) and *Representation* (London, Macmillan, 1972); or J. Lively, *Democracy* (Oxford, Basil Blackwell, 1975). For a later discussion of the pathology of elections see A. Pravda, 'Elections in Communist Party States' in G. Hermet, R. Rose and A. Rouquie, *Elections Without Choice* (London, Macmillan, 1978).

[24] M. Pinto-Duschinsky, *British Political Finance 1830–1980* (Washington, American Enterprise Institute, 1981); updated in 'Trends in British Party Funding 1983–87', *Parliamentary Affairs*, 42 (1989), 197–212.

[25] R. J. Johnston, *Money and Votes: Constituency Campaign Spending and Election Results* (London, Croom Helm, 1987).

[26] R. B. McCallum and A Readman, *The British General Election of 1945* (Oxford, Oxford University Press, 1947). For an account of the origins of this series and a brief but insightful review of changing election campaigns over the next half century see D. Butler's 'McCallum Lecture 1997: Elections, elections' (Oxford, November 1997).

[27] H. G. Nicholas, *The British General Election of 1950* (London, Macmillan, 1951).

Dennis Kavanagh.[28] The series included regular statistical appendices by Michael Steed and later John Curtice. Many others contributed specialist chapters. Indeed the full list of authors and contributors to this series reads almost (if not quite) like a list of 'who was who' in the study of British elections.

The format established early on included a brief history of the preceding parliament; an original 'insider' account of each party's preparations and campaign (Anthony King initiated an elaborate procedure of élite interviewing and cross-checking for this); an analysis of candidates' backgrounds; and reviews of the mass media, the published opinion polls, and the private polls commissioned by the parties.[29] Frequently there were special chapters on the campaign in selected constituencies or in the minority national areas (Scotland, Wales, Northern Ireland) and always a comprehensive statistical appendix which included an analysis of constituency voting patterns, and of the operation of the electoral system.

McCallum's original aim had been modest: to prevent the growth of myths about past elections by documenting as much as possible at the time. Any one volume in the series would have been valuable, but its continuity and uniformity made the series much more than the sum of its parts, particularly because trends and comparisons could be made, easily, by the reader even if they were not made by the authors[30]—

---

[28] D. Butler, *The British General Election of 1951* (London, Macmillan, 1952); D. Butler, *The British General Election of 1955* (London, Macmillan, 1955); D. Butler and R. Rose, *The British General Election of 1959* (London, Macmillan, 1960); D. Butler and A. King, *The British General Election of 1964* (London, Macmillan, 1965); D. Butler and A. King, *The British General Election of 1966* (London, Macmillan, 1966); D. Butler and M. Pinto-Duschinsky, *The British General Election of 1970* (London, Macmillan, 1971); D. Butler and D. Kavanagh, *The British General Election of February 1974* (London, Macmillan, 1974); D. Butler and D. Kavanagh, *The British General Election of 1979* (London, Macmillan, 1980); D. Butler and D. Kavanagh, *The British General Election of 1983* (London, Macmillan, 1984); D. Butler and D. Kavanagh, *The British General Election of 1987* (London, Macmillan, 1988); D. Butler and D. Kavanagh, *The British General Election of 1992* (London, Macmillan, 1992); D. Butler and D. Kavanagh, *The British General Election of 1997* (London, Macmillan, 1997). Although they contain very little discursive text, the various publications of F. W. S. Craig contain an enormous amount of tabular information about British elections, much of which should count as 'analysis'. See for example F. W. S. Craig, *British Electoral Facts 1832–1987* (Dartmouth, Parliamentary Research Services, 1989).

[29] Private polling was also reviewed in F. Teer and J. D. Spence, *Political Opinion Polls* (London, Hutchinson, 1973)—one of the many books written by British commercial pollsters themselves.

[30] Some trends from the series were highlighted in D. Butler, *British General Elections since 1945* (Oxford, Basil Blackwell, 1989).

amongst them, the changing importance of radio and television relative to each other and to the press, the sudden lurch towards partisan imbalance in the press which lasted from the 1970s until the mid 1990s, the changing imbalance of party election expenditures, the slight evidence of an 'underdog effect' by which the party in the lead in opinion polls during a campaign tended to lose ground at the end, the 'decline of the marginals' which made the electoral system less sensitive to voter swings, the increasing regionalization of party support, and the trends in the social background of each party's MPs—in which the degree of continuity was perhaps more surprising than the degree of change.

It was a series that prompted imitation. There was an attempt at a specifically Scottish version by a team at Glasgow University which unfortunately ran to only one volume;[31] and a much more ambitious reconstruction by the Australian Neal Blewett of what a Nuffield election study of the two British elections of 1910 would have looked like—in which the impact of religion was so much more visible in the country and in parliament than in the Nuffield Series themselves.[32] Most ambitious of all, the American Enterprise Institute began a multi-national series of *At the Polls* volumes in 1975 with a study of the two British elections of 1974 which was edited by an American but largely written by former co-authors of the Nuffield Series.[33] It was followed by another 18 volumes in the next five years alone.[34] The format of these volumes was self-consciously different from that of the Nuffield Series—more interpretative, less factual, less comprehensive, less uniform from one volume to the next, more multi-authored, more concerned with electoral behaviour. But, at the same time, the new American Enterprise series was self-consciously inspired by the Nuffield example, as the introduction to *Britain at the Polls 1992* made clear. Under the general title

---

[31] S. B. Chrimes, ed., *The General Election in Glasgow: February 1950* (Glasgow, Glasgow University, 1950).

[32] N. Blewett, *The Peers, the Parties and the People: The General Elections of 1910* (London, Macmillan, 1972). For a less ambitious attempt in the same style see A. Thorpe, *The British General Election of 1931* (Oxford, Oxford University Press, 1991).

[33] H. R. Penniman, ed., *Britain at the Polls: The Parliamentary Elections of 1974* (Washington, American Enterprise Institute, 1976).

[34] A multi-national overview of the first five years of this series was provided by D. Butler, H. R. Penniman and A. Ranney, *Democracy At the Polls: A Comparative Study of Competitive National Elections* (Washington, American Enterprise Institute, 1981). Confusingly, the 1992 volume of *Britain at the Polls* claimed to be 'the first in a projected series on British general elections' although that really only reflected a change of publisher. See A. King *et al.*, *Britain at the Polls 1992* (Chatham, NJ, Chatham House, 1993) p. vii. The century ended with A. King *et al.*, *New Labour Triumphs: Britain at the Polls* (Chatham, NJ, Chatham House, 1998).

of *Political Communications*, a third series of election studies began with the General Election of 1979, focused particularly on the parties' campaign strategies (often written by the parties' spin-doctors themselves), on political advertising, and on the mass media.[35]

British authors also studied elections outside Britain. Peter Campbell's *French Electoral Systems and Elections since 1789*, first published in 1958, concluded that frequent changes of electoral system had done no permanent good.[36] At about the same time, rapid decolonization encouraged studies such as W. J. M. Mackenzie and Kenneth Robinson's *Five Elections in Africa*,[37] and David Butler's somewhat parochially-titled *Elections Abroad*[38] reviewed a heterogeneous set of four elections in France, Poland, Ireland and South Africa. Later Thomas Mackie and Richard Rose produced the standard reference work on international electoral history.[39] Stephen White became the leading authority on Soviet,[40] and then post-Soviet[41] elections—which he found shared

---

[35] R. M. Worcester and M. Harrop, eds., *Political Communications: The General Election Campaign of 1979* (London, Allen & Unwin, 1982): I. Crewe and M. Harrop, eds., *Political Communications: The General Election Campaign of 1983* (Cambridge, Cambridge University Press, 1986); I. Crewe and M. Harrop, eds., *Political Communications: The General Election Campaign of 1987* (Cambridge, Cambridge University Press, 1989); I. Crewe and B. Gosschalk, eds., *Political Communications: The General Election Campaign of 1992* (Cambridge, Cambridge University Press, 1995).

[36] P. Campbell, *French Electoral Systems and Elections since 1789* (London, Faber & Faber, 1958); later updated as A. Cole and P. Campbell, *French Electoral Systems and Elections since 1789* (Aldershot, Gower, 1989).

[37] W. J. M. Mackenzie and K. Robinson, eds., *Five Elections in Africa* (Oxford, Oxford University Press, 1960). It contained extensive accounts of two elections in Nigeria, as well as elections in Sierra Leone, Senegal and Kenya.

[38] D. Butler, ed., *Elections Abroad* (London, Macmillan, 1959). A much later example, in an updated version of the same style, was D. Butler and A. Ranney, eds., *Electioneering: A Comparative Study of Continuity and Change* (Oxford, Oxford University Press, 1992) which covered 14 countries and was written by a team of 17 scholars, including five from Britain.

[39] T. T. Mackie and R. Rose, *The International Almanac of Electoral History* (London, Macmillan, 1974).

[40] See for example, S. L. White, 'Non-competitive elections and national politics: the USSR Supreme Soviet elections of 1984', *Electoral Studies*, 4 (1985), 215–29; 'Reforming the Electoral System', in S. L. White, W. Joyce and H. Ticktin, eds., *Gorbachev and Gorbachevism* (London, Cass, 1989); 'The elections to the USSR Congress of People's Deputies March 1989', *Electoral Studies*, 9 (1990), 59–66; 'Democratising Eastern Europe: the elections of 1990', *Electoral Studies*, 9 (1990), 277–87; 'The Soviet elections of 1989: from acclamation to limited choice', *Coexistence*, 28 (1991), 513–59; or S. L. White *et al.*, 'El'tsin and his voters: popular support in the 1991 Russian presidential elections and after', *Europe-Asia Studies*, 46 (1994), 285–303.

[41] S. White, R. Rose and I. McAllister, *How Russia Votes* (Chatham, NJ, Chatham House, 1997).

many but not all of the characteristics of elections in established democracies, lacking the commitment to parties and the respect for electoral law that were common in the west.

Constituency electoral behaviour

The first-ever publication of official Census data by parliamentary constituencies, in 1966, made it relatively easy to relate constituency voting results to precise indicators of social background, and revealed a surprisingly strong relationship between constituency class and constituency voting—at least twice as strong as that implied by opinion surveys of individuals' voting behaviour. Viewed from a political behaviour perspective this might be described as the analysis of 'ecological', 'environmental', or 'contextual' influences upon individual voting choice.[42] But it had important consequences for the operation, and the changing operation, of a spatially-structured electoral system such as the British, and it helped to explain the increasing rather than decreasing insensitivity of the British electoral system to swings of votes.[43] Electoral geographers who had previously struggled with cumbersome methods of analysis which involved mapping different variables on different maps, now largely abandoned maps and switched to the new more direct methods of statistical analysis.[44]

Experience with the parliamentary volumes of the Census, published from 1966 onwards, encouraged a new look at the possibilities of linking earlier Census data to constituency votes. Although not without its

[42] W. L. Miller, 'Social class and party choice in England: a new analysis', *British Journal of Political Science*, 8 (1978), 257–84. Reprinted in D. Denver and G. Hands, eds., *Issues and Controversies in British Electoral Behaviour* (London, Harvester Wheatsheaf, 1992) pp. 118–29. For an account of the influence of the political and temporal context on individual voting choices see P. Norris, *British By-elections: The Volatile Electorate* (Oxford, Oxford University Press, 1990).

[43] J. Curtice and M. Steed, 'Electoral choice and the production of government: the changing operation of the electoral system in the United Kingdom since 1955', *British Journal of Political Science*, 12 (1982), 249–298. The significance of these findings, although not the findings themselves, was disputed in P. Norris and I. Crewe, 'Did the British marginals vanish? Proportionality and exaggeration in the British electoral system revisited', *Electoral Studies*, 13 (1994), 201–21.

[44] Both the potentiality and the severe limitations of map-based methods of analysis are evident in M. Kinnear, *The British Voter: An Atlas and Survey since 1885* (London, Batsford, 1968). The new alternatives to map-based methods were illustrated well—despite its title—by R. J. Johnston, C. J. Pattie and J. G. Allsopp, *The Electoral Map of Great Britain 1979–87: A Nation Dividing?* (London, Longman, 1988).

problems, this allowed Miller to trace the evolving relationship between social background—particularly class and religion—and political choice from 1918 to 1974 in a study that was soon extended back to 1885 by the American Kenneth Wald.[45]

The electoral behaviour of individuals

The basic principles of survey research were known to statisticians and sociologists before the start of the century though not applied to politics. In Britain they were used by Gallup[46] to forecast by-election results in the late 1930s, but they had to compete with the more anthropological techniques of Mass Observation, which recruited a large panel of volunteers to provide not only answers to standard survey-type questions, but also qualitative (what are now sometimes called 'in-depth') interviews, reports on chance conversations over-heard in public places, and direct observations of relevant behaviour.[47] During the 1945 election campaign, Gallup made the lead story in the *News Chronicle* with what proved to be a remarkably accurate fore-cast,[48] but it was not until the election of 1950 that British academics made serious use of survey research methods for a study of electoral motivation and behaviour.

In America, commercial survey researchers gained enormous publicity with their successful prediction of Roosevelt's re-election in 1936,

---

[45] W. L. Miller, *Electoral Dynamics in Britain since 1918*, (London, Macmillan Press, 1977). K. D. Wald, *Crosses on the Ballot: Patterns of British Voter Alignment since 1885* (Princeton, NJ, Princeton University Press, 1983). McAllister and Rose used similar methods in I. McAllister and R. Rose, *The Nationwide Competition for Votes: The 1983 British Election* (London, Pinter, 1984).

[46] British Gallup, originally known as BIPO (British Institute of Public Opinion) was founded in 1937 by H. Durant, just two years after American Gallup. See R. M. Worcester, *British Public Opinion: A Guide to the History and Methodology of Political Opinion Polling* (Oxford, Basil Blackwell, 1991) p. 3. See also G. Gallup, ed., *The Gallup International Public Opinion Polls, Great Britain 1937–75* (New York, Random House, 1976) in two volumes, which contains many of the early British findings, covering for example, public attitudes to the Munich settlement and the trustworthiness of Adolf Hitler.

[47] Mass Observation techniques are described in Mass Observation, *First Year's Work 1937–38* (London, L. Drummond, 1938); R. Firth 'An anthropologist's view of Mass Observation', *Sociological Review*, 31 (1939), 166–93; and T. Harrison, *Living Through the Blitz* (London, Penguin, 1978). They were criticized in M. Abrams, *Social Surveys and Social Action* (London, Heinemann, 1951).

[48] 'Second Gallup Election Poll: Labour's 6–point lead', *News Chronicle*, 4 July, p. 1.

and impressive survey studies of political motivation and behaviour were carried out by Paul Lazarsfeld and his associates in the 1940[49] and 1948[50] Presidential election campaigns. Both these studies used a panel survey technique which required repeated interviews with the same panel of respondents. It was ideal for measuring change, but very expensive. Lazarsfeld cut costs by restricting the scope of his surveys to a single, small location—a small town on one occasion, a single county of New York State on the other.

In Britain, a team at LSE led by Mark Benney used the same method for their study of the 1950 election. They interviewed a panel of electors in Greenwich three times over the winter of 1949–50.[51] Within its limits, this first attempt at an academic study of electoral behaviour in Britain was a remarkable success. The restricted location not only made it economically possible to use a panel design but also allowed Benney and his team to set the voters' decisions in a political context.

Although Benney and his associates expressed some surprise at the amount of stability in their panel, their findings showed that only two-thirds of Greenwich electors held to the same voting preference over three waves of interviews between December 1949 and February 1950: so much for the classic era of voter stability that later became an accepted myth. Their panel also showed that voters' memories of their vote at the preceding election (1945) were unstable—their memories, as well as their preferences, changed between 1949 and 1950. Moreover, it also showed that between 1949 and 1950 voters tended to bring their memories of their 1945 vote into line with their current preferences—a finding which cast doubt on the use of memories to measure political change, and which encouraged the use of panels in most subsequent academic surveys.

The Greenwich survey also paid close attention to the media, and not just the *mass* media. In the style of Mass Observation, a hundred students reported on the speeches and audience reactions at election meetings, on the number of houses displaying window-cards, on loud-speaker tours, and on the distribution of party literature. Ancillary quota

---

[49] P. Lazarsfeld, B. Berelson and H. Gaudet, *The People's Choice: How the Voter Makes up his Mind in a Presidential Election Campaign* (New York, Columbia University Press, 1944).

[50] B. Berelson, P. Lazarsfeld and W. McPhee, *Voting: A Study of Opinion Formation in a Presidential Campaign* (Chicago, University of Chicago Press, 1954).

[51] M. Benney and P. Gleiss, 'Social class and politics in Greenwich', *British Journal of Sociology*, 1 (1950), 310–27; M. Benney, A. P. Gray and R. H. Pear, *How People Vote: A Study of Electoral Behaviour in Greenwich* (London, Routledge, 1956).

surveys were used to measure reactions to the previous night's radio broadcasts.

But Benney's study had its faults, most of which, like its virtues, it shared with Lazarsfeld's 1948 American study: such a restricted location that its findings could not be generalized to the country as a whole, delays that pushed publication beyond even the 1955 election, and the fact that it was a one-off study. Indeed the LSE team had broken up well before publication.

Throughout the 1950s, there were other local, single constituency surveys of electoral behaviour, the best of which, by Milne and Mackenzie, continued to use a short-term panel design, interviewing respondents at least twice—once at the start of the very short British election campaign, and then again after they had voted.[52] One of their major themes was an empirical investigation of the question that had troubled British theorists in the nineteenth century: would democracy prove to be government by the ignorant, the prejudiced and the un-interested? Much of Milne and Mackenzie's findings supported that view and they pointed to the high participation rates in the 1950 and 1951 elections with some dismay. Worst of all, the system was steered and guided by the changing electoral behaviour of floating voters who, on the evidence, seemed to be the most ignorant and uninterested of all, their vacillation and indecision arising from rootlessness or conflicting pressures, rather than deep reflection, rational judgement or modera-tion—although Milne and Mackenzie did admit that their small sample made it difficult to distinguish between what they termed 'illiterate' and 'intellectual' floaters. Even the rationality of party loyalists was suspect: Benney *et al.* found that 'loyalty to a party appears to be compatible with almost any degree of disagreement with its formal electoral policies'. Milne and Mackenzie found that 43 per cent of voters could give no

---

[52] Milne and Mackenzie surveyed voters in Bristol. See R. S. Milne and H. C. Mackenzie, *Straight Fight 1951* (London, Hansard Society, 1954); and R. S. Milne and H. C. Mackenzie, *Marginal Seat 1955* (London, Hansard Society, 1958). Other surveys in the early 1950s included A. H. Birch and P. Campbell, 'Voting in a Lancashire constituency', *British Journal of Sociology*, 1 (1950), 197–208; A. H. Birch *et al.*, *Small-town Politics: a Study of Political Life in Glossop* (Oxford, Oxford University Press, 1959); P. Campbell, D. Donnison and A. Potter, 'Voting behaviour in Droylesden 1951', *Manchester School*, 20 (1952), 62–4; and F. M. Martin, 'Social status and electoral choice in two constituencies—Greenwich and Hertford', *British Journal of Sociology*, 3 (1952), 231–41. A later flurry of local studies included F. Bealey, J. Blondel and W. P. McCann, *Constituency Politics: a Study of Newcastle-under-Lyme* (London, Faber & Faber, 1965); and L. J. Sharpe, *A Metropolis Votes* (London, LSE, 1962). Some others are discussed below, separately.

reason at all for their vote and another six per cent no reason other than family tradition. Labour voters in particular disagreed with their party on specific policies more often than not. Altogether, the data seemed incompatible with naïve models of democracy.

That, of course, could be the fault of the model rather than the fault of the electorate. Milne and Mackenzie found it easier to explain voting behaviour in terms of broad party 'images' than in terms of attachment to specific policies.

Using similar methods—a short-term panel at election time—Jay Blumler and his associates at Leeds University began a series of opinion surveys at the end of the 1950s that focused primarily on the mass media: its content, its influence, the nature of that influence (more to increase information than to change minds, they found), and the reasons why people chose to 'use' the media at all—the so-called 'uses and gratifications approach'.[53] Like the Nuffield Studies of elections, these studies of television and its audience inspired emulation outside Britain. Almost incidentally, they also showed that voters who drifted towards the Liberals during an election campaign were, contrary to the by-now-received wisdom, not like the relatively ignorant and uninterested abstainers, but actually well-informed before the campaign and interested in acquiring more information during it: these floaters 'seemed to embody some of the classic virtues of the rational democratic voter'.

There were two main problems with the methodology of British electoral surveys up to this point, largely caused by a shortage of funds. First, they were local, not national: so they could tell us something about the dynamics of universal electoral behaviour (insofar as such a thing existed), and something about a particular locality such as Greenwich or Bristol. But Greenwich and Bristol were of no interest in themselves, and any generalization to Britain as a whole was purely speculative. The second problem was that they focused on the last few weeks before election day, by which time the most important questions of electoral choice might already have been decided. Politics and political campaigning were clearly not restricted to the last three or four weeks before an election, and the evolution of public opinion might be very different in the medium or longer term. The most influential academic studies of

---

[53] J. Trenaman and D. McQuail, *Television and the Political Image* (London, Methuen, 1961); J. G. Blumler and D. McQuail, *Television in Politics: Its Uses and Influence* (London, Faber & Faber, 1968).

electoral behaviour in America in the 1950s used nation-wide samples and medium-term inter-election panels.[54]

In 1963 Donald Stokes, from the team at Michigan University that had directed these American studies, joined David Butler at Oxford to begin a sequence of five Britain-wide surveys that spanned the next seven years. Butler and Stokes constructed an elaborate four-wave panel, interviewing the same people in 1963, 1964, 1966 and 1970; and supplemented this with a number of interlocking single wave cross-sectional surveys, and two-wave panels.[55] Their design became the dominant model for subsequent British electoral surveys. The Swedish Bö Sarlvik, newly located at Essex University along with Ivor Crewe, extended the Butler and Stokes series through the two elections of 1974 and up to the 1979 election.[56] Thereafter Anthony Heath, Roger Jowell and John Curtice (with others) continued the series, retaining the same methodology, and many of the same questions, that had originally been devised by Butler and Stokes.[57] Data sets were deposited in the ESRC Data Archive at Essex University and extensively analysed, not just by the original investigators, but by others such as Richard Rose and Ian McAllister[58] who sometimes published their findings before the original investigators.

By repeating the same, or nearly the same, questions at successive elections it was possible to investigate trend and change—most systematically in Heath, Jowell and Curtice's *Understanding Political Change* which could draw by then on almost a quarter-century of surveys.[59]

---

[54] A. Campbell, P. E. Converse, W. E. Miller and D. E. Stokes, *The American Voter* (New York, Wiley, 1960); A. Campbell, P. E. Converse, W. E. Miller and D. E. Stokes, *Elections and the Political Order* (New York, Wiley, 1966).

[55] D. Butler and D. Stokes, *Political Change in Britain: the Evolution of Political Choice* (London, Macmillan, [1st ed. 1969, 2nd ed. 1974]).

[56] B. Sarlvik and I. Crewe, *Decade of Dealignment* (Cambridge, Cambridge University Press, 1983).

[57] See A. Heath, R. Jowell and J. Curtice, *How Britain Votes* (Oxford, Pergamon, 1985); *Understanding Political Change: The British Voter 1964–1987* (Oxford, Pergamon Press, 1991); and, with others, *Labour's Last Chance: The 1992 Election and Beyond* (Aldershot, Dartmouth, 1994). For an attempt to break out of the mould of this series, see P. Dunleavy and C. Husbands, *British Democracy at the Crossroads: Voting and Party Competition in the 1980s* (London, Allen & Unwin, 1985).

[58] R. Rose and I. McAllister, *Voters Begin to Choose: From Closed-class to Open Elections in Britain* (London, Sage Publications, 1986). R. Rose and I. McAllister, *The Loyalties of Voters: A Lifetime Learning Model* (London, Sage Publications, 1990).

[59] For a more recent and more wide-ranging account see P. Norris, *Electoral Change since 1945* (Oxford, Blackwell, 1997). The first quarter century of British Election Studies data is presented accessibly, although without analysis, in I. Crewe, N. Day and A. Fox, *The British Electorate 1963–87: A Compendium of Data from the British Election Studies* (Cambridge, Cambridge University Press, 1991).

There was a cost, of course: continuity was bought at the cost of rigidity, repeating questions and retaining survey methods whose value was increasingly questioned, simply in order to maintain a consistent series of comparable data; or improving question wordings and exploring new survey methods, at the cost of endangering that continuity and comparability. Attempts to use the long-term America National Election survey series for comparative purposes drew a deluge of criticism because insufficient attention was paid to the impact of 'improved' question wordings on the answers respondents gave.[60] The British authors of *Understanding Political Change* did not fall into that trap. Indeed they paid very close attention to changes in question wording over the years, which prevented comparison across certain break points. That made their findings less dramatic, but less spurious, and their cautious and often negative findings firmly established the phrase 'trendless fluctuation' in the lexicon of British electoral analysis.

Butler and Stokes' inter-election panels provided the first direct evidence on the extent to which people changed their voting behaviour between elections. That needs emphasis: before Butler and Stokes there was no evidence (although much speculation) about the degree of voting change between one election and the next. They showed that beneath the surface stability of aggregate party support there was a great deal of 'churning' as many individuals changed in opposite directions. A particularly striking example was revealed in Sarlvik and Crewe's continuation of the Butler and Stokes' panels: over the few months between the elections of February and October 1974 the size of the Liberal vote remained fairly constant although the panel showed that the party lost half its February voters by October, but replaced the defectors with roughly as many converts from other parties or abstention. Equally significant was the finding that 'homing tendencies' prevented individual-level change from cumulating over a sequence of three or more elections: people who changed in one direction between two elections were particularly likely to change back again at the third.

One of Butler and Stokes' most distinctive achievements, however, was their comprehensive and sophisticated treatment of the class alignment in British politics. They investigated what the notion of 'class' meant to the voters themselves rather than to political philosophers; they measured the extent of the class alignment and voters' deviations

[60] N. Nie, S. Verba and J. R. Petrocik, *The Changing American Voter* (Cambridge, Mass., Harvard University Press, 1976).

from it; they made innovative use of 'cohort analysis'—treating age groups as cohorts defined by the period when they entered the electorate—to trace the evolution of British politics from sectarian alignments at the start of the century to class-based alignments; and they showed that the class alignment itself was already past its peak. Going beyond their own survey when necessary, they cumulated 180,000 interviews from NOP polls over a two-year period, and then broke them down into individual constituency samples, to show how the class alignment itself varied systematically with the local concentration of the classes, that is with the local context. In short, they viewed and analysed the concept of class in British electoral politics from many different perspectives; neither prior, nor subsequent studies of the class alignment came near to the richness of their treatment.

Their immediate successors as directors of the election survey series, Sarlvik and Crewe, interpreted the surveys of the 1970s as revealing a sharp decline in the strength of the class alignment, already foreshadowed by Butler and Stokes' cohort analysis; and a corresponding, and partially consequential, sharp decline in the strength of the 'partisan' alignment—that is, the degree of psychological attachment to political parties. But their successors, Heath, Jowell and Curtice, denied the reality of class dealignment and denied the significance of partisan dealignment. There was, in fact, never any conflict of evidence between them—they were analysing the same data-sets after all—but a sharp conflict of interpretation. Both sides of the argument could agree with the summary statement that the partisanship of the middle class had become less distinctive as its size had expanded and its internal composition had changed—although they disagreed about whether this should be described as a 'class de-alignment' or not.

Nor was there any conflict of evidence on the second major point of disagreement. Sarlvik and Crewe had shown very clearly that, while the strength of psychological identification with political parties had declined by half between 1963 and 1979, volatility (switching preferences between parties) had not increased. Sarlvik and Crewe stressed the decline in partisan commitment and the potential, although not the actuality, of increasing volatility. Heath, Jowell and Curtice emphasized the lack of any significant increase in actual volatility, and consequently doubted the significance of declining partisan commitment.

But the utility of the 'party identification' concept did not depend solely on its ability, or inability, to forecast time trends in volatility. Although Butler and Stokes used it throughout *Political Change in Britain* mainly as a dependent variable, its status in the earlier American studies had been mainly that of an independent variable—a cause rather than a consequence. Crewe and Sarlvik were the first in Britain to use this concept primarily in its American role, as an independent variable, but unlike the classic American studies, they focused upon trends in Britain-wide *aggregates* of party identification, implying that declining aggregate commitment to parties opened the way to an era of instability in British politics. And indeed, the surges of Liberal, Nationalist and Social Democrat support in 1974 and 1983 seemed to give that notion some credibility. Heath, Jowell and Curtice on the other hand, produced evidence to suggest that such changes were driven more by the changing electoral options presented by political élites, than by the changing psychology of the voter. Both teams tended to neglect the utility of 'party identification' as an independent variable at the *individual* level, however. Although it was clearly true that the correlation between declining partisanship and growing volatility was weak at the aggregate level, it was equally true that the behaviour of those individuals with a strong sense of party identity was always very different from that of other individuals with a weaker sense of party identity. Individuals with a strong sense of party identity were very much less volatile than other individuals, much less easily swayed by propaganda or events, and much more likely to participate in the electoral process, especially in relatively 'unexciting' electoral contests where the overall rate of participation was low—such as elections to Local Authorities or the European Parliament.

The late 1960s saw the first sustained electoral success for the Scottish and Welsh nationalist parties, and an explosion of political and ethnic violence in Northern Ireland. There was clearly a need to study politics in a '*dis*united Kingdom' although perhaps its focus would have to be less strictly 'electoral' in Northern Ireland than in Scotland or Wales. Richard Rose carried out an extensive survey of public opinion in Northern Ireland in 1968 whose theme was well expressed in the title *Governing without Consensus*.[61] It was followed in 1978 and 1992 by other surveys explicitly designed to measure change since 1968.[62] Amongst other things, these three studies showed how rapidly even the sense of

---

[61] R. Rose, *Governing without Consensus* (London, Faber & Faber, 1971).
[62] E. Moxon-Browne, *Nation, Class and Creed in Northern Ireland* (Aldershot, Gower, 1983); S. Elliott, E. Moxon-Browne and J. Ditch *The Northern Ireland General Election: A Political Attitudes Survey* (Swindon, Final Report on grant L304253005 to the ESRC, 1994).

national/ethnic identity could change under the pressure of events: identification with 'Ulster' collapsed, leaving a two-way rather than three-way split of national identity—'British' versus 'Irish'. A series of Scottish election surveys began in 1974—although as little more than an inflated Scottish subsample of the British election survey, with a handful of special Scottish questions[63] and has continued intermittently since then, revealing the strength of public support for constitutional change, the extent and nature of Scottish national identity, and their relationship to electoral support not only for the nationalist SNP, but for the various other parties as well.[64] They showed that Scottish and British national identities were not, for most Scots, incompatible alternatives: individuals held both identities simultaneously, weighting them differently in different circumstances. There were fewer academic surveys of voters in Wales, although they included a comprehensive Welsh election study in 1979.[65]

The motivation for these sub-United Kingdom studies was quite different from that of the early election studies in localities such as Greenwich, Bristol, Leeds and Manchester. Those early studies used a very restricted local sample to investigate the British voter mainly because a severe lack of funds made a national sample impossible. Greenwich was hopefully sufficiently 'typical' to allow a study of the general characteristics of voters in Britain, which could answer very general questions such as whether there was a strong class alignment, whether voters changed during the campaign, and whether they could be influenced by political propaganda. The analogy was that of a scientific laboratory. Roughly speaking, it does not matter much whether the oscillation of a pendulum is measured in Greenwich or Manchester, or elsewhere. But political behaviour is more variable and more context-dependent than the oscillation of a pendulum. No single

---

[63] See W. L. Miller, *The End of British Politics? Scots and English Political Behaviour in the Seventies* (Oxford, Oxford University Press, 1981). Despite its title, the earlier study by I. Budge and Derek W. Urwin, *Scottish Political Behaviour: a Case Study in British Homogeneity* (London, Longmans, 1966), was based entirely on interviews in Glasgow—which was unfortunately no more typical of Scotland than Liverpool was of England.

[64] Comparisons of the Scottish election survey findings in 1974, 1979 and 1992 appear in J. Brand, J. Mitchell and P. Surridge, 'Will Scotland come to the aid of the party?', in Heath, Jowell, Curtice and others, *Labour's Last Chance: The 1992 Election and Beyond* (Aldershot, Dartmouth, 1994); in L. Bennie, J. Brand and J. Mitchell, *How Scotland Votes: Scottish Parties and Elections* (Manchester, Manchester University Press, 1997); and also in A. Brown, D. McCrone and L. Paterson, *Politics and Society in Scotland* (London, Macmillan, 1996).

[65] P. Madgwick, D. Balsom and D. van Mechelen, 'The Red and the Green: patterns of partisan choice in Wales', *British Journal of Political Science*, 13 (1983), 299–325.

locality was ever likely to be sufficiently typical of Britain as to allow precise inferences. An analysis of the class alignment in Greenwich, for example, might reasonably allow us to infer that the class alignment was strong in Britain-wide politics, but it could not tell us how strong. Similarly, a comparison of the class alignment in Greenwich at the 1950 election with that in Bristol at the 1955 election could provide no clue at all as to whether the class alignment in Britain was strengthening or weakening over time. So when funds allowed, a Britain-wide sample was clearly superior to a Greenwich sample since the object of interest was the British voter, not the Greenwich voter as such.

By contrast, Scottish, Welsh and Irish surveys were motivated by the certainty that context was important, and that it *did* matter *where* the survey was conducted. They focused, not on supposedly uniform generalities, but on certainly different specifics—on unique Scottish, Welsh and Irish issues and parties, or on precise quantitative comparisons between Scotland, Wales and England even on issues and attitudes that were not unique to one particular nation within the United Kingdom.

Public opinion and non-electoral political behaviour

The ability to forecast an election result correctly has always been a key test of public-opinion polling methodology, and the ability to explain that election result in terms of the attitudes, opinions, identifications and perceptions of the voters has been a natural extension of that test. Academic election studies have also provided a useful vehicle for the collection of all manner of political opinions but, inevitably, they have concentrated most on those aspects of political opinion that were thought likely to influence the outcome of the election—on attitudes towards parties, political leaders, and the issues that divided them.

But other aspects of public opinion are also important even if they have little impact on a particular election result. In addition to Butler and Stokes' use of their election surveys to study class alignment, there were some other celebrated attempts to research the politics of class in depth, in particular attempts to evaluate alternative explanations of *why* so many of the working class voted Labour—whether for reasons of deeply ingrained instinctive, almost 'tribal' loyalty, or perceptions of rational self-interest,[66] and *why* so many did not,[67] although neither was based on a fully representative sample.

Another theme in non-election surveys was political action. A survey of Welsh language politics in Cardiganshire by Peter Madgwick and others included a pathbreaking analysis of attitudes towards protest behaviour, direct action and violence.[68] Madgwick worked with Alan Marsh to develop a scale of 'protest potential'—that is, willingness to use various forms of direct action ranging from the mildest (signing a petition) up to the use of violence against people or property. In only slightly modified form, that protest potential scale was used some years later in Marsh's own study of political protest throughout Britain and then in multi-national studies of protest behaviour.[69] Later still, Geraint Parry, George Moyser and Neil Day undertook a more comprehensive study of political participation in Britain, including both electoral and non-electoral participation, and conventional as well as protest behaviour.[70]

The Americans Gabriel Almond and Sidney Verba included Britain in their classic study of democratic values in five countries.[71] Reacting against earlier survey studies that judged the supposedly inadequate British and American electorates against demanding theoretical norms for democratic citizens, they noted that 'British and American democracy somehow weathered the crisis of the 1920s and 1930s [while] Germany and Italy did not'. So instead of judging the British and American electorates against abstract theoretical norms for democratic citizens, they inverted the logic and defined the 'political culture of democracy' in terms of the distinctive characteristics of the actual

---

[66] J. H. Goldthorpe, D. Lockwood, F. Bechhofer and J. Platt, *The Affluent Worker*: vol. 1 *Industrial Attitudes and Behaviour*; vol. 2 *Political Attitudes and Behaviour*; vol. 3 *The Class Struggle* (Cambridge, Cambridge University Press, 1968–9).

[67] R. McKenzie and A. Silver, *Angels in Marble: Working Class Conservatives in Urban England* (London, Heinemann, 1968).

[68] P. J. Madgwick, N. Griffiths and V. Walker, *The Politics of Rural Wales: A Study of Cardiganshire* (London, Hutchinson, 1973).

[69] A. Marsh, *Protest and Political Consciousness* (Beverly Hills, Calif., Sage Publications, 1977). S. H. Barnes and M. Kaase, eds., *Political Action: Mass Participation in Five Western Democracies* (Beverly Hills, Calif., Sage Publications, 1979).

[70] G. Parry, G. Moyser and N. Day, *Political Participation and Democracy in Britain* (Cambridge, Cambridge University Press, 1992). It was also inspired, in part, by S. Verba and N. Nie, *Participation in America: Political Democracy and Social Equality* (New York, Harper and Row, 1972) as well as by Alan Marsh's work.

[71] G. A. Almond and S. Verba, *The Civic Culture: Political Attitudes and Democracy in Five Nations* (Princeton, NJ, Princeton University Press, 1963).

electorates in these two tried and tested democracies. They found the British had the most 'effective combination of the subject and participant roles . . . political competence and participant orientations [combined with] a strong deference to the independent authority of government'. Almond and Verba did not claim that the political culture of the mass public had by itself preserved democracy in Britain and the United States, but they suggested it had at least been 'congruent' and supportive. In the aftermath of the collapse of communism, British academics undertook international surveys to gauge the extent to which political élites and the public in the new democracies of eastern Europe and the former Soviet Union had adopted a culture that was at least 'congruent' with democracy.[72]

Under the Thatcher governments of the 1980s there was increasing concern about over-centralization and the erosion of civil liberties in Britain which, in turn, led to a growing interest in the prospect of significant constitutional reforms such as an entrenched charter of citizens' rights, political devolution to the nations and regions of Britain, and democratization of the Upper House of Parliament. The idea of equating democracy with Britain now seemed unduly complacent, although the fault was more often attributed to inadequate institutions than to an inadequate electorate, and surveys measured institutions against the demands of the public rather than the reverse. They found that in most circumstances, British politicians showed more commitment to citizens' liberties than did citizens themselves, although they were also more willing than citizens to grant discretion to the state in matters of security. Thus, for example, politicians were more willing to defend rights of free speech for citizens and the press and yet at the same time more willing than the general public to allow phone-taps and state inspection of private bank accounts to combat crime or terrorism.[73]

---

[72] See, for example, W. L. Miller, S. White and P. Heywood, *Values and Political Change in Postcommunist Europe* (London, Macmillan, 1998); or G. Evans and S. Whitefield, 'The politics and economics of democratic commitment: support for democracy in transition societies', *British Journal of Political Science*, 25 (1995), 485–514.

[73] See W. L. Miller, A. M. Timpson and M. Lessnoff, *Political Culture in Contemporary Britain: People and Politicians, Principles and Practice* (Oxford, Oxford University Press, 1996). It was partly inspired by a classic American study on a similar theme: H. McClosky and A. Brill's, *Dimensions of Tolerance: What Americans Believe about Civil Liberties* (New York, Russell Sage Foundation, 1983). In limited respects, a British precursor was H. J. Eysenck, *The Psychology of Politics* (London, Routledge & Kegan Paul, 1954).

During the 1980s and early 1990s, elected higher-tier local government structures in London, other English metropolitan areas, and Scotland were abolished. The remaining elected local governments had their autonomy restricted and were, in part, functionally replaced by a variety of non-elected bodies. The traditional assumption that local governance should be controlled by a system of democratically-elected local governments was openly questioned by ministers. Public-opinion studies showed that although local democracy lacked content, in that voting in local government elections largely reflected attitudes to central rather than local government, there still remained a deep ideological commitment to the principle of local democracy amongst the public—and, more surprisingly, even amongst those who had been appointed to the boards that ran alternative, non-elected systems of local governance.[74]

In 1983 Roger Jowell and his associates began an annual series of *British Social Attitudes Surveys* (BSAS)[75] which paralleled the ESRC's *Election Survey* series begun by Butler and Stokes, but focused on non-electoral aspects of public opinion. Despite its title, its content was in large measure political. It was later supplemented by a series of *Northern Ireland Social Attitudes Surveys*,[76] and also by a more restricted *International Social Survey Programme*[77] based on an internationally-agreed module of questions applied simultaneously in 22 countries by attaching the common module to various country-specific surveys. Although focusing on different topics in different years, BSAS attempted to maintain a core of recurrent questions which revealed, for example, the cyclical variation in the strength of party identification across the life of a parliament, and the changing balance of preferences between lower taxes and better public services over the years of the Thatcher governments.[78] By cumulating BSAS data sets—typically 3,000 interviews in any one year—over several years, and then dividing by region, it was

[74] W. L. Miller, *Irrelevant Elections? The Quality of Local Democracy in Britain* (Oxford, Clarendon Press, 1988); W. L. Miller, M. Dickson and G. Stoker, *The New Local Governance: Political Theory and Public Opinion* (London, Macnillan, forthcoming

[75] See, for example, R. Jowell, J. Curtice, A. Park *et al.*, eds., *British Social Attitudes: The 12th Report* (Aldershot, Dartmouth, 1995).

[76] See, for example, R. Breen, P. Devine and G. Robinson, eds., *Social Attitudes in Northern Ireland: The 5th Report* (Belfast, Appletree Press, 1996).

[77] See, for example, R. Jowell and C. Airey, eds., *International Social Attitudes (British Social Attitudes: The 10th Report), (1993–4) (Aldershot, Gower, 1994).

[78] See, for example, L. Brook and others, eds., *British Social Attitudes: Cumulative Sourcebook* (Aldershot, Gower, 1992).

possible to study regional variations in attitudes to such recurrent questions.[79] Thus recurrent questions facilitated spatial as well as temporal analysis.

But, valuable though much of the information collected by the BSAS surveys was for specific investigations, the greater achievement was the creation of a vehicle—similar to the 'omnibus' or 'carrier' surveys of commercial pollsters in which several topics for different clients are combined in the same questionnaire—that could provide a basis for many research projects which individually did not merit, or could not afford, their own full-scale survey.

New methods

The methodology of the main ESRC election survey series, largely unchanged since the Michigan studies of the 1950s, was looking increasingly old-fashioned by the 1980s. Face-to-face interviewing was expensive, inflexible and difficult to supervise. Commercial pollsters and a number of university survey researchers, particularly those at Berkeley, California were experimenting with telephone methods and with computer-assisted telephone interviewing (CATI).

The chief advantages of telephone surveys centred on access and timeliness. Telephone access allowed the first genuinely random national samples—without the heavy clustering of interviews that was the norm in so-called random sampling by face-to-face methods; and it allowed the repeated call-backs to widely-distributed respondents which were needed for time-specific surveys and panels. Since, as Prime Minister Harold Wilson once remarked, 'a week is a long time in politics', political opinions could change much more rapidly than other objects of social science investigations such as education, income, or health. That could make the timing of a political survey quite critical. After a limited experiment with telephone survey methods at the 1982 Hillhead by-election, the ESRC's traditional British election survey was supplemented, in 1987, by a second British election study which used telephone interviewing to construct a five-wave panel running from a year before the election, through the pre-election period, and then day-by-day through the short

---

[79] See for example B. Miller, 'Tax factor and devolution', *Glasgow Herald*, 28 December 1991, p. 9. This comparison of Scottish and English attitudes to tax levels was based on 14,216 interviews in BSAS surveys for 1983, 1984, 1985, 1986, 1987 and 1989. Contrary to suppositions based on voting patterns, this analysis indicated that Scots were not more favourable to a high-tax regime than the English, and did not want devolution simply in order to enjoy higher levels of taxation.

formal campaign, to the week after the election.[80] It showed, for example, how strong party identifiers brought their attitudes more into line with their pre-existing party choice over the winter preceding the election, while weak party identifiers brought their voting intentions more into line with their pre-existing attitudes or their newspaper's party preference. During the final campaign, it showed how the visibility of MPs and candidates increased day-by-day from trivially low levels just four weeks before polling day to quite high levels on the day itself— a matter of some importance in terms of the theory of parliamentary democracy. Ten years later, at the 1997 election, some elements of this methodology were incorporated into the commercial pollsters' opinion polls and into the main ESRC election survey series.

Computer assistance made it possible to administer much more complex questionnaires than before, questionnaires that could easily incorporate experiments in question wording, arguments and dialogue, into the interviews. This too had some importance for democratic theory. Anthony Birch, for example, was highly critical of the value-free concept of pluralist democracy, which he described as 'an American intellectual export'[81] and which was, to some extent, implicit in conventional survey research designs that treated all opinions equally, regardless of their merit. As an example of a more European perspective, Birch quoted Laski's view that 'the underlying thesis of parliamentary government is that discussion forms the popular mind and . . . the legislature translates into statute the will arrived at by that mind';[82] and, more clearly still, he quoted Lindsay's view that democracy 'does not mean that what everyone has to say is of equal value. It assumes that if the discussion is good enough the proper value of each contribution will be brought out in the discussion.'[83] This perspective is sometimes termed 'deliberative democracy'.[84]

---

[80] W. L. Miller *et al.*, *How Voters Change: The 1987 British Election Campaign in Perspective* (Oxford, Oxford University Press, 1990); and W. L. Miller, *Media and Voters: The Audience, Content and Influence of Press and Television at the 1987 General Election* (Oxford, Oxford University Press, 1991). For a brief description of the Hillhead experiment see W. L. Miller, *The Survey Method in the Social and Political Sciences: Achievements, Failures, Prospects* (London, Pinter, 1983) pp. 232–36.

[81] A. H. Birch, *The Concepts and Theories of Modern Democracy* (London, Routledge, 1993) p. 160.

[82] H. J. Laski, *The Development of the Representative System in our Times* (Geneva, Interparliamentary Union, 1928) p. 13—quoted by Birch.

[83] A. D. Lindsay, *The Essentials of Democracy* (Oxford, Oxford University Press, 1935) pp. 40–41—quoted by Birch.

[84] On deliberative democracy see D. Miller, 'Citizenship and pluralism', *Political Studies*, 43 (1995), 432–50 at p. 445; and D. Miller, 'Deliberative democracy and social choice' in D. Held, ed., *Prospects for Democracy*, special issue of *Political Studies*, 40 (1992), 54–67, later published by Polity Press (1993).

Conventional survey methods were too remote and too inflexible to research the development of a consensus through debate—the effect of information, the force of rational argument or, less benign, the power of propaganda and persuasion, whether based on rational or irrational appeals. A series of surveys, or a panel survey, with proper attention to events in the intervals between waves of interviews would be useful but perhaps not sufficient. But computer-assisted interviewing made it possible to measure the influence of political argument, for example on public attitudes to practical issues of civil and political rights—by randomly varying question wordings, including or excluding arguments of many kinds, and measuring the impact on responses. It showed that argument was effective although, of course, the power of argument to influence opinion varied from argument to argument, from issue to issue, and from person to person.[85]

But respondents in computer-assisted interviews were still interviewed one-to-one, as isolated individuals. The development of opinion might be different in the more social context of a group discussion, still more in the context of a crowd or a mob. British television companies pioneered a format of investigation that came even closer to Laski's notion 'that discussion forms the popular mind'. Starting at the election of 1974 Granada Television selected 500 voters from a benchmark constituency (the 'Granada 500'), and got them to study the party programmes, question experts, and question the leaders of each main party on national television. It was described by the American democratic theorist James Fishkin as 'a pathbreaking experiment that laid the groundwork for the national telecast of deliberative opinion polls' although in many respects it did not meet his criteria for a true 'deliberative poll'.[86] In April 1994 however, Fishkin worked with Granada Television, the *Independent*, and SCPR[87] on one that did meet his criteria: 300 previously-interviewed voters, met together for a weekend of discussions in Manchester that transformed them into 'far more

---

[85] See W. L. Miller, A. M. Timpson and M. Lessnoff, *Political Culture in Contemporary Britain: People and Politicians, Principles and Practice* (Oxford, Oxford University Press, 1996). The methods used were pioneered by P. M. Sniderman, J. F. Fletcher, P. H. Russell and P. E. Tetlock, *The Clash of Rights: Liberty, Equality and Legitimacy in Pluralist Democracy* (New Haven, Conn., Yale University Press, 1996).

[86] J. S. Fishkin, *Democracy and Deliberation: New Directions for Democratic Reform* (New Haven, Conn., Yale University Press, 1991), p. 96.

[87] The London polling agency, Social and Community Planning Research.

sophisticated consumers of the competing policy prescriptions' on the selected topic of crime and punishment.[88]

As the century drew to a close, qualitative methods—'in-depth interviews' and especially 'focus group discussions'—which had long been used in commercial product research, became more popular with British political parties, and even with government itself, which proposed to monitor public perceptions of its performance by an extensive programme of focus group discussions. They were also increasingly used in academic research. Partly that reflected a desire for different information rather than just more of the same; but, once again, advances in technology provided part of the impetus: cheap and effective software packages for computer analysis of textual information were spreading as rapidly in the 1990s as had computer packages for the analysis of numerical information in the 1970s and the clear divide between quantitative and qualitative methods was being bridged by technology.[89] Many of the early survey studies in Britain—including McKenzie and Silver's *Angels in Marble*, Butler and Stokes' *Political Change in Britain* and Richard Rose's *Governing without Consensus*—had made some limited use of qualitative methods but now it became much easier to do this on a more extended scale.

The study of constituency voting was one form of aggregate analysis; another was the study of time series. The main concern was to identify the factors, principally economic, which affected trends in overall government popularity as measured by monthly opinion poll ratings. Although opinion poll data were used, in time-series studies it was nearly always used as aggregate percentages, not as information on individuals as such. Goodhart and Bhansali published a lengthy article in the 1970 volume of *Political Studies* analysing the time series relationship between levels of unemployment and government popularity.[90] Their conclusions were almost immediately falsified by events, as were many subsequent findings, but international reviews have rightly

[88] J. S. Fishkin, *The Voice of the People: Public Opinion and Democracy* (New Haven, Conn., Yale University Press, 1995) p. 168.

[89] See, for example, E. A. Weitzman, *Computer Programs for Qualitative Data Analysis: A Software Sourcebook* (London, Sage, 1995). For the use of computer-analysed focus group discussions in public opinion research see W. L. Miller, T. Koshechkina and A. Grodeland, 'How citizens cope with postcommunist officials: evidence from focus group discussions in Ukraine and the Czech Republic', *Political Studies*, 45 (1997) (Special Issue), 597–625.

[90] C. A. E. Goodhart and R. J. Bhansali, 'Political Economy', *Political Studies*, 18 (1970), 43–106.

regarded their article as a key 'pioneering study' in the field.[91] It encouraged many others to attempt to solve the difficult problem of predicting government popularity by using other economic indicators—including 'subjective' as well as 'objective' economic indicators, and more complex statistical models that took account of 'political shocks' such as the Falklands War of 1982, or Britain's withdrawal from the Exchange Rate Mechanism (ERM) in 1992. Although significant research on the popularity of British governments was done outside Britain,[92] notable contributions to time-series studies of government popularity were made by Britishers such as James Alt,[93] Paul Whiteley,[94] David Sanders[95] and others.

Conclusion

What do we now know about elections, voting and public opinion at the end of the century that we did not know at the beginning? Almost everything that we *do* know. At the start of the century there was a great deal of moralizing, theorizing, speculation and assertion but very little actual knowledge based on firm evidence. Indeed knowledge was fairly sparse until the century was half over. Then there was a sharp change however, and progress accelerated throughout the second half of the

---

[91] In the editors' introduction to H. Eulau and M. S. Lewis-Beck, eds., *Economic Conditions and Electoral Outcomes: The United States and Western Europe* (New York, Agathon Press, 1985), p. 2.

[92] See for example H. D. Clarke and M. C. Stewart, 'Economic evaluations, Prime Ministerial approval and governing party support: rival models reconsidered', *British Journal of Political Science*, 25 (1995), 145–70.

[93] J. E. Alt, *The Politics of Economic Decline: Economic Management and Political Behaviour in Britain since 1964* (Cambridge, Cambridge University Press, 1979); J. E. Alt and A. K. Chrystal, *Political Economics* (Los Angeles, University of California Press, 1984).

[94] P. Whiteley, *Political Control of the Macroeconomy* (London, Sage, 1986); P. Whiteley, 'Electoral forecasting from poll data: the British case', *British Journal of Political Science*, 9 (1979), 219–236; P. Whiteley, 'The causal relationship between issues, candidate evaluations, party identification and vote choice—the view from "rolling thunder"', *Journal of Politics*, 50 (1988), 961–84.

[95] See for example, D. Sanders, H. Ward and D. Marsh with T. Fletcher, 'Government popularity and the Falklands War: a reassessment', *British Journal of Political Science*, 17 (1987), 281–313; D. Sanders, D. Marsh and H. Ward, 'The electoral impact of press coverage of the British economy 1979–87', *British Journal of Political Science*, 23 (1993), 175–210; D. Sanders, 'Economic performance, management competence and the outcome of the next General Election', *Political Studies*, 44 (1996), 203–31. D. Sanders, 'Voting and the electorate', in P. Dunleavy, A. Gamble, I. Holliday and G. Peele, eds., *Developments in British Politics 5* (London, Macmillan, 1997) pp. 45–74.

century. As the century closed, rapid technological and methodological advances coupled with the collapse of communism and rising doubts about the British system of government provided both the means and the motivation for new work. The torpor of British electoral research in the first half of the century seemed unlikely to recur in the near future.

Insofar as the attempt to make the study of elections, voting and public opinion more scientific was aimed at uncovering important mechanical 'laws of nature' in politics it failed. Even 'empirical regularities' had a disturbing habit of proving weak or variable. Time-series analyses of the relationship between objective economic conditions and government popularity were perhaps the most sustained and sophisticated attempt in that direction but the failure, for example, of John Major's 1992–7 government to capitalize on improving macro-economic conditions showed how weak or conditional such relationships might be.

In fact, empirical research revealed contingency rather than certainty: it put the 'politics' or even the 'history' back into political science. Careful research proved better at limiting or destroying grand assertions than inventing them. R. B. McCallum's objective of 'destroying myths' was much helped by empirical research. The work of Jay Blumler and his colleagues revealed the weakness of political advertising on state television, not the assumed power of propaganda. At a time when standard texts asserted that 'the basis of British politics is class, all else is embellishment and detail', surveys by Butler and Stokes revealed the limits of the British class alignment and showed that it was already past its peak, while their immediate successors charted its rapid decline. At the same time, Miller showed that class de-alignment amongst individuals was consistent with the continuing strength of the class alignment across constituencies. Similarly, Sanders and others noted the paradox that cross-sectional and time-series patterns need not be similar; so that the key variables that explained differences between voters were not the ones that best explained trends. Rose showed that 'proportional representation' systems did not always produce more proportional results than 'majoritarian' systems, and even on the average, produced only moderately more proportionality. Surveys by Milne and Mackenzie revealed that British voters did not 'vote for' many of the key policies of their preferred party, and that in many other respects they did not conform to the idealized model of the democratic citizen, despite sustaining one of the (at the time) most admired democratic systems in the world. Heath, Jowell and Curtice found that psychological ties to parties weakened dramatically without increasing volatility.

There were of course many positive findings that contained no such hints of paradox. More was known about political attitudes and behaviour, in depth and in detail, by the end of the century than could have been guessed at the beginning. Indeed the very conditionality and contingency of empirical findings meant that they could not be reduced to a few simple truths: fact proved more complex, although no less comprehensible, than fiction.

Electoral research on Britain and by Britishers was fully up to international standards in concept and method and it was well integrated with research elsewhere. Just because of that, it is perhaps less easy to specify what was unique or even distinctive about the purely British contribution. What was distinctive was not necessarily what was most typical or most important. It was, rather, the balance between theory, history, awareness of contingency and sensitivity to context on the one hand, and abstract analysis on the other—a combination that frequently led to limited and modest generalizations and to as much concern for the exception as for the norm.

9: The Analysis of British Political Institutions

GEOFFREY MARSHALL

The analysis of British political institutions in the twentieth century has not emerged solely from the writing of textbooks by political scientists. General ideas about the relationships of the organs of government to each other existed before anything that could recognizably be called political science. There were doctrines and concepts about the nature of the constitution in 1850 or in 1688. Such general ideas arose and have arisen in the twentieth century in the course of public and parliamentary debate, in the deliberations of judges and newspaper editors and from the reports of parliamentary inquiries and Royal Commissions. Thus, the genesis of general thinking about the government of the United Kingdom is to a lesser degree the product of professional reflection than is the development of theories about comparative government. It evolves more directly from the political process itself and from the controversies about government that government itself generates.

With perhaps the striking exception of Jacques De Lolme's *Constitution of England* published in English in 1775, general works on the British political system are a product of the latter years of the twentieth century. The classic texts begin with a rush in the 1860s with the publication of Alpheus Todd's two-volume *Parliamentary Government in England*, Bagehot's *English Constitution*, Russell's *English Government and Constitution* and Sir Thomas Erskine May's *Constitutional History of England*. Todd's two-volume work was written as a parliamentary manual for the guidance of the members of the House of Assembly of Upper Canada. It describes in considerable detail (since unmatched) the development of cabinet government, the royal prerogative and the relations of ministers with Parliament. Nothing on a similar scale was attempted until the president of Harvard University, Laurence Lowell, published in 1908 his work on *The Government of England* running to over a thousand pages. In 1907 Sidney Low's *Governance of England*[1] assumed the more modest proportions of Walter Bagehot's volume.

If we imagine a late twentieth-century political scientist transposed to the first decade of the century and ask in what direction he might have looked for assistance in analysing the nature of British political institutions, we should find him turning not only to the historians and journalists but to the works of the lawyers, in particular that of Albert Venn Dicey, Frederick Maitland and Sir William Anson. From all of these writers the transmogrified political scientist would glean a number of organizing concepts or ideas. From Bagehot he would have learned that the constitution is a kind of façade that conceals reality. It is 'like an old man who stills wears with attached fondness clothes in the fashion of his youth'.[2] It also has efficient institutions and dignified institutions, the dignified institutions being efficient in a different way in appealing to the weak imaginations of an unphilosophical citizenry. From Anson he would have learned much about the transformation of the prerogative powers of the Crown. From Maitland the investigator would have learned that the constitution is everywhere in the law—that it cannot be codified since it is found in aspects of the law relating to local government, land, taxation and crime.[3] From Dicey he would have gathered that the relations between the organs of government are to an important degree determined by habit and convention, that the rule of law requires subjects and officials (but not the Crown) to be answerable in the same courts and that Parliament has the right to make or unmake any law whatsoever (but the House of Commons cannot). All of these ideas have provided a focus for critics, reformers and celebrants of British government over the century.

---

[1] A title later used by Harold Wilson in *The Governance of Britain* (London, Weidenfeld & Nicolson and Michael Joseph, 1976).

[2] W. Bagehot, *The English Constitution* (Oxford, Oxford University Press [2nd ed.] 1928), p. 1.

[3] F. W. Maitland, *The Constitutional History of England* (Cambridge, Cambridge University Press, 1908), p. 538.

The powers of Parliament

Since at least 1900 the role of Parliament has probably been the pre-dominant theme of textbook writers, political commentators and partisans of parliamentary reform. There has been a consensus that the powers of Parliament have declined, but less unanimity on the question whether this matters. The perception that Parliament's role as the pre-eminent and sovereign legislator does not match its political power and influence and that the theoretical subordination and accountability of the Executive to Parliament has been in some sense stood on its head had made itself felt well before the turn of the century. Sir John Seeley in his Cambridge lectures on political science, first delivered in the 1880s, remarked that 'the truth is that the Ministry and the Ministry as such has legislative power in a far higher sense and greater degree than Parliament. The Ministry . . . has a majority in the House; otherwise it would not be a Ministry. In important cases therefore their consent is secured beforehand'.[4] Sidney Low in 1904 agreed: 'The House of Commons no longer controls the Executive; on the contrary the Execut-ive controls the House of Commons'.[5]

The subsequent history of this lamentation has taken some ups and downs and perhaps betrays a degree of ideological bias. In the first edition of his *English Political Institutions* in 1910 Sir John Marriot also saw the role and the representative character of the Commons threat-ened by the increasing popularity of the doctrine of the mandate with the coming of mass democracy. 'If pushed to a logical conclusion, it can have but one issue', he wrote—'the adoption of some species of Refer-endum'.[6] Oddly, at about the same time, Dicey was moving towards the notion of the referendum as a way of protecting the electorate from the excesses of party leaders who had secured control of the Commons and might use that power to force through fundamental constitutional change of a kind unwelcome to Unionists.

In the 1930s and 1940s the theme of parliamentary decline became commonplace. It was voiced in Ramsay Muir's *How Britain is Governed* in 1930, in Leo Amery's *Thoughts on the Constitution* in 1947, and still more strongly in two post-war works, Christopher Hollis's *Can Parliament*

---

[4] Sir John Seeley, *Introduction to Political Science* (London, Macmillan, 1896), p. 219.
[5] S. Low, *The Governance of England* (London, Fisher Unwin, 1902). This is the theme of Chapters IV, V and IX of Low's book.
[6] Sir John Marriot, *English Political Institutions* (Oxford, Oxford University Press [3rd ed.] 1925), p. 228.

Survive? (1949) and Professor G. W. Keeton's *The Decline of Parliament* (1952). On the other hand, some contrasting perspectives could be found in the post-war writings of Harold Laski and Sir Ivor Jennings. In Laski's *Reflections on the Constitution* of 1951 and Jennings's *Parliament* (2nd edition 1957), the legislature is shown in a more favourable light. Laski saw 'no reason to suppose that the status of the House of Commons has deteriorated in the last fifty years'.[7] He added that the House could make and unmake ministerial reputations and 'from the passage of the Second Reading of the Bill to the stage where it is sent to the House of Lords most things that need to be said for and against it will in the course of debate be said'.[8]

Perhaps the signs of an ideological division of opinion can be seen here. The parliamentary pessimists seem almost all to have been towards the right-hand side of the political spectrum. The moderate optimists, such as Laski, Jennings (and, one could add, Herbert Morrison in *Government and Parliament*, written in 1954) have been liberal or left-ish. When the left is in office, its supporters tend to praise the sound sense of the House of Commons whilst its opponents speak of electoral dictatorship and the need for checks and balances (the referendum in Dicey's case and a Bill of Rights in Lord Hailsham's). However, it may be that division of opinion on the powers of Parliament reflects a more complicated split of viewpoints. One is between the left and right. But some liberals, such as Ramsay Muir, were pessimists about the reduced role of Parliament. Another division of opinion is between those who saw the national source of authority as being in Parliament and those, such as Amery, who saw it as inhering in the executive.

Amongst the political scientists, diagnosis has elicited various conceptual schemes for categorizing the role of legislatures. Some have spoken of 'arena' legislatures and 'transformative' legislatures (i.e. of the American variety).[9] The British legislature in this schema may be characterized as veering towards the arena style, or perhaps in Professor Philip Norton's terms, a policy-influencing rather than a policy-making legislature.[10]

[7] H. Laski, *Reflections on the Constitution* (Manchester, Manchester University Press, 1951) p. 36.

[8] Ibid.

[9] A description adopted from M. Mezey's *Comparative Legislatures* (Durham, Duke University Press, 1979).

[10] P. Norton, *Legislatures* (Oxford, Oxford University Press, 1990) p. 177. See also Norton's *Does Parliament Matter?* (New York and London, Harvester Wheatsheaf, 1993).

These differences of viewpoint have in some degree influenced the theory and practice of parliamentary reform, for which the universal recipe has been the creation of a stronger committee system in the House of Commons. Professor Bernard Crick's *Reform of Parliament* (1964), in acknowledging the reality of a governmental entitlement to be the primary legislator, portrayed Parliament's future as that of a would-be effective controller and supervisor rather than policy-maker. The Crossman reforms and the subsequent Conservative strengthening of the Select Committee system have elicited a more favourable response from those who share this standpoint than from those who wish to see the Committee system shift the balance of power in the House between government and Parliament. Amongst academic students of legislative behaviour there seems to be a consensus that although improvements are possible in the selection procedures and logistical support of Select Committees, no substantial increase in powers can be expected in a two-party non-transformational legislature.[11] The dialogue that has taken place between the government and Select Committees reflects a claim by the House to reverse a tendency that has almost, since the time of Gladstone, become an orthodoxy—namely, that policy-making is an internal matter for governments in office—the role of Parliament being merely to keep watch, to oppose and, if possible, to amend or defeat government policy. The House, via its Select Committees, is now, however, claiming in effect to participate in the government's policy-making and to have access to its hitherto private sources of policy advice. This is a major claim, amounting to an attempt to adjust in a significant way the established understanding of the separation of powers between legislature and executive.

The nature of cabinet government

The recent (i.e. 30-year-old) debate about the characterization of British executive government as cabinet or prime ministerial is generally remembered as an argument about a thesis originating with Richard Crossman who, in 1963, wrote of the passing of cabinet government:

---

[11] A number of influential works on various aspects of the work of Parliament has been produced by The Study of Parliament Group since 1964, e.g. M. Ryle and P. G. Richards, eds., *The Commons under Scrutiny* (London, Routledge, 1988); M. Franklin and P. Norton, eds., *Parliamentary Questions* (Oxford, Clarendon Press, 1993); and G. Drury, ed., *The New Select Committees* (Oxford, Clarendon Press, [2nd ed. 1985], 1989).

'The post-war epoch has seen the final transformation of cabinet government into prime ministerial government. Under this system the hyphen which joins, the buckle which fastens the legislative part of the state to the executive part becomes one single man'.[12] However, the theory has antecedents that go back to the beginnings of the century. Sidney Low quoted a speech in the House of Commons on the Licensing Bill of 1904 that rings very similarly to Crossman's words: 'The constitution had undergone a serious change (said Mr. Lawson Walter). It had ceased to be governed by Parliament; it had become governed by cabinet . . . and it was now governed by Prime Minister in Cabinet'.[13] Lord Morley, in his study of Walpole published in 1913, also took a Crossman-like view in calling the prime minister 'the keystone of the cabinet arch'. The flexibility of the cabinet system, he wrote, 'allows the prime minister in an emergency to take upon himself a power not inferior to that of a dictator'.[14]

The latter-day regeneration of the presidential or dictatorship theory of the prime ministerial role began with Crossman's misinterpretation of the theme of Professor John Mackintosh's *Cabinet Government*, published in 1962. Crossman, reviewing Mackintosh's book, hailed him as the discoverer of a new theory of the constitution. Mackintosh's theory was, however, that the country was controlled by the prime minister and cabinet, with the cabinet acting as a clearing-house and court of appeal. The subsequent debate stimulated by Crossman's view ranged over at least three different putative theories. The strongest was the allegation that the system of government was now in effect presidential with the prime minister as president and ministers as his agents. The second (an inconsistent) thesis was that effective power was exercised by inner groups of ministers and by cabinet committees. The third and most

[12] R. H. S. Crossman, 'Introduction' to Walter Bagehot, *The English Constitution* (Glasgow, Fontana, 1963), p. 51. The second edition of this work (London, Watts, 1964) contains a significantly modified and weaker version of the 'one man executive' theory.

[13] Low, *The Governance of England*, p. 77.

[14] Lord Morley, *Walpole* (London, Macmillan, 1913), pp. 157–8. However, compare the account of cabinet/prime ministerial relations in Asquith's *Fifty Years of Parliament* (London, Cassell, 1926) I, Ch. IV. For discussions of the prime ministerial government thesis see P. Gordon Walker, *The Cabinet* (London, Fontana/Collins, 1970) Ch. 5; A. King, ed., *The British Prime Minister* (London, Macmillan, [2nd ed.] 1985); and D. Shell and R. Hodder-Williams, *Churchill to Major: the British Prime Minister since 1945* (London, Hurst, 1985); P. Hennessy, *Cabinet* (Oxford, Basil Blackwell, 1986); P. Madgwick, *British Government: The Central Executive Territory* (London, Philip Allan, 1991); and G. W. Jones, 'Prime Ministerial Government since Bagehot' in R. Blackburn, ed., *Constitutional Studies* (London, Mansell, 1992).

diluted form of the theory was that the power of the prime minister had increased significantly over the past half century, in large part because of an increase in his patronage power and the increasing importance of foreign affairs in national politics. Opponents of the Crossman theory have tended to concede the second and third theses, but (obviously) to oppose the first. A stalwart opponent of the Crossman thesis was Lord Wilson, who devoted several chapters of his *The Governance of Britain* to rebutting it. Crossman himself believed Wilson to be an instantiation of the theory's validity,[15] but his view of the matter was perhaps monocular.

Whether most analysts would now put emphasis on prime ministerial or cabinet authority is not easy to determine. In 1990 a perceptive student of British politics wrote that 'it is very difficult to imagine a British prime minister in good health being deposed by cabinet colleagues. The effect is likely to be politically disastrous even if they can agree on a successor'.[16] Shortly afterwards Margaret Thatcher failed to obtain the united support of her cabinet colleagues and was deposed, although in good health at the time. She was perhaps the very image of Richard Crossman's presidential première. But the dependence on colleagues and party for survival points to a fatal flaw in the Crossman thesis. Under Margaret Thatcher the role of the cabinet was undoubtedly diminished. But she was, on more than one occasion, outfaced by cabinet opposition and it could be said that she extended surprising toleration to dissenting views in cabinet in the case of Michael Heseltine. Although it can be adjusted to suit governmental convenience, the collective responsibility of ministers for policy-making undoubtedly remains a significant feature of parliamentary government on the British model.

In recent years some writers have subsumed the debate about the relations of prime minister and cabinet in a wider enterprise that includes an attempt to view the operations of cabinet government through the medium of various theories and models of administrative behaviour applied to what has been called the 'core executive' (the prime minister, the cabinet and its committees and all the departments and organizations involved in co-ordinating government policy). Some useful information has resulted—for example, about the working of the

---

[15] See e.g. Richard Crossman's *The Diaries of a Cabinet Minister* (London, Hamish Hamilton and Jonathan Cape, 1975–7), I, p. 28: 'After five years of service in the government I was relieved to find that my Cabinet thesis had survived the test of firsthand experience.'
[16] D. Kavanagh, *Thatcherism and British Politics: The End of Consensus* (Oxford, Oxford University Press, [2nd ed. 1990] 1987), p. 261.

Cabinet Office and the behaviour of prime ministers in the House of Commons. However, it is not clear that the translation of the problem into the language of organization theory or the contrast between so-called institutional/historical and behavioural approaches has greatly clarified the questions in issue. It is possible to overdraw the contrast between behavioural studies that rely on the study of documentation, mass media coverage and participant interviews on the one hand and historical or institutional inquiries with 'no developed theoretical perspective' that utilize 'memoirs, diaries and platitudinous observations by ex ministers' on the other. Ministers do not abandon platitudes when subjected to participant interviews and historians are not confined in their documentation to political memoirs. New forms of inquiry should be welcomed and it is possible that the methodology of core executive studies will produce new and enlivening insights. On the other hand, they may be more useful in creating a framework of comparison for the study of executive behaviour in different political systems than in throwing a different kind of light on domestic political behaviour.[17]

The accountability of ministers

The principle that a government and its ministers are responsible to, subordinate to, and removable by, the legislature, is what in formal terms distinguishes the British political system from the system of co-ordinate, non-subordinate and virtually irremovable executive power exemplified in the United States. It can perhaps be called the central organizing principle that fixes (although by convention not law) the relation between the executive and legislative branch of government.

For all that, writers of textbooks have not devoted much space to its analysis as an aspect of the separation of powers.[18] Bagehot's remark that 'the efficient secret of the English constitution may be described as the close union, the nearly complete fusion of the executive and legislative power' relates to the intermix of persons and membership as distinct

---

[17] On all of this, see particularly P. Dunleavy and R. A. W. Rhodes, 'Core Executive Studies in Britain'; A. Seldon, 'The Cabinet Office and Coordination 1979–87'; and P. Dunleavy, G. W. Jones and B. O'Leary, 'Prime Ministers and the Commons: Patterns of Behaviour 1868–1987', in Dunleavy, Rhodes and O'Leary, 'Prime Minister, Cabinet and Core Executive', *Public Administration*, 68 (1990) 1–140.

[18] The best recent discussion of the separation of powers doctrine in its application to the United Kingdom is in E. Barendt's article 'Separation of Powers and Constitutional Government', *Public Law*, 599 (1995).

from the contrast of functions or powers. The functions are not fused. Bagehot's proposition tends to conceal the fact that the accountability of government and the checking and balancing that goes with it is one aspect of the separation of powers. Even the fusion of membership was historically by way of a special exception from the historical principle that the King's ministers as servants of the Crown should not sit in the Commons. The right to force the resignation of ministers as the successor to the procedure of impeachment indicates that some of the virtues of a separation of powers can be found as much in a system of legislative supremacy as in one embodying co-ordinate branches of government.

The staple theme of academic discussion through the century has, however, been that accountability diminishes as party discipline and whipped majorities give ministers security of tenure. So also has been the question whether ministerial responsibility of individual ministers can be an effective sanction where cabinets maintain collective solidarity. Low's chapter on ministerial responsibility in *The Governance of England* is an early statement of the point that 'the delinquent minister' may be protected from dismissal by the assertion of the collective liability of the cabinet backed by a party machine. However, oddly, the major works on British government between the wars do not contain any extended account or analysis of the responsibility convention either in its collective or in its individual aspect. For example, there is little to be found in Harold Laski's *Parliamentary Government in England* (1938) or in the major works of Jennings on *Parliament* and *Cabinet Government*.

The modern debate on the principle of individual responsibility dates from the publication in 1956 of an article by Samuel Finer in which he argued that the supposed convention required that a minister should resign after personal or departmental misdemeanour had resulted in condemnation by the House of Commons. But there were, he argued, no significant precedents for the operation of such a rule.[19] In 1954 Sir Thomas Dugdale had resigned after a public inquiry into the Crichel Down case had given rise to a debate in the House of Commons and also to some much-quoted speeches by Sir David Maxwell-Fyfe and Herbert Morrison, the upshot of which was that ministers should resign only for departmental activities of which they were aware or had participated in. There was some uncertainty at the time about Sir Thomas Dugdale's part

---

[19] S. E. Finer, 'The Individual Responsibility of Ministers', *Public Administration*, 34 (1956), 377.

in the affair[20] but he was certainly blamed for his part in it and resigned. Few subsequent individual resignations have occurred as the result of parliamentary criticism of a minister or his department's policy or administration, although Lord Carrington's resignation in 1982 and Leon Brittan's in 1985 are examples. The line between them and the many ministers who have resigned after various forms of individual misbehaviour is, however, in some degree unclear.

New forms of governmental organization beginning with the post-war public corporations and continuing with the so-called Next Steps Agencies have promoted a good deal of commentary as to the ways in which different forms of accountability may be conceptualized (e.g. executive/explanatory, corrective, sacrificial and the like).[21] Also, a head of the Civil Service, Sir Robin Butler, has promulgated a distinction between the formal answerability of ministers (accountability) and responsibility or culpability which may involve the sanction of resignation. Ministers on this view retain accountability but not responsibility for the actions of non-departmental agencies exercising quasi-independent powers conferred on them in their framework agreements.

All of this perhaps illustrates the potentiality for co-operation between academic and governmental inquiry into questions of governance. Ministerial responsibility has recently been in part the subject of inquiries by the Treasury and Civil Service Committee (now the Public Service Committee)[22] and by the inquiry under Lord Justice Scott.[23] This has in turn stimulated further academic and parliamentary debate on the government's reactions to both sets of inquiries.[24] Perhaps the most significant recommendation of the Scott Report was that freedom of information provisions should be seen as a corollary of ministerial responsibility and a necessary counter-weight to the acceptance of a Civil Service entitled to a shield of confidentiality in its relations with

---

[20] Significant additional information about the participants in the Crichel Down affair appears in I. F. Nicolson's *The Mystery of Crichel Down* (Oxford, Oxford University Press, 1986).

[21] On which, see D. Woodhouse, *Ministers and Parliament: Accountability in Theory and Practice* (Oxford, Oxford University Press, 1993) Ch. 2.

[22] *Rôle of the Civil Service: Interim Report, Minutes of Evidence and Appendices*, H.C. 390–II, 1992–3; and *Ministerial Accountability and Responsibility*, Public Service Committee, H.C. 234, 1996–7.

[23] *Report of the Inquiry into the Export of Defence Equipment and Dual Use Goods to Iraq and Related Prosecutions*, 1995–6, H.C. 115.

[24] See e.g. the articles in [1996] *Public Law*, 179 (Special Number on the Scott Report); also articles in *Parliamentary Affairs* (January 1997); and A. Tomkins, *the Constitution After Scott: Government Unwrapped* (Oxford, Clarendon Press, 1998).

ministers. Problems still unresolved are the limits of the duties of civil servants to serve ministers, the competing and inconsistent claims of ministers and select committees about their respective powers and the limitations on the subject matter of parliamentary questions. Ministerial responsibility is in fact not one but a large bundle of problems. There is a ministerial aspect in the working of almost every institution in the parliamentary system—in the relations of government with the Civil Service, the non-departmental agencies, the police, the security services, the machinery of prosecution and the law and procedure of Parliament.

Some critics (ever since Finer) have argued that the convention of individual ministerial responsibility is a fiction that conceals reality and not a genuine convention. This conclusion was confirmed for some when Lord Justice Scott's inquiry concluded that constitutionally improper things had been done by ministers, but no minister resigned. The correct conclusion is not that the rule or convention is a fiction or that it does not exist, but rather that rules may be broken and that some recent breaches testify to what one critic has called 'the feeble state of our constitutional morality'.[25] The enforcement of our constitutional morality is in such cases in the hands of Members of Parliament and the evidence of post-war experience is that they are not up to the task.

The dignified institutions

The monarchy and the Upper House of Parliament have generally been thought to merit Bagehot's label of dignified rather than efficient institutions in government, although this view would no doubt be disputed by monarchists and by many peers on both sides of the House. Nonetheless the part played by the House of Lords in the British system has been a somewhat peculiar one. Debate about the second chamber has been dominated by the question of its reform. The struggle over the Liberal budget that produced the Parliament Act of 1911 ended with a preamble to the Act that contained the phrase:

> Whereas it is intended to substitute for the House of Lords as it present exists a second chamber constituted on a popular instead of hereditary basis but such substitution cannot immediately be brought into operation.[26]

---

[25] Bogdanor, *Public Administration*, 74, at p. 611.
[26] Recounted in R. Jenkins, *Mr. Balfour's Poodle* (London, Heinemann, 1954). Also in Asquith, *Fifty Years of Parliament* II, part IV. On the Parliament Act, see Ch. XII of Sir Ivor Jennings, *Parliament* (Cambridge, Cambridge University Press, [2nd ed.] 1957).

What conclusion about the nature of British political institutions can be inferred from the fact that despite this manifest intention the second chamber retained its unreformed character at the end of the century? The delay in bringing the House of Lords into full conformity with modern democratic practice has stemmed in the main from uncertainty about its composition rather than its powers. The second Parliament Act of 1949 reduced its delaying powers between successive second readings of a bill in different sessions to one rather than two years, which in practice reduced the period of effective resistance to governmental measures supported by the Commons to a few months.

Over the course of the century two abortive attempts have been made to tackle the issue of composition—one in the Bryce Report on Reform of the Second Chamber in 1918 and the other in the Wilson government's unsuccessful bill in 1969. The Bryce Report is probably the most comprehensive survey of the desired features of the British second chamber. They were the examination and revision of bills brought from the Commons; the initiation of bills of a non-controversial character; the interposition of so much delay (and no more) in the passage of bills affecting the fundamentals of the constitution as to enable the opinion of the nation to be adequately expressed; and full and free discussion of large and important questions such as foreign policy for which the House of Commons cannot find time. After considering nomination by the Crown, direct election by local authorities and selection by a joint standing committee of both Houses, the Conference recommended election of a majority of members by members of the House of Commons (grouped into territorial areas) with the remainder chosen, at first from the existing peerage, by a joint standing committee of the two Houses, with the elected Members holding office for twelve years. The members of the Bryce Conference had in addition some clear views as to the persons who should be elected to the second chamber. They included persons with a knowledge of what were called Imperial Questions and matters affecting the Overseas Dominions and 'a certain proportion who are not extreme partizans, but are the cast of mind which enables them to judge political questions with calmness and comparative freedom from prejudice or bias'. It might well have been thought that if such persons were available for employment as legislators they could be better put to work in the House of Commons. Needless to say, none such have been available and the question of selecting the members of a renovated upper chamber has continued to pose a problem to the Blair reforming government. The interim solution has been life peerages, bolstered by generous attendance allowances. The abortive Labour reform attempted in 1967 featured a complex scheme of voting and non-voting peers, with existing peers by succession having the right to speak but not vote. The new House was to have a delaying power of six months, which in effect would have been no delaying power at all. Until the Blair Government, the most significant development in the role of the Lords was the 1958 Life Peerages legislation and the virtual elimination of hereditary peerages. The prime ministerial patronage involved in the selection of life peers has had as one of its incidental results the augmentation of prime ministerial power.

Not a great deal of descriptive or analytic work on the role of the Lords in the political system has been done by historians or political scientists until relatively recent times. In the 1950s Peter Bromhead's *The House of Lords and Contemporary Politics* (1958) was the standard work. Janet Morgan's *The House of Lords and the Labour Government* (1975) covers the attempted Labour reform of 1969 and the most recent works are Donald Shell's *The House of Lords* (1988) and *The House of Lords at Work* (1993)[27] a case study of the 1988–89 session by Donald Shell and David Beamish. At the time of writing all of this is no doubt about to change with the House of Lords at the centre of the Government's constitutional reform agenda, with legislation to abolish the right of hereditary peers to sit and a Royal Commission on Reform of the House of Lords appointed to consider the powers, procedures and composition of a reformed House.

The House of Lords has played a significant role in the argument over the years about the role of the mandate in British politics. There are two forms of mandates that might be dubbed positive and negative. The positive mandate posits that a government ought to do what at the time of an election it has promised to do. The negative, and commoner, form of the mandate argument is that a government ought not to do what it has not been authorized to do at the time of a general election (or possibly by referendum). As the Bryce Report indicates, the House of Lords has been traditionally defended by the argument that its delaying powers may serve to allow popular opinion to focus on an issue, so creating the required authority necessary for fundamental or

---

[27] There is a good factual chapter in J. A. G. Griffith and M. Ryle, *Parliament: Functions, Practice and Procedure* (London, Sweet & Maxwell, 1989) and in the chapters on the Lords in Sir Thomas Erskine May, *Parliamentary Practice* (London, Butterworth [21st ed.] 1989). A useful exchange on the role of the Lords during the Thatcher Administration is to be found in *Parliamentary Affairs* in 1985 and 1988. D. R. Shell, 'The House of Lords and the Thatcher Government', *Parliamentary Affairs*, 38 (1985), 16, and A. Adonis, *Parliamentary Affairs*, 41 (1988), 380.

constitutional change.[28] In the immediate post-war period the Conservative opposition refrained from opposing on a second reading a number of Labour bills on the ground that they had received the popular mandate by having been included in the Labour Party's 1945 election manifesto. This allegedly gave rise to the so-called Salisbury convention. The convention has not been consistently followed by either party[29] and there might well be doubt as to whether it ever was a genuine convention, since conventions do not normally arise on the basis of a unilateral party practice. It might also be questioned whether the rule, if it is such, is still in force, having been enunciated before the reconsideration of the role of the House of Lords that took place in 1949. The debates on the 1949 Parliament Act led to a compromise between those who wished for longer and shorter periods of delay. It was not at that time stated that the compromise of a one-year delaying period was subject to a convention that the House should never use the powers conferred by the Act in the case of mandated legislation. A binding prohibition of this kind seems in any event inconsistent with the practice of parliamentary government which rests on parliamentary debate. Some time may pass between the placing of a policy in a party's manifesto and its becoming the subject of legislation. Fresh arguments may arise in the course of the Bill's passage which may not have been aired at a general election. So an absolute conventional ban on opposing manifesto items seems difficult to justify. However, some opponents of the Lords appear to adopt the premise that any use of the powers agreed in 1949 provides a justification for threats of abolition or swamping. Although the hereditary basis has been the focus of inter-party disagreement, it is noticeable that no significant arguments have been advanced in favour of a unicameral system of the kind adopted in some Commonwealth countries. Both academic and political opinion supports the institution of bicameral government.

In some degree the monarchy[30] has benefited until recently from a similar institutional conservatism. Republicanism has not been a signi-

---

[28] The development of the mandate argument in the nineteenth century is analysed in G. H. L. Le May's chapter 'The House of Lords and the Doctrine of the Mandate', in his *The Victorian Constitution: Conventions, Usages and Contingencies* (London, Duckworth, 1979).

[29] For examples, see Griffith and Ryle, *Parliament*, pp. 504–5.

[30] For general commentary on the role and powers of the monarchy, see H. Nicolson, *King George V: His Life and Reign*, Ch. VIII (London, Constable, 1952); A. Berriedale Keith, *The King and the Imperial Crown* (London, Longman Green, 1936); E. A. Forsey, *The Royal Power of Dissolution in the British Commonwealth* (Toronto, Oxford University Press, 1943); R. Blackburn 'The Future of the Monarchy', in R. Blackburn, ed., *Constitutional Studies: Contemporary issues and controversies* (London, Mansell, 1992); and V. Bogdanor, *The Monarchy and the Constitution* (Oxford, Oxford University Press, 1995).

ficant element in the politics of the United Kingdom. Criticism has focused on the alleged need to remove the exercise of some prerogative powers from the Crown—particularly the prerogative of parliamentary dissolution and refusal of dissolution, together with the prerogative of appointing prime ministers—powers which affect the way in which governments begin and end.

The points in time at which the exercise by the Crown of a personal prerogative or personal influence has affected the course of politics could be numbered on the fingers of one hand. Even these occasions are controversial, since defenders of the Crown's prerogatives would argue that even at such times the Crown has been guided by a desire to follow responsible political advice or by a clear rule of constitutional convention rather than by personal discretion or preference. That might have been said of George V's part in the party struggle over the role of the House of Lords in the period 1909–11[31] and over the Irish Home Rule issue immediately before the First World War. The views of George V were of some significance in relation to the need for an effective popular mandate for House of Lords reform and in his willingness to give a conditional guarantee as to the creation of peers to coerce the Upper House. The same could be said of his resistance to using the prerogative of dismissal against Liberal ministers in response to Unionist arguments that Irish Home Rule would create a fundamental change in the constitution.

As regards the choice of prime minister, it is doubtful whether much element of personal choice could be said to have been involved in the relevant decisions. In the preference in 1923 for Stanley Baldwin over Lord Curzon as leader of the Conservative Party, George V was following the clear line of Conservative party opinion. In 1931, despite criticism on the Left, the King in seeking a coalition to replace the Macdonald government was fortified by the advice of the party leaders. In 1940 the replacement of Chamberlain by Churchill was essentially the result of inter-party agreement. In the post-war years Eden's succession was not disputed and the choice of Macmillan over Butler again followed a balance of party preference. In 1963, Elizabeth II, in appointing Sir Alec Douglas-Hume, received a strong recommendation from her ex-prime minister but was possibly culpable of accepting it too readily without further inquiry. This is probably the sole point at which the

---

[31] See G. H. L. Le May's chapter 'The Crisis of the Constitution, 1906–1914' in *The Victorian Constitution*.

post-war monarch could be said to have exercised an element of personal choice. When a prime minister resigns or dies in office, the choice of successor is now, since 1965, in practice made by party leadership elections. It could be argued that the British monarchy has an indeterminate set of prerogatives whose extent has been in practice made invisible by the workings of a two-party system in which governments tend to enjoy overall support in the legislature. A more fluid party system might for this reason enhance the political role of the Crown. Much academic and political debate has indeed centred on the possibility that a hung Parliament[32] with no overall majority might face the Queen with exercising a political discretion in the choice of a prime minister in the aftermath of a general election if the incumbent prime minister is defeated by a combination of the other parties. But this difficulty, together with that of refusing a dissolution of Parliament to a prime minister, whether defeated or undefeated, has been much exaggerated. Constitutional practice and convention set fairly clear guidelines and in any problematical situation the Queen would almost certainly prefer to allow a general election to take place rather than to risk the possibility that her action might be presented in an unfavourable light by one of the major political parties. There are some few conceivable situations in which it might be necessary to take the risk. Those who advocate placing the prerogatives of dissolution and choice of prime minister in some other hands have to face the burden of suggesting a person free of all party political connection who would be equally trusted to act impartially by all political parties and interests. It is not easy to imagine who such an executive person might be.

That is a problem which faces reformers who would either create a republican constitution with a presidential head of state or who would retain the monarch with purely ceremonial duties. The first has been proposed by Anthony Benn and the second by the Institute for Public Policy Research in its draft written constitution for the United Kingdom.[33]

The Crown's role in the Commonwealth is worthy of further attention by political analysts. Over the century the Crown has, in the law of

---

[32] On the Hung Parliament problem, see D. E. Butler, *Governing without a Majority* (London, Collins, [2nd ed. Macmillan, 1986] 1983); and V. Bogdanor, *Multi-party Politics and the Constitution* (Cambridge, Cambridge University Press, 1983).

[33] See A. Benn and A. Hood, *Common Sense: A New Constitution for Britain* (London, Hutchinson, 1993) and Institute for Public Policy Research, *The Constitution of the United Kingdom* (London, Institute for Public Policy Research, 1991).

the Commonwealth, become divisible. Thus, as Queen of her various monarchies, the person who is Elizabeth II of the United Kingdom is constitutionally obliged to act in accordance with the law and convention of a number of different jurisdictions. What she can do in each of them may not be on all fours with what she can do in relation to ministers in the United Kingdom. Discovering what in each case this is poses a problem both for academic research and constitutional advisers.

For example, some uncertainty still prevails as to whether the Queen can constitutionally refuse a request by a prime minister of one of the Commonwealth countries of which she is Head of State to dismiss the Governor-General of that country. In relation to those Commonwealth monarchies whose constitutions incorporate or have adopted the Westminster conventions, the answer should be in the affirmative. In exercising such prerogative or reserve powers, the Queen acts as Head of State of the Commonwealth country in question and may need to seek advice in that country. The Crown's powers are a necessary barrier against intimidation of the Governor-General. A rule that the Governor-General is dismissible automatically at the discretion of a prime minister would, in effect, tend to coalesce the office of Head of State and head of government and de-stabilize the constitution.[34]

The re-modelling of Dicey's constitution

It could be argued that the political systems of the Commonwealth have had a significant impact on the basic elements of the British system. If anyone were now to re-write Dicey's classic exposition of the politico-legal structure of British government he might well be struck by the thought that all three elements in that structure—the sovereignty of Parliament, the rule of law and the conventions of the constitution—have developed in ways that have been effected by events that have occurred in the working of the Westminster model of government in Commonwealth countries—particularly Canada, South Africa and New Zealand.

The conventions

In Dicey's classic work[35] the role of convention in the working of the political system was held to be fundamental but the main conventions

---

[34] See V. Bogdanor and G. Marshall, 'Dismissing Governor-Generals', [1996] *Public Law* 208.
[35] *Introduction to the Study of the Law of the Constitution* (London, Macmillan, 1885). Dicey's work has gone through ten editions, the last being in 1959 (ed. E. C. S. Wade).

define the relations between the branches of government (although some relationships, e.g. between the two Houses, rest partly on statute). They also have as a major purpose the effective working of the system of political accountability. They modify in practice the operation of the royal prerogative and other legal rules and also regulate important aspects of the relations between the United Kingdom and the members of the Commonwealth.

Over the century there has been both an evolution of the major conventions, such as the rules of ministerial responsibility[36] and a better appreciation of their relationship to the legal rules of the political system. Critics have contested Dicey's view that conventions are obeyed because disobedience to them causes collision with the rules of law. Dicey drew this conclusion only in relation to the convention of ministerial resignation or dissolution after a confidence defeat in the House of Commons, arguing that a defeated government would sooner or later find its policies, including its financial legislation, unworkable for lack of legal authority. However, no illegality would follow (as Dicey conceded) the breach of other conventions such as those relating to the two Houses of Parliament or to the relations between the Crown and Cabinet. All that it is necessary to say of this is that conventions rest on an acknowledgement by politicians of their moral and political obligatoriness. If politicians do not acknowledge this and a convention is consistently breached, the convention changes.

Authoritative commentators such as Sir Ivor Jennings and Sir Kenneth Wheare[37] have attempted to clarify the way in which conventions are established. Apart from express agreement, conventions arise from precedents, from beliefs by politicians that the precedents are binding and the existence of good reasons for the rule in question. It has become clear, however, that these criteria are potentially inconsistent. The beliefs of politicians are empirical matters of fact; the rational basis of rules and the correct interpretation and identification of precedents are matters of argument. Politicians may draw false conclusions about the justification of rules of political behaviour and there is no independent arbiter as to the correct conclusion to be drawn from a line of precedents. However, some still think that conventions are the

---

[36] See above pp. 8 ff.

[37] I. Jennings, *Cabinet Government* (Cambridge, Cambridge University Press [3rd ed.] 1959). Ch. 1; *The Law and the Constitution* (London, University of London Press [5th ed.] 1959). Ch. 3; K. C. Wheare, *Modern Constitutions* (London, Oxford University Press, 1951) Ch. viii.

rules that politicians in fact believe to be obligatory; others, that conventions are the rules that they *ought* to think obligatory.[38]

A further bone of contention has been the relationship between the conventions and the rules of law. Dicey believed that conventions were in principle rules not enforced or recognized by courts of law. This view has proved to be correct as to enforcement but incorrect as to recognition. Many decisions in British courts have recognized the existence of conventions, particularly those of ministerial responsibility — when interpreting statutes or applying common law doctrines. The line between recognizing a convention and giving it legal effect is in these circumstances a thin one, as became clear in the Crossman Diaries case in 1976 when the High Court, in applying the doctrine of breach of confidence to Cabinet proceedings, heard much evidence about the conventions of Cabinet secrecy and solidarity.[39]

Many of these issues were presented in a novel light during the brief constitutional crisis in Canada in 1980–82 which arose from the Canadian federal government's attempts to change the constitution of Canada by requesting Westminster legislation. This raised the question whether a clear convention required the United Kingdom Parliament to comply automatically with the federal government's request in the face of opposition by eight of the ten provinces. In Canada, the question was whether any local convention existed permitting the provinces to veto federal action of the kind proposed and whether such a convention could be enforced in the courts. The first question was answered in the negative by a Select Committee of the House of Commons. The Canadian question was submitted to a number of provincial courts in Canada and finally to the Supreme Court which held that the federal government's action was lawful but contrary to convention.[40] This was an example of a convention being declared to exist by a court although without any suggestion that it was legally enforceable. It was only possible because statutes in Canada permit references to be made by governments to the courts of any question of law or fact. Since conventions often involve disputed facts and are controversial and, since governments may be disinclined to obey them, a legally unenforceable

---

[38] See G. Marshall, *Constitutional Conventions* (Oxford, Oxford University Press, 1986) Ch. 1, pp. 10–12.

[39] *Attorney-General* v. *Jonathan Cape* [1976] QB 752.

[40] See H.C. 421 (1980–81) *British North America Acts: The Rôle of Parliament*; also 3rd Report H.C. 128 (1981–2) and *Reference Re. Amendment of the Constitution of Canada (Nos. 1, 2 and 3)* (1982) 125 D.L.R. (3rd) 1. Marshall, *Constitutional Conventions*, Ch. XI.

judicial arbitration as to their existence and application might be a useful adjunct to the governmental machinery of the United Kingdom also.

Although the area of convention in the strictest sense of clear and unambiguous rules regarded as politically obligatory is fairly limited, there is a wide area of political behaviour that is governed by customary or convention-like rules of practice. Examples are the parliamentary relations between Government and Opposition, the rules for the allocation of election broadcasts between the parties, the Code of Conduct and Guidance on Procedures for Ministers, and the understandings governing the relations of the Civil Service with the political opposition in the period before general elections. Some proponents of proposals for a written constitution do not make it clear whether all such rules of constitutional practice would be brought within the code or whether they would continue to exist and to accumulate outside it. It is uncertain how a written constitution could either satisfactorily codify all the existing rules of constitutional practice or forbid their further development.

The rule of law

Over the years Dicey's statement of the circumstances necessary for the rule of law to prevail has been continuously debated. Modern liberals and radicals have felt some discomfort with Dicey's contention that the rule of law should preclude the exercise of broad discretions by ministers and civil servants. Many who were not radical also castigated his view that administrative courts of the Continental kind were inconsistent with the equality of all subjects before the law.

Between 1920 and 1939 administrative law became a battleground between lawyers and polemicists of left and right. Lord Hewart's *The New Despotism* of 1929, a Dicey-ite (and forceful and much-maligned) attack on the expansion of bureaucratic power and the growth of delegated legislation, was followed by a series of works by Sir Carleton Allen, Professor of Jurisprudence in Oxford, beginning with *Bureaucracy Triumphant* in 1931.[41] Similar views were expressed by F. A. Hayek in *The Road to Serfdom* published in 1944—a work described by Professor Herman Finer in *The Road to Reaction* (1945) as 'the most sinister offen-

---

[41] C. K. Allen, *Bureaucracy Triumphant* (London, Oxford University Press, 1931). Also later, *Law and Orders: An Inquiry into the Nature and Scope of Delegated Legislation and Executive Powers in English Law* (London, Stevens, 1956). For an extended historical account of the expansion of delegated powers through the century, see W. H. Greenleaf's *The British Political Tradition Vol. 3: A Much Governed Nation*, Part 2 (London, Methuen, 1987).

sive against a democracy to emerge from a democratic country for many decades'. Hayek argued that socialist planning and the rule of law were incompatible.

The LSE lawyers and political scientists took a friendlier view of ministerial powers, arguing that delegated legislation and administrative adjudication were necessary elements in modern administration. This standpoint was expressed at some length in W. A. Robson's *Justice and Administrative Law* (1928) and urged by Harold Laski and Ellen Wilkinson as members of the Committee on Ministers' Powers of 1929–32.[42] The Committee agreed.

In the 1950s the control of administrative powers lost its ideological fervour. In the post-war years the House of Commons had assumed some control of statutory instruments through its scrutiny committee and the source of concern shifted to the need to control administrative decision-making and to the system of administrative tribunals and public inquiries, a system lacking in structural consistency and insufficiently amenable to judicial control. Some order was introduced into the chaos on the recommendations of the Franks Committee on the Administrative Tribunals and Enquiries[43] in 1957 by the Tribunals and Inquiries Act of 1959 and subsequent legislation. In the 1960s, after both Labour and Conservative governments had experienced the necessities of office, a cross-party debate developed on the need to expand the machinery for the redress of citizens' grievances. Some favoured a homemade version of the French Conseil d'Etat as a general forum for administrative appeals. Other reformers looked to Scandinavia where citizens' defenders were to be found operating, albeit in a rather different kind of parliamentary system. Finally, after the Labour Party found itself committed to action by its 1964 election pledges, a version of the Ombudsman was imported via New Zealand and given the more Anglican title of Parliamentary Commissioner for Administration.

In many respects the rule of law is better served by the institutions of British government than it was in Dicey's day. Since 1947 the Crown has been made answerable to actions in tort and contract as if it were a private person, and the courts, after a period of extreme deference to ministerial decision-making from the beginning of the First World War to the late 1950s, have exerted a widening control over administrative action through the machinery of judicial review. In 1985 Lord Roskill

[42] Cmd 4060, HMSO (1932).
[43] Cmnd 218, HMSO (1957).

remarked that 'As a result of judicial decisions since about 1950 . . . there has been a dramatic and indeed a radical change in the scope of judicial review . . . and upsurge of judicial activism'.[44] Over this period, the higher judiciary has resisted the conferring of unreviewable discretions on ministers or civil servants, narrowed the scope of state immunities including the exercise of prerogative powers and virtually invented new grounds of judicial review.

There remains an unanswered question about Dicey's rule of law concept. Is the equality before the law that it embodies merely to do with procedural regularity and keeping all decision-makers within their jurisdictions through the application of the *ultra vires* rule, or does it embrace what might be called due process of law and constitutionalism in the wider sense, namely the idea that law, including that made by Parliament, must respect the rights of citizens? In recent years differing views have been expressed on this point by legal and political theorists.[45] At any rate, Dicey's rule of law theory seems clearly to be the narrower one.[46] Dicey regarded his two principles—the rule of law and the sovereignty of Parliament—as compatible, but legislative supremacy as he expounded it is clearly inconsistent with the wider (or constitutionalism) sense of the rule of law and potentially inconsistent even with the narrower concept of procedural regularity.

Parliamentary sovereignty

How then has the twentieth century treated the doctrine of legislative sovereignty? In 1915, when Dicey completed the eighth edition of his book, the authority of Parliament extended throughout the British Empire. In 1931 when the Statute of Westminster conferred independent legislative powers on the Parliaments of the major dominions, it did not seek to terminate the power of the Westminster legislature, but made it exercisable with the consent of the Dominions. By the 1960s, independence legislation had begun to declare more boldly that the powers of the United Kingdom Parliament should not in future extend to the independent Commonwealth countries as part of their law. This, if

---

[44] *Council of Civil Service Unions* v. *Minister for the Civil Service* [1958] AC 374.

[45] See e.g. J. Raz, 'The Rule of Law and its Virtue', [1997] 93, *Law Quarterly Review*, 195; J. Jowell, 'The Rule of Law Today', in J. Jowell and D. Oliver, eds., *The Changing Constitution* (Oxford, Oxford University Press, [2nd ed.] 1989); T. R. S. Allan, *Law, Liberty and Justice* (Oxford, Oxford University Press, 1993), Ch. 2.

[46] C.f. E. Barendt, 'Dicey and Civil Liberties' [1985] *Public Law*, 590 (All Souls—Public Law Seminar: Dicey and the Constitution).

effective, was a serious revision of Dicey's view of imperial sovereign authority which could not make partial territorial abdications of legislative power while itself remaining in existence. Dicey's theory therefore placed substantial obstacles in the way of the United Kingdom's either creating legal autonomy for previously subordinate legislatures or merging the United Kingdom in any future federal arrangements of states, but the needs of the Commonwealth and later of the European Community have forced the theory to grapple with new situations. Dicey's sovereignty theory, although supported in the courts, had its critics. A number of them, including Sir Ivor Jennings[47] and Richard Latham[48] argued that Parliament's sovereign power was a legal concept and that the rules about the composition and procedure of the sovereign were not created by it but by the common law. The courts might not question the area of power within which Parliament could legislate but necessarily must decide what constituted a valid Act of Parliament. This analysis, which some have called a 'new view' of sovereignty[49] received some support from decisions in Commonwealth jurisdictions, particularly Australia and South Africa.[50] In South Africa in 1952 in *Harris* v. *Minister of the Interior*, the Supreme Court held that certain protective clauses in the constitution, whose repeal originally required Parliament to act by a two-thirds majority in a joint session of both Houses, were still binding on the South African Parliament although it had become sovereign under the provisions of the 1931 Statute of Westminster. It was held that this was not a limitation on the unfettered area of power of the sovereign Parliament but merely a judicial insistence that Parliament must act in the appropriate manner and form laid down by existing law in order to be Parliament. This decision, although it had no direct application to the United Kingdom Parliament, at least raised the question whether the courts would apply the area of power/manner and form distinction if faced by an attempt in the United Kingdom to impose

---

[47] Sir Ivor Jennings, *The Law and the Constitution* (London, University of London Press, [3rd ed.] 1959), Ch. IV.

[48] R. Latham, 'The Law and the Commonwealth', in W. K. Hancock, *Survey of British Commonwealth Affairs*, I, (London, Oxford University Press, 1937).

[49] R. F. V. Heuston, *Essays in Constitutional Law* (London, Stevens, 1964), Ch. 1. Heuston remarks that 'the doctrine of parliamentary sovereignty is almost entirely the work of Oxford men', p. 1. That need not perhaps constitute a conclusive condemnation of it.

[50] *A.G. for New South Wales* v. *Trethowen* (1932) 44 C.L.R. 394 and [1932] AC 526 (PC); *Harris* v. *Minister of the Interior*, 1952 (2) SA 429. Credit should also be given to a short work of great importance: Professor D. V. Cowen's *Parliamentary Sovereignty and the Entrenched Sections of the South Africa Act* (Capetown, Juta, 1951).

such conditions by Act of Parliament on future repeals. Could Parliament entrench a constitutionally important or fundamental enactment such as a Bill of Rights, a European Community Act, or a Scottish devolution measure by changing the future manner and form of law-making for the repeal of such enactments? When the House of Lords set up a Select Committee to consider the need for a Bill of Rights in the United Kingdom[51] they accepted the view that entrenchment of such a Bill was not possible. But the literature on this point is extensive and there are persuasive arguments of principle to the contrary.[52]

Those who hold the revised theory of parliamentary sovereignty and believe that Parliament may impose procedural restrictions on future law-making do not contest the view that Parliament's area of authority (once properly constituted) is unlimited. However, that view has been challenged in Scotland, in the Commonwealth and in Europe. There are Scottish lawyers who believe the Act of Union to be fundamental and beyond the reach of Parliament, although the Scottish courts have never in practice endorsed this view. In Australia in recent years, the judiciary have concluded that, although the federal Parliament's powers are (apart from the federal division) entirely unconstrained, the system of representative government implies the existence of rights such as free speech which legislatures must respect on pain of invalidation.[53] Some British judges (extra-judicially) seem to be edging towards this view.[54] Perhaps most radically the jurisprudence of the European Court of Justice on the question of the supremacy of Community law[55] is flatly inconsistent with Dicey-ite sovereignty which by implication holds that the legislative organs of the Community are in the law of the United Kingdom mere delegates of the United Kingdom Parliament which was incapable in 1972 of abdicating its supremacy to them and therefore did not.

The same problem makes legally effective decentralization or federalization of power within the United Kingdom difficult of achievement. The most that Parliament at Westminster can do for Regional Assemblies in Scotland and Wales or Northern Ireland is to delegate

---

[51] HL 176 (1978). *Report of the Select Committee on a Bill of Rights.*

[52] See the works cited in Ch. 5 of E. C. S. Wade and A. W. Bradley, *Constitutional and Administrative Law* (London, Longman, [11th ed.] 1993).

[53] The cases are surveyed in H. P. Lee, 'The Australian High Court and Implied Fundamental Legal Guarantees', [1993] *Public Law*, 606.

[54] See e.g. Sir John Laws in 'Law and Democracy', [1995] *Public Law*, 72.

[55] E.g. in cases such as *Van Gend En Loos* [1963] ECR 1; and *Costa* v. *Enel* [1964] ECR 585.

or devolve legislative powers. The attempted division of legislative authority between Westminster and Edinburgh caused a welter of practical problems in 1979 and will continue to do so now that powers have been divided on a different plan under the provisions of the Scotland Act 1998.[56] So will the fact that powers devolved to Regional Assemblies will in many cases be in areas for which the United Kingdom as a whole remains responsible under Community law.

At some level of theory the sovereignty of Parliament remains a salient legal feature of the British constitutional system and has been careully preserved under the provisions of the Human Rights Act 1998.

In practice, however, the European dimension is the major transformative influence on British political institutions and on the constitution as it stood in 1900. A basic and possibly never-to-be-reversed decision was taken in the European Communities Act to cede the authority to make law for the United Kingdom to the Community. In consequence virtually every compartment of the law of England and Scotland is subject to a process of constant modification and amendment, not by Acts of Parliament but by statutory instruments introduced to give effect to Community directives and by regulations and treaty obligations having direct effect. Much, although not all, of this law has an impact on the private as well as the public sphere—insofar as these can now be disentangled. The political and social rights of British citizens are to a major degree now shaped by the Community organs, by the European Court of Justice and by the Strasbourg Human Rights Court applying the European Human Rights Convention. It is in effect a major re-shaping of British political institutions into a quasi-federal configuration. Its analysis will be a major task for British political scientists over the next decades.

Political institutions and public inquiry

To a considerable degree the study and analysis of British government in the twentieth century has been forwarded by the efforts of publicly-appointed bodies set up to study particular problems. In many cases their effect on the development of governmental practice has been immediate and obvious; in other cases it has been less visible, at least

---

[56] See J. McEldowney, 'Legal Aspects of Relations between the United Kingdom and the Scottish Parliament: the evolution of subordinate sovereignty', in D. Oliver and G. Drewry, eds., *The Law and Parliament* (London, Butterworths, 1998).

in the short run. The Bryce Committee on the Second Chamber is an obvious example. Another is the Haldane Committee on the Machinery of Government appointed in 1918 to 'inquire into the responsibilities of the various departments of the central executive government and to advise in what manner the exercise and distribution by the government of its functions should be improved'.[57] The Report pointed out that the functions of the departments of executive government have been allocated in response to particular historical needs on no consistent or pre-considered plan. That could still be said—particularly in relation to the haphazard division of administrative powers between local government on the one hand and decentralized agencies of central government on the other. As to the cabinet, whose job was defined as 'the continuous coordination and determination of the activities of the several departments of state', it should, the Haldane Committee said, be small in number—preferably ten and not more than 12. Nothing much came of the Haldane Report, although the question of the appropriate size of the cabinet became the staple of a good deal of academic discussion. It was debated in Leo Amery's *Thoughts on the Constitution* and in Harold Laski's *Reflections on the Constitution*. Amery favoured a small policy-planning cabinet. Laski thought it impractical. The topic has now disappeared from view, partly for political reasons and partly because of the reorganization of cabinet business and the system of cabinet committees.

There have in fact been a number of Royal Commissions whose efforts and analyses have led to little in the way of legislative change. The 1929–1932 Donoughmore Committee on Ministers' Powers is an example. On the other hand some recent Committees of Inquiry have led to relatively rapid government action. The Franks Committee on Administrative Tribunals and Enquiries led almost immediately to the Tribunals and Inquiries Act of 1959 which did much to implement the general doctrine developed by Sir Oliver Franks's Committee that administrative tribunals were to be considered not as an adjunct to the executive branch of government, but as part of the machinery of justice. Similarly, the deliberations of the Kilbrandon Commission on the Constitution of 1973 were, with some modifications, adopted as the basis of the ill-fated Scotland and Wales Acts of 1978. Similar claims might be made for the Reports of the Fulton Committee of 1968 on the Civil Service and the Willink Royal Commission on the Police in 1962 (which

[57] *Report of the Machinery of Government Committees* (Cd 9230, HMSO, 1918).

made a wide-ranging re-assessment of the role of the police service in the United Kingdom and whose recommendations were substantially adopted in the Police Act of 1964).

It is a frequently-made observation that British political scientists, unlike their American counterparts, have not played a major role in the activities of government—in part because of the different character of the federal bureaucracy, in part perhaps because of a different perception of what political science has to offer. Nonetheless, British academics have had a substantial role as members of, and advisers to, Royal Commissions and to parliamentary and governmental inquiries. The Webbs played some part in the deliberations of the Haldane Committee, Beatrice being a member. Harold Laski and Sir William Holdsworth were influential members of the Committee on Ministers' Powers. Sir Kenneth Wheare was a member of the Franks Committee, Sir Oliver Franks (as he then was) being at least by inclination an academic. W. J. M. Mackenzie served on the Royal Commission on London Government. Lord Crowther Hunt was a member of the Fulton Committee and Kilbrandon Commission and Lord Blake a member of the House of Lords Select Committee on the Bill of Rights of 1978. In addition, a large number of academics have acted as special advisers to House of Commons Select Committees on diverse matters, including ministerial accountability, Official Secrets and repatriation of the Canadian Constitution. The published and written evidence of the Study of Parliament Group (a joint study group of academics and officers of the House of Commons) has since the 1960s produced a stream of advice on matters of parliamentary procedure.

Theory and analysis in political institutions

The post-Second World War generation of political scientists whose interest was in the workings of British government had a fairly modest view of their profession. When they formed the Political Studies Association of the United Kingdom in 1950 some hesitation was felt even about the term 'political science' and 'Political Studies' was preferred.[58] In some degree this was because their training was in a miscellany of traditional disciplines. Brogan, Cole, Laski (who died in

[58] See the account by Sir Norman Chester 'Political Studies in Britain: Recollections and Comments' (in *Studies in Politics: Essays to mark the 25th Anniversary of the Political Studies Association*, ed. F. F. Ridley (Oxford, Oxford University Press, 1978) p. 29).

1950), Oakeshott, Chester, Robson, Wheare, Mackenzie, Barker, Smellie, Jennings, S. E. Finer, Hanson, Harrison and Beloff were historians, social and political theorists, lawyers and students of public administration. Most of them probably did not think of political science as a distinct discipline. William Robson was perhaps an exception. He somewhere described political science as a master science or a key to the greater welfare, dignity and happiness of mankind. This provoked Kenneth Wheare into saying that the term itself was harmless; but if he were told that political science was no more than recent or current political and constitutional history, he was prepared to postpone the argument and get on with his work.[59]

That generation of students of the governmental process and many of their successors in the United Kingdom were relatively untouched by the behavioural revolution in political science. Not that they fitted the behaviouralist target of formalistic writers studying mere legal forms or appearances and confining their studies to the state. They were interested in the working of institutions in a wide sense, believing that if the study of politics does not reserve a significant part of its energy for the state it becomes a mere segment of sociology.

However, the question may be raised, and often is, by political scientists whose interests are in theory-making at a fairly general level, particularly in comparative studies or models of electoral behaviour or rational choice theory, what kind of methodology or explanatory conceptualization is appropriate in the study of politics. There may be no single answer that is appropriate to every branch of political inquiry. In the analysis of political institutions, particularly of a single country (and particularly of one's own) it may be needful to reflect that the theorizing or generalizing that typically goes on is not exclusively or even primarily part of a search for explanatory models. Equally common activities are detailed description and classification and comparison, often carried out for purposes of assessment or improvement. The study of institutions is a normative as well as an explanatory activity. But in relatively familiar territory neither explanation nor assessment normally involves the promulgation of hitherto undiscerned models or concepts either of an explicatory or prescriptive kind. We already have most of what we need. The explanatory problem is simply that of describing relevant segments of the system in sufficient detail to expose what happens or happened. When we know enough about what happens, we know why. That

---

[59] K. Wheare, 'The Teaching of Politics', *Political Studies*, 3 (1955) 70.

applies to questions such as why a particular device or institution does not work as well in one place as in another, or why it now works better or worse than it did. (Why do legislative committees have a different impact in British and American government? Why does the United Kingdom national ombudsman system work more effectively than the local system?) When we know enough of the what, the why is obvious.

When it comes to assessment or prescription no deep justificatory theories are normally required. We know already what the relevant moral and political values are—democracy, liberty, equality, due process, rule of law and the like. The problem is not the invention of new categories of evaluation but rather the resolution of stresses between the existing well-known values and delineation of the particular policy consequences that may follow from the application of a particular principle. (Should all executive officers be made accountable to elected bodies? What does the principle of free expression imply for the regulation of electoral expenditure or the criminalization of racial incitement?) Most of the problems are applicatory, not foundational. In the institutional part of political science we may feel that theorizing is not one big kind of thing but a lot of miscellaneous, variably-sized things. What many of them need is not more or deeper conceptual theories but a supply of craftsmen possessed of a sceptical eye for professional jargon and capable of writing interestingly in the English language.

10: British Public Administration
Dodo, Phoenix or Chameleon?

CHRISTOPHER HOOD

Without attempting a detailed narrative history, this chapter discusses three possible interpretations of the development of British Public Administration[1] over the twentieth century, as a way of assessing its contribution to political science. Those interpretations are respectively labelled 'dodo', 'phoenix' and 'chameleon'.

The 'dodo' interpretation is a pessimistic *fin de siècle* view of British Public Administration (hereafter shortened to 'PA' for convenience) as in serious decline from early promise and former greatness. The 'phoenix' interpretation is a more optimistic perception of the subject as advancing in scientific rigour and conceptual sophistication over the century, leaving behind the outmoded styles of the past. A third view, the 'chameleon' interpretation, is a picture not of linear advance or overall decline but of lateral transformation, with the adoption of new intellectual colouring and markings to fit a new era.

There are 'facts' which fit each of these interpretations, and the overall assessment necessarily depends on what weightings are given to which facts. But it is argued here that the 'dodo' interpretation (although probably the commonest of the three) seems rather less plausible than the 'chameleon' or 'phoenix' interpretations.

---

[1] Public Administration is here taken to mean the study of institutional arrangements for the provision of 'public services', broadly defined to include regulation, public policy and the study of the operation of executive government (see V. Bogdanor, ed., *The Blackwell Encyclopaedia of Political Institutions* (Oxford, Basil Blackwell, 1987), pp. 504–7). It is conventional to denote PA as a field of study in upper case, as Public Administration, and as a phenomenon in lower case. In line with the approach taken by other contributors to this volume, 'British' work is taken here to mean studies by scholars based in Britain, although inevitably that criterion creates a grey area calling for line-ball judgements.

The 'dodo' interpretation: a century starting propitiously but ending in decline

The story of twentieth-century British PA is sometimes said (and more often implied) to be one of early promise followed by decline, perhaps paralleling the demise of Britain's imperial and manufacturing supremacy and the waning prestige of its once-admired administrative and governmental system. Late twentieth-century titles such as 'What's Gone Wrong with Public Administration?'[2] and 'Public Administration: A Discipline in Decline'[3] evoke images of loss of direction, loss of respect and loss of intellectual coherence. In the same vein, Rhodes[4] suggests that by the mid 1990s: 'an optimist would describe the future as bleak. A pessimist would be living and working in America'.

Implicit in such titles and comments is a view of British PA as having developed promisingly for some (or much) of the century, only to falter or fizzle out in some way in its final decades. To tell the story this way at least three long-term developments need to be negatively valued and heavily stressed. One is a putative process of 'academic drift', paralleling what Barker[5] claims to be the 'academicization' of political argument in twentieth-century Britain. A second is a 'loss of identity', with what might once have been distinctive about the British approach to PA becoming melded into a combination of American and Continental European approaches. A third is a perceived loss of influence of political science in PA relative to other disciplines (notably economics and management science), reflected towards the end of the century in a widespread tendency to re-title 'public administration' as 'public management'.

The charge of 'academic drift' would hold that PA moved in the last four decades of the century away from its Fabian roots as a humdrum but useful field of study focusing on the 'small print' details of public-service provision, and in the process became less useful as a practical contribution to good government. The charge would be that PA achieved early success by offering a largely practico-descriptive account of admin-

---

[2] P. Self, 'What's Gone Wrong with Public Administration?', *Public Administration and Development*, 6 (1986), 329–38.

[3] J. A. Chandler, 'Public Administration: A Discipline in Decline', *Teaching Public Administration*, 11 (1991), 39–45.

[4] R. A. W. Rhodes, 'From Institutions to Dogma: Tradition, Eclecticism and Ideology in the Study of British Public Administration', *Public Administration Review*, 56 (1996), 507.

[5] R. Barker, *Political Ideas in Modern Britain* (London, Routledge, [2nd ed.] 1997), p. 218.

istration (with a bit of history and philosophy thrown in), which was understandable and useful to public servants. As its language became jargonized and its concepts monopolized by political science academics (so this version of the story would run), alienated practitioners of the art of government understandably turned instead to business–management gurus for enlightenment on how to redesign their organizations or do their job better.

The tradition of PA as the 'practical' end of British political science was established early in the century, particularly by Beatrice and Sidney Webb.[6] For Sidney Webb, according to Beilharz, 'public administration . . . replaced 'utopianism''[7] and its academic study meant mapping out administrative structures, tracing their evolution, evaluating their strengths and weaknesses in historical and comparative perspective, and devising practical schemes for reform and improvement. In sharp contrast to the 'history-of-political-thought' tradition then dominating political science, focusing on the classics, students of PA as viewed by the Webbs and their followers were expected to undertake detailed analysis of government machinery on the ground, from prisons to roads to sewerage. Close attention to the details of organization and provision in public services, and careful discussion of executive arrangements in constitutional debate harks back to the tradition of Jeremy Bentham, whose intellectual 'grandchildren' Manning[8] declares the Fabians to be.

That mission established a special purpose and constituency for PA as a minority enterprise within political science, and in the early twentieth century the field rapidly acquired the conventional trappings of an academic domain—including university chairs (at Oxford and LSE) and lectureships, degree courses and diploma programmes, a learned society in the form of the Institute of Public Administration founded in 1922 (upgraded to the status of 'Royal Institute' from 1954) and its professional journal *Public Administration*. Institutes of Public Administration were set up across the then British empire, particularly for training clerks, tax collectors and inspectors. A purely academic professional grouping, the Joint University Council (JUC) Public Administration Committee emerged to co-ordinate curricula in the

---

[6] Sidney Webb, the founder of LSE, was its first Professor of PA from 1912 to 1927, although LSE did not appoint a full-time Professor of PA (William Robson) until 1947.
[7] P. Beilharz, *Labour's Utopias* (London, Routledge, 1992), p. 56.
[8] D. J. Manning, *The Mind of Jeremy Bentham* (London, Longmans Green, 1968), pp. 1, 97.

training of local government officials (never civil servants) in the 1930s.[9] The teaching of PA was also in rising demand at mid-century. PA was introduced as an option in the Oxford Philosophy, Politics and Economics (PPE) degree in the 1920s,[10] a model later widely copied for honours degrees elsewhere. And the 1930s saw much development of part-time Diplomas in PA, taught mainly through evening classes, as a means for local government officers to gain promotion and status (through the equivalent of a professional qualification) and broaden their grasp of administrative structures and processes. Close to 300 students were enrolled in such programmes in nine universities in 1936–7.[11] After the Second World War more universities began to offer diplomas, and more degree courses developed as well, although degrees in PA as such tended to be offered by the then polytechnics rather than the universities.

Moreover, the approach taken to PA in Britain in the early and middle years of the century was relatively distinctive in international terms. Small as the academic PA community was then, there does not seem to have been any single approach. Chapman and Dunsire[12] argue that the British civil service tradition has always contained two divergent styles: the Benthamite 'scientific management' tradition concerned with operational efficiency and the avoidance of muddle, and the tradition of Macaulay, Bridges and Sisson,[13] concerned with the 'courtier' role of high officials and 'high politics' of policy advice. The Webbs perhaps span both traditions, but their stress on constitutional arrangements to keep bureaucrats in check was distinct from a more 'philosophic' strain which became the mainstream British approach to PA prior to the Second World War.[14] Thomas identifies key contributors to what she terms the 'British philosophy of administration' in that era as Haldane (author of the 1918 Machinery of Government Committee report, a classic essay on principles of departmental organization),[15]

---

[9] R. A. Chapman, *Teaching Public Administration* (London, Joint University Council for Social and Public Administration, 1973), p. 9.

[10] D. N. Chester, 'Political Studies in Britain: Recollections and Comments', *Political Studies*, 23 (1975), 33.

[11] Chapman, *Teaching Public Administration*, pp. 10–11.

[12] R. A. Chapman and A. Dunsire, eds., *Style in Administration* (London, Allen & Unwin, 1973), p. 17.

[13] C. H. Sisson, *The Spirit of British Administration and Some European Comparisons* (London, Faber & Faber, [2nd ed.] 1966).

[14] R. Thomas, *The British Philosophy of Administration* (London, Longmans, 1978).

[15] *Report of the Machinery of Government Committee*, Cd 9230 (London, HMSO, 1918).

Wallas, Beveridge, Sheldon, Urwick and Stamp, and argues that these authors developed distinctive doctrines of administration sharply contrasting with the ruling American ideas of that period. Those ideas included Wallas' social–psychological focus on non-economic incentives and needs, which anticipated the American 'human relations' boom of the 1930s; and the ideas of Haldane, Sheldon and Urwick about applying the 'general staff' principle of military organization to public and other civilian organizations.

Instead of the 'politics–administration dichotomy' at the heart of American Progressive-era PA (and to some extent of the Webbs' design for their 'Socialist Commonwealth'), Thomas argues these 'British philosophers' saw politics and administration as inextricably fused in the process of government. Instead of being conceived as a 'science' in a modernist sense, leading to the discovery of 'laws', administration was seen as a combination of science and ethics, to be approached in a philosophical style rather than in the standard literature/hypotheses/data format of natural science.[16] The tradition, epitomized at mid-century in Samuel Finer's classic *Primer of Public Administration*[17] was to set administrative and machinery-of-government issues in an historical and (quasi-) philosophical context, and not to view the teaching of PA as a narrowly technical training.

The major subfields of PA tended to be defined mainly by 'real estate', in the sense of discrete institutions under study (local government, central government, etc.). And in contrast to both the American and Continental European tradition, 'social administration' became separated from 'PA' early in the century in Britain, and in the process developed largely outside political science. Within 'PA' thus defined much attention was paid to local government (as in the work of the Webbs, Robson[18] and Herman Finer[19]). The civil service was also a focus of attention, albeit to a lesser extent, and as public enterprise began to replace regulated private utilities as a favoured instrument of public policy, it attracted increasing analytic attention. Imperial administration, always closely intermixed with that of the 'island state' (as in the case of Indian civil service recruitment practices applied to the United Kingdom in the nineteenth-century Northcote-Trevelyan reforms) was a major

[16] W. A. Robson, 'The Study of Public Administration, Then and Now', *Political Studies*, 15 (1975), 193–201.
[17] S. E. Finer, *A Primer of Public Administration* (London, Frederick Muller, 1950).
[18] W. A. Robson, *The Development of Local Government* (London, Allen & Unwin, 1931).
[19] H. Finer, *English Local Government* (London, Methuen, 1933).

field of study until the 1960s, and the 'theory of indirect rule' as developed by Lugard, Hailey and others was a distinctive contribution to the theory of government.[20] The study of law and administration, pioneered particularly by Robson from the 1920s,[21] also became a major subfield of PA, much of it outside political science in a narrow sense, but the main academic thrust of British PA was not law-centric, as in the Continental European tradition; nor was it closely linked to the scientific management tradition as in the United States.[22] Although there was much arm-waving about 'the need for theory' in the early pages of *Public Administration*, the favoured style was to keep 'theory' (in the orthodox scientific sense) implicit. Mackenzie[23] (with a philological background and a training in classical rhetoric) saw British PA discourse as argument by enthymeme—based on a decision as to what assumptions to expose and which to suppress—rather than by syllogism or systematic evidence.

PA at this time was conceived more as a co-operative enterprise between 'reflective practitioners' and academics, than as a detached world of scholarship in the traditional style of the humanities or natural sciences. Indeed, much of the work of pioneers such as Robson was highly *engagé*—in his case, seeking to reshape local government and champion local government and public enterprise against what he saw as the malign influence of the civil service.[24] The interchange between academia and Whitehall during and after the Second World War perhaps reinforced this approach, and the changed landscape of executive government after 1945 gave PA academics plenty of 'mapping' work to do. For example, Chester and Robson charted the new world of statutory public corporations which had replaced regulated private or municipal enterprise across the utility sector and beyond. More adventurously, perhaps, Wheare[25] analysed the use of committees in administration (a theme much more stressed in the British than American PA literature at

---

[20] Lord Lugard, *The Dual Mandate in British Tropical Africa* (London, Blackwood, 1922); Lord Hailey, *Native Administration and Political Development in British Tropical Africa* (London, HMSO, 1944).

[21] C. E. Hill, 'A Bibliography of the Writings of W. A. Robson', *Greater London Papers No.17* (London, LSE, 1986).

[22] Cf. G. Drewry, 'Never Mind the Administration, Feel the Justice', Inaugural Lecture, Royal Holloway and Bedford New College, 3 May 1990.

[23] W. J. M. Mackenzie, 'Public Administration in the Universities', in W. J. M. Mackenzie, *Explorations in Government* (London, Macmillan, 1975), p. 8.

[24] See preface by G. W. Jones in Hill, 'A Bibliography of the Writings of W. A. Robson', p. 11.

[25] K. C. Wheare, *Government by Committee* (Oxford, Clarendon Press, 1955).

that time) and Mackenzie and Grove explored central government by a combination of institutional description and analytic themes deriving from Simon's work on organization.[26]

The expansive 1960s produced some big-project studies, notably Griffiths' study of central–local administrative relationships[27] and Chester and Willson's survey of central departments,[28] both sponsored by the Royal Institute of Public Administration (RIPA) and neither fully replicated for 30 years. It was also an era of 'reform commissions' concerned with redesign of both central and local government, in which PA academics were much engaged, prompting a review of theory and evidence.[29] Colonial administration had been taught (for example at LSE and Oxford) in the 1930s, but in the era of decolonization and development assistance to new and emergent states, the new subfield of 'development administration' became established and influential, with work by authors such as Chambers[30] and Schaffer (who played a key role in defining the new field[31] and later pioneered a theory of 'access' to bureaucracy)[32] attracting international attention. Local government studies, always central to the Fabian vision of PA, were revitalized by the formation of the Institute for Local Government Studies at Birmingham University (originally in a mainly 'development administration' context) in 1963, a unique institution which trained a new generation of senior administrators, both by short courses and an innovative Master's programme built around organization theory and policy studies. Specialized centres for the study of health service management developed in the following decade, and the Civil Service College, founded in 1970, might be seen as a certain, albeit equivocal, official recognition of a need to expose civil servants to academic PA ideas.

However, from the 'dodo' perspective, the picture for British PA becomes much bleaker for the last quarter of the century. The 'British

---

[26] W. J. M. Mackenzie and J. W. Grove, *Central Administration in Britain* (London, Longman, 1957).

[27] J. A. G. Griffith, *Central Departments and Local Authorities* (London, Allen & Unwin, 1966).

[28] D. N. Chester and F. M. G. Willson, *The Organisation of British Central Government 1914–1964* (London, Allen & Unwin, [2nd ed.] 1968).

[29] See for example W. J. M. Mackenzie, 'Theories of Local Government', *Greater London Papers No. 2* (London, LSE, 1961); L. J. Sharpe, 'Theories and Values of Local Government', *Political Studies*, 18, 153–74.

[30] R. Chambers, *Managing Local Development* (Uppsala, Institute of African Studies, 1974); *Challenging the Professions* (London, Intermediate Technology Publications, 1973).

[31] B. B. Schaffer, 'The Deadlock in Development Administration', in C. Leys, ed., *Politics and Change in Developing Countries* (London, Cambridge University Press, 1969), 177–211.

[32] B. Schaffer and G. Lamb, *Can Equity be Organized?* (Farnborough, Gower, 1981).

model' of public administration declined in prestige at home and abroad.[33] The 'reform commission' approach to reshaping government (involving PA academics as commission members, consultants, or expert witnesses) lost favour. Academic PA and the civil service, although never close, lost even the social ties constituted by academic leaders (such as Mackenzie or Chester) who had had a 'good war' in Whitehall or former civil servants (such as Brown or Schaffer) who moved from Whitehall to academia during the expansionary post-war years. In the first year of the journal *Public Administration* in 1923, at least 60 per cent of the articles came from public servants and only just over 10 per cent from academics. By the 1970s those proportions were reversed and in some years of the two subsequent decades there were no public servant contributions at all. Diplomas in Public Administration, the main vehicle for university teaching of PA to public servants earlier in the century, began to be dropped by universities from the 1970s, and not one remains today. Such trends might suggest a loss or substantial weakening of PA's traditional 'constituency'.

Other developments might point to a loss of intellectual distinctiveness in the British approach to PA. Some of the most influential new analytic and theoretical developments, notably the 'public choice' approach rediscovered and applied to public bureaucracy from the 1960s, tended to come from the United States. Even the classic study of the United Kingdom public expenditure community in the 1970s, *The Private Government of the Public Money*, employing a new cultural perspective, came from American rather than British scholars.[34] As the Fabian vision of the Webbs and the ethical idealism of the pre-1939 'British philosophers' appeared to fade with the resurgence of New Right visions of institutional design, ideas about 'reinventing government' largely came from outside academic PA in a narrow sense, partly in imports from overseas and partly because other disciplines—accounting, economics, business management—seemed to have more to offer than any politics-based version of PA. Perhaps PA had always been 'a subject matter in search of a discipline';[35] but as the 'public administra-

---

[33] Self, 'What's Gone Wrong with Public Administration?', p. 329.

[34] H. Heclo and A. Wildavsky, *The Private Government of Public Money* (London, Macmillan, 1974).

[35] D. Waldo, in J. C. Charlesworth, ed., *Theory and Practice of Public Administration* (Philadelphia, American Academy of Political and Social Science/American Society for Public Administration, 1968), p. 2.

tion state'[36] of the mid-twentieth century gave way to increasing emphasis on outsourcing public services and privatization of formerly state-owned enterprises, even the subject matter seemed to be disappearing, leaving academic PA in a position akin to that of specialists in the former Soviet system after its collapse.

Perhaps the most potent symbol of decay for those who favour the 'dodo' interpretation was the demise of RIPA in 1992, left to its ignominious fate (bankruptcy, and the purchase of its title by a commercial consultancy firm) by a government which did not think it worth saving at the cost of a few thousand pounds.[37] Other crucial signposts along this putative 'road to ruin' might include the removal of the title 'PA' from Oxford's Gladstone Chair in 1995 after more than 50 years,[38] the disappearance of 'PA' from many undergraduate course titles (for example, at LSE from 1988), the widespread replacement of the term 'PA' by 'public management' and the development of MBA (Public Sector) programmes in business schools, including the adoption of a customized MBA for civil service training in 1995 rather than a more political-science-oriented approach to PA. Uncomfortable parallels might be drawn with the disappearance of 'police science' from German debates about public services with the advent of the *Rechtstaat* in the early nineteenth century, suddenly turning a large and once influential body of academic work into an 'undiscipline'.[39]

The 'phoenix' interpretation: rebirth and advance?

The 'phoenix' view of British PA runs clean counter to the pessimistic 'dodo' vision of terminal decline after early promise. From this perspective a new approach to PA was born out of the ashes of the old at the end of the century, and the new approach constituted a clear intellectual advance on the theoretically understated and apparently

---

[36] A phrase coined by G. K. Fry, 'The British Career Civil Service Under Challenge', *Political Studies*, 34 (1986), 533–55.

[37] R. A. Chapman, 'The Demise of the RIPA — an Idea Shattered', *Australian Journal of Public Administration*, 52 (1993), 466–73.

[38] The Gladstone chair was originally titled 'Political Theory and Institutions' on its creation in 1912, but it was split in 1944, being divided into a chair of Social and Political Theory and the Gladstone Chair of Government and Public Administration, first occupied by K. C. Wheare. (See Chester, 'Political Studies in Britain: Recollections and Comments', p. 158.)

[39] H. Maier, *Die ältere deutsche Staats- und Verwaltungslehre* (München, C. H. Beck, [2nd ed.] 1980), p. 19.

practico-descriptive style of the early years. From the 'phoenix' perspective, it would be absurd to take a more specialized vocabulary, or a more theoretically-driven and methodologically rigorous approach, as indicating decline. On the contrary, such a shift would count as an advance, amounting to a later stage of scientific development and a prerequisite for more general theory.[40] The 'phoenix' view is less commonly articulated than the 'dodo' view, but it seems implicit in the views of those who reject what they see as the 'pre-scientific' traditions of PA[41] and see the subject as growing in professional rigour as it leaves behind the outmoded styles of the past. To sustain a 'phoenix' view, the emphasis needs to go on substance rather than nomenclature and on intellectual 'discovery' rather than academic–practitioner links.

This more optimistic way of telling the tale of twentieth-century British PA implies treating the work of the early twentieth-century 'pioneers' as valuable in a ground-breaking sense but undeveloped beside the theories which came later. That would hardly be surprising, given the small number of full-time PA academics in Britain before the 1960s Robbins boom. Robson in his 1948 inaugural lecture as Professor of PA at LSE argued that adequate coverage of the field was impossible with only two PA chairs in the country.[42] Mackenzie three years later put the total number of 'research-active' academics in the field as not much more than half a dozen.[43] Even in the 1960s it was possible for an assiduous undergraduate to read all the major contemporary British works on PA in a single course, a task which would be impossible today. By comparison, London University alone in 1997 had as many officially-titled Professors of PA as there had been in all of the United Kingdom 50 years earlier, and the PSA 1996 *Directory* included over 30 professorial-grade academics alone working out of political science or related departments whose primary interest was in PA, with well over twice that number of staff in total. Such a huge expansion from the days when PA is said to have been in its prime (for those of the 'dodo' persuasion) is a strange kind of decline (unless it is seen the way some people interpret rising 'A' level passes, as an inevitable sign of falling quality).

From the 'phoenix' perspective, not only has there been quantitative growth, producing a larger and more specialized intellectual 'gene pool',

---

[40] A. Dunsire, *Administration* (London, Martin Robertson, 1973), p. 224.

[41] Cf. K. Dowding, *The Civil Service* (London, Routledge, 1995), p. 1.

[42] W. A. Robson, *Public Administration Today* (London, Stevens, 1948), p. 2.

[43] Mackenzie, 'Public Administration in the Universities', p. 11.

but also a pattern of major 'discoveries' concentrated more towards the end of the century than its beginning. The argument would go that the Webbs, for all their undoubted industry and perceived influence, made relatively few 'discoveries' in a modernist sense. Similarly, the early twentieth-century 'British philosophy of administration', as chronicled by Thomas, might be considered too inchoate and arcane to compete effectively with more explicit American approaches expounding the Progressive vision of PA or to serve as a paradigm on which any 'normal science' (in Kuhn's[44] terminology) could develop. Thomas herself notes the fragmentation, lack of explicit theory and failure by the 'British philosophers' to link their work to international administrative science as possible reasons for its fragility.[45] Even at mid-century Mackenzie argued British PA was descriptive and critical, not 'scientific', and that its intellectual content amounted to 'a smattering of history', 'a little law' and some current affairs.[46] As late as 1972, Fred Ridley complained that British PA lacked strong theoretical elements,[47] a theme which can be traced back 50 years or so earlier to the very first volume of *Public Administration*.[48]

On the 'phoenix' interpretation it might be argued some of the major theoretical 'discoveries' in British PA came only in the later decades of the century, reflecting increasing abstraction and methodological innovation—and, at least equally important, the influence of funding institutions—particularly the SSRC (later ESRC) created in 1965—oriented towards 'team projects' in a natural science 'discovery' mode.[49] Such a development might be viewed negatively through grey-tinted 'dodo perspective' spectacles as 'academic drift', but appears as a positive sign of academic progress through the more rosily-tinted lenses of the 'phoenix' view. Six important late twentieth-century British discoveries in PA are given below, as possible examples

---

[44] T. S. Kuhn, *The Structure of Scientific Revolutions* (Chicago, University of Chicago Press, [2nd ed.] 1970), pp. 23–34.

[45] Thomas, *The British Philosophy of Administration*, pp. 200, 208.

[46] Mackenzie, 'Public Administration in the Universities'. Robson gave a very similar account; see Robson, 'The Study of Public Administration, Then and Now', p. 73.

[47] F. Ridley, 'Public Administration: Cause for Discontent', *Public Administration*, 50 (1972), 65–77

[48] See F. Marson, 'Public Administration: A Science', *Journal of Public Administration*, 1 (1923), 220–27.

[49] D. S. King, 'Creating a Funding Regime for Social Research in Britain: The Heyworth Committee on Social Studies and the Founding of the Social Science Research Council', *Minerva*, 35 (1997), 1–26.

of such an interpretation. They are intended to be illustrative, not exhaustive, and do not appear in any particular order of importance.

An important contribution to bureaucracy theory was Dunleavy's[50] discovery in the middle 1980s of 'bureau shaping' to explain how public servants' preferences shaped institutional architecture. 'Bureau shaping' involved a complete reworking of Niskanen's classic 'budget-maximizing' theory of bureaucracy formulated a decade or so earlier in an application of principal-agent theory from the analysis of the firm to public bureaucracy. 'Bureau shaping' led to a substantial development of 'institutional public choice', becoming one of PA's major research para-digms at the end of the century. Rather than a simple importation of hand-me-down American models to replace a once-distinct British approach to PA, 'bureau shaping' produced a quite new vein of bureaucracy theory, in marked contrast to the traditional style of critical-descriptive work on the civil service.[51]

A second and related major field of discovery in the last quarter of the century was the application of 'contingency theory'—the dimensional study of organizational variation in relation to contextual circum-stances—to public service organization. The first British theoretical devel-opments in contingency theory came from industrial sociologists (notably Burns and Woodward),[52] but British PA scholars contributed notably to the development of what came to be dubbed (by analogy with econometrics) the 'bureaumetric' methodology of institutional analysis. That approach began in local government, with the work of Hinings, Greenwood and others at Birmingham University, who in the 1970s adapted the methodo-logy and 'contingency theory' framework of the famous 1960s Aston studies to the analysis of local government organization,[53] and a modified form of the same approach later developed in central government[54] (albeit with less clear-cut results). The bureau-shaping model, mentioned above, can itself be seen as a form of contingency theory.

---

[50] P. J. Dunleavy, *Bureaucracy, Democracy and Public Choice* (Hemel Hempstead, Harvester Wheatsheaf, 1991).

[51] Dowding, *The Civil Service*, pp. 79–107.

[52] See Dunsire, *Administration*, p. 209.

[53] See R. Greenwood, K. Walsh, C. R. Hinings and R. Ranson, *Patterns of Management in Local Government* (Oxford, Martin Robertson, 1980).

[54] See A. Dunsire, 'Testing Theories: The Contribution of Bureaumetrics', Ch. 5 in J. E. Lane, ed., *Bureaucracy and Public Choice* (London, Sage Publications, 1987), pp. 95–144; C. Hood and A. Dunsire, *Bureaumetrics* (Farnborough, Gower, 1981); R. Rose, *Ministers and Ministries* (Oxford, Clarendon Press, 1987); D. C. Pitt and B. C. Smith, *Government Departments* (London, Routledge, 1981).

Contingency theory in its original form went into recession from the early 1980s, but along with American work on 'iron triangles' and related phenomena, it helped to shape a third area of British PA analysis late in the century,[55] namely the development of the analysis of 'policy networks' and 'policy communities'.[56] Rhodes developed a framework derived from inter-organizational theory, viewing central–local relations as a 'game' in which outcomes depend on resources available to the various players manoeuvring to maximize their relative influence. Although the 'policy network' approach of the late 1980s and 1990s was by no means confined to Britain (similar discoveries were made elsewhere), British scholars contributed substantially to theory building, empirical analysis and critical comment[57] on that approach.

In the analysis of institutional control, Dunsire's application of cybernetics to bureaucracy theory led in the late 1970s to the identification of 'collibration' as a major process of institutional control[58]—that is, processes where control works less like a homeostatic system with negative feedback mechanisms than as an open-ended process of interpolation between pent-up opposed pressures to 'steer an equilibrium'. Dunsire's analysis, which filled a major gap in Weber's classic account of bureaucracy, built in part on the insights of Vickers[59] (whose ideas influenced many British writers on policy and institutions in the 1970s and beyond). The discovery of 'collibration' was an international 'first' for British PA; but (in contrast to 'bureau shaping') there is no 'Dunsire school' in Britain (indeed interest in the approach has come mainly from Germany, where cybernetically-based analysis has a much greater following and Dunsire's ideas have been influential) and there has been scarcely any applied work on collibration.

Fifth, in the analysis of public policy, Rose's approach to longitudinal analysis of British taxation, public expenditure[60] and law over half a century led to his controversial, but internationally important, discovery of

---

[55] According to R. A. W. Rhodes, 'A Plague of Practice: Theory and Methods in British Public Administration', Inaugural Lecture, University of York, 20 February 1991, p. 14.

[56] See R. A. W. Rhodes, *Beyond Westminster and Whitehall* (London, Unwin Hyman, 1988); D. Marsh and R. A. W. Rhodes, eds., *Policy Networks in British Government* (Oxford, Oxford University Press, 1991).

[57] See for example K. Dowding, 'Model or Metaphor? A Critical Review of the Policy Network Approach', *Political Studies*, 43 (1995), 136–58.

[58] A. Dunsire, *The Execution Process, Vol. 2* (Oxford, Martin Robertson, 1978).

[59] Sir G. Vickers, *The Art of Judgement* (London, Methuen, 1965).

[60] R. Rose, *Understanding Big Government* (London, Sage Publications, 1984).

the role of 'inheritance' (relative to 'choice') in policy development,[61] and formed another 'paradigm' for team research on large bodies of financial and legal data. Rose's 'programme approach' to analysis of public expenditure growth and his identification of long-term patterns of comparative government growth grew out of a similar methodology and helped establish Strathclyde University's Centre for the Study of Public Policy (founded in 1972, early in the 'policy studies' boom) as a leading international centre for document-based comparative policy studies.

Finally, British scholars made major international contributions in the final two decades of the century to typological work in a number of areas which included the characterization of policy dynamics,[62] forms of accountability,[63] forms of government rules,[64] policy styles[65] and policy instruments.[66] British debates over the so-called 'New Public Management' style of public service delivery which developed in the last three decades of the century were likewise internationally important.

These six areas of 'discovery' are by no means representative of late twentieth-century British work in PA, nor were they all carried out by scholars with the term 'PA' in their official titles. They are simply cited as areas in which British work on executive government in the last quarter of the century led the field internationally, contrary to the 'dodo' notion of terminal decline. In 1950 Britain had no real equivalent to Herbert Simon as a self-conscious 'theorist' of PA, although British institutional developments (particularly the 'Morrisonian public corporation') were influential outside the United Kingdom. Forty years later, in the era of 'new public management', Britain had become a major international source of PA theory, intermixed with the tradition of tracking and critically commenting on public service developments.

A 'phoenix' interpretation would also point to the growth of specialized PA journals in Britain (such as *The Journal of Public Policy, Public*

---

[61] R. Rose and P. L. Davies, *Inheritance in Public Policy* (New Haven, Conn., Yale University Press, 1994).

[62] See B. Hogwood and B. G. Peters, *Policy Dynamics* (Brighton, Wheatsheaf, 1983).

[63] P. Day and R. Klein, *Accountabilities* (London, Tavistock, 1987).

[64] R. Baldwin, *Rules and Government* (Oxford, Clarendon Press, 1995); J. Black, *Rules and Regulators* (Oxford, Clarendon Press, 1997).

[65] J. Richardson, ed., *Policy Styles in Western Europe* (London, Allen & Unwin, 1981); S. Mazey and J. Richardson, 'Promiscuous Policy-Making: The European Policy Style?', in C. Rhodes and S. Mazey, eds., *The State of the European Union, Vol. III, Building a European Polity?* (Boulder, Col., Lynn Reiner Longman, 1991).

[66] C. Hood, *The Tools of Government* (London, Macmillan 1983).

Policy and Administration, Policy and Politics, Teaching Public Administration, Public Administration and Development and *Public Money and Management*, growing up alongside the longer-established *Public Administration* and *Local Government Studies*), many of them having an international reach. A growth in journals (and, arguably, a growth in the professional standard of articles in those journals from the descriptive–philosophical papers, most by practitioners, which dominated *Public Administration* up to the 1960s) hardly squares with the picture of a discipline in decline. And against the death of RIPA has to be set continuing and expanded activity by the JUC Public Administration Committee, the PA academic 'professional' grouping. Indeed, rather like Hennessy's view of 'Hitler's reform' of Whitehall,[67] the change in political and institutional 'habitat', with a strong ideological assault on the traditional 'public-administration state' from the 'new right' 1980s might be argued to have done the *academic* discipline of PA nothing but good (whatever it did to the quality of public services themselves). Far from killing academic PA, it might be argued, those trends forced British PA academics to re-examine their subject matter from the ground up and gave them a laboratory to assess attempts at 'government by the market'.[68]

From a 'phoenix' perspective, any decline in academic PA influence over practitioners might either be seen as reflecting the passing of a generation for whom the Second World War and its aftermath had created opportunities for lateral moves between public service and academia that virtually disappeared in the 1970s, or as an inevitable price of PA growing into an intellectually rigorous enterprise, with an academic orientation and vocabulary that would inevitably be distasteful to civil servants without a formal education in administrative science. Indeed, tension between government and academic PA might even have been productive, in forcing academics to create more theory than might have developed had they been busier servicing official reform commissions (just as it is sometimes suggested that Keynes' *General Theory* was stimulated by the need to 'theorize' a policy approach in a way that was politically unnecessary in other countries whose finance ministries were more open to departures from economic orthodoxy).[69]

---

[67] P. Hennessy, *Whitehall* (London, Fontana, [rev. ed.] 1990), pp. 88 ff.

[68] P. J. Self, *Government by the Market?* (London, Macmillan, 1993).

[69] Cf. M. Weir and T. Skocpol, 'State Structures and the Possibilities for "Keynesian" Responses to the Great Depression in Sweden, Britain and the United States', Ch. 4 in P. B. Evans *et al.*, *Bringing the State Back In* (Cambridge, Cambridge University Press, 1985), p. 128.

Moreover, it might be argued that even the decline of influence by political-science-based PA academics (as seen from the 'dodo' viewpoint) can be exaggerated. After all, it was not exactly top civil service 'mandarins' who had enrolled in the university night-school Diploma in Public Administration (DPA) classes in the 1930s (a number of which, according to Robson, 'were of a very low standard'),[70] which have in part been replaced by Master's courses, 'public management' diplomas and degrees and post-experience courses, especially for local government and the health service. And the Treasury seems to have been every bit as unenthusiastic about supporting the formation of the Institute of Public Administration (IPA) in 1922[71] as the Cabinet Office was to keep it afloat 70 years later. Any loss of influence was more marked in the civil service than in the National Health Service or local government (where PA academics continued to be in demand), and even for the civil service there was a marked *rapprochement* with academic PA in the early 1990s (for example with Cabinet Office sponsorship of the 1995–8 ESRC programme of research into central government). From a 'phoenix' perspective, a new approach to PA had developed from the ashes of the earlier style, and in some ways British PA at the end of the century had 'never had it so good'. More PhD students were being trained and more research was being conducted, by a larger number of internationally-recognized scholars, from more disciplinary viewpoints, than had applied at any earlier point in the century.

The 'chameleon' interpretation: new colours and markings for a new habitat?

One possible way of reconciling the opposing perspectives of the 'dodo' and 'phoenix' views of twentieth-century British PA is to conceive of the subject as changing its form and focus rather than advancing or retreating along a single track—taking up different intellectual colours under different disciplinary labels in changing circumstances and new intellectual perspectives. Changes in nomenclature, shifting disciplinary bases and complex processes of positive and reverse intellectual colonization may give twentieth-century PA an elusive quality, meaning linear

---

[70] Robson, 'The Study of Public Administration, Then and Now', p. 71.

[71] The Institute was founded solely on the basis of individual subscriptions and contributions by NALGO and civil service staff associations (see Chapman, *Teaching Public Administration*, p. 27).

notions of progress or decline may fail to capture what was going on. From this viewpoint PA looks more like a chameleon than a dodo or a phoenix.

The 'chameleon' effect might have worked in several related ways. First, it might be argued that much of what on a 'dodo' reading looks like 'decline'—notably the relative downgrading of the specialized label 'PA'—simply reflects a 'mainstreaming' of the 'PA perspective' in British political science. What had been a distinctive and minority enterprise at the turn of the century, when the largest part of political science had been concerned with political philosophy and the history of political thought, became integral to the burgeoning study of 'government' within political science and used much the same analytic tools, such as institutional theory and rational choice theory. Such a shift was fore-shadowed even at mid-century in Mackenzie's suggestion that the 'cleanest cut' for shaping PA's future was to merge it with general political science, with the detailed analysis of executive government forming part of more general inquiries as to how states are governed.[72] The 'public policy' approach that swept through American political science in the 1970s brought together the traditional institutional realm of PA with broader questions about policy outcomes. The 'public choice' approach that succeeded 'public policy' as the hot topic in the following decade brought together PA's traditional institutional focus with a different perspective on preferences and interest organizations.[73] If such developments brought about Mackenzie's 'cleanest cut', it means that what some might see as PA's decline can be viewed by others as a partial 'colonization' of the parent subject, even a case of 'nothing fails like success'.

To the extent that such 'mainstreaming' took place, it implies a blurring not only of the boundaries between 'British' and other (notably American) approaches to PA, but also of the boundaries between PA and other branches of political science. For example, the tradition of comparative (and comparative/historical) institutional analysis of executive government, dating back at least to Barker's classic *Development of the Public Services in Western Europe*,[74] has been a notable growth point of

---

[72] Mackenzie, 'Public Administration in the Universities', p. 11.

[73] M. Sproule-Jones, 'Public Choice Theory and Natural Resources', *American Political Science Review*, 76 (1982), 795.

[74] E. Barker, *The Development of Public Services in Western Europe 1660–1930* (London, Oxford University Press, 1944).

the second half of the century, for example in Ridley and Blondel's pioneering study of French public administration,[75] in the later work the British comparative institutional school (incorporating such scholars as Wright, Dyson, Hayward and Page).[76] Historical approaches to the study of executive administration, both in 'broad sweep' exercises in the Ernest Barker tradition (as in Chester's final work and Finer's post-humously-published history of government)[77] and in narrower studies (for instance of administrative biography), have also continued to develop. The boundary between 'comparative government' broadly conceived (in the tradition of Brogan or Bryce) and comparative PA is a fine one, but as students of comparative government have grown more interested in the fine grain of state structures, there has been much emphasis on the administrative institutions of the state in late twentieth-century British work on comparative government.

Second, a 'chameleon' effect (rather than linear progress or regress) might play out through a process highlighted by Rodney Barker[78] for political ideas more generally, in which the 'recessive' themes of an earlier generation become the dominant ones later on. Chapman and Dunsire's argument that British administrative style (in the civil service, at least) has tended to veer between 'administrative politics' and management for efficiency has already been referred to. It may well be that the latter theme, which was perhaps dominant in the early decades of practitioner-dominated discourse in PA, became recessive as professional political scientists took over the subject, only to return to at least partial dominance later on. That is, if there is anything in the idea that British political science became more 'public administration-ized' over the century (if that barbarous term may be allowed), it would hardly be surprising if there was some reciprocal process of colonization of PA by the central concerns of political science—notably how blame and accountability play out in the administrative state, how politics interweaves with administration in shaping policy, the political role of top public servants, the social representativeness and self-interest of bureaucracies. To the extent that such a colonization occurred, making British PA more closely focused on politics-of-bureaucracy issues than its American or Continental European counterparts, a reaction to that

---

[75] F. Ridley and J. Blondel, *Public Administration in France* (London, Allen & Unwin, 1964).

[76] Cf. E. Page, *Political Authority and Bureaucratic Power* (Brighton, Wheatsheaf, 1985).

[77] S. E. Finer, *The History of Government from the Earliest Times*, 3 vols (Oxford, Oxford University Press, 1997).

[78] Barker, *Political Ideas in Modern Britain*, pp. 7, 275.

approach was only to be expected. It came both in the form of the 'development administration' perspective emerging in the 1960s as a reaction against orthodox PA, and much more strongly in the 'public management' perspective developed in the 1980s, largely outside political science. The latter focused on the 'production engineering' aspects of public services delivery and on normative 'recipes' that had been partially sidelined by the politics-of-bureaucracy focus of political-science-dominated PA, and aimed to recreate the sort of dialogue between 'reflective practitioners' and academics that had characterized PA earlier in the century. Such a development reflects a continuing tension between mainstream political science and some fundamental concerns of PA which is not unique to Britain. But it cannot be counted as a simple recessive-dominant flipover: the accountability-focused political-science stream of analysis by no means disappeared, arguments about politics and values rapidly resurfaced in the public management literature and political scientists themselves began to analyse the 'politics of public management',[79] which 'as already noted' has attracted much debate over the past decade or so. Indeed, the relative plausibility of the 'dodo' and the 'phoenix' views over the last decade or two turns heavily on how far 'public management' literature should count as 'political science'.

Third, it might be that the apparent catalogue of 'discoveries' biased towards the end of the century (on which the 'phoenix' argument would need to rest) might be better explained by a combination of a 'modernist' scientific metaphor stressing 'discovery' than of underlying changes in content, and of changing 'production bases' rather than a complete change in the product line. The casually understated style of the early years of the century, in which 'theory' was often implicit and tentative (rejecting what was then commonly dismissed as a culturally-alien American penchant for 'overarching theory'), had been replaced by the opposite emphasis by the end of the century, so it may well be that the 'discoveries' of the early years of the century were not so much absent as not 'packaged' in the scientific style of later years, so that they ceased to be recognized and remembered later. For example, Wallas' 'discovery' of social–psychological elements in bureaucratic work—the idea that 'happiness' in organization included reduction in monotony, collegial working and self-respect[80]—prefigured not

---

[79] Cf. C. Pollitt, *Managerialism and the Public Services* (Oxford, Basil Blackwell, [2nd ed.] 1993).

[80] G. Wallas, *The Great Society* (London, Macmillan, 1932), pp. 320–44.

only the later 'human relations' movement but also the motivational assumptions behind Dunleavy's 'bureau-shaping' analysis, but did not even rate a footnote in either body of work because it had effectively disappeared from PA discourse. The same went for what was perhaps the Webbs' most notable PA 'discovery'—their idea[81] that the way to control the large public service which extended state activity would bring was to divide it into two, with half of the bureaucrats regulating and inspecting the other half. In large part, this discovery anticipated end-of-century United Kingdom fashions for re-engineering central administration through 'executive agencies' under more explicit internal regulatory regimes, but current discourse contains no reference to the Webbs' recipe: it too had disappeared from memory.

Similarly, while some political scientists in the last quarter of the century developed more abstract theoretical characterizations of policy and bureaucracy, the older descriptive tradition re-emerged elsewhere. And that is hardly surprising. After all, one basic task for PA (or PA by any other name) is the prosaic but always necessary job of mapping out the detailed institutional arrangements of government and public services. That work is never complete, because it is like trying to map the sand-bars, lagoons and islands at the mouth of a fast-flowing river, when every storm or high tide changes the configuration, leaving the mapping process to be started all over again. Much of the study of European Union institutions in its early phases, for example, necessarily followed the track of mapping and chronicling applied to central and local government two generations before. Indeed, the transformation of the shape of executive government over the century—from a 'regulatory state' to a 'public bureaucracy state' and (to some extent) back again—meant that mapping of those structures has both been in heavy demand and tending to run behind the changing contours of the landscape (in the 1950s, some of the biggest names in the field were focused on nationalization; 30 years later, regulation of privately-owned utilities had again become a central topic in PA).

But many of the 'map-makers' of the new institutional structures at the end of the century, albeit engaged in much the same kind of work that the Webbs had pioneered early in the century, were not formally part of the discipline of political science. It would perhaps be an

---

[81] Set out in their *Constitution for a Socialist Commonwealth of Great Britain* (London, Longman, 1920).

exaggeration to suggest that the 'political science' end of the business became more concerned with meta-analysis—the study of the underlying hydrodynamic forces (so to speak) shaping the face of government—leaving first-level cartography to other disciplines. There are important exceptions to that pattern, for example in the analysis of 'informatization' in administration,[82] the analysis of 'decision advice procedures',[83] or the continuing quest for an adequate taxonomy of 'quangos',[84] to name only three cases. But it is notable that much of the new map-making has come from outside the formal boundaries of political science—in public law, accountancy, geography, economics, sociology and operational research, and in 'topic-centred', rather than disciplinary, fields such as housing, social policy, health care or transport. Examples include Ogus' work on the 'regulatory state',[85] Heald's work on public expenditure,[86] and studies of detailed institutional responses to reform coming from the 'new critical accounting' (for example, in the work of Miller, Power and Laughlin),[87] drawing from much the same Habermasian critical-theory frame as many 'political science'-based studies. PA in that sense remains an intellectual crossroads (indeed an increasingly busy one), not exclusively 'political science' territory.

Fourth, and relatedly, even within PA in the traditional sense, intellectual fashions and nomenclature have changed over the century, meaning there may be less to 'progress' and 'decline' than at first appears. It may even be a case of reinvention and 'forgetting' processes of the kind that Douglas[88] has argued to be endemic in organized science (contrary to the conventional ideology of cumulative scientific development through 'pygmies standing on the shoulders of giants').[89] As she puts it:

---

[82] Cf. H. Margetts, 'The Computerization of Social Security: The Way Forward or a Step Backwards?', *Public Administration*, 69 (1991), 325–43; J. A. Taylor and H. Williams, 'Public Administration and the Information Polity', *Public Administration*, 69 (1991), 171–90.

[83] See A. Barker and B. G. Peters, *The Politics of Expert Advice in Western Europe* (Edinburgh, Edinburgh University Press, 1992).

[84] Cf. A. Barker, ed., *Quangos in Britain* (London, Macmillan 1982).

[85] A. Ogus, *Regulation* (Oxford, Clarendon Press, 1984).

[86] D. A. Heald, *Public Expenditure* (Oxford, Martin Robertson, 1983).

[87] See for example, R. Laughlin, J. Broadbent, D. Shearn and H. Willig-Atherton, 'Absorbing LMS: The Coping Mechanism of a Small Group', *Accounting, Auditing and Accountability Journal*, 7 (1994), 59–85.

[88] M. Douglas, *How Institutions Think* (London, Routledge, 1987), p. 69.

[89] For the definitive account of 'OTSOG', see R. K. Merton, *On The Shoulders of Giants* (New York, Harcourt, Brace and World, Inc., 1965).

> Every ten years or so classroom text books go out of date. Their need to be revised is in some part due to new work in science or to the deeper delving of historians. Much more, it is because science has come to seem over-religious or scandalously irreligious . . . or because the history of the last decade gives a wrong political feeling . . . In the intervening years, some slogans have become risible, some words have become empty and others too full . . . Some names count for more and others that count for less are due to be struck out. The revisionary effort is not aimed at producing the perfect optic flat . . . The aim of revision is to get the distortions to match the mood of the present times.

Such an analysis may well apply to the shifts and changes in British PA over the twentieth century. For example, Robson, reflecting on changes in PA in the three decades up to 1975, argued that changes in terminology masked some underlying continuities: he claimed 'organization theory' was a new label for institutional analysis and 'policy studies' for politics in the older idiom.[90] But neither the Fabian frame in which the subject was set by the Webbs early in the century nor the hierarchist planning culture of the two world wars which formed the backdrop to the work of the middle decades of the century fitted the prevailing mood from the 1970s, with policy stances becoming more polarized between 'Chicago school' individualism and radical egalitarianism. If received theoretical frameworks have changed with the social backdrop over time, a chameleon-like quality in PA is only to be expected. For example, the language and analysis of radical 'state theory' figured large in the analysis of urban politics in the 1970s, displacing an older institutional style, but by the late 1980s this approach had lost momentum, and the same went for the 1970s' focus on implementation studies,[91] which faltered in the subsequent decade. 'Policy studies' as a post-Vietnam war boom in the 1970s, were somewhat displaced by the resurgence of 'public management' in the 1980s (and also partially incorporated into comparative politics). The focus on contingency theory which was central to the analysis of local (and to a less extent central) government in the 1960s and 1970 was likewise to some extent displaced by the 1980s' idiom of public choice. This somewhat bewildering churning of labels and frameworks—radical state theory yesterday, public choice today, chaos theory and autopoiesis tomorrow—is not readily explicable by reference to neo-Popperian 'crucial experiments' in which one approach outperforms another in

---

[90] Robson, 'The Study of Public Administration, Then and Now', p. 200.
[91] Cf. C. Hood, *The Limits of Administration* (London, Wiley, 1976).

predictive power. Indeed, frequent changes of idiom and nomenclature may make PA, like management science,[92] an area in which Kuhnian 'normal science' development is particularly problematic.

If there is anything in this 'chameleon' analysis, much of what might have been counted as 'PA' within political science in 1900 had by the 1990s become part of mainstream political science, moved into the realm of inter-disciplinary studies or been picked up by specialists working under different disciplinary colours, notably a new breed of public lawyers and accountants. Whether that is to be called 'progress' or 'decline' depends heavily on an assessment of 'what's in a name?' From the 'chameleon' perspective, the point is that if PA did not exist it would be necessary to invent it; and arguably it has been reinvented at least once over the course of the century (if not in every generation), in different nomenclature, much of it no longer 'owned' by political science. The overall picture may be too complex to be adequately characterized by simple notions of 'progress' or 'decline'.

Conclusion

A 'chameleon' perspective certainly has its attractions. It seems to capture some of the shifts in twentieth-century British PA without needing to embrace either the 'metaphysical pathos' of the 'dodo' view or the 'Whig history' of the 'phoenix' view. But, like both of the other two perspectives, it may underplay strong elements of continuity in the field. Not all of British PA has been chameleon-like (or dodo-like, or phoenix-like) over the century. Some of it, it may be objected, has remained in a remarkably stable form, and for that we might need a fourth animal metaphor—giant tortoise, coelacanth or 'living fossil'. For example, the Fabian tradition of championing local against central government stretches directly from the Webbs through Robson down to the work of Jones and Stewart[93] in the 1980s; local government finance and re-organization have been recurring themes throughout the century; and criticism of the shortcomings of the civil service also has a long history, from Demetriadi[94] in the 1920s through the 'what's wrong with the Civil Service?' debates of the 1960s[95] to the critiques of Plowden[96] and others in

---

[92] See A. Huczynski, *Management Gurus* (London, Routledge, 1993) for an account of how 'forgetting' processes work in management thought.

[93] G. W. Jones and J. Stewart, *The Case for Local Government* (London, Allen & Unwin, 1983).

[94] Sir Stephen Demetriadi, *A Reform for the Civil Service* (London, Cassell, 1921).

[95] Cf. B. Chapman, *British Government Observed* (London, Allen & Unwin, 1963).

[96] W. Plowden, *Ministers and Mandarins* (London, IPPR, 1994).

the 1990s. Critical analysis of the complex of quasi-government bodies, to elucidate the architectonics of public service structures, is also a very long-standing 'project' in PA, long antedating the coining of the word 'quango' in the 1970s and going back at least to the first volume of *Public Administration*. So is the study of comparative institutional structures and the development of the study of law and administration.

Even so, there is some *prima facie* evidence to support each of the three different views of the development of British PA considered in this paper, and in that sense each seems to capture a partial truth. Some aspects of the early Fabian design for public administration, and associated assumptions about the role of the state apparatus seem to be in some decline, with change in 'habitat' and intellectual fashions (although some Fabian prescriptions have been revived, as noted above). A weakening of the 'practico-descriptive' approach to PA has certainly meant some loss of the United Kingdom's tradition of rich institutional description. The term 'PA' has to some extent fallen from favour both in academia and the world of practice, and certainly the expansion of numbers of academics working in the field (as with British political science more generally) has inevitably meant some loss of coherence and community. PA (often under other titles) has expanded outside political science and intellectual fashions, paradigms and research teams have become more international, meaning that 'British' PA over the century has become rather like the 'British' motor or computer industries—larger in production capacity than in the past, perhaps, but now inextricably linked with larger cross-national structures, networks, journals and associations. At the same time, there have been some notable advances over recent decades, particularly in theoretical development, with innovative British work attracting international attention. But lateral transformation has also been evident, for example in the succession of paradigms used in the study of local politics and government (such as contingency theory, radical urban politics theory, public choice), in the rebirth of some of the original concerns of the 1920s 'public administration' movement outside political science as 'development administration' in the 1960s and 'public management' in the 1980s and in increased interest in the administrative workings of the state across political science generally.

For the 'dodo' interpretation to be the most plausible account of the development of twentieth-century PA, the heaviest emphasis needs to be laid on the self-conscious use of the term PA rather than the substance of work on institutional arrangements for executive government and public service provision. Stress also has to be laid on the existence of an officially-blessed élite association linking academics and public servants; and on a national intellectual community small enough to read the work of everyone else in the field, to be more closely linked with one another than to related specialists overseas, and to share a broadly common 'paradigm' for studying their subject. Such criteria count for something, but they are not the normal benchmarks of scientific progress.

For the 'phoenix' interpretation to be plausible, on the other hand, just the opposite weightings need to apply. The substance of work concerned with government and public services, however labelled, has to be counted as more important than PA as a title, for 'Public Administration' existed *avant la lettre* and will continue to exist in substance even if the term disappears altogether. Likewise, the proliferation of serious internationally-rated journals—and academic articles to fill them, from a larger intellectual community—must be weighed more heavily than the existence of a national professional institution, and the explosion of different approaches and sub-specialisms must be counted as a testament to scientific progression in the field, with individual scholars knowing more and more about less and less (just what should happen, in the development of 'normal science'). For the 'chameleon' interpretation to be plausible, processes of relabelling, rediscovery, forgetting and intellectual reconfiguration need to be stressed, and it seems hard to deny that such processes have applied to PA. The debateable issue is how far the relabelling matters.

However, if twentieth-century political science is viewed as an essentially American activity, it is possible that the 'phoenix' and 'dodo' interpretations might both be true in a sense, in that even though real 'discoveries' were made in British PA over the century, few of those instanced above have made much impression on the American political science literature. But the story is very different for Europe, Asia and the Antipodes; and overall, unless we choose to use non- or even anti-scientific criteria for the assessment of progress or decline, British PA over the twentieth century looks more like a phoenix or a chameleon than a dodo.

Acknowledgements.　I am grateful to Keith Dowding, Andrew Coulson, Andrew Dunsire, George Jones, Desmond King, Richard Chapman and John Stewart for helpful comments on a preliminary draft of this chapter, as well as to participants in the Birmingham University School of Public Policy seminar group, and the St Antony's College British Academy symposium, to which this paper was originally presented in the Spring of 1997.

11: Nations and Nationalism in British Political Studies

CHARLES KING

To persons only casually familiar with the literature on nations and nationalism, it might seem that the British study of nationalism has been the study of nationalism *tout court*. Such a view would not be surprising, for the most discussed and cited comparative studies of nationalist politics are, at century's end, those of authors tied by birth or education to the United Kingdom. The works of Hugh Seton-Watson, Elie Kedourie, Ernest Gellner, and Anthony D. Smith, to name only a few, continue to be the major guideposts in a now voluminous literature.[1] Despite a long line of studies of nationalism by American historians and a growing interest in ethnicity among American social scientists from the 1960s, the most cited works in the field have long been those by authors who have made their careers within British universities. In the 1990s, with renewed attention focused on the nation-state and its discontents, these authors and their compatriots have been discovered by a new generation of political scientists, international relations specialists, sociologists and journalists. Britain has also been important in the development of a sense of professional camaraderie among scholars

---

[1] H. Seton-Watson, *Nationalism and Communism* (New York, Praeger, 1964); H. Seton-Watson, *Nations and States* (Boulder, Col., Westview Press, 1977); E. Kedourie, *Nationalism*, (Oxford, Blackwell, [4th edition] 1993); E. Gellner, *Thought and Change* (Chicago, University of Chicago Press, 1964); E. Gellner, *Nations and Nationalism* (Oxford, Basil Blackwell, 1983); E. Gellner, *Culture, Identity, and Politics* (Cambridge, Cambridge University Press, 1987); E. Gellner, *Encounters with Nationalism* (Oxford, Basil Blackwell, 1994); A. D. Smith, *The Ethnic Origins and Nations* (Oxford, Basil Blackwell, 1986); A. D. Smith, *The Ethnic Revival* (Cambridge, Cambridge University Press, 1981); A. D. Smith, *National Identity* (London, Penguin, 1991); A. D. Smith, *Nations and Nationalism in a Global Era* (London, Polity Press, 1995).

with an interest in nationalist phenomena. The Association for the Study of Ethnicity and Nationalism, founded under Smith's aegis at the London School of Economics and Political Science (LSE), is the English-speaking world's major professional organization devoted to the comparative study of ethnic, racial and nationalist politics.[2] Two of the most important journals in the field, *Ethnic and Racial Studies* (established in 1978) and *Nations and Nationalism* (established in 1995), are both edited in Britain, the former at the University of Surrey and the latter at LSE.

American scholars educated in the tradition of Carlton Hayes, Hans Kohn, and Boyd Shafer will no doubt balk at the suggestion that Britons have played a leading role in the study of nationalism.[3] The claim seems even more peculiar in light of the upsurge in new research on national identity and ethnonational mobilization by American historians, political scientists and sociologists since the mid-1960s. Karl Deutsch, Louis Snyder, Walker Connor, Ted Gurr, Donald Horowitz and other American-based researchers have become mainstays in the literature on nationalism and the comparative study of ethnic politics.[4] However, while it is difficult to discern a unique 'British tradition' in the study of nationalism, especially when international conferences and e-mail have made scholarship a genuinely global enterprise, one can speak of a substantial and vital British contribution to the field. British writers on nationalism have come from disparate disciplines and have arrived at substantially different conclusions about the origin of nationalist senti-

---

[2] Two of the major American associations dealing with ethnic and nationalist issues — the National Association for Ethnic Studies, based at the University of Arizona, and the organized section on Race, Ethnicity and Politics of the American Political Science Association — remain dominated by persons whose research concentrates on African-Americans, Native Americans, Latinos and other ethnic groups in the United States. Another important American group, the Association for the Study of Nationalities, concentrates mainly on the former Soviet Union.

[3] Classic works by American scholars include C. J. H. Hayes, *Essays on Nationalism* (New York, Macmillan, 1926); C. J. H. Hayes, *The Historical Evolution of Modern Nationalism* (New York, Richard Smith, 1931); C. J. H. Hayes, *Nationalism: A Religion* (New York, Macmillan, 1960); H. Kohn, *The Idea of Nationalism* (New York, Macmillan, 1944); B. C. Shafer, *Nationalism: Myth and Reality* (New York, Harcourt, Brace and World, 1955); B. C. Shafer, *Faces of Nationalism* (New York, Harcourt, Brace, Jovanovich, 1972).

[4] See K. Deutsch, *Nationalism and Social Communication* (Cambridge, MIT Press, [2nd ed.] 1966); L. Snyder, *The Meaning of Nationalism* (New Brunswick, Rutgers University Press, 1954); L. Snyder, *Varieties of Nationalism: A Comparative Study* (Hinsdale, Dryden Press, 1976); D. Horowitz, *Ethnic Groups in Conflict* (Berkeley, University of California Press, 1985); T. R. Gurr, *Minorities at Risk: A Global View of Ethnopolitical Conflicts* (Washington, DC, United States Institute of Peace Press, 1993); W. Connor, *Ethnonationalism: The Quest for Understanding* (Princeton, NJ, Princeton University Press, 1994).

ment, the conduct of nationalist politics, and the future of the nation-state. But among the major contributors to the field, one can discern a particular sensitivity to the power of nationalism and its fundamental connections to other topics of concern to students of politics, from the bases of social identity to party politics, to the causes of violent conflict. Focusing on the national idea at a time when it was largely outside the interest of their political science colleagues in the United States, British scholars carved out a distinct field of study located at the nexus of the humanities and the social sciences.

The literature on nationalism, even that generated by scholars work-ing in a single country, is gargantuan. Nearly every major British historian, political scientist, sociologist and political theorist—whether writing on political interactions within states or between them, or on the normative principles by which such interactions ought to be governed—has touched on the question of nationality. Furthermore, the intellectual openness of British social science has meant that the study of national-ism, like the study of other socio-political phenomena, has been a truly multidisciplinary endeavour; research in the field continues to draw on the expertise of historians, sociologists, linguists and anthropologists, in addition to political scientists. The purpose of this chapter is not to offer a comprehensive treatment of this massive scholarly literature, nor even to attempt the more manageable task of providing a 'reader's guide' to the subject.[5] Instead, this essay aims to explore some of the major trends in the British study of nationalism and to relate these to broader sub-stantive and methodological concerns within the social sciences. The focus will be the most important comparative and conceptual studies of nationalism as a general political and historical phenomenon, rather than research limited to particular countries or periods. The contention here is that British scholars have made profound contributions to our understanding of nations and nationalism, and have aided in the development of a distinct, multidisciplinary field dedicated to research on ethnic and national phenomena. At the same time, however, the

---

[5] Useful bibliographies include K. S. Pinson, *A Bibliographical Introduction to Nationalism* (New York, Columbia University Press, 1935); K. Deutsch, *A Multidisciplinary Bibliography on Nationalism, 1935–1953* (Cambridge, Mass., MIT Press, 1956); K. Deutsch and R. L. Merritt, *Nationalism and National Development: An Multidisciplinary Bibliography* (Cambridge, Mass., MIT Press, 1970); A. D. Smith, 'Nationalism: A Trend Report and Bibliography', *Current Sociology*, 21 (1973), 5–185; D. B. Knight and M. Davies, eds., *Self-Determination: A Multidisciplinary Annotated Bibliography* (New York, Garland, 1987); the annual survey published by the *Canadian Review of Studies in Nationalism*; and periodic issues of the *Bulletin* of the Association for the Study of Ethnicity and Nationalism.

future of multidisciplinary scholarship in this area is by no means clear. The defining features of British political studies, including a respect for methodological eclecticism and historically grounded research, have made British writers uniquely attuned to the importance of nationalism at times when many of their American colleagues dismissed it as the residuum of retarded modernization. But where such an essentially multidisciplinary field might go in an age of increased academic specialization and calls for greater 'professionalism' within the study of politics is uncertain. The chapter concludes with some reflections on possible future directions for research and modest proposals for thinking about the study of nationalism and its relationship to broader debates within political science.

Intellectual traditions and the study of nationalism

In terms of methodology and approach, political scientists may indeed sit at 'separate tables', as Gabriel Almond once mused,[6] but they also sit on separate continents. More so perhaps than other disciplines, the study of politics in Britain and the United States has long borne a national stamp. It is one of the few academic fields whose intellectual fissures have developed along broadly national lines. In the United States, the discipline of political science has evolved in the direction of ever greater methodological self-consciousness; the specification of variables, the stress on falsifiable hypotheses, the generation of testable inferences, and the elaboration of deductive theories of political behaviour have become standard components of political science education and scholarship. These developments, of course, have not been without their critics, and there is today as little consensus as in the past about what constitutes the truly dominant paradigm within American political science.[7] However, 'mainstream' political science, as represented in

---

[6] G. A. Almond, *A Discipline Divided: Schools and Sects in Political Science* (London, Sage Publications, 1990), p. 13.

[7] For recent reports on the 'state of the discipline', see J. Farr and R. Seidelman, eds., *Discipline and History: Political Science in the United States* (Ann Arbor, University of Michigan Press, 1993); R. M. Smith, 'Still Blowing in the Wind: The American Quest for a Democratic, Scientific Political Science', *Daedalus*, 126 (1997), 253–287; M. A. Baer, M. E. Jewell and L. Sigelman, eds., *Political Science in America: Oral Histories of a Discipline* (Lexington, KY, University of Kentucky Press, 1991); and M. I. Lichbach and A. S. Zuckerman, eds., *Comparative Politics: Rationality, Culture and Structure* (Cambridge, Cambridge University Press, 1997).

the discipline's flagship journal, the *American Political Science Review*, remains dominated by scholars for whom a theory's generality is a virtue superior to its empirical accuracy.

In Britain, however, there has long been a tension within political studies between a certain Whiggish traditionalism and the growth of a sense of 'sceptical professionalism'—between scholarship informed by the descriptive or normative concerns of history, law and moral philosophy, and research influenced by the methods and agendas of political scientists in the United States and, perhaps, parts of Continental Europe.[8] While the differences between American and British approaches can certainly be overstated,[9] for the development of scholarship on nationalism, the relative lack of consensus about the scope and methods of political science in Britain was critical, for it was precisely the unsettled nature of the discipline that facilitated the growth of a distinct, multidisciplinary field defined more by its object of study than by its disciplinary pedigree. The pluralism of opinions on the meaning of 'political science' was a catalyst for the development of a professional community of scholars reflecting and writing on the origins of nations and the conduct of nationalist politics.

In British higher education, the relatively permeable boundaries between the various social sciences has generally allowed a greater degree of communication across disciplines than in the United States. There, the growth of a reasonably well-defined discipline of political science, with its own agendas and professional standards, has tended to discourage the development of autonomous areas of research outside the concerns of the discipline's mainstream. Graduate students are socialized in a particular professional tradition, 'trained' as political scientists, at the same time that they are introduced to a body of knowledge associated with the established specializations—American politics, comparative politics, international relations, political theory—in which they choose to concentrate. The chief criterion against which their work is judged tends to be the degree to which it contributes to the theoretical questions at the cutting edge of the established sub-field or of the discipline as a whole; the

---

[8] J. Hayward, 'Political Science in Britain', *European Journal of Political Research*, 20 (1991), 311.

[9] This point is especially applicable to comparative politics, the sub-field in which most studies of nationalism naturally fall. There is little evidence to suggest, at least in the 1990s, that British comparativists are somehow less rigorous, more inclined toward inductive methodologies, or less willing to make general statements about political phenomena than their American colleagues. See E. C. Page, 'British Political Science and Comparative Politics', *Political Studies*, 38 (1990), 438–52.

potential contribution to the literature on a particular region, period or theme is generally of secondary concern. In this respect, what Oakeshott called in a slightly different context the 'sovereignty of technique' has tended to define American approaches to the study of politics.[10]

The enthusiasm for such a programme in Britain has generally been more muted, informed by a suspicion that 'political science', to paraphrase Alfred Cobban, may be merely a label for avoiding the adjective without achieving the noun.[11] The unsettled nature of disciplinary boundaries in the United Kingdom has meant that research tends to be evaluated according to rather different criteria from in the United States. Empirical accuracy, originality, style of argumentation and contribution to existing research on a distinct region, period or theme—the same criteria that might inform the work of, say, an historian or legal scholar—have been paramount. A certain uneasiness about intellectual system-builders and a tendency to judge the worth of political research more in terms of the importance of its conclusions than the elegance of its method have been characteristic of British approaches to the 'master science'.[12] The object of research, rather than the discipline in which research is conducted, has been the major determinant of professional loyalties and standards of scholarship. For many British political scientists, like their American counterparts earlier this century, there is still a propensity to value an interesting utterance over a falsifiable one, whereas in American universities today, rather the opposite has perhaps become the norm. Before his delivery of the Conway Memorial Lecture

[10] M. Oakeshott, 'Rationalism in Politics', in *Rationalism in Politics and Other Essays* (Indianapolis, Liberty Fund, 1991), p. 23.

[11] A. Cobban, 'The Decline of Political Theory', *Political Studies Quarterly*, 68 (1953), 335.

[12] Some of the most articulate expressions of this view have been those of Sir Isaiah Berlin:

> The attempts to substitute machines, methods of mass production, for the slow manual labour of antiquaries and historical researchers have all broken down; we still rely on those who spend their lives in painfully piecing together their knowledge from fragments of actual evidence, obeying this evidence wherever it leads them, however tortuous and unfamiliar the pattern, or with no consciousness of any pattern at all. Meanwhile the wings and the machinery are gathering dust on the shelves of museums, examples of overweening ambition and idle fantasy, not of intellectual achievement.

I. Berlin, *The Sense of Reality: Studies in Ideas and their History* (New York, Farrar, Strauss & Giroux, 1996), pp. 6–7. For Berlin, the attempt to construct a 'science' of politics was not only misguided but potentially immoral as well, in so far as its fanciful conclusions encouraged political leaders to believe that, given the correct system of institutions, they could effectively channel and change the interests and aspirations of their constituents. Such systems, as Berlin often argued, have inevitably led to ruin.

in 1932, Harold Laski, then professor of political science at LSE, was introduced by the chair with the observation that 'He has the training and outlook of the historian. Schemes and projects that lack a basis in history are no more than an exercise of fantasy in a world of dreams.'[13] While one can imagine a similarly complimentary introduction for a British politics professor today, more than a few American political scientists would consider such remarks at best a mild insult.

One result of these differing professional traditions was the relegation of studies of nationalism to the periphery of American political science and, concomitantly, their unusual growth within political studies in the United Kingdom. Until the 1970s, many American political scientists were prone to view nationalism as an atavistic sentiment that would eventually disappear as societies became more variegated and economies more modern. Seeing nationalist movements as either echoes of a premodern past (as in residual ethnic attachments in western democracies) or as masks for the process of modernization itself (as in the nationalism of post-colonial states), mainstream political scientists tended to ignore the power of the national idea and to leave its elucidation to departments of history; when political scientists did turn their attention to questions of ethnicity or nationalism, it was most often in the context of racial, ethnic or regional politics in the United States. Historians, for this reason, have been responsible for the bulk of the scholarship produced in America on nations and nationalism since the First World War. Carlton Hayes' graduate seminar at Columbia University trained generations of prominent scholars, and Hayes' own writings, especially his *The Historical Evolution of Modern Nationalism*, remain the foundational work for American historians of nations and nationalist ideology.[14] The hegemony of historians was not, of course, complete. Karl Deutsch in political science, Rupert Emerson in international relations, Joshua Fishman in linguistics, and Leonard Doob in psychology were early advocates of bringing the techniques of social science to bear on contemporary nationalist phenomena.[15] In the main, however, the study

---

[13] H. J. Laski, *Nationalism and the Future of Civilization* (London, Watts and Co., 1932), p. 5.

[14] Hayes spent his entire academic career at Columbia, from his entrance as an undergraduate to his retirement as full professor in 1950. He also served as Roosevelt's ambassador to Spain during the Second World War. See C. J. H. Hayes, *Wartime Mission in Spain, 1942–1945* (New York, Macmillan, 1945).

[15] See, for example, Deutsch, *Nationalism*; R. Emerson, *Government and Nationalism in Southeast Asia* (New York, Institute of Pacific Relations, 1942); J. A. Fishman, *Language and Nationalism* (Rowley, Mass., Newbury House Publishers, 1973); L. Doob, *Patriotism and Nationalism: Their Psychological Foundations* (New Haven, Conn., Yale University Press, 1964).

of nationalism remained outside the professional interest of most American social scientists, and political scientists in particular, through the late 1960s.

Doubts about the power of nationality were also, of course, to be found in Britain. Both Harold Laski and G. D. H. Cole were convinced that the nation-state was, by the middle of the century, already an outmoded form of political association, while E. H. Carr adopted what now seems the rather infelicitous title *Nationalism and After* for his speculations on sovereignty and international order after the Second World War.[16] But since the study of nationalism was never dominated by a single academic discipline, much less the relatively nebulous discipline of politics, there was no academic 'mainstream' from which it could be marginalized. The methodological pluralism of political studies meant that the object of research, rather than the boundaries of the discipline, defined the field of study; likewise, the stress among British political scientists on empiricism and historically-informed research was especially suited to the study of a phenomenon whose manifestations were both complex and particularistic.

We might say, then, that the study of nationalism in Britain has been marked by a kind of providential anti-professionalism. Intellectuals with interests and expertise difficult to corral within a single academic category have dominated the field, and their eclectic interests have placed them at various times at the nexus of politics and philosophy, history and anthropology, or sociology and cultural commentary. Gellner, who ended his career as the first director of the Center for the Study of Nationalism at the Central European University in Prague, also occupied posts at various stages as a professor of social anthropology and as lecturer in sociology and in philosophy; his academic *oeuvre* (leaving aside his numerous essays and reflections on contemporary events) touches on subjects ranging from linguistic philosophy to the religious beliefs of Berber tribesmen.[17] The

---

[16] See Laski, *Nationalism*; Laski, *A Grammar of Politics* (London, George Allen & Unwin, [3rd ed.] 1934), especially Chs. 2 and 6; G. D. H. Cole, *Europe, Russia, and the Future* (New York, Macmillan, 1942); E. H. Carr, *Nationalism and After* (London, Macmillan, 1945). To be fair to Carr, however, his arguments on the fate of nation-states are far more subtle than the title of his essay might indicate. See Ernest Gellner's charitable treatment of Carr in Gellner, *Encounters*, pp. 20–33.

[17] See, for example, E. Gellner, *Saints of the Atlas* (London, Weidenfeld & Nicolson, 1969); E. Gellner, *Spectacles and Predicaments: Essays in Social Theory* (Cambridge, Cambridge University Press, 1979); E. Gellner, *Relativism and the Social Sciences* (Cambridge, Cambridge University Press, 1985); E. Gellner, *Plough, Sword and Book: The Structure of Human History* (London, Collins Harvill, 1988); E. Gellner, *Conditions of Liberty: Civil Society and Its Rivals* (New York, Penguin, 1994).

same point could be made about any number of other scholars who have made important contributions to the field.

Beyond these considerations, however, there are three other factors that have made British scholars particularly sensitive to the power of nationalism. First, the personal biographies of British writers themselves are important. The study of nationalism has always had a certain *mitteleuropäische* disposition. Gellner and Eric Hobsbawm (as well as their North American contemporaries Hans Kohn, Karl Deutsch and Thomas Spira, the long-time editor of the *Canadian Review of Studies in Nationalism*) were born in various parts of the Habsburg Empire or its successor states. Throughout Gellner's work in particular, the Habsburg experience remained a powerful symbol of the force of national passions and the tragedy of governments that failed to accommodate them. Hugh Seton-Watson, scion of a family whose name is synonymous with the historiography of the Habsburg, Romanov and Ottoman lands, was himself both a student of, and activist for, the peoples of Europe's former continental empires.[18] John Plamenatz, who made a significant, if largely unappreciated, contribution to the debate on nationalism and individualism, was by birth a Montenegrin, while C. A. Macartney, the great historian of nationalism in central Europe, was the grandson of a Bulgarian colonel.[19] Similar points could be made about Isaiah Berlin, J. L. Talmon and others with central and east European connections.[20] It is not difficult to find in their writings an element of the personal, both in

[18] See the survey of the elder Seton-Watson's legacy in H. Seton-Watson and C. Seton-Watson, *The Making of a New Europe: R. W. Seton-Watson and the Last Years of Austria Hungary* (Seattle, University of Washington Press, 1981). Among the family's most important works on east central Europe are R. W. Seton-Watson, *The Rise of Nationality in the Balkans* (London, Constable, 1917); R. W. Seton-Watson, *The Southern Slav Question and the Habsburg Monarchy* (New York, H. Fertig, [1969] 1911); R. W. Seton-Watson, *A History of the Roumanians* (Cambridge, Cambridge University Press, 1934); H. Seton-Watson, *East Central Europe Between the Wars, 1918–1941* (Cambridge, Cambridge University Press, 1945); H. Seton-Watson, *The East European Revolution* (New York, Praeger, 1956); H. Seton-Watson, *The Russian Empire, 1801–1917* (Oxford, Clarendon Press, 1967).

[19] J. Plamenatz, *On Alien Rule and Self-Government* (London, Longmans, 1960); C. A. Macartney, *National States and National Minorities* (Oxford, Oxford University Press, 1934); C. A. Macartney, *Hungary and Her Successors* (Oxford, Oxford University Press, 1934); C. A. Macartney, *The Habsburg Empire, 1790–1918* (New York, Macmillan, 1969).

[20] As Brian Barry notes, this point extends far beyond the study of nationalism. 'Self-Government Revisited', in D. Miller and L. Siedentop, eds., *The Nature of Political Theory* (Oxford, Clarendon Press, 1983), p. 123. For an intriguing argument about the central European origins of modern nationalism studies, see T. Snyder, 'Kazimierz Kelles-Krauz (1872–1905): A Pioneering Scholar of Modern Nationalism', *Nations and Nationalism*, 3 (1997), 143–69.

their appreciation for the ambiguities of national identity and in their reflections on the challenges of assimilation, especially for European Jewry.[21] Born in one collapsing empire and educated in another, many of these thinkers were uniquely placed to recognize the enduring importance of nationality and particularly disinclined to dismiss it as a mere remnant of pre-modernity.

Second, the British study of nationalism has clearly had an important relationship to British politics and foreign policy. The work of scholars in this field has been as much influenced by a practical concern for dealing with the manifestations of nationalism as by an academic interest in its origins. In the last century and a half, crises at home and abroad have attracted the attention of thinkers with a special interest in questions of nationality and self-determination. The Greek crisis of the 1820s, the Bulgarian atrocities of the 1870s, the problem of Ireland, and the fate of India and other colonial possessions have all prompted serious debate among British political theorists and statesmen over the bases of nationality and the claim to national liberation.[22] The well-known Chatham House study group, whose lengthy report on nationalism was published just three months before Hitler's invasion of Poland, addressed both the question of rising nationalism on the Continent as well as the problem of self-determination within colonial states, both of which by 1939 had become of considerable practical importance to British policymakers.[23] Gellner's later writings were similarly concerned with the dangers of nationalism for post-communist governments which ignored the sources and salience of mobilized ethnicity.[24] At the same time a colonial power, a multiethnic metropolis, and the only western democracy in the post-Second World War period to have fought a war in defence of its sovereign territory, Britain perhaps more than other states has experienced first-hand the power of the national idea.[25]

---

[21] See, for example, I. Berlin, 'Benjamin Disraeli, Karl Marx and the Search for Identity', in his *Against the Current* (New York, Viking, 1980), pp. 252–86.

[22] See the classic study of nationalism, domestic politics and British foreign policy by R. W. Seton-Watson, *Disraeli, Gladstone and the Eastern Question: A Study in Diplomacy and Party Politics* (London, Frank Cass, 1962).

[23] Royal Institute of International Affairs, *Nationalism* (Oxford, Oxford University Press, 1939).

[24] See E. Gellner, 'Nationalism and Politics in Eastern Europe', *New Left Review*, 189 (1991), 127–34; E. Gellner, 'Homeland of the Unrevolution', *Daedalus*, 122 (1993), 141–53.

[25] Even the otherwise cosmopolitan A. J. P. Taylor initially found himself a supporter of Mrs Thatcher's policy in the Falklands, a view from which he later, however, recanted. See A. J. P. Taylor, *An Old Man's Diary* (London, Hamish Hamilton, 1984).

Finally, the question of what exactly constitutes national identity in Britain itself has never been straightforward. As Richard Rose has reminded political scientists since the 1960s, the United Kingdom is a multinational state in which the 'territorial dimension' of politics is fundamental.[26] British studies of nationalism have thus existed within the context of debates on the relationship between the unity of the kingdom and the competing national and sub-national identities of its constituent parts. From early debates between Ernest Barker and Hamilton Fyfe over the meaning of 'national character' to discussions in the 1980s and 1990s led by Tom Nairn, John Rex, Bhikhu Parekh and others on the challenges of an increasingly multicultural Britain, questions of nationality have never been purely academic.[27] The same could, of course, be said for North America and Australia, where the problems of forging unified national communities out of an array of linguistic, cultural and religious groups have preoccupied sociologists and political scientists for decades. But in Britain, the problem has perhaps been more acute for one important reason: Britain has been throughout this century at once an old, continuous European nation and a settler community. The political symbols and institutions of the state are part of a specific national tradition; the distinct cultures of the British Isles were blended in the eighteenth and early nineteenth centuries into a hybrid Britishness by the dual forces of war and Protestantism.[28] At the same time, because

---

[26] Rose's contribution on this and related themes is immense. See especially R. Rose, *Politics in England: an Interpretation* (Boston, Mass., Little, Brown, 1964); *The Territorial Dimension in Government: Understanding the United Kingdom* (Chatham, NJ, Chatham House Publishers, 1982); and his successive contributions to the various editions of G. Almond and G. B. Powell, *Comparative Politics Today: A World View* (New York, HarperCollins, [6th ed.] 1996).

[27] On the question of national character, see E. Barker, *National Character and the Factors in Its Formation* (London, Methuen, 1927); H. Fyfe, *The Illusion of National Character*, revised ed. (London, Watts, 1946). The implications of racial, ethnic and nationalist politics, both for the United Kingdom and for social science, are dealt with extensively in T. Nairn, *The Break-Up of Britain* (London, Verso, [2nd ed.] 1981); M. Banton, *Racial and Ethnic Competition* (Cambridge, Cambridge University Press, 1983); J. Rex, *Race Relations in Sociological Theory* (London, Routledge and Kegan Paul, [2nd ed.] 1983); J. Rex, *Race and Ethnicity* (Milton Keynes, Open University Press, 1986); J. Rex, *Ethnic Minorities in the Modern Nation State* (New York, St Martin's Press, 1986); J. Rex and D. Mason, eds., *Theories of Race and Ethnic Relations* (Cambridge, Cambridge University Press, 1986); B. Parekh and J. Dederveen Pieterse, eds., *The Decolonization of Imagination* (London, Zed Books, 1995). For a useful overview of racial and ethnic issues in British social science, see the special issue of *Ethnic and Racial Studies*, 19 (1996).

[28] L. Colley, *Britons: Forging the Nation, 1707–1837* (New Haven, Conn., Yale University Press, 1992). For alternative views, though, see H. Kearney, *The British Isles: A History of Four Nations* (Cambridge, Cambridge University Press, 1989) and L. Greenfeld, *Nationalism: Five Roads to Modernity* (Cambridge, Mass., Harvard University Press, 1992), Ch. 2.

of the legacies of colonialism and the forces of globalization, Britain in this century has also become a highly variegated and multiethnic state, where the bonds of national sentiment and the boundaries of the national community are increasingly indistinct, and where the relationship between Britishness and its various subordinate identities is decidedly problematic. As Hugh Kearney has quipped, at the close of the century, it may be that Britain has become a national analogue of Oxford University: 'Visitors to Oxford, asking "where is the University" are mystified when they cannot be directed to it.'[29] Intellectual debates on the meaning of nationhood, the dilemmas of multiculturalism and the link between nationality and territory have therefore been conducted in a political context in which the answers to these questions continue to have considerable practical relevance. Today as in the past, 'What ish my nation?', as Macmorris asks in the third act of *Henry V*, has no uncontroversial response.

Up to now, I have spoken of the development of a relatively distinct and multidisciplinary field of 'nationalism studies' in Britain which was in part the result of the methodological dispositions of political studies itself, and in part the result of the personal backgrounds of the major scholars in the field and broader features of British academic and political life. The sections below analyse three overarching themes in this field: the ideology of the nation and the relevance of political ideas to nationalist politics; the sources of national identity and communal solidarity; and the legitimacy of claims about nationality and rights to national self-determination.

Nationalist ideology and the relevance of the national idea

One of the major lines of debate in the study of nationalism this century has been the degree to which the content of nationalist thought is itself a legitimate and relevant subject of research. All nationalist ideologies offer at the same time an ontology, a philosophy of history, and a theory of political legitimacy. For nationalists, the world is composed of discrete nations, primordial *Urvölker* whose members share a number of identifiable ascriptive traits, among which might number physical appearance, cultural symbols, shared historical memories, and linguistic

[29] H. Kearney, 'Four Nations or One?' in B. Crick, ed., *National Identities: The Constitution of the United Kingdom* (Oxford, Basil Blackwell, 1991), p. 4.

peculiarities. Each of these groups has an intimate historical connection to a particular piece of land, and it is the effort to assert and defend claims to this territory that forms the chief motor of history. Disputes may arise between rival claimants to the same territory, but there is at the end of the day a fact of the matter to be uncovered; either the direct antecedents of a modern nation occupied a given territory at a given point in history or they did not, and sifting through these contesting claims to uncover the truth is the task of historians, archaeologists, ethnographers and the like. Feelings of solidarity among members of the same nation are natural, for they are based on shared historical memories of the struggle for self-definition and self-determination. Political boundaries that mirror the demographic boundaries of the national group are normal and laudable; borders should be genuinely 'international', setting off one nation from another rather than merely demarcating the horizons of state authority. On this view, political movements that seek to remedy the divide between nations and states are therefore both predictable and praiseworthy.

These basic assumptions about the nature of nations and relations among them underlie all nationalist discourse. For scholars, though, the degree to which these assumptions are appropriate topics of research has proved to be controversial for two reasons. In the first place, the question of nationalist discourse has defined the divide between scholars whose methods and assumptions draw on the traditions of intellectual history and those interested in the search for patterns of social and political behaviour; and second, it has focused attention on the issue of the relative autonomy of the national idea—whether nationalism should be seen as *sui generis* or as an epiphenomenon of more fundamental political or economic processes.

The history-of-ideas approach, which seeks to locate nationalism at the nexus of political philosophy and everyday politics, has had a long tradition in Britain. Alfred Cobban, Elie Kedourie and Isaiah Berlin have been among the foremost chroniclers of the national idea, tracing its origins among German intellectuals at the end of the eighteenth century, its manifestations in eighteenth- and nineteenth-century western Europe, and its spread to the captive nations of east central Europe by the middle of the last century.[30] These writers share at least four conclusions about

---

[30] See A. Cobban, *Nationalism and National Self-Determination* (New York, Thomas Crowell, [rev. ed.] 1969); Kedourie, *Nationalism*; I. Berlin, *Vico and Herder* (London, Hogarth Press, 1976).

the origins and evolution of the national idea. First, the terms 'nation', 'nationality' and 'nationalism' are inherently protean, and any attempt to arrive at an overarching definition for these terms and their derivatives does violence to their essential embeddedness in the historical periods in which they appear. Second, the emergence of the idea of timeless national communities, in which individuals are thought to express their true individuality only as part of a culturally-defined collective, emerged as a response to the rationalism and individualism of the Enlightenment. Nationalism as a political ideology, therefore, is fundamentally anti-rational, 'an off-shoot', in Berlin's words, 'of the romantic revolt'.[31] Third, the national idea—in particular, the concept that sovereignty should lie with 'the people' and that 'the people' are coterminous with a culturally distinct nation—has historically played a major role as a catalyst for liberation. The sense that one's own personal struggle against cultural discrimination is part of a wider injustice visited upon one's nation by alien oppressors has been a powerful guarantor of liberty and a bulwark against tyranny. But, fourth, when dislodged from the concept of democracy, nationalism can itself become an excuse for authoritarianism. As long as the nation remains defined as a community of rights-bearing individuals, nationalism can serve the benign purpose of unifying the community against external threats. Once the perceived interests of the collective are defined in opposition to the interests of its individual constituents, however, the nation becomes inimical to human liberty. The history of nationalism is, therefore, the history of competing definitions of the nation, with purveyors of nationalist ideologies offering their own rival versions of history, culture and identity in the political marketplace.

This focus on the origins and manifestations of the national idea arose from the persistent belief among many scholars that nationalism is, above all, a state of mind, a corporate will which inspires large numbers of individuals within a national group and which lays claim to the allegiance of even more.[32] It is, in the colourful metaphor used by Kedourie, a type of 'political bovarysme', a philosophy inspired by too little reason and too many romantic novels.[33] This view had an important impact on the research agendas of scholars concerned with

---

[31] I. Berlin, 'Nationalism: Past Neglect and Present Power', in his *Against the Current*, p. 355.

[32] H. Seton-Watson, *Language and National Consciousness*, offprint from *Proceedings of the British Academy*, 67 (1981), 2–3.

[33] Kedourie, *Nationalism*, p. 80. See also Kedourie's lengthy introduction to his edited volume *Nationalism in Africa and Asia* (New York, World Publishing Co., 1970).

nationalist politics. Since nationalism was seen as, at base, a mental state, the most that scholars could hope to do would be to trace its development over time and to reveal the ways in which the seemingly natural division of humans into distinct national categories was in fact the product of a particular, historically contingent idea. Changeable and indistinct, the idea of the nation was not, therefore, readily susceptible to anything other than a more or less descriptive account of its origins and evolution. For, as Ramsay Muir reflected at the beginning of this century, '[nationality] cannot be tested or analysed by formulae, such as the German professors love'.[34]

For the study of politics, however, the obvious question is whether any account of the history of the idea of the nation is ever helpful in addressing the questions of most concern to social scientists. The inherent difficulties of tracking the evolution of any political idea, especially one as changeable as 'nation', is only part of the problem. A more basic issue is whether elucidating the history of the concept could ever reveal anything valuable about the politics of nationalism itself. If nationalism is analysed only as an idea—especially, as many writers earlier this century concluded, as an idea whose time has come and gone—then there seems little hope of being able to address some of the key questions about nationalism as a political force. Given the array of possible forms of political association, why has the nation proved to be so persistent and universal? What is it about nationality as a source of group loyalty that sets it off from religion or class? Under what conditions do national allegiances trump all others? Within individual nations, why do some conceptions of national identity endure while others become quaint footnotes in the history of the respective national group? Examining the historical evolution of an idea can be useful as a reminder that no political concepts spring fully formed from the minds of political scientists and, instead, trail behind them a string of multiple and often mutually contradictory meanings. But once this fact is recognized, the history-of-ideas approach seems to offer little in the way of real explanatory power.

The question of the utility of intellectual history to the study of nationalism lay at the heart of a long-running debate between Kedourie and Gellner. Kedourie's *Nationalism* masterfully traced the evolution of 'nation' from Sieyès and Kant through Herder and Fichte to the creation

---

[34] R. Muir, *Nationalism and Internationalism: The Culmination of Modern History* (Boston, Mass., n.p. 1916), p. 51, quoted in Snyder, *Meaning*, p. 56.

of new European national states after the First World War. The book
began as a series of lectures which the author prepared shortly after
joining the Department of Government at LSE, then headed by
Oakeshott. Kedourie approached the subject of nationalism primarily
as a problem in the history of ideas. To treat it otherwise, he argued, was
merely a species of economism; those who give in to the 'sociological
temptation' to seek general explanations for nationalist phenomena,
treating nationalism as a development to be explained away by reference
to economic or other social forces, misunderstand the essentially autonomous character of the national idea and the variety of radically different forms that it has taken over the past two centuries. Like Molière's
Monsieur Jourdain, who discovered that he had been speaking prose all
his life, nationalist thinkers would surely be surprised to hear from social
scientists that their doctrine of nationality was, in reality, 'either an
expression of bourgeois self-interest, or an industrial lubricant, or a
reflection of deep subterranean movements slowly maturing through
centuries and millenia.'[35] Kedourie's attack on social scientific treatments
of nationalism was aimed largely at Gellner, who had earlier questioned
his view that Kant's concept of individual 'self-determination' or 'autonomy' prefigured later nationalist views on the right to self-determination
of culturally defined collectivities.[36] As Gellner argued, while Kedourie
had shown that the nation is a logically contingent concept—that the
national is in no sense natural—the corollary, that nationalism is also
sociologically contingent, was nonsensical. If the nation were a more or
less accidental creation of European thinkers, as Kedourie maintained,
might not nationalism—the appearance of culturally-defined political
units and the proliferation of feelings of connection and attachment to
these units—also be merely accidental? On the contrary, Gellner held,
although the idea of the nation, like any political ideology, was certainly
contingent on the backgrounds and intellectual predisposition of its
authors, its spread and success as an organizing principle were the direct
results of definite changes in social relations on the eve of industrialization. The shift from structurally defined, hierarchical and static forms of
social organization to culturally defined, egalitarian and mobile societies
during the process of modernization created a milieu in which ideas

[35] Kedourie, *Nationalism*, p. 144. For a further defence of the history of ideas and its place in
political studies, see E. Kedourie, 'The History of Ideas and Guilt by Association' in his *The
Crossman Confessions and Other Essays* (London, Mansell Publishing, 1984), pp. 143–7.
[36] Gellner, *Thought*, p. 151, fn. 1. Berlin shared Kedourie's view of the importance of Kant in
the history of nationalist thought. See Berlin, *Sense*, pp. 232–48.

about the unity of the nation could take root.[37] While an account of the tortuous path via which modern concepts of the nation have arrived on the political scene might be a useful corrective to the views of nationalists themselves, such an enterprise cannot explain why those ideas and not others have proved so politically successful since the end of the eighteenth century.

The issue of the utility of intellectual history was only one strand in a much broader discussion about the determinants of nationalism and national identity, a discussion that Gellner once termed 'the LSE debate'.[38] In many ways, it exemplified the divide within British studies of nationalism between historians and social scientists—between an older tradition of seeing nationality primarily as an idea, and a newer approach that sought general explanations for the individual sacrifices and social cohesion that characterized nationalist politics. Even among social scientists, however, questions about the sources of national sentiment and its relationship to the social cohesion of cultural communities have proved no less controversial.

National identity, communal solidarity and the reductionist impulse

Beyond ideology, the question of the solidarity of national groups has also been central to discussions of nationalist politics. Why is it that, given the range of possible foci of human loyalty, groups often coalesce around the particular array of common cultural symbols, linguistic peculiarities, and shared histories represented by the nation? And under what conditions does the nation eclipse other potential symbols of allegiance? The most familiar response to these questions, one often encountered today in discussions about the threat of post-Cold War 'ethnic conflicts', is the view that nationality is as fundamental a component of personal identity as kinship, and that as a result, it represents a uniquely powerful source of group solidarity and a potential mobilizational resource for political élites. On this view, nations, while perhaps not the timeless entities imagined by nationalists themselves, are nevertheless rooted in established patterns of belief and behaviour that bind individuals into communal groups and mark them off from others. A

[37] Gellner, *Nations*, pp. 33–4.
[38] Gellner, *Encounters*, p. 61. The 'LSE group' included Gellner, Kedourie, Anthony Smith and Percy Cohen.

collective name, a common language, shared history, common customs, perhaps distinctive religious beliefs or a sense of allegiance to an ancestral homeland are the key symbols of this collective identity and the major focal points of group solidarity. Modern nations, then, do not arise *ex nihilo*, but are instead the direct heirs of long-standing reciprocal bonds within human communities.[39]

Although variants of this view—now often labelled 'primordialism' or 'perennialism'—have become commonplace in discussions of ethnicity and nationalism after the Cold War, as an account of solidarity within ethnonational communities it suffers from several serious shortcomings, both empirical and methodological. In the first place, the assertion that modern nations have existed in an unbroken line from primordial cultural communities is contradicted by the manifest heterogeneity of populations and the fluid nature of personal identity before the advent of structured systems of mass education. Even today, nations are far less homogeneous than primordialist views allow, and there is rarely a clear and undisputed correspondence between the claims to a particular territory by nationalist groups and the willingness of neighbouring populations to accede to them. Moreover, by reifying nationality and seeing it as the most salient of an entire portfolio of personal identities, primordialists cannot explain how nationalism might intersect with other forms of social mobilization tied to class, gender or regional affiliation.[40]

Of even more concern, however, are primordialism's methodological difficulties. First, primordialist claims beg the question of the sources of communal cohesion and solidarity. While this problem does not mean that primordialists have nothing interesting to say, it does mean that their ability to offer genuine explanation is severely limited. The problem

---

[39] Classic statements of this view include E. Shils, 'Primordial, Personal, Sacred and Civil Ties', *British Journal of Sociology*, 8 (1957), 130–45; H. Isaacs, *Idols of the Tribe: Group Identity and Political Change* (Cambridge, Mass., Harvard University Press, 1975); C. Geertz, 'The Integrative Revolution: Primordial Sentiments and Civil Politics in the New States', in Geertz, *The Interpretation of Cultures* (New York, Basic Books, 1973), pp. 255–310. For more recent books that share many of the assumptions of these earlier works, see R. Kaplan, *Balkan Ghosts* (New York, St Martin's, 1993); R. Kaplan, *The Ends of the Earth* (New York, Random House, 1996); D. P. Moynihan, *Pandemonium* (Oxford, Oxford University Press, 1993); W. Pfaff, *The Wrath of Nations: Civilization and the Furies of Nationalism* (New York, Simon & Schuster, 1993). Traces of this argument can also be found in the widely-read book by M. Ignatieff, *Blood and Belonging: Journeys into the New Nationalism* (London, Vintage, 1993), although it would be unfair to place the author squarely within this camp.
[40] For a discussion of this point, see E. Benner, *Really Existing Nationalisms: A Post-Communist View from Marx and Engels* (Oxford, Clarendon Press, 1995), pp. 222–8.

arises from the fact that primordialists normally fail to make a distinction between solidarity (the ties of culture or custom that bind individuals into relatively cohesive social units) and collective action (the mobilization of these units toward a particular goal). The latter is simply assumed to be more likely in cases in which the former is present. Attempts to test the primordialist hypothesis that nationality is a perennial component of collective identities therefore reduce to tautologies:[41] national solidarity is taken as given and used to explain group behaviour, while cases of collective action—demonstrations, ethnonational violence, wars, etc.—are in turn offered as evidence for the existence of group solidarity.

A second problem is that, because they have no way of identifying solidary groups other than by pointing to cases of collective action, primordialists tend to choose their case studies on the dependent variable—seeking to explain nationalist sentiment by concentrating only on cases in which nationalist mobilization has taken place. 'Nationalisms That Failed' is not a chapter one is likely to find in books that proceed from primordialist premises. The problem with this method is that, since such accounts tend overwhelmingly to focus on cases in which nationalists have succeeded in mobilizing individuals around a given set of ascriptive traits, primordialist arguments can do no more than assume—rather than demonstrate—that nationalism was a necessary outcome of the presence of those traits themselves. From the outset, then, primordialists violate two of the basic tenets of social scientific methodology—proffering a hypothesis which is essentially unfalsifiable, and then attempting to test the hypothesis by choosing cases on the dependent variable. The mere fact that primordialists assume the very thing that most students of nationalism want to explain—group solidarity—should lead one to look with scepticism on the usefulness of such treatments of nationalist phenomena.

Although the debate in Britain has normally been framed in a language less self-consciously scientific, the question of the roots of social solidarity within national groups has been basic to the study of nationalism. Early discussions about the utility of 'national character' as an analytical tool—as well as the rebirth of studies in 'political culture'

---

[41] On this problem, see S. Olzak, *The Dynamics of Ethnic Competition and Conflict* (Stanford, Calif., Stanford University Press, 1992), pp. 5–6. For a further critique of primordialism on social scientific grounds, see the selection by Paul Brass in J. Hutchinson and A. D. Smith, eds., *Nationalism* (Oxford, Oxford University Press, 1994), pp. 83–9.

in the 1970s and 1980s—centred on precisely the issue at stake in debates over the sources of national identity and their relationship to group solidarity: To what extent do culturally-defined communities share identities, norms and values that are useful in explaining political behaviour?[42] Discussion has normally focused on two sets of issues.

First is the question of the reducibility of national identity, that is, the extent to which nationality and national solidarity arise only as epiphenomena of other social processes. The position of Anthony Smith, sometimes mistakenly equated with primordialism, combines an appreciation for the modernity of the national idea with a sensitivity to the more enduring ethnic cores around which contemporary national groups have coalesced. In Smith's view, nations in the modern sense of the term—bounded political entities with a single, over-arching sense of identity and community—are unquestionably of modern vintage. It was not until perhaps the French Revolution that genuine nations appeared on the European scene; before then, localized identities or loyalty to particular political élites formed the bases of group solidarity. The belief in nations as the basic divisions of humanity and in nation-states as the primary components of the international system did not make its appearance until rather late in the day. But as Smith has argued, a recognition of the modernity of nations themselves, or at least the modernity of the concept of nationalism, does not preclude our acknowledging the existence of long-standing cultural and linguistic commonalities as the bedrock on which modern nations have formed. National identities and their attendant sense of communal solidarity are not immutable, but they are enduring; the trappings of nationalism, while themselves surely invented and manipulated by political and cultural élites, are embedded in pre-existing ethnic communities (or *ethnies*, in Smith's usage). The mobilizing power of nationalism can neither be reduced to its adherents' labouring under a false consciousness about their history and identity, nor explained away by the observation, often made by nationalists themselves, that their awakening to a shared

---

[42] As Barker poetically phrased the problem, scholars should investigate 'the house of thought which men have made that their minds may dwell there together'. Barker, *National Character*, p. 18. The study of Communist Europe was especially important in the 'return' of political culture, and studies of the region from the 1970s set the stage for the more wide-ranging discussions of democratization and civil society in the 1990s. Two important examples are A. Brown and J. Gray, eds., *Political Culture and Political Change in Communist States* (London, Macmillan, 1977) and A. Brown, ed., *Political Culture and Communist Studies* (Armonk, NY, M. E. Sharpe, 1985).

identity often results from external oppression. Rather, national appeals have historically been so powerful precisely because the modern versions of national identity rest on long-standing bonds of belonging and obligation, duty and commitment, within relatively homogeneous cultural communities. For Smith, as for Hans Kohn, recognizing the power of these enduring attachments need not lead one down the path of primordialism; indeed, appreciating the ethnic origins of modern nations is primarily an effort to rescue primordialism's sensitivity to nationalists' own pronouncements about their identity and the sources of group solidarity, while jettisoning its propensity to take nationalists simply at their word. Nationality, then, is reducible neither to timeless bonds of blood and land, nor to the cynical manipulation of national symbols by political élites; rather, the mobilizing strength of nationality lies somewhere between the two, grounded in enduring ethnic attachments that have, in the modern era, been infused with a peculiar political salience.

Gellner, like Smith, was firmly opposed to the reductionist impulse. Nations were neither mere modern instantiations of timeless social bonds, nor ephemeral sources of identity whose exit from the historical stage would be hastened by the advance of modernity. The former view, which Gellner termed the 'Dark Gods' theory of nationalism, rested on a naïvely static conception of human society, while the latter failed to appreciate the genuine sentiments of solidarity that bind individuals into distinct culturally defined communities.

> Those who oppose nationalism hope that Reason will prevail, aided perhaps by Student Exchange Schemes, the British Council, foreign holidays, re-written history textbooks and *au pair* girls. Those who favour nationalism, on the other hand, hope that a grey cosmopolitanism and a false bloodless ethos will not submerge the true sources of vitality, and they trust that the old Adam will out.[43]

Both views, Gellner noted, share a belief in the naturalness of national affiliation: One is born into a nation as one is born into a family. They differ only in their evaluation of this fact. For the nationalist, the natural character of national bonds imbues them with an authenticity which other allegiances will always lack; for the anti-nationalist, the fact that national sentiments are a natural part of human existence means

---

[43] Gellner, *Thought*, p. 149.

only that individuals should work even harder to ensure the triumph of reason over their innate national passions.

The relative malleability of these identities has been another question of pressing importance. One of the most enduring problems for students of nationalism, particularly those interested in the process of nation-building in newly-independent states, is the extent to which national myths can be self-consciously constructed. Under what conditions are national symbols most easily manipulated? How far can the historical record be stretched in order to accommodate the exigencies of nationalist history and communal identity? And how, if traditions really are 'invented', can they nevertheless become such powerful rallying points in times of political crisis? Nationalism may well involve getting history wrong, as Ernest Renan famously noted, but how far can nationalists continue getting it wrong before someone calls them to task?

There is clearly no easy answer to these questions, and most political scientists, whether in Britain or elsewhere, have focused mainly on debunking nationalist myths rather than attempting to explain their durability. The literature on the 'invention' of nations and their cultural accoutrements is now immense, and political scientists have been as active as historians and cultural theorists in criticizing the ostensibly timeless character of nationalist mythology and revealing the ways in which national symbols have been forged—in both senses of the word—over the past two centuries.[44] While such 'deconstructionist' accounts of nationalism have shed considerable light on the apparent falsity of many nationalist claims, studies in this genre can sometimes suffer from the defect of telling us little that we did not know already. We know from Marx, for example, that national myths and symbols can be recycled and infused with meanings radically different from those with which they were originally imbued. Detailing still further instances of this phenomenon in the remotest corners of the globe seems to add little to our understanding. More seriously, proponents of this approach often

---

[44] The classic studies in this genre are E. Hobsbawm and T. Ranger, eds., *The Invention of Tradition* (Cambridge, Cambridge University Press, 1983), and B. Anderson, *Imagined Communities: Reflections on the Origin and Spread of Nationalism* (London, Verso, [rev. ed.] 1991). For further examples, by both British and American authors, see W. Sollors, ed., *The Invention of Ethnicity* (Oxford, Oxford University Press, 1989); N. Shumway, *The Invention of Argentina* (Berkeley, Calif., University of California Press, 1991); P. K. Longmore, *The Invention of George Washington* (Berkeley, University of California Press, 1988); J. Katz, *The Invention of Heterosexuality* (New York, Dutton, 1995); M. Pittock, *The Invention of Scotland* (London, Routledge, 1991).

have trouble developing a sustainable research agenda, other than to discover still further fraudulent myths to expose.

As a result, much of the deconstructionist literature on nationalism sometimes represents little more than antiquarianism, interesting for the bizarre nature of the cases it studies but unable to build on previous work to deepen our understanding of the evident power of nationalist myths. Indeed, in many ways the proliferation of deconstructionist studies in the 1980s and 1990s has represented a return to the older history-of-ideas approach to nationalism. Since they are concerned primarily with confronting nationalist mythology and revealing the mutable definitions of the 'nation' over time, such studies normally encounter the same problems faced by historians of ideas. Once all the myths have been debunked and the nation revealed as a social construct, we are still left with the question of why individuals and groups are prepared to sacrifice blood and treasure in defence of an identity so patently ephemeral.

It is concern over the persistent tug of national sentiment—even among liberal intellectuals who ought to know better—that has prompted British scholars to focus on yet another aspect of nationalism: the relationship between nationality and the demands of liberal individualism. How to reconcile feelings of communal solidarity, individual rights and the supposed right to self-determination of national groups has been an enduring theme in British scholarship for the past century and a half, and its resurgence in the late 1990s has sparked renewed debate on the compatibility of communal sentiments, the requirements of the liberal conscience, and the imperatives of international order.

Nationality, liberalism and self-determination

The problems of explaining the origins of the national idea and the sources of national solidarity have been only part of the British study of nationalism. There is, in addition, a long tradition of speculation about to what extent, given that there are things in the world called nations to which individuals seem to attach considerable importance, the demands of nationalism should be accommodated by both political philosophers and policymakers. The concept of 'liberal' or 'civic' nationalism is often considered one of the great contributions of British political thought to this question. From Hume, Acton and Mill through Plamenatz and Berlin, to the upsurge in discussions of communitarianism, liberalism and national self-determination in the 1980s and 1990s, the relationship between communal values and individual rights has been a perennial feature of studies of nationality in the United Kingdom.[45] Acknowledging individuals' need for a sense of community and connectedness, while abjuring culturally-exclusive definitions of the community, 'civic' nationalists are often contrasted with their 'ethnic' counterparts, for whom the collective will of the culturally-defined nation is held to be superior to the wills of its individual constituents. In the case of civic nationalism, love of country and a sense of fellow-feeling with one's compatriots are shields against alien oppression and tyranny at home; in the case of ethnic nationalism, by contrast, the nation takes on a more sinister character, endangering liberty by subjugating individual freedom to the demands of the group.

Of course, the picture has never been as clear as facile distinctions between 'civic' and 'ethnic' forms of the national idea would indicate. In the first place, it is as easy to uncover a distinctive strand of ethnic exclusivism within British discussions of nationalism as it is to find more inclusive, civic conceptions of national identity.[46] What Orwell called prodding 'the nerve of nationalism'—the tendency for otherwise civically-minded individuals to transform overnight into ethnic exclusivists, given the right circumstances—has never been far removed from debates about the nature of the British state, relations within the empire, and Britain's place in Europe.[47] More importantly, however, among liberal intellectuals themselves there has long been a certain ambivalence about nationality. On the one hand, as Acton argued, when combined with a love of freedom, a strong national sentiment could advance the cause of human liberation. Nationality, if tempered by respect for the

---

[45] Key works in these debates, in both Britain and North America, include: W. Kymlicka, *Liberalism, Community and Culture* (Oxford, Clarendon Press, 1989); W. Kymlicka, *Multicultural Citizenship: A Liberal Theory of Minority Rights* (Oxford, Oxford University Press, 1995); W. Kymlicka, ed., *The Rights of Minority Cultures* (Oxford, Oxford University Press, 1995); D. Miller, *On Nationality* (Oxford, Clarendon Press, 1995); Y. Tamir, *Liberal Nationalism* (Princeton, NJ, Princeton University Press, 1993); C. Taylor, *Multiculturalism and 'The Politics of Recognition'* edited by A. Gutmann (Princeton, NJ, Princeton University Press, 1992); J. Spinner, *The Boundaries of Citizenship* (Baltimore, Johns Hopkins University Press, 1994).

[46] For an overview of racialist theories and their relationship to British politics, see F. Hertz, *Nationality in History and Politics* (London, Kegan Paul, Trench, Trubner and Co., 1944), pp. 66–8; and especially I. Hannaford, *Race: The History of an Idea in the West* (Washington, DC, Woodrow Wilson Center Press, 1996), Chs. 8–9.

[47] G. Orwell, 'Notes on Nationalism' in *England Your England and Other Essays* (London, Secker & Warburg, 1953), p. 64. See also Orwell's well-known essay 'England Your England', pp. 192–224.

individual, could assist in throwing off foreign despotism, buttressing self-government, and guarding against the excessive powers of the state. If all members of a political community shared a consistent similarity of character, interest and opinion, then the state's natural tendency towards centralization and absolutism could be checked.[48] If all that is meant by nationality is a sense of fellow-feeling, a positive sentiment of connection with members of one's own national group, then the relationship between nationality and individual freedom seems unproblematic. On the other hand, if nationality refers to an array of special duties and obligations that one owes to fellow countrymen beyond those that are owed to them in virtue of their being human, then the relationship becomes rather more troubling.

Liberals have therefore found themselves faced with a dilemma. Any theory that might encourage a people to prefer the tyranny of their own race to the kindness of strangers—such as nationalism—surely seems worthy of condemnation, but it is precisely this aversion to foreign rule that has often been the most powerful catalyst of liberation and demo-cratization. Liberal critiques of nationalism have thus traditionally sprung as much from uneasiness as from principle—uneasiness about how to reconcile those special sentiments of connection and camaraderie that one feels towards one's compatriots with the wider duties owed to the whole of humankind. Liberals feel instinctively, Mill wrote, that placing one's fellow countryman in a special category of duty and loyalty is more worthy of savages than of civilized beings, but 'grievous as are these things, yet so long as they exist, the question of nationality is practically of the very first importance'.[49] In fact, Mill noted, the evils of nationalism notwithstanding, without some strong sense of cohesion countries tended to fall under the spell of tyrants who impose unity at the expense of individual liberty. It was no accident that among both ancient and modern states the most powerful countries were those in which fellow-feeling was strongest, and there was thus good reason for believing that sentiments of sympathy and union among the inhabitants of a particular country, however unphilosophical, were a necessary precondition of liberty and good governance.[50]

---

[48] J. E. E. D. Acton, 'Nationality', in *Essays in the History of Liberty* (Indianapolis, Ind., Liberty Fund, 1985), pp. 409–33.

[49] J. S. Mill, 'Vindication of the French Revolution of 1848', in *Collected Works of John Stuart Mill*, vol. 20 (Toronto, Toronto University Press, 1974), p. 347.

[50] J. S. Mill, *A System of Logic*, in *Collected Works*, vol. 8, pp. 923–4.

These issues, which have occupied British philosophers and political theorists since the last century, have been of more than academic importance, for they have raised important questions about the degree to which really existing national sentiments ought to be accommodated or, indeed, cultivated by state institutions. In Britain, discussions on this issue have normally proceeded in three directions. First has been the relationship between patriotism and nationalism. The former, associated with a love of country and a sense of community with one's compatriots, has frequently been contrasted with the culturally exclusivist forms of nationalism found in parts of Continental Europe. While devotion to preserving the traditions and institutions of one's country seems a pre-condition to continued independence and the rejection of foreign domination, calls for the union of all co-nationals into a single, culturally homogeneous state invites individuals to mortgage their freedom for the perceived good of the collective.[51] 'If all the various peoples within a clear-cut unit of territory under a common rule suddenly begin to think of themselves as a common nation', wrote Bernard Crick in his *In Defence of Politics*, 'no great harm is done. But if criteria of language or religion or race are accepted, then those who live just over the borders . . . must be brought into the fold.'[52] Such feelings are thus not only potentially harmful to the political communities in which they arise, but may threaten international stability as well.

Second has been the question of the role of state institutions in fostering a sense of communal or national identity. Some sense of fellow-feeling has generally been seen as essential to the smooth working of democracy, but there has been disagreement over whether such feelings arise spontaneously or only through their active encouragement through state intervention. In other words, is multinationality to be prized within states, as Acton argued, or should the boundaries of statehood mirror insofar as possible those of the nationality? This issue became of increasing importance within Britain as the century progressed. Calls from the kingdom's constituent units for greater local autonomy—encapsulated in the devolution debates of the 1970s and the 1990s, as well as the endless Troubles in Northern Ireland—called into question the future of a fully 'united kingdom'. At the same time, Britain's manifest ethnic heterogeneity and the greater attention paid to problems of inter-

---

[51] A. Cobban, *The Nation State and National Self-Determination* (New York, Thomas Y. Crowell, 1970), pp. 127–9. On the varieties of nationalism in Europe, see Gellner, *Encounters*, pp. 20–33.

[52] B. Crick, *In Defence of Politics* (London, Penguin, [2nd ed.] 1962), p. 80.

ethnic discord and invidious racial discrimination highlighted the problematic relationships between Britishness, Englishness and the myriad identities of the country's South Asian, East Asian and Afro-Caribbean communities.

Finally, national self-determination as a principle of international politics has received considerable attention from British scholars, especially international relations specialists. The principle that national groups should be able to determine their own fate has been viewed as a largely progressive force when employed as a means for delivering oppressed peoples from tyrannical rule, but for all its positive components, the principle of self-determination has not generally been seen as absolute. As the experience of Versailles and the League of Nations illustrated, self-determination must in the first place be tempered by the practicalities of creating economically and politically viable states behind internationally defensible borders. In this regard, the meaning of self-determination has been understood in terms of process rather than outcome; members of a national community should be able, in so far as is practicable, to determine their own fate, but the institutional form that such self-determination might take need not be a new, wholly independent state. There is no reason to believe that the only desirable expression of self-determination should be the nation-state, and indeed, given the manifest heterogeneity of most existing states, complete self-determination would contradict the notion of state sovereignty. As Alfred Cobban argued in *The Nation State and National Self-Determination*, there may, in fact, be many other types of association through which communities can express their will to determine their own destiny.[53] Cultural autonomy, regional self-government and the Commonwealth have all been seen as potential models for reconciling respect for nationality with the desire for political stability. The challenges of self-determination after the break-up of multinational federations in eastern Europe, as well as the increased salience of cultural identity in established democracies, gave renewed vigour to all these debates in the 1990s.

Each of these areas—the distinction between patriotism and nationalism, the role of government institutions in multicultural societies, and the place of self-determination as a principle of international politics—has illustrated the broad, multidisciplinary approach that British

---

[53] Cobban, *The Nation State*. This important study, a revised edition of the author's earlier *National Self-Determination* (1945), was published posthumously with the editorial assistance of E. H. Carr.

scholars have taken to the study of nationalism this century. Historians, political theorists and legal experts have joined political scientists in tackling the major issues at the heart of nationalism, and have aided in the development of a distinct, problem-driven field of study influenced more by common research concerns than by common disciplinary affiliations.

Conclusion: The study of nationalism at century's end

In terms of the sheer volume of new scholarship, few fields within political science have been as fertile in the last two decades as the study of nationalism and ethnonational politics. Doctoral dissertations, journal articles, monographs, edited volumes, and conferences on every facet of nationalism have proliferated at a remarkable rate; since the end of the Cold War, the appearance of nearly two dozen new European and Eurasian states and the apparent upsurge in ethnonational disputes within and among them have given increased prominence to the study of nation-building and nationalist territorial claims. On one level, the results have been encouraging. We now know more than ever about the national idea—its historical origins, its various types in the developed and the less-developed world, its relationship to issues of gender and racism, and the contingent character of its manifestations. Generations of graduate students have written case studies of nationalism in every region of the world, and even the most insignificant nationalist movements have found their interpreters in major universities and research institutes. It is perhaps a mark of the field's maturity that it has even generated its own array of conventional truths. That traditions are invented, that nationalism creates nations, that national communities are imagined, and that the nation is a gendered concept have become ideas that are repeatedly reaffirmed, reinterpreted or rejected in countless new publications every year.

Despite the active engagement of a large scholarly community, however, the genuine explanation of nationalist phenomena has, throughout this century, remained elusive. We do know something (although perhaps not nearly enough) about the relationship between electoral systems and party formation, about the paths from authoritarianism to democracy, about the particular advantages and disadvantages of parliamentary and presidential government. But we still know painfully little about why Serbs and Albanians found it preferable to push themselves toward social anarchy and economic ruin than spend another hour in the same state. Indeed, the same questions that concerned scholars earlier this century remain central to the study of nationalism today. Under what conditions do national claims prove a more powerful mobilizing force than appeals to class or other social categories? What is national identity, and how does it shape interactions among individuals? What kinds of institutions are most appropriate for reducing the chances that ethnonational tensions will escalate to violence? One need only compare the most recent books in the field with Frederick Hertz's insightful, although largely unread *Nationality in History and Politics*, first published in 1944, if one needs convincing that the study of nationalism, like the study of politics more broadly, has never been a truly cumulative science.[54]

It is an occupational hazard of studying nationalism that the more one knows about a particular instance of nationalist politics, the less one is willing to generalize to other cases. Studies of nationalism will always be particularly susceptible to the 'Zanzibar phenomenon'. Any generalization about the sources or conduct of nationalist politics drawn from a limited number of cases can always be met with the objection that 'It isn't like that in Zanzibar'.[55] But given that analysing 'n' cases of nationalism will always be inferior to studying 'n+1', there are two practical things that can be done to ensure that the study of nations and nationalism retains its vitality in the coming years.

To begin with, there must be further serious discussion about what precisely the object and scope of the study of nationalism are meant to be. The political utility of the term 'nation', as James Mayall has noted, has never been matched by its analytical clarity.[56] As a result, most studies begin by lamenting the paucity of serviceable definitions of 'nation' and its variants before proceeding to offer new, allegedly more adequate, ones. But the proliferation of definitions, typologies, terms and labels has more often clouded than clarified our understanding of nationalism. It would be difficult to find within political science a field with more definitions and taxonomies, and fewer general theories, than the study of nationalism. While the sorting out of terms and types is surely an important place to begin, the utility of many of

---

[54] See note 46.

[55] H. Daalder, 'Countries in Comparative European Politics', *European Journal of Political Research*, 15 (1987), p. 19, cited in Page, 'British Political Science', p. 44.

[56] J. Mayall, *Nationalism and International Society* (Cambridge, Cambridge University Press, 1990), p. 2.

these definitions and typologies has often been highly dubious. Definitions and terms are often vague and *ad hoc*, arrived at with little thought given to the purpose that the definition is supposed to serve or to the plethora of typologies that have been devised before.[57] Moreover, the types and categories into which nationalist movements and ideologies are separated are often unhelpful. It is common to find, for example, nationalist movements cavalierly divided into such categories as 'colonial', 'diaspora', 'totalitarian' or 'irredentist', a division which is patently nonsensical. Since each category is constructed according to a different criterion, the labels are useless in helping us understand the essential dynamics of the nationalist movements placed under each rubric. The first tells us about where the nationalist movement takes place, the second about the geographical distribution of its target population, the third about the proclivities of its leadership, and the fourth about its political programme. What such categorizations, which can be found in virtually any text on nationalist politics, are meant to achieve remains a mystery.

The chief problem, though, is not that scholars have given insufficient thought to the question of defining such terms as 'nation' and 'national identity', or even that their typologies are based on an inaccurate understanding of the variety of nationalist movements. Rather, it is precisely the focus on the 'vocabulary' of theory-building that has sometimes deflected attention away from the need for further debate on the 'grammar' of a theory itself. In other words, even though confusion about the terms to be used in describing nationalist phenomena has been a serious obstacle, an even more problematic feature of scholarship in this field has been the almost complete absence of debate, much less consensus, about what an adequate 'theory of nationalism' might entail. If it would be difficult to know a nation if we saw one, it would be even more difficult to know a theory of nationalism. Should such a theory tell us something about political mobilization, or about personal identity, or about the origins of ideology? Might it elucidate the power of political symbols, or the determinants of voting behaviour, or the foci of group solidarity? Or should it be expected, heroically, to do all the above? Understanding what nationalism is has not been nearly so problematic

---

[57] For early attempts at settling the typology problem, see S. Handman, 'The Sentiment of Nationalism', *Political Science Quarterly*, 36 (1921), 107–114, and L. Wirth, 'Types of Nationalism', *American Journal of Sociology*, 41 (1936), 723–37. See also the extensive note on the use of words in Royal Institute of International Affairs, *Nationalism*, pp. xvi–xx.

as agreeing on what a 'theory' of it might reasonably be expected to explain.[58]

The British study of nationalism has made a valuable contribution to our understanding of the contingent character of nationalist ideology and the social bases of nationalist movements. British scholars have explored the mutable conceptions of the nation through history, the changing sources of group solidarity, and the relationship between demands for national self-determination and the exigencies of practical politics. Throughout this century, the field has been marked by a respect for multidisciplinary research and an aversion to simplistic theories of nationalist politics. While such an approach has had the laudable effect of focusing attention on nationalism at a time when it was generally outside the interests of 'mainstream' political scientists in the United States, whether it can retain its vitality in the coming decades will depend on combining the legacy of empirical richness with the need for conceptual clarity. British political scientists are themselves divided about the most appropriate methods for studying nationalism; some defend the eclecticism of the past, others call for more statistically-based research, while still others argue for the elaboration of deductive theories of nationalist behaviour. Like Anglicanism, the British study of nationalism has always been a broad church. The central challenge over the coming years, though, will be to create more truly comparative studies of nationalism, organized according to clear conceptions of the aims of the research itself, while continuing to prize the legacies of an empirically- and conceptually-rich scholarly tradition.

Acknowledgements. I am grateful to the participants in the British Academy symposium convened at St Antony's College, Oxford, on 4 and 5 April 1997, and the editors of this volume for their comments on an earlier draft of this chapter. The insights of Erica Benner, the draft's designated reader, were especially helpful. I also thank Pat Lynch for additional comments, Craig Mooney for several intriguing conversations, and Jennifer Garrard for research assistance.

[58] I am particularly grateful to Erica Benner for her thoughts on the question of theory-building in the study of nationalism.

12: The Study of Totalitarianism and Authoritarianism

ARCHIE BROWN

The rise of totalitarian regimes in Russia, Germany and Italy between the two world wars preceded the professionalization of the study of politics. Until the 1950s academic analyses of totalitarian systems, not least the Soviet one, were rare. Insofar as they existed, they were generally weak and unwittingly deceptive. It was, in fact, neither political scientists, who were thin on the ground in the first half of the century, nor historians who were the most influential and perceptive in portraying the realities of power in Stalin's Soviet Union, but creative writers.

It is salutary for scholars to recall that it was a journalist and author who did not even attend university who made the earliest and most persuasive contribution to an understanding of totalitarian, as distinct from authoritarian, regimes. George Orwell's *Animal Farm* (1945) and *Nineteen Eighty-Four* (1949) had a bigger impact, not only in terms of sales, but also on public consciousness in most Western countries (with France remaining something of an exception)[1] than any academic book.[2] While it is arguable that some of Orwell's essays may represent his finest

---

[1] It was as late as the mid-1970s, and more particularly from the time of the publication of the French edition of Alexander Solzhenitsyn's *The Gulag Archipelago*, that totalitarianism became 'a popular item on the [French] intellectual agenda'. (R. Desjardins, *The Soviet Union Through French Eyes* (London, Macmillan, 1988), p. 64).

[2] The first authors to write in a more academic way about the subject Orwell had illuminated so persuasively appeared just after the mid-way point of the century and were Americans of Central or East-Central European origin. Of the works of the early post-war period on totalitarianism the most cited were H. Arendt, *The Origins of Totalitarianism* (New York, Harcourt Brace Jovanovich, 1951); C. J. Friedrich, (ed.), *Totalitarianism* (Cambridge, Mass., Harvard University Press, 1954); and C. J. Friedrich and Z. K. Brzezinski, *Totalitarian Dictatorship and Autocracy* (Cambridge, Mass., Harvard University Press, 1956).

literary achievement, his two most famous novels were works of far greater international political significance. Writing in 1982, T. R. Fyvel, who succeeded George Orwell as literary editor of *Tribune*, observed of Orwell:

> Both in his own life and his writings, he expressed the basic dilemma of his time, and also of our time which has followed his death. The dilemma was that with Hitlerism and Stalinism, with two world wars and the nuclear arms race, an end had unmistakably come to that optimistic belief in man's inevitable progress, about which he had still read and been taught in early youth.[3]

Orwell went on to play a posthumous part in influencing opinion within Communist states themselves, among them the Soviet Union. In the post-Stalin period his works had a telling impact on East European intellectuals who read them clandestinely. To a lesser, but nevertheless significant, extent, Arthur Koestler's powerful novel, *Darkness at Noon* (1940), likewise made a deep impression in both the West and in Communist countries where, as with the works of Orwell, it was read furtively.

George Orwell to the end of his life regarded himself as a 'democratic Socialist' (even to the extent of consistently using the capital 'S').[4] While not all supporters of the British Labour Party were as clear-sighted as was Orwell in their view of Stalin's Russia, it was with good reason that Communist leaders and theoreticians regarded the democratic socialist parties of Western Europe as their most dangerous ideological enemies. It was very late in the Soviet era before reformist Communists in Russia as well as in Central Europe became part of a one-way, East-West convergence whereby they increasingly embraced a social democratic variant of socialism.[5] Hitherto, they had believed their own propaganda

---

[3] T. R. Fyvel, *George Orwell: A Personal Memoir* (London, Weidenfeld & Nicolson, [Hutchinson paperback 1983] 1982), p. 208.

[4] See B. Crick, *George Orwell: A Life* (London, Penguin, 1980); S. Ingle, *George Orwell: A Political Life* (Manchester, Manchester University Press, 1993); and T. R. Fyvel, *George Orwell*. Crick (p. 569) quotes Orwell as writing shortly before his death in January 1950 apropos *Nineteen Eighty-Four*:

> My recent novel is NOT intended as an attack on Socialism or on the British Labour Party (of which I am a supporter) but as a show-up of the perversions to which a centralized economy is liable and which have already been partly realized in Communism and Fascism . . . I believe also that totalitarian ideas have taken root in the minds of intellectuals everywhere, and I have tried to draw these ideas out to their logical consequences.

[5] Some, indeed, in company with a number of West European erstwhile Marxists, even became neo-liberals, while others in the post-Communist era described themselves as Christian Democrats rather than Social Democrats.

to a sufficient extent not to feel threatened by parties of the right. It was with parties of the social democratic left that they competed in Western Europe, and on the whole unsuccessfully, for the working-class vote.

It is remarkable that Orwell, who never visited Russia, understood the Soviet regime infinitely better than some of his fellow-socialists who had been there—including, notoriously, Sidney and Beatrice Webb. The longest book, and a candidate for the most systematically misleading, to be published on the USSR between the wars was the Webbs' *Soviet Communism: A New Civilisation*.[6] This work (a sad come-down especially for Beatrice, the author of the perceptive *My Apprenticeship*)[7] was a prime example of formal institutional description at its worst. It totally failed to comprehend the way in which decisions were taken and implemented in Russia and how large a part was played by the harsh terror which lay behind Soviet laws and the 1936 Constitution. The Webbs' massive misunderstanding of the system was maintained in their much shorter wartime book, *The Truth about Soviet Russia*.[8] They felt able to write:

> Stalin is not a dictator. So far as Stalin is related to the constitution of the USSR, as amended in 1936, he is the duly elected representative of one of the Moscow constituencies to the Supreme Soviet of the USSR. By this assembly he has been selected as one of the thirty members of the Presidium of the Supreme Soviet of the USSR, accountable to the representative assembly for all its activities.[9]

As for the Communist Party: 'unlike the Roman Catholic and Anglican Church, [it] is not an oligarchy; it is democratic in its internal structure, having a representative congress electing a central committee which in its turn selects the Politbureau and other executive organs of the Communist Party'.[10]

This was precisely what such documents as the Soviet Constitution and the Rules of the Communist Party declared to be the case and, at a purely formal level, it was what occurred. But it was only in the post-war period that Western scholars (with the British attaining a

---

[6] It was published with a question mark after 'New Civilisation' in its first edition in 1935, but writing in 1937 (as the Soviet purges reached their height) the Webbs observed: 'What we have learnt of the developments during 1936–7 has persuaded us to withdraw the interrogation mark'. See S. and B. Webb, *Soviet Communism: A New Civilisation* (London, Gollancz, [2nd ed.] 1937), p. 1214.

[7] B. Webb, *My Apprenticeship* (London, Longman, 1926).

[8] S. and B. Webb, *The Truth about Soviet Russia* (London, Longman, 1942).

[9] Ibid. p. 14.

[10] Ibid. p. 15.

prominence disproportionate to their numbers) began to investigate in detail what went on behind the Soviet democratic façade. Until then, there was no serious academic research. Moreover, some of the most distinguished of British socialist thinkers—notably, R. H. Tawney— remained uneasily poised between the confident but utterly divergent views of the Webbs on the one hand, and of Orwell on the other. Beatrice Webb complained that Tawney 'does not share our faith in Soviet Com- munism', even though his 'contempt for our ruling class is more intense than ours'.[11] But Tawney worried, until things became much clearer in the post-war period, about where Orwell got the evidence on the Soviet Union which led him to opposite conclusions from those of the Webbs. 'How', Tawney asked, 'does Orwell *know* Russia is so bad?'[12]

Tawney's LSE colleague, Harold Laski (although he dedicated his *Grammar of Politics* to 'the London School of Economics and Political Science and to Sidney and Beatrice Webb, its Founders'), was, in his earlier work, less uncritical of the Soviet Union than were the Webbs. In the chapter in which he writes of the dangers of nationalism, he is conscious that a good deal of nationalist aggrandizement lay behind Soviet internationalist rhetoric; he is also aware that getting rid of capit- alism would not necessarily put an end to inter-state conflict. Arguing that 'the control of natural resources by the State in the interests of security' would not diminish 'the explosiveness of the atmosphere', he goes on:

---

[11] Ross Terrill, *R. H. Tawney and His Times: Socialism as Fellowship* (London, Deutsch, 1974), pp. 76–7.

[12] Ibid. p. 77. After the war Tawney's views became very close to those of Orwell and a world away from the Webbs' outlook, although he retained his friendship with them. In a chapter in a book edited by W. Scarlett, *The Christian Demand for Justice*, published in New York in 1949, Tawney wrote:

> It is obvious . . . that the suggestion of affinities between Social Democracy and Communism . . . rests, as the relations between the two unfortunately show, on a naive misconception of the characteristics of both. Whatever the case for Totalitar- ianism, it is of its essence that, since only a single party is, in practice, tolerated, no peaceful procedure exists for the periodical supersession of one set of rulers by another . . . opposition to the Government is readily confounded, when convenient to the latter, with treason to the State. Civil liberty, therefore, as experience shows, is necessarily insecure. Political liberty, of which the right of a majority to make and unmake Governments, and of individuals to speak, write and agitate with that end in view, is an indispensable part, is non-existent.

(Reprinted as chapter 10, 'Social Democracy in Britain' of R. H. Tawney, *The Radical Tradition*, edited by R. Hinden, (London, Allen & Unwin, [Pelican ed. 1966], 1964), pp. 144–75, at p. 165.)

That social control may even, as with Russia, assume the form of a communist State. But so long as it remains persistently nationalist in temper, and works through the mechanisms of exclusive sovereignty, it will simply be more powerful for the purpose it has in view. Russian communism was at least imperialist enough to overrun Georgia . . . Socialism is only international as such because capitalism is international. A world of socialist States, independent of . . . each other, might easily become as mutually hostile as the States of the present epoch.[13]

Systematic studies of the Soviet or, for that matter, fascist systems by British students of politics are, however, virtually absent prior to the outbreak of the Second World War. A rare, albeit partial, exception was Herman Finer who, on the basis of first-hand experience, wrote a useful book on *Mussolini's Italy*[14] (first published in 1935) and who in his *The Theory and Practice of Modern Government* discussed totalitarianism and compared monopolistic political parties 'in three dictatorships': Mussolini's Italy, Hitler's Germany and Stalin's Soviet Union.[15] However, most of the serious examination of twentieth century totalitarian and authoritarian regimes has taken place in the second half of the century and it is on the scholarly literature of that period that this chapter largely concentrates.[16] The German and Italian fascist systems were, by then, a thing of the past, and academic work on them has been carried out primarily by historians. An assessment of that historiography is beyond the scope of this volume.[17]

One work by a historian requires special mention, however, because it crosses the divide between the study of fascism and Communism by

---

[13] H. J. Laski, *A Grammar of Politics* (London, Allen & Unwin, [4th ed.] 1937), p. 225. The work was first published in 1925 and the passage quoted dates from then.

[14] H. Finer, *Mussolini's Italy* (London, Gollancz, [revised ed. 1964] 1935).

[15] Herman Finer, *The Theory and Practice of Modern Government* (New York, Holt, 1949), esp. pp. 91 and 302–310.

[16] I exclude discussion of scholarship on the foreign policies of totalitarian and authoritarian states, for a separate chapter of this volume deals with British writing on international relations.

[17] Major works include: A. Bullock, *Hitler: A Study in Tyranny* (London, Odhams Press, [rev. ed. Penguin, 1962] 1952); I. Kershaw, *Popular Opinion and Political Dissent in the Third Reich: Bavaria 1933–1945* (Oxford, Clarendon Press, 1983); I. Kershaw, *The 'Hitler Myth': Images and Reality in the Third Reich* (Oxford, Clarendon Press, 1987); T. Mason, *Nazism, Fascism and the Working Class*, edited by J. Caplan (Cambridge, Cambridge University Press, 1995); A. J. Nicholls, *Weimar and the Rise of Hitler* (London, Macmillan, 1968); R. J. O'Neill, *The German Army and the Nazi Party, 1933–1939* (London, Cassell, 1966); D. Mack Smith, *Italy: A Modern History* (Ann Arbor, University of Michigan Press, [2nd ed.] 1969); D. Mack Smith, *Mussolini's Roman Empire* (Harmondsworth, Penguin, 1976); and J. W. Wheeler-Bennett, *The Nemesis of Power: The German Army in Politics, 1918–1945* (London, Macmillan, 1953).

comparing Hitler and Stalin as leaders and skilfully putting both of them in their political contexts. Alan Bullock, in his *Hitler and Stalin: Parallel Lives*,[18] deliberately eschews the concept of totalitarianism because he wishes to bring out the significant differences as well as the similarities between Hitler and Stalin and between the Nazi and Soviet regimes.[19] A notable distinction was that Stalin had to continue to justify all his actions within terms of the doctrine formulated by Marx as amended by Lenin. This was more than simply lip-service. As Bullock observes:

> [Stalin] could have argued that, under his leadership, Russia was the first country in the world to have carried out the two most important items in Marx's programme: the abolition of private property, in land and agriculture as well as industry and commerce, and the abolition of the traditional classes, with the elimination of the bourgeoisie, the capitalists and landowners, including the rural capitalists, the kulaks.[20]

Yet Stalin, massive cult of his personality nothwithstanding, could not, in fact, take personal credit for this, but had to contend that these things had been possible only because the Communist Party was dutifully applying the science of society bequeathed to them by Marx and Lenin.

In contrast, Bullock notes, while ideology mattered to Hitler, it was not a serious issue for the Nazi Party: 'the majority were content to say 'Adolf Hitler is our ideology', and to leave it to him, as Führer, to proclaim what it was'.[21] Stalin acquired dictatorial power over the Communist Party, but—both for his international following of Communists and for domestic purposes—he had to find some basis of plausibility for his claim to be acting according to the principles of Marxism-Leninism. Even Stalin could scarcely have launched a campaign of privatization of Soviet industry in the 1930s or 1940s. He was enough of a true believer not to have dreamt of doing this, but—although he did many things which would have horrified Marx—he was not entirely free of political and ideological constraints. As Alan Bullock observes, 'Stalin could never admit to himself or the party that, while retaining the original façade, he was changing the substance'.[22] Appositely summing up the differences in the

---

[18] A. Bullock, *Hitler and Stalin: Parallel Lives* (London, HarperCollins, [Fontana ed. 1993] 1991).

[19] The same applies to Richard Taylor in his valuable study of Soviet and Nazi propaganda within the speciality he has made his own—the politics of the cinema. See R. Taylor, *Film Propaganda: Soviet Russia and Nazi Germany* (London, Croom Helm, 1979).

[20] Bullock, *Hitler and Stalin*, p. 450.

[21] Ibid. p. 451.

[22] Ibid. p. 451.

relationship to doctrine of Hitler and Stalin, Bullock writes: 'In the case of Hitler, ideology was what the Führer said it was; in the case of Stalin it was what the General Secretary said Marx and Lenin said it was'.[23]

Fascism itself, of course, embraces regimes and movements which were by no means identical, but there are works which, while recognizing such diversity, attempt to generalize and theorize about fascism. Two notable examples are books by Noël O'Sullivan[24] and Roger Griffin.[25] Fascism, it is generally agreed, is difficult to define, but it is distinguished from conservative authoritarian regimes by its rejection of 'continuity with the recent past or a purely reactionary return to it' and by being 'future-oriented', even though it also tries to establish links with 'the real or imagined historical national tradition'.[26] O'Sullivan argues that fascist regimes are characterized, above all, by 'a condition of permanent revolution, a cult of despotic leadership trapped out in democratic guise, and a highly theatrical form of state-worship ... which makes a programme of conquest and expansion integral to the fascist philosophy'.[27] Yet this 'state-worship' is paradoxical inasmuch as Nazism, in particular, did not regard the state as 'an independently valid form of political organization'. While the leader may hold state office, his claim to legitimacy is based not on that but on his embodiment of 'the historic destiny of the *Volk*', expressed by Adolf Hitler in a speech to a Berlin audience in 1936 in terms of a symbiotic relationship: 'What I am, I am through you; what you are, you are through me'.[28]

Griffin examines, *inter alia*, the conditions which enable a fascist movement to take off and succeed and those which inhibit its triumph. On the basis of comparative study, he points out how rare it is for populist right-wing movements to take a fascist form 'unless elaborate schemes of decadence and rebirth have become as well established as an integral part of the cultural and intellectual tradition as they were in

---

[23] Ibid. p. 451. In a recent book which also compares the Hitler and Stalin regimes, Ian Kershaw and Moshe Lewin likewise highlight significant differences in the relationship of Stalin and Hitler to their respective parties as well as in the social structures and ideologies of those parties. See Kershaw and Lewin, (eds), *Stalinism and Nazism: Dictatorships in Comparison* (Cambridge, Cambridge University Press, 1997), p. 351.

[24] N. O'Sullivan, *Fascism* (London, Dent, 1983).

[25] R. Griffin, *The Nature of Fascism* (London, Pinter, 1991).

[26] J. J. Linz, 'Totalitarian and Authoritarian Regimes', in F. I. Greenstein and N. W. Polsby, (eds), *Handbook of Political Science*, vol. 3, *Macropolitical Theory*, (Reading, Mass., Addison-Wesley, 1975), pp. 175–411, at p. 316.

[27] O'Sullivan, *Fascism*, p. 5.

[28] Ibid. pp. 157–8.

fin-de-siècle Europe'.[29] Fascist rule is, in fact, a rather rare form of auto-cratic regime and, even in structurally weak democracies—its main breeding-ground—the formation of military, monarchical or presiden-tial dictatorships is a much more likely outcome than a fascist take-over.[30] Germany and Italy were the only examples of fully-fledged fascist regimes in inter-war Europe, although 'para-fascist' regimes emerged in Spain,[31] Portugal and Romania. Elsewhere in Europe and Latin America, including Brazil, Hungary, Latvia and Estonia, fascism lost out to anti-fascist authoritarianism.[32] Where conservative authorit-arian forces have a strong presence, as in Imperial Japan, fascism has never succeeded in prevailing over them. Indeed, argues Griffin, 'fas-cism's *only* chance to take off without being crushed is in a relatively advanced liberal democracy undergoing a structural crisis without a strong non-fascist ultra-right to take over'.[33] This applies, of course, only to indigenous political developments. The case of Austria is not an exception to that rule, for it was incorporated in the German fascist state by external intervention.

Communist regimes have been much more numerous than fascist ones and the first and most powerful of them, the Soviet Union, lasted longer than any other major totalitarian or authoritarian regime of the twentieth century. It played a central role in world politics over many decades and was the subject of a vast academic literature. To do justice to that body of work within a single chapter is difficult. It would be down-right impossible were it to be combined with an equal share of attention to other regimes on other continents. Accordingly, the British study of Soviet politics, while far from being my exclusive concern, will bulk larger than the literature on other totalitarian or authoritarian regimes in the discussion which follows.

Much of the published work on authoritarian and totalitarian regimes is in inter-disciplinary journals and by area specialists, although their areas have usually been much larger, and more culturally diverse, than the parts of the world studied by those for whom 'area specialist'

---

[29] Griffin, *The Nature of Fascism*, pp. 208–9.

[30] Ibid. p. 210.

[31] Spain is sometimes considered to be the third major example of a European fascist state. A recent historian of fascism holds, however, that it was 'really a form of authoritarian conservatism and lacked true fascism's social radicalism, though it had some of the stylistic trappings that were so central to classic fascism'. See R. Eatwell, *Fascism: A History* (Harmondsworth, Penguin, 1996), p. xx.

[32] Ibid. pp. 122, 123 and 210.

[33] Ibid. p. 210.

was to become a term of denigration. As compared with, for example, studies of voting behaviour in the state of Michigan, areas studied by specialists on authoritarian and totalitarian regimes included—besides the Soviet Union (which alone covered a fifth of the earth's land surface)—Eastern Europe, Southern Europe, Latin America, the Middle East, Sub-Saharan Africa and China.[34] Even in 1998, as a result, largely, of the contribution of the most populous country in the world, China, citizens of Communist states make up almost a quarter of all living people. What is more, authoritarian and totalitarian regimes remain more numerous than democracies in the contemporary world, although democracies have been gaining ground over the past generation. The collapse of Communism has contributed notably to that tendency, although more than half of the successor states to the Soviet Union are under authoritarian rule.

When the nine-volume *Handbook of Political Science* was published in 1975, it included a 237–page 'chapter' by Juan Linz on 'Totalitarian and Authoritarian Regimes'.[35] This virtual monograph within a collective volume was not only a valuable contribution to its field of study and an impressive illustration of Linz's erudition, but also a recognition that what was 'normal politics' in North America or Western Europe was anything but normal in much of the rest of the world. In sharp contrast, the one-volume *New Handbook of Political Science*, published just over twenty years later, has no chapter on totalitarian and dictatorial regimes and practically nothing to say about the study of authoritarian rule.[36] Thereby it ignores a very large part of the real world and virtually the

[34] For reasons of space this chapter does not consider authoritarian regimes in Africa, the Middle East or most of Asia. It is worth noting, however, that important studies of traditional authoritarian regimes were carried out by British anthropologists who, thanks to Empire, perhaps enjoyed a comparative advantage over their North American colleagues during the first six decades of the twentieth century. Among the more notable work was that of Max Gluckman. See, for example, his *Politics, Law and Ritual in Tribal Society* (Oxford, Basil Blackwell, 1965). Post-colonial regimes tended to be a good deal less accommodating to Western social anthropologists than colonial administrators with an interest in understanding better the society they governed.

[35] Linz, 'Totalitarian and Authoritarian Regimes' in Greenstein and Polsby, (eds), *Handbook of Political Science*, vol. 3. See also Linz's more recent reflections on the subject, 'Totalitarianism and Authoritarianism. My Recollections on the Development of Comparative Politics', in A. Sollner, R. Walkenhaus and K. Wieland, (eds), *Totalitarismus: Eine Ideengeschichte des 20. Jahrhunderts* (Berlin, Akademie Verlag, 1997), pp. 141–57.

[36] R. E. Goodin and H.-D. Klingemann, *A New Handbook of Political Science* (Oxford, Oxford University Press, 1996). There is a chapter by Laurence Whitehead on 'democratization studies' (pp. 353–71), but that touches on the literature on transitions from authoritarian rule rather than on authoritarian politics *per se*.

entire literature on non-democratic polities. The editors of the *New Hand-book*, which in other ways is reasonably eclectic in its subject matter and methodological advocacy, may have over-reacted to the fall of Communism in Europe, enormously important though that sequence of events was.

The concepts of totalitarianism and authoritarianism

Since the terms 'totalitarian' and 'authoritarian' occur throughout the chapter, a brief excursus on their meanings is required. There is far from complete agreement on how they should be defined and demarcated, and the writers whose work is examined in the pages that follow do not, indeed, use these terms in identical ways. But, although there can be marginal cases where legitimate argument ensues as to whether a regime is authoritarian or totalitarian, it remains worthwhile to make an analytical distinction between these two types of political regime.

Authoritarian systems embrace a wide variety of non-democratic polities, among them absolute monarchy, military dictatorship and state corporatism. Their common features, however, are the absence of free elections, the inability of the ruled to hold rulers to account, and the weakness or absence of a rule of law—especially in politically sensitive cases. (Historically, of course, in many European monarchies a rule of law long preceded democracy.) Political freedoms are, at best, strictly circumscribed and political opposition is not accorded legitimacy. Nevertheless, some organizations, such as churches, may acquire an autonomy which they would not be permitted to attain within a totalitarian system. Moreover, as Ralf Dahrendorf has observed (in the context of comparing Stalinism and Brezhnevism), authoritarian, as distinct from totalitarian, rule requires neither 'a regime of terror nor even permanent mobilisation'. People can 'withdraw to their niches of privacy' and while they may be 'pushed about and sometimes harassed . . . they will not be persecuted with the systematic arbitrariness of total rule'.[37]

Totalitarianism is a more extreme case of concentration of power than authoritarianism and may be regarded as the antonym of political pluralism. The term 'totalitarianism', was first used in Italy in 1923, initially

---

[37] R. Dahrendorf, *Reflections on the Revolution in Europe* (London, Chatto & Windus, 1990), pp. 16–17.

and pejoratively by Benito Mussolini's opponents, but by 1925 it had been embraced by Mussolini and his supporters. The philosopher Giovanni Gentile, as the British scholar Leonard Schapiro noted in his book on totalitarianism, spoke in March of that year of fascism as 'a total conception of life'.[38] A few months later the notion was taken up by Mussolini himself.[39] Speaking proudly of 'our fierce totalitarian will', Mussolini went on: 'We want to make the nation fascist, so that to-morrow Italians and Fascists . . . will be the same thing'.[40] In the years immediately following, as Abbott Gleason observes, the term 'totalitarian' increasingly came to be used to convey 'the intent of the state to absorb every sphere of human life into itself'.[41]

Accordingly, the introduction of the concept of totalitarianism pre-dates both 'high Stalinism' (a term used to describe the Soviet Union from the early 1930s until Stalin's death in 1953) and the coming to power of Hitler. Although some German National Socialists at the begin-ning of the 1930s spoke in positive terms of the idea of a 'totalitarian state', Hitler (perhaps, Schapiro suggests, because he did not wish to appear ideologically indebted to Mussolini), attached the prefix 'so-called' to totalitarianism. In Stalin's Soviet Union the term was applied to fascist states, but indignantly rejected as an appellation appropriate to the USSR.[42]

The Stalin and Hitler regimes were, however, to have a major influ-ence on the subsequent elaboration of the concept in Western scholar-ship. Thus, many of the earliest writers on totalitarianism laid great emphasis on the total power concentrated in the hands of an individual dictatorial leader, albeit in conjunction with a number of other features which distinguished totalitarian regimes from old-fashioned autocracies. Later modifications suggested that such power might be wielded by a small ruling group. The common element lies in the totality of power of the ruler or narrow ruling élite over all political, economic and social institutions within the society.

---

[38] L. Schapiro, *Totalitarianism* (London, Pall Mall, 1972), p. 13.

[39] On this and other aspects of totalitarianism, see the recent book by the American scholar A. Gleason, *Totalitarianism: The Inner History of the Cold War* (New York and London, Oxford University Press, 1995), esp. Ch. 1, 'Fascist Origins', pp. 13–30. On the early history of the term, see also Schapiro, *Totalitarianism*, pp. 13–17.

[40] From Mussolini's speech to the Fourth Congress of the Partito Nazionale Fascista in June 1925, as cited by Gleason, *Totalitarianism: The Inner History of the Cold War*, p. 16.

[41] Gleason, *Totalitarianism: The Inner History of the Cold War*.

[42] Schapiro, *Totalitarianism*, p. 14.

If pluralism denotes a system in which power is dispersed, totalitarianism—more extremely than authoritarianism—signifies the reverse. While the ideal type (in a Weberian sense) of totalitarianism may be found in the pages of Orwell's *Nineteen Eighty-Four* rather than within any actual society, the twentieth century has witnessed regimes which approximate sufficiently closely to ideal-typical totalitarianism for application of that term to them to be meaningful. Among the many characterizations of totalitarianism which have been offered, it is worth noting the observations of Hugh Seton-Watson who argued that for a regime to be classified as totalitarian three specific conditions should be satisfied:

> the concentration of political, economic and spiritual power in the same hands; the denial of any moral or spiritual authority independent of the will of the ruler; and the denial of any autonomy to private and personal life.[43]

To these he added 'one non-specific essential condition', namely 'the availability of the most modern means of publicity, communication and coercion'.[44] Elsewhere, Seton-Watson has written: 'The essence of totalitarianism is that its claims are total'.[45]

In practice, a close approximation to such totalitarian power has been realized only when there exist (1) a strictly hierarchical and monolithic organ of mobilization and control, usually (though somewhat misleadingly) called a party; (2) a body of doctrine which professes to explain both history and contemporary society, thereby providing a framework within which all social phenomena can be fitted and ideological deviation anathematized; (3) a political police force employing terror on a sufficient scale to bring about an atomization of society; and (4) the technological resources to impose central control over an entire country—speed of transport and communication, modern mass media of information and propaganda, and the means of surveillance available to twentieth-century security forces.

Although he did not engage in empirical research on totalitarian regimes, Karl Popper had experienced fascism at first hand, and an underlying assumption of much of his theoretical work was that Hitler's Germany and Stalin's Soviet Union had important features in common.

---

[43] H. Seton-Watson, 'On Totalitarianism', *Government and Opposition*, 2 (1966), 157.
[44] Ibid.
[45] H. Seton-Watson, *Neither War Nor Peace: The Struggle for Power in the Post-War World* (New York, Praeger, 1960), p. 216.

Although Popper's *The Open Society and its Enemies* (first published in 1945) and *The Poverty of Historicism* (1957) may not have been his most intellectually distinguished books, they were vastly influential, not least within Communist states where, initially, they were read only by licensed critics or clandestinely but subsequently, as the regimes underwent radical change, cited increasingly openly.[46]

In considering the importance of British scholarship on totalitarianism and authoritarianism, it would be quite wrong to ignore the impact some of it had within Communist countries.[47] Arguing that 'the distinction between open and closed societies is even more important than Karl Popper thought', Dahrendorf has observed that the countries of 'real socialism' were 'largely closed societies', adding: 'Closed does not necessarily mean totalitarian'.[48] In the post-Stalin period, in particular, surreptitious ways were found of circulating arguments which contravened the official ideology. While many Western writers took for granted that all Communist systems at all times were totalitarian, that was a vast oversimplification. There were great differences both over time and from one Communist state to another. Poland and Hungary in the 1970s and 1980s were more authoritarian than totalitarian, whereas it would scarcely be stretching the category of totalitarianism to put Albania and Romania in those years firmly within it.[49] Romania could also be regarded as 'Sultanistic', a category of regime in which immense political power and wealth are concentrated in a single family. In an echo of Stalin's 'socialism in one country', Ceauşescu's Romania was sometimes described as 'socialism in one family'. Such a form of rule is to be found

---

[46] Any consideration of the influence of Popper in combating totalitarian and authoritarian regimes should not neglect the significance of his direct impact on one man, the LSE-educated Hungarian-American George Soros. He has made a remarkable contribution to the support of an open society and political pluralism, backing his beliefs with many millions of dollars and taking risks—from his supply of xerox machines to dissident groups under late Communism to his support for Russian science in the early post-Soviet era and the foundation of the Central European University.

[47] For a thoughtful review of the literature on the open society, including not least the contribution of Popper, by two Russian political analysts, see M. V. Il'in and V. L. Tsymburskiy, *Otkrytoe obshchestvo: ot metafory k ee ratsionalizatsii* (Moscow, Polis, 1997). The authors also devote a chapter to the writings in the 1990s of George Soros.

[48] R. Dahrendorf, 'The Open Society and its Fears', in *After 1989: Morals, Revolution and Civil Society* (London, Macmillan, 1997), pp. 16–17.

[49] J. F. Brown, *Eastern Europe and Communist Rule* (Durham and London, Duke University Press, 1988); L. Holmes, *Politics in the Communist World* (Oxford, Clarendon Press, 1986); G. Swain and N. Swain, *Eastern Europe since 1945* (London, Macmillan, 1993); and S. White, J. Batt and P. G. Lewis, (eds), *Developments in East European Politics* (London, Macmillan, 1993).

only in a small minority of Communist systems, but in a larger minority of non-Communist authoritarian regimes. Juan Linz, who has elaborated the concept, sees Sultanistic regimes as being distinct from authoritarianism and totalitarianism.[50] I see it, rather, as a cross-cutting category. Regimes can be Sultanistic and authoritarian, as, for example, the Pahlavi regime in Iran, or even Sultanistic and totalitarian, as in the case of North Korea under Kim Il-Sung and his son, Kim Jong-Il.

Not only in the somewhat heterodox Communist systems of Poland and Hungary was Western scholarship with a critical bearing on Communism increasingly disseminated, but in the Soviet Union itself. Academics were allowed to read 'subversive' foreign literature within their own specialities in the *spetskhran* (closed section) of major libraries. In the years separating Stalin's death from the coming to power of Gorbachev, many a book and article denouncing bourgeois falsificators was written by authors who had actually been influenced, in ways they could not reveal in print, by the Western writers they criticized. Popper was among those who was extensively quoted on the 'open society' as a way of introducing the ideas of Western analysts to readers who did not have privileged access to the originals.

Dissidents in Communist countries used the term 'totalitarianism' and by the later 1980s in both Russia and East-Central Europe it was becoming entirely commonplace openly to describe the currently existing regime as totalitarian. Some Western observers saw this as the ultimate justification of the description of all societies headed by Communist Parties by this term. A different conclusion might more appropriately be drawn. The fact that both prominent public figures and ordinary citizens could appear on television and radio and denounce the system as totalitarian, or that writers could publish articles in the press to that effect, was the clearest possible demonstration that the system had ceased to be anything of the kind.[51]

---

[50] See Linz, 'Totalitarian and Authoritarian Regimes', in Greenstein and Polsby, (eds), *Handbook of Political Science*; and H. E. Chehabi and J. J. Linz, (eds) *Sultanistic Regimes* (Baltimore and London, Johns Hopkins University Press, 1998), esp. Ch. 1.

[51] In post-Soviet Russia there has been an understandable concern among historians and social scientists to compare totalitarian regimes (into which category authoritarian regimes tend also to be subsumed) with a view to understanding their emergence and consolidation and, not least, ways of avoiding their re-emergence. See, for example, the substantial book on totalitarianism in twentieth-century Europe: Ya. S. Drabkin and N. P. Komolova, (eds), *Totalitarizm v Evrope XX veka: Iz istorii ideologiy, dvizheniy, rezhimov i ikh preodoleniya* (Moscow, Pamyatniki istoricheskoy mysli, 1996).

It is, nevertheless, worth preserving a distinction between a post-totalitarian authoritarian system and an authoritarian regime which has never experienced the comprehensive controls imposed by a Communist state or had to live with a Marxist–Leninist ideology which purported to provide an answer to everything.[52] It is one thing to see elements of pluralism existing within a Communist system (although if they become substantial it ceases to be meaningful to call that system Communist); it is another to wish to continue to apply the concept of totalitarianism, with the notion of total power embedded in the very term, to all Communist states everywhere and to say with Schapiro:

> It [totalitarianism] can co-exist, at all events for a time, with an independent church, as in Poland; with pluralism of institutions, as in some of the other Communist governments in the Central and East European 'People's Democracies'; and with dissent, incipient pressure groups and some pluralism of institutions in the Soviet Union. These instances of co-existence may well be transitional stages towards a different form of dictatorship, towards some kind of liberal democracy, or towards a return of full and unqualified totalitarian power.[53]

Schapiro, writing in the early 1970s, was, uncharacteristically, stretching simultaneously the concepts of totalitarianism and of pluralism in ways which reduced their analytical usefulness.[54] As a number of British scholars demonstrated in their writings, in the post-Stalin years in the Soviet Union, even prior to *perestroika*, and to a greater extent in Poland and Hungary there was esoteric debate on important political issues and more open

---

[52] See J. J. Linz and A. Stepan, *Problems of Democratic Transition and Consolidation: Southern Europe, South America, and Post-Communist Europe* (Baltimore and London, Johns Hopkins University Press, 1996), esp. pp. 42–51 on 'Post-Totalitarianism'. While it would be very unfair to American scholarship to claim this notable book as an example of British political analysis, it is worth observing that while, at the time of its publication, Linz remained at Yale, Stepan had just become Gladstone Professor of Government at Oxford (where, more than a generation earlier, he had studied PPE). For a discussion of post-totalitarianism and authoritarianism in the Chinese context, see D. S. G. Goodman, 'Political Change in China—Power, Policy and Process', review article, *British Journal of Political Science*, 19 (1989), 425–44.

[53] Schapiro, *Totalitarianism*, p. 124.

[54] Giovanni Sartori, in a well-known article, noted specifically the dangers of stretching the meaning of the concept of pluralism, but his strictures could equally well be applied to totalitarianism. See Sartori, 'Concept Misformation in Comparative Politics', *American Political Science Review*, 64 (1970), 1033–53.

argument in journals about less fundamental political reforms.[55] The same, as Vladimir Kusin and Alex Pravda, among others, have shown, was true of Czechoslovakia between 1963 and 1967. Thereafter, the reform movement which had got underway in 1963–4, developed into something far more radical in 1968. The 'Prague Spring', ended only by Soviet military intervention, achieved a higher degree of political pluralism in the spring and summer of 1968 than was to be found in any Communist country prior to the rise of Solidarity in Poland in 1980.[56]

The politics of Soviet studies

After Soviet-type regimes were established throughout Eastern Europe following the Second World War, there was a strong Western governmental and public interest in the study of Communism. But another reason why the Soviet system was examined more by students of politics than Hitler's Germany or Mussolini's Italy, as noted at the beginning of the chapter, was that it lasted into the period when political science as an academic discipline greatly expanded in British universities. With the Soviet Union seen, on the one hand, as a superpower and a potential

---

[55] See, for example, R. J. Hill, *Soviet Politics, Political Science and Reform* (Oxford, Martin Robertson, 1980) and A. Brown, 'Pluralism, Power and the Soviet Political System: A Comparative Perspective', in S. Gross Solomon, (ed.), *Pluralism in the Soviet Union: Essays in Honour of H. Gordon Skilling* (London, Macmillan, 1983), pp. 61–107. On pre-Solidarity East-Central Europe, especially Poland and Hungary, see G. Ionescu, *The Politics of the European Communist States* (London, Weidenfeld & Nicolson, 1967); G. Kolankiewicz and D. Lane, *Social Groups in Polish Society* (London, Macmillan, 1973); G. Schöpflin, *Politics in Eastern Europe* (Oxford, Blackwell, 1993); and A. Brown and J. Gray, (eds), *Political Culture and Political Change in Communist States* (London, Macmillan, 1977), chapters on Poland by George Kolankiewicz and Ray Taras and on Hungary by George Schöpflin.

[56] British-based authors made significant contributions to the study of the origins and aftermath of the Prague Spring. See V. Kusin, *The Intellectual Origins of the Prague Spring: The Development of Reformist Ideas in Czechoslovakia* (Cambridge, Cambridge University Press, 1971); Kusin, *Political Grouping in the Czechoslovak Reform Movement* (London, Macmillan, 1972); Kusin, *From Dubček to Charter 77* (Edinburgh, Q Press, 1978); A. Pravda, *Reform and Change in the Czechoslovak Political System* (London and Beverly Hills, Sage Publications, 1975); and Brown and Gray, (eds), *Political Culture and Political Change in Communist States*, chapter on Czechoslovakia by Archie Brown and Gordon Wightman. The most substantial study of the Prague Spring was by the Canadian scholar, H. Gordon Skilling (*Czechoslovakia's Interrupted Revolution*, Princeton, Princeton University Press, 1977), who many years earlier did his graduate work at Oxford and London. But the first book to analyse the political process in Czechoslovakia in 1968 with the benefit of access to the Czechoslovak Communist Party archives was that of the British political scientist, Kieran Williams, in his valuable study, *The Prague Spring and its Aftermath: Czechoslovak Politics, 1968–1970* (Cambridge, Cambridge University Press, 1997).

threat and, on the other, as the archetype of a significant and distinctive model of political and economic system, self-respecting Politics Departments increasingly regarded it as essential to have at least one specialist on the Soviet system within their ranks. A considerable expansion of British scholars with such expertise took place in the 1960s and 1970s. While the numbers engaged in Soviet studies were small in Britain as compared with the United States, they were influential both nationally and internationally.

The influence beyond the boundaries of academe followed from the expansion of Communism into Eastern Europe and led to closer links between academic students of the USSR and political practitioners than was common with most other branches of political science.[57] Three of the major figures in the study of the Soviet Union and, more generally, of European Communist systems, Leonard Schapiro,[58] Hugh Seton-Watson[59] and the political economist Alec Nove,[60] were not only regarded internationally as among the most outstanding scholars in their field, but also consulted by British Prime Ministers, Foreign Secretaries and successive ambassadors to the Soviet Union.[61] Nove, for example, served for brief spells as an expert adviser in the British Embassy in Moscow in the mid-1950s and in 1989. He was also one of eight British scholars who participated in an important six-hour seminar held at

---

[57] My own involvement, to offer a personal example, included two lengthy Chequers seminars and a Downing Street briefing session with Margaret Thatcher when she was Prime Minister, meetings with three successive Leaders of the Opposition in Britain and with the executive inter-agency Soviet affairs group in Washington, consultation by the Foreign Offices of Britain and several other Western countries, acceptance of invitations to give evidence both to the American House of Representatives Foreign Affairs Committee and its less powerful House of Commons counterpart, as well as several hundred interviews for television and radio.

[58] Schapiro's major works are discussed in the next section of this chapter.

[59] Among Seton-Watson's important books on Communism were *Neither War Nor Peace*; *The Pattern of Communist Revolution: A Historical Analysis* (London, Methuen, 1953); *The East European Revolution* (London, Methuen, [2nd ed.] 1955); and *Nationalism and Communism: Essays 1946–1963* (New York, Praeger, 1964).

[60] Nove's prolific and perceptive writings include *The Soviet Economic System* (London, Allen & Unwin, [3rd ed.] 1986); *Political Economy and Soviet Socialism* (London, Allen & Unwin, 1979); *Stalinism and After* (London, Allen & Unwin, 1975); and *Glasnost' in Action: Cultural Renaissance in Russia* (London, Unwin Hyman, [rev. ed.] 1990)

[61] For lengthy memoirs discussing their lives and works, see 'Leonard Bertram Schapiro, 1908–1983', *Proceedings of the British Academy: Lectures and Memoirs*, 70 (1984), 515–41 (by P. Reddaway); 'George Hugh Nicholas Seton-Watson, 1916–1984', *Proceedings of the British Academy: Lectures and Memoirs*, 73 (1987), 631–41 (by Dimitri Obolensky); and 'Alec Nove, 1915–1994', *Proceedings of the British Academy: 1996 Lectures and Memoirs*, 94 (1997), 627–41 (by A. Brown and A. Cairncross).

Chequers on 8 September 1983 for which the academic specialists wrote papers which were read in advance by the Prime Minister, Foreign Secretary and Minister of Defence, all three of whom took part in the seminar, along with senior officials.[62] Margaret Thatcher devotes two and a half pages of her memoirs to this meeting, while the late Sir Anthony Parsons, the Prime Minister's Foreign Policy adviser at the time, went so far as to say that it 'changed British foreign policy'.[63]

There was a good deal of diversity within Communist studies in Britain, so generalizations must come with a note of caution. On the whole, in contrast with French and also a substantial part of American writing, political analyses in this field were characterized, especially from the 1960s, by pragmatism rather than ideological zeal, and by close study of Soviet publications which involved separating the kernel of truth from the chaff of propaganda by careful reading between the lines. Moreover, a higher proportion of British political scientists with a specialist interest in the Soviet Union spent a substantial amount of time in Russia (and, to a lesser extent, other Soviet republics) than did their American counterparts.[64] Since in the post-Stalin but pre-*perestroika* period, many Soviet citizens would say more than they could write, this assisted their understanding of how the Soviet political system actually worked. In Stalin's time, as the example of Orwell showed, a sharp-eyed distant observer could grasp essential features of the Soviet system better than gullible travellers, but the advantages of first-hand contact with Soviet society were to become apparent from the 1960s onwards.

At the same time there was a good deal of cross-fertilization between American and British scholarship on Communism. Authors of this

[62] The seminar was specifically designed to hear the views of the non-governmental participants. The other paper-givers, apart from Nove, were (in alphabetical order): Ronald Amann, Michael Bourdeaux, Archie Brown, Christopher Donnelly, Michael Kaser, Alex Pravda and George Schöpflin.

[63] M. Thatcher, *The Downing Street Years* (London, HarperCollins, 1993), pp. 451–3; and A. Brown and A. Cairncross, 'Alec Nove, 1915–1994', p. 639.

[64] Peter Rutland, who made a study of all the PhDs on Soviet domestic politics completed in American universities between 1976 and 1987, found that 'incredibly, only seventeen of the eighty-seven had actually studied in the USSR'. See Rutland, 'Sovietology: Notes for a Post-Mortem', *The National Interest* 31 (1993), 109–122, at p. 114. Rutland, after studying PPE at Oxford and teaching at the University of York (where he took his PhD, having duly spent a year in Moscow) is one of many British scholars in Communist studies who moved to the United States. Rutland's assumption that substantial first-hand contact with the object of study paid dividends is supported by the fact that much of the most innovative research on Soviet politics by American scholars was by those who did make extended study visits to Khrushchev's and Brezhnev's Soviet Union.

volume face a general problem of separating a distinctive British contribution to political analysis from that being conducted elsewhere—particularly in North America. The difficulty is especially acute in the case of Soviet and Communist studies because of the huge resources devoted by the United States to increasing knowledge of the other 'superpower'. The leading British scholars were frequent participants in conferences in the US and published extensively in American journals. These included the influential *Problems of Communism*, which, although financed by the American Government, was open to a wide spectrum of views and contrived to be both lively and scholarly. A British journal, however—which, for its part, attracted many well-known North American contributors (especially from the 1960s)—had strong claim to be regarded as the most serious scholarly periodical on Communism, particularly the USSR. That was *Soviet Studies*, edited from its foundation in 1948 at Glasgow University, and still flourishing in the late 1990s, although in the post-Soviet era it changed its name to *Europe-Asia Studies*.[65]

There were probably fewer acrimonious relationships and political animosities within Soviet studies in Britain than in the same field in the United States. But, especially in the first 20 years after the Second World War, this area of research was strongly affected in Britain, too, by the Cold War. There was a deep division between, on the one hand, people who were unremittingly hostile to the Soviet system and, on the other, those who either thought the system should be studied dispassionately or that it was good in parts. It oversimplifies only a little to say that of the four main centres of Soviet studies in Britain in the immediate postwar decades, London University (both LSE and the School of Slavonic and East European Studies) and Oxford (notably St Antony's College) belonged to the first group and Glasgow and Birmingham Universities to the second. Two of the major figures on different sides of the academic divide were E. H. Carr and Leonard Schapiro. Carr, who made a substantial contribution to the study of the history of the Soviet state at a time when access to reliable sources was particularly difficult,[66] was denied academic appointments in both London and Oxford. This doubtless had less to do with the limitations of his academic work than with

[65] Important articles on Communist, transitional and post-Communist politics have appeared also in the *British Journal of Political Science*, (to a greater extent than in the *American Political Science Review* or in that journal's institutional equivalent in Britain, *Political Studies*).

[66] E. H. Carr, *History of Soviet Russia* (London, Macmillan, 1952–1978) in fourteen volumes.

what even his sympathetic biographer calls 'his all but overt acceptance of Stalin's domination of Central Eastern Europe, and his enthusiastic endorsement of Soviet economic planning'.[67]

However, Carr, who in 1955 became a Fellow of Trinity College, Cambridge, was far from being an outsider *vis-à-vis* the British Establishment even in the late 1940s and early 1950s. He had, on the contrary, positions of influence as head of the Russian Studies Committee of the Royal Institute of International Affairs (Chatham House) and as a regular, anonymous reviewer of works on the Soviet Union for the *Times Literary Supplement*. As its reader for several publishers, he played a major part in holding up publication of Leonard Schapiro's first book, *The Origins of the Communist Autocracy*.[68] In particular, he took a strong stand against Schapiro's work in the Chatham House committee and, through his political hostility to the appearance of that scholarly monograph, did 'his best to stop Schapiro's career in its tracks in the early fifties'.[69]

From the second half of the 1960s and the beginning of the 1970s the Cold War divisions within Soviet studies in Britain diminished. There was a *rapprochement* between Glasgow and Birmingham, on the one hand, and Oxford and London, on the other. This was partly a result of the growing prominence of Alec Nove who moved in 1963 from LSE to become Director of Glasgow University's Institute of Soviet and East European Studies and was on amicable terms with both Schapiro and Carr. Still more, it was a consequence of the coming into the field— mainly as a result of the expansion from the early 1960s of funded graduate studentships—of younger scholars who neither harboured illusions about the Soviet Union nor had direct family connections with victims of it.

Thus, from the second half of the 1960s onwards, while there remained disagreements among British specialists studying Soviet politics, these were expressed in civilized academic discourse. From the late 1960s through to the collapse of the Soviet Union the annual conference of the National Association for Soviet and East European Studies (NASEES) provided a forum for high-quality discussion. It

---

[67] J. Haslam, 'E. H. Carr and the Politics of Soviet Studies in Britain' in D. Holloway and N. Naimark, (eds), *Reexamining the Soviet Experience: Essays in Honour of Alexander Dallin* (Boulder, Col., Westview Press, 1996), pp. 7–23, at p. 15.

[68] L. Schapiro, *The Origins of the Communist Autocracy. Political Opposition in the Soviet State: First Phase 1917–1922* (London, Bell, 1955).

[69] Haslam, 'E. H. Carr and the Politics of Soviet Studies in Britain', p. 21.

attracted leading specialists from continental Europe, especially those who found the relative absence of sharp ideological, institutional and personal conflicts a refreshing contrast with France (in particular), Italy and the Federal Republic of Germany. As the Soviet system began to change fundamentally in the second half of the 1980s, a few extremists (not themselves part of the community of scholars who belonged to NASEES), who saw their vocation as anti-Communists under threat, began to use the columns of newspapers and weeklies to transfer their hatred of the Soviet Union to those who had the temerity to notice it was changing. It is difficult, though, to think of a single serious student of Soviet affairs in Britain who joined in such personal attacks.

The analysis of Communist systems

With the collapse of the archetypal Communist system, that of the Soviet Union, and the changes taking place, or in prospect, within the only Communist systems that remain—China, Vietnam, North Korea, Laos and Cuba—the very concept of Communism may soon be a historical term rather than one which has a place in a typology of contemporary authoritarianism or (in the case, at least, of North Korea) totalitarianism. However, throughout most of the period since the Second World War, Communist states represented a distinct subset of the world's political systems, nothwithstanding the changes over time and differences from one Communist country to another. Elsewhere, I have discussed five defining features which, taken together, distinguished Communist systems from other authoritarian or totalitarian regimes and, still more fundamentally, from pluralist systems in which socialist parties of a social democratic type have held office.[70] These characteristics were: (1) the supreme authority and unchallengeable hegemony of the Communist Party, for which the official euphemism was 'the leading role of the party'; (2) a high degree of centralization and discipline within that organization with very narrowly-defined rights of intra-party debate— which was what 'democratic centralism' meant in practice; (3) state, or at any rate non-private, ownership of the means of production, with exceptions sometimes made for agricultural, but not for industrial, production; (4) the declared aim of building communism as the ultimate,

---

[70] The points are elaborated in A. Brown, *The Gorbachev Factor* (Oxford, Oxford University Press, 1996), pp. 310–15.

legitimizing goal; and (5) a sense of belonging to—and, in the Soviet case, of leading—an international Communist movement.

Important political analysis of the early Soviet period was undertaken by Leonard Schapiro and T. H. Rigby. Schapiro's *The Origins of the Communist Autocracy*, like Rigby's study of *Lenin's Government*,[71] covers the period from 1917 to 1922, but neither is a history of the Russian revolution.[72] In common with Schapiro's later and still more important study, *The Communist Party of the Soviet Union*,[73] they are works of historical-institutional analysis. Schapiro, in his first book, elucidates both the numerical strength and the tactical failures of the opposition, including not least socialist opposition, to Lenin as well as Lenin's extreme ruthlessness in dealing with it. With E. H. Carr evidently in mind, he notes: 'I do not share the predisposition of some contemporary historians, upon whom the hand of Hegel still lies somewhat heavily, in favour of the seemingly victorious side in history. Who are the victors, after all, and who the vanquished?'[74] Schapiro was writing little over a year after the death of Stalin; he himself died a generation later—in 1983—when the slightest criticism of Lenin still remained totally taboo in the Soviet Union. Yet before the end of that decade the political system had undergone fundamental change and Lenin was being publicly criticized for dispatching his fellow-citizens on a 'road to nowhere'. By the 1990s Russian academic writing on Lenin had more in common with the views of Schapiro than those of Carr.

The nature of the interaction between the individual top leader, who wielded great power in the Soviet system, and political institutions is a

---

[71] T. H. Rigby, *Lenin's Government: Sovnarkom 1917–1922* (Cambridge, Cambridge University Press, 1979).

[72] Three notable specialist studies of the same period by students of politics are: G. Gill, *Peasants and Government in the Russian Revolution* (London, Macmillan, 1979); M. McAuley, *Bread and Justice: State and Society in Petrograd 1917–1922* (Oxford, Clarendon Press, 1991); and R. Service, *The Bolshevik Party in Revolution 1917–1923: A Study in Organisational Change* (London, Macmillan, 1979). The fullest (and most up-to-date in its use of sources) narrative history of the Russian revolutions is by O. Figes, *A People's Tragedy: The Russian Revolution 1891–1924* (London, Jonathan Cape, 1996).

[73] L. Schapiro, *The Communist Party of the Soviet Union* (London, Eyre and Spottiswoode, [2nd ed. 1970] 1960).

[74] Schapiro, *The Origins of the Communist Autocracy*, p. x. Elsewhere in his Preface (p. xiv), Schapiro refers explicitly and politely to Carr:

> Mr E. H. Carr read the manuscript at a very early stage of its existence and made a number of comments on points of detail which I was glad to adopt, and for which I am most grateful to him. I regret that I was not able to adopt some other suggestions which he was kind enough to make, because our interpretations of the facts diverged too fundamentally.

major focus of Schapiro's writing, and it figures prominently also in Rigby's *Lenin's Government*. Rigby reveals, in addition, how the new Soviet government drew upon institutional arrangements which had prevailed in pre-revolutionary Russia as well as showing how power relations shifted within the Soviet regime as the post-revolutionary government, the Council of People's Commissars (Sovnarkom), gradually lost authority to the Central Committee and Politburo of the Communist Party. It is appropriate to consider Rigby and Schapiro together, for Rigby took his doctorate at LSE in 1954 and, as a Research Officer at LSE in 1956–7, collaborated with Schapiro in gathering information for the latter's most influential book, *The Communist Party of the Soviet Union*. Described by its *Times Literary Supplement* reviewer as 'a definitive record of the growth of the most powerful organization in the world', Schapiro's account was certainly the most authoritative historical–institutional study of the Soviet Communist Party in any language. Even today, when far more information has become available from archives and memoirs, no comprehensive account has superseded it.

Rigby himself, in his study of the Soviet *nomenklatura* system, élites and patron–client relations, was to draw much more upon the approaches of modern political science than did Schapiro, combining the best of the traditional with the best of the new.[75] Political institutions comprise not only formal organizations which play a part in the political process but formal rules. More important than the Soviet Constitution and, when elucidated, a better guide to the realities of power within the Soviet system were the rules of the Communist Party of the Soviet Union. The fullest account of them is by Graeme Gill.[76] But still more important rules were those of the Soviet *nomenklatura* which determined which posts (from the head-teacher of a local school or the head of the

---

[75] See two volumes which bring together many of his major journal articles: T. H. Rigby, *Political Elites in the USSR: Central Leaders and Local Cadres from Lenin to Gorbachev* (Aldershot, Edward Elgar, 1990); and Rigby, *The Changing Soviet System: Mono-organisational socialism from its origins to Gorbachev's restructuring* (Aldershot, Elgar, 1990). See also T. H. Rigby and B. Harasymiw, (eds), *Leadership Selection and Patron–Client Relations in the USSR and Yugoslavia* (London, Allen & Unwin, 1983).

[76] For a useful commentary on these rules as well as the texts of their successive variants, see G. Gill, *The Rules of the Communist Party of the Soviet Union* (London, Macmillan, 1988). The similarities and differences between the rules of the world's ruling Communist Parties just a few years before the collapse of European Communism can be studied in W. B. Simons and S. White (eds), *The Party Statutes of the Communist World* (The Hague, Martinus Nijhoff, 1984).

supplies department of a brewery to the editorship of a national news-paper) came under the jurisdiction of which party committee. Who had to approve the appointment of whom and how people got on to the *nomenklatura* of party committees were issues of prime importance not only in the Soviet Union but in other Communist states, for this institu-tion was adopted throughout the Communist world. For a long time the *nomenklatura* was shrouded in secrecy, so research on it required pains-taking detective work as well as an understanding of its centrality to the governmental process.[77]

In the real world of politics, nevertheless, the way in which rules are implemented is modified by inter-personal relations. Thus, the study of élites, cliques and patron–client relations in Communist political systems complements an examination of the *nomenklatura*. Rigby was perhaps the first to show that when a local patronage boss was transferred to a new organization or a different part of the country, he tended to take a coterie of clients with him.[78] Subsequently, the examination of career patterns and movements of personnel, in which research on both the *nomenklatura* system and patron–client relations played crucial and complementary parts, made some of the most useful contributions to understanding how Communist systems operated. More narrowly, they contributed to the esoteric sub-discipline of 'Kremlinology', indicating who was on the way up and who on the way down within the party or governmental hierarchies.

Some of the most innovative work in this field, aside from that of Rigby, was by John Miller—a product of Cambridge and Glasgow universities—who built up a card index of 20,000 official careers in the Soviet Union before developing an electronic database of Soviet and post-Soviet élites. He was the author of two important articles in *Soviet Studies* in 1977 which shed fresh light on the workings of the

---

[77] On the *nomenklatura*, see T. H. Rigby, 'The Origins of the nomenklatura system', in Rigby, *Political Elites in the USSR*, pp. 73–93; and J. Miller, 'Nomenklatura: Check on Localism?', in Rigby and Harasymiw, (eds), *Leadership Selection and Patron–Client Relations in the USSR and Yugoslavia*, pp. 62–97. See also G. Ionescu, *The Politics of the European Communist States* (London, Weidenfeld & Nicolson, 1967), pp. 60–64; D. Lane, *State and Politics in the USSR* (Oxford, Blackwell, 1985), pp. 220–23; R. J. Hill and P. Frank, *The Soviet Communist Party* (London, Allen & Unwin, [3rd ed.] 1986), pp. 87–89 and 135; S. Whitefield, *Industrial Power and the Soviet State* (Oxford, Clarendon Press, 1993), pp. 82–5, 126–7 and 260–1; and G. Gill, *The Collapse of a Single-Party System: The Disintegration of the Communist Party of the Soviet Union* (Cambridge, Cambridge University Press, 1994), pp. 33–6, 181–2.

[78] See, for example, Rigby, 'The nomenklatura and patronage under Stalin', drawn with only minor editorial amendments from Chs. 7 and 8 of his 1954 doctoral thesis, and published in Rigby, *Political Elites in the USSR*, pp. 94–126, at p. 119.

Soviet political system. In the first, he showed, with compelling evidence, how 'the top party leadership in nationality areas is a carefully designed system in which Russian and native officials act as a check on each other' and, after examining the educational and career records of the officials concerned, was able to demonstrate that 'the Russian presence is built in for political reasons and is no longer a consequence of lack of non-Russian expertise'.[79] In the same year Miller single-handedly did something that the entire CIA had failed to do, by decoding the groups of letters and figures to be found on the back pages of Soviet newspapers and drawing attention to the existence and work patterns of a Soviet top censorship team.[80]

Mention of the work of Rigby, Miller and Gill in the context of a chapter on the British contribution to the study of politics requires some justification. It might be mistaken for academic neo-colonialism, since Rigby and Gill are native Australians who have spent the greater part of their academic careers in their home country and Miller, although English by origin, has also been in Australia for more than a quarter of a century. The danger of causing offence may be lessened when the broader point is made that, although the number of specialists on Soviet politics in Australian universities was small in comparison with those in Britain (not to speak of the United States), a remarkably high proportion of them have produced work which has been both innovative and of broad interest. Moreover, a majority of these scholars spent at least their years of graduate or post-doctoral research in Britain (rather than the United States) and have close ties with their British counterparts.[81] In addition to those whose work has already been briefly discussed, the notable contributions both to the study of Communist politics and to analysis of transitional and post-Communist regimes of Leslie Holmes and Stephen Fortescue deserve particular mention.[82]

[79] J. H. Miller, 'Cadres Policy in Nationality Areas: Recruitment of CPSU first and second secretaries in non-Russian republics of the USSR', *Soviet Studies*, 29 (1977), 3–36, at p. 34.

[80] J. H. Miller, 'The Top Soviet Censorship Team? A Note', *Soviet Studies*, 29 (1977), 590–8.

[81] Gill, who was one of the last graduate students to be supervised by Leonard Schapiro before his retirement, took his doctorate at LSE in 1975.

[82] Leslie Holmes was a graduate student at Essex University and later taught at the University of Kent at Canterbury before moving to Melbourne where he is Professor of Political Science. His major contributions include: *The Policy Process in Communist States: Politics and Industrial Administration* (Beverly Hills and London, Sage Publications, 1981); *Politics in the Communist World* (Oxford, Clarendon Press, 1986); *The End of Communist Power: Anti-Corruption Campaigns and Legitimation Crisis* (Oxford, Polity Press, 1993); and *Post-Communism* (Oxford, Polity Press, 1997). Stephen Fortescue, after completing his

The 'behavioural revolution' had an impact on the study of Communist politics in Britain, but less than in the United States. While it did lead to somewhat greater methodological self-consciousness as well as quantification in areas where numbers were available and it made sense to count, there was far less of a reaction against the study of institutions in Britain than in the United States. As Jack Hayward observed in an earlier chapter, with reference to British political science as a whole, 'bringing the state back in' was not necessary, for the state was never out. Communist countries had powerful institutions—above all, the Communist Parties. The Soviet Communist Party was especially closely studied and significant work was done on its power structure, inner dynamics, recruitment policies, gender balance and ethnic composition.[83]

Most scholars held that Secretaries of the Central Committee of the Communist Party and republican and regional first secretaries wielded great power within their particular domains and that the top party leader, for the greater part of the Soviet period, could veto policies and people he was opposed to and set the tone and, to a large extent, the policy parameters of government. So hierarchical was the system that it was virtually impossible for important new policy initiatives to be launched other than by the party leader. There is ample evidence of Khrushchev, for example, taking major decisions in both foreign and domestic policy, regarding which even his most senior colleagues had grave doubts but were powerless to prevent.[84] This does not, of course,

---

doctorate at the Australian National University in Canberra, was a research fellow at Birmingham University. He is the author of a series of important articles on the relationship between the Soviet Communist Party, on the one hand, and both science and industry, on the other, and he has worked on politics and industry in post-Soviet Russia. Two notable books by Fortescue are *The Communist Party and Soviet Science* (London, Macmillan, 1986) and *Policy-Making for Russian Industry* (London, Macmillan, 1997). Another prominent British scholar at Melbourne University, apart from Leslie Holmes, is Stephen Wheatcroft. Although primarily an economic historian, Wheatcroft is now conducting a substantial research project on Stalin's Politburo.

[83] See, for example, Hill and Frank, *The Soviet Communist Party*; M. Buckley, *Women and Ideology in the Soviet Union* (Hemel Hempstead, Harvester Wheatsheaf, 1989); and J. H. Miller, 'The Communist Party: Trends and Problems', in A. Brown and M. Kaser, (eds), *Soviet Policy for the 1980s* (London, Macmillan, 1982), pp. 1–34.

[84] See Schapiro, *The Communist Party of the Soviet Union*: R. Pethybridge, *A Key to Soviet Politics: The Crisis of the 'Anti-Party' Group* (London, Allen & Unwin, 1962); M. McAuley, *Politics and the Soviet Union* (Harmondsworth, Penguin, 1977); and A. Brown, 'The Power of the General Secretary of the CPSU', in T. H. Rigby, A. Brown and P. Reddaway (eds), *Authority, Power and Policy in the USSR: Essays dedicated to Leonard Schapiro* (London, Macmillan, 1980), pp. 135–57.

mean that Soviet leaders—especially in the post-Stalin era—were *all-powerful*, and Khrushchev himself had to struggle in some cases to get his way against formidable institutional interests.[85] It was not, however, easy to remove a Soviet leader. In the whole of Soviet history only two supreme leaders did not die in office—Khrushchev and Gorbachev. It is no coincidence that they—Gorbachev much more fundamentally than Khrushchev—challenged the norms of the system. Once Gorbachev had removed many of the traditional prerogatives of the Communist Party, including much of the leverage of the General Secretaryship, he suffered a number of political defeats. Until, however, his pluralizing measures took effect and diminished, *inter alia*, his own powers, he was able to introduce dramatic changes, even though they were perceived to be against the interests of, and certainly met resistance from, major institutions within the Soviet system.[86]

A naturalized British citizen and outstanding scholar who was able to generalize about the Soviet Union and Eastern Europe, on the basis of vast personal experience as one of the region's leading economic reformers, was Włodzimierz Brus. After being accused of revisionism and of giving ideological support to rebellious students, Brus was dismissed as Professor of Political Economy at the University of Warsaw in 1968 and emigrated in 1972 to Britain. Following a year at Glasgow University, he moved to Oxford where he made an important contribution to the study of Communist systems, concentrating especially on the interlinkage of political and economic institutions. Observing that 'the étatist model of socialism *étatises the party, too'*, Brus wrote in 1975:

> The party apparatus is basically a component of the state and economic apparatus, but it is, at each level, the superior component. The area and degree of intervention . . . can be subject to change, but always embraces matters of principle, in particular . . . matters of personnel, reserved officially (the *nomenklatura*) for decision by the party apparatus.[87]

---

[85] See W. J. Tompson, *Khrushchev: A Political Life* (London, Macmillan, 1995); Pethybridge, *A Key to Soviet Politics*; and M. McCauley, *Khrushchev and the Development of Soviet Agriculture* (London, Macmillan, 1976).

[86] See A. Brown, *The Gorbachev Factor*; J. H. Miller, *Gorbachev and the End of Soviet Power* (London, Macmillan, 1993); R. Sakwa, *Gorbachev and His Reforms, 1985–1990* (London, Philip Allan, 1990); R. Walker, *Six Years that Shook the World: Perestroika—the impossible project* (Manchester, Manchester University Press, 1993); and S. White, *Gorbachev and After* (Cambridge, Cambridge University Press, [3rd ed.] 1992).

[87] W. Brus, *Socialist Ownership and Political Systems* (London, Routledge & Kegan Paul, 1975), p. 54. See also W. Brus and K. Laski, *From Marx to the Market: Socialism in Search of an Economic System* (Oxford, Clarendon Press, 1989).

That view of the Communist Party's supremacy was not universally accepted. One British scholar who questioned the power of party officials and came to the unusual conclusion that 'politicians and statesmen were weak actors in the Soviet system' was Stephen Whitefield.[88] He was untypical, not only in questioning how real was the power of Communist Party officials, but also in examining the place in the political system of the economic ministries. Soviet ministries were far more consequential institutions than would be suggested by their neglect in Western political science literature. Whitefield's *Industrial Power and the Soviet State* does more than any other book to redress the balance. He argues that in reality, as distinct from principle, Communist Party overlords had to delegate control over economic decisions to those agencies—the industrial ministries—which were in day-to-day charge of property and economic resources. Other writers, including Nove,[89] had earlier recognized the political importance of economic ministries and state committees, above all Gosplan (the State Planning Committee) and the Ministry of Finance, and had pointed out also the extent to which even Gosplan was dependent on information supplied to it by the branch economic ministries. A great deal of information on the operations of industrial ministries was gathered by an impressive team of scholars at Birmingham University in which prominent parts were played by Ronald Amann and Julian Cooper. However, their focus was not primarily on the ministries as political institutions.[90] That task was left to Whitefield who, while somewhat overstating his case for the political centrality of the ministries, nevertheless argues persuasively that 'industrial power severely constrained the politicians, and radical anti-ministerialism was both difficult and dangerous for all actors'.[91]

Other institutions which were clearly important throughout most of Soviet history were the military and the KGB. While far from autonomous from the Communist Party, they were especially influential institutional actors between the death of Stalin and the mid-1980s. They

[88] S. Whitefield, *Industrial Power and the Soviet State* (Oxford, Clarendon Press, 1993), p. 252.
[89] See especially Nove's *The Soviet Economic System*.
[90] R. Amann, J. Cooper and R. W. Davies, (eds), *The Technological Level of Soviet Industry* (New Haven, Conn., and London, Yale University Press, 1977); and R. Amann and J. Cooper, (eds), *Industrial Innovation in the Soviet Union* (New Haven, Conn., and London, Yale University Press, 1982). See also two thoughtful articles by R. Amann, 'Searching for an Appropriate Concept of Soviet Politics: the Politics of Hesitant Modernization', *British Journal of Political Science*, 16 (1986), 475–94, and 'Soviet Politics in the Gorbachev Era: The End of Hesitant Modernization', *British Journal of Political Science* 20 (1990), 289–310.
[91] Whitefield, *Industrial Power and the Soviet State*, p. 180.

were, however, unable to prevent Gorbachev from pushing through policies which reduced their strength and damaged their interests. Accordingly, both the Chairman of the KGB and the Minister of Defence were prominent participants in the failed coup of August 1991. British students of politics who have thrown significant fresh light on the political police, the army and military industry include Peter Reddaway,[92] Robert Conquest,[93] David Holloway,[94] Michael MccGwire,[95] John Erickson,[96] Julian Cooper[97] and Roy Allison.[98] A majority of these prominent specialists moved to the United States after spending the earlier part of their careers in Britain, the exceptions being Erickson, Cooper and Allison. The physical, though not the intellectual, transatlantic traffic has been mainly one-way.

The study of Communist institutions has also involved attention to a phenomenon which the Australian-based Chinese scholar, X. L. Ding, has named 'institutional amphibiousness'.[99] By that he means the 'mutual infiltration' of the party-state on the one hand, and society on the other. It is strongly arguable that not only the Chinese reforms since the death of Mao, but those which were introduced in Czechoslovakia in 1968 and in the Soviet Union by Gorbachev were *not* the result of the development of civil society. Insofar as that has occurred, it happened later. The impetus for change emerged, rather, from political institutions, including research institutes of the Communist Party and the Academy of Sciences, which

[92] P. Reddaway, 'Policy Towards Dissent Since Khrushchev', in Rigby, Brown and Reddaway, (eds), *Authority, Power and Policy in the USSR*, pp. 158–92; and S. Bloch and P. Reddaway, *Russia's Political Hospitals: The Abuse of Psychiatry in the Soviet Union* (London, Gollancz, 1977).

[93] R. Conquest, *The Great Terror* (London, Macmillan, [rev. ed.], 1973); Conquest, *Kolyma: The Artic Death Camps* (London, Macmillan, 1978); and Conquest, *The Nation Killers* (London, Macmillan, 1970).

[94] D. Holloway, *The Soviet Union and the Arms Race* (New Haven, Conn., and London, Yale University Press, 1983); and Chs. 7 and 8 on 'Innovation in the Defence Sector' of Amann and Cooper, (eds), *Industrial Innovation in the Soviet Union*. David Holloway is Irish rather than British by nationality, but he took both his first degree and doctorate at Cambridge and taught at Lancaster and Edinburgh Universities before moving to Stanford.

[95] M. MccGwire, *Military Objectives in Soviet Foreign Policy* (Washington, DC, Brookings Institution, 1987); and MccGwire, *Perestroika and Soviet National Security* (Washington, DC, Brookings, 1991).

[96] J. Erickson, *The Road to Stalingrad* (London, Weidenfeld & Nicolson, 1975); and Erickson, *The Road to Berlin* (London, Weidenfeld & Nicolson, 1983).

[97] J. Cooper, *The Soviet Defence Industry: Conversion and Reform* (London, Pinter, 1991).

[98] R. Allison, (ed.), *Radical Reform in Soviet Defence Policy* (London, Macmillan, 1992).

[99] X. L. Ding, 'Institutional Amphibiousness and the Transition from Communism: The Case of China', *British Journal of Political Science*, 24 (1994), 293–318.

were very much part of the system. By definition they did not exercise the autonomy from the party-state which would make it appropriate to see them as manifestations of civil society. It was, indeed, their very insider status and access to decision-makers which made the gradually developing heterodox ideas of institutional actors so influential. In all three of the cases mentioned it required, though, a *combination* of reformist ideas emerging from the party intelligentsia and leadership change—the emergence of a top leader, in the persons of Dubček, Deng Xiaoping and, most dramatically, Gorbachev, prepared to widen the terms of economic and political discourse—to produce radical policy innovation.[100]

Bringing society back in

If the state did not have to be brought back in, because it was never out, the same cannot be said of society. Apt though the application of the term 'totalitarian' was to the regimes at least of Stalin, Mao,[101] Kim

[100] On Czechoslovakia: V. Kusin, (ed.), *The Czechoslovak Reform Movement 1968* (London, International Research Documents, 1973); Kusin, *Political Groupings in the Czechoslovak Reform Movement*; A. Pravda, *Reform and Change in the Czechoslovak Political System*; and Williams, *The Prague Spring and its Aftermath*. On China see especially G. White, *Riding the Tiger: The Politics of Economic Reform in Post-Mao China* (London, Macmillan, 1993). See also D. S. G. Goodman, *Deng Xiaoping and the Chinese Revolution* (London, Routledge, 1994); and R. MacFarquhar, (ed.), *The Politics of China: The Eras of Mao and Deng* (Cambridge, Cambridge University Press, [2nd ed.] 1997). (MacFarquhar and Goodman are both British scholars who became part of the 'brain drain'. The former, who is now Leroy B. Williams Professor of History and Political Science at Harvard, was the founding editor of the *China Quarterly*, a post he held from 1959 to 1968. That journal, although it did not share the anti-establishment orientation of *Soviet Studies* in the earlier years of the latter, came to occupy a comparably important place for students of China. Goodman is Director of the Institute for International Studies at the University of Technology, Sydney.) On the Soviet case, see the books cited in note 86.

[101] Mao's may be regarded as the most controversial of these cases. For a comparison, in particular, of the leadership of Stalin and Mao, see L. Schapiro and J. W. Lewis, 'The Roles of the Monolithic Party under the Totalitarian Leader', in Lewis, (ed.), *Party Leadership and Revolutionary Power in China* (Cambridge, Cambridge University Press, 1970), pp. 114–45. Drawing on a distinction made by Robert C. Tucker, Schapiro and Lewis argue that under Stalin and Mao (in his later years) the Communist Parties of the Soviet Union and of China moved from being parties of a Bolshevik type to a *führerist* type. For a variety of alternative views of Mao as political leader by British-based or British specialists on China, see D. Wilson, (ed.), *Mao Tse-tung in the Scales of History* (Cambridge, Cambridge University Press, 1977); S. R. Schram, *The Political Thought of Mao Tse-tung* (Harmondsworth, Penguin, 1969); R. MacFarquhar, (ed.), *The Politics of China*, esp. Ch. 4; J. Gray and P. Cavendish, *Chinese Communism in Crisis: Maoism and the Cultural Revolution* (London, Pall Mall Press, 1968); and J. Gray, *Rebellions and Revolutions: China from the 1800s to the 1980s* (Oxford, Oxford University Press, 1990), pp. 287–411.

Il-Sung, Hoxha and Ceauçescu, it tended to inhibit research on society within Communist countries generally, for these societies were assumed to be inert. None of them, in fact, was infinitely malleable and in some cases there was significant spontaneous organization and pressure upon the party leadership from discontented segments of the population. Until the late 1960s and 1970s there was very little attempt to study either social groups in Communist societies or opinion groupings within the intelligentsia.[102] Equally, there was an assumption that all policy consisted of a top–down process and little attention prior to the 1970s was paid to the role of specialists and issue networks.[103] With the fall of Communism, of course, access to hitherto unavailable sources on the policy process became easier, and case-studies, though fewer in number, have become more detailed and authoritative.[104] It was only from the 1960s that overt dissent and opposition became an observable phenomenon in the Soviet Union,[105] although it had been visible earlier in East-Central Europe, especially in Poland and Hungary where its most spectacular manifestation was the 1956 Hungarian revolution.[106] It was in those countries, too (as distinct from China, the Soviet Union

[102] Works which broke new ground in this respect on Soviet society were M. McAuley, *Labour Disputes in Soviet Russia 1957–1965* (Oxford, Clarendon Press, 1969); D. Lane, *Politics and Society in the USSR* (London, Weidenfeld & Nicolson, 1970); and M. Matthews, *Class and Society in Soviet Russia* (London, Penguin Press, 1972). See also the discussion in A. Brown, *Soviet Politics and Political Science* (London, Macmillan, 1974), chapter on 'Groups, Interests and the Policy Process', pp. 71–88.

[103] Among the books which did examine either social and political stratification or influence from below in Communist societies were: C. Humphrey, *Karl Marx Collective: Economy, Society and Religion in a Siberian Collective Farm* (Cambridge, Cambridge University Press, 1983); J. Batt, *Economic Reform and Political Change in Eastern Europe* (London, Macmillan, 1988); Kusin, *Political Grouping in the Czechoslovak Reform Movement*; J. Woodall, (ed.), *Policy and Politics in Contemporary Poland: Reform, Failure and Crisis* (London, Pinter, 1982); A. Brumberg, (ed.), *Poland: Genesis of a Revolution* (New York, Vintage Books, 1983), chapters by W. Brus, L. Kolakowski, A. Pravda, C. Cviic and G. Schöpflin; and J. Lovenduski and J. Woodall, *Politics and Society in Eastern Europe* (London, Macmillan, 1987).

[104] See especially D. Holloway, *Stalin and the Bomb: The Soviet Union and Atomic Energy 1939–1956* (New Haven, Yale University Press, 1994); and S. White, *Russia Goes Dry: Alcohol, State and Society* (Cambridge, Cambridge University Press, 1996). The former examines in depth all stages of the policy process. The main strength of the latter book is on the implementation stage of the anti-alcohol campaign launched in May 1985.

[105] P. Reddaway, *Uncensored Russia: The Human Rights Movement in the Soviet Union* (London, Cape, 1972).

[106] See T. Cox, (ed.), *Hungary: Forty Years On* (London, Cass, 1997).

and even Czechoslovakia once it had been 'normalized' following the Soviet 1968 invasion) that some elements of a civil society began to develop in the 1970s and 1980s, during which time the *concept* of civil society became an increasingly important one for East-Central European intellectuals.[107]

British scholars have been prominent in the study both of overt dissent and opposition under Communist rule and in examining the longer-term changes in society which had a more subtle, but not necessarily less profound, influence on political outcomes in Communist states. Work on the Prague Spring has already been mentioned, but there have been significant studies also of the rise of Solidarity and the Polish crisis of 1980–81, the Yugoslav reforms which preceded that country's disintegration, and the origins and course of development of China's Cultural Revolution.[108]

One of the ways in which the examination of Soviet, East European and Chinese society was conceptualized was in the study of political culture.[109] With a paucity of reliable survey data—and in the case of several Communist states, including China and Cuba, any survey data

---

[107] See, in particular, J. Keane, *Democracy and Civil Society: on the Predicaments of European Socialism, the Prospects for Democracy, and the Problem of Controlling Social and Political Power* (Verso, London, 1988); and Keane, (ed.), *Civil Society and the State: New European Perspectives* (Verso, London, 1988). See also the critique by K. Kumar, who acknowledges the importance of the concept of civil society in East-Central European intellectual discourse but who questions its fruitfulness: 'Civil society: an inquiry into the usefulness of an historical term', *British Journal of Sociology*, 44 (1993), 375–95.

[108] See T. Garton Ash, *The Polish Revolution: Solidarity 1980–82* (London, Cape, 1983); A. Kemp-Welch, (ed.), *The Birth of Solidarity: The Gdansk Negotiations, 1980* (London, Macmillan, 1983); A. Pravda, 'Poland 1980: From "Premature Consumerism" to Labour Solidarity', *Soviet Studies*, 29 (1982), 167–99; A. Carter, *Democratic Reform in Yugoslavia: The Changing Role of the Party* (London, Pinter, 1982); R. MacFarquhar, *The Origins of the Cultural Revolution*, vol. 1, *Contradictions among the People, 1956–1957* (London, Royal Institute of International Affairs, 1974); vol. 2, *The Great Leap Forward* (London, Royal Institute of International Affairs, 1983); vol. 3, *The Coming of the Cataclysm 1961–1966* (Oxford, Oxford University Press for the Royal Institute of International Affairs, 1997); and S. Schram, (ed.), *Mao Tse-tung Unrehearsed* (Harmondsworth, Penguin, 1974).

[109] Brown and Gray, (eds), *Political Culture and Political Change in Communist States*; S. White, *Political Culture and Soviet Politics* (London, Macmillan, 1979); and A. Brown, (ed.), *Political Culture and Communist Studies* (London, Macmillan, 1984). Although it does not employ the concept explicitly, an important contribution to an understanding of Chinese political culture is made by the work of Jonathan Spence, the Cambridge-educated British historian who has taught for many years at Yale. See J. D. Spence, *The Gate of Heavenly Peace: The Chinese and Their Revolution, 1895–1980* (New York, Viking Press, 1981); and Spence, *The Search for Modern China* (New York, Norton, 1990).

at all—these studies had to draw upon a wide variety of alternative sources.[110] They certainly did not meet the exacting demands of positivistic social science, but did provide a useful corrective to the widespread view expressed, for example by the Harvard political scientists Samuel Huntington and Jorge Dominguez, that 'the most dramatically successful case of planned political culture change is probably the Soviet Union' and that Communist systems were the *exceptions* to a more general rule that 'planned political culture change through mobilization has been rare and has fared poorly'.[111] Drawing specifically on British studies of Communist societies with a focus on political culture, Gabriel Almond, who has the strongest claim to have fathered that concept, summed up their findings thus:

> What the scholarship of comparative communism has been telling us is that political cultures are not easily transformed. A sophisticated political movement ready to manipulate, penetrate, organize, indoctrinate, and coerce and given an opportunity to do so for a generation or longer ends up as much or more transformed than transforming.[112]

Political cultures, of course, do change, although not necessarily in the way those who attempt to mould them from above intend. Ideology—even Communist ideology—is also far from immutable. The ideas espoused by the reformist wing of the Soviet leadership and by several of their East European counterparts by the late 1980s had changed so much that they could scarcely be deemed 'Communist'. Even earlier—as the examples of Khrushchev's and Brezhnev's Soviet Union, Novotný's and Dubček's Czechoslovakia and Mao's and Deng's China showed—there was also some elasticity within Marxist–Leninist ideology and significant differences from one leader to another, as well as

---

[110] There are, it should be noted, scholars who take the concept of political culture seriously but who hold that even the best-conducted surveys can make only a modest contribution to the interpretation of cultures. A case in point is Stephen Welch, who pays particular attention to political culture in Communist societies in his thoughtful book, *The Concept of Political Culture* (London, Macmillan, 1993). Welch observes, for example (p. 147) that 'within comparative political science, even when political culture is characterized mainly through survey data, historical findings are frequently alluded to by way of consolidation of the descriptions gleaned from surveys, or indeed by way of accounting for the results they demonstrate'.

[111] S. P. Huntington and J. I. Dominguez, 'Political Development', in Greenstein and Polsby, (eds), *Handbook of Political Science*, vol. 3, pp. 1–114, at pp. 31–2.

[112] G. A. Almond, 'Communism and Political Culture Theory', *Comparative Politics*, 13 (1983) (reprinted in Almond, *A Discipline Divided: Schools and Sects in Political Science* London, Sage Publications, 1990, pp. 157–69, at p. 168).

between countries, in the way received doctrine was interpreted. Since Marxism–Leninism for many years constituted the compulsory language of politics in Communist states, intellectuals—in the post-totalitarian but still highly authoritarian era—tended to construct their own 'Marx' and 'Lenin'. In so doing, they found the prolixity of both men a great boon and, wittingly or unwittingly, took out of context whatever ideas or phrases from these unimpeachable sources needed to be pressed into political service.[113]

Many scholars—notable among them, John Plamenatz and Leonard Schapiro—have seen Leninism as being, in important respects, a Russification of Marxism, and Bolshevism as owing much to a distinctive Russian revolutionary tradition.[114] The most eloquent proponent of the contrary view, that Lenin was an orthodox Marxist, has been Neil Harding.[115] In his words: 'Lenin's thought is to be understood as an essay in the theory and practice of Marxism. Its difficulties and ambiguities are located within the Marxist tradition itself rather than in Lenin's peculiar character or in the Russian Jacobin tradition.'[116]

Harding is at one, however, with Plamenatz and Schapiro in viewing Leninism as hostile 'not only to democracy but to politics' (since Lenin and his followers were under the illusion that they were applying a science).[117] An especially clear exposition of that view had earlier been provided by A. J. Polan, basing his analysis on what has often been regarded as the most 'libertarian' or 'democratic' of Lenin's writings, *The State and Revolution*. Written between the February and October revolutions of 1917, this work is generally contrasted with Lenin's 1902 political tract, the more obviously élitist and authoritarian *What is to be Done?*[118] However, as

---

[113] See S. White and A. Pravda, (eds), *Ideology and Soviet Politics* (London, Macmillan, 1988), especially the chapter by S. Shenfield, pp. 203–24; and A. Brown, 'Ideology and Political Culture', in S. Bialer, (ed.), *Politics, Society and Nationality Inside Gorbachev's Russia* (Boulder, Westview, 1989), pp. 1–40.

[114] See, in particular, J. Plamenatz, *German Marxism and Russian Communism* (London, Longman, 1954), although Plamenatz (p. 7) also suggests that temperamentally 'Lenin was in some ways closer to Marx than any other great Marxist'; and L. Schapiro, 'Lenin's Intellectual Formation and the Russian Revolutionary Background' in Schapiro's post-humously-published book, edited by E. Dahrendorf, *Russian Studies* (London, Collins, 1986), pp. 188–252.

[115] See N. Harding, *Lenin's Political Thought*, vol. 1, *Theory and Practice in the Democratic Revolution* (London, Macmillan, 1977); vol. 2, *Theory and Practice in the Socialist Revolution* (London, Macmillan, 1981); and Harding, *Leninism* (London, Macmillan, 1996).

[116] Harding, *Lenin's Political Thought*, vol. 2, p. 327.

[117] Harding, *Leninism*, p. 275.

[118] A. J. Polan, *Lenin and the End of Politics* (London, Methuen, 1984).

Polan trenchantly puts it: 'The "libertarian" Lenin bears equal responsibility for the Gulag with the "authoritarian" Lenin. Lenin's theory of the state rigorously outlawed all and any version of those political institutions and relationships that can make the triumph of the Gulag less likely.'[119]

What Chinese leaders made of Leninism and what distinguishes Mao Tse-tung's thought from that of Lenin are among the themes taken up by the leading authority on Chinese politics, Stuart Schram who, although American by origin, taught for many years until his retirement at the School of Oriental and African Studies of London University.[120] Whereas, Schram argues, Lenin 'utterly distrusted the spontaneous tendencies of the population as a whole, and even of the working class' unless they were guided and controlled by the Communist Party, Mao, although 'by no means free of Leninist élitism', was to a far greater extent prepared 'to trust the masses and to involve them actively in shaping their own fate'.[121] Cultivating chaos, of course, turned out scarcely less of a tragedy for the people of China than did Lenin's blueprint for Russia. Schram emphasizes 'the Sinification of Marxism' in Mao's thought,[122] for Mao was unusual among Communist leaders in the extent to which he openly drew on non-Marxist traditional thought, in this case especially that of Confucius, and in stressing that 'Marxism must take on a national form before it can be applied'.[123]

The economic reforms introduced in China after Mao's death have been accompanied by what Gordon White has called 'the decline of ideocracy'.[124] In contrast with Ding (cited earlier), White detected signs also of an 'incipient civil society' in China.[125] Earlier studies by British China specialists had examined both the Chinese Democracy Movement of 1979–80[126] and the broader political movement a decade later which culminated in the massive student demonstrations of May–June 1989

---

[119] Ibid. p. 130.

[120] See S. R. Schram, *The Political Thought of Mao Tse-tung* (Harmondsworth, Pelican, [rev. ed.] 1969); and Schram, (ed.), *Mao Tse-tung Unrehearsed: Talks and Letters: 1956–71*, (Harmondsworth, Penguin, 1974).

[121] Schram, *Mao Tse-tung Unrehearsed*, p. 11.

[122] Schram, *The Political Thought of Mao Tse-tung*, p. 170.

[123] Ibid. p. 172.

[124] White, *Riding the Tiger*, p. 147. Gordon White, one of the foremost British specialists on Chinese politics, was based for the last 20 years of his life at the Institute of Development Studies at Sussex University. He died in 1998 at the age of 55.

[125] Ibid. p. 218.

[126] D. S. G. Goodman, *Beijing Street Voices: the Poetry and Politics of China's Democracy Movement* (London, Marion Boyars, 1981).

and the Tiananmen Square massacre.[127] But White points to social consequences of the marketizing economic reforms which could be of still
greater political significance in the longer term—in particular, the
growth of a new 'middle class' of individual entrepreneurs and
economic managers.[128] The trend, he argues, is towards a society
'socially more complex and politically more assertive'.[129]

In a joint work with Jude Howell and Shang Xiaoyuan, White and his
co-authors examine in greater detail what they call the 'embryonic
development of organizational features of civil society', involving
'voluntary participation and self-regulation in their activities, and autonomy and separation in their relationship with the state'.[130] Yet they
admit that at times they felt they had 'set out in search of civil society
only to find corporatism', and observe that 'registered associations were
penetrated by the state' while 'social organizations more truly characteristic of civil society were marginalized or repressed'.[131] There is no doubt
that the role of the Communist Party in Chinese society has undergone
change, although the state has remained strong. Indeed, some British
China specialists have argued that it has been precisely the existence of a
strong state which has enabled China to have greater success in its
transition to a form of market economy—in particular, in its ability to
prevent asset-stripping by vested interests pursuing their own selfish
goals—than post-Soviet Russia.[132] Whether, however, Chinese marketization will be the forerunner of democratization, and abandonment of
those features of a Communist state which it still exhibits, remains to be
seen.

---

[127] T. Saich, (ed.), *The Chinese People's Movement: Perspective on Spring 1989* (Armonk, M. E. Sharpe, 1990).

[128] White, *Riding the Tiger*, p. 229.

[129] Ibid. p. 234. See also S. R. Schram, *Ideology and Policy in China since the Third Plenum, 1978–84* (London, Contemporary China Institute, 1984).

[130] G. White, J. Howell and S. Xiaoyuan, *In Search of Civil Society: Market Reform and Social Change in Contemporary China* (Oxford, Clarendon Press, 1996), p. 208.

[131] Ibid. pp. 211–2.

[132] See H.-J. Chang and P. Nolan, (eds), *The Transformation of the Communist Economies: Against the Mainstream* (Macmillan, London, 1995); J. Howell, *China Opens its Doors: The Politics of Economic Transition* (Hemel Hempstead, Harvester Wheatsheaf, 1993); and J. Gittings, *China Changes Face: The Road from Revolution 1949–1989* (Oxford, Oxford University Press, 1989).

The study of non-Communist authoritarian regimes

The study of Communist and, to a lesser extent, fascist systems has been the major focus of this chapter up to now. In this penultimate section, and in the concluding one, attention is paid to scholarship on selected authoritarian regimes which were neither Communist nor fascist, especially those which emerged in Latin America and southern Europe. Much of the theoretical literature on authoritarianism stems from a study of these regimes, as does most of the writing comparing transitions from authoritarian rule.

Authoritarian regimes dominated by military leaders have been, and remain, familiar features of the twentieth-century political landscape. More generally, the ways in which the military are kept under democratic political control or, on the contrary, seize political power constitute an important subject for analysis. S. E. Finer, at that time Professor of Political Institutions at the University of Keele, published his pioneering *The Man on Horseback: The Role of the Military in Politics* in 1962. Although rather sweepingly judgemental in its categorization of countries as possessing 'developed', 'low' or 'minimal' political culture, Finer's comparisons were as stimulating as they were broad-ranging. His book had a big impact, paving the way for a substantial body of literature on the hitherto understudied topic of the political role of the military. The conclusions reached by Finer combine empirical observation with admonition. While he accepts that there will continue to be cases where the military are so powerful and civilian forces so weak that the former will dominate political life, he warns that 'any immediate gain in stability or prosperity' is likely to be outweighed by wilful and unpredictable rule, together with 'further military threats, blackmail or revolt'.[133] The military, he observes, 'engage in politics with relative haste but disengage, if at all, with the greatest reluctance'.[134] In the majority of cases where soldiers have governed directly or indirectly, they have faced the dilemma that 'they cannot withdraw from rulership nor can they fully legitimize it'.[135]

Transitions from civilian to military rule and back again have been more frequent in the years since Finer wrote, not least in Central and

---

[133] S. E. Finer, *The Man on Horseback: The Role of the Military in Politics* (London, Pall Mall, 1962), p. 243.
[134] Ibid. p. 243.
[135] Ibid. p. 243.

South America. Both the return of soldiers to their barracks and military rule itself have been the subjects of notable analyses by British specialists on Latin American politics.[136] A military takeover which received particular attention was that by General Augusto Pinochet as head of the junta which seized power in Chile in 1973, for this was a country with a long history of civilian government and one in which democratic institutions had been comparatively strong. Chile was, moreover, already a subject of enhanced interest because three years earlier a socialist government had come to power, headed by the Marxist Salvador Allende who had been chosen as President in free elections.[137] This was precisely what was unacceptable to the Chilean military establishment and, in the atmosphere of the Cold War and a continued American concern about a Communist threat in their hemisphere, the Allende regime was treated in conservative circles abroad as if it were another Cuba in the making. The study of Latin American politics has, perhaps, seen more polarization along a left–right axis than has been the case with studies of European fascism or even Communism. It attracted Marxists as well as militant anti-Marxists and was, indeed, given its greatest initial impetus in both Britain and the United States by the Cuban revolution.[138]

Curiously, the 'Pinochet model' of authoritarian political rule combined with marketizing economic reform appealed to a significant minority of economic reformers in the former Soviet Union and in Eastern Europe. As Communism collapsed, they feared that democracy and the new disciplines of the market would prove incompatible. The

[136] See G. Philip, *The Military in South America* (London, Croom Helm, 1985); and P. O'Brien and P. Cammack, (eds), *Generals in Retreat: The Crisis of the Military in Latin America* (Manchester, Manchester University Press, 1986). Major contributions to the study of the military in politics have also been made by Alfred Stepan, albeit some years before he moved from the United States to Britain. See Stepan, *The Military in Politics: Changing Patterns in Brazil* (Princeton, Princeton University Press, 1971) and Stepan, *Rethinking Military Politics: Brazil and the Southern Cone* (Princeton, Princeton University Press, 1988).
[137] See A. Angell, *Politics and the Labour Movement in Chile* (Oxford, Oxford University Press, 1972); A. Angell and B. Pollack, (eds), *The Legacy of Dictatorship: Political, Economic and Social Change in Pinochet's Chile* (University of Liverpool, Institute of Latin American Studies Monograph Series, No. 12, 1993); K. Medhurst, (ed.), *Allende's Chile* (London, Hart-Davis, 1972); D. E. Hojman, *Chile: The Political Economy of Development and Democracy in the 1990s* (London, Macmillan, 1992); P. O'Brien, I. Roxborough and J. Roddick, *Chile: The State and Revolution* (London, Macmillan, 1977); and P. O'Brien and J. Roddick, *Chile: The Pinochet Decade* (London, Latin American Bureau, 1983).
[138] On Cuba, see H. Thomas, *Cuba, or the Pursuit of Freedom* (London, Eyre and Spottiswoode, 1971); and R. Gillespie, (ed.), *Cuba after Thirty Years: Rectification and the Revolution* (London, Cass, 1990).

attraction of the Pinochet model when seen from afar reflected ignorance of the true costs—not only in terms of abuse of human rights but also social costs—of his rule, as a reading of the literature on Chile during those 17 years would have revealed.

Specialists on Latin American politics, like those on the Soviet Union and China, have been to a greater than average extent among political scientists part of the 'brain drain'—overwhelmingly to the United States.[139] (This was the most favoured destination also of the Soviet and China specialists, although in both of those cases, in contrast with the Latin Americanists, a significant minority moved from Britain to Australia.) It is hardly surprising that the study of Latin America should be strongest within the United States, yet the movement of specialists from Britain to the US testifies, not only to the lower rewards and weaker research support characteristic of British academic life, but also to the international reputations of many of the scholars American universities took the trouble to recruit. Nevertheless, as has been the case with Soviet and Chinese studies, the major inter-disciplinary journal in the field, *The Journal of Latin American Studies* (currently edited by James Dunkerley and Laurence Whitehead, both of whom have individually been important contributors to the literature on Latin American politics)[140] is a British one which enjoys at least comparable status with its American equivalent.

Although the study of Latin American authoritarian and hybrid regimes—those which are a mixture of authoritarianism and democracy—has developed in close interaction with work on the region produced in North America, much of the British writing has maintained

---

[139] Dunkerley lists 21 scholars, many of them very prominent figures, in the field of Latin American history and politics 'who left (and sometimes returned to) the UK, principally for the USA'. See J. Dunkerley, 'The Study of Latin American History and Politics: An Interpretative Sketch', in V. Bulmer-Thomas, (ed.), *Thirty Years of Latin American Studies in the United Kingdom 1965–1995*, (London, Institute of Latin American Studies, 1996), pp. 13–61, at p. 28.

[140] Dunkerley has been a prolific writer on Central America. See, in particular, his substantial study, *Power in the Isthmus* (London, Verso, 1988); and also Dunkerley, *Political Suicide in Latin America and other essays*, (London, Verso, 1992). Whitehead's exceptionally broad-ranging work includes his editorship, with Guillermo O'Donnell and Philippe C. Schmitter, and contributions to *Transitions from Authoritarian Rule* (Baltimore and London, Johns Hopkins University Press, 1986), 4 vols; (with R. Thorp) *Inflation and Stabilisation in Latin America* (London, Macmillan, 1979); *Whatever Became of the Southern Cone Model?* (Institute of Latin American Studies, La Trobe University, Occasional Paper No. 5, 1982); and *The Peculiarities of 'Transition' à la mexicana* (Kellogg Institute Working Paper, No. 4, University of Notre Dame, 1994).

an intellectual distance from, even when in physical proximity to, its American counterpart. In particular, there has been a greater reluctance to engage in minute classification on the one hand, and broad generalization on the other. A representative of that sceptical viewpoint is Alan Knight, the leading specialist on the Mexican revolution,[141] who moved from Essex to the University of Texas at Austin and then back to Britain as Professor of Latin American History at Oxford. Not only historians such as Knight, but also some students of contemporary politics, display 'impatience with analyses that begin with a lengthy "naming of parts" peroration', an exercise which 'seems to involve the mass baptism of old ideas with abstract neologisms'.[142] Indeed, much of the British work is concerned with the historically specific features of each Latin American country, Mexico's long-lasting and relatively successful authoritarian regime having been a particular focus of attention. Among the most important studies of the politics of that country are George Philip's analysis of the presidency and Joe Foweraker's account of the teachers' movement in the late 1970s and 1980s as an example of popular mobilization within a corporatist state.[143]

A number of British specialists on Latin American and Caribbean politics have, nevertheless, combined scholarly research on one or two countries with serious interest in comparative and theoretical problems, among them Alan Angell,[144] George Philip,[145] and, more idiosyncratically,

[141] A. Knight, *The Mexican Revolution* (Cambridge, Cambridge University Press, 1986), 2 vols.

[142] Cited by James Dunkerley in his valuable chapter, 'The Study of Latin American History and Politics in the United Kingdom', in Bulmer-Thomas, (ed.), *Thirty Years of Latin American Studies in the United Kingdom 1965–1995*, p. 22.

[143] George Philip, *The Presidency in Mexican Politics* (London, Macmillan, 1992); and J. Foweraker, *Popular Mobilization in Mexico: The Teachers' Movement 1977–87* (Cambridge, Cambridge University Press, 1993).

[144] A. Angell, *Politics and the Labour Movement in Chile*; Angell, *Peruvian Labour and the Military Government since 1968* (London, ILAS Research Paper, No. 3, 1980); Angell, 'The Soldier as Politician: Military Authoritarianism in Latin America', in D. Kavanagh and G. Peele, (eds), *Comparative Government and Politics: Essays in Honour of S. E. Finer* (London, Heinemann, 1984), pp. 116–143; and Angell, 'The Left in Latin America since 1920' in L. Bethell, (ed.), *The Cambridge History of Latin America*, vol. 6 (Cambridge, Cambridge University Press, 1995).

[145] Philip, *The Presidency in Mexican Politics*; *The Military in South American Politics*; and C. Clapham and G. Philip, (eds), *The Political Dilemmas of Military Regimes* (Totowa, NJ, Barnes and Noble, 1985).

David Nicholls.[146] The Latin Americanist whose comparative range has been broadest and whose international influence within the discipline of political science greatest—partly as a result of his collaborative work with two leading American comparativists, Guillermo O'Donnell and Philippe Schmitter—is Laurence Whitehead.[147] His contribution is discussed in the next, and concluding, section of this chapter, which brings together Communist countries and non-Communist authoritarian regimes in the context of studies of the liberalization and democratization of dictatorial political systems.

Transitions from authoritarian rule

The transition from authoritarianism to democracy in Spain has attracted much attention both from historians and political scientists.[148] The major studies devoted specifically to the Spanish case emphasized the growing lack of fit between the Francoist political system and a

---

[146] Nicholls, who died in 1996 at the age of sixty, combined the study (and at various times teaching) of politics with work as a Church of England vicar. His *Times* obituarist noted that 'his tendency towards anarchic views on secular matters made him an uneasy member of the Established Church'. But his broad-ranging scholarship included not only his important book, *The Pluralist State* (Macmillan, London, [2nd ed. 1994], 1975), *Three Varieties of Pluralism* (London, Macmillan, 1974) and significant work on the history of political and religious thought, but also authoritative writings on Haiti, particularly *From Dessalines to Duvalier: Race, Colour and National Independence* (Cambridge, Cambridge University Press, 1979) and *Haiti in Caribbean Context: Ethnicity, Economy and Revolt* (London, Macmillan, 1985). He also published posthumously 'The Duvalier Regime in Haiti', in Chehabi and Linz, (eds), *Sultanistic Regimes*, pp. 153–81. The book is dedicated to his memory. David Nicholls's mischievous sense of humour extended to his scholarship. He owned, and was extremely attached to, a colourful and abusive South American macaw which he named Archdeacon William Paley after the eighteenth-century theologian. Not only were some of Nicholls's most sharply critical letters to newspapers published under the name of William Paley, but on occasion he would write under his own name to disagree mildly with 'Paley' while peppering his real target with more grapeshot. One of 'Paley's' letters to the *Times Literary Supplement* is cited in his book, *Haiti in Caribbean Context* (pp. 217 and 255).

[147] See especially G. O'Donnell, P. C. Schmitter and L. Whitehead, (eds) *Transitions from Authoritarian Rule: Comparative Perspectives* (Baltimore and London, Johns Hopkins University Press, 1986). Although based at the University of Notre Dame, Indiana, O'Donnell is by nationality Argentinian.

[148] Important historical studies were those by R. Carr and J. P. Fusi Aizpurua, *Spain: Dictatorship to Democracy* (London, Allen & Unwin, 1979); J. Foweraker, *Making Democracy Work: Grass-roots Struggle in the South, 1955–1975* (Cambridge, Cambridge University Press, 1989); and P. Preston, *The Triumph of Democracy in Spain* (London, Methuen, 1986). For an earlier study of the political institutions of Franco's Spain, see K. N. Medhurst, *Government in Spain: The Executive at Work* (Oxford, Pergamon Press, 1973).

changing society which, as both the economy and a substantial middle class developed, 'came to demand not merely the consumer goods of the West, but its political goods'.[149] In comparative studies of transitions from authoritarian rule which embrace, *inter alia*, the examples of Spain and Portugal, Laurence Whitehead was the first scholar to emphasize the international dimension.[150] While in the immediate post-war years it was, as Whitehead notes, evident to the newly-liberated peoples of Western Europe that they lacked the means 'effectively to promote democracy either in Eastern Europe or in the Iberian Peninsula (let alone in Latin America)',[151] this changed over time.

Transnational institutions—above all, the European Union—were objects of attraction for democratic reformers within Southern and East-Central Europe. For some, but not other, regimes emerging from authoritarian rule, NATO membership was also seen as a goal worth pursuing.[152] These international organizations attempt to uphold the principle of democracy as a condition of membership, and the European Union also insists on the member states being part of a regulated market economy. Accordingly, once transition from authoritarianism got seriously underway, the prospect of membership of the European Union, in particular, provided incentives for the establishment of democratic institutions and practices in Southern and Eastern Europe. In the case of the East Europeans it also strengthened the hand of those who pushed for a speedy marketization of the economy; that was not an issue in Spain or Portugal where an essentially market economy already existed.

Whitehead, ten years after his first substantial essay on the subject, returned to the theme of *The International Dimensions of Democratization* in

---

[149] Carr and Fusi Aizpurua, *Spain: Dictatorship to Democracy*, p. 257.

[150] See L. Whitehead, 'International Aspects of Democratization', in O'Donnell, Schmitter and Whitehead, (eds), *Transitions from Authoritarian Rule*, pp. 3–46.

[151] Ibid. p. 11.

[152] Public opinion in the Czech Republic has, for example, been distinctly unenthusiastic about joining NATO. In the case of the Spanish transition, 'it was not the differences among member states that delayed Spain's [NATO] candidature until 1981, but rather the political strategy of the Suarez government to sustain a political consensus among the parties. That meant postponing the divisive issue of NATO entry for as long as possible'. See J. Story and B. Pollack, 'Spain's transition: domestic and external linkages', in G. Pridham, (ed.), *Encouraging Democracy: The International Context of Regime Transition in Southern Europe* (Leicester, Leicester University Press, 1991), pp. 125–58, at p. 134.

his edited book of that title published in 1996.[153] In contrast with Samuel Huntington, who identified three historical waves of democratization, Whitehead, with good reason, sees the process of democratization in Eastern Europe as 'a fourth wave'.[154] The trigger for this latest group of transitions from authoritarian rule he identifies as 'the collapse of Soviet power'.[155] The changes in the Soviet Union did indeed constitute both the most decisive impulse and the essential facilitating condition for democratization in Eastern Europe. That is not, however, to agree that it was Soviet 'collapse' which played such a role. There were two crucial changes in Russia which directly stimulated and made possible the dramatic changes of 1989.[156] First, there was the demonstration effect of liberalizing and pluralizing change within the Soviet political system itself. Second, but no less crucial, there was the change of Soviet foreign policy (instigated by a small group of political actors—above all the principal power-holder, Mikhail Gorbachev, but including Alexander Yakovlev, Eduard Shevardnadze, Vadim Medvedev, Anatoliy Chernyaev and Georgiy Shakhnazarov)[157] whereby it was, in the mid-1980s, decided and, by 1988, publicly intimated, that there would be no more military interventions by Soviet troops to uphold regimes in East-Central Europe which could not command the support of their own people. The

---

[153] L. Whitehead, (ed.), *The International Dimensions of Democratization* (Oxford, Oxford University Press, 1996). Although the team of contributors is also appropriately international, half of them are British. Apart from Whitehead, the British authors of chapters are Alan Angell on international support for the Chilean Opposition (1973–1989), Andrew Hurrell on the case of Brazil, Michael Pinto-Duschinsky on international political finance, and Charles Powell on Spain.

[154] 'Three International Dimensions of Democratization', in Whitehead, *The International Dimensions of Democratization*, pp. 3–25, at p. 4. The first wave was that of countries—beginning with the United States—whose democratic institutions developed in the process of decolonization from the British Empire; the second was of states whose political freedoms stemmed from the Allied Victory in the Second World War; and the third was that of the countries which underwent transition from conservative authoritarian rule in the period between 1973 and the (fourth wave) fall of Communism in Europe. (The 'three international dimensions' of Whitehead's title are 'contagion', 'control', and 'consent'.)

[155] Ibid. p. 4.

[156] On 1989 see R. Dahrendorf, *Reflections on the Revolution in Europe*; and, for an eye-witness account, T. Garton Ash, *We the People: The Revolution of '89* (Cambridge, Granta Books, 1990). For a scholarly study by the same author of the process of change in Germany in particular, with a major focus on German unification, see Garton Ash, *In Europe's Name: Germany and the Divided Continent* (London, Jonathan Cape, 1993).

[157] See A. Brown, *The Gorbachev Factor*, esp. pp. 220–5 and 247–51; A. Pravda, (ed.), *The End of the Outer Empire: Soviet-East European Relations in Transition* (London, Sage Publications, 1992); and M. Bowker, *Russian Foreign Policy and the End of the Cold War* (Aldershot, Dartmouth, 1997).

'collapse of Soviet power'[158] was, in *part*, a *consequence* of the rapidity with which Communist regimes were removed in Eastern Europe, *not* an *antecedent* of them. To say that, however, is to lend support to one of Whitehead's main conclusions: 'In the contemporary world there is no such thing as democratization in one country, and perhaps there never was.'[159]

The fall of Communism in Europe has surely been to the long-term advantage of most citizens of the countries concerned, even if, in the short term, enhanced political freedom is offset by greater economic hardship and new social uncertainties for a majority of citizens in the two largest of the post-Communist European states, Russia and Ukraine. But of particular relevance in the present context, the collapse of Communism has also provided new opportunities for political scientists. It has provided many more cases for analysis of transitions from authoritarian rule and of processes of democratization. Students of different political systems and parts of the world—especially Eastern Europe, Southern Europe and Latin America—have to a far greater extent than hitherto found it useful to read each other's work. Specialists on the former Communist states have drawn on the pre-existing 'transitological' literature, while the most intellectually adventurous of their counterparts who study Latin America and Southern Europe—among whom, apart from Alfred Stepan and Laurence Whitehead, Geoffrey Pridham has been especially assiduous[160]—have turned their attention to Eastern Europe. Pridham, for example, has noted the shift in both Southern and Eastern Europe 'from bilateral to multilateral linkages abroad', a tendency which has generally 'been conducive to democratisation'.[161] There has been a more general convergence of academic interests and increasingly fruitful comparison. That has been manifested in collaboration between specialists on authoritarian regimes who never had the opportunity to conduct serious survey research and political scientists experienced in survey techniques but ignorant of the cultures and languages of the countries which have become candidates for inclusion in wider comparative studies. There is a burgeoning literature

---

[158] Whitehead, *The International Dimensions of Democratization*, p. 4.

[159] Ibid. p. 24.

[160] See G. Pridham, (ed.), *The New Mediterranean Democracies: Regime Transition in Spain, Greece and Portugal* (London, Cass, 1984); and G. Pridham, E. Herring and G. Sanford, *Building Democracy: The International Dimension of Democratisation in Eastern Europe* (Leicester, Leicester University Press, 1997).

[161] Pridham *et al.*, *Building Democracy*, p. 27.

on the ways in which authoritarian and totalitarian regimes come to an end, as well as on the conditions for successful transition to, and consolidation[162] of, democracy.

New opportunities have arisen, especially in the case of the former Communist states, for study of constitution-making and institutional design;[163] social cleavages and party competition;[164] continuity and turnover of élites;[165] ethno-politics, nationalism and federalism;[166] and politics in the regions (many of which, in the Soviet case, were, in the most literal sense, forbidden territory for the Western researcher during most of the twentieth century).[167] Among the subjects crying out for research, but which up to now have attracted little attention from British political scientists, are the new interest-based politics and the relations between business and government and employers and workers, topics

---

[162] The *consolidation* of democracy in states formerly under authoritarian rule is beyond the scope of this chapter, but see: Linz and Stepan, *Problems of Democratic Transition and Consolidation*, esp. Part II, 'Southern Europe: Completed Consolidations', pp. 87–147; L. Whitehead, 'Comparative Politics: Democratization Studies' in Goodin and Klingemann, (eds), *A New Handbook of Political Science*, pp. 353–71; and D. Held, *Prospects for Democracy: North, South, East, West* (Oxford, Polity Press, 1993).

[163] See, for example, J. Löwenhardt, *The Reincarnation of Russia: Struggling with the Legacy of Communism* (London, Longman, 1995); R. Sakwa, *Russian Politics and Society* (London, Routledge, [2nd ed.] 1996); S. Whitefield, (ed.), *The New Institutional Architecture of Eastern Europe* (London, Macmillan, 1993); S. Birch, 'Electoral Systems, Campaign Strategies, and Vote Choice in the Ukrainian Parliamentary and Presidential Elections of 1994', *Political Studies*, 46 (1998), 96–114; and A. Brown, 'Political Leadership in Post-Communist Russia', in W. Maley and A. Saikal, (eds), *Russia in Search of its Future* (Cambridge, Cambridge University Press, 1995), pp. 28–47.

[164] See G. Evans and S. Whitefield, 'Identifying the Bases of Party Competition in Eastern Europe', *British Journal of Political Science*, 23 (1993), 521–48; and G. Wightman, (ed.), *Party Formation in East-Central Europe* (Aldershot, Edward Elgar, 1995).

[165] See D. Lane, 'Transition under Eltsin: the Nomenklatura and Political Elite Circulation', *Political Studies*, 45 (1997), 855–74; D. Lane and C. Ross, 'The Changing Composition and Structure of the Political Elites' in D. Lane, (ed.), *Russia in Transition* (London, Longman, 1995); and T. H. Rigby, 'New Top Elites for Old in Russian Politics', *British Journal of Political Science*, 29 (1999), 323–43.

[166] See G. Smith, 'The Ethno-Politics of Federation without Federalism', in D. Lane, (ed.), *Russia in Transition*, pp. 21–51; G. Smith (ed.), *The Nationalities Question in the Post-Soviet States* (London, Longman, [2nd ed.] 1996); Linz and Stepan, *Problems of Democratic Transition and Consolidation*, esp. Chs. 2, 19 and 20; N. Melvin, *Russians Beyond Russia: The Politics of National Identity* (London, Royal Institute of International Affairs, 1995); and C. King and N. Melvin, (eds), *Nations Abroad: Diaspora Politics and International Relations in the Former Soviet Union* (Boulder, Westview, 1998).

[167] See M. McAuley, *Russia's Politics of Uncertainty* (Cambridge, Cambridge University Press, 1997); and N. Melvin, 'The Consolidation of a New Regional Elite: the Case of Omsk 1987–1995', *Europe-Asia Studies*, 50 (1998), 619–50.

which may be of increasing relevance in the Chinese context as well as in the former Soviet Union and post-Communist Eastern Europe.[168]

The two areas of scholarship which, more than any others, have been conducive to collaborative research between students of authoritarian regimes and 'mainstream' political scientists have been value and attitudinal change, on the one hand, and election studies, on the other (although much of the literature naturally explores the linkages between the two). Thus, William Miller and Richard Rose are among the prominent political scientists whose reputations rest in substantial part on their quantitative research who have entered the field of post-Communism, joining forces with a specialist on Russia and the former Soviet Union, Stephen White (as well as with local directors of the surveys, nationals of the various countries within their purview). *How Russia Votes*, written by White, Rose and Ian McAllister, is the most scholarly account and interpretation to be published thus far of Russia's contested elections from 1989 to 1996.[169] Rose himself has also, beginning in 1991, set up and maintained an annual series of 'Barometer' surveys which monitor public opinion concerning political, economic and social change in 15 post-Communist European countries.[170] William Miller, whose interest in comparative research has also extended eastwards, is co-author with White (as well as with the West Europeanist, Paul Heywood) of a major comparative study of *Values and Political Change in Postcommunist Europe*.[171]

[168] Simon Clarke is one of the few British scholars cultivating part of this field. See Clarke, (ed.), *Management and Industry in Russia: Formal and Informal Relations in the Period of Transition* (Cheltenham, Edward Elgar, 1995); Clarke, (ed.), *The Russian Enterprise in Transition: Case Studies* (Cheltenham, Edward Elgar, 1996); and Clarke (ed.), *Conflict and Change in the Russian Industrial Enterprise* (Cheltenham, Edward Elgar, 1996). See also his article, 'The privatization of industrial enterprises in Russia: four case studies', *Europe-Asia Studies*, 46 (1994), 179–214; and his chapter, 'Privatisation: The Politics of Capital and Labour', in S. White, A. Pravda and Z. Gitelman, (eds), *Developments in Russian and Post-Soviet Politics* (London, Macmillan, [3rd ed.] 1994), pp. 162–86. See, in addition, J. Howell, *China Opens its Doors: The Politics of Transition*.

[169] S. White, R. Rose and I. McAllister, *How Russia Votes* (Chatham, NJ, Chatham House, 1997).

[170] See, for example, R. Rose, 'Where are Postcommunist Countries Going?', *Journal of Democracy*, 8 (1997), 92–108; Rose, 'Freedom as a Fundamental Value', *International Social Science Journal*, 47 (1995), 457–71; and Rose, 'Escaping from Absolute Dissatisfaction: A trial-and-error model of change in Eastern Europe', *Journal of Theoretical Politics*, 4 (1992), 371–93. A book which usefully brings together much of the survey research conducted in the Soviet Union during the Gorbachev era and the first two years of post-Soviet Russia (mainly the former, and so somewhat misleadingly titled) is M. Wyman, *Public Opinion in Postcommunist Russia* (London, Macmillan, 1997).

[171] W. L. Miller, S. White and P. Heywood, *Values and Political Change in Postcommunist Europe* (London, Macmillan, 1998).

Another successful partnership has been that of Geoffrey Evans and Stephen Whitefield, which has resulted in a series of important articles based on transnational survey research conducted in formerly Communist European countries.[172] Whereas a number of authors had suggested that the negative legacy of Communism would leave citizens prey to demagoguery and nationalism, and prevent any structured or social basis for political partisanship, Evans and Whitefield adduce evidence which points in the opposite direction for most of Eastern Europe.[173] Other research by the same authors has undermined the widespread assumption that economic performance is the principal explanatory factor of variation in levels of support for democracy in the states emerging from Communist rule. Although both factors were important, recent political experience was found to be of greater weight than economic. When, indeed, support for marketization was controlled for, there was very little link between economic experience and support for democracy.[174] In emphasizing the importance of post-Communist political experience, Evans and Whitefield note two exceptions to their general rule. Romanians (probably in reaction against the peculiar nastiness of the Ceauçescu regime) show strong levels of normative commitment to democracy, even though their evaluation of 'democracy' in practice in post-Communist Romania has been as negative as that to be found in a number of other East European countries. Estonians, in contrast, are less committed to democracy as a norm than their evaluation of their recent democratic experience would suggest, the likely explanation being that democratic arguments point in the direction of

[172] See, for example, S. Whitefield and G. Evans, 'The Russian Election of 1993: Public Opinion and the Transition Experience', *Post-Soviet Affairs*, 10 (1994), 38–60; Evans and Whitefield, 'Social and Ideological Cleavage Formation in Post-Communist Hungary', *Europe-Asia Studies*, 47 (1995), 1177–1204; Evans and Whitefield, 'Economic Ideology and Political Success: Communist-successor Parties in the Czech Republic, Slovakia and Hungary Compared', *Party Politics*, 1 (1995), 565–78; Whitefield and Evans, 'Support for Democracy and Political Opposition in Russia, 1993–1995', *Post-Soviet Affairs*, 12 (1996), 218–42; and Evans and Whitefield, 'The Structuring of Political Cleavages in Post-Communist Societies: the Case of the Czech Republic and Slovakia', *Political Studies*, 47 (1998), 115–39.

[173] G. Evans and S. Whitefield, 'Identifying the Basis of Party Competition in Eastern Europe', *British Journal of Political Science*, 23 (1993), 521–48; and Evans and Whitefield, 'Electoral Politics in Eastern Europe: Social and Ideological Influences on Partisanship in Post-Communist Societies', in J. Higley, J. Pakulski and W. Wesolowski, (eds), *Postcommunist Elites and Democracy in Eastern Europe* (London, Macmillan, 1998), pp. 226–50.

[174] G. Evans and S. Whitefield, 'The Politics and Economics of Democratic Commitment: Support for Democracy in Transition Societies', *British Journal of Political Science*, 25 (1995), 485–514.

political inclusiveness. That would be at odds with the widespread tendency in Estonia to regard the large Russian minority as an alien group who should not be accorded full citizenship rights.[175] Like the work of Rose, what makes the survey research of Evans and Whitefield especially valuable is its systematic replication over time and the cumulative character of its findings.

Some of the contentious issues of political science are now being investigated in a new and unusual setting—that of a set of countries which had very similar political and economic institutional structures up to the point at which their transition from Communist rule got underway. Among the questions being explored and debated are the extent to which Communism has bequeathed values and political cleavages different from those to be found in other post-authoritarian societies; whether value differences can be explained by reference to longer and more culturally distinctive political and religious traditions; or whether attitudinal and value change should be seen primarily as a rational response to the successes and failures of democratization and marketization in particular countries (and as they affect particular social groups).

Whether differences from one country to another should be explained by political culture remains a contentious issue. Miller and his associates suggest that the results of their surveys reflect the different historical experience of East-Central Europe and the Soviet Union. Their case studies were of the Czech Republic, Slovakia and Hungary, on the one hand, and Russia and Ukraine, on the other. Among many interesting differences they note the fact that only half as many respondents in the latter two countries chose abuse of human rights as the worst feature of the Communist regime. Indeed, they were 35 per cent more critical of the effect of the transition *from* Communism on human rights specifically.[176]

It is far from universally accepted that survey research is the best way to get at people's deeper values, the meanings they impart to political activity, or the way they think about politics. One might say that it is the worst way—apart from all the others (to recall Churchill's comparison of democracy with alternative forms of government). At a time of exceptionally rapid political and social change, it would be surprising if there were not also to be attitudinal volatility. But that is an argument for caution and replication rather than for eschewing survey research. In

[175] Evans and Whitefield, 'The Politics and Economics of Democratic Commitment, pp. 507–9.
[176] Miller, White and Heywood, *Values and Political Change in Postcommunist Europe*, p. 7.

the Russian case, excessively optimistic interpretations of the democratic character of Russian political culture were sometimes offered on the slender basis of survey research conducted in 1990, a period in which, for many Russians, democracy was identified with a future that would endow them with both the political stability and the higher standard of living they perceived in the West. Since the practice of what is called democracy in Russia—in which competitive elections are combined with low levels of political accountability, with economic malfeasance and an extremely weak rule of law—has fallen far short of the expectations of those who identified themselves as democrats in 1990–91, there is, unsurprisingly, substantial dissatisfaction with 'actually existing democracy', to the extent that 'democrat' has become a term of abuse. Yet support for democracy at a normative level showed only a modest decline between 1993 and 1995.[177]

The political experience of recent decades suggests that where authoritarian regimes have given way to democratic systems in which politicians can be held accountable and where a rule of law prevails, there is little likelihood of a return to authoritarianism, least of all in the form of Communism or fascism. It is easier to continue to deny political liberties to people who have never experienced them (as seven decades of Soviet rule demonstrated) than to remove freedoms to which citizens have quickly become accustomed. Most of the studies reviewed here, including the best of the survey research, tend to bear out this optimistic conclusion. But much depends on the quality of that political, as well as economic, experience. It seems likely that the post-Communist countries of East-Central Europe will make no less successful a transition to democracy than those states which emerged from conservative authoritarian rule in the Iberian Peninsula. Where a hybrid and malfunctioning political system is combined with economic crisis, as in Russia and Ukraine, the outcome is still in the balance. Whether the world's first Communist state and the largest country on earth, Russia, will succeed in breaking decisively with its authoritarian past remains, perhaps, the most momentous of all the unresolved puzzles. It is one question, among many, likely to keep British students of politics busy into the twenty-first century.

---

[177] Whitefield and Evans, 'Support for Democracy and Political Opposition in Russia, 1993–1995', p. 228.

Acknowledgements. For comments on an earlier draft of this chapter or for bibliographical suggestions, I am most grateful to Ronald Amann, Alan Angell, Brian Barry, Rosemary Foot, Jack Hayward, Jeffrey Kahn, Juan Linz, A. J. Nicholls, Alex Pravda, T. H. Rigby, Alfred Stepan, Steve Tsang and Stephen Whitefield. I benefited also from useful discussion at the British Academy symposium of 27–28 June 1997.

13: A British School of International Relations

TIM DUNNE

International relations is 'an *American* social science'.[1] This short phrase, which has launched countless undergraduate essays, serves as a constant reminder of the affinity between the discipline and American political power. According to most histories of academic international relations, the only British scholar to be ranked alongside American 'giants' such as Hans Morgenthau, Reinhold Niebuhr, George Kennan, Thomas Schelling and Kenneth Waltz, is E. H. Carr. His book *The Twenty Years' Crisis 1919–1939* is treated by both communities of scholars as the principal destroyer of the rampant utopianism characteristic of the first phase of the discipline.[2] After Carr, the history of academic international relations crosses the Atlantic, and focuses on the wave of early post-war realist writers. This privileging of American thinkers in the general historiographies of the discipline published during the Cold War has consistently discounted the importance of international relations in Britain. Paradoxically, this tendency has been equally evident in the

---

[1] S. Hoffmann, 'An American Social Science: International Relations', in S. Hoffmann, *Janus and Minerva: Essays in the Theory and Practice of International Politics* (Boulder, Col., Westview Press, 1987), pp. 3–24. Emphasis added.

[2] E. H. Carr, *The Twenty Year's Crisis 1919–1939: An Introduction to the Study of International Relations* (London, Macmillan, 1939). It is important to note that there is an ongoing debate about whether or not international relations constitutes a distinctive discipline. Some maintain that the absence of a distinctive approach or method casts doubt on the possibility of describing international relations as a discrete discipline. This, however, is a minority view; a cursory examination of leading textbooks in the field highlights the widespread tendency to refer to the 'discipline' of international relations.

reflections on the development of the discipline written from within British international relations.[3]

There is no doubt that the American international relations community continues to exert a hegemonic influence over the discipline. That said, in the last few years, a series of retrospective articles and books have brought to light the contribution made by scholars working in Britain during the first half-century of the study of international relations.[4] These revisionist histories have served as a useful corrective to the Americanization of international relations, as well as making the related argument that many of the latest trends to come out of the leading centres of international relations in the United States were foreshadowed by scholars on the eastern side of the Atlantic. In my contribution to this volume I will seek to sustain both these arguments. After considering the vexed question of whether it is possible to speak of a collective identity shared by scholars working in Britain, the chapter will then examine the debate surrounding the birth of the discipline in the aftermath of the First World War. Here I will discuss the arguments mobilized by E. H. Carr against the so-called idealists. This leads into a discussion of the evolution of a distinctive voice in British international relations which sought to overcome the realist–idealist dualism which defined what has become known as the first 'great debate'. By the 1950s and 1960s there was a growing sense that disciplines such as history and politics had not paid sufficient attention to the unique patterns of power, order and justice which prevailed in world politics. In order to fill the gap, a group of scholars— principally, Herbert Butterfield, Martin Wight, Adam Watson and Hedley Bull—organized themselves into a committee devoted to the elucidation of foundational questions about the nature of the 'international'. The conclusion briefly considers how far contemporary thinking on international relations builds on this attempt to set out an agenda which was both different from politics as traditionally conceived, and different from international relations as pursued in the United States.

---

[3] H. Bull, 'The Theory of International Politics, 1919–1969', in B. Porter, ed., *The Aberystwyth Papers: International Politics 1919–1969* (Oxford, Oxford University Press, 1972).

[4] See, for example, S. Smith, 'The Forty Years Detour: The Resurgence of Normative Theory in International Relations', *Millennium*, 21 (1992), 489–506; J. L. Richardson, 'The Academic Study of International Relations', in J. D. B. Miller and R. J. Vincent, eds., *Order and Violence: Hedley Bull and International Relations* (Oxford, Clarendon Press, 1990). For an attempt to build bridges between American and British interpretations of international society, which also contains a useful discussion of recent British historiographical literature, see O. Waever, 'Four Meanings of International Society: A Trans-Atlantic Dialogue', in B. A. Roberson, *International Society and the Development of International Relations Theory* (London, Pinter, 1998), pp. 80–144.

Labels and boundaries

I have not attempted here to provide a comprehensive history of the development of international relations in Britain over the last 80 years.[5] I have also avoided the temptation to survey all the different sub-fields of the discipline;[6] such an account would have required an extended discussion of some or all of the following contributory sub-disciplines: area or regional studies; foreign policy analysis; gender and international relations; international history; peace studies; international law and institutions; international political economy; and international theory.[7] Instead, I have chosen to reconstruct one particular discourse which was driven by the question whether the institutions of European international society which emerged in the seventeenth and eighteenth centuries could continue to provide international order under conditions of cultural diversity found in contemporary global politics. The justification for concentrating on this broadly theoretical enquiry into international order over other sub-fields is threefold: the work of international society theorists represents the most distinctive strand in British international relations this century; it is currently receiving an unprecedented level of attention and re-evaluation within the profession; and finally, the research programme sketched out by classical international society theorists from the late 1950s to the late 1980s provides us with a moral compass for judging the practices of states and the extent to which these strengthen or weaken the institutions of international society.[8]

---

[5] See W. C. Olsen and A. J. R. Groom, *International Relations Then and Now* (London, HarperCollins, 1991).

[6] See C. Hill, 'The Study of International Relations in the United Kingdom', in H. C. Dyer and L. Mangasarian, eds., *The Study of International Relations: The State of the Art* (London, Macmillan, 1989), pp. 265–74.

[7] The ESRC defines 'the major contributory disciplines in International Studies' as international history, international politics, international economics, international political economy, international law, strategic studies and peace studies. See the 1996 *Research Training Guidelines*, Section C9.

[8] This is a controversial argument and one that some leading figures in the discipline would dispute. Unfortunately, given the constraints, it is not possible to engage with contemporary critics of the English School working in Britain. For an historical materialist critique of the international society perspective, see F. Halliday, *Rethinking International Relations* (London, Macmillan, 1994). For the contours of a response to critics such as Ken Booth, Fred Halliday and Martin Shaw, see N. J. Wheeler, 'Guardian Angel or Global Gangster', *Political Studies*, 44 (1996), 123–35.

From the early 1980s onwards, the international society perspective has been given the label the 'English School'.[9] An explanation is required about the label as it has generated a good deal of debate and provoked considerable criticism. The most frequently cited objection to the label is that a number of its most important protagonists were not English. Some accounts of the history of the School include Charles Manning, who was a South African, in their number;[10] and *all* references to the School have hitherto included the Australian Hedley Bull. For this reason, a number of writers have preferred to denote the Wight–Bull–Watson–Vincent lineage as 'the classical approach' or the 'international society tradition'. These have the advantage of revealing something compelling about the ideas in question (in the same way that realism or liberalism do) rather than simply grouping their representatives according to the nationality of the majority. Set against this, they both suffer from being rather vague, and more importantly, from a lack of widespread recognition in the profession.

Another attempt to generate a more accurate nomenclature for this particular perspective is to use the label 'British' rather than 'English'; this has the advantage of not appearing to endorse the insensitive habit of using English as a short-hand for British. However, there are three reasons why I believe we should continue to use the epithet 'English School'. First, calling it a British School does little to overcome the principal objection laid at the door of those who use the label 'English School' in that those South African and Australian members did not

[9] Somewhat paradoxically, the label was first used in a polemical article by R. E. Jones who argued that the English School had a degenerate research design. In effect, Jones called for the 'closure' of the School which he had helped to invent. See especially R. E. Jones, 'The English School of International Relations: A Case for Closure', *Review of International Studies*, 7 (1981), 1–13. For responses to Jones's argument, see H. Suganami, 'The Structure of Institutionalism: An Anatomy of British Mainstream International Relations', *International Relations*, 7 (1983), 2363–81. S. Grader, 'The English School of International Relations: Evidence and Evaluation', *Review of International Studies*, 14 (1988), 29–44. P. Wilson, 'The English School of International Relations: A reply to Sheila Grader', *Review of International Studies*, 15 (1989), 49–58.

[10] Charles Manning stands in an ambivalent relationship to the English School. He was never invited to participate in the British Committee meetings. The correspondence between Committee members suggests personal prejudices were part of the reason for his exclusion. His characterization of the society of states was to an extent influential on Hedley Bull. Curiously, given that they were both senior figures in the same Department at LSE, Manning's impact on international theory was barely recognized by Wight. Perhaps this was because of their diverging methodologies, Manning's being a unique blend of phenomenology and jurisprudence which was at odds with the philosophy of history adumbrated by Wight.

believe themselves to be British either. Second, from the perspective of political culture, there are aspects of the work of Butterfield, Wight, Bull and Watson which reflect a very English sense of academic enquiry as a form of conversation, one which was conducted according to an elaborate set of written and unwritten rules. It is no coincidence in this respect that all the leading members of the School were attached to one of the three historic English universities of Cambridge, London and Oxford. In other words, the liberal preference for British over English might in fact represent a greater injustice to the Celtic nations of the United Kingdom in so far as their histories and cultures would not have been so hospitable to the enterprise that Wight and Butterfield embarked upon in the late 1950s. The third reason why the term English School is preferable to British is procedural rather than substantive. It is a term which those who have been trained in international relations—irrespective of their national academic location—associate with the writings of Wight, Bull, Watson and Vincent.

The controversy surrounding the appropriate label is likely to continue, despite the fact there are good grounds for deferring to the conventional usage. In the last instance, the important issue is not where the home of the School is, but how far its ideas travel. After all, the Frankfurt School of critical social theory has attracted a growing band of supporters despite the fact that most of them were not born in Frankfurt and have not had any professional affiliation with the famous Institute of Social Research (ISR).[11] By the same logic, we should not be concerned that the link between territory and identity has been severed in connection with the English School in the 1990s. 'Those whose names are associated with it', argues a Canadian member of the School, 'are as likely to reside outside of England: in Wales, Australia, Canada, Norway, Germany, even the US'.[12]

One possible compromise would be to use the term British School to refer to something much broader than the Butterfield–Wight–Bull–Watson–Vincent lineage. Christopher Hill prefers the broader description of a 'British school' which he deploys to describe the entire international studies profession.[13] But to imply some kind of homogeneity across the various sub-fields is problematic, given the high levels of

---

[11] I am indebted to Ken Booth for drawing to my attention both of these arguments.
[12] R. Epp, 'The English School on the Frontiers of International Relations', *Review of International Studies*, Special Issue, 24 (December 1998) p. 48.
[13] Hill, 'The Study of International Relations in the United Kingdom'.

disagreement within each one. Proponents of traditional strategic studies have more in common with 'realist' strategists in the United States than they do with critical security theorists working in Britain.[14] Similarly, the most important methodological dispute among theorists of international relations do not coincide with national boundaries. Alliances among 'post-positivists' or 'positivists' on both sides of the Atlantic are closer than the ties between advocates of these two different approaches within their respective academic communities.[15]

Adam Roberts also maintains, albeit cautiously, that there is some merit in thinking about a British voice in international relations. He notes that a generic British predisposition can be seen to be at work in the theory and practice of international studies. This, he argues, includes the following characteristics: a sense of one's own history and that of others; a recognition that certain patterns are enduring; a resistance to the articulation of universal moral prescriptions; and a scepticism towards proponents of revolutionary change in favour of a more gradualist approach.[16] However, as Roberts recognizes, some or all of these characteristics can be found in the study of international relations in other countries as well. In his words, 'there is no exclusivity here'.

As will become clear in the main body of the chapter, I am deploying a more restrictive definition of what constitutes a 'school' or approach, one that precisely tries to delineate what is distinctive. There are two compelling reasons why it makes sense to speak of the English School as a distinct tradition of enquiry. First, there are the personal ties, particu-

---

[14] Compare, for example, the different meanings and approaches to security studies found in: K. Booth, 'Security and Emancipation', _Review of International Studies_, 17 (1991), 313–26; B. Buzan, _People, States and Fear: An Agenda for International Security Studies in the Post-Cold War Era_ (London, Pinter, 1990); D. Campbell, _Writing Security: United States Foreign Policy and the Politics of Identity_ (Minneapolis, University of Minnesota Press, 1992).

[15] Compare, for example, the broad similarities between the methodologies sketched by the American scholar J. A. Vasquez in his 'The Post-Positivist Debate: Reconstructing Scientific Enquiry and International Theory after Enlightenment's Fall', in K. Booth and S. Smith, eds., _International Relations Theory Today_ (Cambridge, Polity Press, 1995), pp. 217–240 with M. Nicholson's chapter 'The Continued Significance of Positivism?', in S. Smith, K. Booth and M. Zalewski, eds., _International Theory: Positivism and Beyond_ (Cambridge, Cambridge University Press, 1996), pp. 128–45. The transnational convergence among post-positivists can be seen in the same volume. Compare Smith, Booth and Zalewiski, etc., 'Positivism and Beyond', pp. 11–44 with R. Ashley, 'The Achievements of Post-Structuralism', pp. 240–53.

[16] These features are outlined in his paper 'A New Era in International Relations' presented to a conference on 'Facing the Challenges of the Twenty-First Century: International Relations Studies in China', Institute of International Relations, Peking University, 17–19 June, 1991, Beijing. They are elaborated upon in his lecture on 'The Evolution of International Relations', Royal College of Defence Studies, London, 13 January 1998.

larly evident in the pedagogical bond that unites successive generations of English School scholars. The obvious example here is the relationship between Martin Wight and Hedley Bull. Wight was Bull's intellectual mentor when they were colleagues in the Department of International Relations at LSE; Wight provided him with a training in international relations which he had not received as an undergraduate in Sydney or as a postgraduate studying for a BPhil in politics at Oxford between 1953 and 1955. In his memorial lecture for Martin Wight, Bull describes how he had been a 'constant borrower' from Wight's lectures on 'international theory'.[17] The academic relationship between R. J. Vincent and Hedley Bull followed a similar pattern. Vincent openly admitted to borrowing from Bull; he was, after all, a PhD student at the Australian National University in the early 1970s when Bull was head of department. After Bull's death, Vincent noted the influence Bull exerted on 'every page' of his book, *Human Rights and International Relations*.[18] The lineage between Adam Watson, the former diplomat turned academic, and Herbert Butterfield conforms to a similar pattern. Butterfield taught Watson, brought him into the British Committee in 1959 and exerted 'the most long-standing influence' on him.[19]

These common bonds, 'written in the heart' (to borrow Edmund Burke's famous phrase) were a necessary but not sufficient condition for the existence of a 'school' of thought. What was also required was a belief that they were embarking on a common project. Unlike their contemporaries, they believed that international relations had a much longer history than the conventional historiography of the discipline implied. And crucially, it was only by going back to examine the classical writings by philosophers, jurists and princes that the 'international' could be understood in historical and sociological context. Above all, it was the tradition of rationalism which they believed had been overlooked by the discourses on international relations hitherto. By the mid-1960s, the members of the British Committee on the Theory of International Politics were increasingly aware that their approach to the discipline was distinct from mainstream American thinking, and

[17] A related point concerns the remarkable amount of time and energy Bull lent to the project of disseminating Wight's ideas more widely than he had achieved himself during his lifetime. For a flavour of their pedagogical relationship, see H. Bull, 'Martin Wight and the Theory of International Relations', in M. Wight, *International Theory: The Three Traditions* (Leicester, Leicester University Press, 1991), ix–xxiii.

[18] R. J. Vincent, *Human Rights and International Relations* (Cambridge, Cambridge University Press, 1986).

[19] A. Watson, *The Evolution of International Society: A Comparative Historical Analysis* (London, Routledge, 1992), p. 5.

two decades on, both Bull and Vincent publicly defended the idea of a distinctive English School. These two factors suggest that leading members of the School were aware that they were part of a collective enterprise, and consciously sought to carry its debates forward.[20]

The birth of academic international relations in Britain

Intellectual speculation on issues that concern international relations academics—such as war, peace, security, prosperity, justice—stretches back as far as the earliest philosophy. But as a university-based subject, international relations has a much more recent history. Conventional accounts of the 'birth' of international relations begin in 1919.[21] What makes this date significant is the congruence of the dissolution of the old European order, and the human will—flawed though it was—to create a more stable and more just international order. Academic international relations had a mission to promote peace and 'the truer understanding of civilizations other than our own', as the Welsh Liberal MP David Davies hoped, when he inaugurated the first designated chair of international politics at Aberystwyth in 1919.[22]

Two decades later, the missionary zeal of the idealists was in tatters. The scourge of total war was returning, and students of the subject were dedicating their works to the makers of the next peace. E. H. Carr's *The Twenty Years' Crisis* argued that before looking forward to planning the new society, it was vital that intellectuals and policy-makers came to grips with the reasons for the collapse of the League of Nations. The book was written, in Carr's words, with the 'deliberate aim' of counteracting the 'almost total neglect of the factor of power' which had beset Anglo-American thinking in the inter-war period.[23]

---

[20] Alasdair MacIntyre, quoted in H. Bull, B. Kingsbury and A. Roberts, eds., *Hugo Grotius and International Relations* (Oxford, Clarendon Press, 1990), p. 54.

[21] For a stimulating critique of the conventional accounts of the 'birth' of the discipline, see B. C. Schmidt, *The political discourse of anarchy: a disciplinary history of international relations* (Albany, NY, State University of New York Press, 1998).

[22] In November 1919, David Davies and his family contributed £20,000 as an endowment of a Chair in Aberystwyth for the study of those aspects of law, politics, economics and ethics 'which are raised by the prospect of a League of Nations and for the truer understanding of civilizations other than our own'. I. John, M. Wright and J. Garnett, 'International Politics at Aberystwyth 1919–1969', in Porter, *Aberystwyth Papers*, p. 86.

[23] Carr, *The Twenty Years' Crisis 1919–1939: An Introduction to the Study of International Relations*, (London, Macmillan, [2nd ed.] 1946), preface. For a comprehensive examination of Carr's contribution to the discipline, see C. Jones, *E. H. Carr and International Relations: A Duty to Lie* (Cambridge, Cambridge University Press, 1999).

The label Carr gave to the intellectual movement responsible for the nemesis was, of course, 'utopianism'. To be a utopian was to be immature, or naïvely optimistic. Utopians, Carr argued, prefer wishing rather than thinking and the pursuit of ends over means. Carr is clearly painting idealism—to use its less pejorative label—with a very broad brush. It encompasses a variety of not always compatible positions, including pacifism, advocacy of world government, collective security, and a belief in the power of public opinion. Not only is the menu of idealism contested, so too is the list of protagonists. As Peter Wilson notes in his treatment of the inter-war period, Carr was not particularly explicit about who the 'utopians' were. But in the course of *The Twenty Years' Crisis*, the following thinkers and state leaders find themselves in his sights: Norman Angell, Robert Cecil, Hersch Lauterpacht, Arnold Toynbee, even Anthony Eden and Winston Churchill.[24]

The key move in *The Twenty Years' Crisis* is to show how utopianism caused a breakdown in the inter-war order. Here we come across the central explanatory theme which is said to unite all strands of utopianism across different disciplines, namely, the belief in a 'harmony of interests'. In philosophy, utilitarianism holds out the promise that self-interest promotes the general good; neo-classical economics brings together the interests of the individual with the efficient functioning of the market; and finally, liberal internationalism argues that there are no essential conflicts of interest between nation-states. The slow recognition from the turn of the century onwards, that interests collided in international relations (between great powers and small states for example) just as they conflict in the domestic labour market, revealed for Carr the hollow nature of liberal universalism. This brings him to conclude that the 'inner meaning of the modern international crises is the collapse of the whole structure of utopianism based on the concept of the harmony of interests'.[25]

Carr deploys 'realism' to refute the harmony of interests doctrine. The argument that the national interest and the interests of the international community as a whole good can be reconciled was, according to Carr, nothing more than 'the ideology of a dominant group concerned to maintain its predominance'.[26] For example, Britain's arguments in the nineteenth century for universal free trade reflected its particular advantages

---

[24] P. Wilson, 'Introduction' in D. Long and P. Wilson, eds., *Thinkers of the Twenty Years' Crisis: Inter-War Idealism Reassessed* (Oxford, Clarendon Press, 1995), p. 15.

[25] Carr, *The Twenty Years' Crisis*, (1939), p. 80.

[26] Ibid. p. 58.

in securing such an outcome. Similarly, the Treaty of Versailles represented the interests of the satisfied victor powers, and not those of all states.

Carr's critique of moral universalism is one which later English School thinkers challenged. Hedley Bull's critical review of '*The Twenty Years' Crisis* Thirty Years On' claimed that Carr had exhibited a crude form of instrumentalism whereby morality was merely a reflection of the will of the stronger. This position, he continued, is blind to the 'reality' that there are certain interests and values which are held in common by all states. The essence of Bull's dismissal of Carr's moral relativism is the purported existence of some values (for example, order) which may be for the general well-being of all states.[27] In Bull's own words:

> The idea of an international society—of common interests and common values perceived in common by modern states—is scarcely recognised in *The Twenty Years' Crisis*. In the course of demonstrating how appeals to an overriding international society subserve the special interests of the ruling group of powers, Carr jettisons the idea of international society itself.[28]

Bull concluded his critique of Carr's realism with a clarion-call for the orientation of international relations around 'the idea of international society'.[29]

The above passage succinctly demonstrates the way in which English School writers distanced themselves from pure realism.[30] In its place, they sought to construct an international theory that more closely reflected the practices of sovereign states. Bull maintained that the idea of international society had always been present in the minds and the practices of diplomats, lawyers, and state leaders. According to his famous definition, international society exists because the representatives of states are 'conscious of certain common interests and common values' and believe them to be '*bound* by a common set of rules and institutions'.[31]

---

[27] H. Bull, '*The Twenty Years' Crisis* Thirty Years On', *International Journal*, 24 (1969), 629.

[28] Ibid. p. 638.

[29] Ibid. p. 638.

[30] Without engaging in an extended discussion of the interpretation of Carr's work, it could be argued that Bull's reading is unbalanced for two reasons. First, he underestimates the importance of morality in *The Twenty Years' Crisis*, and Carr's prescription that political theory required realism *and* utopianism, power *and* morality. Second, by focusing only on *The Twenty Years' Crisis*, Bull is not sufficiently sympathetic to the strong utopian undercurrent of Carr's other works in international relations.

[31] H. Bull, *The Anarchical Society, A Study of World Order in Politics* (London, Macmillan, 1977), p. 13. Emphasis added. Andrew Hurrell has argued that 'the subjective sense of being bound by a community was the cornerstone of his definition of international society'. A. Hurrell, 'International Society and the Study of Regimes: A Reflective Approach', in V. Rittberger, ed., *Regime Theory and International Relations* (Oxford, Clarendon Press, 1993), p. 63.

It is clear that writers such as Herbert Butterfield, Martin Wight and Hedley Bull saw the immediate task being the transcendence of Carr's dualism, and the re-positioning of international relations in the space between the polarities. In this sense, Carr's single most important contribution to the development of the English School was to instigate a debate about the adequacy of the prevailing categories of thought. It is also important to bear in mind that one positive consequence of Carr's work for the development of the English School concerns his role in broadening the discipline away from its legal institutionalist origins. International relations in Britain after Carr could no longer be accused of being a surrogate of international law or international history.

E. H. Carr resigned his post as Woodrow Wilson Professor in 1947 after falling out with the college authorities in Aberystwyth. After this point, Carr effectively departed from the discipline that he had done so much to create, and began his fourteen-volume work on *A History of Soviet Russia*. Before taking up a Fellowship at Trinity College, Cambridge, in 1955, where he remained until his death in 1982, Carr was passed over for a number of academic positions for which he was well qualified. The most obvious explanation for his exile from the academy is that his sympathy for the Soviet experiment had become a professional liability with the onset of the Cold War. As his biographer, Jonathan Haslam put it, 'Britain, too, had its equivalent of McCarthyism'.[32]

Martin Wight published his pamphlet *Power Politics* a year before Carr's departure from the discipline. It is this work more than any other which led to Wight's association with realism. In a phrase that could have been lifted from *The Twenty Years' Crisis*, Wight argued that states will generally pursue their national interest at the expense of the common good, 'but in the fraction that they may be deflected lies the difference between the jungle and the traditions of Europe'.[33] It is Wight's elaboration of these traditions in his international theory lectures, given at LSE in the late 1950s, which is his distinctive contribution to the English School.

---

[32] J. Haslam, '"We Need a Faith": E. H. Carr 1892–1982', *History Today*, August 1983, p. 39. For an alternative explanation of Carr's 'exile', see the comments in this volume by Archie Brown.

[33] M. Wight, *Power Politics* (London, Royal Institute of International Affairs, 'Looking Forward' Pamphlet No. 8, 1946), p. 68.

This was not the first course that Wight taught. He was asked to teach 'International Institutions', a subject which 'did not greatly interest him'.[34] But it was partly due to his articles on the United Nations written for the *Observer* after the war that prompted Charles Manning to offer Wight a Readership in International Relations at LSE in 1949. Manning hoped that Wight would strengthen the 'philosophical' and the 'scientific' basis of the teaching of international relations. Clearly Wight made a massive contribution to the former, but completely undermined the latter.

From 1957 onwards, Wight lectured on 'International Theory'.[35] Hedley Bull recalls how the lectures 'made a profound impression' on him.[36] The origins of the thinking behind the lectures can be traced to Wight's increasing dissatisfaction with the logocentrism which underpinned Carr's *The Twenty Years' Crisis*. Although profoundly influenced by Carr's work, Wight believed the architecture of realism and idealism was a 'reflection of a diseased situation'.[37] The essential weakness of any dualism is that it engenders the unfortunate tendency of interpreting different ideas as necessarily mutually exclusive. Wight's additional category of 'rationalism' usefully serves the function of a *via media* between the two diametrically opposite political positions.

Proponents of the English School argue that the rationalist tradition provides the most compelling answer to the question 'what is international society?' The English School's exploration into the nature of international society is rightly acknowledged as the 'distinguishing power' of the School.[38] But what does the term *society* mean in the context of relations between states? Clearly it is a different kind of society, one with fewer members than civil societies, where the gap between the strongest and the weakest is far greater, and where there are no supranational institutions which can enforce the will of the collectivity. Despite the differences between domestic and international society, there are also clear overlaps. Both societies can be defined, in a Rawlsian sense, as co-operative arrangements for securing the mutual advantage

---

[34] H. Bull, 'Introduction: Martin Wight and the Study of International Relations', in M. Wight, *Systems of States* (Leicester, Leicester University Press, 1977), p. 6.

[35] The summer term of the academic year 1956–7 is the first time that Wight's 'International Theory' lectures are recorded in LSE's 'Calendar'.

[36] H. Bull, 'Martin Wight and the Theory of International Relations', in Wight, *International Theory*, p. ix.

[37] According to Wight, 'the more it [the two schools analysis] is made the basis for a general international theory the more untrue it seems to become'. Wight, *International Theory*, p. 267.

[38] P. Wilson, 'The English school of International Relations: A reply to Sheila Grader'.

of the members. Both have highly developed systems of rules which start out from the premise of formal equality (at least in democratic societies). In the case of international society, equality is stipulated by sovereignty, a right which implies obligations to (at a minimum) refrain from interference in the affairs of other states and to respect their territorial integrity.

Bound up with the ontology of international society is the idea that states are not, as has often been assumed, strangers to the moral world. Two related arguments contribute to this normative predisposition. The first concerns the recognition that diplomats and state leaders have 'agency'. The society of states has been constructed by 'the handiwork of real people' and is reproduced by their 'ongoing activity'.[39] Recognizing that it is state leaders who have spun the web of international society leads necessarily (as noted above) to an interpretative mode of enquiry which seeks to uncover the principles guiding their conduct and the meanings they give to their actions. To judge their actions, Wight argued, 'means judging the validity of their ethical principles'. The spectrum of choices facing the agents (i.e. state leaders) in formulating their foreign policies is constrained by layers of legal principles and norms which form the structure of international society. A central tenet of the English School is the belief that the agents are socialized by the structure. This comes through strongly in Hedley Bull's often-quoted definition of international society:

> A society of states (or international society) exists when a group of states, conscious of certain common interests and common values, form a society in the sense that they conceive themselves to be bound by a common set of rules in their relations with one another, and share in the working of common institutions.[40]

While the English School focuses on the nature and possibilities for international society, it remains acutely aware that the practices of the society of states are threatened by the ever present realities of the 'state of war' and global transnational relations. Thus, the ideas of realism and revolutionism are not merely the outer boundaries of a rationalist *via media*. The rationalist desire for international order is constantly under-

---

[39] R. Jackson, 'The Political Theory of International Society', in K. Booth and S. Smith, eds., *International Relations Theory Today* (Cambridge, Polity Press, 1995), p. 113.
[40] Bull, *The Anarchical Society*, p. 13.

mined by the realist pursuit of self-interest and the revolutionist quest for transnational justice. Although these positions are intellectually distinct, and internally coherent, they are not mutually exclusive in practice. In Wight's own words, they 'are streams, with eddies and cross-currents, sometimes interlacing and never long confined to their own river bed'.[41]

Wight's own intellectual journey provides a good illustration of the interplay between the three traditions. In the lectures, he likened pacifism—the position he adopted in the 1930s—to 'inverted Revolutionism' (sometimes identified by him as the fourth tradition). At other moments, Wight believed that his deeply-held Christian convictions were compatible with the realist tradition of despair.[42] In his concluding lecture, Wight admits that he finds his own position 'shifting round the circle'. But tellingly, he adds that 'my prejudices are Rationalist' and he was becoming 'more Rationalist and less Realist through rethinking this question during the course of these lectures.'[43]

A striking fact about Martin Wight concerns the inverse correlation between his minimal published output and his influence upon future generations of international relations thinkers. Indeed, it is unlikely that he would feature at all prominently in the historiography of international relations had it not been for the painstaking efforts on the part of his widow Gabriele Wight, and former friends and colleagues such as Carsten Holbraad, Brian Porter, and above all, Hedley Bull, to edit and publish his work posthumously.[44] That said, it was the British Committee which provided the occasion for Wight to deliver his most ambitious and influential papers.

The key figure in setting up the British Committee on the Theory of International Politics was Herbert Butterfield. Given that the dilemmas of international politics occupied his mind from the early 1950s onwards, it is surprising that his contribution to international relations has not been given more prominence. This is particularly the case in Britain

---

[41] Wight, *International Theory*, p. 260.

[42] M. Wight, 'The Church, Russia and the West', *The Ecumenical Review*, 1 (Autumn 1948), 37.

[43] Wight, *International Theory*, p. 268.

[44] The life and work of Martin Wight is known to students of International Relations because of Hedley Bull's considered introductions to *Systems of States* and the revised edition of *Power Politics* (with Carsten Holbraad) and Bull's memorial lecture for Martin Wight. H. Bull and C. Holbraad, 'Introduction', in M. Wight, *Power Politics* (London, Penguin, [2nd ed.] 1978), pp. 9–22. Bull, 'Martin Wight and the Study of International Relations' in Wight, *International Theory*, pp. ix–xxiii.

where there has been no article or book reviewing his contribution to the discipline.[45]

One possible reason why Butterfield has hitherto been seen as marginal to international relations in Britain is because of his reputation as an historian. He published works of narrative history, on historical method, and on diplomatic history. His academic career as an historian began at Peterhouse, Cambridge in 1923, where he was to become Master (1955 to 1968) and Professor in the Faculty of History.

From the point of view of his influence over the development of international relations, it is important to note the extremely high regard in which he was held by other realists in the United States. Unlike Carr and Wight in particular, Butterfield's reputation resonated more widely in the United States than in Britain.[46] His influence on international relations in the United States can be traced back to his close friendship with Kenneth Thompson who wrote a number of pieces on Butterfield[47] and worked closely with him in setting up a parallel 'Rockefeller Committee' in Britain (discussed in more detail below). We should perhaps not be surprised that Butterfield found intellectual allies among Christian realists in the United States during the 1950s. By the mid-1960s however, their voices were being silenced by the forces of secularism and science. Even within the American Rockefeller Committee, where traditionalism continued to reign, the balance of power was shifting from Niebuhr to Waltz, whose 'third image' view of the discipline inevitably marginalized theological thinking.[48] Butterfield had to wait until the neo-conservative revival in the 1980s before his star began to rise once more.[49]

The context of the Cold War and the threat that nuclear weapons posed for human civilization was the principal motivation for his

---

[45] There are signs that there may be a growing interest in Butterfield and International Relations. See R. Epp, 'The "Augustinian Moment" in International Politics: Niebuhr, Butterfield, Wight and the Reclaiming of a Tradition', International Politics Research Occasional Paper No. 10, (University of Wales, Aberystwyth, 1991).

[46] Here of course I am referring to scholars working in Britain not identified with the English School.

[47] K. W. Thompson, *Masters of International Thought* (Baton Rouge, Louisiana State University Press, 1980) and K. W. Thompson, ed., *Herbert Butterfield: The Ethics of History and Politics* (Washington, DC, University Press of America, 1980).

[48] Epp, 'The "Augustianian Moment"', p. 20. For an intellectual biography of Butterfield, see A. Coll, *The Wisdom of Statecraft: Sir Herbert Butterfield and the Philosophy of International Politics* (Durham, Duke University Press, 1985).

[49] Ibid. In a foreword, Adam Watson describes the work as 'the best and most accurate exposition' of the man and his contribution to history, politics and theology (p. xiv).

increasing interest in international politics. Relations between states were, according to Butterfield, even more prone to suffer 'from the cupidities of the wicked, the anxieties of the strong, and the unwisdom of the virtuous'.[50] Moreover, the regularity of conflict is such that international politics can be amenable to intellectual analysis. As Butterfield put it: 'the problems and paradoxes of nations show such constancies of fundamental pattern throughout the ages, it is the realm where man ought to learn most (though in reality he refuses to learn) from the accumulated experience of the human race'.[51] The idealists (or what he more often called 'moralists') in the inter-war period failed dismally to draw from this well of diplomatic experience.[52] One particular aspect of idealism which concerned him was the prevalence of 'war for righteousness' thinking in the legal discourse of the inter-war period. Butterfield applies the same argument to the Cold War, recognizing the dangers of judging Communism as evil and then fighting a 'war for righteousness' against it.

It is less his critique of idealism that marks out Butterfield as a key thinker in British international relations than his analysis of the causes of wars. According to Ken Booth and Nicholas J. Wheeler, Butterfield provides the earliest account of the 'security dilemma' in the literature.[53] Although Butterfield preferred the term 'absolute predicament', the force of the argument is much the same. In their quest for security, states create an irreducible fear in other states, even if their intentions are benign. The Cold War was a classic example of the 'absolute predicament'. For this reason Butterfield recommended that the Soviet Union should be treated as a great power rather than an ideological threat.

Butterfield was not solely interested in the grammar of power. He thought that the 'institutions' of the society of states, such as diplomacy and the balance of power, could potentially infuse order into international politics. In the case of eighteenth-century Europe, 'wise and moderate statesmen' had succeeded in making 'the path of self-interest coincide with the path of virtue'.[54] But in our own century, Butterfield

---

[50] H. Butterfield, 'Morality and an International Order', in Porter, ed., *The Aberystwyth Papers*, p. 343.

[51] Ibid. p. 343.

[52] His description of 'moralists' as 'specialists in wishful thinking' draws from Carr's realist language game; H. Butterfield, *History and Human Relations* (London, Collins, 1951), p. 31.

[53] See K. Booth and N. J. Wheeler, *The Security Dilemma* (London, Macmillan, forthcoming 1999). In America, the father of the security dilemma is John Herz. See J. Herz, *Political Realism and Political Idealism* (Chicago, University of Chicago Press, 1951).

[54] H. Butterfield, *International Conflict in the Twentieth Century: A Christian View* (New York, Harper and Brothers, 1960) p. 51.

believed that excessive moralism had effectively cut international relations loose from the civilizing habits and practices of an earlier age.

It is interesting that Kenneth Thompson attached great importance to Butterfield's writings on European statecraft. It was here, he argued, that 'Butterfield's realism' was 'tempered by his profession as an historian and by Britain's ancient tradition in foreign policy'.[55] The regulation of conflict, and the preservation of the independence of states, demonstrates how the international order can be morally worthy without falling into the righteous moralism of the idealists, or the despair of the pure realists. This desire to turn back the wheels of history from the tragic predicament of the inter-war period and the early Cold War prompted Butterfield to think that he could make a positive contribution to the emerging discipline of international relations.

In 1954, the year after *Christianity, Diplomacy and War* was published, Kenneth Thompson invited him to attend one of the meetings of the recently-formed American Rockefeller Committee.[56] Two years later, Butterfield finally made it to the 'Theory of International Relations Meeting' at Columbia University in June 1956 (where a young Kenneth Waltz was the raporteur). Butterfield later admitted to being somewhat 'heckled' by his audience;[57] but the experience of the meeting was sufficiently rewarding as to instil in him the possibility of a parallel international theory group in Britain.

The arrival of the English School

It is somewhat ironic that the British Committee on the Theory of International Politics was dependent upon both American motivation and financial support. The reason for the generous support of the Rockefeller Foundation was due principally to the interest of Thompson who, as we

---

[55] Thompson, ed., *Herbert Butterfield*, p. 51.

[56] Letter from K. W. Thompson to H. Butterfield (12 April 1954). The letter begins rather modestly: 'I am writing at the suggestion of a small group of scholars, including Reinhold Niebuhr, Hans Morgenthau and Arnold Wolfers. They have been the nucleus of a little group who have been meeting to discuss theoretical approaches to international politics.' All correspondence between Herbert Butterfield and other academics involved in the British Committee can be found in the Butterfield papers at the University of Cambridge Library. I am grateful to the Library and to Peter Butterfield for granting permission to copy them.

[57] Letter from H. Butterfield to M. Wight (6 May 1958).

saw above, was 'sympathetic' to Butterfield in particular and to traditionalist approaches in general.[58]

The American Committee first met in 1954 under the auspices of Dean Rusk and Kenneth Thompson of the Rockefeller Foundation. The group consisted of the most prominent figures in modern American realist thought: Reinhold Niebuhr, Hans Morgenthau, Arnold Wolfers, Paul Nitze, W. T. R. Fox and Kenneth Waltz. Columbia University was the institutional home of the American Committee. In the foreword to their collaborative publication, the editor states the objectives of the American Committee: 'In the course of this work we have come to recognize the importance of developing a theory to comprehend, explain, and guide the study of international relations and the formulation of foreign policy.'[59] The centrality of foreign policy in the American Committee's agenda (and the concomitant view that 'theory' was to serve 'practice') was a crucial difference between the two Rockefeller groups. It is also a principal reason for the failure of the American Committee whose 'deep divisions' between theorists and practitioners, recalls Kenneth Thompson, 'meant it faded away after a couple of meetings'. In contrast to the American group, Butterfield and the British Committee remained detached from policy issues. According to Thompson, Butterfield was 'scrupulous about maintaining the "quiet" nature of the project'.[60]

Between 1954 and 1958, Butterfield and Thompson continued their correspondence about the possibility of setting up a parallel Committee in Britain in order to extend 'the frontiers of thought' about international politics.[61] Following his visit to Columbia to give a paper to the American Committee in June 1956, their discussions shifted from the question whether it made sense to have a British Committee at all, to the more definitive issue of where it should be located and who should be invited to participate. The decision to attach the Committee to the University of Cambridge came about largely because of Thompson's insistence that Butterfield should be the chairman.

---

[58] Kenneth Thompson began his career at the Rockefeller Foundation in 1955, becoming Vice-President to Dean Rusk between 1961–1973, thereby holding considerable power within the Foundation during the heyday of the British Committee. Aside from his work at the Foundation, Thompson was one of the leading realist thinkers on international politics in the post-war era, writing numerous works on politics, diplomacy and ethics.

[59] W. T. R. Fox, ed., *Theoretical Aspects of International Relations* (Notre Dame, University of Notre Dame Press, 1959).

[60] Letter from K. W. Thompson to the author (7 June 1993).

[61] Letter from H. Butterfield to K. W. Thompson (26 April 1954).

The first to be invited was Desmond Williams, a diplomatic historian from University College, Dublin, and long-term academic contact of Butterfield's. Martin Wight was asked to join in May 1958. In a long letter, Butterfield outlined the activities of the American Committee and proposed that Wight be involved in the parallel group, noting that without Wight's participation the venture would not be possible. Butterfield also anticipated that they should proceed cautiously in issuing invitations to join the group. At the time, Wight was Reader in International Relations at LSE, although soon to become Professor of History and Dean of the School of European Studies at the University of Sussex. Wight insisted on the inclusion of a philosopher in order to strengthen the 'ethical dimension'. He chose a colleague from his Oxford years, Donald Mackinnon, then Professor of Divinity at Aberdeen. Michael Howard, then a lecturer in War Studies at the University of London, was brought in to 'balance him by filling in on the military side'.[62]

Given the academic backgrounds of Wight and Butterfield, it is perhaps not surprising that the original cell of the Committee was composed mainly of philosophers and historians, although the two founder members differed on the balance of the committee. More surprising is the inclusion of practitioners, reflecting perhaps the influence that policy-makers held in the American Rockefeller Committee.[63] Adam Watson was suggested by Butterfield because he felt 'it is desirable to have somebody from the Foreign Office'.[64] They also brought in a future Permanent Secretary of the Treasury, William Armstrong, with expertise in economic affairs and the functioning of government. Michael Howard usefully characterizes the purpose of the practitioners, which was 'to provide pragmatic input into our theorizing, not as channels to feed our theories into the real world'.[65] After a couple of the early meetings, Wight became concerned about the direction and composition of the Committee. Butterfield had raised the possibility of bringing a scientist

---

[62] Letter from Sir Michael Howard to the author (7 January 1992).

[63] Butterfield was keenly aware of the presence of intellectuals who were high-ranking 'professionals' in the American Committee. In earlier correspondence with Thompson, Butterfield noted: 'We are unfortunate in one respect here. We haven't a class of people corresponding to George Kennan and Halle. On the other hand, I do know one to two people in the middle ranks of the Foreign Office who are greatly interested in talking about just the kind of thing that I am concerned with.' H. Butterfield to K. W. Thompson (17 October 1956).

[64] Letter from H. Butterfield to M. Wight (10 March 1959).

[65] Letter from Sir Michael Howard to the author (7 January 1992).

into the discussions, no doubt reflecting his interest in the history of science. This suggestion worried Wight, who wanted to put international relations specialists at the heart of the Committee. To appease Wight, his protégé Hedley Bull was drafted into the Committee in 1961.[66] At that time Bull was a lecturer in International Relations at LSE. This group of nine remained the core of the Committee during the 1960s although the Committee received a number of guests throughout this period.

It was a close-knit community of scholars who were almost as interested in the occasion as the content of the papers. They met three times a year to hear a series of papers written specifically for the Committee (and usually circulated in advance) around a particular theme. After a paper had been presented, the Committee would engage in lengthy discussions concerning questions or issues raised. Herbert Butterfield placed more importance on these than Wight;[67] he originally intended to publish both the discussions and the papers, but eventually found this to be too demanding a task.[68] In the preface to *Diplomatic Investigations*, the edited highlights of the early years of the Committee, Butterfield and Wight describe international society as their 'frame of reference'.[69] The main impetus to interrogate international society came from Martin Wight and Hedley Bull. Three of their papers stand out as being particularly influential: Wight's 'Western Values in International Relations'; Bull's 'Society and Anarchy in International Relations', both given in October 1961; and Bull's 'The Grotian Conception of International Relations', presented in April the following year.[70] These were Bull's only two papers given in the first period of the Committee, effectively vindicating Wight's earlier argument that the composition of the

---

[66] Wight had suggested his membership as early as December 1958. Letter from M. Wight to H. Butterfield (30 December 1958). In correspondence with Wight, Butterfield reflected on the wise decision to bring Bull into the Committee: 'All of you know that I did not suggest Bull's membership, because I did not know him, but I understood right away that he was the right man for us. He appears to know exactly what I think about the structural problems in International Relations.' Quoted in B. Vigezzi, 'The British Committee on the Theory of International Politics', (1958–1985), Introduction to *L'Espansione Della Societa Internazionale: L'Europa e il Mondo della fine del Medioevo ai tempi nostri*, (Milan, Jaca Books, 1994), p. 21. Trans. R. Guerrina.

[67] In correspondence with Butterfield, Martin Wight noted that he had 'always thought the discussions more discursive and less constructive than you did—though none the less valuable and enjoyable'. Letter from M. Wight to H. Butterfield (10 August 1965).

[68] Letter from H. Butterfield to K. W. Thompson (5 October 1962).

[69] H. Butterfield and M. Wight, eds., *Diplomatic Investigations: Essays in the Theory of International Politics* (London, Allen & Unwin, 1966), p. 12.

[70] All three were published in Butterfield and Wight, eds., *Diplomatic Investigations*.

Committee needed to be strengthened by the addition of specialists who had been trained in international relations.

In 1963, the Committee resumed with a new agenda centred upon two particular themes.[71] The first was their growing awareness of a distinction between their approach to international relations in comparison to American 'behaviouralism'. Hedley Bull's 'International Theory: The Case for a Classical Approach'[72] is, of course, the paradigmatic English School assault on the wave of scientism sweeping through Departments of Political Science and International Relations in America in the 1950s and 1960s. Given that Bull is rightly portrayed as the 'arch-traditionalist' in the 'new great debate'[73] it is paradoxical that he was perceived by other members of the Committee as their leading expert on the behavioural revolution. In 1965, he gave two papers on 'Recent American Contributions to the Theory of International Relations',[74] motivated in good measure by the Committee's sense that they had to prepare for a visit by the leading American strategist, Thomas Schelling, later that year.[75]

Bull's research for these papers laid the groundwork for his controversial defence of the classical approach. In the first of the two papers, Bull begins by noting the peculiar insularity of the Committee from the new ideas, texts and approaches of mainstream American international relations. Bull's reflexivity here suggests a degree of embarrassment: 'It is very remarkable that the deliberations of our committee on the theory of international politics have been almost entirely unaffected by the vast literature that has grown up in the last ten years, bearing the stamp of the social sciences'.[76]

---

[71] The coexistence of these two themes is recorded in correspondence between Butterfield and Thompson. Letter from H. Butterfield to K. W. Thompson (2 March 1966).

[72] H. Bull, 'International Theory: The Case for a Classical Approach', in K. Knorr and J. N. Rosenau, eds., *Contending Approaches to International Politics* (Princeton, NJ, Princeton University Press, 1969), 21–38.

[73] See M. Kaplan, 'The New Great Debate: Traditionalism vs Science in International Relations', in Knorr and Rosenau, eds., *Contending Approaches*, 39–61.

[74] H. Bull, 'Recent American Contributions to the Theory of International Politics: Part I', British Committee paper (January 1965). H. Bull, 'Recent American Contributions to the Theory of International Politics: Part II', British Committee paper (July 1965).

[75] In the minutes of the 'Business Meeting' (4 October 1964) Butterfield writes: 'It was agreed that the next meeting should be held on 8–11 January 1965 and that Mr. Schelling should be invited to attend. Hedley Bull undertook to produce for that occasion a paper on 'American Developments in the Theory of International Politics'.

[76] Bull, 'Recent American Contributions, Part I', p. 1.

Hedley Bull did not dwell for long on the strengths of the new scientific theories. In September 1966, he presented to the Committee his polemical essay 'International Theory: the Case for a Classical Approach'.[77] By 'scientific approach', Bull was referring to the formulation of propositions based either upon deductive or empirical methods of testing verifiable propositions, evident to varying degrees in the work of Kaplan, Schelling, Deutsch and Boulding.[78] Bull dismisses these ideas with the following words: 'the scientific approach is likely to contribute very little to the theory of international relations, and in so far as it is intended to encroach upon and ultimately displace the classical approach, it is positively harmful'.[79] Bull justifies this sweeping critique of scientism by way of seven counter-arguments.[80] First, their focus on methodology prevents scientific theorists from coming to grips with the central questions of international relations. Second, the status of science cannot provide shelter from the need for judgement. Third, there is the mistaken belief that theory can somehow evolve from a pre-theoretical stage to a final general theory. Fourth, the fashion for constructing 'models' is inappropriate for international politics and can even be harmful because it disengages the theorist from the real world. Fifth, the scientific school's 'fetish for measurement' leads to absurd conclusions about the degree of community between peoples varying according to the cross-references of countries in newspapers: 'Are the figures of "communication flow"', asks Bull, 'an index of political community at the international level, or a cause of it?' Bull's sixth counter-argument is that the so-called scientific properties of 'rigour and precision' are qualities already present in the classical tradition, from antiquity (Grotius and Vattel) to modernity (Aron, Hoffmann, Wight and Waltz). The seventh and final proposition concerns the danger that the practitioners of the scientific approach 'by cutting themselves off from history and philosophy, have deprived themselves of the means of self-criticism.'[81]

[77] The paper was first presented to the 10th Bailey Conference on the teaching of International Relations, LSE, January 1966. Four months later, it was published in *World Politics*. Mary Bull adds an interesting biographical postscript: 'I remember clearly Hedley saying that he would send it to *World Politics*; he wanted to keep up his connection with the journal, and he wanted to bring the article to the notice of the Americans—in England he was too much preaching to the converted. And they did notice it!' Letter from M. Bull to the author (17 January 1993).

[78] Bull provides a long list of works as examples of the 'scientific approach'. Bull, 'International Theory', fn, p. 22.

[79] Ibid. p. 26.

[80] Ibid. pp. 28–37.

[81] Ibid. pp. 35, 37.

The main thrust of Bull's argument rests upon an unqualified rejection of scientific standards as either a realizable or even worthy goal for the humanities. Here Bull is entering a long-standing debate within the philosophy of science between the social scientific positivists (from Auguste Comte onwards) who see no essential difference between natural science and social science, and interpretivists who believe that the natural world and the social world demand different methodologies. By the early 1950s, proponents of the 'unity of the sciences' had triumphed intellectually and institutionally as political science reinterpreted political theory and the behavioural sciences displaced philosophy in the United States.

Although it was only Bull who went 'public' in his condemnation of behaviouralism, it is evident that both Butterfield and Wight were increasingly aware of the differences between their classical approach and the social scientific methodology of theorists such as Deutsch and Singer. With hindsight, these differences between the 'scientists' and the 'traditionalists' do not appear to be as great as the sound and fury of Bull's rhetoric suggested. The scientists of the 1960s were not as methodologically rigorous as the next generation of rational choice theorists of the 1980s and 1990s, and the English School were not as historical as their traditionalism implied. Moreover, these two sides of the debate did not fracture quite so cleanly along national lines. Traditionalists such as Stanley Hoffmann continued to flourish in the United States, while more social scientifically-inclined scholarship was emerging in Britain in the 1970s.[82]

The second theme addressed by the British Committee in this period was their project for a collaborative publication on comparative states systems.[83] Here we see the Committee following Wight's dictum that international society 'can be properly described only in historical and sociological depth'.[84] In January 1964 Herbert Butterfield presented a general discussion paper reflecting on the progress of the British Committee.[85] The

---

[82] See, for example, S. George, 'The Reconciliation of the "Classical" and "Scientific" Approaches to International Relations', *Millennium*, 5 (1976), 28–40.

[83] The terminology used by different English School scholars to denote types of states systems is unclear. I am using states systems generically to include the following: historic or 'ancient' states systems, European international society after Westphalia, and the global international society which emerged by the time of the First World War, see H. Bull, 'The Emergence of a Universal International Society', in H. Bull and A. Watson, eds., *The Expansion of International Society* (Oxford, Clarendon Press, 1984), p. 123.

[84] M. Wight, 'Western Values in International Relations', in H. Butterfield and M. Wight, eds., *Diplomatic Investigations* (London, Allen & Unwin, 1966), p. 96.

[85] H. Butterfield, 'Notes for a Discussion on the Theory of International Politics', British Committee paper (January 1964).

significance of Butterfield's paper is that it encouraged the Committee to apply their conception of 'theory' to the history of states-systems. His preference was for an analysis of the origins of the European states-system, with particular reference to the way in which the maxims associated with the post-Westphalian order 'have retained their validity'.[86] Butterfield concludes by suggesting the British Committee undertake a project of comparing the *internal* properties of historic states-systems. Although the Committee papers did indeed manage to illuminate aspects of the internal relations of communities in historic states systems, some of their most interesting later work focuses upon the *external* dynamics of civilizations and their 'others'.

Interest in comparative states systems persisted after Butterfield relinquished the chair of the group in 1966, passing it on to Martin Wight (from 1967 to 1971) and Adam Watson (from 1972 to 1978, following Wight's death). During this period, the Committee worked towards publishing a second volume of papers on historical states systems, although this never came to fruition. Hedley Bull's return to the Committee in 1977—coinciding with his appointment to the Montague Burton Chair in International Relations at Oxford—injected a greater degree of focus for the final 'round' of their proceedings. As Bull noted in his first paper on the 'expansion of international society' theme, 'the goal of the study that I am proposing is to reach a deeper understanding of the nature of historical change, in which we are still involved'.[87] These words are important because they highlight the way in which, for the first time in its history, the Committee was embarking upon on a journey with a clear idea of the destination—the publication of a volume of essays written by contributors who had been chosen on the basis of their expertise rather than their congeniality.

In evaluating the Committee's papers from 1964 to 1984, there is evidence of a cumulative research programme, albeit one which ebbed and flowed. The early work on states systems, led by Butterfield and Wight, produced useful classifications and raised a number of crucial questions even though their answers are difficult to disentangle from the depth of historical (and rhetorical) detail. Crucially, Wight's study showed that all previous states systems—the Greek, Western and Chinese states—'each arose within a single culture'.[88] This prompted

[86] H. Butterfield, 'Notes for a Discussion', p. 6.
[87] H. Bull, 'From a European to a Global International Order', British Committee paper (September 1978).
[88] Wight, *Systems of States*, p. 33.

Hedley Bull and Adam Watson to question how far post-colonial international society could survive, given the absence of a common culture.

By the end of the 1970s, Bull was becoming increasingly concerned about the 'decline of the element of society' in international relations.[89] The First World War shattered the idea of homogeneity among the nations of Europe which informed Enlightenment thinking on international politics. After 1945, the ideological antipathy of the Cold War weakened further the element of society because the superpowers failed to act as responsible guardians of international order. Bull recognized that decolonization had an ambiguous impact on international society. On the one hand, the acceptance in the 'south' of the rules of sovereignty and non-intervention represented the realization of the first genuinely universal international society. On the other, Bull worried that these constitutive principles might collapse under the weight of cultural diversity. Could a pluralist society of states provide order in the absence of the binding force of common values?

In his more optimistic moments Bull hoped that a new consensus might develop to enable international society to judge and enforce civilized standards of conduct. After all, the near-universal stance taken by international society against the apartheid regime in South Africa suggested that a consensus on substantive values was possible. One of the causal processes bringing about greater justice in world politics was what Bull referred to as a 'growing cosmopolitan moral awareness', leading the West to increasingly 'empathise with sections of humanity that are geographically or culturally distant from us'.[90] These universalist sentiments, however, were checked by an abiding scepticism as to how far they could be realized in practice. Although Bull argued that a commitment to universal human rights must underpin any cosmopolitan culture, he characteristically pointed to the continuing lack of agreement among states as to what is meant by human rights. 'The cosmopolitanist society which is implied and presupposed in our talk of human rights', Bull argued, 'exists only as an ideal'.[91]

Here Bull worried that particular states—setting themselves up as judges of what constituted universal human rights—would threaten the

[89] Bull, *The Anarchical Society*, p. 249.
[90] H. Bull, *Justice in International Relations* (Hagey Lectures: University of Waterloo, 1984), p. 12.
[91] Ibid. p. 13.

ethic of co-existence. After Bull's death in 1984, the torch of the English
School was carried primarily by R. J. Vincent. In the last decade or so of
his life, one which was also ended tragically early by cancer, Vincent
took up this question whether the 'pluralist' framework of international
society should be modified on the grounds of extending justice in world
politics. In the foreword to his 1986 book on *Human Rights and International Relations*, Vincent admitted that one of the motives behind
writing the book was to make 'inroads' into Bull's 'cheerful scepticism'
about human rights.[92] Vincent was more convinced than Bull that international society at the end of the twentieth century had to be modified,
given that the majority of states were obviously not providing for the
security of their citizens.[93] Vincent argued that states should no longer
be assumed to be legitimate just because they were sovereign. Rather,
legitimacy is something which has to be earned.

This modification begs the question: how should the international
community respond to governments who commit acts of violence
against their own citizens? Vincent's solution to this dilemma is to
elaborate a solidarist conception of the morality of states. Two principles
separate the solidarist ethics from the ethics of coexistence which defines
pluralism. In the first instance, individuals are entitled to the 'basic right'
to life, meaning 'a right to security against violence and a right of
subsistence'.[94] Not content to end up with Bull's scepticism about the
possibility of universal human rights, Vincent argued that 'basic rights'
to security and subsistence allow for both unity and diversity. Unity in
the sense that basic rights hold on to the core claim that *all* individuals
have the right to life by virtue of their common humanity; diversity for
the reason that basic rights only 'seek to put a floor under the societies of
the world and not a ceiling over them'.[95]

The second question prompted by the 'solidarist society of states
model' concerns what type of international action is warranted by systematic abuses of basic human rights? Is humanitarian intervention,
either unilateral or collective, a legitimate instrument for the enforcement of basic rights? A right of humanitarian intervention is, in many
respects, a practice which bears witness to the existence of a modified

[92] Vincent, *Human Rights*, p. viii.
[93] For an elaboration of this argument, see N. J. Wheeler, 'Guardian Angel or Global
Gangster: A Review of the Ethical Claims of International Society', *Political Studies*, 44
(1996), 123–35.
[94] Vincent, *Human Rights*, p. 125.
[95] Ibid. p. 126.

morality of states, since humanitarian intervention 'presupposes a solidarist international society'.[96] To what extent, then, did Vincent believe that the principles of international legitimacy should be modified to incorporate a right of intervention in response to cases of extraordinary repression? Even in his last contribution on the subject, when he was at his most sceptical about the dangers of allowing order between states to trump considerations of justice within them, he still falls short of endorsing humanitarian intervention as a legitimate practice. Although recognizing that non-intervention should only apply to protect 'good states from outside interference', this does not mean that rights violations would 'automatically' justify intervention. But crucially, the absence of a legitimate right of humanitarian intervention, does not, in Vincent's words, 'evaporate international concern, and now each state is quite legitimately exposed to the scrutiny and criticism of the international community on the relationship between government and governed within it'.[97]

The guiding thought here—and one which the term 'solidarism' captures—is that the ties which bind individuals to the great society of humankind are deeper than the institutions and traditions which separate them. This does not mean that solidarism opposes the organization of the human species into states. After all, this too develops out of the application of the universal principle of self-determination. Against 'realism', and its more liberal surrogate 'pluralism', solidarism evaluates the society of states according to its ability to deliver the conditions of moral progress for humankind. Respect for universal human rights therefore becomes, for Vincent, the key test for a civilized post-colonial international society.

Conclusion: New directions in the English School

It would be easy to infer from this brief snapshot of the study of international relations in Britain that the English School represented little more than a polite conversation between like-minded scholars, one which has no relevance today. There are persuasive reasons, however, why we might want to draw a different kind of conclusion. The

---

[96] Ibid. p. 104.
[97] R. J. Vincent, 'Grotius, Human Rights and Intervention', in Bull, Kingsbury and Roberts, eds., *Hugo Grotius and International Relations*, p. 255. The question of how far John Vincent advocated humanitarian intervention is discussed in A. Roberts, 'Humanitarian War: Military Intervention and Human Rights', *International Affairs*, 69 (1993), 429–79.

approach to international relations which has evolved through the work of Carr, Butterfield, Wight, Bull, Watson and Vincent, has in the last decade proved to be more resilient than other mainstream theoretical approaches.[98] It is not uncommon to find prominent writers talking about a resurgence of interest in the agenda set out above.[99] By way of a conclusion, I would like to outline three research questions, informed by classical English School thinking, that are at the forefront of contemporary international relations.

The British Committee's attempt to examine the conditions under which pre-modern states systems existed—how they came into being and why they were eventually eclipsed—is a theme which continues to attract historically-minded sociologists of international relations.[100] Central to contemporary research in this area is the relationship between interests and identity. Does a system of states, characterized by minimalist international intercourse, evolve into a society of states as the frequency and density of interactions between units increases? Or do questions of identity play a prior role in determining the boundaries of international society? This suggestion leads us to think about how membership of international society has been regulated and what conditions have been imposed on outsiders before they were permitted to join.[101]

Alongside these historical investigations, other members of the English School today seek to engage directly with present policy concerns. Members of the School have traditionally adopted an ambivalent stance towards those calling for policy relevance. On the one hand, they valued the space between the 'two worlds' of political power and the academy because it enables them, in Edward Said's famous formulation, to speak truth to power. Yet they also recognized the need to 'dirty' their hands by providing advice to those charged with the responsibility of

---

[98] C. Brown, *Understanding International Relations* (London, Macmillan, 1997), p. 54.

[99] H. Suganami talks of 'a resurgence of interest, in the late 90s, in the "English school" perspective'. H. Suganami, 'A Note on Some Recent Writings on International Relations and Organization', *International Affairs* 74 (1998). O. Waever notes how the English School has been 'reinvigorated'. Waever, 'Four Meanings of International Society', p. 131.

[100] Adam Watson's contribution to a historical sociology of state systems developed out of his British Committee work. See his *Evolution of International Society: A Comparative Historical Analysis* (London, Routledge, 1992).

[101] Among others, two important contributions to this debate include: B. Buzan, 'From International System to International Society: Structural Realism and Regime Theory meet the English School', *International Organization*, 47 (1993), 327–52; R. Little, 'Neorealism and the English School: A Methodological, Ontological and Theoretical Reassessment', *European Journal of International Relations*, 1 (1995), 9–34.

carrying out the affairs of state. Hedley Bull, who had experienced what it was like being on the inside of government, was well aware that in the realm of foreign policy, 'terrible choices had sometimes to be made'. This empathy with the moral dilemmas that policy-makers face is one that recurs in contemporary English School works. It is perhaps not surprising therefore to find that one of the strongest claims made on behalf of the international society perspective today is that it is better placed than the alternatives to understand policy-making. Academics working in this area attach particular importance to the relationship between global norms and the individual practices of states.[102] By listening carefully to the language used by diplomats and state leaders, it is possible to see how the norms of international society are reproduced, and on occasions, transformed.

A third line of enquiry constructed on English School foundations is more avowedly normative.[103] International relations, for more critically-inclined scholars, is not just about describing the institutions of international society and the practices of states. The point is to change them. This normative element came to the fore in the later work of Bull and in Vincent's thinking on human rights. Both recognized that the dominant rules and norms of international society had been transformed in the twentieth century to include some notion of common humanity. This can be seen in the widespread international consensus that exists regarding the promotion and protection of universal human rights. As a consequence, there are now clear limits as to what acts governments are allowed to commit behind the veil of sovereignty; moreover, states have obligations to enforce human rights standards where massive violations are taking place. A central requirement for the next stage of normative

---

[102] For examples of this kind of work, see the following: A. Hurrell, 'Society and Anarchy in the 1990s', in Roberson, ed., *International Society*, pp. 17–42. R. H. Jackson, *Quasi-states: Sovereignty, International Relations and the Third World* (Cambridge, Cambridge University Press, 1990); J. Mayall, *Nationalism and International Society* (Cambridge, Cambridge University Press, 1990); H. Suganami, *The Domestic Analogy and World Order Proposals* (Cambridge, Cambridge University Press, 1989).

[103] See especially A. Linklater, *The Transformation of Political Community* (Cambridge, Polity Press, 1998), Ch. 6; N. J. Wheeler, *Saving Strangers: Humanitarian Intervention in International Society* (Oxford, Oxford University Press, forthcoming); T. Dunne and N. J. Wheeler, eds., *Human Rights in Global Politics* (Cambridge, Cambridge University Press, 1998). For a powerful critique of the possibility that the society of states has the capacity for moral agency, see K. Booth, 'Human Wrongs and International Relations', *International Affairs*, 71 (1995), 103–26.

English School theory is to use the discourse of solidarism to hold states accountable to the human rights standards they have agreed. International relations, therefore, has an important part to play in cajoling states into acting—in Bull's striking phrase—as 'local agents of a world common good'.

Acknowledgements. I would like to thank Chris Brown and Steve Smith for encouraging me to write this chapter, and Jack Hayward for his editorial advice. Adam Roberts took the trouble to read closely an earlier draft and provided a number of constructive comments for which I am very grateful. Diligent proof reading and footnote corrections were performed by Maja Zehfuss. As ever, Nick Wheeler read more than one draft and gave me typically adroit advice. I would also like to thank Macmillan for allowing me to draw upon material published in T. Dunne, *Inventing International Society: A History of the English School* (London, Macmillan, 1998).

14: The Study of Politics as a Vocation

BRIAN BARRY

I. Introduction

The preceding chapters are a mine of information about the work done by British students of politics in the twentieth century. They are, however, for the most part quite non-contextual. We learn a lot about the product but not much about the producers. How many of them were there at any given time? How were they distributed among institutions of different kinds? Did they look for audiences and associates to academic colleagues or to groups outside academia, and in the latter case which groups? How were they trained? How did they get appointed and promoted? What was a typical career pattern? And what (a question of norms rather than tendencies) was regarded as an exemplary academic career? How did all of these change over time, and how were these changes interrelated? How may we expect them to continue changing in the future?

Having the answers to these questions is, I suggest, of value in itself. But the primary reason for pursuing them here is the belief that the answers will help to shed light on the past, present and future of the discipline. I am no apologist for the so-called 'strong programme' in the sociology of knowledge, according to which (to put it crudely, but no more crudely than some of its adherents) science is nothing but a branch of politics. I do not believe, for example, that the theory of evolution won out over its rivals simply because Darwin had a more ruthless and better-organized political machine. But it would also seem to me extraordinary if the factors listed above did not have some influence on the way in which the study of politics was carried out and, ultimately, on the content of that study.

Perhaps unnecessarily, I offer the caveat that I have no professional qualifications as a sociologist, though I have read widely if unsystematically in the sociology of the professions, and have availed myself of the amateur's prerogative of lifting useful concepts without going into their provenance.[1] A deficiency that is actually more serious to my mind is that at many points the quantitative data that are needed to fill out the story have not been collected. Some may now be hard to recover, in other cases it could be done with a few years of full-time research. It would be gratifying if this chapter were to provide the stimulus (or irritant) that is needed. In the meanwhile, I should emphasize that this is a personal view, inevitably coloured by my own 40 years of variegated experience of the profession, but one whose idiosyncrasies have been tempered by the exceptionally generous response of others to an earlier draft.[2]

In seeking a point of entry into our inquiry, we cannot do better than to pay attention to numbers. To get an idea of the scale of expansion, it is worth bearing in mind that already by 1964 there were as many university teachers in Britain as there had been university students in 1900 (20,000).[3] The number of university teachers grew two and a half times,

---

[1] It is also a pleasure to acknowledge that, as a Fellow of Nuffield College, I found it most congenial to hang out with two eminent sociologists of education, Jean Floud and A. H. Halsey, and I should like to believe that over the six years something rubbed off.

[2] A preliminary outline of this chapter was presented at one of the seminars organized as part of the book project and I should like to thank the participants for their suggestions about possible lines of development. In the course of writing the first draft, I had helpful discussions with Alan Beattie, Chris Brown, Keith Dowding, Paul Kelly and James Woodward. Written comments on this first draft, a number of which ran to several pages, were supplied by the other two editors and the following: James Alt, Rodney Barker, Vernon Bogdanor, Robert Dahl, Rosemary Foot, Robert Goodin, Chelly Halsey, Dilys Hill, George Jones, Ira Katznelson, Tony King, Robert Lane, Michael Laver, Joni Lovenduski, Geoffrey Marshall, Michael Moran, Matt Mulford, Brendan O'Leary, Bhikhu Parekh, George Philip, Jeremy Richardson, Adam Roberts, Jim Sharpe, Jack Snyder, Albert Weale and Paul Whiteley. All of these comments have been immensely valuable, including one or two that might be regarded as diagnostic rather than constructive, leaving me with a better appreciation of the advantage to anthropologists of writing about non-literate societies. I should also like to acknowledge with thanks the contribution of members of the government department at the LSE who took part in a seminar on my draft, especially (in addition to those mentioned above) Simon Hix, Solomon Karmel and Cheryl Schonhardt-Bailey. The extensively revised and expanded version of the chapter that resulted was scrutinized by the other editors and by Albert Weale, and this final version has benefited from their comments.

[3] A. H. Halsey, *Decline of Donnish Dominion: The British Academic Profession in the Twentieth Century* (Oxford, Clarendon Press, [1995] 1992), p. 62.

from 2,000 to 5,000, between the turn of the century and the outbreak of the Second World War. It then increased fourteen-fold (to 70,000) between 1939 and 1991.[4] Since then numbers have continued to increase in response to a rapid growth in student numbers, despite declining funding per student.[5] As far as the study of politics in particular is concerned, we cannot assume that Jack Hayward's 'rather relaxed community of about a hundred scholars who formed the membership of the Political Studies Association in 1950'[6] included all those engaged in teaching politics in a university, but the figure gives us a good idea of the order of magnitude, and can be compared with a current PSA membership of around 1,100, to which must be added a proportion of the 900 members of the British International Studies Association (BISA), founded in 1975. (The overlap between the two amounts to only about a hundred.)[7]

My hypothesis is that numbers make a difference: a discipline with a hundred or so members must behave in a different way from one with over a thousand. I shall therefore divide the century in the middle in 1950, the date of the PSA's founding. The first period, then, is one of gradual expansion to the small base from which the massive expansion of the second period was launched. I shall look at the first period in the next section, and then in the following one shift to the second, focusing especially on a number of ways in which (for better or worse) the study of politics in Britain became more professionalized. The rest of the chapter will endeavour to trace through the implications of professionalization for the way in which politics is studied, Section IV focusing on the relations among subdisciplines within the subject, and Section V on relations between the discipline in Britain and in the rest of the world. Section VI is a brief conclusion.

---

[4] Data drawn from pp. 62 and 128 of Halsey, *Decline of Donnish Dominion*.

[5] Between the 1989–90 and 1996–7 academic years, full-time equivalent numbers of university students rose from 560,000 to 970,000. See, for a discussion of changes in numbers and funding, N. Barr and I. Crawford, 'The Dearing Report, the Government's Response and a View Ahead', Submission to the House of Commons Select Committee on Education and Employment (LSE, September 1997).

[6] J. Hayward, 'British Approaches to Politics: the Dawn of a Self-Deprecating Discipline', p. 21 (this volume).

[7] I am indebted to the President of BISA, Chris Brown, for this estimate.

II.   The first 50 years

I have already picked out as a leading feature of the first period the very small number of academics involved in the subject. Another feature which is equally distinctive, taking as our standpoint the present day, is the distribution of academics between different kinds of university. In 1900 one third of all academics in Britain were at Oxford or Cambridge. In 1939, despite the more than doubling in overall numbers, Oxford and Cambridge still maintained the same proportion.[8] (The proportion is now only roughly a tenth of that.) As far as politics is concerned, the Oxbridge contribution was almost entirely from Oxford, but that must have been substantial enough to keep the ratio of Oxbridge academics to the total number well up to the national average. For almost all the 40-odd Oxford colleges will have needed a politics teacher to cater for undergraduates reading for the popular Modern Greats (Philosophy, Politics and Economics) degree which was started in 1921. This distribution among institutions will turn out to be significant if (as I shall suggest) certain organizational peculiarities of Oxford have had an impact on the evolution of the discipline in Britain within the first half century and, to a degree, beyond.

I want to approach the first phase by setting out the distinctive ethos that ran through the whole of the period. I shall then ask how far it may have been caused, and how it interacted with, the phenomena of small numbers and the relative weight of Oxford within those numbers. This ethos can best be characterized negatively, by pointing out its almost complete immunity from the German idea of the university as a place primarily dedicated to research. In the United States, this Germanic approach was imported towards the end of the nineteenth century through the medium of the graduate schools of Johns Hopkins and the newly-founded University of Chicago, and thereafter spread to the Ivy League universities, where it lay uneasily alongside their continued mission of educating the next generation of the national élite.[9] In Britain, however, Benjamin Jowett's triumph over Mark Pattison in mid-Victorian Oxford symbolized the hegemony of the ideal of gentlemanly education. Only in the physical sciences did the competing research model make some headway in the first half of the century:

[8] Halsey, *Decline of Donnish Dominion*, p. 62.
[9] The use of the past tense here should not be taken to imply that the same tension does not exist now, as one correspondent pointed out.

as early as 1908, F. M. Cornford remarked on the way in which the Adullamites (alias scientists) would 'hold a caucus from time to time to conspire against the College System'.[10] Where Oxbridge led, the rest followed. Other universities may have tended to pay more attention to the transmission of knowledge and rather less to character formation, but they did not challenge the centrality of teaching and the marginality of research.

The most striking feature of the study of politics in Britain during the first half century is its very weak tendency to disciplinary boundary-maintenance. Jack Hayward refers in his title to a 'self-deprecating discipline', but it is questionable that politics had any of the characteristics of a discipline in the period. As he reminds us, not only had British academics managed until 1950 without a professional association but even then they thought only that an annual meeting 'ought to be possible' and that 'publication . . . perhaps even of a journal' might be considered.[11] This does not, of course, mean that British academics studying politics would never find themselves in a gathering with anybody outside their own institution. But the meetings that there were tended to be ones at which non-academics would also be present, such as those run by the Hansard Society or the Royal Institute for Public Administration. Similarly, there were journals for academics to publish in before the founding of *Political Studies* in 1953. But these journals catered for a readership that was quite largely outside academia, and this would by itself have ruled out the deployment of any analytical apparatus beyond the reach of untutored common sense, even if authors had been inclined to make use of one. Moreover, the contributors themselves were by no means confined to academia: Christopher Hood notes that in 1923, the first year in which *Public Administration* was published, only ten per cent of the articles were written by academics.[12] *Parliamentary Affairs* was similarly non-academic in orientation.

If academics did not engage in lively debate with one another in the pages of journals, still less did they in books. Because of the paucity of journals, books were necessarily more important in relation to articles than they are now. But the books mentioned by the contributors to this volume that date from the period can not easily be seen as forming part

---

[10] F. M. Cornford, *Microcosmographia Academica: Being a Guide for the Young Academic Politician* (London, Bowes and Bowes, [1964] 1908), p. 14.
[11] Hayward, 'British Approaches to Politics', p. 21 (this volume).
[12] C. Hood, 'British Public Administration', p. 294 (this volume).

of any cumulative enterprise, even within subfields of the discipline. In virtue of the time lags involved, books are in any case not very well adapted at the best of times to fostering scholarly exchange, but that is scarcely sufficient to explain by itself the tendency of academics to plough their own furrow, looking neither to left or right. Much has been made of the 'gurus' of political theory, who referred in their work to nobody else—unless that person were safely dead.[13] But, leaving aside the pretensions to hieratic authority that were perhaps unique to the theorists, it could be said that it was a case of every man his own guru. (For this period, 'man' is appropriate. Even today, the professoriate, which reflects the patterns or recruitment of 40 or so years ago, has a very heavy male bias.)

The sheer lack of numbers goes only some way towards explaining these centrifugal tendencies among the academics. It is, of course, true that numbers matter in as far as they translate into sales. If we assume student–staff ratios of ten to one or less, a hundred academics means at most a thousand students. On the further assumption (which I can vouch for back to the 1950s) that British students were always as reluctant to buy books as they are now—in contrast, for example, to American students—it is clear that the sales potential of any book was very limited unless it could either appeal to a wider public or pick up a lot of academic sales abroad. Similarly, conferences and journals with such a limited base of fully-paid-up academics might well seem a precarious undertaking: better, it might seem, to seek non-academic allies to provide the numbers. Yet *Political Studies* has never (thanks to library sales) been a financial burden to the PSA—quite the reverse—and I surmise that the hesitation about starting a journal arose not so much from financial worries as from doubts about the possibility—or perhaps even the desirability—of encouraging academics to publish articles addressed primarily to their peers.[14]

---

[13] See, for example, B. Parekh, 'Political Theory: Traditions in Political Philosophy', in R. E. Goodin and H.-D. Klingemann, eds., *A New Handbook of Political Science* (Oxford, Oxford University Press, 1996), pp. 503–18, p. 505: 'Hardly any of the major figures [in the 1950s and 1960s] engaged in a critical dialogue with others or even referred to them.'

[14] I have no way of showing the pervasiveness of the hostility to the article as a mode of academic communication. However, I can offer some anecdotal evidence from the LSE, which might a priori have been expected to be less hostile to professionalism than Oxford. Reginald Bassett, one of the senior founders of the PSA, took the view that the only appropriate form of scholarly discourse was the book. (I am grateful to Alan Beattie for this information.) And as late as 1987, Elie Kedourie rejected a case for promotion based (in addition to a book) on a number of articles in leading journals such as the *American Political Science Review* with an expressive shrug and the single word 'Articles!'

The peculiarity of politics is highlighted by a comparison with the sister disciplines in PPE of economics and philosophy. The *Economic Journal* and *Mind* both began publication around 1890, and provided a forum for technically demanding work throughout our period. Yet the number of British academics in these subjects was comparable to the number in politics. We may reasonably ask how those other disciplines would have progressed if articles had had to be accessible to anyone with a professed interest in the subject, regardless of their background. The crucial difference appears to be that economics and philosophy both had a core of technique and (albeit disputed) doctrine which those who taught and wrote about them were expected to have mastered. Thus, even though postgraduate qualifications were a rarity, teachers of economics and philosophy had at least normally studied those subjects as undergraduates. This enabled the content of the curriculum to become over time more arcane, accessible only to those with an increasingly specialized background. (The mathematization of economics, although it falls outside our period, is the clearest illustration of the tendency.) In this respect, these disciplines retraced the path taken by the physical sciences two centuries earlier, as the likes of the noble patrons and 'ingeniose' gentlemen such as Aubrey, Evelyn and Wren who formed the bulk of the Original Fellows of the Royal Society in 1662 were gradually displaced by adepts.[15]

Robert Skidelsky has claimed that, after the First World War, 'the disciplines turned inwards; their practitioners talked to each other, not to the world'. As one of nature's generalists, Skidelsky not surprisingly takes a jaundiced view of this alleged development, claiming that it 'had less to do with the explosion of knowledge than with the breakdown of the larger frameworks of thought which had proportioned knowledge to the purposes of human life.'[16] Skidelsky's claim is undoubtedly overstated. Keynes was by no means the only economist to address governments, bankers and the wider public as well as other economists. Similarly, it would be quite wrong to imagine that only Bertrand Russell, a survivor from an earlier age, addressed philosophy to non-philosophers. In quite different ways, for example, L. Susan Stebbing and A. J. Ayer both wrote books that were widely read among non-academics. Nevertheless, there is

---

[15] O. L. Dick, 'The Life and Times of John Aubrey', in *Aubrey's Brief Lives* (Harmondsworth, Penguin, [1987] 1949), p. 39.

[16] Both quotations from R. Skidelsky, *John Maynard Keynes: The Economist as Saviour, 1920–1937* (London, Penguin, [1995] 1992), pp. 407–8.

surely an element of truth in the idea that most disciplines became increasingly concerned with gaining an analytical grasp on problems that were generated internally, and that this inevitably led to a shying away from attempts to mount direct attacks on the 'big issues' that concerned the press, the politicians and the public.

If this is so, the study of politics in the period surely stands out as an exception. Christopher Hood makes much in his chapter in this volume of the close involvement with practical affairs in the inter-war period of academics in the field of public administration. Then during the Second World War many academics were drafted into the Civil Service, and this experience had a lasting effect on the subsequent academic work of, for example, D. N. Chester and W. J. M. Mackenzie.[17] What needs to be emphasized here is that there was nothing peculiar about public administration in the tendency of its practitioners to be heavily engaged in public affairs.[18] This can be illustrated from the careers of a number of leading political theorists—the group within the discipline that might be expected a priori to lead a relatively cloistered existence. Thus, Bernard Bosanquet was active in the Charity Organisation Society; L. T. Hobhouse found nothing incongruous in giving up his academic position to become a full-time leader writer for the *Manchester Guardian*; and A. D. Lindsay's energies were heavily invested in the cause of adult education.

Above all, there is the case of Harold Laski, who regularly topped the poll for membership of the National Executive Committee of the Labour Party, and was a prolific newspaper columnist, to the consternation of the Director of the LSE, Sir William Beveridge.[19] Indeed, it may be said that he wrote very little that was primarily addressed to his fellow academics after his books on pluralism in the early 1920s. That he is represented in this volume primarily by these is, I fear, a valid judgement on his lasting significance for the subject.[20] Beveridge may have been right, even if for the wrong reasons. The journalistic virtues of facility and simplicity when carried over into the writing of books become the vices of haste and lack of care. I would not, of course, wish to deny that the same might be said of one or two contemporaries. The point is, however, that they are peripheral to the overall enterprise of political theory as it is currently conducted. In the earlier period, by

[17] Hood, 'British Public Administration', p. 294 (this volume).

[18] I am grateful to Chelly Halsey for pressing this point on me in correspondence.

[19] The story can be found in I. Kramnick and B. Sheerman, *Harold Laski: A Life on the Left* (London, Hamish Hamilton, 1993), Ch. 13, esp. p. 324.

[20] See particularly R. Barker, 'Pluralism, Revenant or Recessive?' pp. 117–45 (this volume).

contrast, it would not even be possible to talk about a periphery because that presupposes the existence of a centre. Alternatively, the point could be put by saying that, in the absence of strong internal lines of communication, everything is periphery.

We could leave it there, and simply conclude that for some unexplained reason politics did not join those disciplines that created in the period a distinctive analytical apparatus whose development and refinement engaged a substantial proportion of its practitioners. However, it may be possible to get a little further than that by turning our attention to questions of training and recruitment. Thus a crucial aspect of any guild is control over entry: guild members preserve their 'mystery' by insisting that only those trained by existing members of the guild are qualified to become members in turn. Today, even in Britain, a PhD is normally required to practice as an academic. But teachers of politics (in contrast to teachers of economics or philosophy) failed in the first half of the century to make even an undergraduate qualification in the subject a requirement. In Oxford, especially, a large proportion of college Fellows holding appointments in politics had their first degrees in history and, of course, no postgraduate work in politics either. This problem of amateurishness was exacerbated in Oxford by the norm maintained by the undergraduate colleges (now much attenuated by the growth of swap arrangements) according to which the Fellow in a subject was expected to teach all the compulsory papers and a large proportion of the optional ones to the college's undergraduates.

The dispute between the forces (led from the LSE) in favour of 'political science' in the name of the new association and those (led from Oxford) who wanted 'political studies' may thus be related to the organization of the subject at the two institutions. For the specialization implied by professionalism would obviously have created difficulties in Oxford, unless its denizens were prepared to think the (still) unthinkable about the role of colleges in teaching and about the virtues of the tutorial system (a sort of institutionalization of the amateur ethos).[21] It is also

---

[21] Resistance to anything that might be thought to undermine the 'college system' by providing an academic base for those teaching politics has been, it is noteworthy, much stronger than resistance in philosophy and economics. A proposal for something on the lines of facilities already enjoyed by those in those other subjects surfaced at a meeting of the Social Studies Faculty Board in the late 1960s. The idea was scotched by an *ex officio* member (that is to say, the holder of a senior *university* post in politics), on the ground that it would have the effect of weakening the college system. Since this was, of course, the intention, the charge could scarcely be denied. Nothing has changed since: there is still no building that teachers of politics can call their own.

significant that the successful amendment striking 'political science' and replacing it with 'political studies' was moved by an historian.[22]

Patterns of recruitment may help to explain how politics continued to stay out of line with other disciplines in failing to develop a distinctive technique and doctrine. But they leave unresolved the prior question: how did it become possible to maintain throughout the period that no special training was required to teach the subject? Presumably because to begin with it was true anyway, and its truth then became self-fulfilling as a result of recruitment patterns. At that point, however, it appears to me that structural explanation runs out. In the end, the brute fact is that no compelling technique and doctrine did emerge. Has it done so now? That question will be taken up in Section IV.

III. The professionalization of political studies

The picture drawn in the previous section was of an academic culture within which beliefs, institutions and individual behaviour meshed as smoothly as among any interwar anthropologist's islanders in the South Seas. That world has gone for good. Not only has the number of university students and teachers increased greatly, but there are also many more universities, as a result of the creation of the 'new universities' recommended by the Robbins Report in the 1960s and the later incorporation of the polytechnics into the university sector. The balance between institutions of different kinds has thus changed greatly, one aspect being the marginalization (numerically if not in other respects) of Oxbridge. The idea behind the post-Robbins 'new universities' was to spread the Oxbridge ethos of pastoral care and attention to character formation. Subsequent expansion, however, has made these, too, quantitatively of little significance within the system as a whole.

Interacting with these changes in a complex way has been the growth of professionalization. We can find signs of this across the board in universities, but its course has been especially dramatic in the study of politics because (as the previous section argued) there was such a long way to go. One sign of this is the transformation of the PSA itself. In keeping with the low-key prospectus quoted by Hayward, it ran an annual conference and a journal, but was otherwise a pretty somnolent body for its first 25 years. Since then, it has fostered far more academic

[22] Hayward, 'British Approaches to Politics', p. 20 (this volume).

exchange by creating sub-groups, most of which also have annual meetings, and become active in relation to the various funding bodies whose
decisions impinge on members of the profession. It has thus acquired the
kind of representative functions that one might expect of a professional
body.[23] Another index of professionalization is the way in which the
PhD has ceased to be an option, regarded in some quarters with deep
suspicion, and become a virtual necessity for the acquisition of a
permanent appointment, at least in any department with pretensions
to research standing. This change did not occur, again, until a long way
into the second half-century. When I proposed to do a doctorate in 1958
it was explained to me that doctorates were only for people who had
something to hide—the words used by Sir Isaiah Berlin that have stuck
in my memory—such as a second class degree from a first-rate institution or any sort of degree from a second-rate institution. There is no
reason to suppose that Oxford was in this respect peculiar: indeed,
Michael Oakeshott at the LSE was deploying around the same time
exactly the same line of dissuasive argument.[24]

If control over recruitment is critical to the maintenance of any guild,
we can say that in this respect professionalization has now been
achieved. Admittedly, politics is still more hospitable to those with
doctorates outside the subject than its sister disciplines (a phenomenon
that is also observable in the United States and elsewhere), but to a great
extent academics are now reproducing themselves within the discipline.[25] Another aspect of professionalization is the 'turning in' process
denounced by Skidelsky, if we understand this simply as the tendency to
address fellow academics rather than interested outsiders. The explosion

---

[23] This was not a gradual evolution. It came about as the result of the election of an entirely
new set of officers in 1975. Quite understandably, this created lasting ill-will towards the
organizers of the reform slate on the part of a number of senior members of the profession,
but this did not prevent two of them surviving to become editors of this immensely
respectable volume almost a quarter of a century later.

[24] I am grateful to Jim Sharpe for this information.

[25] The only hard figure for endogeneity of recruitment in Europe that I have come across
would suggest that closure in Britain may be relatively high: 'In the Netherlands "about
half of the present full and associate professors of political science initially started in a
different field than political science, usually sociology or law"'. It should be borne in mind,
however, that the internal quotation is from 1982, and does not refer to those in junior
positions. It would be interesting to have comprehensive up-to-date figures for all countries. Quotation from n. 1, p. 101 of M. Dogan, 'Political Science and the Other Social
Sciences', in Goodin and Klingemann, eds., *A New Handbook of Political Science*, pp. 97–130,
internal quotation from A. Hoogerwerf, 'The Netherlands', in W. G. Andrews *International
Handbook of Political Science* (Eastport, Conn., Greenwood Press, 1982), pp. 237–45, p. 227.

of journals in the field of public administration since the 1970s chronicled by Christopher Hood in his chapter in this volume can be matched in all other branches of the discipline in Britain.[26] Publication— and for the most part publication addressed in the first instance to other academics—has become the professional norm.

Here again, the change occurs mostly in the second half of our period, as a new (and larger) cohort moved in to the system and progressed through the ranks. Thus, when the *British Journal of Political Science* (founded in 1971) had been running for a couple of years, Tony King and I, its first two editors, were struck by the absence of contributions from senior academics in Britain. To find out what was going on, we commissioned a count of articles in all journals by British academics of the rank of senior lecturer and above, which showed that very few were publishing articles anywhere: we were not being singled out for neglect. Of course, this finding still requires interpretation. Were we looking at a cohort whose members eschewed journal publication throughout their careers, or was it that promotion led to putting away childish things such as articles? To answer the question systematically would require a reconstruction of the publishing careers of a sample of academics over a long period. This would be a valuable project. In the absence of the information it would yield, I can only offer the guess that it was some of both.

What have been the incentives facing academics who have chosen to pursue a career in the study of politics, and how have they changed in the past half-century? Leaving aside Oxford (to be dealt with below), universities have maintained throughout the period a uniform hierarchy of positions that has remained the same, apart from the relatively unimportant simplification constituted by the abolition of the entry-level post of assistant lecturer. However, this stability in the structure conceals something approaching a revolution in the way in which appointments and promotions are made. In what follows I shall explore the nature of this change, which amounts to a major shift towards professionalization in the form of bureaucratic and publicly-accountable procedures.

In the 1950s and 1960s, a handful of powerful figures dominated appointments to chairs, as assessors, advocates or (most effective of all) both at once. Outsiders were especially well placed to manipulate appointments to chairs in those universities (the vast majority) in which each department had a single professorial head. Since only professors took part in the appointment of professors (universities were a professorial

---

[26] Hood, 'British Public Administration', pp. 300–301 (this volume).

oligarchy), and by convention a professor could not play a part in his own replacement, the committee making the decision necessarily contained no internal members with any competence in the subject of the position to be filled.[27] Even promotions and appointments at other levels gave a good deal of scope for outside influence, since these were normally in the gift of the head of the department, who might well feel that in areas outside his own competence the path of safety lay in deferring to some hierarch.

In these circumstances, the criteria that formed the basis of recommendation had a profound effect on the pattern of appointments. Moreover, beliefs about these criteria, even if unfounded, will have had effects on the calculations of aspiring academics. It was widely held that one eminent professor wrote rave references for all his protégés, regardless of their merits: he was accused by those aware of this foible of 'crying swan'. A solid appreciation of Association Football made up for a lot, with another powerful personage, in the way of lack of academic talent. A third was thought to place little weight—if anything perhaps a negative weight—on publication, and his own record and that of his protégés seemed to support this. A fourth was reputed to have said that the formula for shortlisting was 'First knock out all the women, then get rid of anybody with a foreign-sounding name'. However, as the possessor of a pawky sense of humour, he may well have been making a sly comment on typical practice rather than putting forward a proposal.

Entertaining as the study of what Cornford called the 'peculiarities of powerful persons' may be, it should not conceal the more important systemic point that such persons existed. Advancement at all levels depended as much on having the right background and the right sponsor(s) as on demonstrated achievement.[28] After this lapse of time, it is

---

[27] As late as the end of the 1970s I was interviewed for a chair at a quite well-regarded provincial university by a committee consisting of several local councillors and businessmen plus an assortment of professors from around the university. I shall say of the occasion only that the pen of a Tom Sharpe would be required to do it justice.

[28] Jenifer Hart's autobiography frankly acknowledges and provides examples of the importance of knowing the right people for getting jobs in Oxford in the 1940s and 1950s. Thus, when appointed to a fellowship at New College in 1945, Herbert Hart 'had not written a thesis or published anything on philosophy, and had had nothing to do with academic life for 16 years. The job was not advertised and was in effect engineered by the Warden of New College, A. H. Smith, his old tutor.' Again, when appointed to the Chair of Jurisprudence in 1952, he 'had no law degree and had published almost nothing—one article and one book review'. J. Hart, *Ask Me No More: An Autobiography* (London, Peter Halban, 1998), pp. 111, 131. It goes without saying that both appointments were triumphantly justified in retrospect, but for every Hart there were many others appointed in similar ways who did no more afterwards than before.

doubtful that universities have kept files on the filling of jobs (as against a file on those appointed), so it may be worth offering as personal testimony the fact that I was, as far as I know, the only candidate considered for my first three positions (in 1960, 1961 and 1963) and that during all this time I was still working on my doctoral dissertation—by contemporary British standards, a protracted process. There is no reason for supposing that this was exceptional. It is how things were done. (Berlin's notion that the doctorate was only for those with something to hide is quite comprehensible within this context: why bother if—as the event proved—it was possible to get a perfectly good academic job without it?)

Sponsorship systems are, and always have been, ubiquitous in organizations of all kinds. (So pervasive, indeed, is sponsorship that it tends to find a place—even if attenuated—in overtly meritocratic systems.) There are many advantages to sponsorship systems: they dramatically reduce search costs and make it possible for talent to be recognized on the basis of promise alone—though there is, of course, the drawback that the promise may remain unfulfilled. Moreover, they need not be straightforwardly corrupt, at any rate so long as sponsorship is not based (as in some continental European countries) on party affiliation. What cannot be denied, however, is that a sponsorship system, even if it were in some sense more efficient than any alternative, could never avoid the charge that it is in gross violation of any idea of equal opportunity. And what seems clear in retrospect is that over a period around five years either side of 1980—no doubt at an uneven pace across the whole of the higher education system—the old ways fell into disrepute. It came to be felt that appointments and promotions must be made on grounds that could stand up to public scrutiny, which meant that they must be based on criteria whose fulfilment was verifiable. The 'old boy network' (and they were mostly old boys, let us recall) could no longer be sustained.

How is this sea change to be accounted for? It is hard to see that the spirit of Thatcherism had much to do with it, since one of its manifestations was the extraordinarily ruthless use of patronage. More plausible is the influence of British equal opportunities legislation: though weak in enforcement, it gave personnel departments an opening for the formulation of codes of practice. Perhaps also defensive strategies developed in response to the energetic persecution of American universities by the Office of Equal Opportunity filtered across through professional communication among personnel managers.

Numbers themselves surely made a difference here. As the number of universities grew, the number of jobs and the number of candidates increased, and the candidates came from an increasingly large and heterogeneous set of institutions. It is scarcely, therefore, to be wondered at if the previous cosy arrangements broke down both practically and normatively. A contributory phenomenon—itself largely though not wholly stemming from the increased size of departments in this period—was the replacement of the traditional autocratic head of department appointed for life by more collegial departmental decision-making.[29] Clearly, a sponsor's chance of gaining the ear of a single professor was much greater than his chance of swaying a majority of the senior staff in a department. A committee charged with appointments or promotions wishing to act in a way that is publicly defensible is virtually driven to giving a dominant role to publication. Good teaching, competent administration and the more diffuse virtue of 'good citizenship' are also valid elements in such decisions, but they resist the construction of measures that can be presented with much conviction to outsiders. Once under way, the tendency to weight publications is self-reinforcing. For if all serious candidates have publications, this puts appointing committees in a good position to form a judgement of their relative merits, based on their actual achievement. This leaves correspondingly less room for sponsors' speculation about the potential of candidates to determine decisions.

The implication is that the transformation in the role of publication was already essentially complete by the time that the Research Assessment Exercise (RAE) was introduced in 1986. The RAE reinforced practice that had already emerged rather than effecting the change itself. Nonetheless, it must surely have concentrated the minds of any remaining laggards. For while the RAE ratings of departments did not affect their position directly, because any money earned on the basis of them was paid to their universities, the universities themselves normally reacted by rewarding and punishing departments within them for doing well or badly (by the prevailing local standard) in the RAE. This in turn gave those in departments responsible for making or recommending appointments and promotions strong incentives to pay a lot of attention to publication.[30]

---

[29] The qualifying clause is intended to leave room for the independent influence of a sentiment in favour of democratization. A widespread effect of this was the opening up of membership in the academic Senate to representatives of non-professors.

[30] I am indebted to Albert Weale and Joni Lovenduski (in correspondence) for help with this paragraph and the preceding one.

It is quite possible, however, that—whatever may have been the case in the past—the norm of publication is now self-sustaining. In line with this conjecture, the editor of *Political Studies* has recently remarked on the steadily rising number of submissions to the journal and suggested as one explanation 'a different, more "publication focused" culture among the more recent members of the profession'.[31] Some indirect support for this notion can be drawn from the case of Oxford University, which I have so far left out of the discussion because there is to all intents and purposes a single career grade and emoluments are related to age rather than merit (on any criteria of merit).[32] Thus, although the university as a whole is subject to the financial pressures exerted by the RAE, it has no way of turning these into material incentives for individual college Fellows. Despite this, the university appears among the leaders in the RAE ratings, which suggests that forces independent of hopes of promotion are at work.

What are these forces? To appeal to a norm of publication is too close for comfort to the invocation of the *virtus dormitiva* as an explanation of sleep. We need to account for the norm itself. The explanation most favoured among those with whom I have discussed the question is simply that recent recruits have internalized the expectations of their seniors, which in turn are reactions to the pressures exerted by the RAE. No doubt such a widely shared view, based as it is on observation or introspection (depending on the age of the respondent), deserves credence. But there is another force at work, which operates especially strongly in the most research-orientated departments. This is the way in which highly visible publication is the key to rewards that lie outside an academic's own department or university.[33] These include invitations to present papers at conferences in (sometimes) interesting places, with expenses paid by the organizers, membership in international research networks, and successful competition for externally-awarded research funding, which in turn (by providing free time and other resources) makes it possible to stay in the game for further rounds.

It may be said, with some justice, that playing this particular game is not everybody's idea of a good time. However, the conjecture offered

---

[31] M. Moran, *PSA News*, 9 (1997), 8–9, p. 9.

[32] The recent introduction of titular professorships with no distinctive prerogatives or emoluments does not change the picture significantly.

[33] For some suggestive remarks along these lines, focused mainly on the United States, see S. Rothblatt, 'The "Place" of Knowledge in the American Academic Profession', *Daedalus*, 126 (1997), 245–64.

here is that the choice of playing it or refraining is less and less a matter of personal taste. Conformity to this model is increasingly regarded as what makes for a successful academic career—almost as much among those who are not successful on this criterion as among those who are. This explanation still, it is true, appeals to a norm. But this time it is not simply a norm that corresponds to the behaviour to be explained. Rather, it is a deep norm that goes to the heart of the question of what it means to be an academic. Such a conception of professional identity may be thought of as integrating the organizational aspects of professionalization outlined earlier in this section.

What all this has left out, of course, are the intrinsic rewards of research—*Rerum Cognoscere Causas*, as the motto of the LSE has it—as an end in itself. The title of this chapter amalgamates those of two famous essays by Max Weber, 'Politics as a Vocation' and 'Science as a Vocation'. In the latter, Weber wrote of those who respond to the academic calling most intensely as feeling that they are in the grip of 'a demon who holds the fibres of their very lives'.[34] Many academics (and their families!) can attest to the strength of this compulsion. But even among those in which it is operative, its connection with the regular flow of well-placed publications that is demanded by the professional norm is quite contingent. Some who are driven by the desire to know will be satisfied to get things straight in their own heads. Others will wish to get it straight in some written form but be reluctant to go through the additional efforts required to get the manuscript into publishable shape. Even those who have publication in mind may prefer to wait until an entire large-scale project is completed before letting it see the light of day. But for better or worse (in many ways worse, no doubt), this is incompatible with the emergent professional norm, not to mention the exigencies of the RAE. Among the reasons (a list of which is circulating on the Internet) explaining why God would not obtain tenure at a major American university is one that runs: 'Sure, He created the world, but what has He done lately?' And although tenure is still in most British universities a curiously low hurdle by American standards, the academic anxious to be in the swim had better have done something lately.

In the next two sections of this chapter, I shall be asking about the consequences of the expansion and professionalization that are such marked features of recent decades, and speculating modestly about

---

[34] M. Weber, 'Science as a Vocation', in H. H. Gerth and C. Wright Mills, eds., *From Max Weber: Essays in Sociology* (New York, Oxford University Press, 1946), p. 156.

future development. As a basis for doing that, however, it is necessary to conclude this section with a tentative exploration of the future of the two trends analysed here. As far as numbers are concerned, one point can be established with great confidence: the growth in the number of academics engaged in research and teaching in politics within the British higher education system cannot continue at the same pace into the next century. In this century, the number of full-time university students has increased roughly fifty-fold (from 20,000 to around a million), and the number of academics in the discipline of politics (including international relations) has increased on much the same scale. If the participation rate in university education were to go up to one hundred per cent this would generate only a further tripling of student numbers—a large absolute increase but comparatively picayune as a ratio. Whether it will rise at all is quite problematic. On the one hand, the number has in recent years been held by administrative fiat below that which would have resulted from universities taking all the applicants they would have liked to take. On the other hand, it is not surprising if supply and demand equate only at a very large number if the price is set at zero. How attractive universities will be to students, and how attractive students will be to universities, depends on decisions (by governments, universities and potential students) that it would be rash to anticipate. Even if student numbers were to increase (by, say, a further quarter), however, it is not at all clear that this would result in an increase in the number of academic staff. Moreover, it seems likely that any further expansion will occur mostly in subjects more (supposedly) practical and/or intellectually undemanding than politics.

Leaving aside the distribution of students between subjects, and focusing only on overall numbers of academic staff, it is worth pondering the doubling over the past 20 years of the student–staff ratio.[35] It may seem at first blush absurd to contemplate a continuation of this trend at the same rate over an extended period. What is undeniable is that any large further increase in the student–staff ratio would change the academic role and the nature of university education. But that has happened already, with remarkably little objection in any quarter except that of academics themselves—a producer interest to be automatically suspected of feather-bedding in the still regnant ideology of the past 20 years. Students and their parents appear to be far more concerned with the cost of higher education than with its quality, which suggests that

[35] From 8 : 1 to 16 : 1—see Halsey, *Decline of Donnish Dominion*, p. 304.

downward pressure on costs can be expected to continue. Moreover, no serious participant in the debate on the future of higher education in Britain expects the system ever to return to one in which the vast bulk of university income came from centrally-allocated state funding. The university sector has already become more open to market forces and will become more so. A leading characteristic of higher education is that it can be supplied at almost infinitely varied levels of cost and quality.[36] The élite universities will either levy tuition charges in addition to those set by the government or give up the relatively small sums offered by the government in return for the freedom to charge full costs, seeking to compete for students internationally.[37] At the bottom end of the system, potential students will be reluctant to borrow heavily in order to acquire a qualification with relatively little value in the job market, so these institutions will be forced to cut costs in order to be competitive. As the equalizing tendencies of state funding of students become less significant, we shall see universities offering a balance of costs and benefits at widely different levels, as in the United States. At the top end, cost will be high and quality will have to be internationally competitive, while at the bottom end students will be attracted only by a significant price advantage.

It is hard to say what will be the effects on the discipline of this widening of the divisions among institutions. It presumably means that academic leadership will be concentrated in fewer places, and this makes more feasible in principle the capture of the discipline by some one approach, with publication and research funding becoming difficult for those who do not follow it. But feasibility is one thing and probability another. To ask how likely this is to happen, we need a different kind of inquiry, one directed at the nature of the discipline as it has developed and is developing.

IV. Specialization or fragmentation?

At the end of Section II, it was suggested that the dispute between the advocates of a 'Political Science Association' and those who preferred

---

[36] From the demand side, cost may be a surrogate for quality. The benefits of individual over group tuition, for example, are as debatable (or, if you prefer, intangible) as those of individual over group therapy, but there will be a market for the more expensive forms so long as enough people believe in the benefits and are prepared to pay the extra costs of providing them.

[37] See M. Moran, 'Teaching Political Science in England', *ECPR* Newsletter 8 (1997), 25–6, p. 26.

'Political Studies Association' reflected opposing views of the subject. For the second group, it was a congeries of 'studies' developing a variety of methods (drawn from history, philosophy, sociology, law, economics or perhaps even literary criticism) whose only commonality was they all in some way or another dealt with a loosely-defined family of issues concerning politics, government, public administration, constitutions, relations between states, and so on. It should not be assumed that those in the first group, who preferred 'political science', presupposed that the natural sciences (especially physics) provided the model to be emulated. (This assumption is commonly made by critics and gives them an easy target.) But if 'science' is understood as entailing no more than an organized body of knowledge, the conception of 'political studies' outlined above would seem to defy even that characterization.

If we believed that the dispute about the name of the new association had been simply about the most accurate description of the current state of affairs, we would have to say there is little doubt that the right decision was reached. But the real question was, of course, whether science (however understood) was a feasible or indeed desirable aspiration or whether 'political studies' was prescriptively as well as descriptively the right name for the work done by members of the association. It may appear that, in picking a title for this volume, the editors have come down on one side and against the other in this now-distant dispute. But 'study' may reasonably be claimed to beg fewer questions than 'science', since it need not be taken to preclude the possibility that what is studied may be a science.

What of the current position? In none of the preceding chapters can we be said to have been presented with the picture of a well-developed structure of 'normal science' within which concepts, theories and methods are all tightly integrated. At the same time, some chapters paint a portrait of an active research community engaged in testing and refining theories about their subject matter in a way that could not have characterized any area of the discipline in 1950. Other chapters give more of an impression of change without progress: there is accumulation (in the sense that more is added) but it is not cumulative. At this point, however, anybody who has not been away on the moon for the last couple of decades is bound to be afflicted by the worry that the differences between these accounts may reflect different viewpoints rather than different realities. Would a different choice of authors have produced a quite different set of answers?

As is well known, this problem gives rise to the meta-problem that any attempt to offset the effects of others' perspectives must itself be carried out from some point of view.[38] However, although that is tautologically true, there are ways of at any rate reducing the inconvenience. In some instances, others have published alternative accounts. Perhaps even more valuable for the present purpose is the fact that drafts of all the chapters were presented at seminars at which they were subjected to extensive critical discussion by others working in the area covered by the chapter and cognate areas.[39] Another resource available in the present case consists of the comments on an earlier draft of this chapter (which was sent to all participants as well as some others), since these between them further illuminate the way in which different perspectives can be brought to bear on an area of study.

Focusing on the more empirical chapters (political theory will be discussed in the next section), we might think of a spectrum, from less to more 'scientific'. Christopher Hood, of course, anticipates the problem of multiple perspectives and organizes his own discussion around three competing analyses. However, both the gung-ho 'phoenix' interpretation and the more nuanced 'chameleon' approach that he himself favours would put him towards the same end of the spectrum. There is no doubt in my mind that different authors—in a number of cases alternatives from the same department—would have given accounts that would cause some shift in the placement of these topics on the spectrum. At the same time, however, it is scarcely surprising that phenomena combining large numbers and a lot of natural variation, such as parties and pressure groups, or voters and electoral systems, should invite attempts at generalization and that the sophistication of these attempts should improve over time. 'Public administration' is less of an analytical construct, and in the hands of other authors might have looked rather more of a series of 'studies'. At the other end of the spectrum, it is hard to see how a topic defined simply as 'Britain' could be anything but a bit of a miscellany, though an element of greater rigour might have been introduced by taking up work in local politics and government, carried out, for example, at Birmingham University and the LSE. In contrast, comparative politics is a field riven with methodological disputation, and

---

[38] One correspondent was so taken by the point that on the basis of it he pressed for the withdrawal of this chapter.

[39] The three two-day meetings devoted to discussion of (precirculated) draft chapters grouped them so that the authors and discussants at each meeting came from related fields.

my judgement here is that the position represented in this volume lies toward one end of the range.[40]

Thus, if we say that it is the study of one or more countries other than that in which the writer is normally resident, it is obvious that the subject will be resistant to the development of generalizations for two reasons. One is that the scope of the subject is all countries except one. (Moreover, its scope will vary from country to country, from which immediately follows that there cannot be any internationally valid theory of comparative politics.) The other is that the study of one country cannot, except by definitional fiat, constitute an exercise in comparative politics. It is true that a single-country study can contribute to comparative politics if it forms part of a collective multi-national project and is therefore expressly designed to facilitate comparison by using common categories and addressing common questions. Even in the absence of this kind of institutional framework, a single-country study can still be seen as contributing to comparative politics if it explicitly deploys concepts and ideas that have already developed for comparative use. Unless one or other of these conditions are met, however, a study of a country is liable to be just that and no more.[41]

Assuming that there has been in the last half-century an uneven but unmistakable development of theoretical elaboration, and in some areas (voting studies being the obvious example) technical sophistication, this opens up a further question, which emerges if we reflect that 'political studies' implies a multiplicity of unrelated intellectual endeavours, whereas 'science' suggests a unified body of knowledge. If the study of politics has become more 'scientific', does this also mean that it has become more unified? The question can be further refined if we stipulate a distinction between specialization and fragmentation. The growth of knowledge must entail specialization: Adam Smith, for example, while

[40] The point made parenthetically earlier in the paragraph serves as a reason for being cautious in interpreting the fact that Oxford occupies one end of the spectrum while the other is filled from Essex, Strathclyde and the LSE. At the same time, however, it seems fair to observe that the most plausible alternatives from Oxford are either a good deal younger (and even then mostly come from elsewhere) or if of a similar age moved to Oxford only after completing the bulk of their careers at other universities. Perhaps the most that can be said is that the distinctive Oxonian allegiance to 'political studies' claimed in Section I survived the 1950s but in an increasingly attenuated form.

[41] For this reason, it seems to me that it must be doubtful that Philip Williams really fits. Nobody would wish to question the classic status of Williams's work on the Fourth French Republic. But while there is much in the claim that running through it is an implicit comparison with British Parliamentary institutions (to the disadvantage of French ones) this is perhaps too tenuous a basis on which to argue that it is work in comparative politics.

writing about the division of labour, also contributed to it by furthering the creation of the discipline of political economy. But specialization within a discipline is, roughly speaking, the elaboration and extension of a common body of ideas to different aspects of the subject. The specialities radiate out from a hub like spokes in a wheel. This conception appears to correspond quite closely to the image that economists have of their discipline, and over time they have tended to bring their practice into line by dropping or marginalizing what does not fit, for example economic history and the comparative study of economic institutions. In contrast, fragmentation might be defined as what happens when the centrifugal tendencies inherent in specialization are not reined in by the gravitational pull of the central core. Changing the metaphor, we might say that specialization goes with all those in the discipline having a common map marking out the relations between the different areas, whereas in a fragmented discipline there are a number of different maps each putting a different locality at the centre and surrounding it with *terra incognita*.

For better or worse, the study of politics in Britain surely approximates to the model of fragmentation rather than to that of specialization. I suggested in Section II that in the first half of the century academics in each area of the subject were orientated more to outsiders (different ones in each area) than to their fellows in the same area or *a fortiori* different areas. This entailed, as I argued, that no branch of the subject could afford to develop along lines that would put it out of the reach of a lay audience. It did, however, have the consequence that if academics did choose to talk to one another there were no barriers between different fields: if each field could be comprehended by amateurs then it could equally well be comprehended by fellow professionals. It was therefore quite natural that there should be one association, and that its annual meeting should have only one session in each time period. This was not simply a question of numbers, for a division into four sessions (as occurred in 1975) could still have from the beginning have put more people together in each room than have ever attended a great majority of the sessions at the annual meetings of the PSA in the last decade. The point was rather that there was no pressure to divide up according to fields when the intellectual entry fee to any field was so easily paid.

It is instructive to contrast this simple set of arrangements with what has developed in the following years. Let us start with organizations. In 1975, a number of academics in international relations set up the British

International Studies Association (BISA), which (as I noted in Section I) now has a membership that is largely non-overlapping with that of the PSA. The founding of BISA was no doubt an effect of a pre-existing semi-detached attitude to the PSA on the part of many practitioners of inter-national relations, but it has certainly reinforced that attitude. There are other organizational clues to the loose connection between international relations and the rest of politics. Thus, it is the only area that has had independent departments. It should be added that the two general politics journals, *Political Studies* and the *British Journal of Political Science*, have consistently had great difficulty in attracting publishable work in international relations, despite efforts over the years to redress the balance by successive editors of both.

In comparison with membership in BISA, membership in other spe-cialized organizations is far less likely to be seen as an alternative to membership of the PSA. It is nevertheless quite plausible to suppose that attendance at the meetings of specialized groups (including those of the PSA itself) competes for severely limited travel funds with attendance at the annual conference of the PSA.[42] To the extent that this occurs, it means that some professionally active students of politics will not even be at the same venue as colleagues outside their department who belong to other sub-fields. But in any case, how far can attendance at the annual conference of the PSA now be said to promote disciplinary integration? No doubt eating at the same tables once a year is some sort of contribu-tion to a sense of professional solidarity. But what about the academic part of the experience? Metaphorically, even if not literally, is this a matter of 'separate tables', as Gabriel Almond put it some years ago?[43]

As the academic convenor of a PSA conference who instituted simul-taneous panels—divided along conventional lines into British politics, comparative (i.e. non-British) politics, political theory and international relations—I had better confess that attending one nowadays makes me feel a bit like the Sorcerer's Apprentice. Typically, there are a dozen or so panels at once, and each has three or four papers and one or two

---

[42] Thus, in my own field of political theory, the annual meeting run by the United Kingdom branch of the Conference for the Study for Political Thought has in the last couple of years become less exclusively antiquarian in its focus, and this has resulted in increased atten-dance. There are signs that this is cutting into attendance at the PSA conference, and my own non-systematic inquiries suggest that the two are seen by at least some academics as rivals for their suffrage, especially where travel grants are inadequate to fund attendance at both.

[43] G. A. Almond, *A Discipline Divided: Schools and Sects in Political Science* (Newbury Park, CA, Sage Publications, 1990).

discussants. Cramming all this into 90-minute time slots makes for meetings that, it has to be said, are not well adapted to fostering any very useful intellectual exchange. The large number of formal participants prevents anyone from being able to expound an idea at sufficient length to make it worth discussing, and ensures that there is little or no time for discussion anyway. (The problem would be somewhat alleviated if papers were pre-circulated and taken as read. However, current arrangements manage to secure the worst of all possible worlds by demanding papers months in advance so that they can be reproduced but then distributing them only when those attending the conference have already arrived.) This is a reflection (as well as a reinforcement) of fragmentation. In particular, if the discipline is divided into many different groups with their own distinctive ideas about what is worth doing, this is bound to create a lot of pressure towards the proliferation of panels.

Another indication of the fissiparous tendencies of the subject is the proliferation of journals from about 1970 onward, which still continues despite the tight constraints on university library budgets that make it difficult for new journals to make a profit. 'In the past twelve years one hundred specialized journals in English relevant to political science have been launched.'[44] What is particularly significant is that very few of these journals have been aimed at a wide readership. Rather, almost all have been specialized: they have had a subdisciplinary focus or an area focus; in some cases their scope has been limited in both ways at once. Even before the proliferation of the past 12 years, a profile of the American profession had suggested that this specialization 'may also decrease the value of the *American Political Science Review*'.[45]

It may be true that few choose to read articles in *APSR* that lie outside their own subfield, but publication in *APSR* is still the gold standard for tenure and promotion in American universities. Thus, once again, the organization caters to the interests of academics as producers at the expense of their interests as consumers. Much the same story might, I think, be told of Britain. Here, the two non-specialist journals, the *British Journal of Political Science* and *Political Studies* are the best to publish in from a career point of view, at any rate for those outside international

[44] Dogan, 'Political Science and the Other Related Social Sciences', pp. 99–100.
[45] Ibid. p. 100, quoting N. B. Lynn, 'Self-Portrait: Profile of Political Scientists', in A. W. Finifter, ed., *Political Science: The State of the Discipline* (Washington, DC, American Political Science Association, 1983), pp. 114–15.

relations. But, again, it would be interesting to know how far the readers of these journals pay attention to articles outside their own speciality. I have no systematic evidence to offer, but I have asked quite a number of academics about their journal reading habits, and almost all report that they turn first to the book reviews and survey articles and only then— and very selectively—to the rest. One possible solution would be to press to its logical conclusion the trend away from articles already visible in these general journals, making them akin to the *Journal of Economic Literature*. A less drastic move in the same direction would be to give up on the idea that a general journal is an appropriate place in which to publish state-of-the-art research, and accept only contributions designed to be accessible to those outside the author's area of specialization.

It is hard to tell whether there is a latent demand for such integrative efforts by journals or whether British academics feel they have done enough if they can manage to keep abreast of developments in their own specialization. What I have to admit, however, is that I can find little evidence in Britain for the kind of integrative tendencies that the editors of the *New Handbook of Political Science*, Robert Goodin and Hans-Dieter Klingemann, have claimed to find. Drawing on roughly the same distinction as I have made between fragmentation and specialization within a common framework, they suggest that their book

> provides striking evidence of the professional maturation of political science as a discipline. This development has two sides to it. On the one side, there is increasing differentiation, with more and more sophisticated work being done within subdisciplines (and, indeed, within sub-specialities within subdisciplines). On the other side, there is increasing integration across the separate disciplines.[46]

There are three integrative tendencies for which claims are made. First, 'an increasingly shared overarching intellectual agenda across most of the subdisciplines makes it possible for theoretical innovations to travel across subdisciplinary boundaries.' Second, 'an increasingly shared methodological tool-kit makes such interchange easy.' And, finally, there is 'an increasing band of synthesizers of the discipline, often intellectually firmly rooted in one particular subdiscipline but capable of speaking to many subdisciplines in terms which they find powerfully engaging'.[47]

[46] R. E. Goodin and H.-D. Klingemann, 'Political Science: The Discipline', pp. 3–49 in Goodin and Klingemann, eds., *A New Handbook of Political Science*, p. 3.
[47] Ibid. pp. 3–4.

Taking these in turn, the 'overarching intellectual agenda' referred to by Goodin and Klingemann turns out to be in essence the 'new institutionalism'.[48] With desperate brevity, this might be described as an attempt to bring together the 'behaviouralist' emphasis on looking at what people actually do with the 'old institutionalist' focus on the rules of the game: politics is individual goal-directed behaviour constrained by institutional norms.[49] More formally, within rational choice theory,

> individual action is assumed to be optimal adaptation to an institutional environment, and the interaction between individuals is assumed to be an optimal response to each other. Therefore, the prevailing institutions (the rules of the game) determine the behavior of the actors, which in turn produces political or social outcomes.[50]

Methodologically speaking, it may be said to fall within the realm of 'soft rational choice', the 'softness' lying in the relatively low level of abstraction and formalization of the game theoretical elements deployed. Although this form of analysis has its distinguished practitioners within Britain, it would plainly be absurd to suggest that it provides an intellectual matrix within which most British academics in the subject conduct either their teaching or their research. Indeed, I am prepared to venture a guess that it would be possible to graduate with an excellent degree class from many quite respectable departments of politics in Britain entirely innocent of even the most famous of the names associated with the 'new institutionalism'.

The second element in the tendency to integration discerned by Goodin and Klingemann was, it may be recalled, 'an increasingly shared methodological tool-kit', but here again their description of what is involved is liable to resonate only feebly with the experience of the modal British academic. The authors refer to 'the extent to which practitioners, whatever their particular specialities, share at least a minimal grounding in broadly the same methodological techniques and in broadly the same literature'.[51] Thus 'virtually all political scientists nowadays can make tolerably good sense of regression equations' and 'virtually everyone is at least broadly familiar with broadly the same

---

[48] See especially ibid. p. 11.

[49] See K. Dowding, 'The Compatability of Behaviouralism, Rational Choice and "New Institutionalism"', *Journal of Theoretical Politics*, 6 (1994), 105–17.

[50] G. Tsebelis, *Nested Games: Rational Choice in Comparative Politics* (Berkeley and Los Angeles, University of California Press, 1990), p. 40.

[51] Goodin and Klingemann, 'Political Science: The Discipline', pp. 14–15.

corpus of classics in the field'.[52] The post-1970 'great books' offered as illustrative by the authors all have American authors (in two cases with European co-authors) and it would be intriguing to find out how many British academics have read as many as half of these. To save space, I simply list the authors: Allison, Axelrod, Barnes, Kaase *et al.*, Fiorina, Inglehart, March and Olsen, Ostrom, Skocpol, and Verba and Nie.[53] Those who know the books will be able to work it out; those who cannot do so will serve to defeat the generalization.

The third element in the case made by Goodin and Klingemann is the existence of a set of 'integrators of the profession's subdisciplines', whose job is to overcome 'niche theorizing and boutique marketing' by 'pull[ing] all the disparate bits of knowledge back together'.[54] The evidence for this is a 'bibliometric analysis' based on a count of the number of chapters in the book in which an author or a work is cited. (Note that it is not a count of citations: one or a dozen citations of the same name or item in a single chapter count the same.) This produces a list of ten people who are 'among the most frequently referenced both across the discipline as a whole and within one or more of its subdisciplines' and a further list of seven who are 'among the most frequently referenced across the discipline as the whole but not in any particular subfield'. These names are Almond, Barry, Dahl, Lijphart, Lipset, Olson, Shepsle, Skocpol, Weingast and Verba in the first list, and Downs, March, Olsen, Ordeshook, Ostrom, Riker and Simon in the second.[55]

What stands out here is the extent to which the authors' bibliometric analysis bears out their claim that the integrative core lies in the area of institutional rational choice in that 11 of the 17 are there for their contributions to rational choice.[56] The list of the books that are cited in the largest number of chapters confirms this strikingly, leading off as it does with Anthony Downs's *An Economic Theory of Democracy*, Mancur Olson's *The Logic of Collective Action*, Elinor Ostrom's *Governing the Commons* and Douglass North's *Institutions, Institutional Change and*

---

[52] Goodin and Klingemann, 'Political Science: The Discipline', p. 15.

[53] Ibid. pp. 16–17.

[54] Ibid. p. 14.

[55] Ibid. pp. 40–41.

[56] Nine of the authors are clearly identified with rational choice. I add two others because it turns out that they are cited mostly in a rational choice context. Herbert Simon is mentioned either in general terms, as a public choice economist or specifically (in the context of rational choice analysis) for the concept of bounded rationality. Outside the political theory chapters, almost all references to me are to the rational choice part of my *Sociologists, Economists and Democracy* (Chicago, University of Chicago Press, [1978] 1970).

Economic Performance, all of which have a rational choice orientation.[57] Again, however, the question that forces itself on our attention is: how far are these authors the guiding stars of British academics and these books their bibles? If (as I suppose) the answer to both questions is negative, we cannot offset against the solid evidence for fragmentation the countervailing tendency to integration that Goodin and Klingemann claim to have found.

This leaves open the possibility that integration could simply be focused in a different place in Britain. The reader of these pages will be in a position to do something that is not open to me: using the volume's index, it will be possible to carry out a similar bibliometric analysis of its contents to that carried out by Goodin and Klingemann. It would be surprising if some names, for example those of Richard Rose, S. E. Finer and W. J. M. Mackenzie, did not turn up in several different chapters.[58] But this is a weak criterion of integration: in itself it shows only that certain individuals integrated the subject for themselves, at least in the sense that they wrote things of interest to the denizens of different areas within it. For them to serve an integrative function for the discipline, we have to demand in addition that it should be the same pieces of work that appealed across different areas. By this more exacting criterion, there may be no integrators.[59]

How far out of line does this make Britain? To take a sensible view on that we need to probe the Goodin–Klingemann data. Bibliometry is objective in that different people doing the counting should come out with the same answers. In a larger sense, however, it simply reproduces in quantitative form whatever peculiarities there are in the underlying data as a result of the choice of contributors. The point of this remark is not to rehash the issue in relation to the present volume but to draw attention to its equal applicability to the *New Handbook of Political Science*. Are the results of the analysis the reflection of a distinctive editorial policy? My view, which will have to be stated briefly and dogmatically, is that the international provenance of the contributors (half are from outside the United States) is not a guarantee of representativeness because the contributors tend to be more orientated to American

[57] Goodin and Klingemann, 'Political Science: The Discipline', Table A1.D on p. 32.

[58] I am grateful to Robert Goodin for this suggestion and proposing the names that seem to me too to be the most plausible.

[59] The same question can be asked about the Goodin and Klingemann 'integrators'. The answer is that versatility is not what accounts for their position (with one exception) but rather the recognition of the same key works in a number of chapters.

scholarship than their median national colleague would be, and in particular more drawn towards rational choice approaches. There is, of course, nothing improper, I hasten to add, in the editors calling upon those whose work they think well of. The point is simply that caution must be exercised when interpreting a bibliometric analysis.[60]

A measure of scepticism is also in order in relation to the other two indicators of integration adduced by Goodin and Klingemann. What their account looks like is an idealization of the situation in the United States. But how accurate is it? The 'national essence' always looks clearer in outline to sympathetic outsiders than to those who have to live with the messy reality—this is the essence of diaspora politics—and perhaps something of the kind is at work here. A member of a leading American political science department has remarked to me that he would not like to answer for a majority of his senior colleagues on either knowledge of multiple regression or familiarity with the contents of the booklist, and there is no reason for thinking that his department is peculiar in this way. However, the profile fits most closely those who obtained the PhD most recently and is most likely to represent the way in which these recent recruits think it would be desirable for the discipline to move. This probably means that the picture will become somewhat more accurate over (say) the next 20 years.

This leaves institutional rational choice as the remaining binding force claimed by Goodin and Klingemann. There can be no doubt that this is better established in the United States than in Britain, with hegemonic status in at least one department and a strong representation in most of the leading departments. However, it is a very long way from informing the bulk of what gets done, and it is not plausible to think that it is only a matter of time before it does—though the age distribution of adherents again provides a basis for predicting an increase in its influence. This is because the applicability of this analytical framework is limited to situations in which there are well-established rules that constrain behaviour so as to create a kind of game in the technical sense, and

---

[60] Another quite different reason for doubting the significance of a count of references (put forward by Albert Weale) is that the citations tend to be suspiciously vague—to whole books rather than to pages in them, for example. However, this does not seem to be an objection to their use in the present context. In as far as there is a *lingua franca* in the study of politics, it is surely mediated by the invocation of Olson's theory of collective action, Hirschman's 'exit, voice and loyalty', Rawls's original position, and so on. If this is what is being picked up by the count of references then it is, I would suggest, exactly what should be looked at.

in which it is possible to impute objectives to the participants directly.[61] It is therefore not surprising that the most elaborate applications are to relations between congressional committees, Houses of Congress, or Congress and the President, and in Europe coalition formation in multi-party systems. For these have the multiplicity of actors operating within well-defined rules that give the approach most scope. At the other extreme, the more a situation approaches the condition of anarchy, the less institutional rational choice has to contribute. Where the rules are up for grabs, the most that it may be sensible to aim for is to talk about possible equilibria while leaving it open which of them, if any, will actually come about.

What must be added, however, is that it is very hard to discern any alternative paradigm capable of serving an integrative function, so the limits of institutional rational choice are the limits of integration, at least for the foreseeable future.[62] The only way in which this prediction of permanently limited integration could be falsified is, I would guess, if the discipline of political science in the United States were to be redefined so that it no longer claimed a certain subject matter but actually came to be defined in terms of method. The result would be (as in economics) that recalcitrant phenomena that might be thought of as falling within the province of the political by lay people would simply fall out of view, relegated perhaps to remaining catch-all subjects such as area studies or history or the capacious receptacle of a school of public policy. There are some signs of this happening but it would have to proceed a great deal further to turn political science into a unified discipline.

V. Internationalization or autonomy?

The assumption underlying a volume about the British study of politics is that there is a corpus of work produced in Britain that is at any rate to

---

[61] In the absence of the second condition, there is a danger that the utility functions of the actors will be postulated so as to make the proposed explanation work. A good deal of this point is made by D. Green and I. Shapiro in their *Pathologies of Rational Choice Theory* (New Haven, Conn., Yale University Press, 1994).

[62] The questions raised about the representativeness of the Goodin–Klingemann sample do not seem to me to impugn the significance of their finding that 'integrators' strongly tend to be exponents of rational choice, mostly in its institutional form. My hypothesis is that, if the contributors had been less orientated to this approach, there would have turned out to be fewer 'integrators'. It is not, I suggest, the case that there is some other set of potential 'integrators' who might have been thrown up by a different choice of contributors.

some degree distinctive. Looking back over the preceding chapters, it seems fair to say that they would bear out such an assumption, though to differing degrees in different areas. At the same time, there seems equally little doubt that this distinctiveness is substantially less at the end of the century than it was earlier on. What Christopher Hood writes of the study of public administration can surely be generalized to the rest of the discipline: '"British" PA over the century has become rather like "British" motor or computer industries—larger in production capacity than in the past, perhaps, but now inevitably linked with larger cross-national structures, networks and associations'.[63]

If we were to extrapolate this trend, we would have to conclude that any residual distinctiveness retained by the British study of politics is bound to decline further and eventually disappear. But let us pause for a moment and ask just what might be the source of the 'inevitability' referred to by Hood. The persuasiveness of the case depends on our unhesitating acceptance of the parallel between cars and computers on one hand and academic disciplines on the other. But if we think about the forces at work creating these 'larger cross-national structures, networks and associations' in the first case, it is not at all apparent that they have any similar place in academia. In the case of cars and computers (aerospace would be an even clearer example), the cost of research and development is so great that the market will support only a half dozen or so independent firms in the world: nobody who has ever tried to find the gears on a British Leyland car built after 1970 will have doubted that (to adapt the old slogan) 'Britain can't make it'. But it is hard to see where the parallel is with the study of politics. (High-energy nuclear physics is another matter, as the existence of CERN demonstrates.) No doubt a panel survey with several waves is a more expensive way of doing research on elections than reading the newspapers and interviewing some politicians, but it is not so expensive that it cannot be done using national resources, and such studies typically do rely on local money.

An alternative way of accounting for the decline in national autonomy depicted by Hood, which seems to me to have some merit, is to say that is was the effect of very rapid growth from a very small base. The crucial point for this explanation is that the discipline as it existed in Britain in the 1950s and 1960s could not be said to have offered fertile ground for the development of high-intensity interaction through the medium of journals, working papers, meetings, and eventually all the

---

[63] Hood, 'Public Administration', p. 310 (this volume).

other paraphernalia of contemporary academia such as e-mail and the Internet. The stance of the academic leaders in Britain during that era might be compared with that of the Miller of Dee: 'I care for nobody, not I/ If nobody cares for me'. The American scene was quite different, and provided any number of footholds for the aspiring academic climber. In this respect, our subject reflected the 'stop-go' economy of the period, in which economic expansion led to an unsustainable sucking in of imports as a result of the lack of attractive domestically-produced merchandise. The crucial difference is, of course, that the volume of intellectual imports did not run up against resource constraints.

As was shown in Section II, the headlong rate of expansion of the past thirty or so years cannot possibly continue into the future, and in any case the national base is now large enough to sustain a relatively autonomous discipline. If this line of argument is correct, there is no inevitability about greater international integration. The refreshing implication is that the balance will turn on academically-relevant considerations: how far it makes sense for the subject to be pursued in different ways in different countries. In what follows, I want to suggest some reasons for thinking that the future may bring more rather than less autonomy to the British study of politics.

Michael Moran has recently written of the 'declining parochialism of the English university', and emphasized that 'for political science in England internationalization has meant Americanization'.[64] There are good reasons for this. One is sheer size: 'the American academic profession is the largest in the world, with half a million full-time scholars and scientists'.[65] (This compares with about a million full-time *students* in Britain.) Another, not to be underestimated, is that it operates in English. More subtle but equally important is the extraordinary openness of the American discipline. Noël Coward, in his song 'I like America', remarked on its 'passion for publicity', and Edward Shils, commuting between Chicago and Cambridge, coined the phrase 'the torment of secrecy'. Accustomed to behaving among themselves as a nation of strangers, Americans make it easy for foreigners to join in.[66]

---

[64] Moran, 'Teaching Political Science in England', p. 25.

[65] P. G. Altbach, 'An International Academic Crisis? The American Professoriate in Comparative Perspective', *Daedalus*, 126 (1997), 315–38, p. 316.

[66] Conversely, visiting American academics tend to be bemused by the absence of similar explicitness in Britain: they feel subject to definite expectations but suspect that they will not find out what they were until afterwards.

None of this was true for the continent of Europe during the period of rapid expansion of the 1970s. There was less going on, it was not conducted in English, and in any case it was hard to find out about it. Since then, however, a lot has changed. A large part of this is due to the activities of the European Consortium for Political Research (ECPR). As Jack Hayward pointed out in his introductory chapter, the object of one of the prime movers in setting up the ECPR, Jean Blondel, was to '"Americanize" European political science—beginning with British political science'.[67] Like Frankenstein's monster, however, the beast has acquired a life of its own and become rather an agent for Europeanization by facilitating the exchange of information and cultivating joint European research projects. But there has been an important independent development, and that is the increasing use of English not only as the language of conferences but also of publications. Thus 'increasingly, journals edited and published in such countries as Sweden, Japan, Taiwan, the Netherlands and Germany are in English . . . Even the large multinational academic publishers, such as Dutch-owned Elsevier or Germany's Bertelsmann or Springer, publish increasingly in English'.[68] Moreover, academics in these countries (and others, such as Israel) are increasingly publishing abroad—and, it is worth noting, in Britain rather than in the United States. Given the continuing weakness of British education in foreign languages, the significance of this is hard to overestimate.

Needless to say, the thesis of British autonomy would be undermined just as much by total Europeanization as by total Americanization. But there is a third possibility—to reverse Canning's diplomacy and call in the Old World to redress the balance of the New without thereby being swallowed up by it. Consider the case of comparative politics. There are, prima facie, excellent reasons for comparative politics to be orientated along a European axis. Almost all European countries have parliamentary government, and in the great majority more than one party is required to form a government. This provides a research agenda distinct from any generated in the United States. Again, what is meant by 'ethnicity' in Europe has nothing to do with what is meant by it in a country of immigration such as the United States. A related, though separate, point is that any attempt to transfer the American literature

---

[67] Hayward, 'British Approaches to Politics', p. 27 (this volume), internal quotation from J. Blondel, 'Amateurs into Professionals', in H. Daalder, ed., *Comparative Politics: The Story of a Profession* (London, Pinter, 1997), p. 117.
[68] Altbach, 'An International Academic Crisis?' p. 317.

on race relations to Europe is liable to generate more heat than light unless it is done with a great deal of caution. A third example (though more could be given) is the way in which European systems of social security and social assistance, although they differ from one another, are all different from that obtaining in the United States. In parallel with this, the forms taken by public debate are also very different.

What may be noticed here is, however, that Britain is—as Charles de Gaulle feared—only weakly connected to continental Europe. Its version of a parliamentary system is idiosyncratic, and the terms of its debate about 'welfare' (the term itself being a tendentious and pejorative American import in this context) owe more to Charles Murray and Lawrence Mead than to either social democracy or Christian democracy.[69] Even in race relations, although the caution previously expressed still stands, there are obvious respects in which British Afro-Caribbeans have more in common with American blacks than do Algerians in France or Turks in Germany (or, of course, south Asians in Britain). The implication is, however, that there should be room for a distinctive British study of politics in Britain that draws on both American and continental European models as appropriate.

How does the case stand with that branch of political theory that is not primarily historical in its interests but rather concerned in an analytical way with normative issues in politics? As it happens, recent political philosophy (as I shall call it for convenience) makes only incidental appearances in the substantive chapters of this volume, as a result of the way in which we as editors have divided up the topics.[70] Nevertheless, it is a large and active presence in the discipline, and plausibly can boast more practitioners of international standing than any other single area. I can scarcely undertake to fill the gap here, since doing so could comfortably occupy a whole chapter on its own. Nevertheless, I should like at any rate to take up in relation to political philosophy the question raised in the previous section about integration versus fragmentation and the question opened up in this section about national autonomy. In fact, the answers are closely connected.

---

[69] Hence, a book on the politics of 'workfare', as an outdoor version of the old 'workhouse test', naturally has a British/American focus: see D. King, *Actively Seeking Work? The Politics of Unemployment and Welfare Policy in the United States and Great Britain* (Chicago, Chicago University Press, 1995).

[70] It should be said in fairness to Noël O'Sullivan that the first draft of his chapter did bring his account up to date, and that it was at the behest of the editors (motivated by considerations of space) that the material dealing with the more recent period was cut out.

As far as the first question is concerned, political philosophy is not at all well integrated with any other part of the discipline: references among political philosophers tend to be to the work of other political philosophers, while those outside the field do not very often refer to the work of political philosophers. This is not a peculiarity of the subject as practised within Britain: I believe that in this instance the Goodin and Klingemann bibliometric analysis is valid in not finding any normative political theorists among their list of 'integrators'.[71] At the same time, the field itself is very highly integrated. Anybody who wants to be taken seriously in a meeting of political philosophers needs to be on top of a fairly formidable literature of books and articles published in the last 30 years, as well as having at least a nodding acquaintance with the 'classics'.

If we ask what is contained in this common core, we shall have the answer to the second question. The most striking feature of it is the extent to which it consists of work carried out in north America. An index of citations by British academics in their publications would undoubtedly lead off with the name of John Rawls and would include in leading positions Robert Nozick, Michael Walzer, David Gauthier, Richard Rorty, and Alasdair MacIntyre, also from the United States, and Charles Taylor and Will Kymlicka from Canada.[72] Perhaps the most compelling single piece of evidence for the influence of the north American agenda is that all the chapters in the best-selling (and best-regarded) British-authored textbook are devoted to north American political philosophers, with the exceptions of Joseph Raz and Ronald Dworkin (whose status in this regard I shall address in a moment).[73] In addition, it is worth pointing out that British authors have written books on Rawls and Nozick, while there have been multi-authored books with British authors devoted to MacIntyre and Gauthier.

If all of this suggests that Britain is seamlessly integrated into an anglophone international community, the impression is strengthened if we look at the list of academics based in Britain who would be the highest placed in a citation index based on British sources: Derek Parfit

---

[71] More precisely, no work in normative political theory serves an integrative function: as mentioned in note 56, I get in but only because of a lot of (mostly vague) references to an old book that is not primarily normative; only in the political theory chapters is there any reference to work in normative political philosophy.

[72] MacIntyre is of British origin and Gauthier of Canadian origin, but almost all their work that is currently cited has been published while they have been based in the United States.

[73] S. Mullhall and A. Swift, *Liberals and Communitarians* (Oxford, Basil Blackwell, [2nd ed.] 1992).

and Bernard Williams (though neither is primarily a political philosopher), Joseph Raz, Ronald Dworkin and Amartya Sen (whose official subjects are jurisprudence and economics, but who surely count as political philosophers as well), Alan Ryan, Onora O'Neill, myself, Jerry Cohen, Hillel Steiner and David Miller.[74] All except the last three either have spent a substantial number of years in full-time posts in the United States, or have had a permanent part-time appointment in the United States in conjunction with a British post, or both at different times. No other branch of the discipline has anything like this relation to the United States, nor has any other suffered such a significant loss of talent to the United States, in the persons of Carole Pateman, Jeremy Waldron and (half United States/half Australia) Philip Pettit. The other side of the coin is that in this field Britain has also attracted a lot of talent from elsewhere: of the eleven currently British-based academics listed, five originated outside Britain and the same is true of the three just mentioned who left and did not come back.[75]

What of the European dimension? British political philosophers do form an intellectual community with some of their Continental colleagues, but they do so to the extent that these colleagues are attuned to the same basically American core. A typical ECPR workshop will have heavy British and Dutch participation, with the rest of northern Europe represented more spottily and the rest very little; occasionally, there is a theory workshop in which the proportions are reversed, which is a further illustration of the same point. It is doubtful, therefore, if there really is a European dimension to British political philosophy in any sense that is not misleading. There is a conversation between British political philosophers and their counterparts in the rest of Europe, but it could just as well occur between any of them and their American counterparts. Propinquity and the availability of funding (academic nature abhors a financial vacuum) may lead the satellites to communicate, but they remain satellites.

The great exception to all this, it may be argued, is the prominent position assumed by Jürgen Habermas among British political theorists.

---

[74] It should be noted that all of those in the list are in their fifties and sixties. (I was based in Britain when the chapter was written, hence my inclusion.) The analysis is therefore valid only for this cohort. It seems unlikely that in 20 years' time the same analysis will be found to hold good for those now in their thirties and forties.

[75] By origin, Raz is Israeli, Dworkin American, Sen Indian, Cohen and Steiner Canadian. Waldron originated in New Zealand and Pettit in Ireland, but both spent long enough working in Britain to count as a genuine 'brain drain'.

However, he is the exception that proves the rule. For, although he is, of course, German through and through, his vogue in the United States is a good deal stronger than in Britain. Despite his being referred to quite a lot, no British academic has written a book about him and I am not aware that any British academic would identify himself or herself as a follower. His reception in Britain is, in fact, via his reception in the United States. But for the amazing pertinacity of MIT Press in publishing translations of his voluminous works, and the interpretative efforts of American scholars, it is highly doubtful that Habermas would be referred to as much as he is in Britain.

On the face of it, this is a strange situation. The differences between conditions—material and intellectual—in Europe and those in the United States can hardly be less relevant to political philosophy than to any other aspects of politics. How, then, can we account for this transatlantic hegemony? The simple-minded answer may be the right one: the Americans built a better mousetrap and the world—at least the part of it we are concerned with—beat a path to their door. (In a number of cases, already noted, this involved actual relocation.) John Rawls's *A Theory of Justice* was simply of a quite different order of ambition and achievement from anything in the preceding hundred years.[76] Noël O'Sullivan's portrayal of the preceding situation in Britain makes it apparent that the work being produced, whether heavy-handed ideology or light-footed *belles lettres*, did not lend itself to criticism or development.[77] (The same can be said of the *émigré* American gurus of the same period, such as Leo Strauss, Erich Voegelin and Hannah Arendt.) The only exception was Isaiah Berlin's 'Two Concepts of Liberty', and the remarkable amount of critical discussion that this elicited was a sign of the unappeased hunger for something more rigorous and analytically sophisticated.[78] The point is not that 'Two Concepts of Liberty' scored very well on either criterion: negative liberty was poorly defined and positive liberty was everything left over—a very heterogeneous collection of ideas. The point is rather that, despite these failings, it provided an opportunity to engage in the kind of argument that had become commonplace in the rest of philosophy.[79]

[76] J. Rawls, *A Theory of Justice* (Oxford, Oxford University Press, 1971).

[77] N. O'Sullivan, 'Visions of Freedom: The Response to Totalitarianism', (this volume).

[78] I. Berlin, 'Two Concepts of Liberty', originally delivered as an inaugural lecture (Oxford, 1956), and reprinted in *Four Essays on Liberty* (Oxford, Oxford University Press, 1969), pp. 118–72.

[79] For a more extended presentation of this line of thought, see my 'Political Theory, Old and New', pp. 531–48 in Goodin and Klingemann, eds., *A New Handbook of Political Science*.

There is another reason for the reception of Rawls, which has to do with the substance (as against the style) of his theory. Rawls's first principle of justice and his exposition of it has a very American feel to it: its content closely follows the American constitution, especially as interpreted by the Warren court. But his second principle, which is concerned with social and economic inequality, had more connection with European social democracy than it had with the Democratic Party. Despite the efforts of revisionists from Bernstein to Crosland, social democracy had never been put on a sound footing, and continued to look like an opportunistic compromise between socialism and capitalism. If we leave aside the Swedish social democrats during the period in which they espoused the Meidner plan, Rawls's socio-economic prescriptions were actually more radical than those endorsed by any social democratic party in Europe, since they called for a choice between market socialism and a capitalism in which large private fortunes were broken up. However, they were far closer to political acceptability on a large scale in Europe than they were in the United States.[80]

Predicting the development of new ideas is subject to the limitation famously enunciated by Karl Popper, that he who forecasts the invention of the corkscrew has already invented it. All the same, I believe that it is reasonable to expect the intellectual dominance of north America to lessen in future. Consider, in this context, the rise on both sides of the Atlantic of the politics of identity. This is a development in the real world, but it is paralleled (and to some extent self-consciously furthered) by the construction of new ideas within political philosophy. Roughly speaking, the central claim is that the conceptions of equality and impartiality elaborated over the past two centuries within liberal political thought (to which practice it has gradually approximated) are flawed. It is argued that the conception of equal treatment as identical treatment fails to take account of the way in which the same law or policy applied to all has a differential impact on people, to the disadvantage of members of a number of groups such as women, gays, the disabled, religious

---

[80] This is not to suggest that Rawls's theory of justice is well adapted to real political debate. The annual conference of the Social Democrats (if that counts as real politics) was once harangued by a delegate on the merits of Rawls's theory, but reports of the event suggested that this created a good deal of bemusement. The opening pages of Margaret Drabble's novel *The Witch of Exmoor* promote Rawls's 'veil of ignorance' (rechristened the 'vale of ignorance') as the basis of a good party game. As the mother of Adam Swift, however, her idea of a good party game may be atypical.

and ethnic minorities, and (in countries of European settlement) indigenous peoples.

Let us compare the politics of identity with the kind of political philosophy against which it is presented as a reaction. In contrast to the politics of identity, this focuses on the politics of equal opportunity, equal access to public services, redistribution of income, pensions and benefits, and so on. This agenda is a product of industrialization. Neither the institutions that it analyses nor the ideas for discussing them existed before (except in very primitive forms): the key term for this genre of political philosophy, 'social justice', itself dates only from the 1840s. In essence, it is a response to the rise of the market, the breakdown of forms of social solidarity that (at least to some extent) defended the infirm, the aged, the widows and the orphans from destitution, and the appearance of the novel phenomenon of cyclical mass unemployment.

The bearing of this familiar point on the current issue is that, within western countries, there was a good deal of uniformity in the way in which the problems presented themselves, so it is not surprising that both practical and theoretical discussion revealed a high degree of commonality across countries.[81] Indeed, what if anything is surprising is the extent of divergence, classically illustrated by the conundrum 'Why no socialism in America?' Rawls's great achievement, as I have already suggested, was to pull together the New Deal and the Fair Deal with the European social democracy of the 1950s and 1960s into an impressive intellectual construction. However, as we know, the Owl of Minerva takes her flight as the shades of dusk descend, and within only a few years the settlement rationalized by Rawls was under strain. The politics of identity received its impetus, it may be argued, from the problems experienced by that model. However, and here is the point, the politics of identity is much more culturally specific than the politics of social justice.

What was said earlier in the context of comparative politics applies here with if anything even greater force. The north American literature on the politics of identity is to a large extent conditioned by the problems peculiar to countries formed by European immigration and (in half of the United States) chattel slavery. What north Americans mean by 'eth-

---

[81] A good deal of this similarity flowed from the broad similarity in relations between markets and family structures. The notorious exception among capitalist countries was Japan, hence the need for the qualification in the text limiting the claim to western countries.

nicity' has nothing to do with what anybody else means by it, since it refers to the identities of immigrants with their countries of origin. The breast-beating about indigenous peoples overrun by settlers in the New World has little relevance to western Europe, and the absence of a history of African slavery within Europe makes for a decisive difference in race relations.

So far, we might conclude that the future lies in a unified European theory of the politics of identity. But, as with comparative politics, so here we have to observe that Britain is in all kinds of ways a special case within the western European context. As far as non-European immigrants are concerned, each major country is distinctive: British Commonwealth immigrants are citizens, unlike almost all German Turks, and their loyalties are nothing like as divided as those of French Algerians (who are almost all citizens), many of whom choose to perform their national service obligation in Algeria rather than France, even though the period is longer. In other respects, Britain is more similar to the United States than it is to the rest of Europe. The movements on behalf of women, gays and the disabled, for example, look more to the United States for models than do their Continental counterparts (to the extent that they exist at all), and this difference is reflected in political philosophy too. What all this suggests is that British political philosophy will be related to, but distinct from, both north America and the continent of Europe.

VI. Conclusion

As the end of the next century approaches, will the Politics Section of the British (or will it by then be the English) Academy think it worth commissioning a set of chapters for *The British Study of Politics: The Twenty-first Century Contribution*? Was it worth it this time, if it comes to that? Taking the second question first, the answer seems to be a definite 'yes'. Having entered into the project (I can now afford to confess) rather in the spirit of 'We can but try', I have been persuaded by the cumulative effect of the preceding chapters that our story has been one well worth telling.

At the seminars at which draft chapters of this volume were discussed, an issue that cropped up every so often was: What do we mean by 'contribution'? To say that something makes a contribution implies that there is some object whose flourishing it furthers. But what is this object? The upshot of our collective ruminations, conducted among three groups whose members were only partially overlapping, cannot be reduced to a statement to which all participants can reasonably be held. Nevertheless, it is fair to say that two ideas surfaced repeatedly. One is that we can say there is a British contribution to the extent that British scholars are recognized by those outside Britain as having helped to advance an international enterprise of political studies (or science). The alternative, developed in reaction to this conception, is that (as one advocate put it) a contribution is a contribution to knowledge in the eyes of God: it does not need external validation—at any rate from human beings.

There is no necessity of choosing between these criteria. Both might be accepted as valid for certain purposes. However, it might be asked if the first does not presuppose an international scholarly community that barely exists. (I raised some doubts about this in Section III.) There is an inevitable tendency for the criterion of influence on the discipline as a whole to become in practice one of the reception of British work into American political science. Even on this less than favourable ground, given the insularity of American political science, we can trace a British contribution in most of the preceding chapters. But it is important not to neglect the influential role that British academics have played in the ECPR from its inception, not only in running it and organizing the Summer School that has trained young European academics for a quarter century, but also in instigating many of its most valuable collective projects. There is, however, no reason for people outside Britain to be as interested in British politics as the locals are (and the same goes for all other countries), so contribution in the eyes of God is a perfectly valid additional criterion. Here the evidence is overwhelming. Focusing just on Britain, it is only necessary to compare what was available in print about the workings of British institutions in 1900 with what has been written since to appreciate the distance that has been travelled.

What of the future? I have argued that, taking a long view, the tendency for the discipline in Britain to become a sort of American franchise operation may appear as a blip, the consequence of very rapid expansion from a very small base, plus the accident (if that is what it was) that the only classic of political philosophy written in the twentieth century was written by an American. At any rate, the mood of most of our authors is probably more bullish than it would have been if the book had been published 20 years ago.

How distinctive the British study of politics will be in the future depends, I suggest, on two things: how far British politics remains distinctive and how persuasive ideas for organizing the subject emanating from abroad are found to be. My predecessor at the LSE, Michael Oakeshott, wrote in 1964 of British parliamentary democracy as 'an instrument of remarkable refinement and responsiveness, thrown up in the course of political history, capable of digesting the enterprises of zealots'.[82] Thirty years later, my colleague at the LSE Chun Lin ended her book about the British New Left by depicting (in the late 1970s) 'a return with qualifications, to the root values of the native ethos—clarity, logical rigour, soberness, scepticism and distrust of any dogmatic ideology, maybe even a utilitarian and individualist bent'.[83] Taken as a whole, the preceding chapters suggest that this ethos is alive and well in Britain. It is a commonplace that, since Britain was never captured by the 'behavioural revolution', it did not offer very fertile ground for the postbehavioural reaction that occurred in the United States. (As has been observed, the discipline in Britain did not have to 'bring the state back in', because the state had never left.) Somewhat analogously, Britain has scarcely embraced the project of modernism with enthusiasm, so there is less provocation to fuel postmodernism. Perhaps resistance to intellectual fashion will continue to be the distinctive British trait—for better *and* for worse.

---

[82] M. Oakeshott, 'Introduction' to R. Bassett, *The Essentials of Parliamentary Democracy* (London, Frank Cass, [2nd ed.], 1964), p. xxiv. I am grateful to Rodney Barker for the reference.

[83] Lin Chun, *The New British Left* (Edinburgh, Edinburgh University Press, 1993), p. 191.

Index

Prepared by Margaret Cronan

Note. Subheadings printed in **bold** type indicate contributions to this volume.

British Academy (*continued*)
 Politics Section, xiii, 465
British Committee on the Theory of
  International Politics
 approach distinct from American
   thinking, 401–2
 Butterfield's role in setting up, 411–12
 composition, 401, 402, 413–15
 financial support from Rockefeller
   Foundation, 411–12
 Manning's non-participation, 398n.
 papers given, 414–19
   Bull's assault on scientism, 415–17
   comparative states systems, 417–19
   on international society, 414, 418
 see also English School of international
   relations
British Commonwealth *see* Commonwealth
British Constitution
 continuity of unwritten, 4–5
 conventions of, 258, 271, 272, 273–6
 distinctiveness of, 175
 early works and classic texts on, 257–8
 effect of European Community
   membership on, 280, 281
 House of Lords, 267–70
 impossibility of codifying, 258
 Kilbrandon Commission, 282, 283
 Mackintosh's theory of, 262–3
 ministerial accountability and
   responsibility, 264–7
 monarchy, 270–3
 and national character, 3, 5
 nature of cabinet government, 261–4
 parliamentary sovereignty, 278–81
 powers of Parliament, 259–61
 re-modelling of Dicey's, 273–81
 rule of law, 276–8
 Whiggish interpretation of, 3–4, 9
 see also British political system; political
   systems
British democratic values, xiv
British Empire
 decolonization, 227, 234, 322, 324, 419
 education for administrators of, 6, 289–90
 Indian civil service, 291
 and parliamentary sovereignty, 278–9
 and study of public administration,
   289–90, 291–2
 transformation into British
   Commonwealth, 12n.
British International Studies Association
  (BISA), 427, 447–8
British Journal of Political Science, 226, 363n.,
  448, 449
British political studies

academics
 activities outside academia, 7–9, 432–3
 in government, 7–8, 16, 283, 361–2
 in public administration, 294–5,
   301–2, 432
 incentives, 436–41
 numbers of, 427, 428, 430, 442–3
 publishing abroad, 458
 Americanization, 26, 457, 466
 aversion to grand theories, 148–50, 174,
   219–20
 bureaucratization as threat to, 178
 deductive or inductive, 4, 6
 distinctive approach, 1–2, 29–35, 37, 166,
   178–9, 455–9, 467
   overview, 29–35
 to history of political thought, 48–9
 to pluralism, 121–4, 126–30, 143
 to politics of identity, 465
 to public administration, 290–4
 early history of, 2–21, 428–34
 and founding fathers, 174–9
 Europeanization, 458–9
 future of, 466–7
 and growth in student numbers, 427,
   442–3, 457
 history as foundation of, 2–10, 44, 55, 178,
   283, 433, 444
 influence of Oxford on, 428–9, 433–4
 internationalization or autonomy, 455–65
 journals, 363, 429, 448, 449–50
 lack of doctrine and technique, 429–34,
   444
 little sign of integrative tendencies, 450–5
 not captured by behavioural revolution,
   23, 33–4, 284, 370, 467
 professionalization, 2–3, 433–43
   proliferation of associations, 447–8
   and 'turning in' process, 431, 435–6
 specialization or fragmentation, 443–55
 as sphere of philosphers, historians and
   jurists, 2–3, 433
 training and recruitment, 433–4, 435–6
 without disciplinary frontiers, 2–21,
   283–4, 314–19, 320–1, 429–30, 433
British political system
 democratization, 109
 role of groups, 186–7
 see also British Constitution
British Social Attitudes Surveys (BSAS), 248–9
Britishness, 339
Brittan, L., 266
Brogan, D., 6, 16, 283–4, 304
 An Introduction to American Politics, 16
 sponsor of Political Studies Association,
   20